CRIMINAL JUSTICE MANAGEMENT: THEORY AND PRACTICE IN JUSTICE CENTERED ORGANIZATIONS

MARY K. STOHR

PETER A. COLLINS

New York   Oxford
OXFORD UNIVERSITY PRESS
2009

Oxford University Press, Inc., publishes works that further Oxford University's
objective of excellence in research, scholarship, and education.

Oxford New York
Auckland Cape Town Dar es Salaam Hong Kong Karachi
Kuala Lumpur Madrid Melbourne Mexico City Nairobi
New Delhi Shanghai Taipei Toronto

With offices in
Argentina Austria Brazil Chile Czech Republic France Greece
Guatemala Hungary Italy Japan Poland Portugal Singapore
South Korea Switzerland Thailand Turkey Ukraine Vietnam

Published by Oxford University Press, Inc.
198 Madison Avenue, New York, New York 10016
http://www.oup.com

Library of Congress Cataloging-in-Publication Data

Stohr, Mary K.
   Criminal justice management: theory and practice in justice centered
organizations / Mary K. Stohr, Peter A. Collins.
      p. cm.
   Includes bibliographical references and index.
   ISBN 978-0-19-533761-7
   1. Criminal justice, Administration of—United States.   2. Police
administration—United States.   3. Prison administration—United
States.   4. Court administration—United States.   I. Collins, Peter A.
(Peter Alan)   II. Title.
   HV9950.S743 2008
   364.973068—dc22   2007022983

9 8 7 6 5 4 3 2 1

Printed in the United States of America
on acid-free paper

CONTENTS

FOREWORD

We have all had the experience—scholar, student, and ordinary citizen alike—of visiting a local post office to conduct our business with a ubiquitous element of our government. In one location we encounter happy faces, a helpful "customer-friendly" orientation on the part of the counter clerks, postal service personnel who know the rules and regulations that apply to our particular request for service, and staff who possess the ability and clear desire to translate those strictures into appropriate application to accommodate our request. In another local office of the *very same bureaucracy*, however, we might encounter the faces of seemingly uninspired staff, offering little in the way of concern for our need for assistance, manifesting an attitude that countless rules and regulations constrain their work needlessly, and suggesting in their interactions with us that our request for service is a somewhat unpleasant imposition on them and their colleagues.

Why is this? Why does the same type of organization working with the same structures and system of rules and regulations produce such different work environments for the people employed in them and such different outcomes for the people who have business to conduct with this piece of their government? This is the first book I have seen in over thirty years of college teaching that offers answers to these questions in regard to the principal agencies of the American criminal justice system. As with the fictitious local postal service branch offices portrayed here, our nation's police agencies, prosecutors' offices, courts, and correction facilities range widely in their performance as places in which to work and as organizations carrying out their duties in service to a democratic society. As students in a foundational course in criminal justice, you deserve a text that addresses this fundamental question of variable performance, and in the process prepares you very well for a deeper study of the many specific aspects of this important discipline. This book does precisely this! You are in for a major treat, and if you do your part through diligent study and reflection on what you read here, you will be well prepared for the more specialized courses that await you.

This book reflects a commanding knowledge of the literature in the field; but that knowledge, derived from theoretical refinement and empirical study, is presented in student-friendly, engaging way, where the approach is to put "theory into practice" through the persistent translation into everyday experience of the "best practices" revealed by research in the areas of policing, criminal prosecution and defense, juvenile and adult court operations, and institutional and community corrections. While historical developments and major public policy issues in these principal areas of criminal justice receive their proper due in this fine book, the primary focus through-out is placed on the dynamics of organizations and how the management of those dynamics can lead to healthy and helpful agency settings, as opposed to dispirited and off-putting agency settings, sketched out earlier. Nearly a century of scholarly work on the management of public, private, and nonprofit organizations of all types and sizes has produced a wealth of insight into organizational best practices, and many success-ful criminal justice agency managers in fact carry out their business—in part or in whole—with reliance on these insights derived from thoughtful reflection on practice and careful empirical study.

To date no textbooks in criminal justice have attempted to capture these insights and to frame an introduction to the field in this particular way—largely because of the immense range of knowledge and experience required of authors of such a book. Consequently, you have the privilege of being the first generation of students of crimi-nal justice to enjoy the benefit of this highly ambitious and deeply enriching effort. I urge you to take full advantage of that exceptional privilege. Future textbooks in crim-inal justice will have to take their measure against this book's new high standard.

The authors of this book rightly emphasize the importance for criminal justice agencies of the use of human relations management practices, the provision of support for professional development of staff, the consistent use of proactive, collaborative, and shared-responsibility forms of leadership, the development and maintenance of a deeply embedded belief in ethical practice, the implementation of evidence-based best practices in agency programming, and the building of strong bridges to an engaged and informed community. To the extent that criminal justice agencies make use of these principles and practices in the way they are managed, they are likely to be car-rying out their mandates well and at the same time providing enriching jobs for their employees.

How well the criminal justice system works in a democratic society is a good measure of the health of democracy in that society. In the United States we have much of which we can be justly proud, including the dedication to the public service ethic displayed in much of our criminal justice system. We also have much work before us to move our criminal justice system closer to what it could be vis-à-vis enlightened prac-tice and enriching workplaces. I can't imagine a more appropriate foundational book than this one for preparing students to take up the challenges of making our criminal justice system the best it can be.

Nicholas P. Lovrich, Director
Division of Governmental Studies and Services
Washington State University–Pullman

PREFACE

This book was inspired by the students of, and practitioners in, criminal justice agencies. These people, as well as those interested enough to pick up this book, know the value of effective management and they understand (or soon will) the need for organizations to fit the desires of community members and the needs of workers. We wrote this book as a means of addressing the truths—as we understand them—about justice-centered agencies, their management, and their operation. One such truth is that we believe that workers deserve to be included in the management process, both for their own sake and sanity and to advance the accomplishment of the publicly determined goals of the agency.

Another truth, which unfortunately falls under the heading of "sad, but true," is that students often see management and organizational topics as dry and irrelevant. In recognition of this, we did our best to provide a student-oriented text that gives, serious attention to the relevancy of all topics for people who hope to understand and effectively negotiate their work lives within criminal justice organizations.

We also wrote this book as a means of addressing some critical organizational issues that are not always given sufficient attention in texts, namely: understanding ethics in the organizational environment, personnel processes, the 21st-century workforce, and budgeting. As we indicate in these chapters, such topics are terribly important to the operation of any criminal justice agency and therefore to the education of our students.

As a reader of this text, you should also know that it was pure pleasure for us to write! Writing this book, much like teaching this topic, provided us the opportunity to explore the seminal management issues of our time.

As with any project of this size and scope, there are many, many people to thank for their assistance and inspiration, and we would be remiss if we did not at least attempt to acknowledge some of their efforts. We apologize in advance if anyone is left out of these acknowledgments.

First of all, we thank our editor, Sherith Pankratz, and all of the other Oxford University Press staff who helped us see this manuscript through to its publication. We are also indebted to Claude Teweles and his staff, Scott Carter in particular, from Roxbury Publishing. Claude first convinced us to write this book and then supported our efforts through the revisions. Needless to say, those revisions would not have been as extensive, or as germane, without the thoughtful and very helpful comments of the reviewers that Claude recruited.

We are also indebted to Jennifer Ashley, who as a graduate student helped track down research articles and edit parts of the manuscript. Sancheen Collins was also instrumental in formatting the references. In addition, our writing was informed by several students and entire classes of criminal justice management students, fellow scholars in the criminal justice and public administration fields, and justice-centered practitioners in the field. We are indebted to them all for shaping this work.

Sancheen (wife of Pete), along with Craig Hemmens and Emily Stohr-Gillmore (husband and daughter of Mary), deserve much credit for their forbearance and understanding of the importance of this book for their loved ones. We certainly cannot thank them, or love them, enough for it.

Finally, no acknowledgment for this book on management would be complete without a nod, and really a bow, to the mentorship of Nicholas P. Lovrich, Claudius O. and Mary W. Johnson Distinguished Professor of Political Science, and director of the Division of Governmental Studies and Services at Washington State University–Pullman. Directly for Mary and indirectly for Pete, he has modeled and taught the appropriate role of the academic as a catalyst for the nurturance of the just operation of the public sector organization. His positive contributions to those organizations (including numerous police, courts, and corrections entities), and the people who encounter and labor in them, cannot be easily tallied. As the authors labored on this book, his example of what a decent human being should be in an organizational context, was never far from our minds.

Peter Collins: To my wife Sancheen Collins
Mary Stohr: To my husband Craig Hemmens and
daughter Emily Rose Stohr-Gillmore

CHAPTER 1

CRIMINAL JUSTICE MANAGEMENT: THE BIG, THE BAD, AND THE BEAUTIFUL

INTRODUCTION: SCOPE AND PURPOSE OF THE BOOK

The general public may not always view criminal justice agencies in a positive light, though they may admire people who labor in them. Problems with abuse of force by the police or in corrections, overcrowded courts and corrections services, lapsed supervision of clients by probation or parole officers, violence, and instances of mismanagement are highlighted in the press and become a focus for public policy. In such instances the adjectives "big" and "bad" tend to fit criminal justice agencies and institutions and related management practices. But as people who work in the justice system, and those who study those organizations at any length, know, these institutions serve a vital purpose in this democracy; namely, they not only prevent crime, respond to victims and citizens, and operate the machinery of justice, they hold, supervise, feed, cloth, train, and rehabilitate thousands of inmates and clients daily.

The public is much safer because of the efforts of criminal justice staff who investigate crime, adjudicate cases, keep dangerous and repeat offenders incarcerated or supervised, and extract from the system innocent people inadvertently trapped there. And justice is served for both victims and offenders when the accused are given their day (or half-hour) in court, and when appropriate sentences are carried out in correctional institutions, in juvenile facilities, or in the community. Although some would argue that citizens/victims/offenders are physically or mentally harmed by their experience with the justice system, others, even those who are eventually incarcerated, if they are placed in well-managed institutions or programs, may actually benefit from this exposure. In the latter situation, one might even call that kind of criminal justice management "beautiful."

Therefore, a central theme of this book is that there are a number of paths that lead to the effective management of criminal justice organizations, and it makes all the difference which route is taken. The phrase "best practices" is often bandied about these days to describe how a correctional treatment program or a police rape investigation or a number of other activities might be organized and implemented. We argue in this book that there are indeed "best practices," or better ways of doing things in criminal justice management. These "better ways" are more likely to yield desirable outcomes, such as safety and security for the public, the staff, and the clientele of agencies, a skilled and involved staff and, on balance, an enriching experience for all.

When there are problems in criminal justice, they can often be laid at the door of either public policymakers who ask too much and supply too little in the way of resources to agencies; or in many cases, problems are the direct result of mismanagement by administrators of these agencies. Although public policy will be highlighted in a few places in this book, our primary focus is on the dynamics of organizations and how their management can be big or bad or beautiful. After a century of scholarly focus on the management of public and private sector institutions, the knowledge about how best to operate criminal justice agencies already exists and is practiced in part, or in whole, by the most successful managers. This book serves, then, to provide a theoretical, historical, and organizational context for such management practices.

To that end, this book covers a number of topics of interest to practitioners and students of criminal justice management, including organizational and environmental characteristics of criminal justice agencies (Chapter 1); distinctions between, and definitions of, common criminal justice, management, and organizational terms (Chapter 2); a discussion of the value of public vs. private service (Chapter 2); an examination of ethical issues, including official deviance, corruption, the use of excessive force, and sexual and gender harassment (Chapter 3); common management theories and their application (Chapter 4); interpersonal, organizational, and interorganizational communication and barriers (Chapter 5); the nature of the criminal justice role, socialization, and power issues (Chapter 6); leadership theories and styles (Chapter 7); selection issues such as the workforce 2000, diversity and affirmative action (Chapter 8); personnel practices such as selection, performance appraisal, retention strategies, job enrichment, training, and related issues (Chapter 9); managing and evaluating programming, accreditation, and standards (Chapter 10), and strategic planning and budgeting (Chapter 11).

There follows a chapter devoted to the decision-making challenges in criminal justice management (Chapter 12). The final chapter encapsulates the best of management and organizational practices from the scholarly and practitioner literature in the form of an inclusive and consilient proposal of model management practices for criminal justice agencies (Chapter 13).

Chapters 3 and 6 include research instruments used to "take the temperature" of the work environment. Some chapters showcase a perspective or two on the given topic by a criminal justice practitioner, scholar, or student. Some chapters include classroom or training exercises that reinforce knowledge highlighted in the text, as well as key terms and reference tools such as web links for further investigation. Most chapters also include exercises that can be used in class to reinforce concepts and ideas. At the end of all chapters there are discussion questions to spur creative and analytical thought regarding chapter content.

One other note before we get to the "meat" of the book. The tone of the text, as reflected in our writing, is deliberately conversational at times. Research and scholarly works are highlighted in this book, but so are the experiences of people who work in, and study, criminal justice. We want to bring together the two worlds of practitioners and academe, and the best way we have found to do this while teaching is to present material in the second category in a less formal fashion.

The remainder of this chapter is devoted to setting the stage for the management and organizational topics featured in this book. Although most students will have become acquainted with some or all of the major sectors of criminal justice (i.e., police, courts, corrections) before taking this class, the characteristics of the organizations, their staff, and their clientele bear repeating here to ensure a common understanding of them before we proceed. For example, it is important to recall that all criminal justice agencies are creatures of their environment to some extent, and that characteristic affects practice, policies, and funding. Therefore, to provide a common context from which to view the rest of the topics covered in this book, we begin with what is probably a review for most students of organizational, staff, and clientele characteristics.

SOME DEFINING ISSUES IN CRIMINAL JUSTICE: LAW ENFORCEMENT, COURTS, AND CORRECTIONS

Police and Sheriff's Departments

Despite the emphasis on various federal law enforcement agencies in the media, one of the most distinguishing features of public policing is that it is local. For this reason, most of the discussions of policing in this text focus on local city and state police and sheriff's departments, with some discussion of policing agencies at the state and federal levels mixed in. Virtually every city of any size either has a local police department or contracts for such services from the county sheriff's office. Often small villages and towns also have their own police department. In fact, the sheer variety of policing and the focus of policing are huge and complex (Langworthy & Travis, 1994). The local departments, whether police or sheriff, are the most numerous law enforcement organizations and employ the most public officers.

As of 2000 there were 796,518 local, state, and federal police and sheriff's sworn officers in this country (Bureau of Justice Statistics, 2004b). Of these 440,920 were employed by local police departments and another 164,711 worked as sheriff's deputies; or 76% of all sworn officers work for local departments.

Duties, Mission, and Roles of Law Enforcement   The duties of officers and the mission of such departments are diverse, as they are somewhat connected to the type of community being policed (Roberg, Crank, & Kuykendall, 2000). Traditionally, that mission has been divided between order maintenance, law enforcement or crime fighting, and service delivery. Additional roles for law enforcement agencies and officers might include information gathering and acting as a protector of individual rights (Barker, Hunter, & Rush, 1994). "To serve and protect," the slogan of many departments, captures these duties and the overall mission of the departments, and also encompasses many separate tasks that we see officers do every day, such as investigating a crime, assisting a motorist, responding to a report of a prowler, checking the locks on a business, setting up roadside stops for drunk drivers, problem solving with a local neighborhood group concerned about crimes in the area, and working in the local high school as a resource officer. Long ago, such tasks were collapsed into service delivery, law enforcement, and order maintenance by police scholars (e.g., see Goldstein, 1977; Wilson, 1968).

The patrol divisions perform virtually the same role, as that represents their mission, in both police and sheriff's departments. City or municipal police departments and sheriff's departments all perform basic tasks that include law enforcement, service, and order maintenance. The law enforcement tasks are the ones that come to mind when people think of the police. They include crime control activities that revolve around preventing, detecting, and investigating crime. The police or sheriff's officer in this capacity may apprehend the accused, make an arrest, or issue a citation.

Though we think of the police as primarily engaged in law enforcement activi-ties, for the most part they are not. In fact, the majority of their time is spent in either service delivery (e.g., unlocking car doors, assisting accident victims, locating lost children, helping the injured) or order maintenance (e.g., crowd control, directing traffic, settling disputes between neighbors, keeping an eye on vagrant youth) (Langworthy & Travis, 1994). The police are called to act in these capacities because they are particularly suited for them in that they are community-wide service workers who respond to calls from citizens and have specialized training. Moreover, both service and order maintenance tasks are closely connected to law enforcement in that they may involve interpretation of, or disputes about, the law, and they could be associated with crime in some way. For instance, although in most instances the report of a lost child does not signify that an abduction, hence a violation of the law, has occurred, in some cases it does. Or, although disputes between neighbors are usually resolved amicably, the police presence may serve to calm tempers that otherwise would escalate to the point that one or more parties committed an assault or destroyed the other's property.

We discuss the police/sheriff officer's role more in subsequent chapters, but it is instructive to note that law enforcement organizations, like the other criminal justice agencies mentioned here, determine what they do based on the demands from their environment, the type of department, and the law. As Roberg, et al. (2000:21) indicate, this "expectation–integration model" shapes how the police make decisions about what they do. For example, the community environment determines whether the department is primarily engaged in service, order maintenance, or law enforcement activities (Kelling, 1999). As communities become more diverse culturally, figuring out what the community wants can be daunting for the police.

Second, officers police based on perceptions of the formal and informal expectations of their department. If a supervisor wants them to concentrate on order maintenance duties at the expense of service, that is what they will do as long as the informal subculture does not discourage such prioritization (more about the formal and informal subcultures in organizations later). Therefore, the formal policies of a department and the informal culture of the department can both have an impact on how the police operate.

Finally, the law itself will shape what the police spend time on. As laws vary from state to state and even between counties and cities in the same state, the police role will be shaped to some extent by those differences. The increasing incursion of federal law into local policing, particularly via the modern drug war, has had an impact on local policing to the extent that officers in local police and sheriff's departments are assigned to drug task forces that are often run or facilitated by federal law enforcement. While engaged in these typically law enforcement duties involving the drug war, police and sheriff's officers may have less time to engage in service and order maintenance duties.

These diverse and sometimes competing expectations for police role activity can be "integrated" to some degree when they overlap. That is, for *mala in se* crimes (or those that are evil in and of themselves) such as murder, rape, assault, and robbery, there would be similar expectations for police behavior from the community environment, the organization, and the law. It is when the crime or disorder is less serious (*mala prohibita* crimes, or those that are defined as "evil" because they are disapproved of by society), or the service request is minor, that officers may exercise their discretion to ignore or only respond half-heartedly.

Organizational Structure   Typically, police and sheriff's departments, much like jails and prisons and probation and parole departments, are structurally bureaucratic, with paramilitary regimentation, regalia, and accoutrements (more about these later), and top-down communication. They do differ in that in most cases, if a county jail exists, it is run by the sheriff's department. Though some police departments may run a short-term holding facility, they usually do not operate a full-scale jail. State and federal law enforcement agencies do not operate correctional facilities.

Clientele   On the other hand, the clientele are generally the same, as they are residents of the community the organization is located in or has jurisdiction over. The location and type of crime or incident that compels the resident's contact with law enforcement will determine whether that contact is with a city, county, state, or federal agency. However, the clientele for those who have the most negative contact with agencies of criminal justice tends to differ in most cases from the general citizenry in several important respects. Those who have most negative contact with the police or sheriff's department tend to be male, young, uneducated, and poor, with alcohol or substance abuse problems (Radelet & Carter, 1994). In larger cities, they also tend to be disproportionately minority group members.

Staff Characteristics   Many of the officers employed in police and sheriff's departments are white males with a military background (Hickman & Reaves, 2003). Although the number of minorities and women employed as full-time sworn personnel increased by almost 6% (to 22.7%) and 2.5% (to 10.6 %), respectively, from 1990 to 2000. After passage of the Civil Rights Act of 1964, which prohibits discrimination in hiring based on race and ethnicity, its amendment in 1972, and civil suits by minorities and white women over the course of thirty years, the law enforcement agencies have become more diverse, particularly in urban areas (Hickman & Reaves, 2003). As with other sectors of the criminal justice system, the number of former military personnel may be explained by the attraction to the public sector work and the paramilitary structure of police and sheriff departments.

Location/Jurisdiction   Historically, police departments were located in cities and towns and sheriff's departments were located in counties, often policing rural areas.

This is still true today, although some cities have grown so large in area and in population that they have expanded to encompass the same areas policed by both city and county agencies. State police departments are often headquartered in state capitals, though they usually have offices sprinkled throughout the larger cities and towns in the state. Federal agencies also tend to be located in state capitals and large cities.

Public Institutions   City and state policing and sheriff's departments are by definition publicly created and operated entities. Though there is much private policing in this country, cities, counties, and states (and the federal government) have kept and expanded their public sector agencies (Hickman & Reaves, 2003; Peak, 1993). Because of their standing, public agencies tend to be both politically responsive and subject to the prevailing political winds. Which means, say in the case of a local police department, that if a mayor, who is the boss of the chief, wants to focus on service delivery over crime prevention, the department will shift resources to do that: as not only does the chief's job depend on it, but the departmental budget as well. But should the mayor be gone after the next election, the police department may have to reconfigure its duties based on the demands of the new mayor and the local political culture.

Adult and Juvenile Courts

The courts as agencies act as a both a stopgap and a conduit to criminal justice processing. Persons brought before the courts or reviewed by courtroom actors, such as prosecutors and defense attorneys, may be sifted out of the process, say if the evidence is not strong enough, or their case may be scheduled on the court's calendar. The courts operate at a critical juncture in the loosely connected criminal justice system in that they both control the processing "value" to various correctional agencies and act as a check on police and correctional agencies. In the latter role, courtroom actors make judgments about police and correctional staff actions, including decisions regarding arrest, search and collection of evidence, use of force, and living conditions provided to inmates.

As of 1998 (the latest date for which we have statistics) there were 208 general and limited jurisdiction trial court systems in this country, including the District of Columbia and Puerto Rico (Bureau of Justice Statistics, 2004a). In the judicial and legal field at the federal, state, and local levels there were a total of 488,143 employees. Almost 55% of prosecutors, judges, defense attorneys, clerks, and other court staff were employed at the local level (Bauer & Owens, 2004). Another 33% of court employees work at the state level, and about 12% at the federal level. Adult level courts are operated by counties, states, and the federal government, whereas juvenile courts are usually operated at the county level. As organizations, adult and juvenile courts vary widely, as shown later, but there are some commonalities.

Organizational Structure, the Work Group and Clientele   Both adult criminal and juvenile courts have an organizational structure that is regarded as "looser" than that of the typical law enforcement or correctional agency. They do not have the cohesive, single, paramilitary structure that typifies law enforcement and correctional agencies. Rather, there are two to three organizations that when aligned make up the courts at a given level of government, whether that be city, county, state, or federal. The two main organizations are the court organization itself and the local prosecutor's office, which has actors who regularly participate in the court "organization." In larger cities and counties there is a third organization, the public defender's office, whose attorneys fulfill the constitutional right in court for those unable to pay. In smaller jurisdictions, where separate public defense organizations do not exist, defense attorneys will typically be appointed to work on contract. These three actors and their organizations separately, and together, constitute the judiciary in this country.

Courtroom Work Group   However, other organizations have regular participants who might be regarded as part of the "courtroom work group." Two of the most important of these ancillary groups are health and welfare workers, often social workers, who regularly attend to the needs of children before the juvenile court, and probation/ parole or community corrections officers, who may regularly provide input to both juvenile and adult courts.

Of course, each of these organizations—the court, the offices of the prosecutor and the defense attorney, probation or community corrections, and health and welfare organizations—is bureaucratically structured. But the actors come together to work on cases with only a semipowerful leader (the judge) and statutes, case law, and traditions to guide their practice as a "work group" (see Box 1.1). Unlike a police chief or a prison warden, a judge has no power to "fire" those who work "under" her in her courtroom (with the possible exception of community corrections officers in juvenile court). Nevertheless, a judge usually has the ability to sanction or to limit the practice of actors in her court. Moreover, almost all activities, except notably the plea agreement arrangements, are done in open court, are recorded, and are available for scrutiny by the public and other courtroom actors.

BOX 1.1

THE COURTROOM WORK GROUP

According to Clynch and Neubauer (1981), courtrooms might best be understood as informal work groups that are bound by common attributes and goals. The following circumstances tend to bind courtroom workers to each other: the actors in these work groups (e.g., judges, prosecutors, defense attorneys) work together on a continuing basis; they possess discretion to make important decisions; they are mutually interdependent; they have similar backgrounds and tastes; and they have psychological needs (like friendship and respect) that are met by other members of the group. The resulting work group, which ostensibly and formally should be adversarial, at least at the adult level, is instead concerned with completing the work, keeping to the work group norms for behavior, and engaging in informal arrangements (e.g., plea agreements) that are outside the official realm of the courtroom.

Clientele   Another similarity between adult and juvenile courts, and law enforcement and corrections for that matter, is that they tend to process those who have less education and money than the rest of the population. Leaving aside the middle-class and wealthy defendants who capture the media and American attention for months on end, most defendants who come before the courts are young, poor, male, and disproportionately members of a minority group with less educational achievement than is the norm for the general population (Bureau of Justice Statistics, 2004d). This is not to imply that women and whites do not come before the courts; the women do with increasing regularity. As whites still constitute well over half of the population in most of the country, there tend to be more of them than representatives of other groups in criminal and juvenile courts. Women, too, are entering the system at an increasing rate (e.g., see Lab, Williams, Holcomb, King, & Buerger, 2004). However, minority group members are disproportionately represented, as are males and the poor, as defendants in courts.

The Law, Levels   Adult courts, which at times have accommodated some juvenile defendants, have existed for a few thousand years or so. By comparison, the juvenile courts were created only a century ago. As the conception of childhood changed at the turn of the 20th century, social workers and other progressive reformers felt that children who misbehaved should be treated differently than adults and thus deserved a separate court, which would attend to their needs and act in their best interest (Empey & Stafford, 1991). This ideal, of course, was not always realized. Also some advocates for the creation of juvenile courts may have been more interested in controlling immigrant children than in any purer motives like helping such kids. But to summarize, one can still say that juvenile courts were created to serve a different purpose and population than adult criminal courts.

   In fact, for much of their history (until *In re Gault*, 1967 [387 U.S. 1] and other Supreme Court decisions changed their operation), the juvenile courts in this country operated without the traditional due process protections that are enumerated in the Bill of Rights. Juveniles, for instance, used to have no right to protection against unreasonable search and seizure (Fourth Amendment), no protection against self-incrimination (Fifth Amendment), and no right to counsel (Sixth Amendment). Today they possess these rights and more, though no right to a trial by a jury of their peers (i.e., other children) has been declared.

   Of course, until recently adults in state criminal courts did not necessarily have these rights either. Though some states provided them, the Bill of Rights (Amendments One through Ten) was "incorporated," or applied to state citizens in state courts, only incrementally, over a period of years.

   What this indicates is that the law as it is applied in criminal courts has changed over time and differs by type of court (juvenile or adult), type of client (juvenile or, adult), level of court (courts of limited jurisdiction, courts of general jurisdiction, intermediate appellate courts, and courts of last resort), and type of government (local, state, federal). Courtroom actors are guided by statutory law (the law on the books), case law (past judicial decisions), common law (that establishes precedents or stare decisis) and constitutions (state and federal level). Despite their separation, there is some overlap between state and federal courts in terms of the application of law, mostly because the federal appellate courts, with the U.S. Supreme Court resting at the pinnacle of these, serve as the final arbitrators on some legal questions. That said, the vast majority of criminal cases are decided in state and county level courts. Most appeals are settled in state courts. Should they be appealed to the Supreme Court, their chances of being accepted for review are small (the nine justices typically hear fewer than a hundred of the nine thousand cases that come before them every year) (Walsh & Hemmens, 2007). Therefore, criminal courts at the county and state level, as they are guided by state law, are THE most important organizational unit to consider in terms of management issues in criminal justice.

The levels of these state courts are illustrated in Table 1.1. There is a clear hierarchy to these levels, with the lower-level courts (i.e., courts of limited and general jurisdiction) deferring to the decisions made in the upper-level courts (i.e., the intermediate courts of appeal and the courts of last resort). Note that the names and jurisdictions of these courts are generally the same across the states, but there is some variety too (Smith, 1997). For instance, the names and responsibilities of courts of limited jurisdiction vary widely. Moreover, some states (e.g., Delaware, Maine, Rhode Island, South Dakota, Vermont, and Wyoming) have no intermediate appellate court; rather, their Supreme Court serves in the only appellate capacity. For example, the New York court of general jurisdiction (or general trial court) is called the Supreme Court. All states, however, have a court of general jurisdiction (the trial courts) in some form, and all have a version of a court of last resort (ultimate appeals court). For our purposes we will generally be concerned with the organization and operation of the courts of general jurisdiction, as they are the most involved on a day-to-day basis in criminal matters. These are the courts that loosely supervise plea agreements, and these are the courts where criminal trials are held.

Staffing   Judges in state and local courts are either elected (in partisan or nonpartisan elections), appointed (by governors or legislatures), or selected by committee and then appointed and later elected or retained (Meyer & Grant, 2003; Smith, 1997). Judges in federal courts are appointed with the advice and consent of the Senate in what has become an increasingly politicized process. Students of history note that

TABLE 1.1 State Court Levels

	Common Names	**Jurisdiction**
Courts of limited jurisdiction	County, city, municipal, probate, small claims police, justice of the peace, family, magistrate,	Minor crimes, traffic offenses, misdemeanors
Courts of general jurisdiction	Superior, District, Circuit, Courts of Common Pleas or Supreme Court	Trial courts for felony cases; provide initial processing for a range of criminal and civil cases
Intermediate appellate courts	Court of Appeals, Appellate Court	Hear appeals regarding possible mistakes made in trial courts
Courts of last resort	Supreme Court, Court of Appeals	Consider appeals from intermediate appellate courts or from courts of general jurisdiction

from *Marbury v. Madison* (1803) on, this process of appointment and approval of federal judges has had a political flavor; the feeding frenzy of today is a development of recent years. We will discuss the selection of judges and other court actors later in this text; suffice it to say here that no matter what method is utilized, it is hard to separate politics from a judicial position, whether it is in a local, state, or federal court. Having said this, we would also note that judges, whether selected/elected/appointed or retained, are not always concerned about politics in the operation of their courtroom or about the carrying out of their duties on a day-to-day basis. It is when very public or infamous cases come before a judge that politics might have the most influence.

Similarly, the selection of county and state district attorneys (DAs) and United States attorneys (top federal court prosecutors in their jurisdictions) is usually by election for county and state prosecutors and by political appointment for U.S. attorneys (Meyer & Grant, 2003). In some states the DAs, however, are appointed.

Public defenders are less political in that most are not elected, but rise in their organization through appointment and performance. In large counties public defenders represent about 70% of felons; the rest of defendants in these and smaller counties are represented by either private attorneys or assigned counsel (Meyer & Grant, 2003). In federal district courts less than a third of defendants are represented by a public defender; the rest are served by panel or private attorneys.

However, beneath the political top dogs in the courts—prosecutor's and public defender's/assigned counsel offices—are the bureaucrats who labor in the trenches, so to speak. Assistant DAs, law clerks and bailiffs, and public or assigned defense attorneys are the people who variously prosecute the crimes, or not, record the events in a courtroom, or ensure the security of the proceedings; as noted earlier, public defenders also defend those who cannot afford a private attorney. Currently these employees across the country number in the hundreds of thousands.

Location   The county- and city-level courts are located in the communities they serve. State-level appellate courts tend to be located in larger urban areas and/or in the state capital. Federal courts are also located in large urban areas that serve a region of the country.

Jails/Detention and Prisons/Juvenile Facilities: How They Differ

The fact that the general public, even the news media, does not make distinctions between prisons and jails as institutions is baffling. It is not unusual to hear a newscaster or even a print journalist, refer to the recipient of a prison sentence as being "sent to jail," or vice versa (e.g., see Conover, 2000). A teenager in a detention facility is inexplicably said to be "in prison." Though many readers may have a clear understanding of how adult and juvenile jails and prisons differ, others will not, so we shall note their differences and similarities. Additionally, we will discuss the nature of community corrections, also known as probation and parole, and explain how those organizations fit into the corrections picture.

Although there are some obvious similarities between adult prisons and jails and between juvenile detention and longer-term facilities, they are distinct in several ways that have a vast impact on their management. To simplify matters for this discussion, we will use "jails" to refer to both adult jails and juvenile detention centers and "prisons" to refer to adult prisons and juvenile versions of them (which are variously referred to as facilities, reformatories, ranches, or schools in other contexts). When one of the authors asks students at the beginning of an introduction to corrections class to list the differences between adult and juvenile prisons and jails, numerous items typically are mentioned. The most important are listed in the reminder of this section.

Conviction and Sentence Status   About half of jail inmates are unconvicted, whereas all prison inmates have been convicted in court and sentenced to a year or more (inmates with a sentence of less than twelve months often do their time in a jail). Notably, though, this breakdown between convicted and unconvicted inmates in jails varies widely from year to year (Harrison & Karberg, 2003).

Time Incarcerated   Most jail inmates are released within a week, although some await trial, or sentencing, for several months. The average prison sentence is for a year or more.

Local vs. State Operation   Most jails are operated at the county level, although there are a few city, state (combined with prisons), and federal jails. Most prisons are operated at the state level, although there is a burgeoning federal prison system (Harrison & Karberg, 2003).

Size of the Facility   Most jails are relatively small, holding fewer than 50 inmates, although there are jail systems in large urban areas that hold thousands of inmates: the City of New York and Los Angeles County alone held 34,100 jail inmates in 2002, which was 5% of the U.S. total. Most prisons hold 500 to 1,000 inmates or more, although some types of prisons (e.g., work releases) or juvenile facilities tend to hold fewer than a hundred inmates.

Security Level of the Facility   Most jails hold inmates, representing a mix of security levels, from those who serve their DUI sentence on the weekend to convicted murderers awaiting transfer to the state prison. Laws prevent sight and sound contact between adults and juveniles and males and females in jails. In cities of any size, there is often a separate jail facility for juveniles, but women rarely have a separate jail, though some large cities (e.g., Miami, Florida, Los Angeles County, California) do. Because of the mix of security levels represented, most jails tend to operate like maximum security prisons, but with work release and trustee opportunities for the less serious offenders.

Male prisons, on the other hand, are able to specialize in the classification of security levels by considering current offense, offense history, and behavior in prison. So in most states there are adult male versions of maximum, medium, and minimum security prisons and work releases. Most states have only one juvenile prison and one women's prison. Yet there are likely to be halfway houses and work releases that serve men and women who have been sentenced, or juveniles who are adjudicated offenders.

Age and Gender Separation   As mentioned, prisons also usually separate inmates by age (juvenile vs. adult) and gender (male vs. female), though this is not always done. Sometimes teenagers are processed through the adult system for serious crimes and then do their time in adult prisons, and some states maintain co-ed prisons. Jails also generally separate adults from children and men from women; usually these subgroups are held in the same building, but with provision for sight and sound separation. Also some critics (e.g., Belknap, 2001) note that when populations are combined in corrections, managers, both historically and currently, necessarily tend to focus resources and attention on the largest inmate grouping—adult males—at the expense of females and juveniles.

Location   Jails tend to be physically part of a community, usually conveniently located somewhere in the largest city in the county, whereas most prisons are located in more rural and less accessible parts of the state. The placement of jails in larger cities and towns is done to ensure close proximity to the largest police force in the county and to the county courthouse. Also, since the vast majority of inmates are in and out of jail within a week, it makes sense to have the facility closest to where they are most likely to live and work. The placement of prisons in rural areas, however, has usually been a political decision at the state level, which does not always coincide with the mission of those facilities or the original domicile of most of the inmates. In our home state of Idaho, for instance, the only women's prison per se, excepting work release facilities, is located outside the relatively remote town of Pocatello, in southeastern Idaho, which is a four-hour drive from the largest population center, in Boise. This prison was built less than ten years ago, and if state policymakers had been concerned about its reintegrative function, they would have sited it outside Boise, along with the four male prisons (one public maximum, two medium one public and one private and one public minimum security) located there; instead, political considerations determined its placement. Other states (e.g., Washington and New Mexico) also have chosen to locate their one women's prison away from the population centers. Politics affects the location decision when a community wants the facility because of the jobs it will bring and it officials have enough support at the legislative and gubernatorial levels to get what they want, despite what might best fit the mission of the prison or the circumstances of its inmates.

Jails and Prisons: How They Are Alike?   Despite all these fairly serious differences between prisons and jails, they are also quite similar. For this reason, the errant newscaster who uses "prison" and "jail" interchangeably might be forgiven, a little.

1. **Justifications for Sanctioning or Reasons for Being** Both prisons and jails exist to punish (retribution), incapacitate, deter, rehabilitate, and reintegrate (see Box 1.2). The degree to which they emphasize any one of these depends on a number of factors, including the age of an inmate (juvenile or adult), the status of the inmate (i.e., convicted/sentenced or not), the type of crime the inmate has been accused or convicted of, the type of facility, the length of incarceration, the politics of the day, the availability of resources, and the proximity to rehabilitation programming in communities. Both prisons and jails have complex and multilayered missions that center on the justifications listed.

2. **Locus in the Criminal Justice System** Both prisons and jails are key facilities in the criminal justice system, albeit sometimes at different ends of the spectrum. Both law enforcement and the courts act to provide inputs in the form of inmates into them

BOX 1.2

DEFINITIONS OF POLICE, COURT, AND CORRECTIONAL
JUSTIFICATIONS FOR SANCTIONING

The following justifications, or reasons for the existence of criminal sanctioning, are often cited.

- **Retribution (punishment):** People are in the criminal justice system, either
  in institutions or in the community, either to atone for their crime (retribution: balance the scales of justice) or because of the belief that they should
  suffer (punishment) for the crime they committed.
- **Incapacitation:** People are in the criminal justice system, either in institutions or in the community, because their engagement in criminal behavior
  must be stopped. To ensure that this happens, they must either be watched
  (community supervision) or placed in a prison or jail.
- **Deterrence:** People are in the criminal justice system, either in institutions
  or in the community, because that is deemed the best way to dissuade them,
  and others, from engaging in current or future criminal behavior.
- **Rehabilitation:** People are in the criminal justice system, either in institutions or in the community, because that experience and/or the engagement
  in programming and other activities are likely to lead them to rethink and
  desist from further criminal activity or behavior that is related to their criminal activity (e.g., excessive drinking). A related concept that is intertwined
  with rehabilitation is habilitation, the engagement of a person in self-change,
  rather than the imposition of change.
- **Reintegration:** People are in the criminal justice system, either in institutions or in the community, because that is a means of maintaining pro-social
  ties to, the community, or gradually reintroducing them to it.

either directly in the case of jails and the police and courts, or prisons and courts, or
indirectly in the case of prisons and the police. Both law enforcement and the courts
use the incapacitative function of prisons and jails. Judges also use both of them as
appropriate institutions to address the retributive, deterrent, rehabilitative and reintegrative functions of the system, though for different types of inmates/offenders.

3. **Organizational Structure** Typically, jails and prisons are structurally bureaucratic, with paramilitary regimentation, regalia and accoutrements (more about
these later), and top-down communication. In these ways jails and prisons are also
similar to most police and sheriff's departments.

4. **Inmate Characteristics** The inmates incarcerated in jails tend to be young,
uneducated, poor, and disproportionately members of minority groups with alcohol

or substance abuse problems (Harlow, 1998; Harrison & Beck, 2003; Harrison & Karberg, 2003). Though not as young, the inmates in prisons are, on average, younger than 35; and they are uneducated, poor, and disproportionately minority group members with alcohol or substance abuse problems (Harrison & Beck, 2003; Harrison & Karberg, 2003). In both groups there are likely to be more members than the general population who have suffered from child abuse in all its forms, and there is likely to be a significant subgroup that are mentally disturbed (Harlow, 1998; Harrison & Karberg, 2003) in both types of institutions, but particularly in jails. Nearly half the women inmates in prisons and jails report past physical or sexual abuse (Harlow, 1998; Harrison & Karberg, 2003).

5. **Staff Characteristics**   A significant number of the staff in prisons and jails have a military background, and both types of facilities tend to have a predominantly white male staff (Bureau of Justice Statistics, 2004a). The number of former military personnel may be explained by the attraction to the public sector work and the paramilitary structure of jails and prisons. The relative lack of diversity in some facilities is tied to patterns of discrimination and cultural trends. But since passage of the Civil Rights Act of 1964, which prohibited discrimination in hiring based on race and ethnicity, its amendment in 1972, and civil suits by minorities and white women over the course of thirty years, some real inroads have been made in the hiring of a more diverse staff (Bureau of Justice Statistics, 2004a). Jails and prisons still tend to be staffed predominantly by white males, but this is much less true than even twenty years ago, particularly in urban areas. For instance, in one Florida women's jail visited by one of the authors in 1992 there was a white male administrator, but the second in command was an African American woman, and the majority of the staff were minority group members. In the 21st century, women and minority group men serve in all capacities of men's and women's jails and prisons, from warden or director on down, but they are still underrepresented based on their proportion of the larger population (Bureau of Justice Statistics, 2004a, 2004c).

6. **Public Institutions**   Most prisons and jails (93%) are still operated by the public sector, which means that they must adhere to civil service protections of their states and communities and other laws that regulate public sector institutions (Harrison & Karberg, 2003). They are in some ways more politically responsive and vulnerable as public institutions, and staff members have a service orientation that is likely to differ from that found in the private sector (more about this in the following).

Community Corrections or Probation and Parole: How They Are Different and Similar

The term "community corrections" is often used to refer to a more modern form of probation and parole. Both jails and prisons are tied to the respective adult or juvenile probation and/or parole system in their state or county. Probation sentences are often served before or after, or instead of, a jail or prison sentence. A failed term on probation often precedes a prison sentence. States that still possess parole as a form of release option parole most inmates, and some jails also "parole" inmates (Harrison & Karberg, 2003).

Time Sequencing   A simplistic and overgeneralized difference between adult and juvenile probation and adult and juvenile parole is that probation tends to precede prison and parole tends to follow it. The courts, instead of using incarceration, place people on probation. People on parole are released from prison by a parole board or by a mandatory conditional release after serving their time in prison. In both cases, probationers and parolees are subject to being returned to either prison or jail if they commit rule violations (are "violated") or other offenses.

Types of Offenders   Another related difference, given the time sequencing of proba- tion and parole, is that those on probation tend to be less serious offenders than those who have gone to prison and been paroled. Among adult offenders on probation at the end of 2002, only half had been convicted of a felony, 49% of a misdemeanor, and another 1% of other offenses (Bureau of Justice Statistics, 2004d). In contrast, of those on parole, 96% originally had a sentence of year or more to prison. Probation rolls also tended to include more whites and women than those for parole. By the end of 2002, "Women made up about 23% of the nation's probationers and 14% of the parolees. Approximately 55% of the adults on probation were White, and 31% were Black, and 12% were Hispanic. Thirty-nine percent of parolees were White, 42% Black, and 18% were Hispanic" (Bureau of Justice Statistics, 2004d:1).

Rules   But the similarities between probation and parole are greater than their dif- ferences. If probationers and parolees fail to adhere to certain sorts of rules, their probation or parole status will be "violated" and they may be sent to incarceration, or returned there. Moreover, the rules are usually similar (e.g., prohibition against the use of alcohol or drugs; requirements to avoid criminally engaged friends/family, to participate in programming, to get and keep employment, etc.).

Similar Characteristics of Staff and Organizational Structure   The community cor- rections officers who supervise probationers and parolees have similar backgrounds and training, and in small offices, they may have clients of both types on their caseloads. Probation and parole organizations are usually very similar to police and sheriff's departments and prisons and jails in that they tend to have a traditional management and bureaucratic composition. They differ in that they tend to focus more on the value of programming for their clients than is true of correctional institutions.

Juvenile probation and parole differ slightly from the adult versions in that the for- mer officers tend to be supervised by the juvenile court. Which means that they may have a more ingrained history of attending to the "best interests" of juveniles than the adult community corrections system does for men and women under its supervision.

CONCLUSIONS: THE UNIQUE MANAGEMENT MILIEU OF CRIMINAL JUSTICE AGENCIES

Let us begin with the ending. Bureaucrats get a bum rap. Virtually every successful presidential candidate form Richard Nixon, through George W. Bush has run against big government or the Beltway (area around Washington D.C.) or, in essence, bureau-crats who are apparently messing everything up in America. Yet the bureaucrats in the criminal justice system—those police, probation and parole, and corrections officers; those judges, prosecutors, and defense attorneys—perform work that is of inestimable value to this country. Absent their efforts, the average citizen would not see justice done in this country, not at all.

And that is what this book is about. How justice is done in this country.

Because justice is "done" in large part by people in organizations. Therefore, we will study what those organizations are, who works in them, and how they are led and operated. It is our hope that when the book cover closes after that last page, the reader has a more informed, and perhaps profound, sense of the mechanics of how criminal justice is, and should be, managed.

DISCUSSION QUESTIONS

1. How are court organizations substantially different from police and corrections organizations? How might this difference affect the behavior of the actors within these organizational settings?
2. Why is policing mostly a local affair, and how is that affected by organizational and community factors? Explain your answer.
3. How is policing similar at the city, county, and state levels? Provide examples.
4. Why are courts more like informal work groups than like bureaucracies? Explain your answer.
5. How do jails and prisons differ from each other, and in what ways are they similar? Give an example.
6. What are the greatest differences between probation and parole? Give some examples.
7. What are the common characteristics of the clients in all criminal justice agencies? How might these commonalities affect their treatment by criminal justice actors?

WEB LINK

Bureau of Justice Statistics website: http://www.ojp.usdoj.gov/bjs/

REFERENCES

Barker, T., Hunter R. D., & Rush, J. P. (1994). *Police systems and practices*. Englewood Cliffs, NJ: Prentice-Hall.

Bauer, L., & Owens, S. D. (2004). *Justice expenditure and employment in the United States, 2001*. Bureau of Justice Statistics Bulletin, Office of Justice Programs, U.S. Department of Justice. Washington DC: GPO.

Belknap, J. (2001). *The invisible woman: Gender, crime and justice*, (2nd ed.). Belmont, CA: Wadsworth.

Bureau of Justice Statistics. (2004a). *Sourcebook of criminal justice statistics—2002*. Bureau of Justice Statistics, U.S. Department of Justice. Washington, DC: GPO.

Bureau of Justice Statistics. (2004b). *Law enforcement statistics*. Bureau of Justice Statistics, U.S. Department of Justice, Office of Justice Programs. www.ojp.usdoj.gov/bjs/.

Bureau of Justice Statistics. (2004c). *Expenditure and employment statistics*. Bureau of Justice Statistics, U.S. Department of Justice, Office of Justice Programs. www.ojp.usdoj.gov/bjs/eande.

Bureau of Justice Statistics. (2004d). *Probation and parole statistics*. Bureau of Justice Statistics, Office of Justice Programs, U.S. Department of Justice. www.ojp.usdoj.gov/bjs/panp.

Clynch, E. J., & Neubauer, D. W. (1981). Trial courts as organizations: A critique and synthesis. *Law and Police Quarterly, 3(1)*, 69–94.

Conover, T. (2000). *New Jack: Guarding Sing Sing*. New York: Random House.

Empey, L. T., & Stafford, M. C. (1991). *American delinquency: Its meaning and construction* (3rd ed.). Belmont, CA: Wadsworth.

Goldstein, H. (1977). *Policing a free society*. Cambridge, MA: Ballinger.

Harlow, C. W. (1998). *Profile of jail inmates*. U.S. Department of Justice. Washington DC: GPO.

Harrison, P. M., & Beck, A. J. (2003). *Prisoners in 2002*. Bureau of Justice Statistics, U.S. Department of Justice. Washington DC: GPO.

Harrison, P. M., & Karberg, J. C. (2003). *Prison and jail inmates at midyear 2002*. Bureau of Justice Statistics Bulletin, U.S. Department of Justice. Washington DC: GPO.

Hickman, M. J., & Reaves, B. A. (2003). *Local police departments 2000*. Bureau of Justice Statistics, Office of Justice Programs, U.S. Department of Justice. Washington, DC: GPO.

Kelling, G. L. (1999). *"Broken windows" and police discretion*. National Institute of Justice, Office of Justice Programs, U.S. Department of Justice. Washington, DC: GPO.

Lab, S. P., Williams, M., Holcomb, J. E., King, W. R., & Buerger, M. E. (2004). *Explaining criminal justice*. Los Angeles: Roxbury.

Langworthy, R. H., & Travis, L. F. (1994). *Policing in America: A balance of forces*. New York: Macmillan.

Meyer, J. F., & Grant, D. R. (2003). *The courts in our criminal justice system*. Upper Saddle River, NJ: Prentice Hall.

Peak, K. (1993). *Policing America: Methods, issues, challenges*. Englewood Cliffs, NJ: Regents/Prentice-Hall.

Radelet, L. A., & Carter, D. L. (1994). *The police and the community*, (5th ed.). New York: Macmillan College Publishing.

Roberg, R., Crank, J., & Kuykendall, J. (2000). *Police and society*, (2nd ed.). Los Angeles: Roxbury.

Smith, C. E. (1997). *Courts, politics, and the judicial process*, (2nd ed.). Chicago: Nelson-Hall.

Walsh, A., & Hemmens, C. (2007). *Law, justice and society: A sociolegal approach*. Los Angeles: Roxbury.

Wilson, J. Q. (1968). *Varieties of police behavior: The management of law and order in eight communities*. Cambridge, MA: Harvard University Press.

CASES CITED

In re Gault, 387 U.S. 1 (1967).
Marbury v. Madison, 5 U.S. 137 (1803).

CHAPTER 2

SURVEYING THE LANDSCAPE OF CRIMINAL JUSTICE MANAGEMENT

INTRODUCTION: THE TIES THAT BIND

The criminal justice landscape at times appears vast, as far as the eye can see. In virtually every community, there is public policing, courts of one kind or another, a jail, and increasingly more likely, a prison or two. Among these disparate agencies with their unique and distinguishing characteristics, there are shared common features as organizations operating—for the most part—in the public sector.

In the last chapter the focus was on the differences between and among criminal justice agencies. In this chapter we set down the markers on these common landscape features as they relate to terms and concepts, open and closed organizations, competing values of government operation, and government service. In the course of this survey of criminal justice organizations we may find that what binds organizations and their actors is more than just their mission to formally enforce and uphold the law—it is also the nature of these organizations that makes them similar.

COMMON TERMS DEFINED

Organization, Justice, Bureaucracy, Management, and Formal and Informal Goals and Organizations

As we explore the distinctive nature of criminal justice organizations and the characteristics of their staff and clients, there are several terms and concepts that bear definition, since they will be used with some frequency throughout this text. So that there is a common understanding of language, we define a few of these terms up front.

As long as there have been organizations, or groupings of humans for a reason, there has been management. An **organization** is *a grouping of individuals with a binding purpose.* Gulick (1937:79) first defined the theory of organization as having "[t]o do with the structure of co-ordination imposed upon the work-division units of an enterprise." For Gulick the division of work is the primary reason that an organization exists. He argues that we divide work in organizations because people have different skills and abilities and that those attributes can be fitted to the type of work in an organization. He believes that this work in any organization must be coordinated through some sort of authority and through an understood purpose or reason for the work. Finally, he notes that organizations will develop patterns of operation whereby authority is viewed as coming either from the top down or from the bottom up.

Earlier, however, Selznick (1948:125) had argued, that an organizational system may have either an economic or an "adaptive social structure," both of which have "reciprocal consequences." In other words, an organizational system may exist for both economic and social purposes, as "work" (as Gulick put it) is done in that sense. In combining these perspectives, therefore, an organization could be defined as a grouping of people arranged and coordinated to accomplish some purpose.

Types of organizations might include a family, church, school, private business, country club or political party. As mentioned, criminal justice agencies include such organizations as departments of corrections, police or sheriff's departments, state police departments, the courts (both adult and juvenile), community corrections agencies, and jails and prisons. Organizations of all these types might operate with different structures and boundaries, but they are similar in that each has a focus or goal(s), such as the administration of justice, that drives its activities and justifies its existence. Briefly, justice is defined by the American Heritage Dictionary (1992:456) as "1. [t]he quality of being fair; fairness. 2. The principle of moral rightness; equity. 3. The upholding of what is just, especially fair treatment and due reward in accordance with honor, standards, or law." Distinctions between formal and natural justice (law and morality) and how justice is precisely and fully defined are matters best left to the philosophers. However, in this text **justice** means that those who are guilty are caught, processed, and sanctioned, as befits community, professional, and moral standards, by system actors. We think that justice, for our purposes, exists when those who are innocent are given ample opportunity, and the due process necessary, to ensure they are not caught up in, and sanctioned by, the system. In terms of internal organizational operations, justice might also be a characteristic of a system in which employees are treated fairly and honestly by management and given the opportunity to develop and "give back" to their community. Effective or good decision making (we discuss decision making in Chapter 12) in criminal justice agencies, then, and in our view, has to do with furthering the ends of justice for those processed by, and those who participate in (i.e., criminal justice actors), the system.

Some theorists on organizations (e.g., Blau & Scott, 1962) argue that families are just groupings and are differentially distinct from social organizations such as police or correctional agencies or the courts. They define a formal organization as "[f]ormally established for the explicit purpose of achieving certain goals..." (Blau & Scott, 1962:208).

Families, for instance, usually exist to provide companionship, love, and protection for their members and/or a safe harbor to raise children. The structure of a familial organization (we will discuss structure a bit more later) has historically been hierarchical, with an adult male head and all others subordinate. Nowadays in western cultures there is more fluidity of power, with female co-leaders and children still somewhat under their parents' control, though having certain rights of their own. Although the "traditional" family boundary could include just two parents and children related by blood, in truth families have always been much larger and more complex than that;

they have often encompassed stepparents and stepsiblings, grandparents, aunts, uncles, and cousins. They also need not just be restricted to blood or marriage relations. Where the family boundary ends and the tribe boundary begins has been determined somewhat arbitrarily among human groupings and is not always a clearly defined line.

A prison or a jail, on the other hand, exists for the multiple and, Blau and Scott (1962) would argue, formal purposes of incapacitation, deterrence, retribution, rehabilitation, and reintegration. Police and sheriff's departments were created formally to serve and protect, but also to investigate and prevent crime. Courts also act in a formal sense, to enforce the law, like the police, but also to deliberate, adjudicate, and sentence (for the purposes of incapacitation, deterrence, retribution, rehabilitation, or reintegration). The order of these justifications for existence for all agencies varies by type of institution and policy. For instance, a jail with a shorter-term population may be more likely to focus on reintegration than a prison. By the same token, the influence of political trends that favor lengthier sentences and less rehabilitation is evident, since they have shaped the operation of courts and corrections for the last two and a half decades. Both police and corrections agencies tend to have a "traditional" organizational structure with hierarchy, specialization, and rule of law (all three attributes of a bureaucracy), top-down communication and military accoutrements. Their organizational boundaries are set by who is employed by the institution and by who the clientele are.

Briefly, the term **bureaucracy** refers to how organizations are structured, ruled, or socially organized. According to German sociologist and political economist Max Weber, there are six main characteristics of a bureaucracy. These characteristics are presented in Box 2.1; for more about Weber himself, see later (Box 4.1).

Management of organizations may refer to one or more persons who have formal control over an organization, or, the act or process of operating the organization. Management for our purposes will refer to both. Carlisle (1976) defined management as a process of arranging and organizing elements to achieve organizational objectives. In accordance with this definition, management does not have a set beginning or an end; rather, it is something that continues as long as the organization does. The term "management" as it is used in this text will encapsulate the more modern view that there are multiple sources of power and influence in an organization, and these are not all located at the top of the organizational chart (Micklethwait & Wooldridge, 1996). In other words, in reality management is done by all levels of the organization. Management is also goal oriented, with a focus on achieving both the formal and informal goals of the organization.

The formal goals of the formal organization are easier to discern than the informal goals of the informal organization (Blau & Scott, 1962). This is true because the **formal goals** are those that are written down and reflected in the organization's mission statement, in the organizational chart, in the policy manual, and in training curricula. Formal goals are professed by the directors, court administrators, sheriffs, police chiefs, wardens of prisons, administrators of jails, and community corrections personnel and are reinforced in job announcements, selection procedures, and performance appraisals by supervisors. The formal goals, then, are concrete and often exist officially for the formal organization and for public consumption.

BOX 2.1

WEBER'S CHARACTERISTICS OF BUREAUCRACY IN HIS OWN WORDS

I. There is the principle of fixed and official jurisdiction areas, which are generally ordered by rules, that is, by laws or administrative regulations.

II. The principles of office hierarchy and of levels of graded authority mean a firmly ordered system of super- and subordination in which there is a supervision of the lower offices by the higher ones.

III. The management of the modern office is based upon written documents ('the files'), which are preserved in their original or draught [draft] form.

IV. Office management, at least all specialized office management—and such management is distinctly modern—usually presupposes thorough and expert training.

V. When the office is fully developed, official activity demands the full working capacity of the official, irrespective of the fact that his [or her] obligatory time in the bureau may be firmly delimited.

VI. The management of the office follows general rules, which are more or less stable, more or less exhaustive, and which can be learned.

Source: Weber, Max. (1946). Bureaucracy. In H. H. Gerth & C. Wright Mills, Eds. From Max Weber: Essays in Sociology, pp 196–198. Oxford, U.K.: Oxford University Press.

It should be noted at this juncture, however, that though these goals are formally acknowledged by the organization, they are not always achievable. This is because they often conflict (e.g., for an organization tasked to simultaneously achieve both retribution and rehabilitation), there are too many of them (see, e.g., any policy manual for a large organization), and they do not always fit the informal goals or norms of behavior of organizational members.

Criminal justice employees may strive mightily to achieve these formal goals, but the fact that they are dealing with human beings and subgroupings with alternate informal goals in an informal organization hampers their progress. This occurs for several reasons. All situations cannot be covered by one general rule; instead discretion must be exercised. Humans are also motivated by more than just organizational directives or rewards. So, for instance, they may value more time off (an informal goal of the employee) as opposed to finishing a report on time (a formal goal of the employer). In another example, the police organization itself may informally "tell" the officer, without having to state it explicitly, to ignore certain minor law breaking that clearly violates formal organizational rules, so that the appearance of peace and order in the community might be maintained. Blau and Scott (1962:208) explain well the reasons for the **informal organization**:

> In every formal organization there arise informal organizations. The constituent groups of the organization, like all groups, develop their own practices, values, norms, and social relations as their members live and work together. The roots of these informal systems are embedded in the formal organization itself and nurtured by the very formality of its arrangements. Official rules must be general to have sufficient scope to cover the multitude of situations that may arise. But the application of these general rules to particular cases often poses problems of judgment, and informal practices tend to emerge that provide solutions for these problems. Decisions not anticipated by official regulations must frequently be made, particularly in times of change, and here again unofficial practices are likely to furnish guides for decisions... Moreover, unofficial norms are apt to develop that regulate performance and productivity. Finally, complex networks of social relations and informal status structures emerge, within groups and between them, which are influenced by many factors besides the organizational chart.

In other words, the formal organization, with its stated formal goals, does not completely describe what really happens in, and drives, the organization or its membership. This formal vs. informal juxtaposition in organizations will come up many times throughout this text because we must bear in mind that at all times there is an informal organization operating in tandem in criminal justice agencies, along with the formal one. If we pretend that the organization wholly operates along formal lines, we risk impairing our ability to understand the management of such organizations.

Street-Level Bureaucrats and Discretion

One part of this informal organization that has often been ignored by management scholars is the importance of the line worker in determining how or whether policy is carried out. In his groundbreaking book *Street-Level Bureaucracy: Dilemmas of the Individual in Public Services,* Lipsky (1980) defines a street-level bureaucrat as someone who is a public service worker with much *discretion* to do their job. Key aspects of the street-level bureaucrat's job is that there are too many clients and not enough resources. Such SLBs (we tell students they are training to be SLBs not SOBs!) might include police officers, teachers, public defenders or prosecutors, welfare or employment workers, juvenile or adult probation or parole officers, and jail or prison counselors or officers. SLBs have discretion to make choices about arresting offenders, helping students, defending or prosecuting cases, awarding benefits, recommending for release or parole, or identifying this or that inmate. We define (with the help of Lipsky, 1980) this **discretion** as the ability to make one or more choices and to act, or not act, thereon. The discretion possessed by SLBs allows them, according to Lipsky (1980), not only to carry out policy but to make it. The demands placed on SLBs, such as too many clients and not enough resources, mandate that they make choices about the use of their time and their efforts.

Thus, the existence of SLBs and what motivates them further substantiates the existence of the informal organization at play in the operation of public sector entities like police, courts, and corrections. For example, when one of the authors worked as a counselor in a prison in Washington State, the state wanted her and the other counselors to review inmate files and supply the department of corrections with select information about their clients for dissemination to policymakers. When told that they had to do this by their supervisors and faced with choosing this task or getting their other work done, the counselors chose informally to ignore the departmental directive. In effect, by ignoring a formal directive and thus failing to implement a policy, they as SLBs were making policy.

Ethics

The ethics of a choice that comprises an act of de facto policy making is another matter. In this instance the counselors valued their need to complete tasks more highly than the need of the larger organization to respond to designated policymakers. **Ethics** is often defined as the study of, or the act of, doing the right thing in the professional sphere (Braswell, 1998). Doing the right thing in the private sphere is understood to be morality. Along the same lines, **organizational integrity,** a characteristic of an organization whose actors as a whole are honest, ethical, and can be trusted by their members and the community, is also a sign of ethical operation. Chapter 3 is devoted to a discussion of ethics in criminal justice organizations. Suffice it to say here that a code of ethics can be a set of central guiding principles for the management of criminal justice agencies. It should also be understood that ethical decision making is entangled in the operation of both the formal and informal sides of the organization.

NO ORGANIZATION IS AN ISLAND: OPEN AND CLOSED ORGANIZATIONS

In this definitional section of the chapter, we discuss the nature of closed vs. open organizations. A **closed organization** is not affected by its environment and an **open organization** is. Some scholars have noted a debate over the closed or open nature of various organizations (e.g. see Stojkovic, Kalinich, & Klofas, 1998), but in truth, and depending on the organization, the degree to which an organization is open or closed is relative. If any public sector organization ever fit the designation of closed, then jails, but particularly prisons, did and to some degree still do. In his classic work *Stateville,* Jacobs (1977), investigates fifty years of the history of the Stateville maximum security prison in Illinois. As he describes the institution in the early 1900s, staff were forced to sleep at the facility, outside community contact with inmates was restricted, and media involvement was limited to formal occasions when events and what outsiders saw of the inmates and the organization could be carefully orchestrated by the warden.

This type of prison was a *total institution* in that all activities such as eating, sleeping, and working were strictly controlled and occurred under the figurative roof of the institution (Goffman, 1961). The formal face of the Stateville organization was of an ordered and frugal institution, while the informal operation included abuses of inmates and staff. But the informal operation was allowed to continue because Stateville was so close to the larger communities that surrounded it. Or was it? Jacobs (1977) notes that the strict control over the organization eroded over the years because the outside environment in terms of laws, politics, personnel, and types of inmates—to name a few factors—intruded and led to a recognition by the 1970s of the need to evolve in management and practice.

Most people who study criminal justice agencies today recognize their dual nature, both open and closed. Because of their organizational goals, especially incapacitation, correctional managers have a legitimate interest in restricting some access to inmates and facilities. They cannot throw a facility open on a regular basis without impairing their ability to keep inmates in and to provide for a disruption-free workplace and living spaces. They can, and must, however, allow for visits, albeit often with restrictions, by appropriate friends and family, attorneys, and sometimes the media. Staff are allowed to return home after work if they choose (though some few prisons still have staff quarters), but in any event the institution's employees often bring their own beliefs and values to work. Inmates come from diverse backgrounds, and they too have some limited rights that the management must legally respect.

Police and sheriff's departments, courts, jails, and community corrections have always been more "open" than prisons for several reasons. For example, these facilities are physically located in communities, and their clients and staff move fluidly in and out of the organizations, with the staff having at least a partial mission of serving the public or the public good. The media and other community members are much more aware of, and likely to comment on, their operation. Having said this, it is clear that staff attitudes toward clients/offenders, commonly used jargon, expertise, and legal prohibitions that prevent the full sharing of information make those nonprison facilities "closed" as well. Take for instance the closed nature of some organizational police structures, such as the line-officer/squad system, which has a tendency to isolate officers from the general community while fostering a close-knit subculture within that system (Crank, 1998).

Another instance of the legal prohibitions that prevent the full sharing of information between criminal justice organizations and outside organizations, researchers, or the community happened when one of the authors, while working for a state department of health and welfare on a multiagency research project, was denied access to a state patrol's arrest data. Although there may have been interagency cooperation in this case, a state statute barred the sharing and use of such information by any nonpolice agency or personnel. The physical doors were open, but the electronic information or intellectual doors were closed.

There are several factors that are widely acknowledged to influence criminal justice operation. These influences, though, are relative. To some degree corrections, even the notorious Stateville prison have always been open. For instance, the inmates, staff, and the warden of that prison invariably imported their own values and beliefs, which undoubtedly had no small effect on the operation of the facility. Moreover, one wing of the Stateville prison was not completed on time because the state's policymakers had not come up with the funding. From the beginning, then, even a prison as closed as Stateville was subjected to outside influences such as the imported values and culture of its inmates and staff and the politics of budgeting of its state. Because of changes in law and culture over the last forty years, however, the relative openness of all criminal justice institutions and agencies, even prisons, has only increased in regard to both physical and intellectual access. Common factors that influence criminal justice operation, and its relative open-to-closed nature, are included in the following:

staff: their personal demographics, beliefs and values, and background.

clients/offenders/inmates: their personal demographics, beliefs and values, background, and history.

type of agency or institution mission: as that continues to be shaped and viewed by policymakers, managers, staff, and citizens.

community and/or state or federal political culture: as that determines practices, use of, sentences meted out, and resources given to, the organization.

economic status of the community or state: as this determines staff hired, numbers of cases processed, what facilities can be built, how they are maintained, pay and training for staff and programs for offenders/inmates, and programming available in the facilities and the community.

law: as that directs policing, court consideration of evidence and sentencing, supervision of clients/inmates, access to courts, and treatment of, and for, clients, offenders, and inmates.

technology: as that shapes investigations and detection of crime, behavior and accountability of staff, options for sentencing, and supervisory capacity of staff.

weather: as that determines when crime waxes and wanes, how agencies can respond to community crises, how correctional facilities are built and operated, and how offenders are supervised in the community.

politics: the processes involved in decision making within various organizations, whether they are private or public, formal or informal.

In short because of the inherent connectivity between criminal justice agencies and their external environments, they are indeed reflections of them. To paraphrase the poet John Donne (1623), substituting the word "organization" for the word "man" in his famous Meditation 17 "[n]o organization is an island, entire of itself. Every organization is a piece of the continent, a part of the main. If a clod be washed away by the sea, Europe is the less...any man's death diminishes me, therefore, never send to know for whom the bell tolls, it tolls for thee." Simply put, criminal justice organizations are what their communities make them and must be understood in that context, part of which can be understood by defining the competing public service values of democratic accountability and neutral competence.

DEMOCRATIC ACCOUNTABILITY AND NEUTRAL COMPETENCE: THE VALUE-ADDED DIFFERENCE IN GOVERNMENTAL OPERATION

Management theories in criminal justice (which are the focus in Chapter 4) are best understood by means of contextualizing them in a discussion of the competing values of democratic accountability and neutral competence. An understanding of these two values is necessary because they have influenced the development and conceptualization of the current operation and management of justice-centered agencies.

Democratic Accountability

Democratic Accountability is the value in government that the public sector, or the managers and workers in government, are accountable to those who have been democratically elected and/or politically appointed. Which means that those who serve in government must be responsive, via elected or politically appointed persons, to the people. One of the authors often asks students whether they believe this is a value that should be predominate for government service. Inevitably, most or all of them raise their hands in affirmation of this value. After all, as Americans we often proclaim the merits of democracy. How could we not vote in support of democratic accountability?

Under the absolute version of this value's application, all workers in corrections, from the warden or director or sheriff on down, would be either politically elected (as sheriffs already are, but their underlings are not) or appointed. Before the Civil Service Reform Act of 1883, also known as the Pendleton Act, all federal, state, and local public employees were likely to be beholding to a politically elected or appointed person for their job. Which meant that in some counties, when a new sheriff was elected, the whole department turned over, from the lowliest janitor on up (Haller, 1983; Walker, 1983). Wardens and heads of juvenile facilities could hire and fire employees at will, without considering either qualifications or job performance (Jacobs, 1977). Probation and parole officers also served at the whim of their politically appointed department heads. Essentially, all jobs in jails, prisons, courts, and police forces were political appointments; the qualifications and knowledge of employees, or whether they had worked hard in the public's interest, was of less significance. Instead, in public service, it really mattered "who you knew," not "what you knew."

The purest form of the value of democratic accountability occurred in 19th-century America and led to notable corruption and abuse at all levels of government (Van Riper, 1987). Government employees tried to please political actors and those who supported them, rather than working for the public good. Therefore, government contracts were awarded based on political alliances and contacts; government workers were hired and fired based on political allegiances; and public resources were exploited for private ends. Because of the high value placed on democratic accountability at this time, those who won elections (the victors), collected and awarded the patronage jobs and contracts (the spoils) to their political friends. In fact, President James A. Garfield was assassinated in 1881 by a disaffected campaign supporter who had not received the patronage job he had expected (Morrow, 1987). This assassination lent support to those arguing for the passage of the Pendleton Act a few years later (see Box 2.2).

It is no wonder that in 1887, Princeton professor Woodrow Wilson was arguing for a separation of politics and administration. In that same article the future president made the case for expanding the civil service reforms begun at the federal level with the Pendleton Act to all levels of government as a moral duty; he argued that

BOX 2.2

THE PENDLETON ACT AND THE BEGINNING OF CIVIL SERVICE REFORM IN THE STATES

The Pendleton Act of 1883 was passed in reaction to the assassination of President Garfield by a disaffected campaign supporter who did not get the patronage job he had expected (Morrow, 1987). It was also passed in reaction to the general corruption in government that became apparent after fifty years (since President Andrew Jackson's administration beginning in 1829) of over-politicizing the administration or management of government services (U.S. National Archives & Records Administration, 2005).

The act created an agency called the Civil Service Commission, which separated classified and unclassified jobs at the federal level. Those classified job applicants were to be selected based on merit. In essence, the act established a form of civil service protection for jobs (people could not be fired at will) and required that people be hired based on their qualifications or skills and abilities for the job. Initially this act applied to only 10% of low-level federal jobs (Cayer, 1987). Eventually, its application was expanded to virtually all federal jobs, and all states passed some form of the act. The act was championed by President Chester Arthur, who succeeded Garfield. President Grover Cleveland issued an executive order in 1886 that prohibited political activities by federal civil service employees, an order that was later expanded by President Theodore Roosevelt.

Figure 2.1 This image of Woodrow Wilson courtesy of the Library of Congress, LC-USZ62–13028, Library of Congress Prints and Photographs Division Washington, D.C. 20540.

government work should be more neutral and removed from politics and that it should be more "businesslike":

> [W]e must regard civil-service reform in its present stages as but a prelude to a fuller administrative reform. We are now rectifying methods of appointment; we must go on to adjust executive functions more fitly and to prescribe better action. Civil-service reform is thus but a moral preparation for what is to follow. It is clearing the moral atmosphere of official life by establishing the sanctity of public office as a public trust, and, by making the service unpartisan, it is opening the way for making it businesslike. (Wilson, 1887:18)

Neutral Competency

A competing value for government service that has existed in tandem with democratic accountability is **neutral competence,** according to which government service should be politically neutral and focused on the skills and abilities of workers to do the job at hand, rather than on their political allegiances. In essence, this value emphasizes "what you know" for government service, rather than "who you know." Again, we often ask students whether they think this should be the preeminent value for government work in criminal justice. Inevitably most or all of them raise their hands in support of this value as well. And, of course, given the worth Americans place on hard work and the attainment of knowledge, who would not want neutral competence in government service?

Since passage of the Pendleton Act of 1883, its expansion at the federal level, and passage of similar acts in the states, most jobs in criminal justice, with the exception of elective positions (e.g., prosecutors, state and local judges, sheriffs) or top jobs that are political appointments (e.g. wardens, directors of juvenile corrections, undersheriffs, police chiefs, etc.), are protected by civil service. It is because of civil service reforms, for instance, that after a probationary period, most deputy sheriffs and deputy prosecutors, public defense attorneys, police officers, correctional security staff, and counselors in juvenile and adult facilities, cannot be fired without cause, and that cause cannot be related to political affiliation or support. Which means that civil servants, again with the exception of top-level positions, must be politically neutral. Not only do people in these positions enjoy some protection from arbitrary firing, under civil service requirements, they are also hired based on job-valid qualifications. We will discuss these issues more in Chapters 8 and 9, but suffice it to say that there are a series of tests that civil servants in criminal justice must pass and qualifications they must meet, before they can be hired, all of which speaks to their competency to do the job.

Another means of reinforcing the political neutrality of government workers manifested itself in the passage of the Hatch Act of 1939. This federal act, and state versions of it that followed, restricted specific forms of political activity in the workplace (see Box 2.3; Cayer, 1987). According to the current version of this act, government workers at the federal level can register, vote and campaign for their chosen candidate, among other political activities. But government workers may not run for office or campaign for others in partisan elections, among other political activities.

BOX 2.3

THE HATCH ACT REQUIREMENTS

The Hatch Act contains the political activity dos and don'ts (actually mays and may nots) for federal employees. Essentially, covered government workers may not coerce political involvement or compliance or engage in political campaigns in an intensive way, such as by running for partisan political offices, making or handling political contributions, or managing a political campaign. A version of this act exists in the states, and most include the essential elements of the federal law. According to the U. S. Office of Special Counsel website (2003), covered federal workers may:

- be candidates for public office in nonpartisan elections
- register to vote as they choose
- assist in voter registration drives
- express opinions about candidates and issues
- contribute money to political organizations
- attend political fundraising functions
- attend and be active at political rallies and meetings
- join and be an active member of a political party or club
- sign nominating petitions
- campaign for or against referendum questions, constitutional amendments, municipal ordinances
- campaign for or against candidates in partisan elections
- make campaign speeches for candidates in partisan elections
- distribute campaign literature in partisan elections
- hold office in political clubs or parties

On the other hand, they may not

- use their official authority or influence to interfere with an election
- solicit, accept, or receive political contributions unless both individuals are members of the same federal labor organization or employee organization and the one solicited is not a subordinate employee
- knowingly solicit or discourage the political activity of any person who has business before the agency
- engage in political activity while on duty
- engage in political activity in any government office
- engage in political activity while wearing an official uniform
- engage in political activity while using a government vehicle
- be candidates for public office in partisan elections
- wear political buttons while on duty

Reconciling Democratic Accountability and Neutral
Competence in Government Service

The cumulative effect of the civil service reforms and the Hatch Act has been to remove government workers from most of the political fray that can tend to influence their work. In its purest form, this removal can mean, however, that government is unresponsive to the democratic forces of the time. In fact, as noted in Chapter 1, virtually every successful presidential candidate since Richard Nixon in 1968 has originally run as a political "outsider" who is bent on coming to Washington D.C. to "fix" those supposedly lethargic and nonresponsive bureaucrats who were essentially charged with being antidemocratic for not heeding their political masters (Wamsley et al., 1987).

This sense that government was operating without the proper or sufficient political controls led President Jimmy Carter—who first ran as a political outsider in 1976—to use much political capital to gain passage of the Civil Service Act of 1978. This act, when implemented by the Reagan administration that followed Carter, tended to "politicize" more of the high level federal positions (Cayer, 1987). Moreover, President George W. Bush—who also ran as someone "outside the beltway"—engaged in a campaign to lessen the civil service protections in all of the federal service (*New York Times*, 2003). These latest activities by American presidents may portend a move back toward a greater emphasis on democratic accountability in government service.

This brief review of the competing values of neutral competence and democratic accountability indicates that either value, when rendered in its purer form, can lead to undesirable consequences. Of course, neither value has been emphasized exclusively in its "pure" form. Rather each has enjoyed more emphasis at certain periods of our history than at others. For instance, no one would argue that there was no neutrality or competence among government workers during the Jacksonian period (circa 1820s to 1880s) when democratic accountability as a value was most emphasized. Nor would any careful observer of current federal, state, or local government fail to notice the influence that political masters have on the operation of criminal justice agencies, despite the greater emphasis on neutral competence. Thus, students usually conclude that both values have worth for our government, but they must be balanced to prevent the deleterious consequences of overemphasis on either.

GOVERNMENT SERVICE IS DIFFERENT

One integral way in which criminal justice agencies are tied to their communities, or open, is through the service they and their employees do as public sector organizations. About sixty years ago the political scientist Paul Appleby (1945) argued in an often-cited article that "government is different." He noted that there were many characteristics of government work that distinguish it from work in the private sector. Before we embark on a discussion of ethics and management theories, in Chapters 3 and 4, it will be useful to review those reasons and to consider whether government service in criminal justice agencies is indeed different.

A *higher calling* for those drawn to government service is apparent. Appleby (1945) notes that some government employees regard their work as a vocation, as something they were meant to do and as a way of contributing to, and connecting with, their communities. In his Pulitzer–Prize winning book *The Call of Service: A Witness to Idealism*, Robert Coles (1993) makes the related point that a call to service is an attempt at outreach toward others in need, but it is also inwardly motivated to bring good into our lives. He concludes his book (1993:284) by musing over this matter: "[a] call to oneself, a call that is a reminder: 'Watchman, what of the night?'—the darkness that defines the moment of light in us, the darkness that challenges us to shine for one another before, soon enough, we join it."

Whether motivated outwardly or inwardly, we have found this claim that some are called to service to resonate among those who are considering the broader field of criminal justice. Every semester we ask our new students to list reasons for their interest in this field. Every semester at least 60% of those students include a statement such as "I want to contribute," "I want to give back," or "I want to make my community safer." Of course, they say that they want steady employment, excitement and activity in their work, and a decent wage, too, but that does not negate the fact that many of them appear to be "called" to government service to some degree.

That government work focuses on such big-picture issues as the environment, waging war, defending the homeland from terrorism, maintaining the road system, and incarcerating people accused or convicted of a crime, imparts a breadth and scope to such service that Appleby sees as another way in which government is different. As we have seen with the privatization movement over the last thiry years, there is a role that the private sector can play in some of these tasks, including in policing and corrections; for the most part, however, we have assigned these kinds of projects to government organizations because they are best equipped with the power and the resources to accomplish them.

Appleby also argues that government is different from the private sector because of the huge impact of government programs and practices and the need for organized action. Government can deny or award citizenship to nonnatives, wage war, or grant or deny liberties. The impact of justice system workers in this sense is enormous, even though for the most part, police, court, and correctional employees have little power over who their client is and who is committed to their facilities, or who in their communities comes under their supervision. However, criminal justice workers do have power over how these clients are treated, whether they are arrested or prosecuted and, at times, when they are released from supervision or an institution. Again, because the public sector is still predominant in the criminal justice field, they wield much more power over citizens in this area than the private sector does or can. Currently, as a people we have determined that this power is best organized, for criminal justice functions, by government entities and employees.

For Appleby, government is, and should be, different because of the need for accountability when the issues are big and the impact is vast. Because government agencies and initiatives are created and funded in a political context, they can also be held accountable by political actors when they make mistakes. We see this in criminal justice when administrators and wardens are let go or sheriffs are not reelected after illegal shenanigans are discovered in their agencies or facilities. Public sector workers are ultimately held accountable when their offenses surface. The trouble is that much of what happens in criminal justice is relatively hidden because of the closed nature of those facilities, and thus accountability may be present only in an uneven fashion.

Finally, Appleby argues that government is different because it is so political. Criminal justice agencies are practically suffused with politics (the processes involved in decision making about and within various organizations, whether they are private or public, formal or informal). Political actors, whether judges, sheriffs, police chiefs, prosecutors, direct- ors or secretaries of corrections, wardens, or even administrators of public sector juven- ile facilities, usually are directly elected or appointed, or they serve at the pleasure of a politician or political appointee. Budgets for criminal justice agencies are debated in a public forum (e.g., county commission meetings or legislative sessions) and critiqued in the press. If egregious mistakes made by staff have led to a failure to arrest or prosecute, or an escape, somebody is usually going to be held politically accountable. People are hired, trained, maintained, and fired based on rules and laws that were determined in a political environment. Suspects are processed and prosecuted based on laws, crimes, and sentences that vary to some degree by community, state, and nation, which means they were politically designed. Therefore, government is different because it is all about pol- itics and criminal justice agencies and institutions are in the midst of this milieu.

Additionally, government is different because it both holds the ability to mandate compliance through various legal channels, and as we all know, has the power to tax and fund various public and private endeavors (Moore, 1995). For example, when a city statute is passed, members of the public who fail to comply may be found in vio- lation of the statute, and therefore subject to its provisions, such as getting a parking ticket and having to pay a fine. We as community members are forced to pay taxes, such as property tax and income tax, the proceeds of which go toward the budgets of government organizations, which in turn function to benefit our community.

Of course, the distinctions between government work and the private sector noted by Appleby and others have a defining impact on criminal justice organizations and service by their employees. If people are in part motivated to work in the justice sys- tem because of a calling to "do good" in their communities, that motivation can be fruitfully employed by managers to improve their organizations. It might be remem- bered that the most long-term cynical employee at one time joined the profession in part because he was drawn to that work. Managers and employees in criminal justice agencies can be tasked to reinvigorate that original enthusiasm for government work and its grand role in justice administration.

CONCLUSIONS: WHY IT IS IMPORTANT NOT TO TELL JOKES ABOUT BUREAUCRATS

"How many bureaucrats does it take to screw in a lightbulb?" The answer is none; the requisition paperwork has not been put in yet...or three—one to order it, another to study it, a third to screw it up! Yes, bureaucrats get a bum rap, some of it deserved, but most of it is not.

What people who aspire to work in criminal justice agencies sometimes do not recognize is that they are studying and planning themselves,—heck, they are paying for college so that they can be a dreaded bureaucrat, an SLB as Lipsky (1980) put it.

And what people in the profession already know all too well is that their work is often not appreciated by the public, politicians, or even their own management.

Yet criminal justice agencies, both because of, and in spite of, their relatively closed nature—yes, environmental factors have an enormous influence, but these entities and their practices are still hidden to some degree from public view—its paramilitary and bureaucratic structure, its committed employees, and its overwhelming caseloads and overloaded cellblocks is ripe for a management and paradigmatic shift. For instance, courts have adopted restorative justice approaches and mediation as means of reducing formal adjudication, clearing backlogged caseloads and increasing community involvement in processes and sentences (Bohm & Haley, 2005). The paradigm for corrections is shifting back to a greater rehabilitative/habilitative focus and away from incapacitation alone (Clear, 2001). For policing, proactive, prevention/problem-oriented models have come to predominate over a more reactive approach (Kelling, 1992).

These changes are spurred by changing sentiments, by new research on court and police practices and strategies, by a sense that locking up people for relatively minor crimes is pointless, even immoral, and by cost considerations. Even in flush budget years, governors and state legislators cannot ignore the escalating cost of the drug war and the bite it is taking out of other valued programs: schools, health care, parks, and road projects, to name a few alternative funding venues. Within these public agencies, the competing values of democratic accountability and neutral competence tend to shape the role and motivation of workers, and further influence change.

Evidence of this shift can be found in the establishment of drug courts in many states, and the resurrection of treatment in communities and corrections. States like Michigan, which instituted one of the first and most stringent sets of mandatory sentences, repealed those laws in December 2002 and lessened the length of sentences (Families Against Mandatory Minimums, 2003). Other states are also restructuring their sentencing and risk assessment instruments to allow them to reduce, or at least not increase, the use of incarceration (Wilhelm & Turner, 2003).

The paradigm for criminal justice management needs to shift as well. For fifty years now the private sector has toyed with a move toward greater involvement by workers in the operation of companies (Drucker, 1954, 1964; Maslow, 1998). Some private sector companies have made meaningful changes in their organizational structure to reflect this change in philosophy to more democratic participation in the workplace. Some of them have reaped positive outcomes as a result (Peters, 1987; Schein, 1993). It is our contention that there are very powerful reasons for criminal justice management to move further in a similar direction toward democratic participation. These reasons will be highlighted throughout the text and encapsulated in the management model presented in Chapter 13.

DISCUSSION QUESTIONS

1. After reviewing how public service in criminal justice might be different, list and describe the ways in which it is similar to service in the private sector.

2. If government activity is more likely to be honest when under public scrutiny, discuss the ways in which jails or prisons might become more "open" to the public.

3. Why are the values of "democratic accountability" and "neutral competence" in conflict? What is their appeal, and what is their weakness? Can you describe any current examples of either value being emphasized in public service today?

4. As mentioned in the text, criminal justice managers must confront numerous environmental factors. What, then, are some tactics those managers might employ to control their environment? How might they be proactive in this endeavor?

5. Why do you think that old modes of management, by the top only, might be outdated? Explain your answer.

6. Who is likely to know most about how the organization operates—the top-level managers or the lower-level workers? Explain your reasoning.

7. What are some ways in which SLBs make policy in police or court organizations? Give an example.

8. In addition to their shared vision to enforce and uphold the law, what drives criminal justice organizations and their actors, both formally and informally?

9. Using the web links provided following the list of key terms, analyze the various organizational mission statements and design your own mission statement as if you were working for or managing a criminal justice agency of your choice.

10. Using the web links, chose one of the organizations and describe the various organizational actors and the various formal and informal goals those individuals may or may not reflect.

KEY TERMS

bureaucracy: refers to how organizations are structured, ruled, or socially organized and includes hierarchy, specialization, and rule of law.

closed/open organization: a closed organization is one that is not affected by its environment; an open one does experience influences from its enviroment.

democratic accountability: the value in government that the public sector, or the managers and workers in government, are accountable to those who have been democratically elected and/or politically appointed.

discretion: the ability to make choices and to act, or not act, on such selections.

ethics: the study of, or the act of, doing the right thing in the professional sphere (Braswell, 1998). Morality, on the other hand, is understood to be doing the right thing in the private sphere.

formal/informal goals: formal goals are those that are written down and reflected in an organization's formal mission statement, organizational chart, policy manual, memoranda, and training curricula. Informal goals are those that reflect the norms of behavior of organizational members.

formal/informal organization: reflects the goals, values, and beliefs that are officially acknowledged and authorized (formal organization) and unofficially sanctioned (informal organization).

justice: in this text, the term is understood to mean that those who are guilty are caught, processed, and sanctioned, as befits community, professional, and moral standards, by system actors. Justice, for our purposes, also means that those who are innocent are given ample opportunity, and the due process necessary, to ensure that they are not caught up in, and sanctioned by, the system.

management: one or more persons who have formal control over an organization; or, the act or process of operating the organization.

neutral competence: the value that government service should be politically neutral and focused on the skills and abilities of workers to do the job at hand, rather than on their political allegiances.

organization: a grouping of people arranged and coordinated to accomplish some purpose.

organizational integrity: characterizing an organization whose actors as a whole are honest, ethical, and can be trusted by their members and by the community.

WEB LINKS

Corrections Corp. of America: http://www.correctionscorp.com/theccaway.html
FBI website: http://www.fbi.gov/quickfacts.htm
Pittsburgh Bureau of Police: http://www.city.pittsburgh.pa.us/police/
Philadelphia Police Department: http://www.ppdonline.org/hq_mission.php
U.S. Department of Justice: http://www.usdoj.gov/02organizations/

REFERENCES

American Heritage Dictionary. (1992). *American Heritage Dictionary* (3rd ed.). New York: Delta/Houghton Mifflin.

Appleby, P. (1945, reprinted in 1987). Government is different. In J. M. Shafritz & A. C. Hyde (Eds.), *Classics of public administration* (pp. 158–163). Chicago: Dorsey Press.

Blau, P. M., & Scott, W. R. (1962, reprinted in 2001). The concept of the formal organization. In J. M. Shafritz, & S. J. Ott (Eds.), *Classics of organization theory* (pp. 206–210). Fort Worth, TX: Harcourt College Publishers.

Bohm, R. M., & Haley, K. N. (2005). *Introduction to criminal justice* (4th ed.). New York: McGraw-Hill.

Braswell, M. C. (1998). "Ethics, crime and justice: An introductory note to students." In M. C. Braswell, B. R. McCarthy, & B. J. McCarthy (Eds.), *Justice, crime and ethics* (pp. 3–9). Cincinnati, OH. Anderson Publishing .

Carlisle, H. M. (1976). *Management: Concepts and situations.* Chicago: SRA.

Cayer, N. J. (1987). Managing human resources. In R. C. Chandler (Ed.), *A centennial history of the American administrative state* (pp. 321–344). New York: Free Press.

Clear, T. (2001). Ten unintended consequences of the growth in imprisonment. In E. J. Latessa, A. Holsinger, J. W. Marquart, & J. R. Sorensen (Eds.), *Correctional contexts: Contemporary and classical readings* (pp. 497–505). Los Angeles: Roxbury.

Coles, R. (1993). *The call of service: A witness to idealism.* Boston: Houghton Mifflin.

Crank, J. P. (1998). *Understanding police culture.* Cincinnati, OH: Anderson Publishing.

Donne, J. (1623). No man is an island. *Devotions upon emergent occasions.* Meditation XVII.

Drucker, P. F. (1954). *The practice of management.* New York: Harper & Row.

Drucker, P. F. (1964). *Managing for results.* New York: Harper & Row.

Families Against Mandatory Minimums. (2003). Michigan Legislature Repeals Mandatory Sentencing Laws. www.november.org/razor wire/2003–01/winter/mich.html.

Goffman, E. (1961). *Asylums: Essays on the social situation of mental patients and other inmates.* New York: Doubleday.

Gulick, L. (1937, reprinted in 2001). Notes on the theory of organization. In J. M. Shafritz, & J. S. Ott (Eds.) *Classics of organization theory* (pp. 79–87). Fort Worth, TX: Harcourt College Publishers.

Haller, M. H. (1983). Chicago cops, 1890–1925. In C. B. Klockars (Ed.), *Thinking about police: Contemporary readings* (pp. 87–99). New York: McGraw-Hill.

Jacobs, J. (1977). *Stateville: The penitentiary in mass society.* Chicago: University of Chicago Press.

Kelling, G. L. (1992). Toward new images of policing: Herman Goldstein's 'problem-oriented policing'. *Law & Social Inquiry, 17,* 539–559.

Lipsky, M. (1980). *Street-level bureaucracy: Dilemmas of the individual in public services.* New York: Russell Sage Foundation.

Maslow, A. H. (1998, first published in 1967). *Maslow on management.* New York: Wiley.

Micklethwait, J., & Wooldridge, A. (1996). *The witch doctors: Making sense of the management gurus.* New York: Random House.

Moore, M. H. (1995). *Creating public value: Strategic management in government.* Cambridge, MA: Harvard University Press.

Morrow, W. L. (1987). The pluralist legacy in American public administration. In R.C. Chandler (Ed.), *A centennial history of the American administrative state.* New York: Free Press.

New York Times. (2003). Editorials/op-ed: The civil service faces an overhaul. *New York Times.* June 12, 2003. website: www.nytimes.com.

Peters, T. (1987). *Thriving on chaos: Handbook for a management revolution.* New York: Harper & Row.

Schein, E. H. (1992). *Organizational culture and leadership* (2nd ed.). San Francisco: Jossey-Bass.

Selznick, P. (1948, reprinted in 2001). Foundations of the theory of organization. In J.M. Shafritz, and J. S. Ott (Eds.), *Classics of organization theory* (pp. 125–134) Fort Worth, TX: Harcourt College Publishers.

Stojkovic, S., Kalinich, D., & Klofas, J. (1998). *Criminal justice organizations: Administration and management* (2nd ed.). Belmont, CA: Wadsworth.

U.S. National Archives & Records Administration. (2005). Pendleton Act. (1883). Accessed at www.ourdocuments.gov, December 20, 2005.

Van Riper, P. P. (1987). The American administrative state: Wilson and the founders. In R. C. Chandler (Ed.), *A centennial history of the American administrative state,* (pp. 3–36). New York: Free Press.

Walker, S. (1983). *The police in America: An introduction.* New York: McGraw-Hill.

Wamsley, G. L., Goodsell, C. T., Rohr, J. A., Stivers, C. M., White, O. F., & Wolf, J. F. (1987). The public administration and the governance process: Refocusing the American dialogue." In R. C. Chandler (Ed.), *A centennial history of the American administrative state* (pp. 291–317). New York: Free Press.

Weber, M. (1946). Bureaucracy. In H. H. Gerth & C. W. Mills (Eds.), *From Max Weber: Essays in sociology.* Oxford, U.K.: Oxford University Press.

Wilhelm, D. F., and Turner, N. R. (2003). Is the budget crisis changing the way we look at sentencing and incarceration? Vera Institute of Justice Publications. www.vera.org/publications/publications

Wilson, W. (1887, reprinted in 1987). The study of administration. In J. M. Shafritz and A. C. Hyde (Eds.), *Classics of public administration* (pp. 10–25). Chicago: Dorsey Press.

CHAPTER 3

MANAGING TROUBLE—DEVIANCE, ABUSE OF FORCE AND SEXUAL/GENDER HARASSMENT— USING ETHICS

Our findings indicate that being a woman prisoner in U.S. state prisons can be a terrifying experience. If you are sexually abused, you cannot escape from your abuser. Grievance or investigatory procedures, where they exist, are often ineffectual, and correctional employees continue to engage in abuse because they believe they will rarely be held accountable, administratively or criminally. Few people outside the prison walls know what is going on or care if they do know. Fewer still do anything to address the problem. [Dorothy Q. Thomas (1996) reporting on prison practices in eleven states from March 1994 to November 1996 for Human Rights Watch]

We live in a country where the authority of the police to intervene in the affairs of the citizenry is on the ascent. Traditional due process restrictions on police authority are being relaxed. Citizens sometimes encourage illegal police behavior to "do something about crime." And with these changes, opportunities for noble-cause corruption are increasing [Crank & Caldero, from Police Ethics: The Corruption of Noble Cause, *(2000:3)]*

A corrupt judiciary means also that the legal and institutional mechanism designed to curb corruption generally will be handicapped. The judiciary is the public institution that is mandated to provide essential checks on other public institutions. A fair and efficient judiciary is the key to anti-corruption initiatives. [Langseth (2001) reporting on the findings of the United Nations Conference on strengthening judicial integrity against corruption.]

INTRODUCTION

It is an axiom of criminal justice work that staff and administrators will be exposed to temptations to violate rules, procedures, laws, or standards of ethics. This is true because much such work is hidden from public view, or ignored, and involves the secure care of people who are regarded as social outcasts and are relatively powerless. As staff possess enormous amounts of *discretion*, they become the linchpin upon which the just, or unjust, nature of their organization turns.

In fact, the history of criminal justice operations and current practice tells us that there have been numerous instances of corrupt and abusive individuals, institutions, or whole systems (Clear & Cole, 1997; Courtless, 1998; Feeley, 1983; Friedrichs, 2001; Gaines, Worrall, Southerland & Angell, 2003; Gray, 2002; Bennett & Hess, 2001; Holten & Lamar, 1991; Mays & Winfree, 2002; Silverman & Vega, 1996; Welch, 1996). More recent infamous instances of abuse, such as those that occurred in Texas private jails (see Box 3.1), those described by a researcher for the international organization Human Rights Watch (in the quote that opens this chapter), or the 110 documented cases of disciplinary removals of judges in the United States between 1990 and

BOX 3.1

AMNESTY INTERNATIONAL REPORT ON SEXUAL ABUSE OF
INMATES IN THE STATES

The authors of a report published electronically by Amnesty International
(2004:29, 75, 211–213, 229) compiled newspapers reports of sexual misconduct
in state prison systems. The following random sample taken by one of the
authors, surveys the most egregious incidents in such accounts from Alabama,
New York, Connecticut, and North Dakota.

Alabama

"A former city jailer who had quit his job the month prior was arrested for
sexually assaulting inmates at the jail." (AP, December 19, 2000)

"A lieutenant in the police department resigned as his hearing began
over allegations that he solicited sex from a female inmate in the city jail."
(AP, April 15, 2000)

"A deputy threatened to transfer an inmate to a facility far away from her
children if she did not perform oral sex, according to claims filed in circuit
court." (AP, December 10, 1999)

New York

"Albion Correctional Facility: A city councilman working as a prison guard
was suspended for having sexual relations with a female inmate. Has not been
charged with any criminal offense." (*The Buffalo News,* August 19, 2000)

"Albion Correctional Facility: Former officer sentenced to 3 years probation and fined $1,000 for having sexual relations with a female inmate." (*The
Buffalo News*, August 19, 2000)

"Westchester County Jail: Officer 1 was arrested and charged with raping
and sodomizing an inmate. Officer 2 was charged with raping an inmate in a
supply closet. Officer 3 was charged with sexual abuse and official misconduct
for forcing women inmates to strip. Officer 4 was charged with making an
inmate strip for Tylenol. All the officers were released on bail. Charges were
dropped against Officer 2, Officer 1 pled guilty. Charges were pending against
the officers. Male officers were banned from female living quarters." (*The New
York Times*, January 27, 2000 and January 28, 2000)

"Rensselaer County Jail: Officer pleaded guilty to rape and sodomy. He
was sentenced to two years in jail and five years probation. The female inmate
was 16 years old at the time, and she sued the officer and the county." (*The
Times Union, Albany,* December 9, 1999)

"Adirondack Correctional Facility: A former NY State prison guard was sentenced in September 1998 to three years imprisonment after admitting he forced a male prisoner to perform oral sex. When the male inmate filed complaints with the corrections department and state police he was transferred to Clinton correctional facility. He saved the semen in a small vial, which he turned over to the correction's department inspector general's office. Tests verified the DNA matched the officer's. Faced with the strength of the DNA evidence, the officer pleaded guilty to the charge of felony sodomy." (*Prison Legal News*, February 1999)

Connecticut

"In March 1999, a former state probation officer pleaded no contest to 31 criminal charges including sexual assault, racketeering, kidnapping and unlawful restraint. He was originally charged with 224 counts of sexual misconduct stemming from the rape of 15 men and young boys who were on his caseload. He threatened to have the victims imprisoned if they did not submit to his attacks." (AP, August 1999)

"York Correctional Institution: A former counselor was sentenced to serve 18 months in prison for having sex with three female inmates who came to him for help with their problems." (*The Day,* October 19, 2000)

"York Correctional Institution: Prison worker convicted of sexual assault on female inmate. A jury found a food supervisor at the facility had sex with an inmate he supervised." (AP, April 19, 2000)

North Dakota

"North Dakota State Penitentiary: Former guard charged with seven counts of sexually abusing female inmates." (North Dakota headlines, December 6, 1999)

2001 reported by the American Judicature Society (Gray, 2002; see Box 3.2), further serve to remind us that vigilance is needed to ensure that criminal justice agencies, their actors, and their clients remain safe, secure, and just for all.

The development of ethical codes, the professionalization of staffs, and the routinization of procedural protections are often regarded as providing some protection against the temptation to engage in corrupt or unethical behaviors. These codes and processes might be seen as inoculating an organization, as if it were a living organism, against such viral infections.

In this chapter we begin with a discussion of two studies on the public image of the police and courts as social institutions and how that image is tied to ethical practices. We then discuss the explanations for, and types of, deviance, abuse of force, and harassment problems that can plague criminal justice organizations. We will then

BOX 3.2

AMERICAN JUDICATURE REPORT: "A STUDY OF STATE JUDICIAL DISCIPLINE SANCTIONS"

The American Judicature Society, an independent, nonprofit organization, sponsored a study (Gray 2002) of judicial misconduct and discipline in the United States. The purpose of this discipline, as established in numerous court cases, is not necessarily to punish a judge, but to preserve "[t]he integrity of the judicial system and public confidence in the system and, when necessary, safeguarding the bench and the public from those who are unfit" (Gray, 2002:3). In most states a reviewing court (usually the supreme court) hears cases regarding judicial misconduct from a judicial commission. Types of misconduct identified in the report for which judges were removed included "lack of competence," "failure to comply with a sobriety monitoring contract" [he was on probation], "failure to disqualify from a case," "misuse of powers to benefit a family member," "filing false travel vouchers," "neglect or improper performance of administrative duties," "failure to remit court funds," "abuse of contempt powers," and "sexual harassment" among others (Gray, 2002:8–11). Types of sanctions given for misconduct ranged in severity from counseling and letters of caution to suspension or outright removal from the bench. It was established in numerous court cases that the removal sanction was reserved for misconduct only that was "truly egregious" or "flagrant and severe" (Gray, 2002:4).

Having said this, Gray reported that from 1990 to 2001, 110 judges were removed owing to misconduct. As this is the most severe sanction, it can be projected that hundreds more judges may have been given lesser sanctions for judicial misconduct during this time period. As an indication of how widespread misconduct might be, another 625 judges resigned, retired, lost reelection, or died between 1990 and 1999 with a judicial misconduct complaint pending before a reviewing court.

Gray reported that several factors were common themes in removal cases. Recurring factors in these cases included "dishonesty," "a pattern of misconduct" whereby the judge was usually involved in more than one incident of misconduct, presence of a "prior discipline record," the claim that an established "judicial reputation" should mitigate against any sanction, "proportionality," or ensuring that similar cases are handled similarly, and the judge's "conduct in response to investigation" (Gray, 2002:59–66).

review the concept of ethics and its philosophical underpinnings, we will also consider how ethical practice, when inculcated into the organizational structure, might serve as a partial remedy for such abuse and deviance. These topics are in sync with those covered in Chapters 7, 8, and 9, which have to do with the importance of leadership and personnel practices and the power of leaders to further professionalize criminal justice agencies.

PUBLIC DISTRUST

The public perception of criminal justice agencies often hinges on how professional they perceive those entities to be. In two separate studies of the courts and policing there is some indication that those perceptions could be improved (Gallagher, Maguire, Mastrofski, & Reisig, 2001; National Center for State Courts [NCSC], 1999).

In a 1999 national public opinion poll of American adults, the 1,826 respondents were asked to indicate their level of "trust and confidence" in several American institutions (NCSC, 1999:12). Only 43% of the respondents indicated that they had a "great deal" of trust or confidence in the local police, and only 23% had the same level of belief in courts in their communities (NCSC, 1999:12).

In their report to the International Association of Chiefs of Police on the public image of the police, Gallagher and her colleagues (2001) found, after reviewing over forty years of research, that the public generally has a very positive perception of the police. However, this perception is shaped in part by one's minority/majority status, with African Americans and other racial minorities having a less positive perception than whites. The authors of the report also found that the public's tolerance for the use of force by the police has decreased as time has gone on. Significantly, though, "The public image of honesty and ethical standards of police has fluctuated over the years, but has improved substantially from 1977 to 2000" (Gallagher et al., 2001:5).

In the National Center for State Courts (1999:7) study, the findings were less rosy, as indicated by the following sampling:

- "Only 10% of the survey respondents felt the courts in their communities handled cases in an 'Excellent' manner, with 20% indicating criminal cases and family relations cases are handled in a 'Poor' manner and nearly 30% indicating juvenile delinquency cases are handled in a 'Poor' manner."
- "The vast majority of respondents (81%) agree that politics influences court decisions. This pattern holds across racial and ethnic groups."
- Over 75% of the respondents thought that the need to raise campaign funds influences elected judges.
- Hispanics were most positive about court performance, with African Americans being least positive and whites falling in between.

These studies clearly indicate that the public has some concerns about fair treatment at the hands of both the police and the courts, though the courts were rated higher in the NCSC study (the respondents were not queried about corrections in this study). Some of these concerns center on use of force, disparate treatment based on racial or ethnic status, and political influences, as all these factors might shape the perception that justice is or is not done in criminal justice agencies. Clearly, a low public image warps the ability of these agencies to do professional work. After all, in a democracy it is only with public support and trust that the police and the courts exist, are funded, and achieve any success. It is crucial then for criminal justice agencies to garner the trust and confidence of the people; one means to this end is through ethical practice.

DEVIANCE EXPLAINED

It is often assumed that staff or administrators who violate the law, organizational rules and procedures, or ethical codes in and of criminal justice do so for personal profit or gain or from an *egotistical* perspective. An example might be a prosecutor who accepts a bribe from the family of the accused in exchange for a reduced charge. Or we might view the exchange of sexual favors between a police officer and a prostitute hoping to avoid arrest, as another example of deviance for personal gain. Or perhaps a private treatment provider might bribe a correctional administrator to ensure they get the contract to provide food services to juvenile facilities in that state.

But in actuality, *deviance* by staff in a criminal justice organization should be more broadly defined to include other *explanations* for misbehavior and abuse of authority. **Deviance by staff** might be defined as involving behavior that violates the statutes, institutional rules or procedures, or ethical codes for individual *or* organizational gain *or* even as a means of serving a "noble cause" (Bartollas & Hahn, 1999; Crank & Caldero, 2000: Lee & Visano, 1994). Although it is difficult to determine how often staff or management deviance might be motivated by organizational or noble cause purposes, experience tells us that it is likely that people misbehave in organizations for reasons other than personal profit alone.

Corruption for Individual Gain

But people misbehave for personal profit too! Indeed, the profit motive corruption at the individual level in criminal justice is quite powerful and is also easy to understand and recognize. Some people will be drawn to work in a criminal justice agency because they see the opportunity to make extra money or to get illegal services. Others might recognize these opportunities once employed. New hires might be especially tempted when they see that some colleagues are taking advantage of a situation. Because of the hidden nature of much of this corruption and the subcultural prohibition against "ratting" in most criminal justice agencies (Pollock, 2004), it is difficult to determine how much deviance there is and what behaviors are involved. But stories of the corruption and abuse, many much worse than the ones one of the authors describes from her experience in working in a prison (see Box 3.3), are rife among staff, and many agencies have had to grapple with scandals caused by the unethical or illegal behavior of their workers (see Box 3.4).

Those who have worked in or studied criminal justice agencies relate instances of parole dates being sold for political favors by board members, of FBI lab technicians misrepresenting their findings in court (Pollock, 1998, 2004), of beatings of inmates by staff or inmate–to–inmate fights that are allowed by staff (Conover, 2000; Marquart, 1995), of sexual abuse of women inmates by staff (Amnesty International, 2004; Thomas, 1996), and of numerous other abuses (Crank & Caldero, 2000; Muraskin, 2001a, 2001b). As one of the authors has observed in visits, and as students working in

BOX 3.3

PERSONAL OBSERVATIONS OF DEVIANCE IN A PRISON SETTING

by Mary K. Stohr

In the prison I worked at in Washington State from 1983 to 1986 there were stories of a maintenance supervisor getting his cars serviced for free and of a security sergeant with unauthorized inmate artwork in his home. I don't know if these stories were true, but staff gave them credence because the environment was so unprofessional in other respects.

For instance, a Hispanic officer told me that he was continually passed over for promotion by the warden because of his ethnicity. I found this plausible because the officer was highly qualified for positions that came open and because the warden himself told me that the Affirmative Action Committee he wanted me to be on was only a sham and he didn't really want to recruit, hire, or promote minorities. The warden also said that he had hired me, and the few other white females who worked there, only because he was forced to after five years of pressure by central office.

Other instances of unprofessional behavior by staff occurred when I worked an escape on a July 4th evening and three of the supervisors had to be driven by subordinates because the were seriously inebriated and unable to safely operate a vehicle. I also witnessed the retaliation against a female correctional officer who refused to go out with a male sergeant; she was eventually hounded out of her job by the man, who also verbally harassed all the other female staff in his orbit, including myself. This was one of two sergeants who told me after I was just hired that he did not think women should work in male prisons.

Despite the reputation the harassing male sergeant had among male and female staff—most of the male staff disliked him as well because of his unprofessional behavior in other respects—and the complaints by the female staff he harassed, the man was never formally reprimanded or disciplined for his behavior. He was eventually fired, however, for an unrelated case, after he pled guilty to four counts of child sexual abuse with his preteen daughter's friend.

criminal justice agencies have told us over the last eighteen years, juveniles in a detention center have been openly and routinely referred to as "little criminals" by some staff; police officers get overly excited and throw extra punches at resistant suspects; prosecutors who suspect police have insufficient evidence to produce an indictment overcharge to secure a plea to some crime; prison staff regularly use foul and abusive language to address inmates; and a few jail officers in one facility routinely allowed unauthorized personnel to participate in strip searches of admittees.

BOX 3.4

TAPE PUTS FOR-PROFIT PRISONS BACK IN SPOTLIGHT

Video shows guards abusing inmates

"In the next few days, 165 Missourians will leave a long, red wedge of a metal building surrounded by Texas prairie and coils of razor wire to return to a prison in their home state. They are drug-pushers, burglars and car thieves; medium-security convicts Missouri shipped off to a for-profit prison far from their homes, relatives and friends. Until two weeks ago, not too many people thought or cared about them.

But then a videotape of a different set of Missouri inmates in Texas—men forced to crawl on the floor, shocked with electric prods, bitten by police dogs—surfaced. The tape from the Brazoria County Detention Center 200 miles to the south has shaken the Groesbeck prison, the leading industry in town, focused national attention on the Texas penal system and prompted Missouri to remove 800 prisoners from Texas.

As a result of that tape, prison-for-profit plans are being reviewed by states nationwide—studies that could lead to the early release of prisoners, millions more in tax money for new state-run prisons or laws to stem the flow of non-violent offenders to prison. And in Texas, the tape has devastated a small town that had hooked its future on prison money. Tim Kniest, spokesman for the Missouri Department of Corrections, doesn't have much sympathy for Groesbeck's plight. 'This is not an economic development issue,' he said. 'This is an issue of conditions of confinement.' [A]lready in Brazoria, 100 Capital Corrections employees have been laid off."

Excerpt Schofield (1997).

Idaho inmates tell of assault in Texas: Nurses, who inmates say fondled them, have been arrested and fired

"Three Idaho inmates have said they were sexually assaulted at a private Texas prison, leading to the arrest and firing of two prison nurses. The two male nurses allegedly fondled the prisoners in April at the Frio County Detention Center infirmary, south of San Antonio. They were indicted by a grand jury and arraigned last week, and now are out on bond."

Excerpt Steve Bard (1997).

For more information on the ethical dilemmas present within the private vs. public prison debate see Reisig and Pratt (2000) Perrone and Pratt (2003); and Shichor (1998).

In well-documented court cases, a prison was afflicted by individual corruption when female inmates in Georgia were forced into prostitution by prison staff (Thomas, 1996). And whole prison systems in Arkansas and Texas were placed under court order for years for numerous individual and systemic violations of constitutional protections of inmates (Welch, 1996).

In Eugene, Oregon, two officers were accused of over sixty counts of sexual abuse and rape (Seligman, 2004). Specifically, the officers were accused of forcing women to perform sex acts in exchange for roadside assistance. One officer was convicted of ten charges, and the investigation was ongoing on the other officer as of January 2004. As of fall 2005 the City of Eugene was facing millions of dollars in liability from civil suits brought by the victims of these crimes.

Such unethical behavior may be committed out of stupidity, ignorance, prejudice, the desire for sex or to exert power, for convenience sake, or to obtain some other gratification that cannot be easily quantified monetarily, or otherwise, by an observer or participant. The behavior might also be motivated by greed. Whereas it is fairly clear how personal profit or gratification might motivate misbehavior in criminal justice, the influence of the organization and its subculture, and of a noble cause, in motivating such behavior is less clearly understood.

Official Deviance

Official deviance may be one other explanation for staff corruption or abuse. Lee and Visano (1994:203) defined **official deviance** as *"[a]ctions taken by officials which violate the law and/or the formal rules of the organization, but which are clearly oriented toward the needs and goals of the organization, as perceived by the official, and thus fulfill certain informal rules of the organization."* What they found in their analysis of the behavior of criminal justice actors in several agencies in Canada and the United States is that many deviant acts are not committed for personal gain; rather, the motivation is found in an organizational or subcultural end. It is believed that at times the *informal* subculture of an organization not only encourages official deviance, but punishes or excludes those who refuse to participate. According to Lee and Visano (1994), the agencies most susceptible to official deviance are those in which decision making and practice are most hidden and the clients have the least power, such as criminal justice agencies.

Examples of deviant behavior include lying in court by a police officer, withholding evidence by a prosecutor, and misrepresenting information on a revocation report by a probation officer, all for the sake of ensuring that the "presumed guilty" receive the desired verdict. Official deviance also encompasses lying for, ignoring, or covering up the wrongdoing of others in an organization. Those who refuse to participate in official deviance might be shunned, or worse, by members of the subculture. Some officers might refuse to back up people who will not play along or even harass them.

As remedies for official deviance, Lee and Visano (1994) recommend that criminal justice agencies open up their operations to the scrutiny and study of scholars, citizens, the media, and other interested stakeholders. They are fans of freedom of information acts, assessment and evaluation of programs by outside and independent reviewers, civilianization of certain aspects of agency functioning, and investigation of wrongdoing by disinterested third parties. They warn against solutions for official deviance that include the creation of more bureaucracy and law, which would provide more opportunities for deviance and secrecy. They also argue that those who work within the criminal justice system can neutralize the effects of official deviance by changing their language and behavior so that the system can be regarded as legitimate by those outside it.

Noble Cause

A related concept that explains the motivation for some deviance by criminal justice staff is "noble cause" corruption. Crank and Caldero (2000:35) define the **noble cause** for police officers as "[a] profound moral commitment to make the world a safer place to live. Put simply, it is getting bad guys off the street. Police believe they're on the side of angels and their purpose in life is getting rid of bad guys."

Crank and Caldero (2000:35) identify two noble cause themes that explain police officer behavior: "[t]he smell of victim's blood and the tower." What they mean by "smell of victim's blood" is that police officers are intimately aware of the suffering of the victims of crime as symbolized by their blood. Therefore, the officers' behavior is motivated in part by the desire to see offenders "pay" for the crimes they commit, particularly against victims who are the most defenseless, such as children.

Relatedly, Crank and Caldero (2000) and others (e.g., Bartollas & Hahn, 1999; O'Connor, 2001) theorize that police officers are motivated in their everyday practice by a desire to do something to make the world right. Caldero presents a scenario that illustrates this point in a police staff training session. In the scenario a sharpshooter in a university tower has already killed twelve students. Rather than running away from the tower like regular citizens, the police will literally run toward the tower, and not just because it is their job to do so. The police will "run toward the tower" because they want to actively make things right; they want to be proactive. This is, Crank and Caldero feel, yet another distinguishing motivating feature of a noble cause perspective for the police.

The desire by the police to defend victims and to be proactive are laudable traits in any officer. These noble causes are corrupted, however, when the police look on these *ends* as more important than the *means* to achieve them.

According to Crank and Caldero, those who engage in *noble cause corruption* are prone to see the world in black and white. They think that in their pursuit of what they perceive as just ends, they may, with impunity, use corrupt means. Therefore, a police officer might excuse excessive force, manufacturing evidence, lying on reports, or commiting perjury in court if such an action were seen as serving their noble cause.

Although Crank and Caldero's book (2000) is about deviant practices of the police, the threat of noble cause corruption might be fruitfully applied to courts and corrections, since those who are drawn to other criminal justice work are just as likely to be as interested in a "just end" as police officers. Though the experience of the victim is more removed from them, prosecutors, judges, and even correctional managers and staff know something of the crimes and circumstances surrounding the various offenses. As with the police, their sympathies are also likely to be with the victim or potential victims, particularly for the most brutal or offensive crimes.

For example, when one of the authors was first hired to work as a correctional officer in that adult male prison in 1983, the sergeants and the other officers quickly told her who was in for "child molesting" as well as other crimes. It was implied, and at times explicitly stated, that she was to treat the child molesters, or "those scumbags," as they were often openly referred to, differently from other inmates—with more disrespect or more disdain, at a minimum. Subsequent interactions with correctional staffs at other prisons and jails and in other states have reinforced the perception that correctional staff are also motivated to action by the "victim's blood," especially that of the more defenseless victims, such as children. Although this motivation is understandable, as it is human, it also makes correctional staff susceptible to noble cause corruption.

Similarly, in her article on criminal defense attorneys, which McIntyre (2004) tellingly titles "But How Can You Sleep Nights?" even the defenders of the accused are troubled by their concerns over what was done to the victims. If defense attorneys are attuned to the suffering of the victims, imagine how the prosecutors, whose job it is to have contact with them, may be bothered and perhaps swayed to act in unethical fashion by the "smell of the victims' blood."

Criminal justice staff are also likely to be "doers" who are interested in rectifying wrongs and stopping criminality: in the parlance of Crank and Caldero (2000), they are the type of people who will run toward the tower. The observations of social scientists would serve to reinforce the perception that criminal justice personnel will behave in this manner. While in graduate school, one of the authors attended a lecture by an anthropology professor who had just returned from a sabbatical spent working as a correctional officer at a federal prison in California.[1] One of the behaviors of staff that the professor remarked on was the adrenaline rush and the excitement that followed an emergency summons. Whether it was to break up a fight or to deal with a lesser verbal dispute, he was surprised at the unadulterated thrill he experienced, and noticed in others, when asked to respond to an emergency situation. Similarly, an older correctional officer friend of one of the authors recalled that when he was a young man working at the Walla Walla prison in Washington State in the 1960s, the most fun he had was racing to a cell to quell a disturbance or to do a cell extraction.

Conover (2000) makes the same point about correctional officers responding to a disturbance at the Sing Sing prison in New York State. Or probation officers we know relate how excited they get when going to arrest a client who has committed a new crime or has otherwise seriously violated his terms. Or jail officers work hard to qualify so they can join the Emergency Response Team and engage in the same "fun" the Walla Walla officer had forty years ago. Or a police ombudsman noted that back when he worked as an officer, he and his colleagues were invariably excited when responding to an emergency call. Clearly, this metaphorical "racing to the tower," which would be regarded as peculiar behavior by regular citizens but may be one of the attractions of criminal justice work, might also lead to some abuses in the use of force.

The chance for noble cause corruption might also be heightened in the criminal justice environment because the work is often hidden from public and official view. Scrutiny by actors in the rest of the criminal justice system or by political leaders is still relatively rare and is usually related to infamous cases of abuse or deviance that come to public attention. What this means is that corrupt behavior and deviance are not often known outside the institution or the agency and are sometimes easy to hide within it.

For this reason, criminal justice work provides fertile ground for those who resort to illegal or unethical means, which they attempt to justify by citing a "just end."

In addition, "noble cause" staff members in criminal justice generally might view their clients, or at least some of them, as "deserving" abuse at the hands of other staff or, in corrections, clients. Therefore, keeping the accused or offenders off the streets or away from lesser offenders, or further enhancing their punishment for wrongdoing, might inspire noble cause corruption by criminal justice staff.

Examples of noble cause corruption in criminal justice work include the same types of behaviors that constitute official deviance, but the motivation for the staff member is not to satisfy informal institutional or subcultural demands, but to mete out the individual's perception of a just end. This "justice" could take the form of excessive force used on a suspect, accused person, or inmate; lying in court or on reports; abusive emotional treatment; overcharging or withholding evidence by prosecutors; exceptional sentences by judges; unjustified violation/infraction resulting in the imposition of administrative or disciplinary segregation; or the unwarranted loss of privileges or good time, or any action the staff member might excuse by saying that the action would lead to a "just end," even if at the expense of "just means."

TWO INSIDIOUS TYPES OF ABUSE

Excessive Use of Force

One particular type of unethical behavior deserves special attention because the harm can be so serious for the person abused: the excessive use of force in the criminal justice system (also discussed in Chapter 10). Whether the excessive use of force was due to a desire for personal gratification, official deviance, or noble cause corruption is rarely knowable. Moreover, the actual amount of excessive use of force in policing, courts, or corrections is difficult to determine.

An attempt was made by Hemmens and Atherton (2000) to investigate the use-of-force issue in correctional institutions. In a questionnaire sent to the fifty state corrections departments, the Federal Bureau of Prisons, U.S. military organizations and the Canadian provinces, Hemmens and Atherton (1999) found that about 55% of the U.S. departments of correction (DOCs), 40% of the Canadian DOCs, 63% of the jails, and 45% of the juvenile detention facilities surveyed reported a range of 1 to 25 excessive use of force incident(s) for 1997. Although there are no data available regarding the incidents themselves the correctional agencies that responded did indicate that a range of 73% of the incidents (in the jails) to 33% (in the Canadian DOCs) resulted in disciplinary action for the correctional personnel involved.

Hemmens and Atherton (1999:80–81) identify the key indicators of excessive use of force in corrections that managers and staff should pay careful attention to as follows:

- Staff and/or inmate rumors, incident reports, and inmate grievances
- Unexplained injuries
- An increase in the frequency in the overall uses of force without a reasonable explanation

- A history of burnout and no rotation of staff in facilities that contain high-risk, disruptive inmates, affording a higher potential for excessive use of force
- Staff who fail to provide sufficient information, are clearly mimicking one another in incident reports, or are reluctant to discuss conditions surrounding a use of force, signaling the possibility that excessive force is being used
- Significant and extreme changes in inmate behavior (and in inmate group behavior)

These authors recommend a proactive use-of-force program as an effective means by which excessive use of force can be avoided. The elements of this program, which would also fit a police or court organization, involve administrative oversight, training, development, and implementation of a use-of-force policy, clear and complete documentation of incidents and training, and competency in force technology that allows for de-escalation, as well as escalation, when appropriate (see also the remedies for abuse of force discussed in Chapter 10).

Sexual and Gender Harassment

Sexual and gender harassment (or just general harassment) is a particularly problematic and pernicious category of abuses practiced by a few criminal justice staff against each other and their clients. Although one might expect that it is usually motivated by personal profit or gratification, there may be official deviance both by the perpetrator of such offenses and by coworkers and supervisors, who either do nothing to stop the offenses, encourage them, or facilitate their occurrence. As the vast number of studies indicate that sexual and gender harassment in the workplace usually, but not always, involves a male perpetrator and a female target (e.g., see U.S. Merit Systems Protection Board, 1981, 1988; Erdreich, Slavet, & Amador, 1995), there are some who believe such behavior is really motivated by a dislike or hatred of women or at least a distaste for working with them.

Sexual and gender harassment are defined by the U.S. Equal Employment Opportunity Commission in the Code of Federal Regulations (2006) as:

> "Unwelcome sexual advances, requests for sexual favors, and other verbal or physical conduct of a sexual nature constitute sexual harassment when: (1) submission to such conduct is made either explicitly or implicitly a term or condition of an individual's employment; (2) submission to or rejection of such conduct by an individual is used as the basis for employment decisions ... or (3) such conduct has the purpose or effect of unreasonably interfering with an individual's work performance or creating an intimidating, hostile or offensive working environment."

Behaviors that characterize sexual or gender harassment can range from unwelcome requests for dates or for personal information to unwelcome touching (e.g., arms around the shoulder) to stalking or physical or sexual assault. When the request for a sexual favor is tied to keeping or advancing in a job, that harassment is termed *quid pro quo* ("something for something" in Latin).

When the behavior is aimed at making the job uncomfortable for a specific gender, those actions are believed to create a *hostile environment* and are often more general gender, rather than sexual, harassment. Such behaviors might overlap with sexual harassment, but typically they include displaying pornographic materials in the work-place, comments about the inabilities of a particular gender, personal comments about body parts of one gender, jokes that focus on the ineptitude or objectification of one gender, undesirable assignments for a particular gender, and exclusion of one gender from the more desirable assignments that lead to promotion, to name a few.

The research on sexual and gender harassment in the workplace indicates that it is not uncommon. In the three largest sampling frames of public employees ever done for a personnel issue, the U.S. Merit System Protection Board (Erdreich, et al., 1995; U.S. MSPB, 1981, 1988) found that the incidence of sexual harassment among federal employees remained almost identical over a fifteen-year period. In these studies of tens of thousands of clustered, randomly assigned employees, conducted in 1980, 1987, and 1994, the rate of sexual harassment among women was 42% (1980 and 1987), and 15% (1980) and 14% (1987) among men employees in the first two studies; in 1994 44% of the women and 19% of the men reported such harassment. Other studies of state government employees report similar results (McIntyre & Renick, 1982).

In a more recent study of sexual and gender harassment among residents of Idaho, the researchers found that 68.8% of the women and 31.2% of the men reported such harassment in their workplace for the year 2000 (Stohr, et al., 2001).

Studies of sexual or gender harassment in the criminal justice workplace are less commonplace. However, the available evidence, anecdotal reports, plaintiff suits, the closed nature of some workplaces, and the tendency for such environments to be dominated by males would suggest that sexual and gender harassment is not uncommon in the criminal justice field (Amnesty International, 2004; Belknap, 2001; De Amicis, 2005; Marquart, Barnhill, & Balshaw-Biddle, 2001; Martin 1980, 1990; Pogrebin & Poole, 1998; Scarborough & Garrison 2006; Stohr, Mays, Beck, & Kelley, 1998; Thomas, 1996; Zimmer, 1986; Zupan, 1992). The evidence does indicate that the vast majority of the serious and violent sexual abuses of community members, suspects, accused persons, and inmates are by male staff of female victims (see, e.g., Box 3.1) and recall the case of the two police officers in Eugene, Oregon, who engaged in quid pro quo harassment of female community members they stopped.

However, Marquart and his colleagues (2001:892) found in their study of the Texas prison system that most of the staff who committed "general boundary violations" with inmates (e.g. "accepted or exchanged food products or craft work/materials with prisoners, or wrote letters to prisoners") were Anglo and female, interacting with male inmates. The researchers also found that staff involved in dual relationships with the inmates were overwhelmingly female (80%). But they note that in fifteen cases of sexual contact between employees and inmates, which involved "predatory situations," all the employees were male and all the inmates were female (Marquart et al., 2001). What these findings indicate is that sexual and gender harassment is not the exclusive province of men; rather, it is practiced by both male and female staff members in the criminal justice system.

The monetary costs of gender and sexual harassment are horrendous for state and local facilities and agencies. Although the charge is very difficult to "prove" in a court of law, and in most cases the plaintiff does not prevail, the court costs and staff time devoted to defending a solid case constitute a black hole of funds for a criminal justice facility or agency. One of the authors was an expert witness for the successful plaintiffs

BOX 3.5

THE UNITED NATIONS REPORT: "STRENGTHENING JUDICIAL
INTEGRITY AGAINST CORRUPTION"

In the year 2000 the United Nations convened a conference on worldwide judicial corruption. While noting that judicial corruption was a global problem,
and that no country was immune from its taint, developing nations were found
to be particularly susceptible. Yet the conference attendees recognized that
judicial corruption and the lack of integrity as "[o]ne of the main obstacles
to peace, stability, sustainable development, democracy, and human rights
around the globe" (Langseth 2001: 3). "Indicators" of corruption in any given
court included inefficient or overly efficient processing of bail, prisoners, or
charges; suspicious treatment of cases and clients; and exceptions in sentences
and charges.

Preliminary remedies suggested by the conferees included "increased pay
for judicial officers so that they might be less tempted to engage in corruption; transparency in judicial appointments and case assignments to ensure that
judges were selected based on merit and that cases were not assigned based on
corrupt influences; the adoption of a code of conduct by judicial officers; public disclosure of officers own and family assets; computerization court files;
use of alternative dispute resolution when at all possible; use of peer pressure
to encourage appropriate behavior; and punishment or disbarment of those
who engage in corruption" (Langseth 2001:3).

on two sexual harassment claims in the 1990s: the state of California was ordered to
pay over a million dollars to the plaintiffs in each case. California is just one state, it is
probable that hundreds of such cases and judgments passed through other state courts
in the last decade.

Couple the monetary costs with the time commitment and emotional turmoil and
distress these claims raise, and it becomes clear that the most prudent policy for managers and staff is to try very hard to ensure that such violations do not occur. To this
end, managers and staff should consider whether they need to enhance their policy,
procedures, and practices in the following ways

- Ensure that there is a formal policy specifically prohibiting behaviors of the types
  that comprise sexual and gender harassment. Ensure that this policy also includes
  a description of the specific disciplinary actions that violations of this policy might
  elicit.
- Model the appropriate and respectful treatment of all employees/clients.
- Train employees on the policy.

BOX 3.6

CASES IN POINT

Albany Judge recommended for Dismissal

"A state commission has recommended that a State Supreme Court judge from Albany be removed for soliciting tens of thousands of dollars in contributions from lawyers to help pay legal bills.

According to the panel, the New York State Commission on Judicial Conduct, [www.scjc.state.ny.us/] the judge, Thomas J. Spargo, had sought to stop the commission's investigation into a number of complaints by filing lawsuits in both federal and state courts. In the process, he incurred $140,000 in legal expenses and turned to lawyers with cases before him for donations."

Excerpt from an article by Lisa W. Foderaro, The New York Times, April 1, 2006. For more information on judicial corruption, see *Greylord: A Study in Judicial Corruption* (Jordan, 2006).

"Police Lose Badges After Sex Offenses"

"SALT LAKE CITY—Utah police officers most frequently lose their certification or are suspended from their jobs after sexual misconduct offenses.

Officers from agencies small and large commit sex offenses more than any other offense, including excessive force, falsifying reports or driving under the influence, according to data from the state's Peace Officers Standards and Training Council (POST) [http://post.utah.gov/index_flash.html].

An analysis of records by The Salt Lake Tribune showed that of 94 officers whose certifications were revoked between 2000 and 2005, 42 were accused of sexual offenses. Over the same five-year period, another 22 officers were suspended for the same reason."

Excerpt from an Associated Press, article in The Idaho Statesman, October 30, 2006.

"Ex-Border agents get prison for bribes."

"SAN DIEGO—Two former supervisory Border Patrol agents were sentenced Tuesday to more than six years in prison for taking nearly $200,000 in bribes from what authorities say was eastern California's largest smuggling ring of illegal immigrants from Mexico.

Mario Alvarez and Samuel McClaren released smugglers and their customers from jail while working on a prisoner transfer program with the Mexican government. They released one prisoner in a Wal-Mart parking lot for a fee of $6,000, according to court documents.

The agents, based in El Centro, once smuggled two illegal immigrants across the border themselves in a government vehicle and released them for cash, according to court documents. They turned over the location of surveillance cameras and other Border Patrol intelligence to smugglers."

Excerpt from an article by Elliot Spagat, Associated Press, The Idaho Statesman, November 1, 2006.

• Evaluate employees based on their adherence to the policy and on their respectful treatment of colleagues and clients.
• Promote only those employees who abide by the policy and model the respectful treatment of all employees/inmates/clients.
• Provide a mechanism by which employees can complain (blow the whistle) in privacy and without retribution when the policy is violated.
• Investigate all complaints of violation of the policy.
• Discipline those who fail to abide by the policy and/or facilitate the retribution against whistleblowers.

ETHICS DEFINED AND DISCUSSED

Whether deviance in the criminal justice environment is motivated by personal gratification or gain, official deviance, or noble cause, and whether the deviance takes the form of excessive use of force, sexual or gender harassment, or some other abusive behavior, the inculcation of ethical practice into the workplace is one possible way by which the manager can focus on prevention.

Ethics is *the study of what is right and wrong behavior in the professional sphere. Morality* is *the same basic concept as ethics, but it involves the private sphere.* **Ethical behavior** is action that is regarded as "right" in accordance with the ethical codes, rules and procedures, and statutes that govern the professional sphere. Again, as stated in Chapter 2, we have both ethical behavior at the individual level and *organizational integrity*—that is, an organization exhibits integrity when its actors as a whole are honest, ethical, and can be trusted by their members and the community. In a study that examined the enhancement of police integrity, the National Institute of Justice (2005:ii) found that "[a]n agency's *culture of integrity*, as defined by clearly understood and implemented policies and rules, may be more important in shaping the ethics of police officers than hiring the 'right' people" (emphasis added).

Ethical behavior often is guided by one's own beliefs about what is right and wrong. It is possible, however, that one's ethical beliefs will conflict with organizational rules and procedures and/or with state law. This was likely a greater problem in the past, when rules and procedures were rarely written down and standardized, and the informal culture promoted or ignored unethical behavior. Where racist and other discriminatory or brutal practices were part of everyday life in some agencies, there would be general condemnation today and a sense that the condoning of such behavior was unethical as was the action itself. In other words, most of us would say that it is understandable, even desirable, for staff to ignore agency edicts that are unethical, hence contrary to, or in conflict with, state law, formal procedures and policies, or current ethical practice.

Because of court challenges to criminal justice practices and procedures, over the last thirty years, however, one is less likely to find unethical behavior that is officially sanctioned, or *formally* accepted, nor are rules and procedure manuals, which are much more in evidence today, likely to promote it, all of which supports organizational integrity. Nowadays when one's personal beliefs conflict with ethically acceptable behavior in a criminal justice work environment, it is more likely that the individual, rather than the organization, is dismissive of ethical behavior and so is on the wrong side of ethical practice. Of course, some criminal justice agencies might *informally* promote or facilitate official deviance, and in this case the individual staff member should choose a more appropriate ethical path (Conover, 2000).

The Origin of Ethics

Most of the research on ethics includes some discussion of philosophical bases for decisions regarding right or wrong behavior (Braswell, McCarthy, & McCarthy, 1991; Pollock, 1994, 1998, 2004; Rohr, 1989; Solomon, 1996). Our ethical beliefs are shaped by life experiences, the prevailing culture, and important social institutions like the family, religion, and schools and perhaps by the work environment. The philosophical touchstones that are usually mentioned as guiding human decisions regarding ethics are ethical formalism, utilitarianism, religion, natural law, the ethics of virtue, the ethics of care, and egoism. These "ethical frameworks" for criminal justice agencies are buttressed by ethical systems that are the source of moral beliefs (Pollock, 1998).

There are both deontological and teleological ethical systems that shape moral behavior. **Deontological ethical systems** are concerned with whether the act itself is good, whereas **teleological ethical systems** are focused on the consequences of the act. If the act is moral or ethical, then the consequences are unimportant according to someone who is guided by a deontological system. But if an act that is immoral or unethical results in a "good" outcome, someone guided by a teleological system would be satisfied. Pollock defines the ethical frameworks that fall under these ethical systems in her book *Ethics in Crime and Justice: Dilemmas and Decisions* (1998).

She first defines **ethical formalism** as "[w]hat is good is that which conforms to the categorical imperative" (Pollock, 1998:48). There is a universal law of what is right or moral and what is wrong or immoral. One must do ones duty in order to comply with this law. According to Immanuel Kant (1724–1804), who defined the *categorical imperative* as the requirement for each person to act as the individual would wish all people to. Kant believed that people must resort to their higher reason to shape decisions. This is a deontological approach because there is a focus on the act and its rightness, rather than on the consequences of the act. Ethical formalism is an absolutist position, where all acts are either and always right or wrong. Therefore, acts such as murder, lying, and stealing were always wrong even when the end they purportedly serve might be morally good.

Utilitarianism is described as "[w]hat is good is that which results in the greatest utility for the greatest number" (Pollock, 1998:48). An individual's actions are moral if they maximize the greatest good for the greatest number of people. The British philosopher Jeremy Bentham (1748–1832) believed that because individuals will seek pleasure over pain, they will do a "utilitarian calculus" to determine what action will result in more pleasure. When an individual's pleasure conflicts with a desirable societal outcome, then the greater good for the larger number should prevail. This is a teleological perspective because the focus is on the good or bad end or the pleasure or pain, rather than on the good or bad means, or the intent of the actor, as it was with ethical formalism. In criminal justice work, one would focus on acting so that the greatest good might be served for the greatest number.

A **religious perspective** would include the belief that "[w]hat is good is that which conforms to God's will" (Pollock, 1998:48). This type of perspective guides beliefs about what is right and wrong, how to treat others, and the meaning and purpose of life. Religions approach these topics in different ways with a focus on both means and ends, depending on the circumstances. Most religions have reference to a higher power, a spiritual being, or beings, as a source for the belief system. For example, the teachings of Christianity, Judaism, Islam, Hinduism, and Buddhism include explicit or implicit reference to a universal set of rights and wrongs. Most religions teach some form of the categorical imperative, often formulated as "Do unto others as you would have done unto you." Although there is some agreement about what constitutes right and wrong among most religions, there is disagreement about certain social practices such as drinking alcohol, dancing, foods, behavior on holy days, and the appropriateness of types of clothing, and about the political status of women and other political minorities such as gays or lesbians.

Someone who adheres to a **natural law** ethical framework believes that "[w]hat is good is that which is natural" (Pollock, 1998:48). Behavior is guided by a universal set of rights and wrongs that are knowable for all of us. The major difference between a natural law framework and a religious framework of moral beliefs is merely that in the former case there is no supreme being for reference. According to a natural law perspective, we know what truth and decency are; we merely have to act on our existing natural inclinations to do good. "Morality is part of the natural order of the universe. Further, this morality is the same across cultures and times" (Pollock, 1998:41). Out of these natural laws flow natural rights, or so the authors of the U.S. Constitution believed.

Proponents of the **ethics of virtue** ethical framework propose that "[w]hat is good is that which conforms to the golden mean [the middle ground between extreme positions]" (Pollock, 1998:48). Whether a person is good or virtuous is more important than whether an action is. The important teleological end to achieve is living a good and moral life by performing virtuous acts. "Virtues that a good person possesses include thriftiness, temperance, humility, industriousness, and honesty" (Pollock, 1998:43). Morality is learned from models or "moral exemplars" and is reinforced when the law is just. To determine what a virtuous act is, an individual must find the "golden mean." A person who develops a "habit of integrity" does not even consider acting unethically.

BOX 3.7

POLICE ETHICS AND PUBLIC TRUST: GETTING ALL THE SYSTEMS RIGHT

By Pierce Murphy, Boise Community Ombudsman

"At the beginning of 1996, the population of Boise, Idaho, stood at 140,000 and its police force employed 240 sworn personnel. Boise was a quiet city, certainly by national standards, and no one was prepared for the events of the next 21 months. Between January of 1996 and September of 1997, the Boise Police Department experienced seven officer-involved shootings. Eight deaths resulted, one of them the tragic death of Officer Mark Stahl, the first Boise officer killed in the line of duty. With each new shooting, more and more questions were raised in the media and on the street. By the sixth incident, the Idaho State Police were asked to jointly investigate, along with the Boise Police, in an effort to address growing questions about the police department's ability to investigate itself. Two separate citizen groups formed, each one calling for some form of police commission or citizen oversight of the police. Editorials were written demanding answers and scores of people showed up for town hall meetings. Battle lines were drawn between those calling for support of the police and others saying the police could not be trusted.

Boise's mayor and the City Council responded to these events by announcing the creation of a new position in the mayor's office: an ombudsman who would mediate between the community and the police and have a role in resolving citizen complaints. Their goal was to restore public trust and confidence in the police department; and they wanted to calm a volatile political situation. Precisely how the ombudsman's office would function and the specific duties assigned to it were not clear. These details were left to the first ombudsman to work out and recommend to the City Council.

I was appointed Boise's first ombudsman in March of 1999 and immediately began work drafting empowering legislation and detailed procedures. In July the City Council unanimously passed an ordinance specifying the ombudsman's duties and ensuring sufficient authority and independence to perform them. The ombudsman reports to both the mayor and the City Council and can only be removed for cause following a public hearing and a vote for removal by five out of six council members, or four council members plus the mayor. The independence of the ombudsman is assured by a section of the ordinance making it unlawful for anyone to undermine or attempt to undermine that independence. This same ordinance requires the ombudsman to perform the following duties: receive and investigate complaints about law enforcement, independently investigate police incidents involving the use of deadly force or resulting in death or serious injury, audit internal affairs investigations, make policy recommendations, act as a mediator, issue public reports, and conduct community outreach.

To assure the community and the police that the ombudsman had the tools necessary to arrive at the facts and reach reasonable findings, the ordinance requires all city employees to truthfully answer questions put to them by the ombudsman and to provide him with any documents, information, and evidence he requests in the course of an ombudsman investigation. The ordinance also gives the ombudsman unfettered access to any and all police records and files. At the same time, the ordinance requires the ombudsman to respect the privacy of all parties and follow state and federal privacy laws.

I took this position because I believe that, in order to enjoy the blessings of a safe and stable community, individuals must be willing to contribute to that community in an active and even sacrificial manner. I saw how trust in the Boise Police Department had been damaged by unsubstantiated and overly generalized assertions. A serious and substantial breach of trust existed between some members of the community and the police officers serving and protecting them. There was, to borrow a phrase, an "alienation of affection" between the public and the police. However, divorce was not an option; something needed to be done to rebuild the relationship and get the partners in public safety working together again.

As the ombudsman, I share in the responsibility of maintaining public trust in the police. The public possesses a healthy suspicion of those in the government who possess the power to take away their property, their freedom, and their very lives. Trust and suspicion cannot coexist. The ombudsman's office is an objective and independent source of information about police activities. I am an advocate for accountable, professional, and ethical policing. Through my public reports and community outreach I am able to lift the veil of secrecy that often shrouds law enforcement, to open a window through which the public can view its police department. At the same time, the police receive vital feedback and learn more about the concerns of their community.

Based on my experience as a human resources professional and, more recently, as a police oversight official, I am convinced that a key strategy for maintaining the trust of the community is to take a "whole system" view of police ethics. Law enforcement agencies must hire people whose core character is inherently directed towards service and ethical behavior. Recruiting efforts and the applicant screening process should identify candidates who, given adequate encouragement and controls, will act responsibly and ethically. Investing in thorough and high-quality pre-employment background investigations will produce better officers and reduce future civil liability. The organization's culture, policies, and human resource systems must be aligned to encourage and reward behavior that rises to the highest ethical and professional standards. These systems, in addition to selection, include promotions, training, performance management, compensation, informal rewards, feedback (from both internal and external "customers"), internal audit and investigations, and complaint resolution."

Pierce Murphy earned a master of pastoral studies degree from Loyola University of New Orleans, a master of arts degree in counseling psychology from Gonzaga University in Spokane, Washington, and a bachelor of science degree in commerce from Santa Clara University in Santa Clara, California. He began his career in 1972 as a law enforcement officer with the City of Menlo Park in California. Prior to work in the private sector, beginning in 1994, as manager of human resource development, he maintained a human resource management consulting practice.

One who believes in the **ethics of care** ethical framework subscribes to the statement that "[w]hat is good is that which meets the needs of those concerned" (Pollock, 1998:48). This perspective is focused on the feelings, needs, and care of others, rather than on whether action is, or should be, guided by universal conceptions of right or wrong. It is known as a more feminine perspective, since women are regarded as viewing the wrongness of actions undertaken to care for or nurture others as being attenuated by the human needs of those involved. Carol Gilligan (1982) found in her work on moral development that women, more than men, have a moral perspective that differs from that enunciated in western ethics. They are more likely to identify the care and concern for others as more important to guiding ethical practice. Peacemaking justice and restorative justice are believed to flow from this ethical system. The goal of these perspectives is to meet the needs of all actors, while at the same time preventing further criminality.

Pollock (1998) also describes a more individualistic ethical framework titled **egoism**. Someone who believes in this framework thinks that "[w]hat is good is that which benefits me" (Pollock, 1998:48). Egoism is focused on what is best for an individual. In this framework, an individual who acts to satisfy needs or wants is acting ethically. It is believed that humans evolved and survived only because of this drive to satisfy their needs, therefore, acts in service of self are not only ethical, they are natural and the only way humans can act. A form of this system, *enlightened egoism,* predicts that even when people are acting in what appears to be a selfless manner, they are in fact acting egoistically to ensure that others treat them similarly.

A WARNING SIGN: TOO MUCH FOCUS ON ENDS OVER MEANS

Because the motivations and ethical frameworks for unethical and deviant behavior vary in criminal justice agencies, the remedies vary as well. It is relatively easy to recognize and dispense with corruption at the individual level, as the attentive manager can see that it usually involves both corrupt ends and means.

At times, however, the ends of official deviance and noble cause corruption may be good, or perceived as such by the actor and even the organization, but the means are corrupt. One thing is certain, if staff are inordinately focused on the ends of the system and dismissive of the need to have just means, managers have a clear warning signal that staff are prone to engage in official deviance, noble cause corruption, or both.

Of course, as with any violation, there are degrees of seriousness that should govern the response to, or remedy for, the deviance. Some research on jails and prisons does indicate that staff seem to be able to identify clear violations. In 1998 and 1999 Stohr, Hemmens, Kifer, and Schoeler (2000) administered a 33-item "ethics instrument" to 467 correctional staff members at three prisons, two jails, and a jail detention academy class in a western state (see the chapter appendix for a revised version of this instrument for the jails). They found that for some types of deviance there are "bright lines" of perception for staff, or behaviors that respondents generally agree are wrong. Usually the strongest agreement was found on items that violate state laws, as well as organizational policies and ethics codes. For instance, there was a high level of agreement about the wrongness of theft or contraband smuggling by staff. But there was less certainty regarding items concerned with respect of inmates or other staff members, which are typically violations of organizational procedures and ethics codes, but not statutes.

THE WAR ON TERROR PRESENTS THE PERFECT CONDITIONS FOR ETHICAL ABUSE

After the September 11, 2001, attack by terrorists on American soil, the country experienced an understandable, sense of urgency to catch and prosecute those guilty of planning the offences. A "war on terror" was declared, and military might was exercised in pursuing terrorists around the world and at home. In democracies, however, wars can lead to suppression of speech and suspension of due process even when the battleground is not necessarily in the homeland. But when people have reason to feel threatened at home, this felt need to single out the wrongdoers takes on a whole new urgency.

Witness, for example, the suspension of due process rights by President Lincoln during the Civil War (Currie, 1985). Or the internment of Japanese Americans during World War II (when there was the false impression that American citizens of Japanese descent were engaged in wartime espionage in the states) (Irons, 1999). Or even the "war on drugs" that has led to an unraveling of some case law regarding property rights (asset seizures and forfeitures) and privacy rights (search and seizure) (Cole, 1999).

We do not yet know the long-term effect of the "war on terror" on criminal justice agencies at the local, state, and federal levels. Thus far, however, the war seems to have created the perfect admixture for ethical abuses to occur in agencies. First and foremost, the motivation for ethical abuses is there: What more noble cause is there than saving the homeland? What organization would not encourage deviance to catch terrorists? When matters are conducted in secrecy, with little outside review by the courts, the media, the public, or its representatives, what is to stop individual actors from profiting from this war? Second, secrecy is emphasized in this war, which would tend to provide cover for wiretapping and torture, to name a few abuses highlighted in news reports (see Box 3.8). Third, there is evidence of suppression of speech and due process rights, liberties and protections that free peoples typically rely on to prevent the rise of tyrantnical goverments.

At the federal level, law enforcement agencies are most susceptible to ethical abuse because of their proximity to the war and their primary responsibility for executing it. Witness, for example, the widespread secret wiretapping of American citizens without a warrant or without prior court approval a practice that many legal scholars are calling illegal behavior (Lichtblau & Risen, 2005; Strobel & Landay, 2005). Or the accusation (under investigation in December 2005) that the FBI falsified documents to cover up mistakes made in a Florida terror investigation and then punished a whistle-blower (an FBI agent himself) when he called attention to those mistakes (Lichtblau, 2005:25):

> "The agent who first alerted the F.B.I. to problems in the case, a veteran undercover operative named Mike German, was "retaliated against" by his boss, who was angered by the agent's complaints and stopped using him for prestigious assignments in training new undercover agents at F.B.I. schools, the draft report concluded."
>
> Mr. German's case first became public last year, as he emerged as the latest in a string of whistleblowers at the F.B.I. who said they had been punished and effectively silenced for voicing concerns about the handling of terror investigations and other matters since Sept. 11, 2001.

Mr. German reluctantly left the FBI even as he proclaimed his respect for the people who worked there. But he claimed his career had been ruined because he spoke out. Senator Charles E. Grassley, an Iowa Republican, agreed with Mr. German, stating in a *New York Times* article that "[u]nfortunately, this is just another case in a long line of FBI whistle-blowers who have had their careers derailed because the FBI couldn't tolerate criticism" (Lichtblau, 2005:25).

Local law enforcement is likely to experience some of the same challenges, though to a lesser degree, to ethical behavior because of the "war on terror" as those in federal agencies. One way in which local law enforcement has become involved in this war is via the FBI-organized Joint Terrorism Task Forces (FBI, 2004). The JTTFs are composed of FBI agents and state and local law enforcement and other federal agency members situated in over a hundred cities nationwide. Some JTTFs existed before September 11, 2001, and sixty-five were created afterward. The task force, collaborate on secret investigations of alleged terrorist activities in cities and states. The FBI claims that the JTTFs were involved in the identification of terrorist cells in Portland, Oregon, and northern Virginia, for example (FBI, 2004). It remains to be seen how this collaboration will play out at the local and state levels. However, experience suggests that certain factors, such as secrecy, lack of review by the courts, intolerance of dissent, and the urgency that a "war" implies, will set the stage for ethical abuses motivated by personal greed/benefit, organizational deviance, and/or noble cause corruption, (as indicated in Box 3.8.)

Box 3.8

THE *LOS ANGELES TIMES* REVIEWS ABUSE OF MUSLIM PRISONERS

9/11 Prisoner abuse suit could be landmark: rounded up, muslim immigrants were beaten in jail. Such open-ended detentions and sweeps might be barred

"NEW YORK—Five years after Muslim immigrants were abused in a federal jail here, the guards who beat them and the Washington policymakers who decided to hold them for months without charges are being called to account.

Some 1,200 Middle Eastern men were arrested on suspicion of terrorism after the attacks of Sept. 11, 2001. No holding place was so notorious as Brooklyn's nine-story Metropolitan Detention Center. In a special unit on the top floor, detainees were smashed into walls, repeatedly stripped and searched, and often denied basic legal rights and religious privileges, according to federal investigations.

Now the federal Bureau of Prisons, which runs the jail, has revealed for the first time that 13 staff members have been disciplined, two of them fired. The warden has retired and moved to the Midwest.

And in what could turn out to be a landmark case, a lawsuit filed by two Brooklyn detainees against top Bush administration officials is moving forward in the federal courts in New York.

Five investigations by the Department of Justice inspector general's office, most of them never publicized, documented wholesale abuse of the Muslim detainees at the Brooklyn detention center. In the months after the Sept. 11 attacks, 84 men were held there. None was charged in the attacks. Most were deported on immigration infractions.

One disturbing incident, repeated over and over, is particularly haunting—inmates head-slammed into a wall where the staff had taped a T-shirt with an American flag printed on it. The motto on the shirt proclaimed: "These colors don't run." In time, that spot on the wall was covered with blood.

Guards at the detention center first denied there was any mistreatment, then slowly came forward. Finally videotapes were uncovered that showed abuse, including detainees head-butted into the T-shirt on the wall.

Traci Billingsley, a spokeswoman for the federal Bureau of Prisons, said 13 staff members have been disciplined. Two were fired, two received 30-day suspensions and one was suspended for 21 days. Two more were suspended for four days, three for two days, and three were demoted."

Excerpt from an article by Richard A. Serrano, Los Angeles Times, November 20, 2006. For the full story, see http://www.latimes.com/news/nationworld/nation/la-na-jail20nov20,0,4583237.story?coll=la-home-headlines.

THE ETHICAL REMEDY TO ALLEVIATE THE DEGREE OF ABUSE, DEVIANCE, CORRUPTION, AND HARASSMENT

As the preceding review of the ethical frameworks indicates, most of us derive our conception of moral behavior from several sources. Therefore, the approach used to ensure that ethical behavior is practiced in the workplace must also adjust. What is clear from the discussion of official deviance and noble cause explanations for abuse and corruption is that the manager interested in inculcating ethics into the criminal justice workplace must be as concerned with just means as with just ends (Muraskin & Muraskin, 2001). In addition to the solutions to alleviate abuse and corruption that have already been suggested throughout the chapter, and grievance procedures and whistleblowing mechanisms that will be reviewed in other chapters, we shall also explore the inculcation of *ethics* as a preventive measure for the criminal justice environment. For the inculcation of ethics to have any effect on the workplace, however, there needs to be a level of commitment by managers to meaningfully engage their colleagues in a discussion of what an ethical work environment would be like and how to make it the reality.

As part of two ethics training exercises for thirty state probation and parole managers conducted in 1994 and 1995,[2] one of the authors, along with a colleague, explored just this topic. First, they asked the managers to identify barriers to ethical practice in their workplace. Most of the barriers identified also had been noted by Kauffman (1988:85–112) in his study of correctional officers and included by Pollock (1994:195) in her text on ethics and concerned the reinforcement of negative behaviors by the subculture. The sometimes problematic behaviors identified by Kauffman, and reaffirmed as applicable by the managers, included the following:

1. Always aid your coworker.
2. Never rat on coworkers.
3. Always cover for a coworker in front of clients.
4. Always support the coworker over the client in a disagreement.
5. Always support the decision of a coworker regarding a client.
6. Don't be sympathetic toward clients. Instead be cynical about them (to be otherwise is to be naïve).
7. Probation/parole officers are the "us" and everyone else is the "them," including administration, the media, and the rest of the community.
8. Help your coworkers by completing your own work and by assisting them if they need it.
9. Since you aren't paid much or appreciated by the public or the administration, don't be a rate buster (i.e., don't do more than the minimal amount of work).
10. Handle your own work and don't allow interference.

Notably, a few of these subcultural values are positive, such as aiding your coworker or doing your work so others do not have to. But most of the values, if adopted by staff, would foster unethical work practices. In fact, most of the managers in those training sessions admitted that they regularly encountered unethical behavior on the job, from the relatively benign and more common rudeness to clients and their families to the rarer lying on reports or verbal or physical abuse of clients. In addressing these issues, the managers were stymied by the negative subcultural values that reinforced unethical behaviors by some and then prevented others from confronting or reporting it.

Of course, a number of professional criminal justice organizations have developed codes of ethics that promote an ideal workplace (e.g., see Box 3.9). But just having

BOX 3.9

THE LAW ENFORCEMENT CODE OF ETHICS

"As a law enforcement officer, my fundamental duty is to serve the community; to safeguard lives and property; to protect the innocent against deception, the weak against oppression or intimidation and the peaceful against violence or disorder; and to respect the constitutional rights of all to liberty, equality and justice.

I will keep my private life unsullied as an example to all and will behave in a manner that does not bring discredit to me or to my agency. I will maintain courageous calm in the face of danger, scorn or ridicule; develop self-restraint; and be constantly mindful of the welfare of others. Honest in thought and deed both in my personal and official life, I will be exemplary in obeying the law and the regulations of my department. Whatever I see or hear of a confidential nature or that is confided to me in my official capacity will be kept ever secret unless revelation is necessary in the performance of my duty.

I will never act officiously or permit personal feelings, prejudices, political beliefs, aspirations, animosities or friendships to influence my decisions. With no compromise for crime and with relentless prosecution of criminals, I will enforce the law courteously and appropriately without fear or favor, malice or ill will, never employing unnecessary force or violence and never accepting gratuities.

I recognize the badge of my office as a symbol of public faith, and I accept it as a public trust to be held so long as I am true to the ethics of police service. I will never engage in acts of corruption or bribery, nor will I condone such acts by other police officers. I will cooperate with all legally authorized agencies and their representatives in the pursuit of justice.

I know that I alone am responsible for my own standard of professional performance and will take every reasonable opportunity to enhance and improve my level of knowledge and competence.

I will constantly strive to achieve these objectives and ideals, dedicating myself before God to my chosen profession...law enforcement."

Code provided courtesy of the International Association of Chiefs of Police website www.theiacp.org. *Reprinted here with permission from the IACP.*

such codes on a wall does little to reinforce them in the workplace, though their very existence is a first step. What is really needed is some co-option and remolding of the subculture so that the ethical values that an organization wants to promote are supported by most workers in the organization.

Here lies the difficulty for the criminal justice managers and staff: How does one get all or most staff to buy into completely ethical practice when they have multiple motivations and may adhere to different ethical frameworks? Pierce Murphy, the Community Ombudsman for the City of Boise Police Department, faced just this issue when he undertook this role (see Box 3.7). He needed to first define his position and authority; then he could proceed to recommending organizational changes that were more likely to lead to an ethics-based subculture at this agency.

Relatedly, the probation and parole managers at the training sessions we conducted thought that the first step was to define what an ethical manager is.[3] The "Model of An Ethical Manager" that evolved from those discussions contained the following items.

THE ETHICAL MANAGER IS:

1. Respectful and civil in treatment of staff, clientele, the department, and community members.

2. A person who knows that personal relationships should not be allowed to interfere with professional treatment or merit considerations affecting others.

3. A person who adheres to legal standards, including due process protections for staff and clientele, and works to ensure their maintenance and facilitation.

4. A person who ensures that monies are expended in the most efficient and effective manner.

5. A person who ensures that staff are assigned where and when they are most needed to provide the optimal program delivery.

6. A person who ensures that program substantive content is valid.

7. A person who ensures that staff are allocated the time, training, and the resources to successfully fulfill their assigned tasks.

8. A person who ensures that program outcomes are measured and measurable.

9. A person who models ethical behavior.

10. A person who is fair and forthright in all dealings with staff, clientele, administration and community members.

11. A person who listens emphathetically.

12. A person who is accountable for actions of self and team members in the workplace.

13. A person who has integrity in that he or she will not be swayed by what is politically expedient, but is guided by concerns for justice and adherence to legal requirements.

14. A person who reinforces and rewards ethical behavior by other staff in all personnel processes (selection, training, performance appraisals, promotions, and assignments).

15. A person who disciplines violators of ethical and professional standards of behavior.

BOX 3.10

AN EXPERIENCED COUNTY JUDGE REFLECTS ON ETHICS,
SUPERVISION, AND STANDARDS

By Judge John A. Bozza

"The best oversight of ethics is done by supervision. Likewise, the best control
of discretion is supervision. Managers (of all units) have to ensure that standards are met and enforced. The process for resolving any disputes that might
arise has to be clear to the point of outlining the particular steps in the process.
Moreover, each organization has to have a management system that supports
the standards. All employees need to be trained on the policy manual and then
become acquainted with all policies that apply to their specific area.

After my many years of service in the courts, I have found that the most
common ethical lapses vary depending on the type of case you are talking
about. On the criminal side, the most common professional lapses by defense
attorneys include a lack of communication with clients (communication is
inadequate because of caseload pressures). In turn, a common prosecutorial
professional lapse would be the inadvertent failure to disclose evidence (also
largely due to caseload pressures).

Furthermore, I believe that defense and prosecuting offices suffer from
a lack of performance standards that permeates the rest of government.
Inadequate supervision in those organizations and the lack of performance
standards can lead to the common ethical and professional lapses seen in the
field. Unfortunately, too often governmental agencies do not often provide
much incentive to do the job more efficiently. Because of this lack, poor performance is related to the notion that what is good performance is not very
clear."

*Judge Bozza works for the Erie County Court of Common Pleas in Pennsylvania.[4] He
has been on the bench since 1989. He has taught criminal justice for seventeen years
and was the director of a criminal justice program at Gannon University, in Erie.
He also has an extensive history as a practicing attorney doing civil work and as an
assistant prosecuting attorney and a public defender. He once worked as a probation
officer. He earned his MA in criminal justice from the State University of New York at
Albany in 1972 and his law degree from DePaul University in 1979.*

*While on the bench Judge Bozza has undertaken a number of administrative
assignments; namely, he has served as both the president judge and, separately, as the
administrative judge, for his court on more than one occasion. The president judge for
each district makes policies and the administrative judge implements them. The size
of the court determines exactly what their respective roles are. In these roles Judge
Bozza has been called upon to handle budgetary, personnel, ethical, and political
matters.*

16. A person who provides a mechanism by which personnel can report violations.

17. A person who ensures that whistleblowers are not punished.

18. A person who gives employees developmental feedback so that they might know what is and isn't ethically acceptable in the department.

19. A person who communicates openly and freely with employees.

20. A person who values and facilitates employee input and decision-making processes.

21. A person who ensures that output from self and others is qualitatively high.

22. A person who facilitates the growth of others.

23. A person who is concerned with the human dignity of the clientele.

24. A person who is concerned about the safety of the community.

25. A person who seeks first to understand and then to be understood.

Clearly, this model reflects a number of the ethical frameworks defined by Pollock (1998) and encompasses a recognition of the influence that official deviance and noble cause perspectives can have on the subculture of any criminal justice agency. It also reflects not just what an ethical manager *should do*, but what a good manager generally *should be*. But even if managers in criminal justice adopt this model, a problem still remains: How does the ethical manager reform a subculture so that it reflects ethical values?

One possible way to reshape the subculture is to engage the workforce in an open discussion about the development of a code (using the relevant professional codes as models) (Barrier, Stohr, Hemmens, & Marsh, 1999; Pollock, 1994). That discussion would be followed with training throughout the workplace on that code and how to implement it (use of related scenarios would be instructive). Then the code would need to be reinforced in all selection, performance appraisal, and promotion decisions. In this way, the *formal* workplace (rules, procedures, processes) would shape the *informal* subculture of that agency because those who bought into the ethical values would be rewarded in a number of ways.

CONCLUSIONS

In this chapter we have discussed the explanations for abuse and corruption with some focus on two particularly destructive types of deviance in criminal justice agencies— excessive use of force and sexual and gender harassment. A review of the nature and origin of ethics was included, as was the proposal that the inculcation of ethics into the workplace is one possible means management might choose in trying to improve the work environment for staff and their clients.

As was mentioned at the beginning of the chapter, and as history would instruct us, criminal justice agencies and the honorable work performed in them are particularly susceptible to corruption and abuse. But with a clear-eyed focus on "just" means and ends, and attention to the need to keep the subcultural forces on the side of angels, the task of reinforcing ethical work behavior and creating organizational integrity in criminal justice is always doable.

EXERCISE : THE STUDENT'S ETHICS QUIZ[5]

One of the authors has conducted this informal quiz once, but with interesting and highly relevant results, so proceed at your own risk! On the single occasion of its use, the quiz was administered at the beginning of class to sharpen students' interest in a discussion of ethics.

1. Ask students to take out a blank sheet of paper and tell them they are going to take a little quiz. Once the outcry dies down, say that the quiz will not be graded and is meant only to be illustrative of the topics that can be discussed in terms of ethics.
2. Tell them not to put their names on their papers.
3. Ask them to respond to the following six questions regarding their college career:
    (a) Do you know someone who has cheated on a test? (yes/no)
    (b) If yes, how many times have you been aware that someone has cheated on a test? (put the raw number down)
    (c) Do you know someone who has cheated on a paper? (yes/no)
    (d) If yes, how many times have you been aware that someone has cheated on a paper? (put the raw number down)
    (e) What sorts of measures do you think would keep a student from cheating on a test or paper? (list up to five)
    (f) What sorts of measures do you think would keep a police officer, courtroom actor, or corrections actor from engaging in corrupt behavior while on the job? (list up to five).
4. Collect the response sheets from the students.
5. Ask for six student volunteers and assign a question to each of them.
6. Line the six up by question order and tell them how to keep track of the responses to each question (for twenty five people in my class this took about five minutes).
7. Have each student write the responses to his or her question on the board and discuss the findings.

DISCUSSION QUESTIONS

1. What might motivate unethical behavior by criminal justice actors? Why?
2. What is the difference between the official deviance and noble cause motivations? Give an example.
3. How might the "smell of victims blood" and the "tower" be associated with unethical behavior by criminal justice actors? Give an example.
4. Under what circumstances are abuse of force and sexual/gender harassment more likely to occur and why? Explain.
5. How is ethics different from morality? Why? Explain your answer.

6. What is the difference between informal and formally sanctioned ethical lapses in behavior? Give an example.

7. What is the difference between deontological and teleological ethical systems for the control of ethical practices in criminal justice? Give an example.

8. How do the different origins of ethics affect people's view of them? What origins seem most suited for ensuring that criminal justice staff and administrators adhere to ethical codes? Why?

9. How are the means and ends of criminal justice work tied up in the discussion of ethics? What is the importance of each? Explain your answer.

KEY TERMS

deontological ethical systems: concerned with whether an act itself is good. To someone who is guided by a deontological system, if an act is moral or ethical, then the consequences are unimportant.

deviance by staff: involving behavior that violates the statutes, institutional rules or procedures, or ethical codes for individual *or* organizational gain *or* even as a means of serving a "noble cause" (Bartollas & Hahn, 1999; Crank & Caldero, 2000: Lee & Visano, 1994).

egoism: the belief that "[w]hat is good is that which benefits me" (Pollock, 1998:48).

ethics: the study of what is right and wrong behavior in the professional sphere; morality is the same basic concept as applied to the private sphere;

ethical behavior: action that is regarded as "right" per the ethical codes, rules and procedures, and statutes that govern the professional sphere.

ethical formalism: "[w]hat is good is that which conforms to the categorical imperative" (Pollock, 1998:48).

ethics of care: "[w]hat is good is that which meets the needs of those concerned" (Pollock, 1998:48).

ethics of virtue: "[w]hat is good is that which conforms to the golden mean" (Pollock, 1998:48).

natural law: "[w]hat is good is that which is natural" (Pollock, 1998:48).

noble cause: for police officers, "[a] profound moral commitment to make the world a safer place to live. Put simply, it is getting bad guys off the street. Police believe they're on the side of angels and their purpose in life is getting rid of bad guys" (Crank & Caldero, 2000:35).

official deviance: "[a]ctions taken by officials which violate the law and/or the formal rules of the organization, but which are clearly oriented toward the needs and goals of the organization, as perceived by the official, and thus fulfill certain informal rules of the organization" (Lee & Visano, 1994).

religious perspective: includes the belief that "[w]hat is good is that which conforms to God's will" (Pollock, 1998:48).

teleological ethical systems: focused on the consequences of the act. But an immoral or unethical act that results in a "good" outcome would satisfy someone guided by a teleological system.

utilitarianism: "[w]hat is good is that which results in the greatest utility for the greatest number" (Pollock, 1998:48).

NOTES

1. The professor was Mark Fleischer, who spoke at Washington State University in spring 1987.
2. Drs. Robert L. Marsh and Mary K. Stohr conducted two ethics training sessions for probation and parole managers in the state of Idaho in 1994 (half-day session) and a follow-up in 1995 (day-long session).
3. This model of an ethical manager was also informed by Stohr and Marsh's reading of a number of texts on ethics and/or management, our interpretation of the Idaho Code of Ethics for Field and Community Service Officers, and comments by students in Stohr's Criminal Justice Management class (spring 1995). The last item in the model was also influenced by the "Prayer of Saint Francis." Frankly, for most of these items, it is difficult to determine who said what!
4. Interviewed by phone by Mary K. Stohr on April 26, 2006.
5. Some colleges and universities will expect that student surveys be subjected to institutional review because the work entails human subjects.

REFERENCES

Amnesty International. (2004). *Abuse of women in custody: Sexual misconduct and shackling of pregnant women, a state-by-state survey of policies and practices in the United States.* Accessed at www.amnestyusa.org on April 5, 2005.

Bard, S. (1997, July 31). Idaho inmates tell of assault in Texas: Nurses, who prisoners say fondled them, have been arrested and fired. *The Idaho Statesman,* p. B1.

Barrier, G., Stohr, M. K., Hemmens, C., & Marsh, R. (1999). A practical user's guide: Idaho's method for implementing ethical behavior in a correctional setting. *Corrections Compendium, 24*(4), 1–3, 14–15.

Bartollas, C., & Hahn, L. D. (1999). *Policing in America.* Needham Heights, MA: Allyn & Bacon.

Belknap, J. (2001). *Invisible woman: Gender, crime, and justice* (2nd ed.). Belmont, CA: Wadsworth/Thomson Learning.

Bennett, W. W., & Hess, K. M. (2001). *Management and supervision in law enforcement.* Belmont, CA: Wadsworth Thomson Learning.

Braswell, M. C., McCarthy, B. R. & McCarthy, B. J. (1991). *Justice, crime and ethics.* Cincinnati, OH: Anderson Publishing Co.

Clear, T. R., & Cole, C. F. (1997). *American corrections.* Belmont, CA: Wadsworth.

Code of Federal Regulations (2006).Title 29, 4: 198–204. Washington, D.C.: U.S. Government Printing Office. Citation: 29CFR1604.11.

Cole, D. (1999). *No equal justice: Race and class in the American criminal justice system.* New York: New Press.

Conover, T. (2000). *New Jack: Guarding Sing Sing*. New York: Random House.

Courtless, T. F. (1998). *Corrections and the criminal justice system: Laws, policies, and practices*. Belmont, CA: West/Wadsworth.

Crank, J. P., & Caldero, M. A. (2000). *Police ethics: The corruption of noble cause*. Cincinnati, OH: Anderson Publishing.

Currie, D. P. (1985). *The Constitution in the Supreme Court: The first hundred years 1789–1888*. Chicago: University of Chicago Press.

De Amicis, A. P. (2005). An ethical dilemma in corrections. *American Jails, 19*(5), 77–82.

Erdreich, B. L., Slavet, B. S., & Amador, A. C. (1995). *Sexual harassment in the federal workplace*. U.S. Merit Systems Protection Board. Washington, DC: GPO.

Federal Bureau of Investigation. (2004). Protecting America against terrorist attack: a closer look at the FBI's joint terrorism task forces. Federal Bureau of Investigation. Accessed at www.fbi.gov/page2, December 2005.

Feeley, M. M. (1983). *Court reform on trial*. New York: Basic Books.

Friedrichs, D. O. (2001). *Law in our lives: An introduction*. Los Angeles: Roxbury.

Gaines, L. K., Worrall, J. L., Southerland, M. D. & J. E. Angell (2003). *Police administration, second edition*. Boston: McGraw Hill.

Gallagher, C., Maguire, E. R., Mastrofski, S. D., & Reisig, M. D. (2001). *The public image of the police*. Final report to the International Association of Chiefs of Police. Accessed November 11, 2005, www.theiacp.org.

Gilligan, C. (1982). *In a different voice: Psychological theory and women's development*. Cambridge, MA: Harvard University Press.

Gray, C. (2002). *A study of state judicial discipline sanctions*. Des Moines, Iowa: American Judicature Society.

Hemmens, C., & Atherton, E. (1999). *Use of force: Current practice and policy*. Lanham, MD: American Correctional Association.

Holten, N. G., & Lamar, L. (1991). *The criminal courts: Structures, personnel and processes*. New York: McGraw-Hill.

Irons, P. (1999). *A people's history of the Supreme Court: The men and women whose cases and decisions have shaped our Constitution*. New York: Viking Press.

Johnson, R. (2002). *Hard time: Understanding and reforming the prison*. Belmont, CA: Wadsworth/Thomson Learning.

Jordan, R. L. (2006). *Greylord: A study in judicial corruption*. Paper presented at the Annual Conference of Western and Pacific Association of Criminal Justice Educators, Reno, NV, October 11, 2006.

Kauffman, K. (1988). *Prison officers and their world*. Cambridge, MA: Harvard University Press.

Langseth, P. (2001). *Strengthening judicial integrity against corruption*. Vienna: United Nations Global Programme against Corruption. Accessed at www.unodc.org, November 2, 2005.

Lee, J. A., & Visano, L. A. (1994). Official deviance in the legal system. In S. Stojokovic, J. Klofas, & D. Kalinich (Eds.), *The administration and management of criminal justice organizations: A book of readings* (pp. 202–231). Prospect Heights, IL: Waveland Press.

Lichtblau, E. (2005). Report finds cover-up in an F.B.I. terror case. *The New York Times* pp. 25, Sunday, December 4.

Lichtblau, E., & J. Risen (2005). "Spy agency mined vast data trove, officials report." *The New York Times*, p. A1, A12.

Marquart, J. W. (1995). Doing research in prison: The strengths and weaknesses of full participation as a guard. In K. C. Haas & G. P. Alpert (Eds.), *The dilemmas of corrections: Contemporary readings* (pp. 166–182). Prospect Heights, IL: Waveland Press.

Marquart, J. W., Barnhill, M. B., & Balshaw-Biddle, K. (2001). Fatal attraction: An analysis of employee boundary violations in a southern prison system, 1995–1998. *Justice Quarterly, 18*(4), 877–910.

Martin, S. E. (1980). *Breaking and entering: Policewomen on patrol.* Berkeley: University of California Press.

Martin, S. E. (1990). *On the move: The status of women in policing.* Washington, DC: Police Foundation.

Mays, G. L., & Winfree, L. T. (2002). *Contemporary corrections.* Belmont, CA: Wadsworth/ Thomson Learning.

McIntyre, L. J. (2004). But how can you sleep nights? In S. Stojkovic, J. Klofas, & D. Kalinich (Eds.) *The administration and management of criminal justice organizations: A book of readings* (pp. 167–198). Long Grove, IL: Waveland Press.

McIntyre, D. & J. Renick (1982). Protecting public employees and employers from sexual harassment. *Public Personnel Management,* 11(13), 282–292.

Muraskin, R. (2001a). Probation and parole officers: Ethical behavior. In R. Muraskin & M. Muraskin (Eds.), *Morality and the law* (pp. 119–129). Upper Saddle River, NJ: Prentice Hall.

Muraskin, R. (2001b). Corrections/punishment/correctional officer. In R. Muraskin & M. Muraskin (Eds.), *Morality and the law* (pp. 140–150). Upper Saddle River, NJ: Prentice Hall.

Muraskin, R., & Muraskin, M. (Eds.). (2001). *Morality and the law.* Upper Saddle River, New Jersey: Prentice Hall.

National Center for State Courts. (1999). *How the public views the state courts: A 1999 national survey.* Report presented at the National Conference on Public Trust and Confidence in the Justice System, May 1999, Washington, DC. Accessed at www.ncsconline.org, November 11, 2005.

National Institute of Justice. (2005). *Enhancing police integrity.* NIJ Research in Practice, December, 2005. U.S. Department of Justice, Office of Justice Programs. Washington, DC: GPO.

O'Connor, M. L. (2001). Noble corruption—police perjury—what should we do? In R. Muraskin & M. Muraskin (Eds.), *Morality and the law* (pp. 91–106). Upper Saddle River, NJ: Prentice Hall.

Perrone, D., & Pratt T. (2003). Comparing the quality of confinement and cost-effectiveness of public versus private prisons: What we know, why we do not know more, and where to go from here. *Prison Journal, 83*(3), 301–322.

Pogrebin, M. R., & Poole, E. D. (1998). Women deputies and jail work. *Journal of Contemporary Criminal Justice, 14*(2), 117–134.

Pollock, J. M. (1994). *Ethics in crime and justice: Dilemmas and decisions* (2nd ed.). Belmont, CA: Wadsworth.

Pollock, J. M. (1998). *Ethics in crime and justice: Dilemmas and decisions* (3rd ed.). Belmont, CA: West/Wadsworth.

Pollock, J. M. (2004). *Ethics in crime and justice: Dilemmas and decisions* (4th ed.). Belmont, CA: Wadsworth Thomson Learning.

Reisig, M., & Pratt T. (2000). The ethics of correctional privatization: A critical examination of the delegation of coercive authority. *Prison Journal, 80*(2), 210–223.

Rohr, J. A. (1989). *Ethics for bureaucrats: An essay on law and values.* New York: Marcel Dekker, Inc.

Scarborough, K. E., & Garrison, C. (2006). Police women in the twentieth-first century. In A. V. Merlo, & J. M. Pollock (Eds.), *Women, law, and social control* (pp. 91–110). Boston: Allyn & Bacon.

Schofield, M. (1997). Tape puts for-profit prisons back in spotlight: Video shows guards abusing inmates—and jeopardizes system. *The Idaho Statesman,* August 24, pp. A1, A16.

Seligman, A. (2004). Betrayal: How will the EPD win back women's trust? *Eugene Weekly,* p. 1. Accessed at www.eugeneweekly.com, November 2, 2005.

Shichor, D. (1998). *Private prisons in perspective: Some conceptual issues. Howard Journal of Criminal Justice, 37*(1), 82–100.

Silverman, I. J., & Vega, M. (1996). *Corrections: A comprehensive view.* Minneapolis/Saint Paul: West Publishing.

Solomon, R. C. (1996). *A handbook for ethics.* Fort Worth, TX: Harcourt Brace College Publishers.

Stohr, M. K., Mays, G. L., Beck, A. C., & Kelley, T. (1998). Sexual harassment in women's jails. *Journal of Contemporary Criminal Justice, 14*(2), 135–155.

Stohr, M. K., Hemmens, C., Kifer, M., & Schoeler, M. (2000). We know it, we just have to do it: Perceptions of ethical work in prisons and jails. *The Prison Journal, 80*(2), 126–150.

Stohr, M. K., Vazquez, S. P., Prescott, C., Green, D., Smith Daniels, S., Fellen, S., Elson, R., Gloerchinger-Granks, G., Aydelotte, J., Musser, W., Uhlenkott, R., Wulfhorst, J. D., Foltz, B. & S. Raschke (2001). *Idaho crime victimization survey-2000.* Meridian, ID: Idaho state police.

Strobel, W. P., & J. S., Landay (2005). Backlash lowers spy agency morale. *The Idaho Statesman,* December 25, (2001) p. 10.

Thomas, D. Q. (1996). *All too familiar: Sexual abuse of women in U.S. state prisons.* Human Rights Watch. Accessed at www.hrw.org/summaries, April 5, 2005.

U.S. Merit Systems Protection Board, Office of Policy Evaluation. (1981). *Sexual harassment in the federal government.* Washington DC: GPO.

U.S. Merit Systems Protection Board, Office of Policy Evaluation. (1988). *Sexual harassment in the federal government.* Washington DC: GPO.

Welch, M. (1996). *Corrections: A critical approach.* New York: McGraw-Hill.

Zimmer, L. E. (1986). *Women guarding men.* Chicago: University of Chicago Press.

Zupan, L. (1992). The progress of women correctional officers in all-male prisons. In I. L. Moyers (Ed.), *The changing roles of women in the criminal justice system* (pp. 232–244). Prospect Heights, IL: Waveland Press.

THE ETHICS INSTRUMENT VERSION FOR JAILS*

Developed by M.K. Stohr and C. Hemmens (1997). Use of this instrument requires the permission of the authors (mstohr@boisestate.edu or chemmens@boisestate.edu).

Jail staffs are often faced with difficult choices that affect inmates, their job and their organization. Therefore, this instrument was developed to allow jail staff to determine which are the most pressing issues they face. Please read each question carefully and put the number that best reflects your response in the space provided in front of that question.

```
1 ----------------- 2 ------------- 3 ------------ 4 ------------5 ----------- 6----------- 7 --------------8 -------
strongly      disagree      slightly      neutral      slightly      agree      strongly      don't know
disagree                    disagree                   agree                    agree
```

_____1.   Jail staff have an obligation to report thefts by other staff.

_____2.   The only thing that inmates respect is a show of force.

_____3.   Special favors done for inmates by staff do not need to be taken seriously by the administration.

_____4.   Making sexual comments in the workplace about other staff is not harassment.

_____5.   Coworkers provide a major source of emotional and physical support on the job.

_____6.   Inmates who have committed sex offenses deserve poor treatment in jail.

_____7.   Most inmates, in most instances, will respond to an order with no force needed.

_____8.   Jail administrators should provide a means for other jail staff to have input into the operation of the institution.

_____9.   The first loyalty of jail staff is to their coworkers, not to uphold the law for the public.

_____10. Staff who bring in contraband should be disciplined.

_____11. Abusive or offensive language is sometimes appropriate when addressing inmates.

_____12. When staff see other staff abusing inmates they should report that abuse.

_____13. A jail staff member should simply listen to orders and rarely offer input.

_____14. An officer who reports the harassment of inmates by other staff is doing the right thing.

_____15. It is expected that officers on the graveyard shift will fall asleep from time to time.

_____16. Putdowns of people of the opposite sex in the workplace are usually meant to be funny.

_____17. Reasoning with inmates is usually the best way to gain their cooperation.

_____18. Use of stronger inmates by jail staff to control other inmates presents the potential for corruption.

_____19. Staff should avoid making personal comments about other staff in front of inmates.

_____20. Jail staff members have a duty to protect inmates.

_____21. Sexual relations between staff and inmates are sometimes acceptable.

_____22. Jail staff are the only people who can really understand why institutional rules often can't be followed by staff.

_____23. Staff who treat inmates with respect rarely get respect from inmates in return.

_____24. Jail staff at all levels have much knowledge to contribute to the operation of the jail.

_____25. Minority staff members should not be so sensitive about racial or ethnic slurs made by others in the workplace.

_____26. Hitting a disruptive inmate a few more times than is strictly necessary is understandable.

____27. When a jail staff member is consistent and fair with inmates they are more likely to be respected by inmates.

____28. Addressing inmates in a respectful manner may give them the idea that they can manipulate staff.

____29. Jail staff should above all concern themselves with upholding the law.

____30. Jail staff have the skills and abilities necessary to solve problems in the workplace.

____31. If most of your coworkers choose to disregard policies and procedures then it is okay for you to do so as well.

____32. Jail administrators are usually willing to listen to the concerns raised by inmates.

____33. Minority group inmates are naturally less reliable as trustees than white inmates.

____34. Staff should be most concerned about their duty to uphold the law, rather than about what their coworkers will think.

CHAPTER 4

SERVICE VALUES, THE ADMINISTRATIVE STATE, AND MANAGEMENT THEORY IN PERSPECTIVE

Administration is the most obvious part of government; it is government in action; it is the executive, the operative, the most visible side of government, and is of course as old as government itself.

(Woodrow Wilson, 1887:11)

[P]roper management of the work lives of human beings, of the way in which they earn their living, can improve them and improve the world and in this sense be a utopian or revolutionary technique.

(Abraham Maslow, 1961:1)

INTRODUCTION: A BIT OF BACKGROUND

Much of management theory regarding the operation of corrections, policing, and courts derives from the private sector. Despite Appleby's (1945) claim that government is different, management theories applied to the public and private sectors usually have been developed and tested in businesses. This is not to say that scholars in universities have not written extensively on public sector "administration." In fact, back when Woodrow Wilson was a political scientist at Princeton (1887), the future president wrote one of the first articles about how the administration, or management, of government is a separate issue from the politics of it. He also maintained that there should be a "science of administration" (Henry, 1987).

Of course any scientific approach requires theories, and some of the first of these to develop arose from the private sector and were only later, and sometimes awkwardly, applied to public organizations. A theory is "a set of ideas, concepts, principles, or methods used to explain a wide set of observed facts" (Webster, 1992:1098). Generally, this definition suits our purposes. As we review the major theorists on management in this chapter, however, we will find that such folk often believe that theories not only describe what is, in accordance with Webster's (1992) definition, but prescribe what should be.

As we found in the discussion of the influence of environmental factors on management practices, theories exist in a context. In Chapter 2 we saw that part of that context or overlay consists of the competing public service values of *democratic accountability* and *neutral competence,* which tend to shape the role and motivation of workers. Another key piece of that context is the extent to which the attributes of an administrative state exist. In this chapter, we discuss in detail these attributes, along with the predominant management theories that operate within this larger criminal justice framework.

THE ADMINISTRATIVE STATE

A thorough understanding of management theories also requires some grasp of the nature of an administrative state. By *state* here we are referring generally to the government. By *administrative* we mean that part of government, usually the executive branch, which is engaged in day-to-day operations of government. Such an understanding of the administrative state is necessary because modern management cannot exist without some sophistication in it. In other words, there needs to be a superstructure and purpose and means for government to operate and for management to be adequate. Throughout human history, the degree to which such a state existed and its level of complexity, given the time period, varied widely. Van Riper (1987:6) notes there are six attributes of an administrative state that derive from the work of the German philosopher Max Weber (see Box 4.1). Those first six attributes are as follows:

1. A workable organization in the classical hierarchical sense
2. The recruitment of expertise by merit
3. Rational decision making
4. The rule of law, with an emphasis on equality before the law
5. Written procedures and records
6. Not only a money economy, but also sufficient public funds to support a complex administrative apparatus (Van Riper, 1987:6)

BOX 4.1

A BRIEF SYNOPSIS OF THE LIFE AND TIMES OF MAX WEBER

Max Weber (1864–1920) was a German citizen, trained in the law, who taught at Berlin University for most of his life (Pugh, Hickson, & Hinings, 1985). His intellectual and philosophical explorations were quite broad and included a study of the then predominant religions (i.e. Judaism, Christianity, Buddhism) and economic development. His work on organizations was focused on "authority structures" and their categorization. He observed that the dominant rational-legal institution in modern society had a bureaucratic structure. He thought that a bureaucratic structure led to greater efficiency and regularity in organizational operations, which in turn paved the way for the spread of the capitalistic economic system, the smooth functioning of which had order and objectivity as prerequisites. Most modern studies of organizations and authority begin with Weber, though his influence was not felt in the United States till after his death, when his writings were translated into English.

Max Weber

To these six Van Riper adds the following four:

1. At least a modest base in quantitative data and technique
2. Adequate supporting technology, especially pertaining to records, communications, and numeracy
3. The enforcement of responsibility and ethical standards
4. All of the above in a moderately developed and mutually supporting arrangement (1987:6).

Let us review these ten attributes in order. The first attribute refers to the basic structure of the organizations in the state. For Weber and Van Riper this structure should be hierarchical in what one might visualize as a pyramidal shape. In organizations with a hierarchical shape there is a clearly defined leader at the top who has most of the power, and the rest of the organizations members are followers. Similarly, in the larger state there are leaders who also wield most of the power and followers who abide by their decisions. Of course, this power in a democracy is far from absolute and is tempered by the electoral process, the role and mission of organizations, and the motivation of workers and citizens.

A related attribute, which illustrates a distinct preference for neutral competence by Van Riper, is that of recruitment based on merit. This attribute, as well as the first, the third (rational decision making), and the fourth (rule of law and equality before the law), may provide the administrative state and the organizations that operate in that context with a degree of legitimacy. If the public believes that people are hired because of what they know, not who they know (attribute 2), that decisions are made in an explainable way with a consideration of tradition, benefits, and drawbacks (attribute 3), that the law, not a person, determines what the law is and how individuals are treated (attribute 4), and that there is someone to take responsibility for that decision (attribute 1), then people may be more likely to regard the operations of the state and its organizations as fair and just.

Written rules and procedures, as required in attribute 5, are necessary as the administrative state and its organizations become more complex. It would be impossible to operate a courtroom without such written directives, let alone the larger governmental apparatus. Such an argument also holds true for attribute 6, which requires a money economy, plus a surplus. Governmental entities—indeed, private organizations of any size—cannot operate efficiently on a barter economy, nor can they continue to operate on a volunteer basis. Hence there must not only be a money economy, but enough money to pay for government operation to exist, even, dare we say it, flourish.

Attributes 7 and 8 are necessary to provide vital information to governmental entities. If there is no information on the number of citizens (a census), the recidivism rate, and the programs that work best, and/or the technology does not exist to collect it, then organizations operate in the dark in terms of decision making.

Attribute 9 is particularly critical if there is to be a sense of order and justice in an administrative state and among the organizations that must operate in that context. If unethical behavior is allowed to continue unchecked either in the private sector (if, e.g., some Enron officials had not been apprehended, tried, and punished for their crimes), or in the public sector if the governmental official who revealed the identity of a CIA operative has his sentence commuted, then people have the perception that government is not acting in a manner that is in accord with our core beliefs. In other words, it appears that when ethical standards are ignored because of the money and power of the offender, the legitimacy of the government and its organizations (including those in criminal justice) come into question.

Finally, the last attribute is believed to be necessary because it ameliorates all the others. For instance, and by way of example, an administrative state these days cannot operate well without a money economy, which makes it possible to attract and train qualified personnel to operate technology to determine whether the organization is applying the law in an equal fashion. In other words, all these attributes of an administrative state are interwoven and have provided the backdrop for the development of management theories and their implementation.

MANAGEMENT THEORIES

Some see tracings of management theory in ancient and medieval writings on organizations and government: "After all, it was Aristotle who first wrote of the importance of culture to management systems, ibn Taymiyyah who used the scientific method to outline the principles of administration within the framework of Islam, and Machiavelli who gave the world the definitive analysis of the use of power" (Shafritz & Ott, 2001:21). Socrates remarks on the similarities between an organizational structure that functions as well for the public and the private sector, and the basic structure of hierarchy and specialization are laid out by Moses in the Bible.

Adam Smith in the first chapter of *The Wealth of Nations*, discusses the value of the "division of labour." His basic contention is that an individual depends on the joint labor of any number of workers to make modern life possible, "[w]e shall be sensible that without the assistance and cooperation of many thousands, the very meanest person in a civilized country could not be provided, even according to, what we very falsely imagine, the easy and simple manner in which he is commonly accommodated" (Smith, 1776:12). In other words, the production of food, clothing, housing, transportation, and entertainment for the collective good require the individual work and specialization of thousands.

For the purposes of simplification and clarity, we like to categorize management theories into two main paradigms, or ways of viewing the management world. These two paradigms are *traditional*, or *classical*, *theories* and *human relations*, or *resource*, *theories*. Some theories do not neatly fit these categorizations, and so we note at the outset that, much like the public service values of *democratic accountability* and *neutral competency* explored in the preceding chapter, few organizations in criminal justice are managed in a way that fits only one of these theories at any given time. Moreover, public administration and business scholars describe a number of theories and philosophies that reach beyond, and improve upon, both traditional and human relations theories; examples include structural organization theory, systems theory, power and politics organization, organization culture critiques, organization culture reform movements, and the influence of the information age on organizations (Shafritz & Ott, 2001). We will discuss these two sets of theories and theorists and then add some of the most influential theories, such as systems theory, which represent hybrids and extensions of traditional and human relations theories. Establishing a rough demarcation line between these theories does serve to put their more outstanding differences in sharp relief, to facilitate an analysis.

Traditional Theories of Management

Max Weber (1864–1920) and Frederick W. Taylor (1856–1917) are often thought of as the two thinkers who, when their contributions are combined, created the basis for traditional management theory. Weber's contribution is seen in his conceptualization of what a *bureaucracy* is. As an astute social observer of his time, Weber (2001, first printing in English in 1946) noticed that a distinct type of organization, a *bureaucracy*, was becoming predominant in his home country of Germany and in Europe. Because he described this phenomenon, some have made the mistake of believing that he advocated it, which is not true (Shafritz & Ott, 2001; Weber, 2001). He merely remarked on its existence, and its resilience, and defined it. For Weber, there are several, but at least these three, essential components of a *bureaucracy*:

- hierarchy
- specialization of roles
- rule of law (including formal administrative rules)

The first term refers to a pyramidal structure of the organization whereby authority, power, and communication are centered at the top and diffused down through the organization. Specialization is important as it allows the bureaucracy to compartmentalize so that each person, rather than being a generalist, becomes an expert in a narrowly defined task. Rule of law and/or adherence to formal rules is important to ensure order and predictability of operations in the organization. Rules provide the blueprint for all workers to follow.

Frederick W. Taylor's book *The Principles of Scientific Management,* published in 1911, provided some of the other essential ingredients to the traditional management mix (see Box 4.2). As an engineer, Taylor was concerned with the mechanics of the operation of the organization. His thoughts, culminating in his book, were shaped by the great American progressive period (roughly 1880s to 1920s) and reflect the hope that many in those years placed in social engineering. He also subscribed to the idea of *bureaucracy* as described by Weber. That is, he clearly believed in a hierarchical structure for the private sector businesses he analyzed, and he believed in compartmentalized tasks and orderly, rule-bound organizations.

What Taylor added was the application of the scientific method to organization study—hence the title of his book, *Scientific Management*—coupled with a theory on how best to *motivate* workers. **Motivation** for our purposes will be defined as "[to] impel, incite; or a stimulus prompting a person to act in a certain way" (Webster, 1986:1475). *In one sense or another, all management theories, are at least in part*

BOX 4.2

FREDERICK W. TAYLOR, SCIENTIFIC MANAGEMENT, AND THE PIG IRON STORY

Frederick Winslow Taylor (1856–1917) was trained as an engineer. He began his work as a laborer in a steel mill and eventually rose through the ranks to become chief engineer (Pugh et al., 1985). Later he became a consultant, as his ideas were published and gained currency. He began publication with an article in 1895, then a book in 1903, and, in 1911, the publication of his oft-cited *Principles of Scientific Management.* Taylor was the founder of the *scientific management* movement and believed that the careful study of workers and the workplace would yield an understanding of the "one best way" to do the work and the "first rate worker" or "high-priced man" who performs it that way. He thought that management techniques could be improved to achieve the greatest profit for both management and workers. His work was often seen as controversial, even in his lifetime, and was characterized as inhumane. To be fair, Pugh and his colleagues (1985) note that one of Taylor's basic tenets, which was never implemented in American business, was unlimited earnings of the "first rate or first class man." The "pig iron story" was included in Taylor's 1911 book to illustrate how managers should interact with workers to motivate them to perform at a higher level (see the exercise at the end of the chapter).

Frederick W. Taylor

about how best to motivate workers. That motivation may come in the form of internal or external forces for the individual, depending on the theory.

In general, the scientific method is an approach to discovering the truth about phenomena. Taylor believed that if managers wanted to know the truth about how best to manage workers, they should apply this method of study. Thus, he recommended that managers study the work and the workers, formulate theories about how the work is best done and who is the "first rate worker," test those theories, and then align the information they collect as support for, or refutation of, the theory. By engaging in this scientific approach, Taylor thought that managers could identify what is the "one best way" of doing the work of any enterprise.

By way of illustrating the components of *Scientific Management,* one of the authors asks for volunteer actors to take on the two parts in the "Pig Iron Story." When students act out the parts of Taylor and the hypothetical worker, "Schmidt," the class is able to discern the essential elements of Taylor's theory. Students note that this story demonstrates both Taylor's belief in the manager as "scientist" and his means of motivating workers. Taylor believed that the "first rate worker" could be motivated through a "piece rate" approach by using "money" to more efficiently increase worker output. In turn, this "first rate worker," who is receiving better pay and will become a "high-priced man," will serve as a model for other workers on how to do work "the one best way" and thus receive better pay. A worker under this theory becomes much like a machine part, which once greased with money, functions quite predictably. To recap, the essential elements of Taylor's *Scientific Management* are as follows:

- use of the scientific method by managers
- discovery of the "first rate worker"

- discovery of the "one best way"
- motivation of workers with money
- use of a piece rate to encourage more work output
- workers seen as machine parts

Students also note some values that come through the "pig iron story" that Taylor did not perhaps intend. For instance, the content of the story makes clear that Taylor does not think much of the intelligence of the worker "Schmidt," who speaks broken English with an obvious German accent. Students are rightly put off by the assumption that immigrants are stupid and easily manipulated by money. Indeed, that critics charge other progressives of the period of harboring the same patronizing sentiment (Rothman, 1980). Moreover, the dictatorial approach of Taylor vis-à-vis Schmidt, whom he orders about, does not play well with the students either. But then, the students are part of a culture of a century away from Taylor's world, and that may make all the difference for them and for workers of today.

Of course, the traditional management theory has been quite influential in both the public and the private sectors. Ford Motor Company's assembly line, as well as virtually any business of any size, was, and is, influenced by the bureaucratic and scientific management components of traditional theory (Kanigel, 1997; Shafritz & Ott, 2001). Virtually all public sector criminal justice agencies have been and are organized as bureaucracies, with some elements of scientific management embedded in their formal and informal cultures. Historically, managers treated correctional workers almost as badly as the latter treated inmates. And some managers in policing and corrections still take a dictatorial and hierarchical approach toward their workers. As with our students, however, such an approach is off-putting to modern workers and may not enhance their motivation, if it ever did.

A number of scholars, both before and since Weber and Taylor, wrote about and/or supported a traditional approach to management. In France, in 1916, Henri Fayol, a private sector executive engineer, and a contemporary of Taylor, lauded some of the essential elements of traditional management in terms of division of labor, unity of command, centralization, rate pay, and discipline (Shafritz & Ott, 2001). He developed one of the first sets of principles of management and believed that these principles could be applied successfully in any workplace, public or private. Luther Gulick (1937), building on the work of Fayol, outlined the seven major functions of executive management or POSDCORB(E): planning, organizing, staffing, directing, coordinating, reporting, budgeting, and (some may like to add) evaluating.

But Fayol moved beyond the traditional theorists too. He noted that in practice, hierarchy, or the "scalar chain" as he describes it, does not always work efficiently for businesses. Sometimes it is necessary for organizations to communicate horizontally, for instance, and this is not a rare occurrence in organizations, despite their formal hierarchical structure. Also, unlike Taylor, Fayol recognized the value of "equity" in the workplace, a concept that, for him, combined the use of kindliness and justice in relations between workers and managers. In fact, he finished his 1916 article on management by extolling the virtues of teams as a means of creating and maintaining an esprit de corps among workers. Although Fayol noted that it is easy to build dissension and jealousy in the workplace, such sentiments tend to hamper productivity rather than enhance it (a thought that presages the Hawthorne experiments that began a little over a decade later).

Criticisms of the Traditional Theory of Management   Critics of the traditional management theory identify several false assumptions in the approach (Kanigel, 1997; Klofas, Stojokovic, & Kalinich, 1990; McGregor, 1957; Ouchi, 1981). For one, people at work are motivated by factors in addition to money (e.g., respect, a sense of accomplishment, social needs). The traditional approach acknowledges only the formal, and not the informal, subcultures at play in the workplace, which means that any analysis of the workplace based on a traditional approach is liable to be inaccurate.

Second, the traditional approach to management ignores all the talent, creativity, and insight found among lower-level workers. Such workers and their abilities are devalued in a traditionally operated organization, which means that the business entity is not making the best use of its human resources. Since in criminal justice agencies, about 80 to 90% of the cost of doing business resides in payroll, this may add up to a substantial loss.

Finally and relatedly, the traditional approach to management ignores the human needs of workers and the larger community environment. Where is the evidence of the recognition of the need for kindliness and justice in relations between workers and managers that Fayol identified in 1916? In the postscript to the "pig iron story," students have wondered aloud what happened to the workers who could carry pig iron like Schmidt? What happened when workers were sick or old? For that matter, what happened to Schmidt in his old age? Are all workers really expendable? Where, they ask, is the human care in that? And what about those workers who may be older, who cannot carry the weight of the pig iron, either literally or, when applied to other workplaces, figuratively, but who carry the traditions and knowledge vital to the work in their heads? Do not the organization and the work suffer when they are let go? What responsibilities do organizations, both public and private, have to individuals and communities beyond just the provision of jobs? In other words, the traditional theory of management is too mechanistic and cold. It makes workers expendable and the promise of the "good life" for most American workers a fable.

But, the traditional approach to management has been so ubiquitous in both the private and the public sectors in part because it works for someone (Jacques, 2001 [first printed in 1990]); (Shafritz & Ott, 2001). Though its flaws are apparent in its mechanistic, and some might say soulless, manipulation of workers, the truth is that bureaucracies exist because they can be an efficient way of organizing workers and work (Jacques, 2001). A scientific approach to analyzing how the work is done and who does it best also seems to make sense. And, to a point, at least, people are mighty motivated by money; some are motivated by nothing else.

Systems Theory

Although Taylor's scientific approach provided a framework for the effective measurement of workers and organizations to unearth "the one best way," the onset of the technological age brought forth more complex methods for finding out "optimal solutions" to organizational problems (Shafritz & Ott, 2001). *Systems theory* represented a departure from classical organization theory (which viewed the *closed* organization as static and predictable). This is true because under sytems theory the organization is considered to be *open* to dynamic, unpredictable environmental influences, as well as to internal forces, and is viewed as much more complex, and in a constant state of flux (Gordon & Milakovich, 1998; Shafritz & Ott, 2001). Moreover, the systems approach has provided a nice segue into the modern human relations/resources theoretical paradigm.

One way the difference between the two eras of scientific measurement can be delineated is simply by understanding the level of quantitative rigor used to analyze causality in organizational problem solving. With this change in rigor came the refocusing of organizational goals away from trying to control and predict everything (Gordon & Milakovich, 1998). The advent of the computer made available the powerful statistical software needed to analyze increasingly large numbers of people and organizations systematically. The simple cause-and-effect statement has become infinitely complex, while numerous other variables can be added to the problem equation almost effortlessly. Which means that this ability to analyze and organize a vast amount of data has impacted the way we think about organizations.

Just about every social setting can be dissected into various working components, the whole of which may be referred to as a system. Take, for example, the Adam Walsh Child Protection and Safety Act of 2006, which was passed to expand the national sex offender registry, toughen federal laws against sex offenders who prey on children, and support law enforcement efforts to dampen the negative effects of child pornography on the Internet (White House, 2006). We shall consider the passing of this act as an *input*, which may consist of *demands* on local police organizations to conform to the legislative requirements and may also provide *support* in the form of resources. The police organization as a system then reacts to these inputs and make adjustments or *outputs*. For example, these adjustments may surface as new organizational goals and funding for new police training and staff. These outputs are then given environmental *feedback*, which then influences the inputs, and the *process* begins again (see Figure 4.1 for a simple schema of this theory).

Briefly, the systems perspective can be understood as an ever-changing ecosystem. According to Norbert Wiener (1948 [in Shafritz & Ott, 2001]), there are five main active components within the model (eco)-system: the *environment*, the *process*, *outputs*, *inputs,* and *feedback*. Along with these components there are two main information-processing systems, the biological (human) and the mechanical (technology) (Shafritz & Ott, 2001). Self and organizational regulation and change can be monitored and dealt with "[t]hrough biological, social, or technological systems that can identify problems, do something about them, and receive feedback to adjust themselves automatically" (Shafritz & Ott, 2001:243). This multifaceted interplay between the *environment* and the organization is labeled a *process*, which constantly receives *feedback* through informed reciprocal bursts of *inputs* and *outputs* (Shafritz & Ott, 2001). This pattern is absorbed and analyzed through technology and its utilization and implementation by people; this cycle, in turn, affects the processes. The acknowledgment of the workplace or organization as a complex and dynamic system of ever-changing reciprocal processes, which are interlocked in a constant battle for homeostasis or equilibrium, has forced scholars to analyze the "organization" as such.

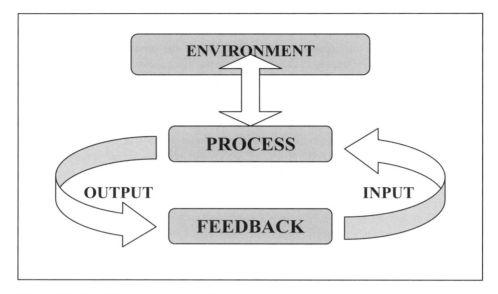

Figure 4.1 Simplified systems theory diagram.

Human Relations or Human Resource Theories

Just as the traditional theory of management gained currency in all sectors of American society, the germ for an opposite set of theories began to develop. Mary Parker Follett in 1926 was the first to recognize the value of a participatory management style for leaders that is dependent on the situation. Situational leadership will be discussed in much more detail in Chapter 7, but suffice it to say here that the precept flies in the face of traditional management theory, which values hierarchy and top-down, not bottom-up communication. Parker Follett recognized that not only does giving orders rarely work practically, without the consent and involvement of people in receipt of those orders, but that it is bad business policy (Parker Follett, 1926). For Parker Follett, the giving of orders will be more effective and the dignity of the worker will be maintained when all are involved in work decisions. Moreover, workers will take responsibility for their activity if they are given some say in it. Notably, at the time that Parker Follett wrote these words she was virtually alone in her beliefs, but that was soon to change as managers began to assimilate the findings of the Hawthorne experiments.

The Hawthorne Experiments   The *Hawthorne experiments*, which took place from 1927 to 1933 in the Hawthorne plant of Western Electric, near Chicago, were ostensibly set up to test scientific management. These experiments were conducted by Harvard professor Elton Mayo, along with his colleagues Frederick Roethlisberger, George Homans, and T. N. Whitehead. The Hawthorne experiments, and the conclusions drawn from them, set the stage for conceptualizing the management of work in an alternate fashion.

The experiments began in 1924 as a series of productivity studies, conducted from a scientific management perspective, which tinkered with environmental conditions such as lighting, room temperature, and humidity to increase worker productivity. Mayo and his colleagues were called in to take over the research in 1927 because the reasons for the outcomes were not clear (Shafritz & Ott, 2001). As Roethlisberger (1941:158) recalled later, "The purpose was to find out the relation of the quality and quantity of illumination to the efficiency of industrial workers." Experimental conditions were imposed and a "test group" and a "control group" were identified. In the initial set of studies the test group was subjected to more illumination by candles, less illumination by candles and they were led to believe that illumination was increased or decreased when it was not. In each of these cases, no matter what was done in terms of illumination, the workers output in the test group remained the same as the control group whose illumination remained constant throughout these experiments. As Roethlisberger recalls, it was not until the illumination for the test group was reduced to the equivalent of moonlight—or when it became physically impossible to see—that the output of the test group declined.

The researchers were not sure what to make of these findings. Scientific management principles would have predicted a direct cause-and-effect relationship between the conditions of work and the output of workers. Thus, if lighting increased, so should productivity; if lighting decreased, so should productivity. The experimenters were not sure whether the problem lay in the workers, the experiment, or themselves. More research was planned, and Roethlisberger notes that there was some suspicion that the real culprit was an analytical approach that ignored the human situation in work. "The experimenters had obtained no human data; they had been handling electric-light bulbs and plotting average output curves. Hence their results had no human significance" (Roethlisberger, 1941:159).

So the researchers set up another set of experiments on a segregated test group of five women that lasted for five years. They varied the work breaks from one to two, they gave the women Saturday morning off (they usually worked 48 hours per week), they decreased the length of the working day, and they provided lunch during one break. During this whole period productivity increased. Then the researchers took all of these amenities away and PRODUCTIVITY STILL INCREASED. The researchers had to ask: What is going on here?

One conclusion was that what is now known as the **Hawthorne effect** was at play. This is the belief that when humans know they are being studied or watched, they will react to that observation. In other words, the women were reacting to the presence of the experimenters, not to the experimental conditions.

Another reason for the improved output by these women may be that management practices during the experiment completely changed. The input of the women was taken into consideration in terms of experimental conditions, and the women's welfare and health was of concern. In effect, the workers received positive attention from management and their input was valued. "Inadvertently a change had been introduced which was far more important than the planned experimental innovations: the customary supervision in the room had been revolutionized. This accounted for the better attitudes of the girls and their improved rate of work" (Roethlisberger, 1941:161). The experimenters realized that worker output was tied to workers' attitudes and feelings about their labor.

The next stage of the research was to develop a uniform interviewing technique whereby experimenters could go into any plant and listen to the workers' concerns and complaints. Then the social behavior of a group of men was studied separately over a period of time, and it was determined that in groups, there are norms for worker output that operate independently of management decrees. For instance, workers were socialized to avoid being either "rate busters" (people who outperformed others by substantial amounts) or "chiselers," who worked too little. Nor should you be a "squealer," who tattles on group members, or act in an "officious" manner. From these collective efforts, the researchers concluded the following vis-à-vis management (Roethlisberger, 1941:162–166):

1. They found that the behavior of workers could not be understood apart from their feelings or sentiments.

2. They found that sentiments are easily disguised, and hence are difficult to recognize and to study.

3. They found that manifestations of sentiment could not be understood as things in and by themselves, but only in terms of the total situation of the person.

4. Management should listen to workers.

5. Workers operate within the accepted social standards or norms for group output. You must not be a "rate buster" or a "chiseler." Worker output will vary, but it will tend to fit within an acceptable group range.

6. People are social animals and want to be part of a group.

7. Worker output is not always directly related to intelligence or ability.

8. The social functions of the group influence worker behavior.

9. Though pay is important, it is only part of the social recognition that motivates workers.

10. Most of us want the satisfaction that comes from being accepted and recognized as people of worth by our friends and associates.

11. People want meaningful work and skills that give social recognition.

12. Management practices are archaic and need to recognize that workers are social animals and operate in that context. If this civilization is to survive, we must obtain a new understanding of human motivation and behavior in business organizations—an understanding which can be simply but effectively practiced.

The Hierarchy of Needs

The Hawthorne experiments set the stage for the development of a theory of human motivation, or Abraham Maslow's *hierarchy of needs theory* (also known as the actualization theory), first published in 1943 (see Box 4.3). This theory provides the framework for understanding the motivation of employees in most of the management theories that followed it. Its importance in shaping the modern understanding of behavior in organizations cannot be overestimated.

Maslow believed that there is a hierarchy of needs that motivates human beings in their lives and in their work behavior. The needs appearing at the bottom of this hierarchy

---

BOX 4.3

ABRAHAM MASLOW

In a description of Maslow (in *Maslow on Management* (first printing 1961, reprinted in 1998)), Stephens and Heil note that Maslow taught Psychology at Brooklyn College. He then worked at Brandeis University and later served as president of the American Psychological Association. In his career he published hundreds of articles and books, but is is best known for his development of the "hierarchy of needs." "Maslow believed that human beings aspired to become self-actualizing" (Stephens & Heil, 2001:xx). He died in 1970 at the age of 62.

---

were seen as the most important motivators, or "prepotent," and until they were satisfied, at least relatively, a person was not as likely to be motivated by the upper-level needs. The needs in order of importance were as follows (Maslow, 1943:167–172, 1961):

- physiological needs (food, water, sex)
- security needs (physical safety, job security, provision for old age, etc.)
- love needs (need to belong, the need to give and receive love, the need to be accepted by associates)
- self-esteem needs (also known as self-respect—need for achievement, recognition, importance and for confidence in the world, the desire for a reputation or prestige)
- self-actualization needs (need to be creative, to fulfill one's potential, becoming what you were meant or fitted to be)

Maslow believed that people who were relatively satisfied in these needs were the most creative and resilient of all. A precondition to the satisfaction of these needs, he thought, was the existence of freedom (Maslow, 1943:172):

> Such conditions as freedom to speak, freedom to do what one wishes so long as no harm is done to others, freedom to express one's self, freedom to investigate and seek for information, freedom to defend one's self, justice, fairness, honesty, orderliness in the group are examples of preconditions for basic need satisfactions. Thwarting in these freedoms will be reacted to with a threat or emergency response.

Management's role was to provide a work environment where people could meet these basic needs (Maslow, 1961). If management succeeded in fulfilling this role, Maslow believed, workers' motivation to produce was likely to improve.

He did note, however, that achievement of these needs was not as fixed as it might appear (Maslow, 1943). For instance, he thought that for some the achievement of some needs (e.g., self-esteem) might be more important than others (e.g., love). Or that some people who are driven by the need to be creative (the starving artist cliché), might bypass the satisfaction of some needs and be motivated primarily by self-actualization.

He also believed that there are others who have had their need for love, respect, or self-actualization in the workplace deadened by chronic unemployment or other uncertainty and who then are satisfied and motivated by steady employment. Relatedly, he thought that those who were starved for love as children are not motivated by love as adults. Maslow also acknowledged that behavior is motivated or acted out for other reasons than these needs (e.g., ignorant people sometimes act stupidly), that there are multiple motivations for behavior (e.g., people eat for hunger and for love), and that sometimes people ignore the importance of their needs.

Maslow states unequivocally that those who have relative satisfaction of the basic needs all their lives are the most likely to be able to withstand adversity:

> They are the "strong" people who can easily weather disagreements or opposition, who can swim against the stream of public opinion and who can stand up for the truth at great personal cost. It is just the ones who have loved and been well loved, and who have had many deep friendships who can hold out against hatred, rejection or persecution. (1943: 173)

Theories X and Y

A number of theories in the human relations genre followed the Hawthrone experiments and the publication and promulgation of Maslow's hierarchy of needs. One of the most well known of these was Douglas McGregor's *Theory X* and *Theory Y,* as explicated in his 1957 article "The Human Side of Enterprise." (Box 4.4 supplies a brief synopsis of McGregor's life.) In that article he laid out the traditional view of management's task, or Theory X: "in harnessing human energy to organizational requirements" (McGregor, 1957:179). According to proponents of Theory X, both materials and people must be organized, controlled, and motivated by management to achieve organizational ends. The management and control of the workers is central to Theory X because people are assumed to be passive and are assumed to not like, or want, to work. McGregor

---

BOX 4.4

DOUGLAS McGREGOR

Douglas McGregor (1906–1964) was a social psychologist who for a time served as president of Antioch College. For ten years in later life he was a management professor at the Massachusetts Institute of Technology (Pugh et al. 1985). McGregor is best known for explicating the traditional assumptions and style of management (Theory X) and those of human relations (Theory Y). He used the Maslowian concepts of human needs as a framework for his belief that modern organizations were those that provided a supportive environment for staff.

(1957:179) identifies additional beliefs that underpin the traditional Theory X:

- The average man is by nature indolent—he works as little as possible.
- He lacks ambition, dislikes responsibility, and prefers to be led.
- He is inherently self-centered, indifferent to organizational needs.
- He is by nature resistant to change.
- He is gullible, not very bright, the ready dupe to the charlatan and the demagogue.

McGregor (1957; Heil, Bennis, & Stephens, 2000) believed that those who managed under the precepts of Theory X were just fundamentally wrong. He believed that they confused cause and effect in terms of motivation and thus misinterpreted the resultant behavior in the work-place. Instead he believed that a Theory Y manager, who understood the human side of enterprise, hence McGregor's title, would build on the hierarchy of needs theory proposed by Maslow. He believed that those who did not have these needs satisfied were in effect "sick" and that this sickness will be apparent in their behavior. In fact, he believed that many negative work behaviors such as passivity, hostility, and the refusal to accept responsibility were symptoms of this sickness and not inherent characteristics of human nature, as those of the Theory X persuasion might think. McGregor's (1957:183) Theory Y included the following concepts:

- Management is responsible for organizing the elements of productive enterprise—money, materials, equipment, and people—in the interest of economic ends.
- People are *not* by nature passive or resistant to organizational needs. They have become so as a result of experience in organizations.
- The motivation, the potential for development, the capacity for assuming responsibility, the readiness to direct behavior toward organizational goals are all present in people. Management does not put them there. It is a responsibility of management to make it possible for people to recognize and develop these human characteristics for themselves.
- The essential task of management is to arrange organizational conditions and methods of operation so that people can achieve their own goals *best* by directing *their own* efforts toward organizational objectives.

McGregor (1957; Heil et al., 2000) recommends that managers create these optimal conditions by decentralizing and delegating, enlarging jobs to make them more meaningful to workers, by engaging in participatory and consultive management, and by ensuring worker involvement in performance appraisals. He disparaged managers who only added the window dressing of participatory management or delegated tasks without truly recognizing the worth and abilities of their workers.

Other Human Relations–Related Theories

Other related theories in this genre followed such as Chris Argyris's *immaturity-maturity theory* and Frederick Herzberg's *motivation-hygiene theory* continued in a similar vein (Gordon & Milakovich, 1998). In Argyris's view, subjecting workers to traditional management practices keeps them "immature," and thus management should work to develop the responsibility and skills of workers by providing the right conditions. Similarly, Herzberg noted that workers tend to be motivated by both the levels of needs identified by Maslow. For Herzberg "hygiene factors" such as organizational policies, working conditions, interpersonal relationships, and the quality of supervision all affect job satisfaction either positively or negatively (Schermerhorn, Hunt, & Osborn, 1982). Herzberg hoped, though studies did not always confirm, that satisfaction in turn affected performance, hence managers needed to ensure a high level of satisfaction for workers.

Peter Drucker (1954, 1964), a contemporary of McGregor's and a management luminary, was also instrumental in spreading the human relations approach to management, both in the United States and abroad. In the context of a larger reform of the business enterprise, he cajoled executives to systematically study and research their businesses (a scientific management approach), but to be cognizant of the needs and wants of their staffs and the effect that a business has on the larger community (Drucker, 1954, 1964). Drucker, in effect, bridged the gap between the traditional and human relations theories of management and between the first version of the latter and all subsequent versions.

Criticisms of Early Human Relations Theories of Management   Of course, human relations theories have had their share of critics (Gordon & Milakovich, 1998). One weakness that is identified is that the democracy assumed under human relations is excessive and may lead to inefficiencies. Jacques (2001) remarks that hierarchy in organizations tends to "work" because it makes the lines of command and tasks explicit. If there are too many people involved in making decisions, then it is difficult to accomplish much.

Some have critiqued the suppression of individuality that might occur when people are urged to always work in groups or teams. Janis Irving L. (1972) in his seminal book titled *Victims of Groupthink,* outlines the dangers of "groupthink" for organizations that put too high a premium on group engagement at the expense of individual thought and critique.

A third criticism is that there is an overemphasis on employee happiness and well-being. After all, it is the first responsibility of an organization to get the job done, not to fret about whether the workers are content.

And, finally, some have argued that the assumption by Theory Y-ers that people are generally kind and naturally exercise self-control is false. This assumption is part of the larger belief system that people are good at heart and should be given freedom, as opposed to the assumption that human nature is basically evil and in need of control. These opposing assumptions lie at the heart of the centuries-old debate about the nature of human nature, and for the more traditional manager the belief that people need no control is just plain false.

Despite these criticisms and concerns about human relations theories, most modern management theories advocate a version of them. Theory Z, teams, total quality management, management by objectives, and learning organizations theories all hold as their basic premise a human relations approach to management. But what is interesting is that in practice such an approach is often still carried out within an organizational structure that is bureaucratic and includes other elements of traditional theories. In other words, modern management in practice, whether in a computer chip manufacturing firm or a police department, is really an amalgamation of traditional and human relations theories.

Modern Human Relations Theories and Techniques: Theory Z, TQM, MBO and Learning Organizations

The *Theory Z* management approach advocated by Ouchi (1981) and others represents a conscious choice to combine some of the important elements of both traditional and human relations theories of management. It also recognizes the importance of the larger environment in influencing and motivating human behavior at work. In fact, Theory Z is distinguished from Theories X and Y because Ouchi centers the organization in the context of the larger social, political, and economic environment. Other social institutions such as schools, families, and religious organizations also influence the work setting for Z proponents.

Theory Z is also a "bridging" theory between Theories X and Y because it recognizes the production needs of X along with the human needs of Y (Klofas, et al., 1990). To summarize, Theory Z management is concerned with the production needs of X, the human needs of Y, and the environmental impact and influence—the unique contribution of Z. Ouchi (1981) highlights the team approach to work in organizations, a concept that he believed distinguished the Japanese workplace from the American workplace of the 1970s. Other attributes included the shared decision making central to other human relations theories, but combined with a distinct career path to motivate workers up the organizational ladder (both X and Y theories).

The logical extension of Theory Z was **total quality management** (TQM) or the idea that the greater the involvement of workers or teams in developing and delivering organizational goals, the higher their level of commitment to achievement of those goals. The key elements of TQM are (Gordon & Milakovich, 1998:374) as follows:

- top-level support and commitment
- focus on customer satisfaction
- written productivity and quality goals and an annual improvement plan
- productivity and quality measures and standards that are consistent with agency goals
- use of the improvement plan and measurement system to hold managers and employees accountable
- employee involvement in productivity and quality improvement efforts
- rewards for quality and productivity achievement
- training in methods for improving productivity and quality
- retraining and out-placement for any employees who might be negatively affected by improvement efforts
- reducing barriers to productivity and quality improvement

Another derivative of the human relations approach, which was key to Theory Z, was the advent of *quality circles* in American management practice of the 1980s. Developed in the 1960s in Japan by an American (W. Edwards Deming), **quality circles** are just groups of workers who consider all the data available to them and make decisions. Such circles, in all-important respects, closely resemble the *team approach* to management and worker engagement that has been popular since the 1980s, in both the public and private sectors (Fink, Jenks, & Willits, 1983; Larson & LaFasto, 1989). In quality circles and teams we see the full recognition of the importance of the work group and its dynamics as first documented in the Hawthorne experiments some fifty years beforehand. There is also a clear and obvious link between quality circles/teams and TQM (Gordon & Milakovich, 1998). In all such practices and philosophies, including management by objectives (MBO), there is an emphasis on employee involvement and empowerment in the workplace as an integral piece of the successful management puzzle.

Management by objective is a philosophy of management that also contains the elements of both the traditional and the human relations theories, with particular emphasis on the latter in terms of employee relations. It really caught fire in the private sector in the 1970s and 1980s, but was developed by Drucker (1954) almost 20 years earlier. It is a collaborative approach by all members of the organization to achieve objectives. Fink and his colleagues (1983:36) note:

> [MBO] says, in essence, that commitment to organizational goals can best be achieved by allowing and encouraging members of the organization to play an active role in setting their own work objectives. Through a collaborative process in which superiors and subordinates jointly articulate work objectives, with targets and timetables mutually agreed upon. This approach to management keeps all members focused on the achievement of specific outcomes, which converge over time toward general goals and purposes.

Another, and more recent, innovation in the application of human relations theories has been the conceptualization of organizations as living, evolving, and learning entities (Kaufman, 1985; Gordon & Milakovich, 1998). The **learning organization** is believed to be one that operates in an open environment, as defined in Chapter 1. For an organization to be effective in such a dynamic milieu, it must learn from that environment. Because the environment of the organization is continually changing, the organization must grow, learn, and adapt as well. "Learning organizations are built on many of the same assumptions as those of earlier theories, including shared vision, consistent values, dedication to customer service, and competence" (Gordon & Milakovich, 1998:137).

A related concept that has gained credence in the management literature and that has been particularly espoused by management guru Tom Peters (1987, 1992) is the expectation that organizations and their members will have to take risks and make mistakes to learn. Under traditional management systems, Peters claims, people are punished for their mistakes; so as rational beings, when they make mistakes they hide them. The problem is that those hidden mistakes do not provide any opportunity for learning. Instead, other organizational members continue to make the same mistakes, and hide them. Moreover, it is only through the taking of some risks that innovation and growth can be achieved. Though under this perspective some mistakes are expected, even welcomed as they provide a learning opportunity, they make innovation and growth possible for the organization.

Taken in tandem, all the more recent organizational theories and practices require some semblance of the following:

1. A fatter and flatter organizational structure, or a less pyramidal shape to the organization than is traditional.
2. Shared decision making by all sectors of the organization.
3. A mechanism or mechanisms for sharing those decisions.
4. Empowered employees who are willing and able to participate fully in decision making that affects their workplace.
5. Enhancement of top-down communication with bottom-up, horizontal, and diagonal communication avenues.
6. Acceptance and expectation that the organization and its members must adapt, grow, and even take risks, if they hope to achieve objectives.

Of course, any organization wishing to shift from a more traditional format to become a TQM, MBO, or learning/risk-taking organization has much work in front of it. Change of this magnitude takes time, patience, commitment, and persistence over a period of years. Such a change requires a paradigm shift that affects all aspects of management.

CONCLUSIONS: THE APPLICATION OF MANAGEMENT THEORIES TO CRIMINAL JUSTICE AGENCIES

Some writers on organizations have been skeptical regarding the application of old and new human relations theories to criminal justice. They think that although agencies of criminal justice would undoubtedly benefit from greater sensitivity to employee well-being, their organizational missions preclude them from adopting a modified "fatter and flatter structure." Moreover greater employee engagement in decision making is impractical for organizations that must react to emergencies, adjudicate difficult matters, and house and supervise people who sometimes have little concern for the niceties of behavior. Such skepticism may be misplaced, however, for two reasons: (1) criminal justice organizations have as great a need for effective management as any other private or public sector organization and (2) human relations management practices are already ubiquitous, in them as else where. *It is not a matter of whether criminal justice organizations will adopt human relations practices, but how much they will adopt them.* Therefore, our focus for the management of criminal justice should center on the latter issue, as the former is already settled.

As a case in point, consider the existence of inmate team unit management in corrections. Since the 1970s and continuing into the 2000s many prisons, jails, probation and parole departments, and juvenile facilities have implemented a team process for classifying and managing inmates/offenders. We can also include police and sheriff's departments that engage in team policing in neighborhoods. What is this process but a replication of quality circles?

Or consider most performance appraisal systems in courts, corrections, and police departments. Most supervisors ask employees for their input before, during, or after an appraisal. Oftentimes a supervisor will sit down with the employee beforehand and develop appropriate goals for that person. What is this engagement but a version of MBO?

Training in criminal justice often includes recognition of the importance of employee participation and shared leadership and decision making. Because human relations practices have become so ingrained in the thinking on management, leaders in such agencies will often claim they are transparent or open even if they are not.

That said, there is much that can be done to move criminal justice organizations further toward the adoption of modern management principles and practices as represented by Theory Z, TQM, MBO and learning organizations. There are some areas and instances when these principles will not or cannot apply, but for the most part, they can and do. Much of the rest of this book will be concerned with the application of modern human relation's theories and practices to management of criminal justice organizations. Suffice it to say that as all management thought on organizations has made the shift to a human relations perspective; criminal justice agencies and institutions will inevitably move to a greater extent in that direction as well.

EXERCISE: TAYLOR'S PIG IRON STORY[1]

Ask for two student volunteers. If more than two students volunteer, choose the pair who seem to have a flair for drama. Go into the hallway so that the class cannot hear the discussion and brief them on their roles. One is to adopt the role of "Schmidt," aka "the high-priced man," a worker who speaks broken English with an exaggerated "foreign" accent. The other is to adopt the role of the industrial engineer and theorist Frederick Taylor. Taylor should speak with forceful authority and Schmidt should be just a bit clueless. Hand the volunteers a copy of the script and have them read over it once and then run through it together (this takes at most five minutes).

After briefing the student volunteers, return to the classroom and explain to the class that pig iron is a kind of metal that has been produced by American companies since the turn of the nineteenth century. Taylor (point to the student representing him) is involved in a discussion regarding the loading of pig iron with a worker in the factory named Schmidt (point to the student representing Schmidt). This dialog was printed in Taylor's 1911 book *Scientific Management* as a way of illustrating the author's approach to management, workers, and motivation. Ask the class to be careful observers of the interaction between Taylor and Schmidt.

Then, without further ado, the students stand in front of the class and perform/read from the script. Afterward, the class discusses what they noticed about the dialog and the two characters. The two student performers also remark on what they noticed about the dialog and how they felt about their characters. The collective observations provide a very nice rampart from which to discuss Taylorism and traditional management theory. Depending on the acting ability of the respective students and the liveliness of the audience, this exercise is usually fun as well as instructive.

The Dialog

THIS DIALOG IS REPRINTED WITH PERMISSION OF TAYLOR'S PUBLISHER, (1911: 44–46) AND MAY BE DUPLICATED FOR CLASSROOM USE

T: Schmidt, are you a high-priced man?

S: Vell, I don't know vat you mean.

T: Oh, come now, you answer my questions. What I want to find out is whether you are a high-priced man or one of these cheap fellows here. What I want to find out is whether you want to earn $1.85 a day or whether you are satisfied with $1.15, just the same as all those cheap fellows are getting.

S: Did I vant $1.85 a day? Vas dot a high-priced man? Vell, yes, I vas a high-priced man.

T: Oh, you're aggravating me. Of course you want $1.85 a day—everyone wants it! You know perfectly well that has very little to do with your being a high-priced man. For goodness sake answer my questions, and don't waste any more of my time. Now come over here. You see that pile of pig iron?

S: Yes.

T: You see that car?

S: Yes.

T: Well, if you are a high-priced man, you will load that pig iron on that car tomorrow for $1.85. Now do wake up and answer my question. Tell me whether you are a high-priced man or not.

S: Vell—did I got $1.85 for loading dot pig iron on dot car tomorrow?

T: Yes, of course you do, and you get $1.85 for loading a pile like that every day right through the year. That is what a high-priced man does, and you know it just as well as I do.

S: Vell, dot's all right. I could load dot pig iron on the car tomorrow for $1.85 and I get it every day, don't I?

T: Certainly you do—certainly you do.

S: Vell, den, I vas a high priced-man.

T: Now, hold on, hold on. You know just as well as I do that a high-priced man has to do exactly as he's told from morning till night. You have seen this man here before, haven't you?

S: No, I never saw him.

T: Well, if you are a high-priced man, you will do exactly as this man tells you tomorrow, from morning till night. When he tells you to pick up a pig and walk, you pick it up and you walk, and when he tells you to sit down and rest, you sit down. You do that right straight through the day. And what's more, no back talk. Do you understand that? When this man tells you to walk, you walk; when he tells you to sit down, you sit down, and you don't talk back at him. Now you come on to work here tomorrow and I'll know before night whether you are really a high-priced man or not.

DISCUSSION QUESTIONS

1. Why does Van Riper argue that an administrative state is more sophisticated and functional if there is a money economy and at least a modest semblance of quantitative data and technique? Do you think that an administrative state existed before the computer, at the turn of the 20th century, or at the founding of the country? Why or why not?

2. What portions of traditional management theory apply to the operation of courts? Explain your answer.

3. How do the five major components of a system work together? Give an example of a system and explain your answer.

4. What portions of human relations theories apply to the operation of police and corrections? Explain your answer.

5. How would Maslow's theory of human needs apply to explain the behavior of staff and inmates in a juvenile correctional institution? Give an example.

KEY TERMS

hawthorne effect: the belief that when humans know they are being studied or watched, they will react to that observation.

learning organization: one that operates in an open environment. For an organization to be effective in such a dynamic milieu, there must be learning from that environment. Because the environment of the organization is continually changing, the organization must grow, learn, and adapt as well.

management by objective: a philosophy of management that also contains the elements of both the traditional and the human relations theories, with particular emphasis on the latter in terms of employee relations.

motivation: (for our purposes): "[to] impel, incite; or a stimulus prompting a person to act in a certain way" (Webster, 1986:1475).

quality circles: worker groups whose members consider all the data available to them and make decisions.

theory: "a set of ideas, concepts, principles, or methods used to explain a wide set of observed facts" (Webster, 1992:1098).

total quality management: (TQM): idea that the greater the involvement of workers or teams in developing and delivering organizational goals, the higher their level of commitment to achievement of those goals.

NOTE

1. The idea for this exercise was suggested many years ago by Dr. Tara Gray of New Mexico State University.

REFERENCES

Appleby, P. (1945, reprinted in 1987). Government is different. In J. M. Shafritz & A. C. Hyde (Eds.), *Classics of public administration* (pp. 158–163). Chicago: Dorsey Press.

Drucker, P. F. (1954). *The practice of management.* New York: Harper & Row.

Drucker, P. F. (1964). *Managing for results.* New York: Harper & Row.

Fayol, H. (1916, reprinted in 2005). General principles of management. In Shafritz, J. M., Ott, S. & Jang Y.S. (Eds.). *Classics of organization theory.* pp. 48–60. Belmont, CA: Thomson/Wadsworth.

Fink, S. L., Jenks, R. S., & Willits, R. D. (1983). *Designing and managing organizations.* Homewood, IL: Richard D. Irwin.

Gordon, G. J., & Milakovich, M. E. (1998). *Public administrtaion in America* (6th ed.). New York: St. Martin's Press.

Gulick, L. (1937, reprinted in 1978). Notes on the theory of organization. In J. M. Shafritz & A. C. Hyde (Eds.), *Classics of public administration* (pp. 79–95). Chicago: Dorsey Press.

Heil, G., Bennis, W., & Stephens, D. C. (2000). *Douglas McGregor revisited: Managing the human side of the enterprise.* New York: Wiley.

Henry, N. (1987). The emergence of public administration as a field of study. In R. C. Chandler (Ed.), *A centennial history of the American administrative state* (pp. 37–85). New York: Free Press.

Janis, I. L. (1972). *Victims of groupthink. A Psychological study of foreign- policy decisions and fiascres.* Boston: Houghton Mifflin.

Jacques, E. (2001, first printed in 1990). In J. M. Shafritz & J. S. Ott (Eds.), *Classics of organization theory* (pp. 152–157). Fort Worth, TX: Harcourt College Publishers.

Kanigel, R. (1997). *The one best way: Frederick Winslow Taylor and the enigma of efficiency.* New York: Viking Press.

Kaufman, H. (1985). *Time, chance, and organizations: natural selection in a perilous environment.* Chatham, NJ: Chatham House Publishers, Inc.

Klofas, J., Stojokovic, S., & Kalinich, D. (1990). *Criminal justice organizations administration and management.* Pacific Grove, CA: Brooks/Cole.

Larson, C. E., & LaFasto, F. M. J. (1989). *Teamwork: What must go right/What can go wrong.* Newbury Park, CA: Sage.

Maslow, A. H. (1943, reprinted in 2001). A theory of human motivation. In J. M. Shafritz & J. S. Ott (Eds.), *Classics of organization theory* (pp. 152–157). Fort Worth, TX: Harcourt College Publishers.

Maslow, A. H. (1961, reprinted in 1998). *Maslow on management.* New York: Wiley.

McGregor, D. (1957, reprinted in 2001). In J. M. Shafritz & J. S. Ott (Eds.), *Classics of organization theory* (pp. 152–157). Fort Worth, TX: Harcourt College Publishers.

Ouchi, W. (1981). *Theory Z: How American business can meet the Japanese challenge.* Reading, MA: Addison-Wesley.

Parker Follet, M. (1926, reprinted in 2001). The giving of orders. In J. M. Shafritz & J. S. Ott (Eds.), *Classics of organization theory* (pp. 152–157). Fort Worth, TX: Harcourt College Publishers.

Peters, T. (1987). *Thriving on chaos: Handbook for a management revolution.* New York: Harper & Row.

Peters, T. (1992). *Liberation management: Necessary disorganization for the nanosecond nineties.* New York: Knopf.

Pugh, D. S., Hickson, D. J., & Hinings, C. R. (1985). *Writers on organizations.* Beverly Hills, CA: Sage.

Roethlisberger, F. J. (1941, reprinted in 2001). The Hawthorne experiments. In J. M. Shafritz & J. S. Ott (Eds.), *Classics of organization theory* (pp. 158–166). Fort Worth, TX: Harcourt College Publishers.

Rothman, D. J. 1980. *Conscience and convenience: The asylum and its alternatives in progressive America.* Glenview, IL: Scott, Foresman.

Schermerhorn, J. R., Hunt, J. G., & R. N. Osborn. (1985). *Managing organizational behavior* (2nd ed.). New York: Wiley.

Shafritz, J. M., and J. S. Ott (Eds.). (2001). *Classics of organization theory* (5th ed.). Fort Worth, TX: Harcourt College Publishers.

Smith, A. (1776, reprinted in 1937). *The wealth of nations.* New York: Random House.

Stephens, D. C., & Heil, G. (1998, in reprinted text by Maslow, 1961). Abraham Maslow: The man and his work. *Maslow on management.* New York: Wiley.

Taylor, F. W. (1911). *The principles of scientific management.* Norcross, GA: Engineering and Management Press.

Van Riper, P. P. (1987). The American administrative state: Wilson and the founders. In R. C. Chandler (Ed.), *A centennial history of the American administrative state* (pp. 3–36). New York: Free Press.

Weber, M. (2001, first printing in 1946). Bureaucracy. In J. M. Shafritz & J. S. Ott (Eds.), *Classics of organization theory* (pp. 152–157). Fort Worth, TX: Harcourt College Publishers.

Webster. (1992). *Webster's new world encyclopedia.* New York: Prentice Hall.

Webster. (1986). *Webster's third new international dictionary.* Springfield, MA: Merriam-Webster.

White House. (2006). *Fact Sheet: The Adam Walsh Child Protection and Safety Act of 2006.* Office of the Press Secretary, July 27, 2006. http://www.whitehouse.gov/news/releases/2006/07/20060727–7.html

Wilson, W. (1887, reprinted in 1987). The study of administration. In J. M. Shafritz & A. C. Hyde (Eds.), *Classics of public administration* (pp. 10–25). Chicago: Dorsey Press.

CHAPTER 5

COMMUNICATIONS: WHAT YOU SAY AND DO IS WHAT THEY THINK YOU MEAN

A successfully functioning jail environment is one where good communications are the basic requirement.... Good communications flow in both directions—from the top to the bottom of the organization and vice versa.

(Kerle, 2002:5)

Changes in response to the growing workload demands have negatively affected communication between judges and probation officers... the independent voice probation officers can provide to judges is in jeopardy.

(MacDonald and Baroody-Hart, 1999:49)

INTRODUCTION: THE MESSAGE AND THE MEDIUM

Some criminal justice managers may think that if their intent is pure and their ideas are superior, positive change is inevitable in their organization. They could not be more wrong. If we have learned nothing else in the last century, it is that effective communication abilities and techniques, whether in a sophisticated microwave conferencing format or in an informal tête-à-tête at lunch, are key to moving a management agenda. It is not just the message that is important when communicating; it is the medium.

But, of course, for the receivers of your message, what they think you mean is what you both say *and* do. Thus, **communication** is often defined as a sharing or exchange of information, via a medium, between a sender and a receiver (McLuhan, 1964). As indicated by this definition, information is not just shared; it is at times exchanged for something from the receiver. In other words, communication can be tied to expectations within the organization that the process will entail a quid pro quo (something for something).

Obviously, the medium of communication can be accomplished verbally, in writing and in other nonverbal forms (e.g., body language, symbols, etc.) or electronically (McLuhan, 1964). Moreover, the message in organizations is sent and received through both *formal* and *informal* channels, and sometimes the latter can be as important as the former. **Formal communications** are usually found in the policies and procedures, the mission statement, the training sessions, and the training manual, and in official communiqués or memorandums. **Informal communications**, on the other hand, are in the one-on-one-conversations, the asides, and the jokes that permeate the workplace (Morash & Haarr, 1995). These informal communications can even come across in formal training venues in the form of examples or tropes ("stories, ironies, and metaphors") that are used to illustrate how criminal justice works in the real world, as opposed to training situations (Crank, 1996:265).

In this chapter we discuss the multiple purposes of communication, the types of communication within, between, and across organizational boundaries, the barriers to effective communication, and some means by which they might be tackled. Both formal and informal communications occur in the organization and shape its operation, so both will be discussed in this chapter.

We note at the outset that in criminal justice organizations that have adopted a human relations management perspective, there is a greater need to understand the techniques that enhance communication. Under traditional theories, formal communications are presumed to move from the top down, although informally there is much unrecognized activity. In contrast, in organizations focused on human relations, there is formal recognition that communications should come from and move in all directions: from the top down, from the bottom up, horizontally, diagonally, within a group, between groups, and so on. As most modern organizations have moved to some extent in the human relations direction, a thorough discussion and understanding of communication becomes even more paramount for managers and workers in criminal justice agencies.

THE PURPOSE OF COMMUNICATION

People undertake communication in criminal justice for any number of reasons. Each of these purposes for communication is tied in some way to multiple missions of those organizations. For example, communication is used differently when the "protect" mission of policing is the primary focus and when "service" has taken center stage. Typical purposes of communication that are mentioned by other authors (e.g. see Klofas, Stojokovic, & Kalinich, 1990; Peters, 1992; Souryal & Killinger, 1985) and us include the following:

- to solicit information
- to train
- to explain/inform
- to command or give an order
- to reassure
- to educate
- to stimulate
- to motivate
- to facilitate
- to understand
- to listen
- to unite
- to persuade
- to mediate
- to reduce anger or stress

- to debilitate/harm
- to denigrate
- to problem solve
- to brainstorm
- to empower
- to document

For instance, when a correctional officer in a prison is supervising inmate workers, she might communicate to motivate, to persuade, or to command. In other circumstances, when explaining the rule regarding use of art supplies, she might be communicating to solicit information about the use of these materials, to educate people regarding any applicable rules, and to explain expectations concerning compliance with the rules. At another point in the day she might communicate to mediate a dispute between two inmates or to avert violence by working to reduce an inmate's anger or stress. Managers, in turn, might train that same officer on supervision techniques and practices, anger/stress management, and how to spot nonverbal preparations for a riot or the body language of inmates who are on the brink of violent behavior. The inmates might educate each other about what the best job assignments are, who the best staff supervisors are, how hobby work is done, and how to defend themselves in the event of attack.

Police officers and court personnel also use communication during all aspects of their work. During a domestic violence call, an officer may communicate to solicit information, to mediate, and to problem-solve. Later, that same officer will most likely document what he observed during the call, both to describe the situation and to inform others of the incident. He may be summoned to court to testify to the facts of the case.

These illustrations of the purposes of communication in corrections, policing, and courts indicate that there are multiple reasons or motives for communication and that these vary by the situation and with the role of the sender and the receiver. Communication can be either formal or informal. People engage in communication for many reasons, most of which are tempered by each person's intent, his or her place in the organization, the type of organization (its mission), and the situation existing at that point in time.

For instance, in a study of the victimization of youthful prison inmates, Maitland and Sluder (1998) found that the most common form of victimization by inmates of other inmates was verbal harassment. Here communication was used to debilitate or harm a group of younger and more vulnerable inmates in a setting where they felt particularly threatened. In a related study, Belknap, Holsinger, and Dunn (1997) used a particular communication/research device, the focus group, to listen to both young female inmates and correctional personnel so that the latter might better understand the lives of incarcerated girls in Ohio. In both cases, the type of communications used, its intent, and its effects were situation based and dependent on the particular senders and receivers.

Such situations, for instance, sometimes drive the formal responses of agencies to public or media inquiries. Motschall and Cao (2002) found from a convenience sample survey of public information officers (PIOs) for police departments that PIOs primarily see their role as media oriented and reactive to inquiries. They communicate to inform the community and to reassure people regarding police activities. But communication from the police to the public sometimes reverses direction. The researchers noted that PIO personnel also bring information into the organization from the public and the media; in this sense they act as a "liaison" between the public and the police (Motschall & Cao, 2002:175).

COMMUNICATION WITHIN AND ACROSS ORGANIZATIONAL BOUNDARIES, AND COMPLAINTS

In any organization both the sender and the receiver may be participants in communication within a group, between groups, or across groups or organizational boundaries. In any of these instances, the sender and the receiver might engage in either formal or informal communications.

Communication Within and Between Groups

As the Hawthorne experiment findings indicated (see Chapter 4), the communication that occurs within groups and between them is vital to not only those groups but also to the organization. The researchers at the Western Electric plant found that they themselves both set the pace and moderated it, in terms of work produced. Likewise, and more recently, Ouchi (1981), the proponent of Theory Z, sees work groups, as they function internally and in their interactions with others, as important incubators of ideas and solvers of puzzles. In fact, the fascination with grouping and teaming concepts as means of problem solving has become quite popular as organizations have evolved (Gordon & Milakovich, 1998; Larson & LaFasto, 1989; Lipnack & Stamps, 2003; Peters, 1992, 1995; Wageman, 2003). Witness, for instance, the adoption of quality circles and teams in both the public and private sectors since the 1980s.

In criminal justice over the last thirty years, we have seen the proliferation of classification teams, policy and procedure development teams, prosecution and defense teams, crime task forces, informal courtroom work groups, training teams, neighborhood policing teams (as part of community policing efforts), organizational change teams, emergency response teams, treatment teams, and selection teams, among many others (Bennett & Hess, 2001; Clear & Cole, 1997; Gaines, Southerland, & Angell, 1991; Meyer & Grant, 2003; Phillips & Orvis, 2000; Pollock, 1997; Seiter, 2002; Stojokovic & Lovell, 1997; Swanson, Territo, & Taylor, 1998; Tewksbury, 1997; Thibault, Lynch, & McBride, 1998; Whisenand & Rush, 1998). The very existence of these teams and their viability over time in criminal justice organizations signals the importance of their communication function. Depending on their mission, their role in the organization, and the team members, such teams can be a vital means of both sending and receiving communications.

By classifying juveniles in a given way, the team sends a message to detainees that the youths' current behavior and criminal history determine their living unit placement, or not, in the detention center. By formalizing policies regarding the respectful treatment of others in the workplace, a policy and procedures team at a police department puts on notice those who are inclined to abuse force in the workplace. In other words, the concepts of teams and within-group communication are so compelling and so pervasive in the workplace now because they can be used as tools to enhance communication in the workplace (Wageman, 2003). Teams can generate information by problem solving and brainstorming, and they can convey it by educating their members and others about organization policies and practices.

Teams might also serve the purpose of empowering workers who do not feel they have enough say in the workplace (Wageman, 2003). Not only may those who feel they have a say in the development of policies and plans in the organization be more likely to engage in the implementation of those ideas, they may try and convince others as well (Ouchi, 1981). In this sense, teaming is an effective management tool for enhancing communication in the workplace.

Communication Across Organizational Boundaries

Communication between organizations—say between the local police department and the prosecutor's office, or the courts and the parole board, or the detention facility and the juvenile court—can be tricky. As with communications that occur within the organization, there are both formal and informal communications between organizations and their members. The difference is that people within an organization have at a minimum a shared mission, enabling legislation and statutory requirements, leadership, culture, and traditions to at least loosely bind them with others in their organization, consequently forging a common understanding. Though a cooperative spirit might pervade communications between organizations, the differences between them, on so many levels, may present an obstacle to effective communication. Some have argued that such organizations, though still part of the criminal justice system are only "loosely coupled" in terms of their communication and shared goals (King Davis, Applegate, Otto, Surette, & McCarthy, 2003:23).

The difficulties in establishing open lines of communication between criminal justice organizations, can lead to any number of problems, such as duplication of efforts and cost overruns. Giacomazzi and Smithey (2001) found just such problems as they chronicled an effort by several diverse agencies (including a large police department and relevant service provider agencies) to collaborate on solutions to problems stemming from violence against women in one metropolitan area. They noted that organizational factors sometimes hampered communication and collaboration, and at other times an unwillingness to engage by personnel created difficulties. Disputes over turf, philosophy of approach (e.g., preventive vs. law enforcement), and disorganization were just some of the obstacles to effective collaboration and communication.

Coleman (1998) describes a different experience with interagency collaboration, one that involved the King County Jail in Seattle, Washington, in the 1990s. As in the rest of the country, jail populations in Seattle were exploding. When the relatively new jail was filled shortly after it was opened, the manager of the facility knew he had to do something. That something involved engaging the major actors from other organizations in a discussion of the best means of addressing the overuse of jail facilities. So he developed a monthly interagency meeting over dinner; the participants, who went

BOX 5.1

TEAMING TO CREATE AN ETHICS CODE

In a western state prison, one of the authors witnessed the use of teaming to assist management and staff in getting buy-in on an ethics code (Barrier, Stohr, Hemmens, & Marsh, 1999). A medium security prison wanted to open a discussion among staff regarding ethical and unethical behavior in the prison. The author and a colleague were called in to facilitate the training of staff on the current procedures and policies that existed regarding ethical behavior. The management staff required attendance at this training by all staff, including managers, support, treatment, and security. We used a mix of lecture, exercises, and surveys to elicit information from and among attendees. The open nature of these sessions provided a forum for staff to vent about ethical violations they had observed and about the general inadequacy of the policy manual vis-à-vis ethical violations.

As an outgrowth of those sessions, management decided to create a team to develop an ethics code for the institution. A progressive associate warden was given the task of creating this team. He asked that the author serve as a consultant to the team, and the associate warden declined to participate himself, though he did observe team operation. To his credit, the man selected team members who were representative of all facets of the prison (medical, kitchen supervisors, security, treatment) and from different levels (supervisors, line staff, sergeants and lieutenants) and who represented multiple perspectives (those who were enthusiastic and those who were skeptical). During the first meeting the group vented their frustrations and concerns and chose a chair (a young officer who was well respected). During the second meeting there were some continuing complaints and venting, but mostly there was a sense that we should get on with the task. Thus information was collected and disseminated to group members regarding other state codes and those of the American Correctional Association and the American Jails Association. The team also reviewed the comments of their fellow staff members that had been provided anonymously on the surveys gathered by the trainers.

From this information, and over a period of a couple of months, with weekly meetings, an ethics code was developed for this prison. Once there was consensus regarding the code, the members engaged in a campaign to promote it among their colleagues. To do this they placed the code in several issues of the institution newsletter and promoted it by providing examples of its application. The group leaders also met with the warden and the associate wardens to emphasize the importance of allowing code compliance to guide selection, but particularly performance appraisal and promotion decisions. In other words, if management truly believed in the process and wanted staff buy-in on the values expressed in the code, then those who abided by it should be rewarded, to send the message that the ethics code values were an integral part of the organization. Management agreed enthusiastically, and the author received reports later indicating that promotion and performance appraisals had been affected by this code and relative adherence to it. But the best indication of success of this teaming exercise occurred when one of the more curmudgeonly members of the team, who had been a complete skeptic about the code and the process at the beginning, told the group in a later meeting that he had defended both the code and its development process to coworkers.

dutch, included representative and influential judges, police officials, prosecutors, public defenders, jail administrators, and other relevant stakeholders. The agenda for these meetings was both to educate members about the limited jail resources and to engage them in a problem-solving discussion, with the goal of developing an informal plan for limiting use of the jail. The jail manager reported that as a direct result of these discussions over dinner, the use of the jail dropped or remained steady for several years and the building of another jail was temporarily averted (Coleman, 1998).

This example demonstrates that interorganizational communication is as important to the effective operation of some criminal justice agencies as is intraorganizational communications. Other examples of interorganizational teaming between criminal justice organizations abound: drug task forces, community policing teams that include other stakeholders besides the police, youth councils, and many more. These groups exist and flourish because they play a major role in enhancing communication between organizations and allow those organizations, in turn, flexibility in meeting the demands of their environment.

Another important element of the enhancement of both inter- and intraorganizational communications is embedded in how these organizations deal with complaints from the community and other organizations. First, it is important to note that there are several sources and outcomes of complaints. For example, police *respond* to the complaint of loud noise originating from a party near campus, or to a victim's complaint of an assault. In these examples, the complaints could result in drunken underage partygoers being cited as MIPs (minors in possession), or the assault victim's attacker being identified and arrested. However, here the focus is on complaints directed *at* the police, court, or correctional agency from within, or originating from, the community. There are several issues within the realm of intra-agency and community complaints, especially when it comes to police use of excessive force, correctional officer misuse of power (inmate coercion), or arbitrary sentencing practices (such as those based on race), and whether such conduct is intentional or negligent (Langworthy & Travis, 1994; B. W. Smith & Holmes, 2003).

In each of these scenarios the criminal justice agency (or community ombudsman) must effectively field and deal with citizen complaints and assess whether each one is founded. A complaint filed against a police, court, or corrections officer may spur an internal investigation, which may include assessment of criminal or civil liability, as well as disciplinary action, and may also address some form of restitution (individual and/or community) (Smith & Holmes, 2003; Smith, 2004).

Complaints filed from within a criminal justice agency are ideally treated in similar ways. However, because of "office politics," power differentials between managers and staff, and close personal ties, not always amicable, among and between various employees, some form of complainant anonymity must be allowed. One way to curb the arbitrary backlash that may arise when an employee reports abuse (whether physical, emotional, or financial) has been the implementation of "whistleblower" programs, which are described shortly. When one considers that most criminal justice agency mission statements purport some form of "service to the community," it is easy to see why effectively dealing with citizen and employee complaints becomes paramount to public relations and the success of the agency.

BARRIERS TO EFFECTIVE COMMUNICATION

Effective communication, which has occurred when the receiver comprehends the message sent by the sender, is often stymied by intentional or unintentional barriers. As noted in the discussion of interorganizational communication, different organizations may be prevented from engaging in productive communication by their formal and informal policies, procedures, missions, politics, turf, and traditions (Giacomazzi & Smithey, 2001; King Davis et al., 2003). But there are barriers that exist at both the interpersonal and organizational levels for organizations (Klofas, Stojokovic, & Kalinich, 1990). Some common barriers at the interpersonal level, or in the communications between individuals, which are identified by Klofas et al. (1990:66–67), Whisenand and Rush, (1998:102), and the authors, include the following:

- preconceived ideas
- denial of contrary information
- filtering
- emotions
- noncredibility of the source
- personality differences
- use of personalized meanings
- use of complex channels
- lack of motivation or interest
- lack of communication skills
- nonverbal signs
- poor organizational climate
- information overload
- fear of embarrassment
- fear of reprisal
- time pressures

When people have "preconceived ideas" about others or deny "contrary information" or information that conflicts with preconceived beliefs, there is more likely to be a breakdown in communications. These conditions can in turn lead to a belief that the source is not credible. All these perceptions might be conveyed both verbally and non-verbally. Of course, as with all organizations in which there are regular interactions among individuals, these barriers are common. Categorizations based on personal characteristics, family and friend associations, income, role, and any number of other factors would appear to be common among humans. The bias and prejudicial attitudes that result, however, can lead to an inability and even an unwillingness to communicate with people unlike you: the "other" or "outsider." Such attitudes can also lead to discriminatory behavior. For instance, it is not uncommon for inmates to claim that staff look down on them, ignore them, and treat them with disrespect in large part because of their inmate status (Belknap et al., 1998; Johnson, 1996). Some police officers may claim that their race, age, or gender is the basis for discriminatory behavior by colleagues (Morash & Haarr, 1995). The preconceived ideas about others that result, or those regarding projects or policies, can also hamper communication in the workplace. Relatedly, filtering of information can result from deliberate twisting of information by either the sender or the receiver. Perhaps the best management remedy is to ask staff to have an open mind and then to train them on diversity issues and organizational initiatives as a means of overcoming these communication barriers.

A related barrier, but one that is less obvious, may be the clash that comes from divergent personalities working together. Emotions might also get tangled up in this delivery of information when people do not understand each other. For instance, an extroverted probation officer and an introverted supervisor will act differently in the workplace. These differences may lead to a breakdown in communication as the introvert prefers a quiet workplace where she can reflect on written material and the extrovert is most comfortable with dialog and diversions in the workplace. The measurement of personality types in the workplace has become popular management practice (e.g. see Box 5.2) and may serve to enhance communication and understanding between these divergent personality types.

The use of personalized meanings as a barrier to effective communication is also common to criminal justice agencies. The police, with their coded designations of criminal events, but particularly the legal profession and their use of Latin (lawyers resuscitate this "dead" language throughout their careers!), for all intents and purposes limit the number of people who can understand them. Though corrections is not quite as esoteric in its use of language, the slang and abbreviations used throughout the system create barriers to effective engagement with others not on the inside, so to speak. What is a kite, a shank, or a rap in a correctional setting? (Answer: a grievance, a knife, and a charge, respectively.)

Relatedly, the need to use complex channels of communication makes it difficult to convey information from the bottom up. It also makes the accurate transfer of information from the top down questionable. Often a simple communication must pass through several layers of bureaucracy—a problem that is particularly acute when the bureaucracy has not been flattened in terms of levels of supervisors.

Interpersonal communications can also break down when there is little motivation to communicate and/or either sender or receiver has poor skills in this area. The

BOX 5.2

THE MYERS-BRIGGS PERSONALITY TEST AND THE WORKPLACE

The Myers-Briggs personality test helps one to identify which of sixteen personality types a person tends to fit into. The original short form of the test includes seventy questions, which are used to diagnose whether a person is an extrovert or an introvert (E/I), has a preference for intuition or sensing (N/S), for thinking or feeling (T/F), and for judgment or perception (J/P). There are no preferred or superior personality types, just different ones. Some types are much more common in the population than others.

Isabel Meyers and her mother, Katherine Cook Briggs, developed the instrument called the Myers-Briggs Personality Type Indicator to enhance learning and understanding of personality types in all kinds of venues (for more information and recommended Internet, or in-person, providers of the test, log onto www.MyersBriggs.org). The Indicator is based on the work of Carl-Gustav Jung and his book *Psychological Types*. Myers, influenced by both her mother's and Jung's work, began devising the Indicator in 1942.

In the workplace the Indicator has been used in a number of ways to improve understanding and matching of personality types. For instance, if you google "Myers-Briggs" you will find there are numerous business entities promising to use the tests, or a version of it, to assist organizations in teaming, diagnosing communication styles, career planning, pre-employment testing, turning managers into coaches, and improving sales, among other things. Myers-Briggs has also been put to use in the social and familial spheres in the matching of dates and mates and as a means of improving understanding between parents and children. Over the years, millions of people have taken the personality test.

latter problem can usually be addressed with training. But lack of motivation is a more difficult issue and may be related to a poor organizational climate that neither fosters communication nor rewards its effective use. This climate might further hamper communication when there are time pressures. Again, the remedy is to provide open and accessible lines that allow for the ready communication of ideas and information.

College students, particularly before an exam, often remark that they are overloaded with information, and they are. Police staff faced with tomelike policy and procedures manuals and weekly, if not daily, memoranda regarding initiatives and policies, are likely to feel the same way. The solution, of course, requires that college teachers and police administrators limit the test or training to a review of the most relevant topics. But it also means that the students and policing staff, given the complexity of the information and their role in the processing of it, engage in a continuous course of learning. For students this means they study much and often throughout the semester or quarter, not just before an exam. By the same token, police staff, including administrators, must take on the role of "learner" throughout their careers.

Some staff and clients/inmates may be reluctant to communicate in corrections because they fear either reprisal or the embarrassment that might result from the disclosure of certain information. In the depositions of female and male staff who had witnessed sexual harassment, one of the authors has seen both these fears expressed as motivators for keeping quiet and not confronting the harasser or reporting the improper behavior. Likewise, inmates sometimes express the fear that they will be punished if they report the wrongdoing of staff (Belknap et al., 1998). Wells, Horney, and Maguire (2005) found in their study of citizen responses to an audit on police practices in Lincoln, Nebraska, that even when given performance feedback by community members, officers might not alter how they interact with the public.

Given these problems in communicating problems by clients, one solution of long standing that enhances the reporting of the more egregious abuses of management or staff is the development of "whistleblower" programs in government. Many states have such programs because there is a recognition of the reluctance of staff to report wrongdoing when punishment might result (Hananel, 2002). The best of such programs allow the whistleblower to remain anonymous. Although, this must surely invite abuse and vindictive behavior by some who make spurious claims, it also means that people who would not report real abuses will now do so.

There are similar barriers to communication at the organizational level, including the checks and balances between organizations, the personalized meanings of words as discussed earlier, the fact that agencies will intentionally withhold information because they are in competition with each other or because they are required to by statute, and built-in conflict between the roles of the actors (Klofas et al., 1990). The checks and balances between organizations—for instance, the courts monitoring police searches or overseeing consent decrees in jails—can stymie communication between organizations. This is not to say, of course, that these checks and balances are wrong, just that they may hamper communication. Similarly, the formal adversarial role of the actors in criminal justice (e.g., the prosecutor and the defense attorney) can lead to a breakdown in communications. This would certainly be true when attorneys for plaintiff inmates are advocating before the courts for improvement in conditions of confinement. It is unlikely in this instance that communications between the plaintiff's attorney and the warden or director of the correctional facility would be warm and friendly, or even allowed.

IMPROVING COMMUNICATIONS

Several authors of texts on criminal justice or police or corrections management have proposed solutions to the communication barriers that bedevil all criminal justice organizations (Champion, 2003; Klofas et al., 1990; Seiter, 2002; Souryal & Killinger, 1985; Whisenand & Rush, 1998). These authors provide some solutions for overcoming the barriers to communication that occur at both the individual and organizational levels. We know that some barriers are beneficial to our system of governance and are constitutionally mandated, such as the checks and balances between the branches of government (e.g., the courts reviewing the actions of the police and corrections).

Having recognized this, though, we will discuss the solutions to overcoming the illegitimate barriers that are offered by other authors and then mention a few of our own.

Klofas et al. (1990) propose organizational change as a means of improving communication. These authors believe that the change to a more participatory form of management along the lines of Theory Z is most likely to lend itself to open lines of communication and more avenues of communication.

Champion (2003) details the functional and dysfunctional aspects of communication in organizations, especially as it occurs in to informal and formal groups. His message, like that of Whisenand and Rush (1998), is that despite the pitfalls of over-reliance on either informal or formal communications, both should be recognized and utilized by managers.

Whisenand and Rush also emphasize the need for greater clarity in the message and the medium. Repeating the message, delivering it verbally as well as in written form, and reducing ambiguity are some of the suggestions they provide.

Seiter's (2002) and Souryal and Killinger's (1985) suggestions are more situationally based, but also indicate a bias toward organizational change. They recommend that managers who are interested in improving communications should consider the situation and tailor their communication style and message to it. Souryal and Killinger also suggest emphasizing requests and de-emphasizing orders in interactions with staff. They argue that managers should be respectful of staff and avoid threats; in addition, they should "avoid excessive solicitousness" but focus on cooperation. Seiter would have the supervisor be interested in positive verbal communication, be knowledgeable about the subject, and know the facts and the background of the recipient. He would ask that senders keep their remarks specific and use language that is clear.

Seiter (2002) goes further, however, to recommend an active listening process for those who work in criminal justice as a means of enhancing communication. He believes that two-way communication in corrections is sometimes stymied because supervisors view questions by staff as a threat to their authority or are ill prepared to provide adequate information. Ironically, Seiter notes that the same person who will be held responsible if an inferior job is done by those under his or her supervision often ignores vital information from subordinates. His prescription for effective listening is as follows:

- ask questions
- concentrate
- listen for main ideas
- listen for the rationale behind what the other person is saying
- listen for key words
- organize what you hear in your own mind in a way that is logical for you
- take notes if the issue or request is complex (Seiter, 2002:356)

An Additional Prescription for Communication Enhancement

Clearly, the secret to enhancing communication in an organization and to overcoming barriers is *more communication*. How more communication is achieved depends on the situation, and the sender and the receiver in those circumstances. Fortunately, there are techniques and processes that can be used in the criminal justice workplace to improve communication.

Training   One method of transmitting the formal message of the organization is to TRAIN, TRAIN, and TRAIN. Consult any successful manager, management text, or a text on organizational change and the importance of training will be prominently featured. Training is used to inform, to prevent mistakes, and to address misconceptions. In a sense, it levels the playing field of knowledge and empowers workers to negotiate in their workplace more effectively: the old cliché is true, "Knowledge is power."

Teaming   To make positive change in any organization, training is part of the solution and teaming is another (see Box 5.3). Teams perform collective problem-solving, solution-building, and even implementation-monitoring functions that are vital in the 21st-century workplace. They destructure the hierarchy of the organization by opening up avenues of communication that are too narrow in traditional organizations (Lipnack & Stamps, 2003; Peters, 1992; Wageman, 2003). Teams also lend credibility to the process and make employees feel that they have a voice in organizational operation. They can provide a mechanism for bridging the divide between organizations within the same system that may have interests in common.

Listening   Seiter (2002) makes an excellent point and one echoed in some fashion in many management texts: if you want to know your organization and your workers, develop effective listening skills. Perhaps because they think they must, managers may propose initiatives or support programs without first taking the temperature of the organization or, for that matter, truly knowing the organization. It is the height of arrogance for a new manager to come in and propose changes without knowing why or how the current policies or practices work. Such managers, who are more inclined to tell or sell their initiative without listening first, risk losing not only the chance to successfully implement their own ideas (because people will sabotage them) but the allegiance of the workers; we will discuss leadership issues much more in Chapter 7. One last point here. Sometimes "listening" means paying attention to the nonverbal communication as much as the verbal (see Box 5.4).

Newsletters   It is a given that written communications of all kinds proliferate in bureaucratic organizations. Formal communiqués flutter down from the top, and incident reports filter up through the ranks, while more informal e-mails zigzag throughout the organization. The value of departmental newsletters is that they can be used to cross hierarchical lines and capture the most salient of both the formal and informal information filtering through the organization. At their best, they can serve the purpose of training, passing along general staff information while also influencing the subculture. They are more likely to be seen as a means for input if all levels and types of staff have a say in their content. In other words, if newsletters are produced by the top for the bottom, they will be viewed as merely a more developed memorandum rather than as a vehicle for interactive communication between ranks and roles.

BOX 5.3

LEADERSHIP TEAMS AT THE ADA COUNTY SHERIFF'S OFFICE

By Sheriff Gary Raney

As I rose through the ranks, I so often thought to myself, "If only they would have sought input from those of us who are *doing* the job, we could have offered some good ideas." Even as a deputy I wanted to see things run well across all of the organization. Often when I felt we had good ideas, I was frustrated that there was no mechanism to share them other than the chain of command, who were often wrapped up in their own issues and didn't want to take on more.

When I became sheriff, I was convinced that forming focus groups to provide feedback from within the agency presented many benefits. I wanted to offer that attentive ear to my employees that I wished I could have had. I also wanted to make changes in the organization. I knew that a feedback loop would be necessary to monitor those changes, and what better feedback loop than the front line? Lastly, I also knew that I wanted employees to feel engaged with management and that a great instrument for that would be the honest and open, but respectful, discussion of how supervision and management were doing from a front line perspective.

I assembled focus groups, later to be called leadership teams, and intentionally sought a cross section of employees within each major area of the agency. I included them all—young and old, males and females, new and veteran, happy and unhappy. Mostly, I tried to identify the employees who had the personal maturity to think outside their own agendas and to be honest with me.

Some executives insulate themselves to only listen to upper management. I have to ask if they think they'll actually hear the bad news from the person in charge of it. It's doubtful. That said, I also set ground rules for the leadership teams to qualify that these meetings were not a "bitch session" or a convenient opportunity to circumvent the chain of command with personal agendas, but an opportunity for employees and management to work together.

I think success requires that someone at the top listen to the bad news, filter out what's accurate, and act upon it. The outcome of these groups has been as simple as getting many small irritating issues taken care of (from regular inspections of laptops in patrol cars to replacement of missing keys). More significantly, the open dialogue brought forward some specific examples of supervision and management inconsistencies in policy and practice, and it was ultimately the catalyst for some sound operational changes like how we deliver medication in the jail—a high liability and time-consuming issue— and our patrol training program. Last but not least, rumors can drag an organization down. Each time we met I solicited the rumors from out of the group and addressed them very directly, which both greatly decreased the negative rumors and reinforced the idea that people should verify what they hear.

This process really helped me know what reality was at the line level. Equally true, it became very meaningful to them when they could see something happen as a direct result of their discussion and conclusions. I think it was the realistic application of the buzzwords we like to use: empowerment, participative leadership, buy-in, etc. I believe an organization can operate by completing necessary tasks, but an organization can only run well when communication becomes more important than the tasks. The leadership teams have bridged that communication gap better than anything else I know of, and they have made the whole system work better.

Gary Raney began his career with the Ada County Sheriff's Office in 1983, rising through the ranks to become sheriff in 2005. The agency, based in Boise, Idaho, has 530 employees and provides full-service law enforcement, jail, and support services.

Grievance Procedures and Whistleblowing Programs   Though grievance procedures and whistleblowing programs tend to engender negative communications within the organization, they are central to preventing abuses by employees. To enhance legitimacy, they need to be handled in the most professional, objective and formal way possible. The programs should afford anonymity to whistleblowers, and provisions for punishing retaliation against whistleblowers (Hananel, 2002).

Technology   It is well known that technology has revolutionized communication in so many aspects of our lives, including in the criminal justice arena. It is also a truism that telephones, cars, radios, and computers have all made the management of staff and clientele more efficient and effective in criminal justice organizations (Langworthy & Travis, 1994). In a more recent example of the powerful effect of technology to improve communications, appellate decisions, previously available only through private companies, are now published widely on the Internet for free (Shelton, 2000). Furthermore, through the use of e-mails, listservs, and web pages, courts and the police and correctional agencies are able to provide information to the public that was heretofore difficult or impossible to access.

Inside and Outside Research   Even the best manager in the world may lack information about the workplace that workers are afraid to report, purposefully withhold, do not know they know, or do not consider relevant; still other information is not self-evident to the manager. Several states and localities have research entities in their criminal justice organizations (usually in state level or large metro area agencies), but unfortunately most small municipalities and states have little or no research capacity. Yet there is no substitute for a fresh and unbiased eye for examining any phenomenon, and the criminal justice organization is no exception. To the extent that a criminal justice entity can embrace the value of research and encourage it, the validity of

BOX 5.4

NONVERBAL COMMUNICATION

In a training session for prison classification counselors that one of the authors attended in the mid-1980s in Washington State, the facilitators had attendees engage in a group problem-solving process. Those present were given a problem to tackle and the circumstances surrounding it and told to discuss solutions among themselves. Unbeknownst to the participants, the trainers used this exercise as an opportunity to diagnose the interpersonal and group communication styles within each group by focusing on the nonverbal communication that was exhibited.

When the discussion of the problem was complete, the facilitators asked the groups to identify who in each group had been most engaged, most disengaged, and most thoughtful in their interactions in the group. Many times, but not always, the group perceptions of an individual member's activity conformed to their observations of nonverbal communications. They found that those who were leaning forward toward the group, with arms somewhat loose and open, or leaning on elbows and maintaining eye contact with other group members, were also those identified as most involved. Likewise, those who sat back away from the group and had their arms folded, legs crossed, and eyes anywhere but on other group members, were, of course, identified as disengaged. The training facilitators also noticed that some group members exhibited a mix of these behaviors, depending on what part of the exercise the group was engaged in. The explicit and verbal message at the time by the facilitators was to pay attention to the nonverbal communications by both coworkers and clients/inmates in the workplace, as these behaviors include a message as well.

Relatedly, Brougham (1992), in an *FBI Law Enforcement Bulletin* article, discusses the importance of nonverbal communication in his work as a police sergeant in Chicago. He notes that attention to body movements (movement of feet and hands, folded arms, etc.), personal distance (increasing and decreasing proximity from others people), facial expressions (asymmetry in the face that occurs when people lie, increased eye blinking, etc.), physiological symptoms (perspiration, flushing, etc.), and paralanguage (the pitch and rate of speech, etc.) all convey an involuntary message about the truth to the astute observer of nonverbal communications.

the information cycling through the communication channels will improve (Fleisher, 1996; Kerle, 2003).

A related point is that even if the criminal justice agency cannot initiate its own research, there are studies in both the professional and academic press that should be regularly accessed by the savvy manager and staff. Professional magazines should be subscribed to and passed around the workplace as they often feature relevant research. Managers should also subscribe to, read, and make available to their employees the relevant academic journals. Not all the articles in these journals will be directly related to a particular workplace, but many of them will. However, even articles without direct application can be used to broaden the understanding of research, functions, and innovations in other criminal justice agencies.

Organizational Change   Underlying most prescriptions for the improvement of communications in organizations (e.g., Champion, 2003; Klofas et al., 1990; Peters, 1992, 1995; Seiter, 2002; Whisenand & Rush, 1998) is the belief that we must move beyond the natural constrictions placed by a bureaucratic organization on people's ability and willingness to communicate (Stohr, Lovrich, Menke, & Zupan, 1994). Many modern observers of organizations also argue for a more human relations-oriented management style (e.g., see Chapter 4).

As discussed previously in this chapter and others, bureaucracy and a traditional management perspective favor communication from the top down and provide no formal mechanism for bottom-up or horizontal or, for that matter, diagonal communication. As bureaucracy is here to stay in terms of the basic shape of most criminal justice organizations (although they can definitely get fatter and flatter—see Chapter 4) and courts are a notable exception, there can and must be some change in traditional management if we are to see measurable improvement in communications in such organizations. In fact, a basic assumption of our prescription for improving communication is that criminal justice organizations will further move to embrace a human relations perspective on management.

From such a perspective, the knowledge and skills that workers bring to their jobs are recognized, and managers who do not value that information or provide vehicles for its transmission are seen as handicapping their organization. There is also clear evidence that criminal justice workers will be more committed, more satisfied, less stressed, and less likely to quit if they are given the chance to meaningfully develop and participate in workplace decision making (Alarid, 1999; Brody, DeMarco, & Lovrich, 2002; Kiekbusch, Price, & Theis, 2003; Lipnack & Stamps, 2003; Slate, Vogel, & Johnson, 2001; Stohr et al., 1994; Witte, Travis, & Langworthy, 1990; Wright, Saylor, Gilman, & Camp, 1997; Wageman, 2003).

CONCLUSIONS

Communication in criminal justice organizations is formal and informal, verbal and nonverbal; it is rarely as straightforward in delivery or interpretation as we might like. People and their jobs, roles, and organizations differ, and this just makes communication problematic. Yet, there is plenty of evidence that effective communication is key to organizational success and positive work perceptions (Flanagan, Johnson, & Bennett, 1996). As discussed in the chapter, there are techniques and processes that can serve to improve the amount of communications, and their accuracy. Though there is nothing particularly new about the prescriptions for improving communication in criminal justice that are offered by ourselves and others, these measures are likely to provide the kind of environment in which communications flow most freely.

EXERCISE: THE SPACE INVADER

Just for fun, we include a version of a communication exercise that is ubiquitous in classroom and training environments. The exercise has no clear author that we are aware of, and the name invented for it here is not to be confused with the video game. We have found the exercise useful in the classroom and in training as a means of conveying the nuances in communication. Without giving the game away, so to speak, we note that the exercise usually yields interesting insights from participants about the nature of communication. It also serves to liven up lecture or training sessions on communication in a way that mere lecturing cannot always accomplish.

The Space Invader

1. Ask the group to form two facing lines about five feet apart; it works best if there is enough room so the lines do not have to double over or twist around. You can have men in one line, women in the other, or use another criterion.
2. Ask everyone to identify a specific person in the other line as a point of reference.
3. It is okay if every woman is not matched with a man, and vice versa, as it actually is interesting to have a mix of male/female and female/female and male/male matchings for comparison (which means you may have to move some of the excess males to the female line or some of the excess females to the male line; you could do this even if there is the same number of males and females).
4. Ask all to pay careful attention to their own reaction and that of their point-of-reference person during the exercise.
5. Ask the people in one line to walk slowly toward their respective point-of-reference partners and ask the people in the other line to put one hand forward (palm facing the point-of-reference person) when they are starting to feel uncomfortable. (We usually have the male line walk and give the female line the power to stop them— the reason should become obvious as you complete this exercise!).
6. When all in the "walking" line have been stopped, ask the members of both lines to note mentally, and WITHOUT SPEAKING, the distance they are from their point of reference and then glance around the room to see how far other people are from their points of reference.
7. You could stop here and ask for observations by people regarding the different amounts of space between given individuals and why that might be so, or you could delay the observations until after the group has repeated the exercise with the opposite line walking toward their point-of-reference people.
8. Inevitably, the observations include some discussion about how people react differently to the proximity of others based on the personal characteristics of those in the

"walking" and the "stopping" lines (gender is an important variable here, but so are many others).

9. Participants are asked how these differences in proximity comfort levels might affect and color communication interactions in the workplace.

DISCUSSION QUESTIONS

1. Why and how would the style of communication vary when the issue is service versus protection in policing? Explain your reasoning.

2. Why are barriers to communication within and between organizations sometimes a good thing? Explain your answer.

3. What are the best methods for surmounting organizational barriers to communication within the organization? List and explain your answers.

4. What are the best methods for surmounting the organizational barriers to communication between organizations? List and explain your answers.

5. What is an approach to improving the flow of "negative" communications within the organization? Give a real-world example of this method.

6. What set of organizational theories serves as the underpinning for many recommendations for improvements in communications? Why is this so?

7. If you had to devise a "system" for enhancing communication within a given criminal justice organization, what would be its components?

KEY TERMS

communication: often defined as a sharing or exchange of information, via a medium, between a sender and a receiver (McLuhan, 1964). As indicated by this definition, information is not just shared; it is at times exchanged for something. In other words, communication can be tied to expectations within the organization that there will be a quid pro quo (something for something) in the process.

formal communications: usually found in the policies and procedures, the mission statement, the training sessions, and the training manual, as well as in official communiqués or memorandums.

informal communications: the one-on-one conversations, the asides, and the jokes that permeate the workplace.

WEB LINK

Myers-Briggs Personality Test website: http://www.myersbriggs.org

REFERENCES

Alarid, L. F. (1999). Law enforcement departments as learning organizations: Argyris's theory as a framework for implementing community-oriented policing. *Police Quarterly, 2*(3), 321–337.

Barrier, G., Stohr, M. K., Hemmens, C., & Marsh, R. (1999). A practical user's guide to ethical practices: Idaho's method for implementing ethical behavior in a correctional setting. *Corrections Compendium, 24*(4), 1–12.

Belknap, J., Holsinger, K., & Dunn, M. (1997). Understanding incarcerated girls: The results of a focus group study. *The Prison Journal, 77*(4), 381–404.

Bennett, W. W., & Hess, K. (2001). *Management and supervision in law enforcement* (3rd ed.). Belmont, CA: Wadsworth/Thomson Learning.

Brody, D. C., DeMarco, C., & Lovrich, N. P. (2002). Community policing and job satisfaction: Suggestive evidence of positive workforce effects from a multjurisdictional comparison in Washington State. *Police Quarterly, 5*(2), 181–205.

Brougham, C. G. (1992). Nonverbal communication: Can what they don't say give them away? *FBI Law Enforcement Bulletin, 61*(7), 15–18.

Champion, D. J. (2003). *Administration of criminal justice: Structure, function and process.* Upper Saddle River, NJ: Prentice Hall.

Clear, T., & G. F. Cole. (1997). *American corrections* (4th ed.). Belmont, CA: Wadsworth.

Coleman, R. J., (1998). A cooperative corrections arrangement: A blueprint for criminal justice in the 21st century. *Corrections Now, 3*(1), 1.

Crank, J. P. (1996). The construction of meaning during training for probation and parole. *Justice Quarterly, 13*(2), 265–290.

Flanagan, T., Johnson, W. W., & Bennett, K. (1996). Job satisfaction among correctional executives: A contemporary portrait of wardens of state prisons for adults. *The Prison Journal, 76*(4), 385–397.

Fleisher, M. S. (1996). Management assessment and policy dissemination in federal prisons. *The Prison Journal, 76*(1), 81–91.

Gaines, L. K., Southerland, M. D., & Angell, J. E. (1991). *Police administration.* New York: McGraw-Hill.

Giacomazzi, A. L., & Smithey, M. (2001). Community policing and family violence against women: Lessons learned from a multiagency collaboration. *Police Quarterly, 4*(1), 99–122.

Gordon, G. J., & Milakovitch, M. E. (1998). *Public administration in America* (6th ed.). New York: St. Martin's Press.

Hananel, S. (2002). Whistle-blower report cites abuser. *Washington Post.* www.washingtonpost.com, September 1.

Johnson, R. (1996). *Hard Time: Understanding and reforming the prison.* Belmont, CA: Wadsworth.

King Davis, R., Applegate, B. K., Otto, C. W., Surette, R., & McCarthy, B. J. (2003). Roles and responsibilities: Analyzing local leaders' views on jail crowding from a systems perspective. *Crime and Delinquency, 49*(10), 1–25.

Kerle, K. (2002). Editorial: Communications. *American Jails, 15*(6), 5.

Kerle, K. (2003). Editorial: Keeping your best employees? *American Jails, 17*(4), 5.

Kiekbusch, R., Price, W., & Theis, J. (2003). Turnover predictors: Causes of employee turnover in sheriff-operated jails. *Criminal Justice Studies, 16*(2), 67–76.

Klofas, J., Stojokovic, S., & Kalinich, D. (1990). *Criminal justice organizations.* Pacific Grove, CA: Brooks/Cols.

Langworthy, R. H., & Lawrence F. T., III. (1994). *Policing in America: A balance of forces.* New York: Macmillan.

Langworthy, R. H., & Travis, L. F., III (1994). *Policing in America: a balance of forces.* New York: Macmillan.

Larson, C. E., & LaFasto, F. M. J. (1989). *Teamwork: What must go right/What can go wrong.* Newbury Park, CA: Sage.

Lipnack, J., & Stamps, J. (2003). Virtual teams: The new way to work. In J. S. Ott, S. J. Parkes, & R .B. Simpson (Eds.), *Readings in organizational behavior* (pp. 297–303). Belmont, CA: Wadsworth/Thomson Learning.

MacDonald, S. S., & Baroody-Hart, C. (1999). Communication between probation officers and judges: An innovative model. *Federal Probation, 63*(1), 42–51.

Maitland, A. S., & Sluder, R. D. (1998). Victimization and youthful prison inmates: An empirical analysis. *The Prison Journal, 78*(1), 55–73.

McLuhan, M. (1964, reprinted in 1994). *Understanding media: The extensions of man.* Cambridge, MA: MIT Press.

Meyer, J. F., & Grant, D. R. (2003). *The courts in our criminal justice system.* Upper Saddle River, NJ: Prentice Hall.

Morash, M., & Haarr, R. N. (1995). Gender, workplace problems, and stress in policing. *Justice Quarterly,* 12, 113–140.

Motschall, M., & Cao, L. (2002). An analysis of the public relations role of the police public information officer. *Police Quarterly, 5*(2), 152–180.

Ouchi, W. (1981). *Theory Z: How American business can meet the Japanese challenge.* Reading, MA: Addison-Wesley.

Peters, T. (1992). *Liberation management: Necessary disorganization for the nanosecond nineties.* New York: Knopf.

Peters, T. (1995). *Two complete books: Thriving on chaos and a passion for excellence* (with Nancy Austin). New York: Random House.

Phillips, P. W., & Orvis, G. P. (1999). Intergovernmental relations and the crime task force: A case study of the East Texas Violent Crime Task Force and its implications. *Police Quarterly, 2*(4), 438–461.

Pollock, J. M. (Ed.). (1997). *Prisons: Today and tomorrow.* Gaithersburg, MDA: Aspen Publishers.

Seiter, R. P. (2002). *Correctional administration: Integrating theory and practice.* Upper Saddle River, NJ: Prentice Hall.

Shelton, D. E. (2000). Communicating with lawyers on the Internet. *The Judges Journal, 39*(1), 26–27.

Slate, R. N., Vogel, R. E., & Johnson, W. W. (2001). To quit or not to quit: Perceptions of participation in correctional decision making and the impact of organizational stress. *Corrections Management Quarterly, 5*(2), 68–78.

Smith, B. W., & Holmes, M. D. (2003). Community accountability, minority threat, and police brutality: An examination of civil rights criminal complaints. *Criminology, 41*(4), 1035–1063.

Smith, G. (2004). Rethinking police complaints. *British Journal of Criminology, 44*(1), 15–33.

Souryal, S., & Killinger, G. G. (1985). *Police organization and administration.* Cincinnati, OH: Pilgrimmage.

Stohr, M. K., Lovrich N. P., Jr., Menke, B. A., & Zupan, L. L. (1994). Staff management in correctional institutions: Comparing DiIulio's 'control model' and 'employee investment model' outcomes in five jails. *Justice Quarterly, 11*(3), 471–497.

Stojokovic, S., & Lovell, R. (1997). *Corrections: An introduction* (2nd ed.). Cincinnati, OH: Anderson Publishing.

Swanson, C. R., Territo, L., & Taylor, R.W. (1998). *Police administration structures, processes, and behavior* (4th ed.). Upper Saddle River, NJ: Prentice Hall.

Tewksbury, R. A. (1997). *Introduction to corrections* (3rd ed.). New York: Glencoe.

Thibault, E. A., Lynch, L. M., & McBride, R. B. (1998). *Proactive police management* (4th ed.). Upper Saddle River, NJ: Prentice Hall.

Wageman, R. (2003). Critical success factors for creating superb self-managing teams. In J. S. Ott, S. J. Parkes, & R. B. Simpson (Eds.), *Readings in organizational behavior,* (pp. 285–296). Belmont, CA: Wadsworth/Thomson Learning.

Welch, M. (1996). *Corrections: A critical approach.* New York: McGraw-Hill.

Wells, W., Horney, J., & Maguire, E. R. (2005). Patrol officer responses to citizen feedback: An experimental analysis. *Police Quarterly, 8*(2), 171–205.

Whisenand, P. M., & Rush, G. E. (1998). *Supervising police personnel: The fifteen responsibilities* (3rd ed.). Upper Saddle River, NJ: Prentice Hall.

Witte, J. H, Travis, L. G., III, & Langworthy, R. H. (1990). Participatory management in law enforcement: Police officer, supervisor and administrator perceptions. *American Journal of Police, 9*(4), 1–24.

Wright, K. N., Saylor, W. G., Gilman, E., & Camp, S. (1997). Job control and occupational outcomes among prison workers. *Justice Quarterly, 14*(3), 525–546.

CHAPTER 6

SOCIALIZATION, ROLES, AND POWER ISSUES

Power corrupts and absolute power corrupts absolutely.

(Lord Acton, 1887, in a letter to Bishop Creighton)

This analysis argues that, instead of being a simple matter of putting on a uniform and learning about schedules, becoming and being a prison officer is a complex process. Behind the walls, through constant interaction that is typically informal and subtle, yet sometimes frighteningly bold and sudden, the recruit learns the contours of the prison world and his place in it....

(Crouch & Marquart, 1994:327)

Not only does justice require the prosecutor to "weed out" cases where the evidence is weak, but the practical need to conserve scarce legal resources for only the most serious cases demands this....

(Meyer & Grant, 2003:116)

Cops are selecting modes of adaptation that they prefer, that they sometimes, to use a term uncommon to scholarly studies, simply like... they make choices that are pleasing to them, that make them feel good, or that at appropriate times make them angry.

(Crank, 1998:21)

INTRODUCTION: WHAT IS MY JOB AND HOW DO I DO IT?

The topics of socialization, roles, and power issues in criminal justice organizations are really concerned with what the job of the professional is (roles), how people learn about it (socialization), and how they exercise one of the most important tools at hand (power). In the multicontextual environment of criminal justice organizations, where politics, economics, crime levels, and stakeholder expectations all affect the operation of the multilayered agency, the answer to our questions (What is my job and how do I do it?) may not be as clear in practice as it is in the formal job announcement.

In this chapter, we will discuss the criminal justice workers at the base of the management chart. They, like managers, and others within their larger organizations, are professionals who are often asked to do too much with too little. Recall that these types of workers, including police and correctional officers, counselors, probation and parole officers, prosecutors, and defense attorneys, fit the description given in Chapter 1 of street-level bureaucrats—SLBs (Lipsky, 1980). Or public service workers who have more demands on their time and agency resources than they can meet, and who also have the discretion to make choices about their work.

This chapter is framed with a focus on the SLBs because how they are socialized into the role they adopt essentially defines criminal justice policy in practice. As all who are likely to read this book know, work in the criminal justice field is fascinating because of the human element that defines it. The roles of detention and reform school officers, prosecutors, and counselors are diverse, but bound by the nature of the socialization into those roles, and by the presence of power. How socialization is accomplished and the choice of roles adopted really defines criminal justice agencies, and justice dispersal, in the United States.

SOCIALIZATION

Occupational socialization, like any form of socialization, involves learning and teaching. A child in school is taught what and how to learn by teachers and fellow classmates. A new member of a book club is initiated into the ways of the club operation and focus by the other members. Likewise, the new police recruit learns from organizational members and others who teach him or her the job and how to do it. But recruits learn not just the particulars of the job itself, they learn what the prevailing and conflicting values and beliefs are for the organization. This learning curve is steepest at the beginning, but the officer gains knowledge, and sometimes relearns his role, throughout his career.

Therefore, according to Klofas, Stojkovic, and Kalinich, (1990:150) **occupational socialization** is "[t]he process by which a person acquires the values, attitudes, and behaviors of an ongoing occupational social system." Socialization is a process and it is ongoing. What is not said here, but is implied, is that socialization is not done by organizational members only; rather, as we will discuss later in the chapter, clients and other stakeholders also teach the criminal justice worker about the job (Crank, 1998; Lipsky, 1980; Lombardo, 1989). The socialization process may also vary based on individual personal characteristics; for instance, the gender and race/ethnicity of the jobholder have been shown to influence how criminal justice staff view and perform their jobs (Camp, Saylor, & Wright, 2001; Haarr, 1997; Jenne & Kersting, 1998; Morash & Haarr, 1995).

This socialization process is believed to take place in three stages: *anticipatory*, *formal*, and *informal*. Each stage entails learning, but the first and the third particularly involve some socialization by others outside the organization.

Anticipatory Socialization

The **anticipatory socialization** stage begins before the criminal justice worker even starts the job. It occurs as the person *anticipates* perhaps someday working in law, police, or corrections. Those involved in anticipatory socialization for this prospective criminal justice recruit could include family, friends, teachers, and the media. In fact, this process may begin in childhood as a person is influenced by friends and family who are employed by, or in contact with, the relevant agencies or by popular media depictions of that kind of work. Although family and friends who work in corrections may be able to supply important and relevant information about work in corrections, depictions of such work in the popular media are usually grossly inaccurate and almost uniformly misleading.

The same holds true, of course, for policing and legal work. Though many of us might be aficionados of the various *Law and Order* series, the reruns of the *NYPD Blue* drama, or even the very silly *Reno 911*, someone unacquainted with actual police or legal work may be led to believe by these shows that detectives and prosecutors have the luxury to pursue every lead and to prosecute every case to the fullest extent of the law. Or, as is depicted on *Reno 911*, that the police are complete incompetents. Moreover, the defense of cases in such programs is usually vigorous even if the defendant is poor and socially powerless. Although, of course, police, prosecutors, and defense attorneys do at times behave in accordance with the TV dramas, these descriptors hardly represent every case. As Ford (2003:87) writes regarding the "media tales" told about policing: "Gleaned from the epic stories recounted in police lore, media tales take rare events and magnify and describe heroic stories as the everyday grist of police work." But once on the job, those new recruits "[s]ense that what they will be doing is a far cry from the media's promise" (Ford, 2003:87).

Just as misleading, if not more so, are the depictions of corrections in the movies and on television. The inmates, most of whom are murderers and rapists, are inevitably housed in dirty large city jails or in maximum security prisons overseen by staff who are uncaring and sarcastic in their demeanor.

A related problem with anticipatory socialization and the criminal justice system is that much of the work is done outside the view of the public, which heightens the credence afforded media depictions, since those are often the only intimate exposure people have to criminal justice agencies. It is somewhat rare to find a community member who has taken a tour of the local jail, has sat through a trial, or knows how the parole office supervises parolees. Because of this general lack of knowledge, and because many people do not know anyone who works in the system and have not taken related classes in college, those who anticipate working in criminal justice–related positions tend to be most influenced by inaccurate media depictions, which do not give a complete or true picture of the work.

College students considering a career in criminal justice are also socialized into the nature of the work when they take related classes. Forty percent of criminal justice programs and departments include an introductory survey class on the system (police, courts, and corrections) and a research methods class (Southerland, 2002). Fewer, but still a significant number, require law, juvenile justice/delinquency, and policing courses. Not as many programs, however, require a corrections class. These classes may or may not include much discussion of the actual work done in the field; but to the extent that they do, anticipatory socialization occurs through classroom lectures, readings, criminal justice professionals who give guest lectures, or visits to local work sites. Inevitably, students note on the class evaluations that they found the guest speakers and on-site visits to be the most enlivening parts of our criminal justice classes!

Perhaps because of the media depictions, a lack of knowledge, and some notable abuses of power that tend to make the headlines, some types of criminal justice work today (e.g., correctional officers) have not achieved the professional status enjoyed by police, lawyers, teachers, and firefighters. Criminal Justice will have arrived as a profession when a little boy or girl responds to the ubiquitous adult question, "What do you want to be when you grow up?" with " I want to work in a prison" or "I want to work with kids at the detention center." When children begin to provide such responses, the popular image of corrections will have changed to reflect an understanding of the work and recognition of its professional status. At this point, anticipatory socialization may more accurately reflect the positive side of work in corrections. Because of generally higher educational and training requirements, not to mention pay, for policing and law, workers in those organizations are more likely to be regarded as "professionals."

Formal Socialization

Formal socialization occurs when a worker is exposed to the legal or officially sanctioned requirements of a job. Formal socialization can begin in the job interview and in criminal justice agencies usually occurs in the initial on-the-job training conducted by a designated official, during the academy training (for corrections and policing), and in ongoing training sessions throughout the career of those workers.

The amount of academy training corrections and police workers receive varies widely across job types, between the states, and between positions at the federal, state, county, and city levels. The average length of a police recruit training program is 640 hours (Thibault, Lynch, & McBride, 2004), although a number of agencies provide far less. For instance, according to their respective websites (accessed in summer 2005), the Michigan State Police Training Division provides only 400 hours and the Georgia State University Police Department provides only 335 hours. On the other hand, the websites of the police departments of Tulsa, Oklahoma, and Mobile, Alabama (also accessed in summer 2005) indicates that new recruits receive 23 weeks, or 920 hours, of training.

Required recruit training for corrections jobs is usually far less. Unfortunately, there is no easily accessible national compilation of training requirements for corrections work as there is for policing in the *Sourcebook of Criminal Justice Statistics 2002* (Maguire & Pastore, 2004). However, individual states and organizations do publish their entry-level training requirements.

For instance, the private Corrections Corporation of America (CCA) provides all staff with 40 hours of training; correctional officers get an additional 120 hours of training during their first year (CCA website, 2004). Those first 40 hours of training include such topics as corporate history and practice, facility and personnel policies and procedures, employee standards of conduct, communicable diseases, institutional safety, special management of offenders, suicide prevention, unit management, use of force, emergency procedures, and sexual harassment. The 120-hours specialized training course for correctional officers includes such topics as count procedures, cultural diversity, defensive tactics, direct supervision, emergency procedures, facility policy and procedures, firearms training, hostage situations, first aid/CPR, and inmate disciplinary, grievance, and classification procedures.

Though they do not indicate what the training topics are, the Maine Criminal Justice Academy (MCJA) website notes that 80 hours of academy training in a two week period are provided for correctional officers (MCJA, 2004). The Maine officials also do not indicate on their website what training is required for probation and parole or juvenile justice workers.

In Delaware, a nine-week set of basic training for probation and parole officers is required. The state website does not indicate whether this nine-week training period is at 40 hours per week, but if so, then Delaware requires 450 hours of entry-level training for these officers (Delaware Department of Correction, 2004).

In contrast, in California, probation officers and parole agents are treated somewhat differently. Counties in California hire the probation officers and the state hires the parole agents who work for either the Department of Corrections or for the Youth Authority (California Employment Development Department, 2004). Both positions, as is often true for adult and juvenile probation and parole officers, require a four-year degree. Probation officers in California must also complete a 200-hour basic training within their first year, and the parole agent must complete a four-week (possibly 160-hour) training in the same time period. In Nevada, the probation and parole officers are afforded 480 hours of training in their first year of employment, but that includes both classroom and field training hours (Nevada Department of Public Safety, 2004).

Attorneys laboring in the criminal courts usually get on-the-job mentoring by more experienced colleagues, much like those in policing and corrections who participate in FTO programs. Of course, three years of law school, particularly if a clinic is required, might be regarded as providing some formal training, in addition to education. Smith (1997) notes that law school students often do not enroll in clinical programs, though such programs might help them become better lawyers, because they are not tested on bar exams. The stark truth is, law students feel the need to focus on those courses that will help them pass the bar exam and the bar exam is not based on clinical practice. In fact, the bar exam, tends to be preoccupied with business law (Smith, 1997). Therefore, some might argue, ironically, that the profession with perhaps the highest regard in the criminal justice system, and arguably exerts the most power, has the least practical training.

Reddington and Kreisel (2003) found in their research on training requirements for juvenile probation officers that thirty-six states mandate some form of training, which varies widely in amount and type. They noted that one to two weeks of fundamental skills training was typical for most of the states providing any. They note that "[t]his average amount of training for juvenile probation officers is somewhat lower than the average for adult probation officers, which is 125 hours, or for law enforcement officers" (Reddington & Kreisel, 2003:45).

Needless to say, the amount of training for entry-level positions varies widely by position and organization. But generally, correctional workers get less formal socialization via training at the beginning of their career than do police officers and much less anticipatory socialization via education than attorneys (particularly those who take a criminal law clinic) working in the criminal court system.

Ongoing training offered by criminal justice agencies also varies widely by jurisdictions and jobs. Some workers are required to take 10 to 20 hours per year to remain current in their field, while others may be offered little or no training, or participation is viewed as entirely optional. We will discuss training more in subsequent chapters, but clearly, the extent to which training is provided and required for criminal justice workers is a measure of the professional stature that a field has acquired.

In addition to the academy and ongoing training that police and corrections workers are exposed to, they, and often new prosecuting and defense attorneys, are often also formally socialized by an on-the-job trainer/mentor or a field training officer, either before or after their initial training. The FTOs, who often have years of tenure in the job, are detailed to teach the relatively new employee about how things are "officially" done in the organization. If selected correctly, the trainer/mentor/FTO can impart valuable knowledge about how to translate formal education and training to actual job practice. They can both model professional work and allow the new employee the opportunity to learn and practice skills, while gradually transitioning into full practice on the job (Sun, 2003).

The policing field first adopted FTO programs in the 1970s (Thibault et al., 2004). Critics of these early programs noted that instead of being the water walkers of the organization, too often FTOs are those who get stuck with the extra task of on-the-job training without instruction in how to do it, without the necessary time to do it right, and without any particular predilection to teach on the part of the officers. Hence, recommendations for current programs hinge on training for the trainers or FTOs and adherence to official policies, procedures, review, and evaluation requirements (Thibault et al., 2004). Bradford and Pynes (2000) also note that police academy training has not kept up with changing focuses in police work. Specifically, they note that few academies provide training in problem-solving or interpersonal and decision-making skills, though such knowledge is key to working in an organization that is focused on community policing.

Informal Socialization

Informal socialization is teaching and learning that takes place on the job. It is outside the official strictures of law and procedure and away from the officially recognized instructors. It is learning how the job is actually done, and many times that means learning the official and the unofficial versions. The divide that sometimes separates the official and unofficial versions of how the job is done, is represented by the experience of many correctional and police practitioners upon finishing the academy: they were taken aside by an old-timer and told something like "Okay, now forget that bullshit you heard at the academy, I'll show you how we REALLY do things around here." This happened to one of the authors after a week with an FTO, when she first started as a correctional officer, and she saw it happen to correctional officers returning from academy training. Our students report having had the same experience when they began work in corrections and policing after academy training.

The means of transmitting this informal socialization can take many forms. In his study of community corrections, Crank (1996) noted that it may happen under the guise of "official" training when stories or "tropes" are told to illustrate how "real" work is done. In Crank's observation of training for probation and parole officers in Nevada, commonsense advice about how to do the job was transmitted to new hires via a linguistic device he termed a *trope*, which he defines as a "[s]tory, an irony, a metaphor, or some combination of these, constituted from everyday experience" (Crank, 1996:271). For example, one instructor was trying to illustrate the importance of body searches and the inherent danger if they are not done correctly:

> This is the place [the groin area] where people hide all kinds of stuff. There was a case in California where a guy was up for parole. He went before the board, and they turned him down. He bent over and pulled a stabbing tool out of his anal cavity. He jumped over the desk and stabbed a parole board member that he didn't like in the shoulder a couple of times. (Crank, 1996:227)

A different instructor uses a trope to illustrate the understandable sympathy probation and parole officers have when their clients cannot meet their P and P conditions because they are too poor:

> We have a bad situation in our country. A lot of times it is impossible to find work for an unemployed mother. There's no way minimum wage can provide the support she can get from unemployment and ADC. However, a condition of parole is employment. You may have to talk to your supervisor. A low-skill offender with three children, her children will literally starve if she has to take a minimum-wage job. They can't afford childcare. You can write it up so that they have to work, but you can write it up so that they can take care of their children at home. (Crank, 1996:282)

In both instances, the academy instructors for probation and parole are informally socializing the new recruits to the nature of the work. In the second trope, the instructor is even advocating that the officer ignore a formal condition out of compassion for the circumstances some clients face.

Neophyte criminal justice workers are also informally socialized by their colleagues. They observe what is common practice in given situations and they sometimes model that (Pollock, 2004). If juveniles in the detention center are treated with respect in speech and deed by the majority of the other counselors, then the new counselor understands that this is the norm for behavior. If, however, the kids are referred to as "little criminals" or worse by staff, if their requests for assistance and information are ignored and their privacy is repeatedly violated for no purpose, then new counselors will detect a conflict between the official version of their job and the informal socialization being provided on the job.

In addition to the stories or tropes and observations of common practice, informal socialization may occur when clients train workers. Lipsky (1980) noted that clients will tell SLBs what behavior they expect either directly or indirectly. They might do this with intent or inadvertently. It is possible that the more prolonged and intense the contact with clients, the more likely they are to be able to "shape" the behavior of the workers. If this is true, those who work in corrections are probably more likely to experience the influence of the client than are police officers or criminal attorneys, whose exposure is likely to be short term and more remote. For instance, an inmate in a prison or jail might shape the behavior of the correctional officer by refusing to follow an order, by following the order, or by just ignoring it. If the same person refused an order by a police officer, the officer would handle it as she does all such circumstances, without the constraint of knowing that she will have to deal with the person over and over again over a span of days, months, or years.

Even so, repeated exposure to the same victims and offenders, or persons in similar circumstances, surely shapes the reactions of both the police and criminal attorneys. It is often noted in the police literature, for instance, that officers can become cynical about domestic violence because they are called to the same house to mediate the same disputes again and again. Likewise, the literature on sentencing indicates that criminal attorneys and judges will develop "norms" for sentencing, or like sentences for like offenders and offenses even when the law allows a wide range of sentencing options. In both the domestic violence and sentencing examples just given, it is possible that coworkers and supervisors are also shaping the behavior of the police and attorneys; but we must not forget that the clients in these circumstances, or their "type," may also be exerting some influence (Lipsky, 1980).

In corrections, a counselor is subtly reminded to hurry up with the current client by the line of inmates waiting outside the office. The repetitive requests of a juvenile's parents make for an alcohol or drug program placement may persuade a probation officer to be a particular advocate for that child's case. Recurring mistakes by correctional industry (inmate) workers may lead their supervisor to rethink the amount of training and pay they receive. A defense attorney may be persuaded by a client 's fervent claims of innocence to allocate more time for that case. The point is that clients, and their friends and family, can also serve in a socialization capacity vis-à-vis the criminal justice worker.

Crouch and Marquart (1994:303), in their classic article "On Becoming a Prison Guard," note that the decision to work in institutional corrections comes later in life for many, and it "[o]ften appears to be somewhat accidental, a rather unplanned response to a fortuitous opportunity or a need for immediate employment." Once on the job, the authors found that the inmates and the "guard" subculture were key to the socialization of the new recruit.

The new officer reacts to and is shaped to some degree by the inmate subculture, which may be foreign to him, as the inmates react to his official status and authority (Crouch & Marquart, 1994). Some officers are tested by inmates and some who fail the test are then corrupted in ways that Sykes (1958) identified a half-century ago: officers become too friendly with inmates; they engage in reciprocity with inmates (such as ignoring enforcement of one rule to secure inmate obedience in another matter); officers concede some tasks to inmates (such as mail delivery); and inmates use the officer's transgressions to blackmail them.

In the prison one of the authors worked at in the 1980s, a sergeant she admired told her to ignore the bulldogging by one powerful inmate. This inmate, who we'll call Jim, collected soda and potato chips and other store items from inmates in a dorm one Saturday after store. The sergeant wanted his younger colleague to ignore the bulldogging because the inmate was an important ally for staff in keeping younger and rowdier inmates in line. Greatly influenced by the wisdom of this sergeant the new officer did not infract Jim for the proscribed behavior; it was a decision she later came to regret. Eventually, the bulldogging inmate was infracted and transferred out, but only when he went too far in his collection and enforcement efforts—he was involved in a serious assault on an inmate, which could not be officially ignored.

Crouch and Marquart also note the influence of the correctional subculture in informally socializing the new officer: "The recruit learns how to be a guard most directly by observing, listening to and imitating the veterans with whom he works" (1994:312). This subculture teaches the officer how to perceive and manage inmates and how to anticipate and handle trouble. Old-time officers tell the newer officers that if they heed such advice they are less likely to find themselves in a bad spot with inmates and more likely to garner the respect of other officers.

In addition to the circumstances of the job and the socialization that criminal justice workers receive from clients and coworkers, there is evidence that other factors influence socialization. For instance, the personal characteristics and framework that criminal justice workers bring to their jobs have been found to influence how they feel about the work and how they behave in their role. Martin (1990) was one of the first to note that men and women police officers experienced their jobs differently. Jurik

(Jurik & Halemba, 1984; Jurik, 1985) also noted this difference between the genders in her research on job perceptions and performance of correctional officers in Arizona in the 1980s. Notably, since that time, and building on Jurik and Halemba's research, others have found both similarities and differences between the genders in how they experience and perform corrections and police work (Belknap, 1995; Farkas, 1999; Lawrence & Mahan, 1998; Martin, 1990; Lutze & Murphy, 1999; Pogrebin & Poole, 1997; Zupan, 1986). Research has also documented that people of diverse races and ethnicities and/or with diverse backgrounds (e.g., military service) may differ in their views of the work and how they perform it (Hemmens, Stohr, Schoeler, & Miller, 2002; Van Voorhis, Cullen, Link, & Wolfe, 1991). When there are differences between groups, however, it is not always clear whether they are the result of a framework people bring to the job or the result of socialization on the job (Ford, 2003): Is it nature or nurture? The perennial question, which, alas, as yet, has no clear answer!

THE CRIMINAL JUSTICE ROLE

Anticipatory, formal, and informal socialization in the workplace are geared toward defining what the job is for the criminal justice worker or what his or her *role* is. According to Katz and Kahn (1978) role behavior is essentially what people do over and over on the job. What you do on the job is your **role**, be that officially outlined by statutorily defined tasks, position descriptions and policies, and procedural require-ments, or unofficially defined by the actual work that is done and required. As we have seen from our discussion of socialization, the criminal justice role is both officially and unofficially defined in the organization (Purkiss, Kifer, Hemmens, & Burton, 2003). But oftentimes those official requirements for the role are in conflict with unofficial requirements.

Role Conflict: The Service vs. Security/Serve vs. Protect Dichotomies

Role conflict occurs when there are competing expectations for the role that are dif-ficult to fulfill. A related concept is **role ambiguity**, which occurs when expectations for the role are not clear or are confusing. In corrections and policing there is a classic dichotomy of roles for workers between the informal and formal demands of service work and rehabilitative tasks and the competing requirement that they always be atten-tive to security, protection, incapacitative, and even punitive requirements (Buerger, Petrosino, & Petrosino, 1999; Cullen & Gilbert, 1982; Johnson, 1996; Lombardo, 1989; Maahs & Pratt, 2001).

Prosecutors and defense attorneys have clearer roles formally than their sisters and brothers in policing and corrections. Nevertheless, it can be said of them, as is true of the police and corrections, organizational demands on attorneys time—caseloads principally—can serve to informally reduce their ability to perform their defense or prosecutorial roles adequately (Smith, 1997). According to Smith, lawyers must both defend the client (in the case of prosecutors, this would be the state) and serve as gatekeepers to the court system, keeping out complaints that do not merit prosecution and pursuing those that do. Their role also includes the ability to transform grievances into legal claims, develop new legal theories and arguments, serve as decision makers, exert influence over public policy, and control entry into the legal profession (Smith, 1997). In the larger sense lawyering includes these grander activities, but down in the trenches of the criminal court, the role of the defense or prosecuting attorney is primarily to advocate for the client or case and to get through the caseload.

Lombardo (1989) found in his research on officers working in the state prison in Auburn, New York, in the 1970s and 1980s that institutional rules sometimes prohibited an informal role that was weighted toward rehabilitative services. The roles for corrections workers are often in conflict and at times ambiguous. Similarly, Buerger et al. (1999:125) note the difficulties that arise when police officers who are more traditional in their expectations for law enforcement (e.g. "favoring confrontation, command and coercion") are suddenly working in a community policing–based organization where interactions with citizens might be expected to include more "participation, promotion and persuasion."

Role conflict occurs because of the differing expectations for corrections and policing work. Research shows that the general public and many system actors strongly support punishment as the primary goal of corrections (Norman & Burbridge, 1991; Zimmerman, Van Alstyne, & Dunn, 1988). On the other hand, several studies indicate strong support for rehabilitation among the general public and correctional actors (Cullen, Cullen, & Wozniak, 1988; Flanagan & Caulfield, 1984; Gordon, 1999; Kifer, Hemmens, & Stohr, 2003; McCorkle, 1993; Moak & Wallace, 2000; Moon, Sundt, Cullen, & Wright, 2000). The result is that in correctional settings, role conflict is more common because of this bifurcated interest in rehabilitation and punishment.

In an analysis of the statutorily defined role for probation officers, Purkiss et al. (2003) found that state legislatures required officers to perform twenty-three tasks in 2002. These tasks included a mix of law enforcement, rehabilitative, and other requirements. The authors note that a comparison of 1992 through 2002 statutes in the states clearly shows, that the law enforcement role for probation officers gained primacy in the early 1990s, whereas rehabilitation and a restorative justice focus became more popular as the decade ended and the new century began.

The service or rehabilitative role, also known as the human service role, requires a trust relationship between correctional worker and client and a willingness of the worker to advocate for the client. On the other hand, a security or punitive role, also known as the custodial role, for the correctional worker requires distrust and suspicion of clients and the need to maintain distance from them. Johnson, in his important book *Hard Time: Understanding and Reforming the Prison*, starkly defines these two roles, first describing the custodial officer working in prisons this way (see also Box 6.1):

> "Smug hacks"...typically account for about a quarter of the guard force. They are custodial officers in the pejorative sense of the term. They seek order at any price, and violence—their own or that of inmate allies—is one of the tools of their trade. Their stance of toughness is exalted in the guard subculture, and is the public image (though not the private reality) adopted by most officers. Smug hacks find their counterparts in the convicts of the prison yard. The combative relations that ensue between these groups account for much of the abuse and even brutality that occurs in the prison (1996:197).

In contrast, Johnson defines human service officers as those who

[u]se their authority to help inmates cope with prison life; they provide human service rather than custodial repression. They do the best they can with the resources at their disposal to make the prison a better place in which to live and work. In contrast to their merely custodial colleagues, these officers cope maturely with their own problems as well as with the problems experienced by prisoners. They serve, by their helping activities and by example, as true correctional officers (Johnson, 1996:223).

Clearly, there cannot always be a clear demarcation in these roles. Police and correctional staff often adopt one role or the other depending on the situation. Sometimes police officers need to exercise a law enforcement role to maintain the safety of the community. Sometimes a human service role might be misinterpreted by inmates and/or might compromise the ability of the correctional officer to objectively supervise. Certainly mindless brutality is never called for in policing or corrections; but an emphasis on protection, security, and order often is. It is the degree to which criminal justice

---

BOX 6.1

THE HUMAN SERVICE AND CUSTODIAL ROLES FOR CORRECTIONS

Johnson in Hard Time (1996) and Lombardo in (*Guards Imprisoned: Correctional Officers at Work*) (1989), both following in the footsteps of Toch (1978), discuss the human service and custodial roles for correctional officers. Primary attributes of each are as follows:

Custodial Officer

- mindless
- brutal
- custodian
- emphasis on order maintenance

Human Service Officer

- provider of goods and services
- referral agent or an advocate
- assistance with institutional adjustment

Both men thought that human service work was common practice for most correctional officers and that the custodial officer role was the exception rather than the rule.

staff fall on one or the other end of this continuum of roles and how they respond to a given situation that should be of interest.

Whereas, Johnson (1996) and Lombardo (1989) each developed an understanding of these roles from studies of adult prisons, similar distinctions have been made officially and unofficially for other sectors of criminal justice. Juvenile justice has traditionally had the greatest focus on a service or rehabilitative role for its staff (Rothman, 1980). As the juvenile court, juvenile probation and parole programs, and detention and prison facilities were established to function formally in "the best interest of the child," there has naturally been a greater focus on rehabilitation.

In research on the attitudes of juvenile correctional facility directors, Caeti, Hemmens, Cullen, and Burton (2003) administered a questionnaire measuring role orientation, job satisfaction, and stress to the 406 facility directors across the nation. They had a 63.5% response rate and found that most directors (61.2%) ranked rehabilitation as the number-one goal of juvenile corrections with deterrence (25.6%), incapacitation (12.0%), and retribution (0.4%) following. In that same publication, Caeti and his colleagues compared these responses to those by prison wardens (to a questionnaire administered in the early 1990s); the wardens' ranking was in the following order: retribution, deterrence, rehabilitation, and incapacitation.

Not surprisingly, then, there tends to be a more formal orientation toward a rehabilitative role for criminal justice workers who have juvenile clients or who work in that system. Informally, however, the actual role that the police, attorneys for juveniles, and their probation and parole officers or detention workers or prison counselors adopt is shaped by their roles as SLBs (with too many clients and not enough resources) and by the clients themselves, the ambient subculture, and the political winds. In his book describing the work of juvenile probation officers, Jacobs (1990) notes that because of the crush of young clients on the caseload, the officer often has to make a King Solomon-like choice, whether to focus her energies on those who need them most or on those who show the most promise.

As with criminal justice workers who labor in the juvenile justice system, the traditional role of probation and parole officers who work with adults has also differed somewhat from that of adult correctional institution workers. Probation and parole departments were established based on the belief that clients were in need of a helping hand to settle into a job and put a roof over their heads (Rothman, 1980). Probation and parole officers were expected to help and counsel their clients. In reality, probation and parole officers, termed community corrections officers now in some states, also function as SLBs, with too many demands on their time and too many clients. Their role is also shaped by their clients, by the subculture, and by the politics of the day (Lipsky, 1980).

For both the juvenile justice system and adult probation and parole, there has been a move toward a more custodial role, in large part because of a shift in the political winds toward a more conservative approach to criminal justice in general (Benekos & Merlo, 2001; Seiter, 2002). Crowded correctional institutions and crowded caseloads for court personnel and probation and parole officers at both the adult and juvenile levels are a direct consequence of the greater willingness to punish by putting more and more people under some kind of correctional supervision in the last thirty years (e.g., King Davis, Applegate, Otto, Surette, & McCarthy, 2004). Until recently, this also meant that the dollars available to fund correctional programming were scarce in most states and communities. In the late 1990s, as governments were more flush in terms of tax dollars and as there was a dawning realization that the cost of locking so many people up would eventually claim any extra revenue, there was renewed interest in rehabilitation programming in many states and at the federal level. Unfortunately, funding has been uneven and sometime inadequate at all levels in the first decade of the 2000s.

Moreover and relatedly, juvenile and adult probation and parole officers lament their client overload and the lack of programming options for the indigent clients they supervise (Jacobs, 1990; Seiter, 2002). What this means is that even if they were inclined to perform a more rehabilitative or service role, their efforts would be stymied by the nature of the work and the lack of funding in their communities.

Seiter (2002) in a survey and interviews of adult parole officers in Missouri found that despite the crowding and despite political pressures to focus on the security/surveillance and control role, many officers thought that the most important aspects of their job involved helping and assisting parolees. When officers were asked to identify the most important aspects of reentry programs for parolees, they listed employment, treatment, and support from loved ones first, second, and third, and supervision/monitoring and controlling and holding offenders accountable fourth and fifth. Likewise, when parole officers were asked to identify the most important aspect of their job that leads to successful completion of parole, they provided similar responses. Specifically, they listed the supervision/monitoring and controlling activities first, but the assessment of needs and referral to agencies and the support for employment, second and third, with accountability fourth.

Criminal justice workers at both the juvenile and adult levels are faced with similar limitations on their ability to adopt a service or rehabilitative role. There is little rehabilitative programming in adult corrections in many states and facilities (more about this in subsequent chapters). What does exist is too often delivered in a nonstructured way, by volunteers or by staff who have received little training to conduct it. Moreover, the programming is rarely subjected to rigorous evaluation. The "best practices" research provides some hope for improvement in this area, but funding, delivery, and evaluation of programming in correctional institutions and in the communities are problematic, though not hopeless. In policing, and as indicated earlier, the training for officers has not kept up with the move to a more service and problem-solving role for officers working in community policing–oriented organizations.

Not surprisingly, role conflict and ambiguity have been tied to several negative outcomes for workers in the criminal justice system, including alienation from their work, cynicism, lowered job satisfaction and commitment, a less favorable attitude toward service and treatment, and stress and turnover (Brody, DeMarco, & Lovrich, 2002; Crouch & Marquart, 1994; Lombardo, 1989; Maahs & Pratt, 2001), which might, in turn, be interrelated (Bennett & Schmitt, 2002). For the criminal justice manager interested in minimizing role conflict, the answer may lie in greater clarification of the role, and reinforcement of the appropriate role both officially and unofficially. Personnel practices such as selection, training, performance evaluation and promotions should reinforce the expectations for the role. Bennett and Schmitt (2002) find that cynicism among police officers is intimately tied to job satisfaction. In turn, in the other studies just mentioned, levels of job satisfaction have varied depending on role conflict

BOX 6.2

A DISCUSSION OF THE CORRECTIONAL ROLE INSTRUMENT

By Mary K. Stohr

We developed the thirty-six-item "correctional role instrument" for several reasons (Hemmens & Stohr, 2000; 2001; Hemmens et al. 2002). First, we wanted to measure the extent to which correctional staff in jails and prisons identified with either a human services or a custodial role for corrections. We were also interested in perceptions of the use of force by staff and perceptions of male and female staff of the work of women as correctional officers. We were measuring perceptions, not actual behavior.

The instrument items were developed based on a review of the relevant literature and prior work experience (by Stohr), and on comments provided by a correctional role scholar (Robert Johnson). After face validity analysis by a warden and a deputy warden in a medium security prison (Barrier, Stohr, Hemmens, & Marsh, 1999; Stohr, Hemmens, Marsh, Barrier, Palhegy: 2000), the items were rewritten and the instrument was pretested at a medium security prison in Fall 1997, then refined in 1998 in response to those findings (Hemmens & Stohr, 2000, 2001). The questionnaire and the research process were subjected to Human Subjects Review before the instrument was pretested and administered.

Respondents were asked to indicate their level of agreement or disagreement with each given statement. Responses could range from 1 (strongly disagree) to 7 (strongly agree). Respondents also had the options of answering "don't know" or leaving a particular item blank. A number of items were reverse coded. This was done to ensure that staff completing the questionnaire were truly reading the questions and responding with some degree of consistency. As recoded, for all items, the higher the mean, the greater the agreement with the human service role.

The study was conducted in 1998 and 1999. At each institution, including male minimum and male maximum security prisons, a female prison (combined minimum, medium, and maximum security), two mixed-gender jails, and a jail training academy, the research team administered and collected the questionnaires. Facility administrators scheduled training or meetings at different times of the day, so that all shifts were given the opportunity to complete the questionnaire. Attendance at the meeting was mandatory, but, completion of the survey was entirely voluntary. For most of the facilities, the research team returned on different days and at different times to complete the administration of the questionnaire.

The findings are more fully summarized in the publications cited earlier, but here are the basics: most correctional staff tended to favor a human services role orientation; women were less likely to value the use of force in their work; men and women tended to positively perceive the work of women in corrections, but women had a higher regard for their abilities to do corrections work than men; military service tended to have a negative effect on the perception of the abilities of female staff; and, as other research has determined regarding cynicism and alienation (see Toch & Klofas, 1982), those in midcareer (6–10 years) tend to be less human service–oriented than those at the beginning and end of their careers.

The jail version of the instrument is provided in the appendix at the end of this chapter. Readers may use it, the cover page (without our names!), and the demographics sheet. We would caution anyone who uses the instrument to closely follow the data collection procedures outlined in the cited publications and to secure human subject approval by an accredited university or institution prior to administration of this questionnaire. We would also urge users to abide by accepted methodological practices in terms of questionnaire administration and data analysis. Item means might be compared with those in the publications, though we made slight changes in a few items over the course of the instrument development and testing. Pleased notify Hemmens and Stohr if you intend to use the instrument, and share your methodology and findings with us afterward.

NOTE: ITEMS 3, 6, 9, 10, 12, 14, 16, 18, 20, 21, 24, 27, 28, 30, AND 33 NEED TO BE REVERSE CODED AFTER THE DATA HAVE BEEN COLLECTED. ALSO, ENSURE THAT THE QUESTIONNAIRE AND THE RESEARCH PROCESS ARE REVIEWED BY THE 'HUMAN SUBJECTS COMMITTEE' AT YOUR INSTITUTION.

and ambiguity. Johnson (1996) argues that officers who adopt a more human services role in corrections have a more enlarged and enriched job and are more likely to gain satisfaction from it. In turn, Lombardo (1989) argues that human service work in corrections reduces the alienation that officers feel from their work. Relatedly, Brody and his colleagues (2002) found that police officers report more job satisfaction when they work in agencies most supportive of a community policing role.

An alternative perspective is that criminal justice staff *integrate* the roles of security/law enforcement and service/rehabilitation/treatment, rather than experience role conflict as a result of the existence the different sets of requirements. In a study of two probation-intensive supervision sites, one in Ohio and the other in Georgia, Clear and Latessa (1993) found that individual officers' behavior was influenced by the policy of each person's organization. They also found that within the same organization, some officers may display an interest in one role over the other, but that the roles were not incompatible, as "[a]n officer's preference for one attitude will not cause avoidance of tasks consistent with the other" (Clear & Latessa, 1993:457).

Our colleague Craig Hemmens and one of the authors (Stohr) developed the "Correctional Role Instrument" as a means of diagnosing role preference in jails and prisons (see Box 6.2 and Section 2 of the chapter appendix). This instrument, or a version of it, might be used by correctional managers to research which role preference tends to predominate in their facility. We think that most of these instrument items could be reworded to fit the work of those in probation and parole and the juvenile justice system.

POWER

The popular perception of criminal justice staff is that their role is heavily invested with power, and to some extent this is true. Such staff do have the ability to limit the liberty and freedoms of those they are entrusted to investigate, hold, try, sentence, watch, supervise, treat, and care for. These are awesome powers when situated in a democracy such as ours, where regular citizens are guaranteed a certain level of protection from their government via the Constitution and the Bill of Rights. Given how important power is to the role of criminal justice workers, especially in a democracy, some discussion of its nature is warranted.

Power *is the ability to get others to do what they otherwise wouldn't* (which is very close to Dahl's 1957 definition). This definition works at the individual level, but it does not encompass the power that organizations wield in their environments. In other words, power is exerted at the individual level and at the organizational level in criminal justice agencies and, of course, within the organization. There is power that attaches to individuals because of their charm, charisma, or other personal abilities. There is power that attaches to a given job or project or team, and supervisors and staff have the power to wield raw coercion over suspects, accused, persons, inmates, and clients.

Weber (1947) noted that there were three types of **authority** (defined by the American Heritage Dictionary (1992:56) as "[t]he right and power to enforce laws, exact obedience, command, determine, or judge"), which he equated with *legitimized power*. The first type of authority he identified is **traditional,** or the power held by royalty or a head of state, or power that is vested with a sense of tradition and history. The second type is **charismatic,** or based on the personal charm and leadership qualities of the individual. The third type of authority is **legal,** or that based in laws and rules that are generally accepted. These three types of authority give those who wield them the legitimized power to operate without resort to the other types of power.

Relatedly, French and Raven (1959) identified the following five types or bases of power (along with legitimized power).

- Reward (or the perception that the power holder can give some kind of reward). In criminal justice agencies actors have the power to decline to arrest, investigate, or prosecute; they can prefer charges or grant sentence reductions; they can secure better housing or job placement, direct that someone receive a positive write-up, or decline to infract or violate a person's probation or parole.

- Coercive (or the perception that the power holder can use force to get what he or she wants). In criminal justice agencies this can range from the threat of force if the power recipient does not comply with commands to the actual use of force.

- Legitimate (or the perception that the power holder has legal or official status). In criminal justice agencies this means a position as an attorney or officer or counselor or work supervisor or health care provider is recognized as empowering the holder.

- Referent (or the perception that the power holder is a reference for the power recipient). In criminal justice agencies this means that the worker is looked upon as a model for the power recipient, which in turn empowers the worker.

- Expert (or the perception that the power holder has qualifications that confer this status). In criminal justice agencies this means that the power holder is recognized as possessing experience or knowledge that makes him or her qualified to exert power.

Hepburn (1990) did a study of these bases of power in the correctional environment in the 1980s. He administered questionnaires that included five items related to each type of power. Officers in five prisons in four different states were asked to indicate, by ranking these items, why inmates obey the correctional staff. In the same study he collected background information on the officers, as well as their attitudes toward work and toward inmates. What he found was that the officers thought that inmates did what they otherwise would not do because of the legitimate and expert power of the officers. "Legitimate power was ranked first by over one-third of the guards, and three of every five guards ranked legitimate power as either the first or second most important reason why prisoners did what they were told" (Hepburn, 1990:291). The types of power were ranked as follows: legitimate, expert, referent, coercive, and reward. This ranking was relatively stable across the different institutions and states. Hepburn notes that Lombardo (1981) also found that 44% of the prison officers he interviewed attributed their base of power to legitimacy.

Hepburn did find that the more experience an officer had, the more likely he or she was to rank expert power as more important and coercion and legitimacy as less. He found little effect for education, formal contact with inmates, or attitudes toward work. He also found that the higher the custody orientation of the officer, the more likely was the officer to see coercion as an important power base.

Hepburn (1994) explains these findings by drawing attention to the regular duties of correctional staff. On a day-to-day basis and in the context of the normal operation of the institution, officers give direction to inmates based on their legitimate role. Rarely do they need to give orders that are starkly coercive. Rare, too, are the rewards they can give for ordinary compliance with rules and requirements. Hence, there is little need for reliance on coercion or rewards as bases for power in the usual operation of institutions.

Moreover, the use of coercion on a day-to-day basis would be highly inefficient and disruptive in corrections work. If a correctional officer was continually having to use force or, its threat, it would be very difficult to get through the day, and hard feelings and resistance would accumulate among the inmates (experiment with the role exercise at the end of the chapter to see how this dynamic might play out). As an officer is usually outnumbered by at least 30 to 1 when out and about with inmates, he could easily be overpowered if the inmates were to choose to cooperate in such a maneuver. Calling backup continually to get inmates to comply with basic rules would throw the whole institution into disarray and would not be positively viewed by coworkers or administration. The ability to supervise of an officer who makes frequent calls for backup will very quickly be called into question.

On the other hand, corrections work is inherently coercive inasmuch as those who are supervised or incarcerated rarely volunteered for this status. Instead, the state, in the form of criminal justice actors like the police, prosecuting attorneys, and correctional workers, uses the threat of, or actual, force to gain compliance (Hemmens & Atherton, 1999). Yet it is curious that in the day-to-day relations with inmates, the officers do not perceive coercion as the reason for inmates' general compliance with institutional rules and directives. One wonders whether inmates would respond in a similar manner to the ranking of power bases by Hepburn. Would they mark "legitimacy" as the primary power base for correctional officers?

In policing, the use of force, or coercive power, has been the subject of much scholarly discussion and study (Alpert & Smith, 1999; Crank, 1998; Griffin & Bernard, 2003; Kaminski, DiGiovanni, & Downs, 2004; Terrill, Alpert, Dunham, & Smith, 2003). In their discussion of the police use of extra legal force, Griffin and Bernard argue for the salience of the angry aggression theory. They posit that officers who do not learn coping mechanisms to handle the multiple sources of stress that are inherent in police work (e.g., citizen hostility, danger) are physiologically aroused by this stress, which tends to lead to more fear of threats and eventual aggression. A feedback loop develops (as in systems theory) whereby this chronic physiological arousal leads to the perception of more threats, then to aggression and the development of an "authoritarian" personality, back to still more perceived threats and more aggression. Other related negative outcomes, which only serve to reinforce the perception of threats and the concomitant aggression, are social isolation and displaced aggression (Griffin & Bernard, 2003).

Another angle to the discussion of power is the fact that some criminal justice staff feel relatively powerless in their jobs. For instance, in his research on prisons Lombardo (1989:145) noted frequent job dissatisfaction among correctional staff because officers had a perceived "[i]nability to influence [their] work environment in an effective manner." He found that the most mentioned reason for this feeling was a "lack of support" by administrators, supervisors, and coworkers, who not only were not always helpful but sometimes worked at cross-purposes with the officer. The officers thought that they were too often obliged to work short-handed; that administrators tended to resolve problems by focusing on short-term rather than on long-term solutions; that officers were not always backed up regarding inmate discipline; and that the behavior of other officers was at times "lax and non-cooperative." Griffin and Bernard (2003) also mention the helplessness that police officers feel vis-à-vis their inability to change aspects of their job, a condition that adds to their stress and ultimately, for some, leads to the abuse of coercive power.

Sometimes it is not just the criminal justice actor who feels powerless in the system. Smith (1997) notes that though 13% of the American population falls below the poverty line, less than 2% of lawyers do legal work for agencies representing the poor. Clearly, this maldistribution of legal resources has led to an imbalance of advantages when the poor are drawn into the criminal courts.

For workers, however, this sense of powerlessness is to some degree attached to the type of management theory practiced in particular institutions, as was discussed in Chapter 4. If criminal justice workers had the opportunity to participate to a greater degree in decisions affecting their workplace, it is unlikely that they would feel so powerless.

CONCLUSIONS

Criminal justice work is composed of complex tasks requiring multiple skills and favoring those with certain propensities. The criminal justice organization has the opportunity to shape the outlook and habits of workers through both informal and formal socialization. The role such workers adopt is determined to a large extent by the emphasis that managers place on it. People generally will do what they are rewarded for. To the extent that a service or security or advocacy role for staff is acceptable to, and supported by, management, organizational members will recognize this fact and respond accordingly.

How criminal justice workers wield power is also shaped by the socialization process and the role the workers have adopted. Officers in Hepburn's study were quite clear in their belief that legitimacy, followed by expertise, constituted their main bases of power. The bureaucratic nature of the job, and the inefficiency of force usage, precludes the regular use of force to gain compliance. Thus, almost by default, criminal justice workers are more likely to need human service role skills to maintain the daily routines of their work. Studies of power in police organization confirm that the organizational culture, along with stressors inherent to the job, can lead to the routinized abuse of power by officers.

EXERCISE: THE ROLE–ORDERING PEOPLE ABOUT

One of the authors first observed and participated in a version of this exercise in a mandatory anger management training session for correctional staff. She saw another version of it done in a training session with the state police years later. The purpose of this kind of exercise is to illustrate different styles of supervision and their relative success, or lack of it.

1. Select six to ten people (you need a minimum of three pairs) and pair them off without respect to demographics. Ask the rest of the class to observe the proceedings.
2. Ask one person from each pair to be "the inmate" and the other to be "the correctional officer."
3. Have the inmates and officers meet separately to discuss their approach to being supervised (inmates) or their approach to supervision (officers).
4. Have the pairs meet up again and have the "officer" direct the "subject" to simulate sweeping the floor. The "inmates" may respond as they will (within reason!).
5. Stop the action after a few minutes and ask the "inmates" and "officers" to recount their experiences. Ask for audience comments. There should be obvious tie-ins with the role and power discussions in this chapter. Perhaps some linkage may be made to socialization and training (or lack thereof).

DISCUSSION QUESTIONS

1. How does socialization affect the role that criminal justice workers adopt? Give an example.

2. What are the main components of the human service and the custodial roles for corrections?

3. What are the main components of the service and the protection roles for policing?

4. Why would the use of coercion be inefficient in most situations encountered in the criminal justice environment? Explain your answer.

5. Which types of power tend to fit into the roles? Why would this be so?

6. How is the socialization for lawyers in the criminal courts substantially different from that for the police and corrections workers?

7. Do you think that inmates would rank legitimacy first and coercion next to last if they were asked what were the most important bases for correctional power? Why or why not?

8. Do you think that probation and parole officers would respond similarly to the correctional officers in Hepburn's study? Why or why not?

9. How do you think police officers can reduce stress to prevent themselves from engaging in angry aggression? Give an example.

KEY TERMS

anticipatory socialization: begins before the criminal justice worker starts the job. It occurs as the person *anticipates* that someday working in law, police, or corrections.

authority: "[t]he right and power to enforce laws, exact obedience, command, determine, or judge" (American Heritage Dictionary, 1992:56).

charismatic authority: based on the personal charm and leadership qualities of the individual.

formal socialization: occurs when the worker is exposed to the legal or officially sanctioned requirements of the job.

informal socialization: the teaching and learning that take place on the job. It is outside the official strictures of law and procedure and occurs away from the officially recognized instructors.

legal authority: based in laws and rules that are generally accepted.

occupational socialization: "[t]he process by which a person acquires the values, attitudes, and behaviors of an ongoing occupational social system" (Klofas et al., 1990:150).

power: the ability to get others to do what they otherwise wouldn't (Dahl, 1957).

role: what you do on the job, be it officially outlined by statutorily defined tasks, position descriptions, and policies and procedural requirements, or unofficially defined by the actual work that is done and required.

role ambiguity: occurs when expectations for a role are not clear or are confusing.

role conflict: occurs when there are competing expectations for a role that are difficult to fulfill.

traditional authority: the power one holds in a position (e.g., as royalty or an elected head of state) or which is vested with a sense of tradition and history.

REFERENCES

Alpert, G. P., & Smith, M. R. (1999). Police use-of-force data: Where we are and where we should be going. *Police Quarterly 2*, 57–78.

American Heritage Dictionary (1992). *American Heritage Dictionary*. New York: Houghton Mifflin.

Barrier, G., Stohr, M. K., Hemmens, C., & Marsh, R. (1999). A practical user's guide to ethical practices: Idaho's method for implementing ethical behavior in a correctional setting. *Corrections Compendium, 24*, 1–12.

Belknap, J. (1995). Women in conflict: An analysis of women correctional officers. In B. R. Price & N. J. Sokoloff (Eds.), *The criminal justice system and women: Offender, victims and workers* (pp. 195–227). New York: McGraw- Hill.

Benekos, P., & Merlo, A. V. (2001). Three strikes and you're out: The political sentencing game. In E. J. Latessa, A. Holsinger, J. W. Marquart, & J. R. Sorensen (Eds.), *Correctional contexts: Contemporary and classical readings* (pp. 454–463). Los Angeles: Roxbury.

Bennett, R. R., & Schmitt, E. L. (2002). The effect of work environment on levels of police cynicism: A comparative study. *Police Quarterly, 5*, 493–522.

Bradford, D., & Pynes, J. E. (2000). Police academy training: Why hasn't it kept up with practice? *Police Quarterly, 2*, 283–301.

Brody, D. C., DeMarco, C., & Lovrich, N. P. (2002). Community policing and job satisfaction: Suggestive evidence of positive workforce effects from a multijurisdictional comparison in Washington State. *Police Quarterly, 5*, 181–205.

Buerger, M. E., Petrosino, A. J., & Petrosino, C. (1999). Extending the police role: Implications of police mediation as a problem-solving tool." *Police Quarterly, 2*, 125–149.

Caeti, T., Hemmens, C., Cullen, F. T., & Burton, V.S., Jr. (2003). Management of juvenile correctional facilities. *The Prison Journal, 83*(4), 1–23.

California Employment Development Department. (2004). *Probation officers and parole agents*. Employment development department: Labor market information. Accessed at www.calmis.cahwnet.gov, April 1, 2004.

Camp, S. D., Saylor, W. G., & Wright, K. N. (2001). Research note, racial diversity of correctional workers and inmates: Organizational commitment, teamwork and workers' efficacy in prisons. *Justice Quarterly, 18*(2), 411–427.

CCA. (2004). Careers. *Corrections Corporation of America website*. Accessed at www. correctionscorp.com/training, April 1, 2004.

Clear, T. R. & Latessa, E. J. (1993). Probation officers' roles in intensive supervision: Surveillance versus treatment. *Justice Quarterly, 10*(3), 441–462.

Crank, J. P. (1996). The construction of meaning during training for probation and parole. *Justice Quarterly, 13*(2), 265–290.

Crank, J. P. (1998). *Understanding police culture*. Cincinnati, OH: Anderson Publishing.

Crouch, B., & Marquart, J. (1994). On becoming a prison guard. In S. Stojkovic, J. Klofas, & D. Kalinich (Eds.), *The administration and management of criminal justice organizations: A book of readings* (pp. 301–331). Prospect Heights, IL: Waveland Press.

Cullen, F., Cullen, J., & Wozniak, J. (1988). Is rehabilitation dead? The myth of the punitive public. *Journal of Criminal Justice, 16*, 303–317.

Cullen, F. T., & Gilbert, K. E. (1982). *Reaffirming rehabilitation.* Cincinnati, OH: Anderson Publishing.

Dahl, R. (1957). The concept of power. *Behavioral Science, 2*(3), 201–215.

Delaware Department of Correction. (2004). Probation and parole officer 1. *State of Delaware Department of Correction website.* Accessed at www.state.de.us/correct, April 1, 2004.

Farkas, M. A. (1999). Inmate supervisory style: Does gender make a difference? *Women and Criminal Justice, 10*, 25–46.

Flanagan, T., & Caulfield, S. (1984). Public opinion and prison policy: A review. *The Prison Journal, 64*, 31–46.

Ford, R. E. (2003). Saying one thing, meaning another: The role of parables in police training. *Police Quarterly, 6*, 84–110.

French, J., & Raven, B. (1959). The bases of social power. In D. Cartwright (Ed.), *Studies in social power.* Ann Arbor: University of Michigan.

Gordon, J. (1999). Do staff attitudes vary by position? A look at one juvenile correctional center. *American Journal of Criminal Justice, 24*(1), 81–93.

Griffin, S. P., & Bernard, T. J. (2003). Angry aggression among police officers. *Police Quarterly, 6*, 3–21.

Haarr, R. (1997). Patterns of interaction in a police patrol bureau: Race and gender barriers to integration. *Justice Quarterly, 14*(1), 53–85.

Hemmens, C., & Atherton, E. (1999). *Use of force: Current practice and policy.* Lanham, MD: American Correctional Association.

Hemmens, C., & Stohr, M. K. (2000). The two faces of the correctional role: An exploration of the value of the correctional role instrument. *International Journal of Offender Therapy and Comparative Criminology, 44*(3), 326–349.

Hemmens, C., & Stohr, M. K. (2001). Correctional staff attitudes regarding the use of force in corrections. *Corrections Management Quarterly, 5*, 26–39.

Hemmens, C., Stohr, M. K., Schoeler, M., & Miller, B. (2002). One step up, two steps back: The progression of perceptions of women's work in prisons and jails. *Journal of Criminal Justice, 30*(6), 473–489.

Hepburn, J. R. (1990). The exercise of power in coercive organizations. In Stojkovic, S., Klofas, J. and D. Kalinich (Eds.) *The administration and management of criminal justice organizations.* pp. 249–265. Prospect Heights, IL: Waveland Press.

Jacobs, M. D. (1990). *Screwing the system and making it work: Juvenile justice in the no-fault society.* Chicago: University of Chicago Press.

Jenne, D. L., & Kersting, R. C. (1998). Gender, power, and reciprocity in the correctional setting. *The Prison Journal, 78*(2), 166–186.

Johnson, R. (1996). *Hard time: Understanding and reforming the prison* (2nd ed.). Belmont, CA: Wadsworth.

Jurik, N. (1985). Individual and organizational determinants of correctional officer attitudes toward inmates. *Criminology, 23*, 523–539.

Jurik, N., & Halemba, G. (1984). Gender, working conditions and the job satisfaction of women in a non-traditional occupation: Female correctional officers in men's prisons. *Sociological Quarterly, 25*, 551–566.

Kaminski, R. J., DiGiovanni, C., & Downs, R. (2004). The use of force between the police and persons with impaired judgment. *Police Quarterly, 7*, 311–338.

Katz, D., & Kahn, D. (1978). *The social psychology of organizations* (2nd ed.). New York: Wiley.

Kifer, M., Hemmens, C. & Stohr, M. K. (2003). The goals of corrections: Perspectives from the line. *Criminal Justice Review, 28*(1), 47–69.

King Davis, R., Applegate, B., Otto, C., Surette, R., & McCarthy, B. (2004). Roles and responsibilities: Analyzing local leaders' views on jail crowding from a systems perspective. *Crime and Delinquency, 50*(3), 458–482.

Klofas, J., Stojkovic, S., & Kalinich, D. (1990). *Criminal justice organizations administration and management.* Pacific Grove, CA: Brooks/Cole.

Lawrence, R., & Mahan, S. (1998). Women correctional officers in men's prisons: Acceptance and perceived job performance. *Women and Criminal Justice, 9*, 63- 86.

Lipsky, M. (1980). *Street-level bureaucracy: Dilemmas of the individual in public services.* New York: Russell Sage Foundation.

Lombardo, L. X. (1981). *Guards imprisoned: Correctional officers at work.* New York: Elsevier.

Lombardo, L. X. (1989). *Guards imprisoned: Correctional officers at work* (2nd ed.). Cincinnati, OH: Anderson Publishing.

Lutze, F. E., & Murphy, D. W. (1999). Ultramasculine prison environments and inmates' adjustment: It's time to move beyond the 'boys will be boys' paradigm. *Justice Quarterly, 16*, 709–734.

Maahs, J., & T., Pratt. (2001). Uncovering the predictors of correctional officers' attitudes and behaviors: A meta-analysis. *Correctional Management Quarterly, 5*(2), 13–19.

Maguire, K. & Postore, A. L. (Eds.). *Sourcebook of criminal justice statistics*, Accessed at www.albany.edu/sourcebook, April 12, 2004.

Martin, S. E. (1990). *On the move: The status of women in policing.* Washington, D.C.: Police Foundation.

McCorkle, R. (1993). Research note: Punish and rehabilitate? Public attitudes toward six common crimes. *Crime and Delinquency 39*, 240–252.

MCJA. (2004). Basic corrections training program. *Maine Criminal Justice Academy website.* Accessed at www.state.me.us/dps/mcja/training/mandatory/corrections. April 1, 2004.

Meyer, J., & Grant. D. R. (2003). *The courts in our criminal justice system.* Upper Saddle River, NJ: Prentice Hall.

Moak, S., & Wallace, L. (2000). Attitudes of Louisiana practitioners toward rehabilitation of juvenile offenders. *American Journal of Criminal Justice, 24*(2), 272–284.

Moon, M., Sundt, J., Cullen, F., & Wright, J. P. (2000). Is child saving dead? Public support for juvenile rehabilitation. *Crime and Delinquency, 46*(1), 38–60.

Morash, M., & Haar, R. N. (1995). Gender, workplace problems, and stress in policing. *Justice Quarterly, 12*, 113–140.

Nevada Department of Public Safety. (2004). Officer training. *Nevada Department of Public Safety website.* Accessed at http://dps.gov/pandp/training.htm, April 1, 2004.

Norman, M., & Burbridge, G. (1991). Attitudes of youth corrections professionals toward juvenile justice reform and policy alternatives—A Utah survey. *Journal of Criminal Justice, 19*, 81–91.

Pogrebin, M. R., & Poole, E. D. (1998). Women deputies and jail work. *Journal of Contemporary Criminal Justice, 14*, 117–134.

Pollock, J. M. (2004). *Prisons and prison life: Costs and consequences.* Los Angeles: Roxbury.

Purkiss, M., Kifer, M., Hemmens, C., & Burton, V. S. (2003). Probation officer functions—A statutory analysis. *Federal Probation, 67*(1), 12–33.

Reddington, F. P., & Kreisel, B. W. (2003). The basic fundamental skills training for juvenile probation officers—Results of a nationwide survey of curriculum content. *Federal Probation, 67*(1), 41–46.

Rothman, D. J. (1980). *Conscience and convenience: The asylum and its alternatives in progressive America.* Boston: Little, Brown.

Seiter, R. P. (2002). Prisoner reentry and the role of parole officers. *Federal Probation, 66*(3), 50–55.

Smith, C. E. (1997). *Courts, politics, and the judicial process* (2nd ed.). Chicago: Nelson-Hall.

Southerland, M. D. (2002). Presidential address: Criminal justice curricula in the United States: A decade of change. *Justice Quarterly, 19*(4), 589–601.

Stohr, M. K., Hemmens, C., Marsh, R. L., Barrier, G. & Palhegyi D. (2000). Can't scale this: the ethical parameters of Correctional Work. *The Prison Journal. 80*(1): 40–56.

Sun, I. Y. (2003). A comparison of police field training officers' and non-training officers' conflict resolution styles: Controlling versus supportive strategies. *Police Quarterly, 6,* 22–50.

Sykes, G. (1958). *The society of captives.* Princeton, NJ: Princeton University Press.

Terrill, W., Alpert, G. P., Dunham, R. G., & Smith, M. R. (2003). A management tool for evaluating police use of force: An application of the force factor. *Police Quarterly, 6,* 150–171.

Thibault, E. A., Lynch, L. M., & McBride, R. B. (2004). *Proactive police management* (6th ed.). Upper Saddle River, NJ: Prentice Hall.

Toch, H. (1978). Is a correctional officer, by any other name, a screw? *Criminal Justice Review, 2,* 19–35.

Toch, H., & Klofas, J. (1982). Alienation and desire for job enrichment among correctional officers. *Federal Probation, 46,* 35–44.

Van Voorhis, P., Cullen, F. T., Link, B. G., & Wolfe, N. T. (1991). The impact of race and gender on correctional officers' orientation to the integrated environment. *Journal of Research in Crime and Delinquency, 28,* 472–500.

Weber, M. (1947). *The theory of social and economic organization.* New York: Free Press.

Zimmerman, S., Van Alstyne, D., & Dunn, C. (1988). The national punishment survey and public policy consequences. *Journal of Research in Crime and Delinquency, 25,* 120–149.

Zupan, L. L. (1986). Gender-related differences in correctional officers' perceptions and attitudes. *Journal of Criminal Justice, 14,* 349–361.

THE CORRECTIONAL ROLE INSTRUMENT: JAIL RESEARCH DESCRIPTION SHEET

Dear Jail Staff Person:

This questionnaire was developed by Mary K. Stohr and Craig Hemmens, professors in the Department of Criminal Justice at Boise State University. BSU students Mary Schoeler and Misty Meyer are assisting in this research. Information obtained from responses to the questionnaire will be kept COMPLETELY CONFIDENTIAL and PARTICIPATION IS COMPLETELY VOLUNTARY. No names should be mentioned on this questionnaire, and all responses will be combined by the research team so that it will be impossible to identify specific persons.

We developed this questionnaire so that staff perceptions of jail roles might be better understood by people working in the field and by researchers. In essence, we are trying to determine what people think about their work in jails and why. We would really appreciate it if you would take the time to complete this questionnaire (it should take about 15 minutes).

If you have any questions about this research, you are more than welcome to call us at our offices at Boise State 426–1378 (Mary Stohr), 426–3251 (Craig Hemmens).

YOU MAY KEEP THIS SHEET FOR REFERENCE IF YOU LIKE. ALL RESPONSES TO THIS QUESTIONNAIRE WILL BE KEPT COMPLETELY CONFIDENTIAL AND PARTICIPATION IS VOLUNTARY.

THERE IS NO REASON TO PROVIDE YOUR NAME. QUESTIONNAIRES SHOULD BE RETURNED DIRECTLY TO THE BSU RESEARCH TEAM. ALL RESPONSES WILL BE GROUPED TOGETHER IN ANY REPORT OR PUBLICATION PRODUCED USING THESE DATA.

THANKS SO MUCH FOR YOUR KIND PARTICIPATION.

SECTION ONE: *Demographics*
Please provide us with some general information about yourself.

1. Position: _____

2. Years of service: _____

3. Military service:
___ Yes
___ No

8. Age:_____

9. Education
___ Less than GED
___ GED
___ High school graduate
___ Some college
___ BA or BS degree
___ Master's degree or more

4. What is your current shift? _____
   (i.e., night, day, swing, other)

5. Did you choose your current shift?
   ___ Yes
   ___ No

10. Ethnicity:
    ___ Hispanic
    ___ Non-Hispanic

6. Gender:
   ___ Male
   ___ Female

7. Race:
   ___ White
   ___ Black or African American
   ___ Asian
   ___ Other
   ___ Multiracial

SECTION TWO: *Jail Role Instrument*

The role of jail staff presents many challenges and opportunities. This instrument was developed so that the various parts of that role might be identified by staff. Please read each question carefully and put the number that best reflects your response in the space provided in front of that question.

1	2	3	4	5	6	7	8
strongly disagree	disagree	slightly disagree	neutral	slightly agree	agree	strongly agree	don't know

_____1. Jail staff should make an effort to answer the questions of inmates.

_____2. Jail staff should do what they can to make sure inmates have reasonable access to counselors.

_____3. Jail staff should ignore most inmate complaints.

_____4. Inmates should receive their store/commissary goods on time.

_____5. When an inmate doesn't get the correct medication, a staff member should contact medical staff.

_____6. Anyone who would visit an inmate is likely to be engaged in illegal activity.

_____7. Staff should ensure that inmates have the appropriate access to legal material they have a right to.

_____8. Ensuring that inmates have reasonable access to visitors is a responsibility of jail staff.

_____9. Using force is usually the best method to get inmates to follow orders.

_____10. Most inmates are trying to manipulate staff.

_____11. Explaining the reason for an order will usually gain inmate cooperation.

_____12. Inmate access to medical personnel should be limited to emergency situations.

_____13. When staff members make a mistake, they should admit it.

_____14. Promises made to inmates by staff are promises made to be broken.

_____15. Mail service should be regularly provided to inmates by staff.

1 ----------------- 2 ------------- 3 ------------ 4 ------------ 5 ----------- 6 ------------ 7 --------------- 8 ------
strongly   disagree   slightly   neutral   slightly   agree   strongly   don't know
disagree   disagree   agree   agree

_____16. Sometimes a little extra physical force is needed to let inmates know they can't get away with things.

_____17. Providing a set of written rules (dos and don'ts) to inmates at the beginning helps to avoid problems and misunderstandings later.

_____18. An inmate who fails at one task is likely to fail at another.

_____19. Helping inmates to find a suitable work situation is a responsibility of jail staff.

_____20. Inmate complaints are often just whining about nothing in particular.

_____21. Inmates usually choose to attend religious services, not because they have any faith, but so that they can appear to have changed.

_____22. Staff should assist inmates in gaining access to educational, drug/alcohol, and other programming.

_____23. It is part of the jail staff's job responsibilities to provide important information to inmates.

_____24. Staff should rarely have friendly conversations with inmates.

_____25. Use of physical force is not the easiest way to get an inmate to obey an order.

_____26. Staff should act how they want inmates to act.

_____27. It is okay if staff bend the rules every now and then, given that they have to supervise criminals.

_____28. Inmates often claim they are sick just to get out of school or work details.

_____29. When inmates succeed in jail, staff should be happy for them.

_____30. Jail staff should not guide or mentor inmates during their incarceration.

_____31. Staff are in part responsible for whether inmates "succeed" while incarcerated.

_____32. Female staff are as capable in working with inmates as male staff.

_____33. Inmates who complain about their medication are usually trying to get access to more drugs than they need.

_____34. Jail staff should have a voice in determining how their workplace operates.

_____35. Problem inmates can be more effectively handled when staff communicate and work as a team.

_____36. Female jail officers can carry out their duties just as well as male officers.

SECTION THREE: *Additional Comments*
Please feel free to provide additional information or to comment on all or part of this questionnaire in the space provided below or on the back of this sheet (or give the researchers a call at BSU):

CHAPTER 7

LEADERSHIP AND CRIMINAL JUSTICE ORGANIZATIONS

To some men the matter of giving orders seems a very simple affair; they expect to issue their own orders and have them obeyed without question. Yet, on the other hand, the shrewd common sense of many a business executive has shown him that the issuing of orders is surrounded by many difficulties; that to demand an unquestioning obedience to an order not approved, not perhaps understood, is bad business policy.

(Parker Follet, 1926:152)

The manager is the dynamic, life-giving element in any business. Without his leadership the "resources of production" remain resources and never become production. In a competitive economy, above all, the quality and performance of managers determine the success of the business, indeed they determine its survival.

(Drucker, 1954:3)

When approaching team leadership, however, many [supervisors] revert to their underlying beliefs about control and direction. They argue that leadership can be taught and learned, but team leadership is suspected of being a fleeting fad....Team leaders instill heart, passion, spirit, and vision in the work group.

(Whisenand, 2004:115)

INTRODUCTION: AFTER YOU'VE WORKED FOR "BAD" LEADERS, YOU BEGIN TO APPRECIATE THE IMPORTANCE OF "GOOD" LEADERSHIP

It is really true: people rarely appreciate competent, caring, and effective leaders until they are saddled with the opposite. During their teen and college years, both authors worked in orchards or berry fields, for fast food restaurants, in the business office of a resort, and as security guards in an art museum and a silicone wafer plant. Of course, in these experiences we could not help but notice how our supervisors and bosses behaved, what management practices seemed to work and what did not. But at that time it did not matter much because we were not going to make a career in any of these enterprises. If we liked a supervisor or if we did not, if a boss seemed effective or not, was of no long-term consequence since we were going to be gone soon.

After college, however, one of the authors was hired as a correctional officer and then a counselor—because she was considering a career in corrections—and leadership began to matter a great deal. While working in the prison, she noticed that the supervisors displayed a number of leadership styles and abilities. When she worked a shift with a supervisor who was corrupt, and after she had had many opportunities to observe how the warden and some of his minions led, she began to appreciate the value of the well-intentioned leadership of most of the other supervisors. Integrity, intelligence, vision, and the ability to connect with people in a meaningful way, all of a sudden were vitally important as attributes of a leader. She also began to appreciate from that prison work, research, and her later jobs in academe, that an organization is successful as a result of the efforts of all its members, but that a "bad" leader or two can quickly sour the culture and productivity of the best of work units.

The role of the leader in a criminal justice organization has always been pivotal. In part because much of the work proceeds outside the public eye and because of the nature of the clientele, criminal justice leaders have enjoyed more power and latitude to shape their domains than is true for other public or private sector leaders. Some criminal justice agencies in the past operated as mini-kingdoms with the police chief, prosecuting attorney, judge, warden, juvenile facility, jail or probation, and parole administrator functioning with little or no oversight by the rest of the legal system, the media, or the public. At times, this lack of oversight led to notable abuses.

Since the civil rights movement and Supreme Court decisions of the 1960s and 1970s, with the cycles of riots that heighten media attention and court interventions and the growth in the number of professionally trained administrators entering criminal justice positions, in concert with the professional movement by practitioner organizations, criminal justice leadership has moved closer to the principles governing other public sector leaders. In this chapter we define leadership and discuss its theoretical bases. This definition and these theories will be fleshed out to include such topics as leadership styles, techniques, responsibilities, roles, teaming, and shared leadership. We will also discuss research on the relative satisfaction of criminal justice leaders and two possible pitfalls for them and their organization: organizational decline and groupthink. All these topics, of course, are shaped by our beliefs about who leaders are and what they should be.

LEADERSHIP DEFINED

Leadership has been defined in a number of ways. For instance, oftentimes leadership and management concepts are combined as expectations for leaders of public organizations. Peter Drucker (1954) tended to mix the conceptions of public sector leaders with those of managers in the private sector. He highlighted the skills of the leader or manager as *"organizer of resources," "manager of the organization* (rather than as a politician)", and *"decision maker."*

Maslow (1976:82) argued that "enlightened management" or leadership was necessarily concerned with the "[p]roblems of human beings, with the *problems of ethics*, of the *future of man*." He stated unequivocally that enlightened management in the workplace was the only patriotic way for leaders to behave, as it was prodemocracy. Stojkovic and his colleagues (1998) note that leadership is not static, but is a *process* (like management) that can be learned and must be keenly attuned to the accomplishment of organizational goals. In his book *Organizational Culture and Leadership*, Schein (1992) describes the central role of leaders in *"creating, embedding, and transmitting culture.*" He argues that leadership is intimately tied with culture making and sustenance in organizations.

In their book *Correctional Leadership: A Cultural Perspective,* Stojkovic and Farkas (2003) also recognize the "*cultural creating function*" of leadership, and their definition encompasses the *cooperative nature* of leadership (involving line and management staff) in modern correctional organizations. These authors argue (2003:7) that leadership is "[f]undamentally a process by which an organizational culture is engendered such that tasks, objectives, and goals are achieved through the coordinated efforts of supervisors and subordinates." Whisenand, who further adds to our understanding of leadership, links being a leader in policing to *team building* or being one who creates, empowers, and maintains teams. In *Supervising Police Personnel,* he lists (2004:124) "seven common traits and practices" that a team leader is born with or acquires over time:

1. Accentuate the positive.
2. Know what's going on.
3. Rivet one's attention through vision.
4. Create meaning through communication.
5. Build trust through positioning.
6. Deploy themselves through positive self-regard and trying.
7. Master change.

Relatedly, Gordon and Milakovich (1998) distinguish between political and administrative leadership. A **political leader** is someone who is either elected or appointed by elected individuals. Such leaders in criminal justice typically include sheriffs, prosecuting attorneys, and sometimes judges. In this book we are concerned with both political and administrative leadership. It should be recognized that since even heads of criminal justice agencies who are typically not elected (e.g., police chiefs, wardens, public defenders, judges, directors of probation and parole or juvenile facilities) necessarily have a political component to their work; as, for instance, they must garner resources from politicians. Gordon and Milakovich (1998:231–238) also identify several critical activities for the leader, including the following:

- *leader as director*: reconciling personal and organizational goals
- *leader as motivator*: the carrot or the stick?
- *leader as coordinator/integrator*: meshing the gears
- *leader as catalyst/innovator*: pointing the way
- *leader as external spokesperson*—and gladiator
- *leader as manager of crisis* in the organization

What is notable about all these definitions and descriptors of leadership is that they tend to mesh what a leader *is* and what a leader *does*. For the purposes of this book and in the interest of being somewhat comprehensive in the consideration of criminal justice leadership's past, present, and future, we define **leadership** *as an ongoing process of activity involving organizing, decision making, innovating, communicating, team building, culture creation, and molding that is engaged in by workers and supervisors* *to achieve organizational goals.* Note that this definition borrows and combines concepts about leadership from the work of others (those cited earlier and many more). It also is value neutral in the sense that someone who operates according to this definition of leadership in criminal justice is not necessarily a likable leader, though he or she may be an effective one. And an effective leader is not necessarily one whose practices are regarded as moral or decent (as will become evident in our discussion of "born vs. made" leaders).

Our definition is *not* value neutral in some respects, though, because it encompasses the human relations perspective of criminal justice management. Although the tertiary head of the agency and the supervisors under her are typically regarded as "leaders" for the organizations, this definition recognizes that those on the line and in support activities are necessarily involved in leadership activities. Of course, it is another matter whether the leadership of those at the lower levels of the organization is widely recognized in the organization or outside it. Moreover, the greater this involvement by all who perform meaningful leadership activities, the less likely it is that the decision-making process in the organization will degrade into a "groupthink" situation (more about this concept at the end of the chapter).

ARE LEADERS BORN AND/OR MADE?

Are leaders born with all the traits that make them effective, or do they learn them over time? Many administration and management scholars in criminal justice and public administration tend to think that this matter is settled: leadership skills can be learned, and so leaders are "made" (Gordon & Milakovich, 1998). Certainly the assumption that workers can be molded into leaders fits the treasured American value of equality. It also provides the rampart upon which many management training programs in the public and private sector stand. After all, if the traits of effective leaders are innate, there would be no sense in trying to develop leadership skills through training. Instead, if leaders were born, those who happened to possess the requisite leadership traits/skills—whatever those were determined to be—would merely assume the mantle of leadership.

But it is hard to believe that just any of us can be, or want to be, leaders. Let us assume that courage, gregariousness, thoughtfulness, intelligence, wisdom, and candor are desirable leadership traits. Can any or all of these traits be taught? Or are some people more inclined toward them?

Let us also assume that communication techniques (e.g., verbal or written), time and resource management, planning and policy development, and "walking-around management" are some desirable leadership skills. Again, cannot these skills be taught? Or are some people just better at these activities both because they have received appropriate training and because they have some innate ability in these areas?

In other words, the research on leaders and leadership in organizations has not established that leaders are born or made. The assumption, of late, has been that they are made. Again, perhaps current scholars accept the "made" theory of leadership because organizations have no ability to influence the innate leadership skills that a person might possess. But both cases might be true. The best leaders, and most of us have a few people in mind as "American (or Foreign) Leadership Idols" (see the exercise at the end of the chapter), may have a combination of desirable leadership traits and skills, some innate and some gained through experience or training.

Leadership Theories

The first theories regarding leadership focused on the "traits" that a leader was assumed to be born with (Gordon & Milakovich, 1998). Such traits were linked to the leader's personality and included courage, intelligence, ability to motivate, interpersonal skills, and drive. Yet whether a person was born with such traits or gained them from life experience was difficult to establish with research. Therefore, the *traits theory of leadership* was essentially abandoned in the 1950s, and the research shifted toward situational characteristics that were related to how a leader did or should behave. Notably, the conventional wisdom has continued to support the belief that at least some critical leadership skills are heritable, and the recent (last twenty years) interest in personalities and their relationship to leadership smacks of the old trait theory too (note the discussion of the Myers–Briggs personality test in Chapter 5). Some personality types identified by such indicators as the Myers-Briggs test would appear to better fit the typical requirements of a political or administrative leader (as well as many other roles and professions in organizations).

An alternate way of viewing leadership is the **behavioral model** (Stojkovic, Klofas and Kalinich 1998). Under this model it is believed that the most effective leaders are those who balance concern for the needs of the people they supervise with concern for getting the mission accomplished, or production. One critique of this model offered by Stojkovic et al. (1998) is that it fails to take into consideration the situation that the leader is facing. Would the concern for the needs of the employees be the same, for instance, if the leader was faced with a budgetary shortfall and the need to make staff cuts? On the other hand, would the need for production be paramount for leadership when people were demoralized by the lack of raises during a recession?

Therefore, a new set of theories regarding leadership that builds on the behavioral theory surfaced on the academic plain. Despite the sidelight interest in personality traits as related to leadership and other roles, and the behavioral study of leaders themselves, much of the interest in the study of leadership has shifted toward **situational leadership theories**. These theories focus on leader–member relations, the needs presented by the group, organizational circumstances, and the skills and abilities of the followers. The belief is that different situations require different leaders or leadership skills.

Situational leadership theories are popular because it is obvious that in the normal course of events in an organization the leader is called upon to shift to varying skills sets based on what is happening at the time. The juvenile probation officer must use different skills with those he supervises in an emergency—say, a child on a serious crime spree—and when the members of the work unit are developing their component of the county's five-year plan. Likewise the police officer on the beat must use different leadership skills when one juvenile is threatening others with a knife and when she is training school children on bicycle safety. Similarly, the juvenile court judge is likely to view differently the recommendations of an experienced probation officer and the opinions of one who has just started the job. In all these situations, the theory goes, the leadership skills and techniques need to fit and adapt to the situation.

Change and Maintenance Leadership to Fit the Situation

Some believe, for instance, that the different leaders and leadership skills required when an organization is involved in change are different from those needed in a more status-quo mode. A "change" leader must know how to marshal enthusiasm, assemble and redirect resources and, perhaps most damaging of all to his survival in that organization, be willing to upset some people, who are perfectly satisfied with the status quo and may even benefit from it. Once the change process has been completed, the leader will need to shift gears to focus more on stability and order in the organization and the routinization of practices. To effect this change—that is, to become a "maintenance leader"—requires a whole different skill set and maybe a whole different leader.

Participants at the leadership conference of the International Association of Chiefs of Police (IACP) presented a radical view of the leader as responsible for change (IACP, 1999). As the chief of police for Marietta, Georgia, and a past president of IACP (Bobby Moody) wrote, the participants "recognized the emerging potential, need for, contribution, and acceptability of the 'transition chief'—a comparatively 'short tenure' executive to engineer painful and radical organizational transformation" (Moody, 1999:ii). Not only would "change leaders" develop in the organizations that needed them, but the IACP members recognized that they *should* develop. They also realized that there would be repercussions for such leaders in the form of shortened tenure in office and greater conflict while there. But the point of such change leaders would be to move the organization in a more professional direction.

Perhaps predictably a "change leader" who tries to move into a "maintenance leader" role will find it difficult or impossible to mend fences with those he had upset previously. He also may not be as comfortable in exercising the skills needed for the sedate and orderly operation of the organization as he was in moving it in a new direction. This is why one of the authors often tells students that "change leaders" typically DIE—organizationally, of course. Case in point: Jerome Miller, supervisor of the Department of Youth Service in Massachusetts in the early 1970s, closed most of the large training schools in that state. He did so in response to numerous reports of abuse of juveniles at the hands of staff and other incarcerated youth (Welch, 1996). In the face of resistance by the bureaucracy to change, and political pressure, he resigned. Notably, the long-term effect of his action has been the decreased use of incarceration for delinquent youth. But Miller suffered an organizational "death" to achieve this feat.

Another case in point: the fictional Brubaker, from the movie of the same name, when he agitated for reform of a prison in Arkansas in the 1970s. This 1980 Robert Redford movie includes a synopsis of what happened to Thomas Murton, the practitioner/academic after whom Brubaker was largely modeled, when he tried to change the backward Arkansas prison system in the 1970s (see also Murton, 1976). He too died, organizationally. In both cases political and organizational force was applied to remove a leader of reforms. Some such change leaders, even should they not suffer an organizational death, may find that they do not fit the new situation for their organization, or are unwilling to adopt the skill set needed to be a "maintenance" leader (e.g., see Box 7.1).

Fred Fielder and his colleagues (1969) developed a form of situational leadership theory called **contingency theory**. This theory is based on the consideration of three

BOX 7.1

LEADERSHIP STYLES IN POLICING AND MANAGEMENT AS SEEN BY A LOCAL POLICE MANAGER

By John C. Connolly

Good law enforcement managers must merge several leadership styles to succeed. There are too many scenarios that play out daily to rely on one mode of supervision. Additionally, the nature of the line of work dictates this: while there are many responsibilities that are similar to what managers in other areas face, the law enforcement supervisor/manager has to possess the ability to lead in a command-and-control mode at times. Emergency situations need quick and authoritative decisions. However, the majority of a police manager's leadership challenges are nonemergency, pertaining to personnel issues and problem solving. The good manager will, over the course of a career, develop his or her own unique style, which is a smorgasbord of what that leader has experienced in life. The accomplished manager will have also forsaken those observed styles that have not been effective. Parents, teachers, coaches, bosses, as well as the sergeants, lieutenants, chiefs, field-training officers, met on the way up the ladder, all provide examples of leadership skills.

The police chief has another leadership challenge: as a team leader, he wants his subordinate supervisors to be his representative on the street, in his absence. The chief wants the sergeants, lieutenants, and captains to be "singing from the same sheet of music." This is important in an organization that will have several, if not many squads and divisions, and is prone by its nature to fragmentation. Many police departments have been accused by insiders of being actually many mini-departments, due to a multiplicity of supervision styles. Officers who work relief shifts that cross over between two standard shifts know all too well that "this sergeant wants this, and the other sergeant wants that." Such diversity of style, in this instance, can be counterproductive to a police department's efficiency, and the chief's effectiveness. There is a paradox for this chief: he wants consistency from his staff, but if he is a true leader, he will allow for personal growth and expression out of each of those supervisors.

The chief is not the only manager in a police department to face leadership angst along the way. Sergeants, the first-line supervisors, have a formidable task in leading. Often the sergeant is a new supervisor, as this is typically an entry-level position in police management. This street supervisor is suddenly thrust into an environment where she is expected now to manage six or seven other individuals, whereas, prior to being promoted, she only had to worry about herself. Additionally, the chief has communicated very clearly that she is expected to carry out his mission, to lead in his absence. However, and this is particularly true in smaller agencies, she is now supervising people that were recently her peers, squad mates, friends. Those peers many times expect her to continue to be on their side. She still is out there with the beat cars, working the same shifts, assisting on the same calls. Surely, she is still one of us, they think.

A good sergeant must learn quickly how to strike the proper balance between rank-and-file and manager, with a slant toward management. That will take courage and integrity at 3 a.m. on a Sunday when one of her officers launches a vehicular pursuit of a stolen vehicle, when in fact that pursuit will violate department policy. Or, having to face the unpleasant task of taking to task the officer who has been visiting the female clerk at the gas station too much lately, even though he has not missed any radio calls and is otherwise doing a fine job.

Those sergeants that excel in their duties, and aspire to move up in the organization, may find themselves in a more pure management position, as a lieutenant or captain. While this may appear from the outside to be a purer managerial environment, and as such would solve the identity crisis that a sergeant endures, there are many new lieutenants who soon lament the absence of police work in their daily duties. This is a challenge for many, to switch gears from crimefighter to "pencil pusher."

A philosopher once declared: "Nothing endures but change." The successful police managers have and will continue to adjust to whatever organizational change comes their way, just as they are expected to do in their ever-changing personal lives.

John C. Connolly, Chief of Police of the City of Manchester, Missouri, wrote this essay in August 2005.

situational dimensions: leader–member relations, task structure, and the position power of the leader. According to this theory, the leadership style employed should adapt to, or be *contingent* on, these three considerations: whether the leader and the members have positive relations (or not), whether the task structure (what to do and how to do it) is clear and set (or not), and whether the leader is powerful (or not). Another dimension of this theory is that the leader is believed to have a more "human relations" orientation to management depending on how she describes her least favorite worker. If that worker is described unfavorably, the leader is believed to have a more traditional approach to leadership and management; and, if the opposite is true, then her management and leadership styles will be less traditional. Notably, this theory encompasses the trait theory in that it recognizes the attributes of the situation (e.g., the relations, the task, the power of the leader) that can be manipulated, but the leader is understood to react to a situation based on his or her personality (Gordon & Milakovich, 1998).

BOX 7.2

THE LEADERSHIP SKILLS NEEDED FOR THE CHANGE PROCESS FROM
A TRADITIONAL TO A NEW GENERATIONAL JAIL

One of the most notable changes to occur in corrections in the last two decades
of the 20th century was the transformation of traditional jails to "new generation" or podular/direct supervision jails. A number of jails made this move;
many are still implementing it; and some claimed to have made the switch
when they had not or could not. Even some prisons have adopted forms of
the supervision and architecture that distinguish new-generation jails from traditional facilities.

A *traditional jail* is one that has intermittent or remote supervision and
linear architecture. What this means is that the correctional officer sees the
inmates by walking by their cells or looking through a window, or via an electronic device, only about once per hour. The rest of the time the straight lines
of the architecture and the windows, doors, and bars that separate inmates
from staff prevent the staff from supervising. These architectural obstructions
also allow the more powerful inmates to fill the leadership void created when
staff aren't around. As the jail-building boom exploded over the last twenty
years, many counties and cities replaced old jails or added new jails.

Some of these newly constructed jails were *new-generation jails* with distinct characteristics, the two most important of which were direct supervision
by staff and podular architecture. Direct supervision means that the officer
joins the inmates in the living unit (which ideally houses from forty to sixty
inmates). The architecture is podular (think pea pod and modular) in that it is
open and rounded. The officer in the living unit should ideally be able to stand
in the middle of the unit and see all that is going on with only a few architectural obstructions (shower rooms, etc.). In new-generation jails the architecture
complements the supervision or makes direct supervision possible.

As jails began to engage in this huge change, many of the staff used to
little, and often brief, contact with inmates were very concerned about the
change to podular/direct supervision facilities. Many were not just apprehen-
sive, they were downright fearful of how they would handle themselves and
inmates when they were face to face with the inmates for the duration of a
shift. Clearly, the correctional officers supervising inmates in these jails were
going to need a whole different skill set to be able to operate effectively. In
some of the jails making this change in the early 1980s and 1990s, and particularly before the benefits of podular/direct supervision jails had become established in the literature, staff quit or rebelled openly against this change.

While in graduate school one of the authors had the opportunity to observe
a western state county jail involved in this change. The savvy jail manager was
very cognizant of the concerns of his staff regarding the move. In addition to

having to sell the local political leaders and the community on the virtues of this jail (he liberally used the media and media events—such as a jail sleepover for community members before its opening),to "sell" his staff. His leadership style became one of advocacy and of selling the idea to staff and community members. This "selling" involved sending key staff to other such jails already in operation, distribution of the current research on podular/direct supervision jails that was emanating from the National Institute of Corrections, and training staff not just on the concept, but on the leadership and interpersonal communication skills that would be needed to run the pods. Despite his efforts, some of the correctional officers quit and others never "bought" the idea until they actually had worked in the facility for a time and had their fears and concerns allayed. A very few never got used to the change.

Once the change was complete and the kinks had been worked out organizationally, the jail manager noticed that his leadership style did not fit the maintenance phase the organization had entered. Moreover, the correctional officers, who now exercised more developed leadership and interpersonal skills during their workday with inmates in the pods, were less amenable to the traditional management that had fit the old traditional jail. In other words, the jail administrator needed to adjust his style not only to the new maintenance phase of his facility, but to the new "mature" style of the staff. The jail manager retired from his position after a few years and a newer manager came in with a leadership style that fit the new reality of that jail.

Under Fielder's contingency theory the leader should be more "directive" when leader and member relations are positive, task structure is clear, and the leader is positive. In other words, the leader has high situational control when these factors are present (Stojkovic et al., 2003). But if these circumstances do not obtain, the leader's behavior should reflect concern with keeping or enhancing relationships, clarifying the task, and sharing or building the power. Proponents of this theory seem to assume that leaders tend to be either task oriented or human relations oriented, but not both. When the leadership moves to a greater consideration of the members, Gordon and Milakovich (1998) describe this as a new model of *relational leadership* that better fits the evolving learning organization described in Chapter 4.

A problem with Fielder's contingency theory is that the three factors identified as enhancing the situational control for the leader often are not present in criminal justice organizations. The tasks and roles in criminal justice work are very complex and are often unclear (e.g., see the discussion of roles in Chapter 6). Moreover, leadership styles are often mutable in that some leaders do switch from a task focus to a concern for the workers, depending on the situation; they are not necessarily rigidly married to one style or the other in every situation. It is also hard for the public sector leader who has only limited ability to hire and fire people (recall those pesky civil service rules) to exert much position power. Finally, leadership styles may lie on a continuum, with style use varying by situation; dichotomies involving only a production- or task-driven style and a human concerns style may be inadequate to describe an organization.

A second *contingency theory* that appears to address these concerns about the need for congruence, or a fit, between leader style and the situation is the "path-goal" theory (House & Mitchell, 1982). Leadership behavior under **path-goal theory** includes the following four styles: directive, supportive, participative, and achievement oriented. The *directive style* focuses on the task and the need to get the job done. Rules and regulations are valued under this style and are cited to subordinates as a means of increasing job performance. The *supportive style* combines the task orientation of the directive style with a concern for employees. This concern manifests itself in an open and friendly approach to workers. A *participative style* emphasizes the engagement of the leader and workers in organizational decision making; here the workers' input and standing in the organization are valued. Under the *achievement-oriented style* high goals for production are set for the workers, and the leader expects that those goals will be met when the workers are motivated.

These four styles vary and are contingent on the characteristics of the workers and on environmental factors (House & Mitchell, 1982:522). The subordinates' *locus of control* (are they self motivated or do they need direction?), *orientation to authoritarianism* (do they like to be told what to do or would they like to participate in decision making?), and *ability* (how competent they are to do the job?) determine the appropriate leadership style. *Environmental factors* also determine which leadership style might be appropriate to a given situation, including such variables as the nature of the task (is it clear and understood?), the formal authority system (does it reward accomplishment of goals or serve as a barrier to it?), and the primary work group (can coworkers serve as a catalyst for the accomplishment of tasks or do they comprise another barrier?). Stojkovic and his colleagues note that the path–goal theory is particularly useful for the administration of criminal justice organizations because it delineates a way in which leaders can shape the organizational environment that makes the accomplishment of tasks more likely.

> First criminal justice administrators need to spell out clearly the types of rewards that subordinates can receive if and when they follow specific paths designed and structured by the organization.... Second, path–goal theory suggests, correctly, that no one style of leadership is sufficient for all the situations faced by criminal justice administrators and supervisors. This point cannot be stated too often.... Third, path–goal theory requires that criminal justice administrators design paths and goals for criminal justice employees that are reasonable and attainable. Path–goal theory assumes active leadership on the part of supervisors. (Stojkovic et al., 2003:176–178)

The difficulty, as Stojkovic and his colleagues admit, is that administrators in the criminal justice system cannot always make the changes necessary to ensure effective leadership. For instance, they cannot always control the linkage between performance and rewards. Performance measures and expectations are sometimes confusing and contradictory, and administrators do not always have ready control over the rewards. Nevertheless, the path–goal theory does provide means of matching style to situation and improving the situation.

A related leadership instrument, known as the *LEAD (leader effectiveness and daptability description)* was developed by Hersey and Blanchard (1972, 1974) and is based on the contingency theories of leadership. This instrument is situation based and measures leaders' *style range* or "[d]ominant style plus supporting styles" and *style adaptability* or "[t]he degree to which leader behavior is appropriate to the demands of a given situation" (Hershey & Blanchard, 1974:28). While style range indicates a willingness to use multiple styles, it is less related to leader effectiveness than is style adaptability. Style adaptability was determined based on which of the four alternative actions a leader might choose in twelve different situations. Each alternative action was "weighted" by Hersey and Blanchard (1974) based on theory, concepts, and research in the behavioral sciences.

Those responding to this instrument were thought to adjust their leadership style based on the situation, whether the case at hand required *task or relationship behavior,* and the *maturity* of the followers. *Task* and *relationship* behavior by the leader are juxtaposed in the LEAD instrument (Hersey & Blanchard, 1972). **Task behavior** is much like the directive style discussed under the path–goal theory: the leader is focused on getting the job done and keeping production up. **Relationship behavior** is also much like the supportive leadership style under the path–goal theory; here the leader is concerned about the well-being of the followers. Effective leaders will vary their style based on what the situation requires (e.g., Farkas, 1999; Murataya, 2006).

The *maturity* of the followers refers to their psychological age or their knowledge base and performance in the past, rather than their chronological age. Thus 16-year-old McDonald's worker can be "mature" in her job if she has been at the shop for a time and has a history of displaying competence in required tasks.

The *four styles of leadership* measured by the LEAD instrument are *telling* (high task/low relationship), *selling* (high task/high relationship), *participatory* (low task/high relationship), and *delegating* (low task/low relationship). A leader should adopt a style on the basis of what the situation requires. For instance, the first of the twelve situations included in the LEAD instrument and the alternative actions are as follows (Hersey & Blanchard, 1974:30):

1. Subordinates are not responding lately to the leader's friendly conversation and obvious concern for their welfare. Their performance is in a tailspin.

2. Alternative actions:

The leader would...

(a) emphasize the use of uniform procedures and the necessity for task accomplishment.

(b) be available for discussion, but do not push.

(c) talk with subordinates and then set goals.

(d) intentionally not intervene.

Hersey and Blanchard (1974) would rank the effectiveness of responses to this situation in the following order: a, c, b and d. They rated action (a) the highest because they thought the situation required directive (or telling) leadership, and they also gave the (C) response a positive weight, albeit less than (a), because this response is also directive, but it recognizes the value of relationship concern if the followers are mature enough (something we can't determine from the short description of the situation).

Taken in tandem and once tallied, all the responses indicate whether a given respondent has a proclivity for telling, selling, participatory, or delegating leadership styles (most people have at least a couple of strong style preferences) and how effective that person is in adapting to the given situations.

Hersey and Blanchard administered this instrument to over twenty thousand middle managers in all kinds of organizations (Kuykendall & Unsinger, 1990). They found that a participating–selling style combo is the most prevalent among leaders in the United States.[1]

Kuykendall and Unsinger also administered the LEAD instrument to police managers in the early 1980s. They found at that time that 155 police managers tended to prefer a selling style, with about 80% rating "somewhat effective" to "very effective" on the instrument. The selling style is regarded as the "safest" by Kuykendall and Unsinger (1990), because it allows police managers to focus on the task, while not ignoring the relationship needs of workers. Of course, in policing, as in corrections and courts, with high-accountability situations, rare but important emergency situations, and due process requirements, a directive style does appear to be called for. But what about when the "maturity" of the workers increases? How should the style of criminal justice managers change then? Hersey and Blanchard (1974) would argue that there are consequences for the leader and the organization when the leader fails to recognize the need to shift from telling to selling, participatory, or even delegating styles. One consequence they mention is that the inflexible leader will be less effective in accomplishing goals.

LEADERSHIP STYLES vs. TECHNIQUES

Leadership styles are not the same as techniques. A criminal justice manager might employ several techniques at the same time. Techniques are subsumed under styles in that any given style might include several techniques. For instance, a leader might use some of the techniques identified by Yukl (1981:12–17), such as reminding the followers that the request is legitimate, while also trying to persuade them of the rationality of a given action. Or a police chief may try to indoctrinate followers regarding acceptable behavior vis-à-vis relationships with suspects while also threatening his people with suspension and/or firing should they cross that line. Thus, either singly or in combination, the following are some techniques Yukl (1981:12–17), identified: "legitimate request, instrumental compliance, coercion, rational persuasion, rational faith, inspirational appeal, indoctrination, situational engineering, and personal identification."

THE RESPONSIBILITIES OF LEADERSHIP

Criminal justice leaders and managers, much like their comrades in the public and private sector, are faced with a myriad of responsibilities and duties that make the roles very challenging. Ultimately, as they usually work in traditionally structured bureaucracies, the buck stops with them: that is, they are accountable for the work done by those they supervise. In the state of Idaho a few years ago we saw a salient reminder of this fact when the director of corrections resigned under pressure when an inmate work programs was found to be seriously mismanaged (inmates assigned to deliver furniture in the community were making personal stops with staff knowledge). Although there was no indication that the director knew all along of these activities, there was an expectation that he *should have*. Because of this belief that leaders are accountable for what happens in the facilities for which they are responsible, and as our definition of criminal justice leadership indicated, they often have a diverse stewardship role that spans the breadth of the organization or organizations (Boin, 2001; Carlson & Simon Garrett, 1999; Giever, 1997; Metz, 2002; Schein, 1992; Seiter, 2002; Stojkovic & Farkas, 2003; Thibault, Lynch, & McBride, 2004; Webb & Morris, 2002; Whisenand, 2004; Zupan, 2002).

Typical responsibilities for this role include the following:

- community relations
- internal communications
- maintenance of professional standards
- conflict resolution
- control of violence and deviance
- human resource management
- training management
- collective bargaining
- inmate and client management
- planning, policy implementation, and budget oversight
- culture creation and maintenance
- employee empowerment and team building
- change agent

Of course, in all these tasks the criminal justice leader works with others in the organization. Oftentimes the leader can delegate the supervisory role in these tasks. Also, in some tasks the leader has a role that is merely supervisory; for others the leader's involvement is very hands-on. The extent to which criminal justice leaders are actually involved in the activities just listed depends on the type of organization, the level of government in which it functions (city, county, state, or federal), the size of the organization (whether it is large enough for staff specialization in these tasks), and the supervisory style of the leader (hands-on, intermediate involvement, or removed).

The role of leader as *communicator* to a large extent shapes all the other activities he is involved in (for a review of the importance of communication, see Chapter 5). For example, the director of a halfway house for troubled youth may be actively engaged with governmental entities that oversee the institution and have ultimate responsibility for the youth. He will also be cognizant of the need to communicate with employers, family members, school officials, the police, the juvenile court, and others who are connected with, and have concern and responsibility for, those youth. He might also be in close contact with the city council or county commissioners and local zoning officials about the placement and continued existence of his facility. Of course, and in general, as with all public sector leaders of organizations that create public concern over safety, he will have a broad public relations responsibility to build and keep support for his facility.

As with external communications, the criminal justice leader has a central role in shaping and maintaining internal communications (again see Chapter 5). At a minimum such a responsibility encompasses supporting open communication throughout the organization in any number of ways, including newsletters, transparency in administration, grievance procedures and whistleblowing, training, promotion of research, and teaming. Of course, communication flows more freely internally when the organization and its leaders tear down barriers to its transmission. In this sense, an organization that is focused on human relations management and has a learning focus is an organization that is more likely to promote positive internal communication.

Criminal justice leaders often serve as the symbolic and literal *model of professionalism* for their organization. They set the tone for the organization in what they say but, more importantly, in what they do. If the sheriff upholds standards of professional conduct herself, it is more likely that her deputies will follow suit. She also needs to ensure that personnel and other practices in the organization reinforce the value placed on professional behavior. Thus, those who behave professionally are also those who get positive performance evaluations and promotions.

The criminal justice leader is also apt to be engaged in the role of *mediator* between conflicting interests within the organization. Whether the prosecuting attorney for the county resolves conflicts over issues like resources will determine how other staff experience their work. Most conflicts in the organization are resolved at its lower levels informally and more rarely, formally; for the big-picture issues, however, the prosecuting attorney may be the only person who has the stature and the authority to meaningfully intercede in some conflicts in his office.

The criminal justice leader is also engaged as the *controller of violence and deviance* by both staff (see Chapter 3 for a more detailed discussion of this) and those they process. Adult and juvenile jail and prison administrators are more likely to have to grapple with problems of violence, although other correctional entities in the community, and the police, are afflicted with similar issues of deviance by staff and clients.

Jails and prisons, but particularly prisons, perhaps more than any other social institution, contain the ingredients for the use of excessive force and other forms of deviance. The institutions themselves are total and removed from public view much of the time, they house unhappy people, many of whom are prone to violence; and the staff are often stressed by the attributes of the work. Ironically, given public indifference to the existence of these factors and efforts to ameliorate them, nothing catches the attention and disturbs the public more than the use of excess force in public institutions like prisons and jails. Again, the warden, administrator, or sheriff, as the head of the organization, is ultimately responsible for ensuring that the amount of violence and deviance is under control in his or her facility, bearing in mind that given the clientele, and the need to control it, there is little hope of completely eliminating all violence and deviance in correctional institutions.

The criminal justice leader is also engaged as the *human resource manager,* the *training manager,* and the *collective bargainer* (in agencies where staff are unionized). Of course, if the organization is of any size, there are separate people assigned as the formal managers of these tasks. But in the end, how these areas are managed is the responsibility of the leader. Such tasks will be discussed in much more detail in later chapters; at a minimum, they involve selection, performance appraisal, promotion, disciplinary actions, firing, mediation, negotiation, and training activities of all kinds. In smaller court jurisdictions, staffed by fewer than fifty, the judge may make these decisions personally and sometimes will participate in the delivery of training. In such instances, he will be shaping the organization with his own hands, so to speak. But whether directly involved or not, the judge is best situated to influence human resource, collective bargaining, and training management.

Similarly, the criminal justice leader has some responsibility as the manager of suspects/clients/inmates, though except in the very tiniest of facilities and programs, (say in a home for troubled youth), this responsibility is rarely direct. For instance, how juvenile inmates are managed in a detention facility is determined by the leadership-sanctioned policies, procedures, and practices. If the leader is not concerned about ensuring privacy for the youth, then staff are likely to be lackadaisical in this area. If the leader insists on the provision of high school level classes for the detention inmates, then the schools and the school board are more likely to find a way to support that programming. Again, the leader sets the tone and has enormous influence over how clients and suspects are treated in the system.

Planner, policy implementer, and *budget manager* are also responsibilities of the criminal justice leader (these topics will be discussed in greater detail in Chapter 11). Though criminal justice policies are often set these days by statute and the mission statements of the organization, the extent to which they are adhered to in practice can be greatly influenced by the leader or manager. The budget process necessarily involves and overshadows both the planning and policy implementation considerations for organizations of any size. The criminal justice leader needs to take an active part in this role, since it is intertwined with just about everything else in the organization.

The criminal justice leader is a central figure in *empowering employees* and as a *team builder* in her organization. She is the one who ensures there are avenues for input, and she gives the go-ahead for team creation, viability, and relevance. For instance, the manager of a court-supervised juvenile probation department can ensure that employees involved in case management teaming have the opportunity to meet and that their decisions are respected by the department.

Finally, the criminal justice leader has the pivotal responsibility as *change agent* for the organization. Though this responsibility might be shared formally or informally with others, it is the criminal justice leader who must buy into the need for change and supply the resources for it to actually happen. Without this buy-in and support, change may still occur, but it will be stymied as long as the leader does not engage fully in the enterprise.

TEAMING AS A MEANS OF SHARING LEADERSHIP RESPONSIBILITIES

Teaming presents one way of sharing and channeling the leadership responsibilities in an organization. Criminal justice organizations, like most other public and private sector organizations of the 21st century, tend to dabble in the use of teams. Some criminal justice agencies are particularly adept in their use; others use them only in a rudimentary and perfunctory fashion. Giber, Carter, and Goldsmith (2000) argue that the most important of leadership competencies is the ability to build teamwork. In their research in the private sector, they found that this competency of leaders had the most impact on the leadership development program in the corporations they studied. Lambert, Hogan, Barton, and Clarke (2002) found that the organizational commitment and job satisfaction of correctional officers increased when the work environment had greater group cohesion and cooperation.

Larson and LaFasto (1989) synthesized some of the research on the effectiveness of all manner of teams from public, nonprofit, and private sector organizations. They then did a series of interviews of leaders and members of a sample of teams that they deemed noteworthy for their achievements or for insights they could provide regarding successful teams. In their book *Teamwork: What Must Go Right/What Can Go Wrong,* Larson and LaFasto (1989:19) defined a *team* as "[t]wo or more people; (with) a specific performance objective or recognizable goal to be attained;...coordination of activity among the members of the team is required for the attainment of the team goal or objective." So on the basis of this definition, we could say that criminal justice teams are groups of people whose activity is coordinated to achieve objectives and goals of the organization.

Larson and LaFasto (1989) posit that teams need some key ingredients to be successful:

- Not just a clear goal, but one that inspires passion and action.
- The team must be structured so that it can achieve results.
- The team members need to have the competency that befits the type of goal or objective, the team must address.
- The team needs to be unified in their commitment to the achievement of the goal or objective or they need that elusive quality of "team spirit."
- For the team to function effectively there needs to be a collaborative and supportive climate in the organization.
- High standards of excellence need to guide the team's work.
- External support and recognition make the success of team activity more likely.
- Leadership of the team is principled and "transformative" and creates other leaders.

The authors found that the most common reason for team failure was the inability to stay focused on a clear performance goal. Perhaps because of concern over control issues, or because of personal or organizational political factors, team members sometimes get sidetracked and are rendered incapable of attending to their goals. Of course, in criminal justice, as has been emphasized throughout this text, the definition of clear goals can be problematic for organizations that have multiple missions. However, if the goal can be stated in a clear declarative sentence or two, and if focus on goal attainment, can be maintained, the team is less likely to succumb to failure from this source.

Relatedly, Larson and LaFasto (1989) found that if the goal itself was inspiring or "elevating," as they put it, team members were more likely to be focused on its attainment. Of course, teams in criminal justice, much like other bureaucratic organizations in the public sector, do not have the luxury of dealing with only "elevating" goals, a fact that the authors acknowledge. To the extent possible, however, they think that teams handling matters of some import are more likely to be focused on, and successful in, goal attainment.

Larson and LaFasto (1989) also found that team structure and competent team members were key to team success in achieving its goal. They describe a "results-driven" structure for the team that has clear communication lines, division of tasks, and assigned authority for team members. They also found that opportunities for feedback among team members and a rule that judgments are based on facts reinforces a collaborative environment and allows for the exercise of the competencies of all members. "Competency of members" describes an attribute of people who are best equipped in terms of knowledge and skills to perform in the structure and to achieve the goal of the team. Larson and LaFasto were referring both to skills and abilities related to technical aspects of the job and getting along well with others.

Team members need to be unified in their commitment to achievement of the goal, and the environment should be collaborative. Larson and LaFasto (1989) found that a sense of enthusiasm, dedication, and loyalty to the team would bind individual members with others and to their collective purpose. All these aspects should also allow team collaboration on projects. Rather than competition with each other, the prevailing objective in team operation should be the welfare of the group and group work.

Teams that were most successful were guided by high standards of excellence. That level of excellence was also supported by the organization with the necessary resources and time to get the job done.

Finally, Larson and LaFasto (1989) discuss the importance of "transformative" leadership in teams and organizations as central to the success of any endeavor. Such leaders, who were first identified by Bennis and Nanus (1985:3) and others, are those who not only "commit people to action" but transform "followers into leaders" and "leaders into agents of change." In essence, Larson and LaFasto (1989:121) conclude that the effective leader in a team and an organization should do the following:

- establish a vision
- create change
- unleash talent

Of course, to accomplish these tasks, the leader of a team must have all the other criteria in place (e.g., clear and elevating goal, competent team members, etc.). Wageman (2003:285) argues that a *self-managing team* in private and public organizations would ensure that these key ingredients are acquired and maintained; she defines self-managing teams as those that "take responsibility for their work, monitor their own performance, and alter their performance strategies as needed to solve problems and adapt to changing conditions." The benefits of employing such teams for the organization is potentially heightened performance, more learning and flexibility vis-à-vis the environment, and greater commitment by employees to the organization.

THE RELATIVE SATISFACTION AND STATUS OF CRIMINAL JUSTICE LEADERS/MANAGERS AND SUPERVISORS

In several studies of relative job satisfaction, stress, and performance among wardens and police chiefs' (Caeti, Hemmens, Cullen, & Burton, 2003; Flanagan, Johnson, & Bennett, 1996; Rainguet & Dodge, 2001), some common themes emerge. Personnel issues and the work climate, stress from the responsibilities of the role, and political pressures are all tied into satisfaction levels and the likelihood of an extended tenure as a leader in a given organization.

Flanagan et al. (1996) in their study of 641 wardens of state prisons for adults found that wardens as a group are quite satisfied with their work. But they found that the level of satisfaction may have decreased from 1980 to 1995. They also found that minority wardens tended to be more satisfied than whites; a warden's age, gender, education, military service, and experience were unrelated to job satisfaction, however. The political ideology or political party affiliation of the wardens was also not associated with job satisfaction. Nor did the authors find any relationship between job satisfaction and the size of the institution or the gender of the inmates supervised. What they did find, however, was that relationships with colleagues at the prison had an effect on the wardens' job satisfaction. Satisfaction increased when the wardens had "positive relationships" with their coworkers. "The direction of these relationships suggests that supportive, trusting, and professional relationships with the staff of the prison are a more important correlate of wardens' job satisfaction than other organizational attributes such as population size" (Flanagan et al., 1996:393).

Caeti and his colleagues (2003) conducted a national survey of juvenile correctional facility directors to determine how they felt about a number of individual, managerial, and organizational matters, including their level of job satisfaction. What they found from the 258 respondents (they had a 63.6% response rate) was that on a scale of 1 to 10, the facility directors had an average job satisfaction level of 8.48, with a range in scores from 3.6 to 10. In other words, and in general, they are a very satisfied group. In comparisons with similar studies in and outside corrections, Caeti et al. (2003:397) found that "[j]uvenile facility directors were a little less satisfied than prison wardens, more satisfied than correctional officers, and much more satisfied than the general public." They also found that salary, stress, years as a director, and level of support for rehabilitation all affected reported job satisfaction. The greater the salary and the less the stress, the higher the job satisfaction. The longer the service as director, however, the less the job satisfaction. Also, interestingly enough, the more emphatically a director supported rehabilitation as a primary goal for corrections, the higher his or her level of job satisfaction appeared to be.

Rainguet and Dodge (2001), in their in-depth interviews of ten former and incumbent police executives, found that the major reasons reported for police chief turnover could be collapsed into a few categories. The authors found that stress due to long hours and worry, the resultant health concerns, human resource issues (including unethical behavior of personnel and disciplinary actions), and political pressures exerted by local officials all contributed to the early exit of police chiefs. It did not appear from the interviews that these chiefs were satisfied with their work.

Although a study of the relative satisfaction of prosecutors, defense attorneys and judges was not available for comparison, we suggest that the findings from the studies of correctional and police leaders may be applicable. In general, these findings for all criminal justice managers might be summarized in the following way: the greater the salary, autonomy from political control, and resources to do the job, the less stressed and the more satisfied a leader will be.

CRIMINAL JUSTICE LEADERS: SUCCESS, FAILURE, AND THE DANGERS OF GROUPTHINK

Organizational and Leader Success and Measurement

The relative satisfaction of criminal justice leaders and managers is one measure of organizational success. A few other measures, of organizational and leadership success, named in no particular order, might include the satisfaction of the other workers, low levels of stress and turnover for staff, fewer complaints from the community about the police/courts/corrections personnel, greater satisfaction with services by community members, the prevention of escapes, reduction or elimination of assaults between inmates/clients/with community members or between inmates/clients and staff, the reduction in the use-of-force incidents involving community members, numerous and valid programming options for clients, successful completion of programs, an abundance of training opportunities for staff, criminal justice managers who encourage input and engagement by staff (and to a limited degree community members and clients) in the operation of the organization, and resource acquisition that allows for the normal operations of the organization. Unfortunately, in the criminal justice organization, many of these measures of success are rarely taken, and some defy true estimation.

For instance, and the studies cited earlier regarding criminal justice leaders and satisfaction notwithstanding, managers in most organizations have little idea whether staff are truly satisfied with their work. Few engage in regular assessment over a enough time to allow for comparisons. Rather, they might note the turnover of staff (whether high or low) and use that as a rough barometer of staff sentiments regarding job satisfaction. But turnover (and stress if measured) are only approximately related to organizational operation because these variables might be influenced by opportunities for employment elsewhere (in the case of turnover) or family as well as work responsibilities (in the case of stress). Although a lack of escapes or people jumping parole/probation to a lesser extent might be validly aligned with prevention efforts, it is difficult to know how much of this activity is averted because of organizational efforts. This is true because we cannot know or measure what did not happen. For instance, over a four-month period in a correctional institutions, the sergeant and one of the authors had no escapes during their shift, but, the same shifts during the other half of the week had two. The successful officers attributed their good result to incessant and unpredictable bed and perimeter checks during the shift (2 A.M.–12 P.M.); but they could not know for sure that those efforts had prevented escapes in the period in question.

Can we use the lack of complaints of the community regarding court personnel as a real measure of success? Perhaps no good mechanisms for complaining exist. Perhaps court personnel actively discourage complaints or obstruct the process. Maybe the courtrooms that receive more complaints about their personnel are actually providing better service to their communities because the people feel free to complain and are given the opportunity to do so.

Nor is it always possible to know how many assaults occur between juveniles in a training school. Given the informal organizational culture prohibition against "ratting" on others, and perhaps fear of retribution, most detainees (of any age) will not report the wrongdoing of others. As juveniles are not likely to advertise the assaults, staff are not always aware of their occurrence either. Rather, blood on the sidewalk or in the bedsheets may be the first, only, and purely accidental, indication that an assault may have occurred. This is not to say that prevention efforts should not be aggressively pursued to forestall efforts to escape, jump supervision or assault others. We say simply that one can't always know whether prevention measures are working, hence whether the organization is successful in this regard.

In other words, some measures of success of the organization, and indirectly leadership, can be counted—for example, escapes, official assaults, turnover, use of force, programming options and training opportunities, avenues for input, and whether the budget increases to cover rising costs from year to year. But the intangibles like satisfaction and stress levels, whether programming, training, and prevention efforts work, and whether people feel comfortable communicating openly and honestly with the leader and in the organization are not always known and sometimes are not knowable. Of course, this does not mean that a criminal justice leader should or can abandon her responsibilities in these areas; it does mean that measuring the success of efforts by her and by the organization is not always possible.

Two Leadership Pitfalls: Organizational Decline and Failure and Groupthink

Organizational Decline and Failure Another measure of the success of an organization, and indirectly, of a leader, is the organization's continued existence and its ability to garner more resources (Kaufman, 1985). Meyer and Zucker (1989), in their book *Permanently Failing Organizations,* observed that the mortality of organizations actually declines with age (the longer an organization exists, the longer it will continue to exist) and that the performance of organizations generally does not improve with age. They argue that when the performance for the organization is high, there is agreement between the two groups that control the organization: group 1, the politicians and top-tier managers and those who benefit from organizational existence; and group 2, managers, employees, community members, clients (though no suspects, inmates, or supervisees), and other stakeholders. But when performance for the organization is low, those who control the organization, who also usually wield the most power, are apt to want to change it or even end it. In contrast, those who benefit from its existence will fight to keep it or even increase its resources (Jacoby, 2002). The longer an organization exists, the more groups and individuals—the group entities—are likely to benefit from its continued existence. Group 2 power grows as the organization ages. Hence, self-interest keeps some organizations in operation even though they are "permanently failing," as Meyer and Zucker (1989) put it. Jacoby (2002:169) explains this dynamic in his article on the "endurance of failing correctional institutions":

> Any given criminal justice agency established to fulfill a stated purpose...evolves and survives by serving a variety of other purposes. Among these would be providing patronage opportunities, providing construction and maintenance contract opportunities, providing jobs, and controlling potentially troublesome segments of the population. The participants who depend upon these latent functions of a criminal justice agency and the degree of consciousness of this dependency vary enormously.

Meyer and Zucker (1989) believe that the longer an organization persists, the less likely it is to be "high performing." They note that this is true because efforts at innovation are resisted by those who benefit from the status quo. Also, in the public sector, there are competing goals for the organization, which often conflict and are difficult to quantity (How does one measure "justice," for instance?). Because of this goal focus and conflict problem, it is almost impossible to demonstrate that the status quo is not working just fine, and thus the organization and its leaders find it difficult to make the case that change is needed.

Of course, the leadership role is key to preventing this slide into a "permanently failing" organization. The leader(s) are positioned in the organization to connect the followers with the political masters. They have the means both formally and informally to ensure high performance by staff. As management and staff's self-interest is only natural as a motivator, one way of maintaining high performance is to make it in people's best interest to excel. One way of accessing the power of this motivator is by evaluating, training, and promoting with high-performance criteria in mind. We will discuss personnel practices more fully in Chapters 8 and 9 as both motivational and culture-shaping tools.

Groupthink   The groupthink phenomenon represents another type of organizational pitfall that is best addressed by a leader. Irving Janis, in his well-known 1972 book *Victims of Groupthink*, described the phenomenon at work in decision making in the executive office of the president during the Franklin D. Roosevelt, Truman, Kennedy, and Johnson administrations, as a means of understanding some major policy fiascoes. But "groupthink" as a concept can be fruitfully applied in other organizational contexts that involve group processes. Borrowing from the type of speech that George Orwell used in *1984,* Janis (1972:9) defined **groupthink** as "[a] mode of thinking that people engage in when they are deeply involved in a cohesive in-group, when the members' strivings for unanimity override their motivation to realistically appraise alternative courses of action." Janis (1972:9) believed that groupthink results in a "deterioration of mental efficiency, reality testing, and moral judgment that results from in-group pressures."

Groupthink does not occur, say, in a policing context, because the leader does not appreciate critical thinking. The leader may genuinely wish for the group members to question and critique his decisions. Thus groupthink is an invidious, subtle process that occurs because of at least six defects in group decision making (Janis, 1972:10):

1. The group considers only a few alternative actions (usually just two).

2. The group does not always consider the "non-obvious risk and drawbacks" of the course of action preferred by the majority.

3. The members ignore courses of action that are not popular with the majority.

4. Members do not seek out expert advice on courses of action.

5. Members filter out the facts and information that do not support their preferred course of action.

6. Members do not consider how the implementation of the decision might be stymied by common obstacles such as bureaucratic inertia, sabotage by political opponents, or temporary derailment by the common accidents that beset the best-laid plans.

Finally, Janis found in his analysis of fiascoes resulting from groupthink that another danger is the members' high level of group loyalty: "in a sense, members consider loyalty to the group the highest form of morality. That loyalty requires each member to avoid raising controversial issues, questioning weak arguments, or calling a halt to softheaded thinking" (Janis, 1972:12). This group loyalty, along with group cohesion and conformance to group norms, are only reinforced when the group can identify an "enemy" or "opponent(s)."

In criminal justice, as in other public and private organizations, there is a continuing interest in maintaining and even accelerating the use of groups and group decision making (more on decision making in Chapter 12). For instance, see the earlier discussion of teaming as a responsibility of leadership. Some criminal justice actors may also have an "us vs. them" attitude toward suspects/clients/inmates, but also toward groups or organizations that are considered "outsiders." Decision making is often the province of cohesive groups who, given the hierarchical nature of the organizations and the deference to authority, may self-police out any dissent from the party line. Hence, the danger that groupthink represents for criminal justice decision making is real. Janis's message to us is that without the proper safeguards and vigilance, groups can and do descend into groupthink, sometimes with disastrous results.

Therefore, Janis recommends that preventive measures can be taken to forestall the development of groupthink within group processes. Needless to say, the leader's role in preventing groupthink is key. Specifically, Janis (1972:209–216) offers eight prescriptions for healthy group decision making.

1. The leader needs to ensure that each member takes on the role of critical evaluator and that the group allows for and airs their doubts and concerns. This means that the leader needs to be ready to accept and process any criticisms of his own judgments as well.

2. The leader of the organization should be objective and refrain from expressing any preferences for action or decisions at the outset of the group's formation. Group members should not be swayed before they have had a chance to deliberate by the leader's stated or inferred preferences.

3. On matters of some moment, independent parallel groups with different leaders should be formed to simultaneously consider the same issues.

4. As part of the group process, the main group should subdivide when necessary to work on particular problems and then re-form to work out any differences.

5. Members of the group should talk out group decisions with others in the organization, as well as people outside the group, and then take their input back into the group.

6. Outside experts or "qualified colleagues" should be asked to attend pertinent group meetings and encouraged "to challenge the views of the core members."

7. One member at every meeting should play the role of devil's advocate.

8. When the matter under consideration is in opposition to another organization or entity, at least one of the group's meetings should be devoted to considering "all the warning signals" from that "rival" and "constructing alternative scenarios of the rival's intentions."

Janis (1972) believes that if the organization and leader proactively engage in these preventive measures, they have a chance of avoiding the fiascoes that sometimes result from groupthink. If they do not, they risk making and abiding by decisions that may be disastrous for the organization and for those who are affected by its operation.

CONCLUSIONS

Criminal justice leaders occupy a linchpin and pivotal position in their organizations. As such, they can wreak havoc or be the harbingers of change, progress, and stability for the organization. Leadership in organizations, whether it is recognized or not, is performed by members at the top, on the bottom, and throughout its structure. It is not just a static act, but an ongoing process of organizing, decision making, innovating, communicating, team building, culture creation, and molding to achieve organizational goals. We also need to be cognizant, though, of the individual and group goals that leaders pursue both formally and informally under the aegis of the organization.

In this chapter we discussed the contention that leaders are born and made, though we can really test only the latter, and so that is where the research is focused. Most current writers on leadership tend to see the appropriate style and techniques as tied to the situation the leader faces. If the followers are well versed in their work and have a history of high performance, it would not be productive for the leader to continue to "tell" them what to do; in fact, that might breed resistance and resentment and lead to a decline in morale and productivity. Likewise, the leader of a group that is apathetic and unskilled, or faces an emergency situation, should not be delegating tasks. Leadership, it is believed, is *contingent* on the situation.

As was also discussed in this chapter, leadership carries with it several responsibilities. These responsibilities might be shared to some degree among organizational members, but formally the fame or blame for their accomplishment resides at the top tier. One means of sharing responsibilities and building the competence of organizational members, and in the process helping them to "mature organizationally," is to engage in shared problem solving and decision making, or "teaming" in the organization. It is thought that teaming promotes individual and group communication, development, and innovation by using the human resources and leadership capabilities of all organizational members.

The satisfaction of criminal justice managers is typically high. Research indicates, however, that job satisfaction is contingent on characteristics of the leader and the job.

One pitfall that confronts organizations is their tendency toward demise in effectiveness over time, even as support for their continued existence grows. In addition to recognizing this phenomenon, the criminal justice leader should actively work to prevent the organization from sliding into a state of "permanent failure."

The criminal justice leader must also be mindful of the tendency of management groups to fall into "groupthink" in matters of decision making. The danger of such a phenomenon may be doubly likely in organizations that are most hidden from the community and whose decisions are most removed from critical review. Remedies to prevent the occurrence of groupthink in criminal justice were offered and discussed.

EXERCISE: THE AMERICAN (LEADERSHIP) IDOLS

This discussion helps to illuminate the two sides of the debate over whether leaders are "born" or "made." Usually, we like to do this in-class exercise before the students have had a chance to read the chapter—for instance, at the end of the lecture on roles and socialization. Despite the name of the exercise, no singing is required, though the instructor or students may be inspired to break into song should their favorite singer make the list as an important leader!

1. Ask class members to identify some of the most important American (or foreign) leaders (their idols and others). The leaders may be from any time period.
2. Write the leaders' names on the board as they are mentioned in class.
3. Tell students to note the demographics of the leaders mentioned and ask them to explain why persons of certain races, ethnicity, gender, occupations, and so on tend to prevail (if such a pattern appears).
4. If these are our idols, what does that say about societal values?
5. Probe students to discover why they identified a particular leader as important. What were the particular skills and abilities that made that person stand out?
6. In a separate column, list those skills and abilities.
7. Then ask students whether they think important leaders were born with those skills or at some point learned them.
8. Reexamine the list of leadership idols on the board. Ask students to make judgment calls about whether a given leader accomplished good or evil in this world. (*Note*: We've had students mention some really morally abhorrent leaders.) All the leaders listed on the board may be "important," but were they all "good"?
9. Ask students if the same skills and abilities are necessary for an "important" leader as for a "good" one. The difference between such leaders is not always readily apparent, so ask what it is.
10. Ask students to discuss how leaders in a given field of criminal justice might acquire the necessary skills of both an important and a good leader.

DISCUSSION QUESTIONS

1. What theory of management is in sync with the behavioral model of leadership? Why?
2. How are leadership styles tied to management theories? Explain your answer.
3. Which of the four leadership styles you would (or do) use in a criminal justice setting. Why have you chosen this style? In what situations do you think this style best fits? Are those situations common or uncommon in criminal justice settings?
4. How does "teaming" affect leadership decisions in organizations? Who is best equipped to make leadership decisions in organizations?
5. Explain how "permanent failure" in organizations occurs. How would we know if a criminal justice agency was sinking into this state?
6. What is groupthink? List and explain five reasons *why* it might be more likely to happen in criminal justice organizations versus other public or private sector organizations.

KEY TERMS

behavioral model: under this model it is believed that the most effective leaders are those who balance concern for the needs of the people supervised with concern for getting the mission accomplished, or production (Stojkovic et al., 1998).

contingency theory: based on the consideration of three situational dimensions: leader–member relations, task structure, and position power of the leader. According to this theory, the leadership style employed should adapt to, or be *contingent* on, three considerations: whether the leader and the members have positive relations (or not), whetherf the task structure (what to do and how to do it) is clear and set (or not), and whether the leader is powerful (or not).

groupthink: "[a] mode of thinking that people engage in when they are deeply involved in a cohesive in-group, when the members' strivings for unanimity override their motivation to realistically appraise alternative courses of action" (Janis, 1972:9).

leadership: an ongoing process of activity involving organizing, decision making, innovating, communicating, team building, culture creation, and molding followers and co-workers that is engaged in by workers and supervisors to achieve organizational goals.

path-goal theory: leadership behavior incorporating the following four styles: directive, supportive, participative, and achievement-oriented leadership.

political leader: influential person who is either elected or appointed by elected officials. Such leaders in criminal justice typically include sheriffs, prosecuting attorneys, and sometimes judges.

relationship behavior: characteristic of a leader who is concerned about the well-being of his or her followers.

situational leadership theories: focus on leader–member relations, the needs presented by the group, the organizational circumstances, and the skills and abilities of the followers. The belief is that different situations require different leaders or leadership skills.

task behavior: describes the actions of the leader who is focused on getting the job done and keeping production up.

NOTE

1. If you are interested in learning more about the LEAD instrument and would like to use it in your classroom or work situation, see the website for the Center for Leadership Studies (established by Dr. Paul Hersey in the 1960s) at www.situational.com. You might also consult the original Hersey and Blanchard (1974) article published in the *Training and Development Journal* and cited in the references. A more recent source is the 1988 book by Hersey and Blanchard, also cited in the references for this chapter.

REFERENCES

Bennis, W., & Nanus, N. (1985). *Leaders: The strategies for taking charge.* New York: Harper & Row.

Boin, A. (2001). *Crafting public institutions: Leadership in two prison systems.* Boulder, CO: Lynne Rienner Publishers.

Caeti, T., Hemmens, C., Cullen, F. T., & Burton, V. S., Jr. (2003). Management of juvenile correctional facilities. *The Prison Journal, 83*(4), 1–23.

Carlson, P. M., & Simon Garrett, J. (Eds.). (1999). *Prison and jail administration: Practice and theory.* Gaithersburg, MD: Aspen Publishers.

Drucker, P. F. (1954, reprinted in 1993). *The practice of management.* New York: HarperBusiness.

Farkas, M. A. (1999). Inmate supervisory style: Does gender make a difference? *Women and Criminal Justice, 10*(4), 25–45.

Fielder, F. E. (1969). Style or circumstance: The leadership enigma. *Psychology Today, 2,* 39- 43.

Flanagan, T., Johnson, W. W., & Bennett, K. (1996). Job satisfaction among correctional executives: A contemporary portrait of wardens of state prisons for adults. *The Prison Journal, 76*(4), 385–397.

Giber, D., Carter, L., & Goldsmith, M. (2000). *Linkage Inc.'s best practices in leadership development handbook.* San Francisco: Jossey-Bass.

Giever, D. (1997). Jails. In J. Pollock (Ed.), *Prisons: Today and tomorrow* (pp. 414–465). Gaithersburg, MD: Aspen Publishers.

Gordon, G. J., & Milakovich, M. E. (1998). *Public administration in America* (6th ed.). New York: St. Martin's Press.

Hersey, P., & Blanchard, K. H. (1972). *Management of organizational behavior: Utilizing human resources* (2nd ed.). New York: Prentice Hall.

Hersey, P., & Blanchard, K. H. (1974). So you want to know your leadership style? *Training and Development Journal, 28*(2), 22–37.

Hersey, P., & Blanchard, K. H. (1988). *Management of organizational behavior: Utilizing human resources* (5th ed.). Englewood Cliffs, NJ: Prentice Hall.

House, R. J., & Mitchell, T. R. (1982). Path–goal theory of leadership. In H. L. Tosi & W. C. Hammer (Eds.), *Organizational behavior and management: A contingency approach* (pp. 517–526). New York: Wiley.

IACP. (1999). *Police leadership in the 21st century: Achieving and sustaining executive success*. Recommendations from the president's first leadership conference, May 1999. Alexandria, VA: International Association of Chiefs of Police.

Jacoby, J. E. (2002). The endurance of failing correctional institutions: A worst case scenario. *The Prison Journal, 82*(2), 168–188.

Janis, I. L. (1972). *Victims of groupthink: A psychological study of foreign-policy decisions and fiascoes*. Boston: Honghton Mifflin.

Kaufman, H. (1985). *Time, chance, and organizations: Natural selection in a perilous environment*. Chatham, NJ: Chatham House.

Kuykendall, J., & Unsinger, P. C. (1990). The leadership styles of police managers. In S. Stojkovic, J. Klofas, & D. Kalinich (Eds.), *The administration and management of criminal justice organizations: A book of readings* (pp. 162–175). Prospect Heights, IL: Waveland Press.

Lambert, E. G., Hogan, N. L., Barton, S. M., & Clarke, A.W. (2002). The impact of instrumental communication and integration on correctional staff. *The Justice Professional, 15*(2),181–193.

Larson, C. E., & LaFasto, F. M. J. (1989). *Teamwork: What must go right/What can go wrong*. Newbury Park, CA: Sage.

Maslow, A. H. (1976, reprinted in 1998). *Maslow on management*. New York: Wiley.

Metz, A. (2002). Life on the inside: The jailers. In T. Gray (Ed.), *Exploring corrections: A book of readings* (pp. 64–68). Boston: Allyn & Bacon.

Meyer, M. W., & Zucker, L. G. (1989). *Permanently failing organizations*. Newbury Park, CA: Sage.

Moody, B. (1999). *Police leadership in the 21st century: Achieving and sustaining executive success*. Alexandria, VA: International Association of Chiefs of Police.

Murataya, R. (2006). An examination of the leadership style of the chief of police of a small town in central Washington. *Police Forum: Academy of Criminal Justice Sciences Police Section, 15*(2).

Murton, T. O. (1976). *The dilemma of prison reform*. New York: Praeger.

Parker Follett, M. (1926, reprinted in 2001). The giving of orders. In J. M. Shafritz & J. S. Ott (Eds.), *Classics of organization theory* (pp. 152–157). Fort Worth, TX: Harcourt College Publishers.

Rainguet, F. W., & Dodge, M. (2001). The problems of police chiefs: An examination of the issues in tenure and turnover. *Police Quarterly, 4*(3), 268–288.

Schein, E. H. (1992). *Organizational culture and Leadership* (2nd ed.). San Francisco: Jossey-Bass.

Seiter, R. P. (2002). *Correctional administration: Integrating theory and practice*. Upper Saddle River, NJ: Prentice Hall.

Stojkovic, S., & Farkas, M. A. (2003). *Correctional leadership: A cultural perspective*. Belmont, CA: Wadsworth/Thomson Learning.

Stojkovic, S., Kalinich, D., & Klofas, J. (2003). *Criminal justice organizations: Administration and management* (3rd ed.). Belmont, CA: Wadsworth/Thomson Learning.

Stojkovic, S., Kalinich, D., & Klofas J. (1998). *Criminal justice organizations: administration and management*. Belmont, CA: West/Wadsworth Publishing Company.

Thibault, E. A., Lynch, L. M., & McBride, R. B. (2004). *Proactive police management* (6th ed.). Upper Saddle River, NJ: Prentice Hall.

Wageman, R. (2003). Critical success factors for creating superb self-managing teams. In J. S. Ott, S. J. Parkes, & R. B. Simpson (Eds.), *Readings in organizational behavior,* (pp. 285–296). Belmont, CA: Wadsworth/Thomson Learning.

Webb, G. L., & Morris, D. G. (2002). Working as a prison guard. In T. Gray (Ed.), *Exploring corrections: A book of readings* (pp. 69–83). Boston: Allyn & Bacon.

Welch, M. (1996). *Corrections: A critical approach.* New York: McGraw-Hill.

Whisenand, P. M. (2004). *Supervising police personnel: The fifteen responsibilities* (5th ed.). Upper Saddle River, NJ: Pearson/Prentice Hall.

Yukl, G. (1981). *Leadership in organizations.* Englewood Cliffs, NJ: Prentice-Hall.

Zupan, L. L. (2002). The persistent problems plaguing modern jails. In T. Gray (Ed.), *Exploring corrections: A book of readings* (pp. 37–63). Boston: Allyn & Bacon.

CHAPTER 8

PERSONNEL PROCESSES AND PRACTICES

Selection, performance appraisal, training and motivation principles are four key systems necessary for insuring the proper management of an organization's human resources.

(Latham & Wexley, 1981)

What's not important is the [appraisal] form or the [measuring] scale. What's important is that managers can objectively observe people's performance and objectively give feedback on that performance...[says] Ronald Gross, a Maitland, Florida industrial psychologist and human resources consultant.

(Wessel, 2003:CB 1)

INTRODUCTION: YOU'VE GOT TO PROTECT YOUR INVESTMENT!

Criminal justice agencies are labor-intensive enterprises. People do virtually everything. Personnel costs, then, are by far the greatest expense for criminal justice organizations. Depending on the type of agency, the selection, training, pay, performance appraisal, promotion, disciplinary, stress, and turnover costs or operating expenses can eat up most of the budget of a criminal justice organization and much of the time of employees (Austin & Irwin, 2001; Mays & Winfree, 2002; Thibault, Lynch, & McBride, 2004). For this reason alone, criminal justice organizations, managers, and members need to make sure their investment in personnel is well placed and well protected.

By "well placed" we mean that the best people are selected, promoted, and retained in the organization. By "well protected" we mean that employees are prepared adequately to do their work (trained) and supported by the organization in their efforts to excel (mentored and provided with resources); in addition, the best of these workers are encouraged to pursue a career with the agency (via performance appraisals and promotions).

Of course, the opposite is true as well. As with other public and private agencies, once a selection mistake has been made, poor performers in criminal justice, need to be remotivated and, if that does not work, encouraged to leave the organization.

The point is that mistakes in areas of personnel processes are extremely costly financially. But there are less tangible costs as well for the criminal justice organization with flawed personnel processes. There are human costs for the organization in terms of morale, stress, and overwork when the organization cannot retain competent staff. Clients also suffer when valued staff leave or are demoralized. There are also human costs for employees and community members and clients when staff are selected who are unwilling or incapable of doing their jobs. Such employees can truly wreak havoc in the workplace. Corruption and abuse are just some of the behaviors that can be visited on the organization, coworkers, and community members/clients

179

when personnel processes fail to keep the best and weed out the worst. Of course, the lawsuits that result from harassment and abuse can greatly increase the costs of failure in the personnel area.

In this chapter we review the personnel processes at play in criminal justice agencies. These processes, and the practices that emanate from them, present a real opportunity to shape the organization using human capital. Since the success of criminal justice organizations, holding environmental factors constant, depends to a large degree on who works there, managers and policymakers would do well to ensure that such processes are valid, cost effective, and just.

SELECTION

Job-Valid Qualifications

Typical qualifications for criminal justice work revolve around personal characteristics such as age, height, weight, physical ability, eyesight, and hearing, among other attributes. What people often do not understand is that discrimination based on some *job-valid* characteristics is perfectly legal. For instance, in most states a person under age 18 cannot be hired to work in any criminal justice facility, even though this age requirement discriminates against capable 17-year-olds. Indeed, we shall see in Chapter 9 that in Illinois and North Carolina, prospective criminal justice employees cannot be younger than 18 and 20, respectively.

A qualification is **job valid** if it is related to attributes or abilities that are needed to get the job done. The word *validity* just means *truth*. A qualification is job valid, which means that those who do not have it can be eliminated from the candidate pool, if it is *truly* related to what is to be done on the job. Being a legal adult (18 or older) is a job-valid qualification for some jobs and for virtually all criminal justice jobs. In fact, the law enforcement agencies in the federal government have established in court cases that being younger than 37 when first hired is a job-valid qualification for them because they want to retire agents at a fairly young age (usually within 20 to 25 years). They want to hire before age 37 because they have argued that they need people at the peak of their physical ability, which for most of us, and sadly, declines with age.

Being too short or too tall or too overweight might also be job-valid qualifications if these characteristics prevented people from fitting into standard issue uniforms or using existing equipment or facilities. Being in shape might also be a job-valid qualification if otherwise one could not engage in regular required aspects of the job. Having a known history of drug use or alcohol abuse are job-valid disqualifiers, as may be a serious (sometimes any) criminal history or several traffic offenses. As you might expect, most of these determinations of job validity of requirements have been established over a period of time through practice, by means of adjustment, and in the courts. Criminal justice agencies have to establish that any skill or attribute they require is one that is regularly exercised on the job. If it is not, then that skill or attribute cannot be required of applicants.

In this regard, we like to ask our older students who have worked in law enforcement for years how many times in their career they have been required to jump and pull themselves over an eight- to ten-foot fence? Typically, they say never. Yet until the 1990s, the state police academy in a western state required that applicants be able to do this as part of the test for new recruits. If you could not perform this feat, you were out. Many women, and some men, failed at this task, perhaps because they did not have enough upper-body strength or perhaps because they were short (Lonsway, 2003). Since such fences usually do not exist in the real world, and since police officers claim they have rarely, if ever, had to try to scale one, this would not be a job-valid requirement. (A seasoned male officer who had never faced this dilemma in police work told one of the authors that if he had, he would have gone around it!)

But what of other physical agility and ability tests? Is it reasonable to expect that a person be able to run a mile in 12 or 13 minutes? If you might need to chase down juvenile suspects on the street, maybe it is. Is it reasonable to expect that people be able to complete 25 sit-ups or push-ups in a certain amount of time as a measure of general physical fitness? If you need to be able to engage in the occasional physical altercation with inmates in a jail, perhaps it is. Do such requirements discriminate more against women than men; yes they do (Lonsway, 2003). But the courts have said, and probably most reasonable people would agree, that if a requirement or attribute is actually related to real work on the job, or job valid, then even if it discriminates against certain groups disproportionately, it is allowable because the ability to do the job is more important (but see, Box 8.1).

BOX 8.1

THE AMERICANS WITH DISABILITIES ACT (ADA): A BRIEF SUMMARY

By U.S. Equal Employment Opportunity Commission

Barriers to employment, transportation, public accommodations, public services, and telecommunications have imposed staggering economic and social costs on American society and have undermined our well-intentioned efforts to educate, rehabilitate, and employ individuals with disabilities. By breaking down these barriers, the Americans with Disabilities Act (ADA) will enable society to benefit from the skills and talents of individuals with disabilities, will allow us all to gain from their increased purchasing power and ability to use it, and will lead to fuller, more productive lives for all Americans.

The Americans with Disabilities Act gives civil rights protections to individuals with disabilities similar to those provided to individuals on the basis of race, color, sex, national origin, age, and religion. It guarantees equal opportunity for individuals with disabilities in public accommodations, employment, transportation, State and local government services, and telecommunications.

(U.S. Equal Employment Opportunity Commission, U.S. Department of Justice, May 2002. http://www.usdoj.gov/crt/ada/q%26aeng02.htm).

Legal Disqualifiers

Most criminal justice agencies, but not all, will not hire applicants with felony convictions (Vohryzek-Bolden & Croisdale, 1999). Most agencies also do drug tests at some point in the hiring process, and if illegal drugs are detected, they will not hire the applicant. A pattern of traffic offenses or serious traffic offenses may also disqualify an applicant. The appearance in a background check of a known and recent history of alcohol abuse will usually suffice to disqualify an applicant.

All these reasons—criminal history, illegal drug use, alcohol abuse, and traffic offenses—are either prohibitions established in state or local statutes or practices developed by criminal justice agencies to avoid legal liability problems with new hires (and old hands). But there are exceptions to these rules. For instance, in Idaho one of the authors has seen several students hired as substance abuse counselors in public correctional agencies and in human services private sector type agencies despite a history of drug use or alcohol abuse; these individuals had successfully completed treatment and had been clean and sober for over a few years. That author also knows of a manager of treatment programs for a state department of corrections who had a known history of extensive use of illegal drugs, including heroin. In these instances, a history of abuse, with an emphasis on *history*, is sometimes seen as a qualification for a treatment position and may not limit a person's career options, particularly in the treatment field.

Moreover there is a real variation among agencies within and across the states. For instance, one of the authors knows of a college student with a juvenile history of robbery who was not hired by a jail facility in a small rural state. The same young man was told that this history would be overlooked, in light of more recent accomplishments (completing college, success on the football field), by an urban sheriff's department in a larger state.

Cost

Another major consideration in the devising of a selection process is cost. If you review the typical steps in this process, as we will shortly, you will note that the process for hiring staff for criminal justice agencies is usually geared toward reducing the cost and ensuring the effective management of time. As the number of applicants is largest at the beginning, and as many applicants will not be suited for criminal justice work, the task in selection is to weed out most of the applicants at the beginning and middle stages of the process. Cost and time considerations also dictate that the most expensive portions of the selection process, such as medical exams, psychological exams, and individual oral interviews, are reserved for the applicants who survive the weeding-out process.

Typical Selection Practices

The selection process for criminal justice positions varies widely by type of position, locality, and qualifications (see Tables 8.1 and 8.2). Generally speaking, the jobs that required more education and experience are less likely to require a lengthy selection

TABLE 8.1 The Selection Process

Application form: if you meet the qualifications, have filled out the form completely, and submitted it on time, then proceed; otherwise you're out)

Written test: if you pass, then proceed; otherwise you're out

Medical exam: if you pass, then proceed; otherwise you're out

Physical ability/agility test: if you pass, then proceed; otherwise you're out

Background investigation: if you pass, then proceed; otherwise you're out

Psychological test: if you pass, then proceed; otherwise you're outPolygraph test: if you pass, then proceed; otherwise you're out

Oral interviews: if you pass, then proceed; otherwise you're out

Ranked on hiring list/register: if you are selected when a position opens, you may be hired *conditionally* or unconditionally, but it doesn't stop here…

Probationary period and/or graduation from the academy: the process continues

Training/continual education: the process continues Performance appraisals and evaluation: the process continues

process and training period afterward. In other words, jobs with a more "professional" mantle are more likely to depend on the applicant's extant qualifications rather than on tests of suitability for the job. Since the length and content of a selection process for any given criminal justice job *depends* on such factors as educational and experience qualifications the following discussion of typical selection components should be considered with that in mind.

The Application Form   As public sector entities that are guided by civil service requirements, criminal justice agencies typically have applicants fill out a form listing personal data (name, address, social security number, etc.). Applicants might be asked to provide information about their education and degrees, current or past employment, and where they have lived over the years. Because some application forms are very detailed, covering virtually the person's whole life, it is important for potential applicants to keep organized and accurate records of where they have worked and lived, along with the names and phone numbers of supervisors and apartment managers. They will be grateful to have such information if it is required.

As a starting point in the selection process, the application form serves at least two purposes. It allows the agency to eliminate applicants who do not meet the minimum job requirements as outlined in the job announcement. It also allows the agency to eliminate those who do not fill out the form correctly or completely and those who fail to turn in the application on time. Because the selection process is guided by concerns about job validity and cost, as well as selecting the best applicants, the application form is perfect for fulfilling these multiple purposes.

It is worthy of note that for prosecuting attorney and public defender offices the selection process typically skips over the other steps to the personal interview. For such jobs, then, and as an indication of their "professional status," past work-related experiences, academic success (particularly in law school), and recommendations/references become paramount. Judges are "selected" either by the voters through the election process or "appointed" through other means entailing varying degrees of political influence. Bailiffs, court recorders, and other support personnel usually fill out application forms and are interviewed, but are unlikely to have to submit to all the other steps described in the sections that follow.

The Written Test This portion of the process is also geared toward ensuring that those who do not have the minimum qualifications for the job are eliminated early so that no more organization money is expended on them. To that end, written exams typically include standardized multiple-choice questions that can be easily graded.

The written test may also test analytical skills, math ability, and reading comprehension. The written tests sometimes include situational questions that tend to favor those who have already done the job or are familiar with how the job is done in this particular agency. Such questions also allow the agency to screen out those who would be unsuited for police or corrections work—for instance, those who might favor the overuse of force in certain situations. The California State written test for correctional officers includes 40 questions; 15 devoted to spelling, punctuation, and grammar; 10 to reading comprehension, and 15 to basic math skills (www.edc.state.ca.us). But obviously, the content and use of such tests varies to some extent. For example, some tests include a short essay question that allows the examiner to quickly note deficiencies in relevant areas.

The variability in content creates a need for the criminal justice agency to validate the testing tool. Test validation is done to ascertain the neutrality (e.g., race/ethnicity, gender) of content, with a view to thwarting any possible discrimination lawsuits. Validation can be outsourced to another public or private vendor that specializes in testing, or an agency can develop and validate its test in-house. Both methods are acceptable; however, there are pros and cons for both. Keep the test in-house, and the agency accepts more responsibility for validation but has more control and may save some expense. Outsource the test, and the possibility of the agency falling under a discrimination lawsuit lessens, but the agency may lose some control over the process, and expenses may rise.

A western state's written test for adult probation and parole officers includes a self-assessment of skills and abilities for the job. The problem with such a self-assessment is that some applicants are too modest about their accomplishments and some less qualified applicants provide an inflated evaluation of their skills. In other words, the agency using such a self-assessment test may be compromising its ability to select the best applicants.

Since all portions of the written exams for criminal justice jobs must be job valid, the components of this test need to measure, at least indirectly, skills and abilities that would be required on the job. Cost considerations also determine to some extent the content and use of this test.

Medical Exam Most agencies require that applicants be drug tested as part of the selection process. For instance, North Carolina requires a drug-screening test. Some agencies also require that the hearing, eyesight, and general physical health of the applicant be assessed before a hiring decision is made. Sometimes people do not realize that certain physical ailments may prevent them from gaining employment in criminal justice agencies. For example, although color blindness is usually not assessed for jobs

TABLE 8.2 Interviews, Tests and Examinations Used in Selection of New Officer Recruits in Local Police Departments, By Size of Population Served, 2003

Population Served	Interviews, Tests, and Examinations Used (%) to Select New Officer Recruits									
	Personal Interview	Medical Exam	Drug Test	Psychological Evaluation	Physical Agility Test	Written Aptitude Test	Personality Inventory	Polygraph Exam	Voice Stress Analyzer	Second Language Ability Test
All sizes	98	85	73	67	50	43	26	25	4	1
1,000,000 or more	94	100	100	100	94	81	56	81	0	0
500,000–999,999	100	100	95	100	86	84	48	64	11	11
250,000–499,999	95	93	98	98	93	83	51	78	10	2
100,000–249,999	95	97	86	95	88	82	50	77	11	1
50,000–99,999	99	97	90	97	83	80	47	57	7	3
25,000–49,999	99	99	88	96	76	76	45	47	12	2
10,000–24,999	99	98	88	89	71	72	40	42	6	1
2,500–9999	99	91	74	71	52	48	26	25	3	—
Under 2500	98	73	63	47	31	20	16	11	2	—

Note: List of selection methods is not intended to be exhaustive. Dash—indicates less than 0.5%.

Adapted from Bureau of Justice Statistics, U.S. Department of Justice. (2006). Law Enforcement Management and Administrative Statistics: Local Police Departments, 2003. May 2006, NCJ 210118, Office of Justice Programs, Washington, DC.

in institutional corrections, students should be aware that color blindness may prevent them from working in most police departments, and some probation and parole jobs, where operation of a vehicle is a job requirement (but not all agencies test for this).

Physical Ability/Agility Tests   Only some correctional agencies have these tests, but they are de rigueur for police officer positions. Their purpose is to weed out those who do not meet basic fitness levels and to keep those who meet those requirements. Some states and counties may reserve these tests for the academy, recognizing the decreased emphasis on this ability for institutional and community corrections. One critique of such tests in the past has been that they discriminate against women without measuring job valid qualifications. Because such tests have been debated in the courts, they now tend to measure just the basic fitness of individuals to do the job, including such measures as timed runs, sit-ups, and push-ups. Since such tests can be administered en masse, they usually are relatively low cost and tend to weed out those who would not have the physical capabilities to be able to complete job tasks.

Background Investigation   Once an agency gets to the background investigation, the cost of the selection process begins to escalate, although the cost of the investigation varies in accordance with its thoroughness. It is expensive to review current employment, living arrangements, references and social relationships, and credit history, let alone going back a few years. Generally speaking, those who apply for federal positions are most extensively investigated, but some counties and states do an in-depth job here too. The most important issue from the agencies' perspective is the criminal history of the applicant. Agencies will also check the driving record of the applicant, work history, and personal references, and will review a credit/financial history report to look for irregularities such as bankruptcies or bad checks/credit.

   A thorough investigation proceeds in "snowball" fashion: references listed on the application form constitute only the starting point for the investigator. Past and present employers, landlords, family members, friends, teachers and professors, roommates, coworkers, clerks at an applicant's neighborhood video store (just kidding), or virtually anyone with significant contact with the applicant will be contacted. And this includes people beyond those listed on the application form because the investigator will ask who else the applicant was friendly with or who else the person liked or disliked. Investigators will ask questions relevant to a person's relationship with the applicant; for example, landlords will be asked if the applicant paid her rent on time. There will also be questions about what was observed or known about the applicant: Did you ever see the person engage in unethical behavior or know of it? Did you ever know of the person to lie? Do you have any concerns about this person working with children? Do you have any concerns about this person working with vulnerable populations at all? Have you ever seen the person use illegal drugs or known of it? Did you ever see the person drunk? In other words, thorough background investigations can be quite time consuming and costly, but they can also be very effective in weeding out those who might not be suited for work in criminal justice agencies.

Psychological Test   Psychological exams take many forms. Some include the use of the (Minnesota Multiphasic Personality Inventory) (MMPI), to screen out those who are obviously unsuited for criminal justice work. Responses on the MMPI and other forms of such tests are usually analyzed by a trained psychologist. Other forms of such exams include writing a story in response to a fairly innocuous picture. An applicant whose story features a violent or deviant theme presumably would be rejected. Sometimes applicants are interviewed by an actual psychologist who asks standard questions about their childhood and perceptions of the world. Other versions of psychological exams are also employed. Typically, however, since these tests are time-consuming and must be evaluated by a skilled professional, they are costly. Unfortunately, it is not always clear how effective psychological tests are in terms of targeting future employees. They are probably better at screening out obviously psychotic or antisocial applicants who are not crafty enough to figure out why. For example, if they are asked if they like to see small animals suffer, do not answer yes!

Polygraph Testing   Although polygraph exams are not admitted as evidence in courts, police and corrections agencies are allowed to use them as a means of assessing applicants. If done correctly, they are time-consuming, complex, and costly. The applicant is hooked up to several monitors that record his physiological responses to questions. The polygraph or lie-detector test is done to determine whether the applicant exhibits physical reactions to questions that may not be consistent with honest answers. The accuracy of the assessment to the responses depends to some extent on the training and ability of the examiner. Examiners should be highly skilled practitioners with hundreds of hours of training to ensure a professional assessment of responses. Typically, the applicant is told the questions beforehand. To establish a baseline for responses, the applicant will be asked innocuous questions first. The primary questions, however, will touch on legal issues, criminal involvement, relationships, and any ethical lapses that may lie in the applicant's background.

But sometimes polygraph exams include outrageous and unrelated questions. (The students of one of the authors have told of being asked about sex with animals and whether they have ever engaged in homosexual acts) in the course of applying for jobs as police officers. Clearly, not all criminal justice managers use these tests responsibly.

The professional examiner will ask the primary questions while the applicant is hooked up to the machine. Should there be an aberrant response, the examiner usually explores this with the applicant, who is allowed to respond again. If it is the assessment of the examiner that the applicant has answered truthfully on all the questions then he will have passed the polygraph.

Oral Interviews   Usually but not always the oral interview falls at the very end or toward the end of the selection process. Because these interviews may include an oral board, usually consisting of three or four high-ranking staff members with years of experience, they can be quite costly for the organization to administer. If used at the beginning of the selection process, the sheer number of applicants should be daunting and could be unnecessarily disruptive for the organization.

The types of questions asked at these interviews are usually standardized at the beginning, though follow-up questions may explore the specific responses of individuals. Applicants are usually asked to respond to questions regarding situations they might encounter on the job. Possible responses may be provided to the applicant, and/ or he or she may be asked to formulate a response. Applicants may be asked not only how they would respond to a given situation, but also why they would respond that way. They may also be asked to explain why they did not choose an alternate response. Sometimes oral board members will play "good cop" or "bad cop" as a means of throwing people off and seeing how they respond to stress.

Oral interviews are also likely to include questions that are commonly asked in other job interviews: Why do you want to work here? What skills do you bring to this job? What was the biggest mistake you ever made in your life? What are your greatest strengths and weaknesses? The applicant may also be asked to provide an example of a difficult situation she handled well and then another instance in which the opposite was true. She may then be probed about why she thinks she was successful or unsuccessful in these instances.

In addition, the applicant may be asked about her perceptions of the client population she would be working with. Would she be comfortable working alone in a patrol car? What, if any, concerns would she have about working in a male prison? Does she have any qualms about going into the shower room, should this be necessary ? What is her attitude toward juvenile offenders? What would she consider the appropriate relationship between the public and the police? She may be asked to provide examples of her experiences supervising the relevant population.

Finally, the oral interviewers may ask the applicant about her personal habits as a means of getting a sense of who she is. When does she get up in the morning? What kind of music does she like? Who serves as a model for her life and why?

SELECTION FROM THE APPLICANT'S PERSPECTIVE

As our discussion of the selection process indicates, it can be an arduous affair. It is often said that looking for a job is a full-time job, and there is some truth to that claim. If you are a student reading this book and are interested in working in corrections, policing, the legal field, or some other public sector job, consider applying for such jobs early in your senior year of college or in your last year of law school. It takes at least six months to a year to get a job in the public sector, and some agencies advertise only once per year. Of course, if a degree is required of all who submit applications, then you will have to wait until you have one. But some agencies do not require a degree or allow employees to complete degree requirements while they are on the job.

It possible you may consider applying for jobs before you graduate. Do this because of the length of most selection processes, but also because it is good practice. People who have taken written tests or have been before oral boards may be more likely to do better the second or third time around. The whole selection process for agencies can be intimidating, but it will be less so for the experienced applicant.

Another point for students and/or prospective criminal justice employees to consider is that employers are more likely to look favorably on applicants who have experience (Vohryzek-Bolden, & Croisdale, 1999). Too often students get to the point of graduation with little real-world experience related to their profession. To build your résumé and contacts in the community, consider doing volunteer or internship or part-time work in the agency you want to work for. If this is not possible to work for that agency consider doing volunteer/internship or part-time work with a like agency. Or consider doing volunteer work that builds up your human service experience and prepares you for the kind of work you expect to be doing. For instance, if you are interested in working with juveniles, consider volunteering or part-time employment at the local Boys and Girls Club, or do an internship with the juvenile court, detention center, or drug court.

A final piece of advice is to apply widely for jobs. It is rare for college graduates get the exact position they want right out of school. Therefore, consider applying for the job you want, should it be open, but also for jobs that might be your second or third choices. Such jobs are likely to be more plentiful and less sought after by skilled applicants. It is possible you will get your dream job right away; but it is more likely that you will have to take something else until you can build your résumé to be more competitive. Besides, applying for several jobs gives you more options for employment and more experience with the application process. The whole idea is to have employment options after graduation and/or soon thereafter.

ON THE JOB, THE SELECTION PROCESS CONTINUES

Once hired, the applicant is in a sense still just that, an applicant, as tenure in the job is usually contingent on successful completion of a probationary period (typically six months to a year) and graduation from the agency's academy (we will discuss the content of the academy training more shortly). The ordering of these experiences is not always uniform. Many correctional agencies will not spend thousands of dollars to send a new hire to an academy setting until they are sure that the person is going to work out. So in corrections you often have people who have not completed any training course working for up to a year in jails, prisons, and juvenile facilities, and in community corrections (e.g., Ruddell & Main, 2006). In policing there is a greater concern regarding liability. As a police lieutenant once put it "It is scary, and dangerous to give an inexperienced person a gun and a car and send them out on the street with no training." Therefore, other than very small rural departments in financially straitened circumstances, most police recruits complete the academy after they are hired, but before they are sent on patrol alone.

Most police and correctional agencies also pair up the new hire with one or more on-the-job training (OJT) officers to show them around. The skills and abilities of such FTOs (field training officers) vary widely, but the best, obviously, are those who have many years of experience in the job and are the most professionally oriented toward the work. The cliché, as noted in Chapter 6 in our discussion of socialization, is for an old hand to take the new hire aside and say, "Forget what you learned in the academy (or from administration), I'm going to show you how it is really done." Of course and again obviously, and assuming that the academy training or any other preliminary training befits the organizational mission and priorities, an FTO who delivers this message to trainees, is not the right person to socialize new hires.

TRAINING

The importance of training in socializing and instilling values in new hires (recall this discussion in Chapter 6) and in reorienting in-service workers should not be underestimated. Training represents the most common and official means of transmitting the organizational mission and socializing new hires and old hands (Ford, 2003). It is also the best way to "professionalize" the workforce and to thus prepare people for all the challenges they will inevitably encounter in the workplace.

Historically, those who worked in criminal justice received little more than OJT and sometimes not even that (Thibault et al., 2004). Law school was not required for attorneys to practice in many states until the 20th century; instead, novice attorneys were given the option of serving as an apprentice for an older hand for a number of years. Likewise, most police and corrections departments did not have academies for their recruits until later in the 20th century. It is still true that some corrections departments and jails, even smaller police departments, do not send their recruits to academies until they have been on the job as long as a year.

Back in the early 1980s, when one of the authors was hired as a correctional officer, she received one week of OJT and then was put on a regular shift in the prison. She never did attend the academy for correctional officers, but probably would have if she had not been promoted to the counselor position after eight months. After several months in that role she was sent to a two-week academy.

The offices of prosecutors and public defender often regard law school as one long training academy and couple that experience with on-the-job mentoring by skilled attorneys. Many state bar associations promote or require ongoing training for practicing attorneys, and some states provide formal annual training for judges and court administrators (National Center for State Courts, 2004).

Today police agencies typically require 600 to 800+ hours of training (this includes field training or OJT), whereas prisons, jails, juvenile facilities and probation and parole agencies have a mix of training requirements. Table 8.3 gives a breakdown of average number of new police officer training hours required by population size. In an analysis of 1993 Bureau of Justice Statistics data, Gaines, Worrall, Southerland, and Angell (2003) found that the larger the population served (and presumably the larger the agency itself), the longer the classroom and field training hours required for police recruits.

Training required and provided varies widely in the criminal justice system. For instance, Utah's Weber County Jail requires that correctional officers complete 12 weeks of academy training, or 480 hours. In contrast, the Utah State POST Academy for law enforcement requires 14 weeks, or 560 hours, of training for new hires in police departments. Correctional officers hired by the federal government undergo 320 hours of formal and specialized training. The New Agents' Training Unit for FBI agents requires 17 weeks, or 680 hours, of instruction at the FBI Academy in Quantico, Virginia.

Correctional officers in New York State are required to complete 8 weeks of training, or 320 hours. In Illinois the correctional officers and youth supervisors are required to complete 6 weeks of training, or 240 hours. In California, the minimum core training standard for adult corrections officers is 176 hours, for probation officers

TABLE 8.3 Training Requirements for New Officer Recruits in Local Police Departments, By Size of Population Served, 2003

| Population Served | Average Number of Hours Required | | | | | |
| | Academy | | | Field | | |
	Total	State-Mandated	Other Required	Total	State-Mandated	Other Required
All sizes	749	593	156	546	270	276
1,000,000 or more	1,171	735	436	779	329	450
500,000–999,999	966	605	361	835	288	547
250,000–499,999	1,030	620	410	933	372	561
100,000–249,999	953	650	303	991	503	488
50,000–99,999	834	658	176	977	522	455
25,000–49,999	826	657	169	894	447	447
10,000–24,999	788	644	144	759	372	387
2500–9999	733	598	135	522	269	253
Under 2500	695	552	143	333	178	155

Note: Average number of training hours excludes departments not requiring training.

Adapted from Bureau of Justice Statistics, U.S. Department of Justice (2006). Law Enforcement Management and Administrative Statistics: Local Police Departments, 2003. May 2006, NCJ 210118, Office of Justice Programs, Washington, DC.

it is 170 hours, and for juvenile corrections officers it is 126 hours.[1] In New York the state troopers take 26 weeks, or 1,040 hours, of basic training. In Illinois, new police recruits around the state must complete 400 hours of academy training.[2]

In a survey by *Corrections Compendium* 2003, a publication of the American Correctional Association, the researchers found that 31 of the reporting U.S. agencies required at least 200 hours of preservice training for those destined to work in a correctional institution (Corrections Compendium, 2003a, 2003b).

In a quick survey of 150 directors and staff trainers, with responses received from 13 states or agencies in April 2004, the Juvenile Justice Trainers Association found that about 140 to 180 hours of preservice, academy-like training is required for most new hires in juvenile facilities.[3]

In yet another survey of all states regarding adult and juvenile correctional academy training requirements, researchers for the state of California found that the range in hours required for those correctional officers working with adults was 120 to 640, for parole agents it was 40 to 440, and for correctional officers working with juveniles the range was 54 to 450 (Vohryzek-Bolden & Croisdale, 1999). Moreover, probation, staff, parole officers, and counselors in adult prisons and juvenile facilities may or may not be required to complete a formal academy training course. This may be partly because these employees are required to have more college education (Vohryzek-Bolden & Croisdale, 1999). But in that case, they are likely to have to take a test to become "certified" at the end of that training (Bureau of Labor Statistics, 2004b).

This difference in training provided to those who work as adult and youth officers in corrections versus those who work in policing or attorneys in courts (if we
regard law school as training oriented) reflects the lack of professional status accorded
some parts of correctional work. Another reason for decreased requirements is probably that different populations are served by correctional staff, versus the police or
even the courts. There may be less concern about correctional populations from the
general public and funding bodies such as state legislatures and county commissions
than there is about the people who come in contact with the police or in the courts, all
of whom are until/unless proven guilty. Most people in the community and the courts
can also vote, and they have more access to the courts in the event of real or perceived
improprieties on the part of the police or prosecutors.

Yet there is research that indicates training is key to building skills of staff, maintaining staff, and delivering services for all persons served by the criminal justice
system, including inmates and supervisees. For example, in a small study of probation
and parole officer attitudes, Fulton, Stichman, Travis, and Latessa (1997:295) found
that training made a difference in how officers related to those they supervised. They
concluded that "[a] comprehensive approach to training and development can effectively instill in officers the supervision attitudes that are most conducive to promoting
offender change."

Academy Training

Academy training typically includes a mix of topics (Bennett & Hess, 2001; *Corrections
Compendium,* 2003a, 2003b; ; FBI Training Academy, 2005; Ford, 2003; Gaines et al.,
2003; Haberfeld, 2002; Jordan, 2003; Vohryzek-Bolden & Croisdale, 1999). Typically
emphasized are first aid, CPR, interpersonal skills, communication skills, writing,
legal issues and restrictions, firearms proficiency, self-defense and physical tactics,
and supervision techniques. More specialized courses are provided for positions with
counseling, investigative, interrogation, treatment, or tactical team responsibilities
(Bureau of Labor Statistics, 2004a; FBI Training Academy, 2005; e.g., Peak, Pitts, &
Glensor, 2006).

Especially prevalent in the *Corrections Compendium* (2003a:11) survey of institutional corrections' academy training were the presence of the following topics: inmate
manipulation, report writing, and self-defense. In 100% of the responding facilities,
these three topics were covered in the academy. Next important—that were covered
by 90% or more of the responding agencies in their academies were communicable
diseases (93%), communications (98%), CPR (96%), crisis management (98%), ethics
(98%), fire/safety (96%), first aid (98%), hostages (93%), inmate classification (98%),
inmate gangs (91%), race relations (91%), security devices (96%), stress reduction
(91%), suicide prevention (93%), and use of force (98%).

In that survey of all states on amount and type of correctional training for the state
of California, Vohryzek-Bolden and Croisdale (1999) found that only eighteen states
had training academies for parole agents who supervise adults. Of those, eight states
provided training curricula to the researchers. The researchers (1999:12) found that
the training topics could be divided into the following categories: "overview, narcotics
issues, use of force, firearms training, legal, communications, departmental, parole

process, community resources, health issues, computer training, academy, and other." Of course, there was some variation in topics included and excluded from these academies. For instance, some states included extensive training on legal issues, while others barely touched on the topic. Other states included officer survival training, training on how to manage habitual offenders, sex offenders and offenses, defensive driving training, and courses on sexual harassment, stress management, ethics/professionalism, personnel, and cultural diversity (Vohryzek-Bolden & Croisdale, 1999:12–13).

Only one state (California) provided information to the researchers regarding the training curriculum for parole agents who work with juveniles. The courses offered in California include the following topics: legal issues, use of force, firearms, planning arrests and arrests, search and seizure field exercise, crisis intervention/communication, sexual harassment, labor union, mission/values, intake procedures, revocation and writing violations, and training on the California Law Enforcement Telecommunications Systems.

In the same survey, the researchers were able to determine that sixteen states had an academy for correctional officers who work with juveniles (Vohryzek-Bolden & Croisdale, 1999). Ten of those states provided training curricula to the researchers, who divided those courses into the following fifteen categories: "correctional issues, law enforcement, safety procedures, staff/ward relations, security operations, ward control, use of force, firearms training, communication, departmental, academy, ward rights, health and welfare, on-the-job training, and other" (1999:14). Again, the responding states varied greatly in the amounts and types of training provided. Moreover, the quality of the training provided is another matter entirely; it is not addressed by information on types and amounts.

In her book-length review of police training, Haberfeld (2002) found that academy training typically included the following general categories: "administrative procedures" (academy skills), "administration of justice" (history of the police and other affiliated agencies), "basic law" (types of law that affect policing and police practices), "police procedures" (the whole range of what the police do and confront), "police proficiency" (firearms and other skills and techniques necessary for success), and "community relations." Some agencies, she found, delivered their academy training in-house (e.g., Washington D.C.; Charlotte, North Carolina; Indianapolis, Indiana; New York City), while others sent their new recruits to a regional academy (e.g., the police departments of St. Petersburg, Florida, and Northern Virginia), while still others sent their new officers to the state academy (e.g., Charleston, South Carolina).

The FBI "New Agents' Training Unit" includes three components in its curriculum: "investigative/tactical, non-investigative and administrative" (FBI Academy, 2005:1). Under these components are concentrations in "academics, firearms, operational skills" and what is called "the integrated case scenario" (FBI Academy, 2005:1). New agents need to pass their academic exams with a score of 85% or better in such subjects as behavioral science, ethics, forensics, and interrogation. Physical training is also quite rigorous and requires that new recruits pass both physical agility and defensive tactics exams (see the FBI Academy website: fbi.gov/hq/td/academy/sat/sat.htm).

Beyond academy training, almost all criminal justice agencies require some form of OJT with an experienced coworker or supervisor. The Bureau of Labor Statistics (2004b), for instance, notes that most probation and parole officers, as well as counselors in prisons, work for up to a year in trainee status and on probation before they are given a permanent position.

Ongoing Training

In addition to OJT training, many criminal justice agencies require that their employees be trained as they progress through their career (Bennett & Hess 2001; Haberfeld, 2002; National Center for State Courts, 2005; Stohr, Lovrich, & Wood, 1996; Vohryzek-Bolden & Croisdale, 1999). Sometimes particular training is required, such as use of new equipment, restraint techniques, and training on sexual harassment or ethics, and sometimes it is optional. Some agencies require that their employees complete a requisite amount of training per year. Obviously, the more training required and offered, assuming that most of it is useful, the more opportunities there are for the employee to develop and to further the aims of the organization to be a "learning organization," as was discussed in Chapter 4. Training subjects offered depend to a large degree on the position one occupies and the resources of the organization. Such training might include the following:

- first-line supervisor training
- dealing with special populations (e.g., mentally ill, aged, gangs.)
- interpersonal communication skills
- building of counseling skills
- interviewing and interrogation
- treatment best practices
- terrorism/homeland security
- community relations
- diversity training
- sexual harassment
- firearms
- anger management and de-escalation
- report writing
- security techniques
- use of technical equipment
- data management
- evaluation techniques
- supervision and management theory and techniques

Common Deficiencies in Training

The substance and relevance of training varies widely from jurisdiction to jurisdiction and from job to job (Bennett & Hess, 2001; Bradford & Pynes, 1999; Cornett-DeVito & McGlone, 2000; Gaines et al., 2003; Haberfeld, 2002; National Center for State

Courts, 2005; Vohryzek-Bolden & Croisdale, 1999). Often a correctional officer at a jail will receive more or less training than a correctional officer in a juvenile facility in the same state. Larger police departments may be able to fund more ongoing training than smaller jurisdictions. Probation departments may value a more human service curriculum for training than is the case at maximum security prisons for men. The prosecutor's office may be able to fund more training than the public defender organization, should it exist. It is natural, then, for training levels and content to vary depending on the mission, available funding, and size of an organization.

It is safe to say that in too many organizations, the training for some staff is insufficient. As we have discussed throughout this book, the roles for those involved in criminal justice are complex, at times contradictory, and very challenging. The work is often hidden from public view. Therefore, the best organizations provide the training necessary to do the work in the most professional manner. Until funding bodies such as state legislatures and county commissions acknowledge these facts, however, the amount of training is not likely to increase. We are not saying that simply throwing money at the problem will fix everything, but to address serious deficiencies calls for resources (both monetary and human capital) to be directed toward this issue.

Other problems associated with the training offered in criminal justice have been concerned with the trainers and the training facilities. Concerns have been raised about the qualifications and teaching skills of trainers, both at academies and on the job, and about the lack of adequate and well-maintained facilities. The content of training offerings is not always of the best quality, either. Given the paucity of training offered to staff in some jurisdictions, there is sometimes a tendency to focus on "security" and "control" topics that while necessary do not provide the other skills that staff need daily; often lacking, for example, are training in ethics and opportunities to acquire interpersonal, anger management, or problem-solving skills (Bradford & Pynes, 1999). If managers of criminal justice agencies truly want to engage staff in meaningful dialog and receive useful input, training must precede such engagement, both for staff and for management.

One last point regarding deficiencies in training has to do with the fact that training is not a cure-all for anything that might ail an organization. As Buerger (1998:52) writes regarding police training "as a Pentecost," police managers too often rely on training for "[m]iraculous transformations on the basis of too little [words alone], too late [well after the audience is already steeped in police culture]."

PERFORMANCE APPRAISALS

Performance appraisals are typically administered formally and informally in most criminal justice and other types of agencies (see Box 8.2). The "Atta Boys" or "Atta Girls" used by the affirming manager, or the "You'd better shape up" or "Let's reconsider that decision" lectures that managers must use from time to time are very important. Such feedback is central to maintaining productivity, morale, and enthusiasm and, in the latter case, instilling discipline. The provision of regular and mostly positive, or at least supportive, feedback on the job—when that is warranted—cannot be overestimated. The research indicates that there are numerous beneficial outcomes that

BOX 8.2

JUDGE JOHN A. BOZZA ON PERSONNEL ISSUES

By Judge John A. Bozza

Courts as an administrative agency need to pay closer attention to personnel matters and efficiency. Standards have to be high to ensure performance is correspondingly elevated. Because of the nature of what courts do, even the *perception of fairness* is important. Conduct issues for personnel are very significant.

In 1994 when I became the president judge for Erie County, there were no unified personnel policies for the court; In fact, there were very few personnel policies at all. In the past political influence had been used to influence personnel decisions. So the first thing I did was to get the county to adopt a comprehensive personnel manual. The county did just that in 1995 and 1996.

Because of the special nature of courts, I feel that it is imperative that personnel policies be tailored to court-based personnel. For example, acceptance of a gift by court personnel has different implications than it may have in the legislative branch. Therefore, the Erie County Court and its units adopted a policy of not accepting gifts! This absolute prohibition on gifts faced strong opposition at first. There were practices before where attorneys provided liquor during holidays. There was not any big graft, just these kinds of favors and special treats by people for court personnel who may have to practice in front of them at some future date. Therefore, the appearance of accepting gifts or special favors, regardless of the size of the gifts, was not acceptable. Other policies put limits on partisan activities and ex parte communications in lawsuits.

I believe that all court personnel have to follow same sort of policies as judges, so the code of ethics should extend to all employees. The important point is that the policies have to accommodate those particular concerns of the courts and then be adopted in writing and, finally, they must be enforced consistently. Enforcement by the president judge in Erie County has been done consistently. Each judge, as a separately elected official, also has an obligation to enforce these rules for their own staff.

Notably, in the Erie County Court system we have no backlog. We also have more jury trials in Erie County than any other county in Pennsylvania. I attribute these efficiencies in Erie County to the establishment of standards and their enforcement throughout the court's various units.

See Box 3.10 for the extensive qualifications of Judge Bozza.

derive from the provision of regular feedback (Brody, 2004; Hackman & Oldham, 1974; Zupan & Menke, 1988). Such positive outcomes might include increased productivity, enriched jobs for staff, the recognition that what people are doing and how they are doing it is important, the confidence to continue to strive, and/or the corrective action needed to get employees back on the right track.

Performance appraisals serve the same function of affirming good work, noting any areas that might need improvement and setting goals for the next appraisal period. Performance appraisals also serve as formal departmental documents that can be used to establish a track record of work, whether outstanding or dismal, or more likely, somewhere in between. The performance appraisal may stay in the employee's file throughout his or her entire tenure. Thus, performance appraisals are often reviewed when promotions are discussed and referenced when disciplinary action is being considered.

Typically, performance appraisals are done by one's immediate supervisor after the first six months for new employees and then at, or near, the yearly anniversary of hiring. They take many forms, sometimes involving self-appraisal by the employee and then comments by the supervisor, or appraisal by the supervisor with meaningful input from the employee. At the other end of the spectrum, appraisal by the supervisor with little or no input from the employee, is sometimes the norm.

The types of items included in the appraisal form also vary; some are general statements about performance, others are related to actual job behaviors and sometimes, as mentioned in the foregoing, they encompass larger categories. General areas of evaluation might include whether the supervisee "was supportive of coworkers" and "responded appropriately to directives," among other items. Or the items might be anchored to actual job behaviors, such as "employee conducts four treatment groups per week" or "employee provides medications to inmates in a timely fashion" or "employee made ten traffic stops per week." Some instruments assess only general dimensions of behavior like "communication" or "use of resources," with subquestions that are addressed by either the supervisor or the supervisee. Or, again, the appraisal form may include general areas, which have no set response categories but instead are completed by the supervisor or the supervisee in a more free-form manner.

The responses allowed on the appraisal can take many forms as well. There may be multiple-choice questions requiring a yes or no answer. Or the possible responses might have a range of 1 to 5 or 1 to 7, covering "strongly agree" to "strongly disagree" as responses to the given statements.

In sum, performance appraisals take many forms in terms of employee involvement in the process, content of the form, and response categories. The different facets of the form tend to reflect the management style preferred by leaders and supervisors in the organization. A more traditional manager would believe in supervisor evaluation and perhaps little input—an opportunity provided at the end of the process—by the employee. A human relations or learning-oriented manager, on the other hand, would opt for greater involvement by staff in their own evaluation. Such a manager might encourage an initial self-evaluation, followed by review by the supervisor and then joint evaluation in a face-to-face interview.

The form of the appraisal instrument and its type of questions also reflect organizational traditions. Older performance appraisal instruments tend to have generalized statements about job performance that could apply to several positions. But since the 1960s and 1970s and the movement to remove bias in hiring and promotions, there has been a parallel movement to ensure that the items one is evaluated on in a performance appraisal are actually related to the job one is doing (Latham & Wexley, 1981). We might label these efforts as attempts to increase the validity of performance evaluations. What a novel idea! So, for instance, if a major task for a counselor at a Boys' Ranch is to facilitate groups on substance abuse, several items on the evaluation must be actually related to this central part of the role.

Job analysis represents one approach to increasing performance appraisal validity. A **job analysis** allows the employer to determine what tasks are routinely required for the job and to ensure that those are then evaluated on the performance appraisal instrument (Latham & Wexley, 1981). One version of a job analysis is the Critical Incident Technique (see Box 8.3). The advantages inherent in the development of the instrument in this manner are that employees are intimately engaged in deciding the content of the evaluation. Thus, since they developed the instrument, a general sense of fairness and ownership attends the process. Moreover, should a performance appraisal be challenged in an administrative proceeding, it is more likely to be seen as fair if the items are job valid. The disadvantage of developing such an instrument is that it can be time-consuming to work through each major job category. Notably, some items on this instrument could be shared by several jobs when there are responsibilities and tasks that are shared across roles (e.g., security), thus obviating the need to develop wholly different instruments for each job.

BOX 8.3

USING THE CRITICAL INCIDENT TECHNIQUE TO DEVELOP A JOB-VALID PERFORMANCE APPRAISAL INSTRUMENT

Typically, this technique, which is also used to develop selection instruments, requires that several people who actually do the job, and those who directly supervise them, describe situations in which they witnessed job behavior that they regarded as particularly effective (Latham & Wexley, 1981). Then those people are asked to describe situations that afforded examples of particularly ineffective job behaviors. From these examples, items are developed that reflect actual job behaviors. These behaviors are reviewed by the jobholders and their supervisors for validity purposes and then pretested in an appraisal process. Once the bugs have been worked out, an appraisal form emerges that actually measures real job behaviors (Latham & Wexley, 1981). The advantage of developing the instrument this way is that the instrument is job valid. However, this technique is time-consuming if it must be applied to every position in the institution.

Best Practices in Performance Appraisal

All this discussion of the performance appraisal instrument and its validity presupposes that the knowledge level about job performance is sufficient to permit a valid appraisal. But sometimes it is not. Sometimes supervisors and managers are too busy to pay attention to what their supervisees are doing. When this happens, there can be no valid evaluation. Therefore, in the interest of establishing and reiterating some basic parameters for performance appraisals, or best or optimal practices, the authors, along with others, (Coutts & Schneider, 2004; Latham & Wexley, 1981; Wessel, 2003; see also Box 8.4), offer the following.

1. Allow high involvement of subordinates in the whole process; this will enhance their satisfaction with the appraisal process, and consequently their productivity.

2. Supply supportive behavior throughout employment; this will increase the employee's satisfaction with the appraisal.

3. Engage in joint problem solving about specific goals with the employee; this will increase productivity in those areas.

4. In the evaluation of high-performing individuals, minimize critical comments on the performance appraisal.

5. For those who are struggling in the workplace, provide feedback on problem behavior that is clearly documented in the performance appraisal.

6. Observe employee behavior on a regular basis (daily if possible).

7. Interact with supervisees on a regular basis (daily if possible) and know or find out what they are doing and how they are doing it.

8. Observe the workplace or work setting of supervisees on a regular basis (sometimes supervisors do not work in the same physical location as the supervisee).

BOX 8.4

JUDICIAL PERFORMANCE EVALUATIONS AND JUDICIAL ELECTIONS

In an effort to improve judicial performance, some states began instituting judicial performance evaluation programs in the 1970s. In a study of evaluation programs for judges in Washington State, Brody (2004) administered surveys to witnesses, jurors, and attorneys appearing before participating judges. The responses garnered from the witnesses and jurors did not match the perceptions of the same judges the attorneys had rated. Nevertheless, Brody (2004) noted that judges found the information collected from these surveys useful for improving their performance, and the cost of the study was relatively low. Brody argues that such evaluations can be a beneficial instrument for improving judicial performance and voter knowledge of it.

"Walking-around management" is frequently cited as an effective technique. Managers need to know at a minimum such things as how the job is being done by each supervisee, whether he or she needs more resources or training to do the job effectively, and how he or she interacts with coworkers and those under his or her supervision.

9. Make yourself available to those you supervise. The old "open door policy" is a good one. Supervisees should feel they can approach the supervisor with problems and issues related to job performance and job tasks.

10. Provide regular and informal feedback to employees. As most work by employees is done well, most of this feedback should be positive. But employees going down the wrong track need to be corrected, if possible, before or in addition to, the formal evaluation.

In other words, employees need to be actively engaged in the process, and managers and supervisors need to be proactive in their supervision. If managers do not allow for participation in the process and neglect to engage in active observation and walking-around management, they may succumb to basing evaluations on exceptional and nonrepresentative incidents, gossip, or the production of poor performers who substitute obsequious behavior for real work. Nothing is more demoralizing for outstanding performers than to see poor performers rewarded because they have charmed a supervisor, rather than because of merit (Coutts & Schneider, 2004).

A Final Problem in Appraisals

If these best practices are adopted, the criminal justice manager or supervisor is more likely to be able to fairly evaluate job performance and less likely to encounter the problems associated with appraisals. Similarly, if mangers or supervisors allow for employee input into the process and make sure that the instrument itself fits the job it is being used to evaluate, there will be fewer problems. But a final problem with appraisals, which can be alleviated, but not eliminated if these other issues are attended to, is the matter of over or underevaluating performance. This is a problem that is associated with the manager.

Some managers tend to rate their employees too harshly, and others are too soft in their ratings (Wessel, 2003). This is the Mama Bear, Papa Bear, and Baby Bear problem of performance appraisals. It is hard for managers to settle on the "just right" bed of evaluation. If "too hard" on employees, particularly those who are doing an excellent job, people tend to become discouraged. If "too soft," some employees may slack off, and the best employees may lose heart as even poor performers are rated highly. These disparities in ratings will seem particularly unfair if supervisors in the same unit or organization tend to vary a great deal in their evaluations. People will see and feel how unfair this situation is. Moreover, the problem of disciplining poor performers will be made harder because their evaluations will be lacking the feedback that would be necessary to support disciplinary action. Any manager or supervisor who has been on the job for more than a year is likely to have seen the deleterious effects of failing to evaluate accurately.

One means of alleviating the problem and moving supervisors closer to the "Baby Bear" perspective is to train supervisors on how to do the evaluation and how to use the performance appraisal instrument (Latham & Wexley, 1981). Such training should allow some time to discuss appraisal scenarios and to play-act evaluation perspectives and techniques.

RETENTION STRATEGIES

Our final area of personnel policies and practices is keeping the best and the brightest working in criminal justice agencies. These strategies must be multifaceted, incorporating, at a minimum, adequate pay, career paths, and a fulfilling job design (e.g., McCampbell, 2006).

Pay Isn't Everything, But It Is Something

Turnover can be acute when the economy is humming along and the pay for criminal justice staff is not competitive with other public or private sector work. As is often said by those who espouse a human relations perspective on management, "pay isn't everything." But we would argue it is "something" and figures largely in the decision making of employees (DeFrances, 2002; Patenaude, 2001; Yearwood, 2003; Smith, 1997; Stohr, Self, & Lovrich, 1992; Whisenand, 2004). As discussed earlier, working in some sectors of criminal justice (e.g., institutional corrections) is not the first career choice for some people (Conover, 2001). Therefore, competitive pay for public sector work will keep employees on the job and motivated, even when other opportunities for employment are presented.

For instance, in a national survey of prosecutors, DeFrances (2002) found that low salaries were regarded as the primary reason about a third of the offices were experiencing problems with recruitment and retention of deputy prosecutors. Yearwood (2003) found in an analysis of recruitment and retention issues in North Carolina detention centers that an annual pay increase was rated as the most effective retention technique an agency can employ. Similarly, in a study to explain a high turnover rate of correctional staff (35% from 1998 to 2001) working in Arkansas prisons, Patenaude (2001:58) reported that "[p]ay and benefits were two primary concerns identified in the surveys and discussed by each focus group." About 18% of the respondents in Patenaude's study said they worked in the Arkansas Department of Corrections because they needed a job to support their families, and only about 10% saw that work as a long-term career choice. Meanwhile about 22% would leave if their pay and benefits did not increase and another 18% would leave if they could get better pay elsewhere. Patenaude (2001:58) concluded that: "Pay remains the major contributor to resentment and discontent within the correctional ranks and must be regarded as a major contributor to turnover."

Moreover, staff may be less likely to engage in corrupt activities and be more committed to their work if they are paid decently (Patenaude, 2001). Recall, for instance, that on Maslow's hierarchy the bottom two rungs include needs that are met primarily through financial compensation. For example, an employee of a criminal justice organization whose family qualifies for food stamps is a good indication that pay levels are far too low to motivate workers.

According to the latest figures from the Bureau of Labor Statistics (2004a), many work characteristics affect hourly wages: whether the job is considered white collar, blue collar, or service related; whether it is full or part time, union or nonunion: the size of the organization; its location in a metropolitan location, or not, and the geographic area. As one might expect, white-collar positions, those in union shops, and in metropolitan areas of New England, mid-Atlantic or Pacific regions of the country tended to pay the most. Unfortunately, prosecutors and defense attorneys are not separated out in these data, though mean hourly wages for lawyers ($46.11) and judges ($56.65), or roughly $95,908 and $117,832, are listed under the white-collar category. Of course, these figures grossly exaggerate what public sector defense attorneys and prosecutors make in most jurisdictions. Police officers and detectives, listed under the service category, had a mean hourly wage of $23.57; sheriff's deputies, bailiffs, and other law enforcement personnel had a mean hourly wage of $18.64; and correctional institution officers had a mean hourly wage of $16.70. The annual salaries were roughly $49,026, $38,771, and $34,736, respectively.

There is some variation in pay depending on the level of government. According to another report by the Bureau of Labor Statistics (2004b), in 2002 the median pay for federal correctional officers was $40,000, for states it was $33,000, and for localities it was $31,000. Private sector employment for correctional officers paid much less, with a median salary of $21,000. Starting salaries for these positions ranged in the low $20,000s, with federal correctional officers starting at $23,000. The Bureau of Labor Statistics (2004b) also reports that the median salary for first-line supervisors and managers in corrections was $44,000 in 2002.

Probation officers and correctional treatment specialists tended to make more than correctional officers (Bureau of Labor Statistics, 2004c). The median salary for these two positions in 2002 was approximately $38,000. The mean range of salaries was $30,000 to $50,000, with the lowest paid making about $25,000 and the highest paid taking home about $62,000. Surprisingly, those in local government, often in urban areas, had higher median earnings ($39,000) than those employed by the states ($38,000).

Maintenance, medical, and kitchen personnel make various wage averages dependent, to some extent, on the marketability of their skills. Generally, and in terms of the whole pay and benefit package, those working at the federal level make more than those working in the states; those working in the adult system make more than those working with juveniles; those working in the state system make more than those working for counties or municipalities; those working in a union shop make more than those who do not; and those working for a public sector organization make more than those working for the private sector. But, having said this, there is a wide range of pay across states and localities and job types that make these averages somewhat misleading. Of course, the cost of living in a given area of the country also accounts for some of these compensation differences (Bureau of Labor Statistics, 2004a, 2004b, 2004c). But, not surprisingly, in a survey on pay by *Corrections Compendium* the researchers concluded (2003:8) that "[t]he only common pattern or trend regarding correctional staff wages is the lack of any common pattern or trend."

Another generality is that correctional work tends to pay less than other public sector work like policing or work for the courts. But this does not always hold. One of the authors remembers being shocked when a lieutenant in a Nevada jail told her in 1990 that his compensation package was about $70,000 per year. When she indicated her surprise, he said that correctional officers who frequently worked overtime in his facility made even more. Not surprisingly, we found in research on that jail that the officers and other staff in his facility were some of the most satisfied with their work.

However, pay does not represent *all* the issues surrounding turnover for many criminal justice professionals. For example, Sexton (2006) found in a survey of police chiefs that rapid turnover was due, in part, to five main reasons: health, stress, personnel issues, politics, and job advancement. So pay isn't everything, but it is something.

Career Path

Once the basic compensation needs of staff are met, and if Maslow (1998) is correct, there are other elements of the job that serve as motivators. One such element is whether there is a clearly defined and attainable career path for staff. If staff are motivated by the higher-level needs of respect, belonging (love), and self-actualization at work, as one might expect the best and brightest employees, in particular, to be, they will stay on the job if there is a future for them up the ranks. Specifically, they will be increasingly interested in shouldering greater responsibility and opportunities to make decisions about their work. To some extent, these needs can be met by structuring democratic participation into the work. Eventually, however, some of the best employees are going to want to become managers, or at least supervisors.

Current managers need to provide a clear and identifiable means for such people to advance by outlining for them work expectations (via performance appraisals and other means of feedback) and background requirements (training, work experience, and education levels) and by providing the training and work opportunities that allow people to develop the skills that will be needed for advancement. Likewise, some agencies even provide funding for employee continuing education or have cooperative agreements with local professional schools, colleges, and universities. For instance, Kiekbusch, Price, and Theis (2003:67) found in their examination of five jail settings in the United States that there was a positive influence on retention when the sheriff in a jail communicated "realistic promotion support." Mentoring of the "water-walkers," by current managers will go far toward keeping those best and brightest employees motivated and on the job.

Job Design: Criminal Justice Work for the 21st Century

The topic of job design tends to encompass all the other personnel practices discussed in this and some of the other chapters. **Job design** just refers to how a job or task is structured. A job is said to be *enriched* if it provides opportunities for meaningful work and input. Hackman and Oldham (1974) developed one of the most well-known and often used measures of job design in their Job Diagnostic Survey. To use this survey, respondents estimate on a seven-point scale the degree to which certain attributes presently apply to their own job. Included in the instrument are questions geared toward deciphering the degree of *task identification, autonomy, skill variety, task significance,* and *feedback* perceived to exist in one's work; these characteristics represent the attributes of an "enriched" job. According to Hackman and Oldham (1974), these five "core job dimensions" translate into three "critical psychological states," which result in personal and work outcomes of high internal work motivation, high quality of work performance, high satisfaction with the work, and low absenteeism and turnover.

Skill variety, task identity, and task significance compose the critical psychological state of "experienced meaningfulness of the work"; autonomy measures the critical state of "experienced responsibility for outcomes of the work"; and feedback measures the critical psychological state of "knowledge of actual results of the work activities." Each of the job characteristic scores is weighted to reflect the relative importance of each dimension, and all the scores are combined to create a single "motivating potential" score. The motivating potential scores range from 0 to 360, with 0 reflecting a total absence of motivating potential and 360 indicating a total fulfillment of said potential.

Some colleagues and one of the authors used this instrument in a study of turnover and stress among correctional staff working in five jails around the country (Stohr, Lovrich, Menke, & Zupan, 1994). They found, among other things, that job enrichment, when combined with other model personnel and management practices, is associated with less stress and turnover. Furthermore, in a study including over seventy-three federal prisons, Wright, Saylor, Gilman and Camp (1997:525) found that "[j]ob autonomy and participation in decision making (by employees) are associated with enhanced occupational outcomes including higher job satisfaction, stronger commitment to the institution, greater effectiveness in working with inmates, and less job-related stress."

When we discuss job enrichment and job design in our criminal justice management classes we always ask students to consider what would be their "ideal" attributes of a job (see the 8.1 on job design at the end of this chapter). They often mention such issues as pay, work hour flexibility, variety, and the ability to make a difference in the lives of others or in their community—not necessarily in this order. As our discussion of these personnel practices in this chapter would indicate, good people will be, and are, attracted to criminal justice work when the compensation is reasonable; but they will stay on the job, even in an economy where jobs are plentiful, if they have some control and say in their work and if it is designed to give them opportunities to make their mark in the world.

The research indicates that an enriched job tends to result in distinct and measurable outcomes (Bennett & Hess, 2001; Sims, 2001; Slate, Vogel, & Johnson 2001; Stohr et al., 1994; Zupan & Menke, 1988). Lower turnover, greater job satisfaction, and less stress are some of the outcomes that are believed to accompany a more enriched job and longer tenure in criminal justice professions (e.g., Strickland, 2006).

CONCLUSIONS

Managing the personnel processes in an organization is always difficult; it is doubly so in criminal justice agencies. The multilayered mission of these agencies makes personnel processes vitally important, as the very liberty and safety of other staff and community members/clients/inmates are at risk if serious mistakes occur. In this chapter we discussed all major aspects of personnel processes.

We discussed the selection process, training, and performance appraisal in this chapter. These processes can certainly tax the resources of the organization; but if they are not done right, the cost can be very high. The staff *are* the organization when it comes to criminal justice agencies. They comprise over 60 to 80% of costs, and the organization that fails to select, train, evaluate, and keep the best of their recruits is not achieving what would otherwise be possible. If the selection process is not valid, if the training is not useful or nonexistent, and if the appraisal process is inaccurate, the best staff will not be selected, nor will the better workers be persuaded to stay.

Organizations that do these things right (or as near to right as they can be done) must also make sure that the job itself pays a reasonable wage, has a clear career path that allows for, and even promotes, the advancement of the best and brightest, and provides as many enriched jobs as possible. Not all jobs in criminal justice can meet the ideal of "enrichment." Most, however, can provide avenues for advancement, training, or some variety to allow staff to appreciate their work and the meaningful contributions they are making.

EXERCISE: JOB DESIGN

Before we discuss job design in our management classes, we ask the students to fantasize about the attributes of their dream job. We think that this mental exercise, followed by some listing of these attributes on the board and discussion, helps people both to understand what job design is and to focus on what kind of work environment and tasks appeal to them. Finally, we ask the students to relate their desirable job characteristics to those described by Hackman and Oldham: Are the two sets similar in content?

Although we think these goals are best achieved if we do this exercise before the lecture on job design, the exercise might fruitfully be employed at the end of the lecture as well. As most of these students have some kind of work experience (few are "silver spooners" at the urban state school we currently teach at), our discussion usually includes references to jobs people have already held.

DISCUSSION QUESTIONS

1. Why is the cost consideration so important in personnel processes? Explain your answer.

2. How does the cost of each step in the selection process determine when those steps are taken? Explain your answer.

3. What does the term "job validity" mean, and how does it apply to selection and performance appraisal processes? Give an example of how it applies.

4. Why do correctional workers tend to receive less training than those who work for police departments? What does this difference in training mean for those respective roles?

5. What are the best methods for selecting and keeping the "water-walker" workers in criminal justice? Why don't all criminal justice organizations engage in more of these strategies?

6. Why does the selection process differ for criminal attorneys and for policing and corrections personnel?

7. How do management theories influence the way that selection, training, and performance appraisal are done in criminal justice agencies? Give an example.

KEY TERMS

job analysis: allows the employer to determine what tasks are routinely required for the job and to ensure that those are evaluated on the performance appraisal instrument (Latham & Wexley, 1981).

job design: refers to how a job or task is structured.

job-valid qualification: related to attributes or abilities that are needed to get the job done (age, weight, eyesight, etc.).

performance appraisals: typically administered in most criminal, justice and other types of agencies, both formally and informally; they serve the same function of affirming good work, noting areas that may need improvement, and setting goals for the next appraisal period. performance appraisals serve as formal departmental documents that can be used to establish a track record of work.

NOTES

1. These figures were supplied in response to an email request sent to the California Board of Corrections in April 2004 (webmaster@BdCorr.CA.Gov).
2. Numbers of required training hours were gathered from the relevant agency websites.
3. Barbara Collins, executive director of the Juvenile Justice Trainers Association, kindly provided these figures after quickly surveying her contacts via e-mail. The Juvenile Justice Trainers Association in Ben Lomand, California, may be contacted by calling (831) 336–0611 or e-mailing www.jjta.org.

REFERENCES

Austin, J., & Irwin J. (2001). It's about time: America's imprisonment binge. Belmont, CA: Wadsworth/Thomson Learning.

Bennett, W. W., & Hess, K. M. (2001). *Management and supervision in law enforcement* (3rd ed.). Belmont, CA: Wadsworth/Thomson Learning.

Bradford, D., & Pynes, J. E. (1999). Police academy training: Why hasn't it kept up with practice? *Police Quarterly, 2,* 283–301.

Brody, D. C. (2004). The relationship between judicial performance evaluations and judicial elections. *Judicature, 87,* 168–192.

Buerger, M. (1998). Police training as a Pentecost. *Police Quarterly, 1*, 27–64.

Bureau of Justice Statistics, U.S. Department of Justice. (2006). *Law enforcement management and administrative statistics: Local police departments, 2003.* May 2006, NCJ 210118, Office of Justice Programs, Washington, DC.

Bureau of Labor Statistics, U.S. Department of Labor. (2004a). *National compensation survey: Occupational wages in the United States, July 2003.* Accessed at http://www.bls.gov/oco/ncs/ocs/sp/ncbl0658.pdf, August 29, 2005.

Bureau of Labor Statistics, U.S. Department of Labor. (2004b). *Occupational outlook handbook, 2004–05 edition, correctional officers.* Accessed at http://www.bls.gov/oco/ocos156.htm, April 8, 2004.

Bureau of Labor Statistics, U.S. Department of Labor. (2004c). *Occupational outlook handbook, 2004–05 edition, probation officers and correctional treatment specialists.* Accessed at http://www.bls.gov/oco/ocos265.htm, April 8, 2004.

Conover, T. (2000). *New Jack: Guarding Sing Sing.* New York: Random House.

Cornett-DeVito, M. M., & McGlone, E. L. (2000). Multicultural communication training for law enforcement officers: A case study. *Criminal Justice Policy Review, 11*, 234–253.

Corrections Compendium. (2003a). Correctional officer education and training. *Corrections Compendium, 28*(2), 11–12.

Corrections Compendium. (2003b). Wages and benefits paid to correctional employees. *Corrections Compendium, 28*(1), 8–9.

Coutts, L. M., & Schneider, F. W. (2004). Police officer performance appraisal systems: How good are they? *Policing: An International Journal of Police Strategies and Management, 27*, 67–81.

DeFrances, C. J. (2002). *Prosecutors in state courts.* (2001). Bureau of Justice Statistics Bulletin. U.S. Department of Justice, Office of Justice Programs. Washington, DC: GPO.

FBI Training Academy. (2005). *New agents' training unit.* Accessed at www.fbi.gov/hq/td/academy/sat/sat.htm, August 26, 2005.

Ford, R. E. (2003). Saying one thing, meaning another: The role of parables in police training. *Police Quarterly, 6*, 84–110.

Fulton, B., Stichman, A., Travis, L., & Latessa, E. (1997). Moderating probation and parole officer attitudes to achieve desired outcomes. *The Prison Journal, 77*(3), 295–312.

Gaines, L. K., Worrall, J. L., Southerland, M. D., & Angell, J. E. (2003). *Police administration* (2nd ed.). Boston: McGraw-Hill.

Haberfeld, M. R. (2002). *Critical issues in police training.* Upper Saddle River, NJ: Prentice Hall.

Hackman, J. R., & Oldham, G. R. (1974). *The job diagnostic survey: An instrument for the diagnosis of jobs and the evaluation of job redesign projects* (Tech. Rep. No. 4). New Haven, CT: Yale University, Department of Administrative Sciences.

Jordan, L. (2003). *Physical fitness standards in law enforcement.* Paper presented at the Western and Pacific Association of Criminal Justice Educators Conference, Park City, UT, October 2003.

Kiekbusch, R., Price, W., & Theis, J. (2003). Turnover predictors: Causes of employee turnover in sheriff-operated jails. *Criminal Justice Studies, 16*(2), 67–76.

Latham, G. P., & Wexley, K. N. (1981). *Increasing productivity through performance appraisal.* Menlo Park, CA: Addison-Wesley.

Lonsway, K. A. (2003). Tearing down the wall: Problems with consistency, validity, and adverse impact of physical agility testing in police selection. *Police Quarterly, 6*(3), 237–277.

Maslow, A. H. (1998). *Maslow on management.* New York: Wiley.

Mays, G. L., and Winfree L. T. (2002). Contemporary corrections. Belmont, CA: Wadsworth/ Thomson Learning.

McCampbell, S. B. (2006). Recruiting and retaining jail employees: Money isn't the long-term solution. *American Jails, 20*(2), 9–15.

National Center for State Courts. (2005). *National Center for State Courts Newsletter, 7*, 1–11.

Patenaude, A. L. (2001). Analysis of issues affecting correctional officer retention within the Arkansas Department of Correction. *Corrections Management Quarterly, 5*(2), 49–67.

Peak, K. J., Pitts, S., & Glensor, R. W. 2006. *From FTO to PTO: A contemporary approach to post-academy recruit training.* Paper presented at the Western and Pacific Association of Criminal Justice Educators Annual Conference, Reno, Nv.

Ruddell, R., & Main, R. 2006. Evaluating E-learning for staff training. *American Jails, 20*(3), 39–43.

Sexton, D. 2006. Tenure and turnover of small town police chiefs. *Police Forum, 15*(3), 13–20.

Sims, B. (2001). Surveying the correctional environment: A review of the literature. *Corrections Management Quarterly, 5*(2), 1–12.

Slate, R. N., Vogel, R. E., & Johnson, W. W. (2001). To quit or not to quit: Perceptions of participation in correctional decision making and the impact of organizational stress. *Corrections Management Quarterly, 5*(2), 68–78.

Smith, C. (1997). *Courts, politics, and the judicial process* (2nd ed.). Chicago: Nelson-Hall.

Stohr, M. K., Lovrich, N. P., & Wood, M. J. (1996). Service v. security concerns in contemporary jails: Testing behavior differences in training topic assessments. *Journal of Criminal Justice, 24*(5), 437–448.

Stohr, M. K., Lovrich, N. P., Menke, B. A., & Zupan, L. L. (1994). Staff management in correctional institutions: Comparing DiIulio's 'control model' and 'employee investment model' outcomes in five jails. *Justice Quarterly, 11*(3), 471–497.

Stohr, M. K., Self, R. L., & Lovrich, N. P. (1992). Staff turnover in new generation jails: An investigation of its causes and prevention. *Journal of Criminal Justice, 20*(5), 455–478.

Strickland, M. J. (2006). Causations of stress among correctional officers. *American Jails, 20*(3), 69–77.

Thibault, E. A., Lynch, L. M., & McBride, R. B. (2004). *Proactive Police Management* (6th ed.). Upper Saddle River, NJ: Pearson–Prentice Hall.

U.S. Equal Employment Opportunity Commission, U.S. Department of Justice, Civil Rights Division. (2002). *Americans with Disabilities Act: Questions and answers.* Accessed at http://www.usdoj.gov/crt/ada/q%26aeng02.htm, December 10, 2006.

Vohryzek-Bolden, M., & Croisdale, T. (1999). *Overview of selected states' academy and in-service training for adult and juvenile correctional employees.* Conducted for the California Commission on Correctional Peace Officer Standards and Training. National Institute of Corrections, Longmont, CO.

Wessel, H. (2003, December 28). In search of the perfect performance appraisal. *The Idaho Statesman,* p. CB 1.

Whisenand, P. M. (2004). *Supervising police personnel: The fifteen responsibilities* (5th ed.). Upper Saddle River, NJ: Pearson–Prentice Hall.

Wright, K. N., Saylor, W. G., Gilman, E., & Camp, S. (1997). Job control and occupational outcomes among prison workers. *Justice Quarterly, 14*(3), 525–546.

Yearwood, D. L. (2003). Recruitment and retention issues in North Carolina. *American Jails, 17*(4), 9–14.

Zupan, L. L., & Menke, B. A. (1988). Implementing organizational change: From traditional to new generation jail operations. *Policy Studies Review, 7*, 615–625.

CHAPTER 9

SELECTION ISSUES: WORKFORCE 2000, DIVERSITY, AND AFFIRMATIVE ACTION

Today we hold that the Law School has a compelling interest in attaining a diverse student body.... Major American businesses have made clear that the skills needed in today's increasingly global marketplace can only be developed through exposure to widely diverse people, cultures, ideas and viewpoints.

(Justice Sandra Day O'Connor, writing for the majority in
Grutter v. Bollinger et al., June 2003)

Even though nearly two-thirds of respondents [in a 2003 Gallup Poll] say that race relations will always be a problem in America, when confronted with the prediction that in 2050, a majority of people in the U.S. will be non-white, the vast majority said it wouldn't matter or that it would be a good thing.

(Civil Rights Coalition for the 21st Century 2004:1)

INTRODUCTION: THE 21ST-CENTURY WORKFORCE

The workforce of the 21st century will meld the talents, beliefs, and cultures of a diverse population. And that future is now.

In most criminal justice workplaces the number of women employed has increased significantly, and the number of minority men sometimes mirrors their representation in the larger population (Maguire & Pastore, 2004). Criminal justice client populations for some time now have tended to include a much more ethnically and racially diverse group than those who were hired to handle them. Though there are not anywhere near the number of minority group members among employees as among typical client populations (Joseph, Henriques, & Ekeh, 2003; Lester, 2003), there is a greater congruence in this regard than there once was.

That criminal justice workplaces are much more diverse racially, ethnically, and genderwise can be laid squarely at the door of affirmative action. In practical terms, **affirmative action** simply means *that an organization takes positive steps to ensure that its hiring practices are fair and do not disparately impact a targeted underrepresented group.* The integration of the workplace generally, and specifically in criminal justice, did not occur until affirmative action plans had been mandated and implemented, first on a limited scale affecting government contractors and universities. Because of the importance of this manifest change in criminal justice employment in the last thirty years, we spend some time in this chapter discussing diversity, its importance, and affirmative action as they pertain to personnel processes. But first, it is worth discussing now, as we are squarely in the new millennium, Workforce 2000 and the job market generally.

WORKFORCE 2000

In the 1990s there were a number of studies of "workforce 2000" as the new century approached (Workforce Development Strategies, 2004; see also Workforce 2000 reports on the web). Typically, such reports indicated that the workforce of the future would be more ethnically and racially diverse and would include more females. Furthermore, such studies indicated that there would be a shortage of competent, educated, and qualified people to fill all the available jobs. Currently, we shall see, there is a surplus of applicants for many positions advertised in criminal justice, though the vast majority of those applicants may not fit the qualifications for the jobs. But the authors of the Workforce 2000 reports thought this trend would reverse itself in the first decade of the new century as baby boomers retired and the next two generations, which are proportionately smaller, took their place in the workforce. Of course, the hope is that the new generations will have received the proper education necessary for these jobs.

DEALING WITH DIVERSITY

As the larger community becomes more diverse, so will that workforce. A key to dealing with or managing diversity in the workplace is raising awareness and understanding of diverse groups and cultures (Cox & Beale, 1997). This need will become doubly important, literally, as the century proceeds. The U.S. Census Bureau (2004) projects that from 2000 to 2050 the proportion of minorities in the population will skyrocket. Specifically, the number of Hispanics and Asians as a percentage of the population will double, and the number of African Americans will increase, as will the percentage of other nonwhite racial and ethnic groups. By 2050 about 52% of the population (including white Hispanics) will belong to what we refer to now as a minority group, but by then (2050) may not be (U.S. Census Bureau, 2004).

Cox and Beale (1997), in their book *Developing Competency to Manage Diversity,* argue that managing diversity is a business strategy that is key to increasing organizational effectiveness and performance. For instance, greater diversity in the workforce may contribute to the ability to problem-solve and innovate for public sector organizations faced with diverse clientele. They cite research that indicates that a failure to "manage" diversity, or to build awareness and understanding, leads to such negative organizational outcomes as absenteeism and turnover, harassment, discrimination suits, and stymied communications. They recommend that organizations interested in managing diversity develop individual and organizational level competencies that dispel myths, misconceptions, and stereotypes about minority groups and at the same time build skills in handling situations in which diversity becomes an issue. Individuals, for instance, would need to be trained to do the following:

- understand group identities and how those affect self-concepts, perceptions of historical events, and cognitive styles
- recognize stereotyping and understand how stereotypes can act as a barrier to teamwork

- acknowledge cultural, age, and cross-gender differences and how these may affect perceptions of the quality of life

- see the existence of prejudice and discrimination and their effects in organizations, including those revolving around race, ethnicity, and gender, but also disabilities and sexual orientation (Cox & Beale, 1997:49–198)

Likewise, organizations and managers, need be mindful of, and trained, regarding the following factors:

- organizational culture, or the bicultural experience for minorities and religious diversity, as that affects the organizations' culture

- formal and informal structure of the organizations including affirmative action and mentoring programs

- how to change the organization through education and a plan so that diversity is positively managed

- how the organization and the individual can engage in continuous learning to ensure that diverse groups are well managed (Cox & Beale, 1997:199–332)

In sum, employees and managers in the private and public sector will be more diverse in the near future. To tap into the talent and skills that diverse groups bring to the table, criminal justice managers will need to anticipate this trend and develop strategies and plans to accommodate the changing workforce. As indicated in Table 9.1 and 9.2, and by way of example, first-line supervisor/managers of correctional officers are currently a diverse lot, with approximately 31% of workers from minority groups and 25% female (see also Box 9.1). As the population shifts in its proportion of minority group members, the corrections workforce for the 21st century will undoubtedly shift in the same direction.

SELECTION PROCESSES: WHO WANTS TO WORK IN CRIMINAL JUSTICE?

The answer to the question, "Who wants to work in criminal justice?" is: quite a few people. For every correctional officer position offered in (the Ada County Jail) our local county jail in Boise, Idaho, there are usually twelve applicants.[1] According to Norm Brisson, Legal Administrator for the Denver Prosecutor's Office, when a prosecutor's job becomes available in Denver, the office reviews the résumés on hand (usually 40 to 90) and interviews up to ten applicants. By extension, thousands of people apply for jobs in criminal justice agencies every year. What is worthy of note, however, is that many of these applicants may not be qualified for the job and some may not truly want to work in those positions permanently, but see them as stopgap employment until the factory reopens or as steady employment in a state that has lost timber or manufacturing jobs (Bennett & Hess, 2001; Conover, 2000; Crouch & Marquart, 1994; Lombardo, 1989). Of course, in the latter case of downsized workers looking for steady employment, there can be successful work arrangements even though the job was not a new hire's first career choice.

BOX 9.1

AN ORGANIZATIONAL EXPERT DISCUSSES THE "BUSINESS CASE"
FOR DIVERSITY IN JUSTICE ORGANIZATIONS

By Jan Salisbury

For the past ten years, the most successful companies and businesses have willingly implemented diversity programs that vastly exceed affirmative action programs. Their efforts include ongoing training, active recruiting and mentoring, and measuring management on their ability to retain and manage. Their primary "business case" for this new strategic focus is that to sustain a competitive advantage, they need to recruit the best and the brightest and respond to an increasingly diverse customer and client base. Further, these organizations have realized that a functional diverse work force enhances creativity and innovation in a diverse global economy. The "business case" for managing diversity in justice organizations is indisputable. Not only is there an escalating increase of people of color and women vying for jobs, but the population served in the justice system is overwhelming nonwhite, particularly in large urban areas.

The business of implementing justice is above all a people business, and effective justice professionals must have superior communications skills with which to rehabilitate and control diverse populations. For example, until women began entering corrections and policing in great numbers, there was a stereotype that the indirect, relationship style of women would be disastrous for conflict situations. The result, however, has been the opposite. Women have been very effective in de-escalating conflict with inmates and creating relationships with the community that have led to more control, not less. Other dimensions of diversity are adding value as well. As in business, employing African Americans, Asians, different generations, and people with a variety of backgrounds creates a kaleidoscope of perspectives mirroring the diverse population served and encouraging culturally relevant solutions to workplace and institutional problems. For example, the more direct style of African Americans is less threatening to someone whose own upbringing sees it as a style, and not as an invitation to a fight. As immigrants continue to enter the justice system, the need for multilingual employees also increases.

During the past decade, research has consistently shown that teams who are diverse in problem-solving styles, ethnicity, gender, etc. are more effective and successful than homogeneous groups in solving problems and accomplishing tasks. While homogeneous teams may be more emotionally comfortable for individuals, they do not encourage thinking "out of the box." However, this research also notes that diverse groups need the training and skills to recognize, appreciate, and utilize their diversity. Otherwise, teams may polarize and stereotype their differences! In addition, leaders need coaching and training to understand the value of their diverse teams and to lead them through conflict to cohesiveness. Creating an inclusive work environment also helps institutions retain great employees. When people know that they have an equal opportunity to contribute and where that input and backgrounds are appreciated, they are less likely to withdraw from work or to look for work elsewhere.

Finally, because that which gets rewarded tends to result in work completed, leaders in the justice community should consider articulating the skills and behaviors required for working with diverse populations (e.g., empathy, self-reflection, flexibility, and tolerance for ambiguity) in their performance evaluation systems. The commitment to implement diversity in justice organizations cannot be a strictly "training" effort, but must be part of leaders' strategic plan that implements inclusive policies and values working effectively with diverse "others" as much as it does interrogation methods and other technical skills.

Jan Salisbury is president of Salisbury Consulting,. which specializes in organizational development with a focus on developing leaders, team building, emotional intelligence, and implementing diversity. Salisbury's research is published in psychological journals, and she is the coauthor, with Bobbi Killian Dominick of Investigating Harassment and Discrimination Complaints: A Practical Guide (2004).

TABLE 9.1 U.S.: Census 2000 Data: Employment by Occupation, Sex, and Race/Ethnicity.

Number of First-Line Supervisors/Managers of Correctional Officers					
Total	**W-NH**	**H**	**B-NH**	**AIAN-NH**	**A-NH**
45,730	30,705	3,539	10,130	345	314

Percentages						
	Total	**W-NH**	**H**	**B-NH**	**AIAN-NH**	**A-NH**
Male	74.7	52.5	5.8	14.3	0.5	0.5
Female	25.3	14.7	1.9	7.9	0.2	0.2
Total	100	67.1	7.7	22.2	0.8	0.7

Key: W-NH white non-Hispanic; H Hispanic; B-NH black; AIAN-NH American Indian/Alaskan Native; A-NH Asian.
Note: Some categories were left out due to lack of reported data. Also, percentages may not add to total due to rounding. For information on confidentiality protection, sampling error, nonsampling error, and accuracy of the data, see http://www.census.gov/prod/cen2000/doc/
Table adapted from U.S. interim projections by age, sex, race, and Hispanic origin. U.S. Census Bureau. Accessed at www.census.gov, August 2005.

TABLE 9.2 State Government Employment Data, by Criminal Justice Occupation of U.S. Workers as of: March 2005

Occupation	Full-Time Employees	Part-Time Employees
Judicial and legal	159,335	9,708
Police protection	62,716	744
Officers	39,036	1,974
Other		
Correction	458,365	10,734

Table adapted from: State government employment and parole data, March 2005, U.S. Census Bureau. http://www.census.gov/govs/www/apesst05dl.html, Accessed January 25, 2007.

In fact, data from the U.S. Department of Labor (2004) indicate that government worker turnover is at least half that of the private sector (there are not specific figures for the different criminal justice positions in the public or private sectors). Interestingly, among all workers in the public and private sectors, however, workers are likely to hold an average of 9.6 jobs in a lifetime. These two facts, though on their face contradictory, may mean that people once drawn to work in criminal justice positions may be less inclined to leave it; but, given the transient practices of the American worker, there are no guarantees that they will stay.

But people can, and should be, excluded from work in criminal justice when they lack obvious qualifications such as the requisite education or age or if they have a criminal background that disqualifies them. Moreover, if the various jobs available in criminal justice are to be considered part of a desirable "profession," by the vast majority of Americans and by those who have prepared themselves for professional level careers (e.g., those earning a college or university degree), then the standards for hiring need to reflect that aspiration.

Most of the students one of the authors has talked to over the years (in the states of Washington, New Mexico, and Idaho) are not interested in pursuing a career in institutional corrections, although some ended up working there because of the availability of positions (Mays & Winfree, 2002). Many students *are* interested in working in policing, probation, and parole (adult or juvenile) and/or going to law school as preparation for employment as a prosecutor or defense attorney. However, one of the authors has been given the following reasons for this attraction to policing, courts, and community corrections work over correctional officer work in prisons and jails and juvenile facilities:

1. Better pay
2. Perception of a more professionalized workplace (qualifications require a college degree and more training comes with the job)
3. More perceived excitement and diversity of tasks in policing
4. Less regular contact (of the total institution kind) with inmates/clients
5. Dangerousness of prison and jail work (less true for juvenile facilities)

6. Better hours

7. Unattractiveness of the idea of being "shut in or incarcerated along with" inmates

8. Negative public image of institutional corrections

Of course, the students are not factually correct about all these issues. And these perceptions are true or false depending on the locality, the level of government, and the type of job. In some states and localities, correctional officers and counselors are paid quite well, a certain amount of college credits or a college degree is required or encouraged, and most work in the institution is not inherently dangerous. Also correctional institution workers with any tenure in the job can have as good or better hours than attorneys in private practice, who when starting out can put in 60-hour work weeks. But the necessity for regular contact with inmates, the sense that staff are enclosed like inmates, and the poor public image of institutional corrections are hard to dispute.

Moreover, the students are partially correct about the other issues as well. Generally speaking, in any given state and locality, police and probation and parole officers, and attorneys do make more money, and they have more education and more freedom than workers in institutional corrections (see the Illinois and North Carolina examples provided in the sections that follow). The noncorrections jobs are also viewed as more "professional," in the sense that because of their education and training, jobholders are accorded more discretion in their work and more respect by the community. But regardless of whether the students' perceptions are always correct, the existence of such beliefs has implications for selection processes in criminal justice work. Some agencies may tend to get better or less qualified applicants because of these perceptions (see also the discussion of pay and training levels of criminal justice jobs in Chapter 8).

Entry-Level Corrections and Police Work in Illinois and North Carolina

To illustrate some of our points about jobs and hiring in criminal justice, let us examine some typical job offerings in Illinois and North Carolina, two states chosen at random from those listing jobs on the Internet. Job qualifications and salaries in the courts, for prosecuting attorneys, and for public defenders are not presented here in greater detail because they are not usually conveniently available on the Internet. Salary and qualifications for the police and corrections jobs in Illinois and North Carolina, relatively populous states in which the pool of applicants is theoretically more educated and more numerous, are likely to compare favorably with those elsewhere in the country.

Illinois   Correctional officer (CO) and youth supervisor trainee (YST) positions were advertised on the Illinois Department of Corrections website in April 2004. The basic qualifications for both jobs were that the applicant be an Illinois resident, 18 years of age; he or she should possess a valid driver's license, have a high school diploma or GED, be a U.S. citizen or an authorized alien, and be able to speak, read, and write English.

The starting salary for a correctional officer trainee (as of July 2003) in Illinois was $32,028 and for a youth supervisor trainee it was $31,080. During the first three months on the job, new hires are required to attend and pass a six-week corrections training academy, and then they are on probation for another four and one-half months. During the probationary period their salaries rise to \$34,572 (CO) and \$33,360 (YST), and the benefits are actually quite generous (100% of life insurance); (small co-pay on medical and dental).

To apply, applicants fill out a data form and then begin a series of tests, much like those described in Chapter 8. Preference in scoring and ranking applicants is given to applicants with some post–high school education and to those with applicable work and military experience.

In contrast, in July 2005 the website of the Chicago Police Department indicated that an applicant to be a police officer in that city must be between the ages of 21 and 40, have a valid driver's license, be a resident of the City of Chicago (at least by the time of hiring), and have at least 60 semester hours of college from an accredited university or college or 45 hours and one year of military service.

New officers are on probation and make \$40,830. They make \$52,798 after one year and \$55,794 after 18 months. Probationary officers also are required to complete 480 state academy and 300 additional hours of training with the Chicago Police Department. The department offers very generous benefits of health, prescription drug, and vision and dental insurance and plans, 100% tuition reimbursement, even on advanced degrees, paid sick leave, 20 vacation days, and a retirement plan.

North Carolina   In April 2004 the North Carolina Department of Corrections website posted several corrections-related jobs. Positions as correctional case manager (CCM), correctional officer (CO), probation/parole officer I (PPOI), community services district coordinator (CSDC), and substance abuse counselor II (SACII) are only some of the jobs that were listed.

These jobs called for applicants who were at least 20 years old, had passed a medical examination, possessed a high school diploma or GED, and were citizens of the United States. In addition to those basic qualifications, the website listed the following specifics.

- For the CCM position the applicant also had to have a two-year associate's degree in criminal justice or a related discipline or a high school degree and two years experience as a CO or in a human services position or some similar combination of training and experience. The applicant also had to be certifiable by the North Carolina Training and Standards Council.

- No additional educational, training, or work experience requirements were listed for the CO position, though those with college degrees were encouraged to apply.

- The CSDC position required a college degree and one year of experience, a two-year degree and two years experience, or some combination of, though the advertisement indicated that a trainee position required a four-year college degree.

- The PPOI position required a four-year degree in criminal justice or a related field and one year of experience as a PPO trainee, or another combination of experience and education.

- For the SACII position, a four-year degree and/or a master's degree were required with different levels of experience, primarily as a substance abuse counselor.

As might be expected, given the different levels of required education and experience, the beginning pay for these positions varied. The benefits package offered by North Carolina was also generous by current standards in that employees had full health insurance coverage for themselves with dependent coverage available.

- CCM range in pay was $22,037–34,962.
- CO range in pay was $22,894–34,962.
- CSDC range in pay was $23,819–38,052.
- PPOI range in pay was $25,781–41,569.
- SACII range in pay was $25,781–41,569.

To apply for these positions in North Carolina, applicants fill out the state's application form and then proceed through a selection process that varies by position.

By way of contrast, in July 2005, the website of the City of Chapel Hill, North Carolina, listed the following requirements for a police officer; a valid driver's license, a high school diploma or GED, and U.S. citizenship; persons so qualified must then pass all the selection tests. A college degree and military experience are preferred. The starting salary is $32,600 (there is no mention of pay increases after probation). The city would also prefer to hire people after they have completed the academy. Benefits are generous, with health, disability, and life insurance for the recruit paid by Chapel Hill and optional dental insurance and tuition assistance. There is longevity pay that begins after five years.

Two-State Comparison   This comparison of criminal justice jobs available in Illinois and North Carolina confirms the belief that the jobs that require more education also tend to pay more. It also indicates that for some positions the minimum requirements for employment are very basic and may make it difficult to regard those positions as "professional." This may mean that people may not be adequately prepared to engage in the decision making and the use of discretion that befalls professional level positions. Also of note, the policing positions tend to pay more and provide more benefits than those positions in corrections. Sometimes this is related to educational requirements (e.g., the Chicago police officer vs. the Illinois correctional officer), but sometimes it is not (e.g., the entry-level Chapel Hill police officer pay vs. the entry-level North Carolina probation officer pay). The explanation for the latter difference might rest with the professional regard and responsibilities that are vested in the police officer position over the corrections position.

QUALIFICATIONS

It used to be possible to get a job in criminal justice in many areas of this country if you were "connected" through family or friends or politics. As we discussed in Chapter 4, criminal justice jobs, like all public sector work before the institution of civil service reforms, were handed out based on patronage and the spoils system. Recall that with the passage of the Pendleton Act or the Civil Service Reform Act of 1883, at the federal level, and the passage of similar civil service reforms in the states and localities, criminal justice jobs began to come under civil service requirements. The main purpose of civil service laws and protections is to ensure that people are hired, promoted, and fired based on their qualifications and how they behave rather than on who they know or support in some way.

Nowadays, as discussed in Chapter 8, applicants for criminal justice positions are selected primarily based on merit. Agencies have a set application that queries for personal descriptors (e.g., gender, age), past employment, qualifications such as education and experience, and any criminal involvement or serious traffic offenses. Attorneys are required to have graduated from law school and to have passed, or be willing to take, the relevant state bar exam. In addition, military experience is often prized by criminal justice agencies, and men and women who were honorably discharged may receive extra ranking points at the beginning or end of the process. This is not to say, of course, that "who you know" is completely irrelevant in the selection process. But it does mean that if you do not meet the basic requirements for the job, personal contacts will usually not be enough to get you a job in criminal justice agencies.

EQUAL OPPORTUNITY AND AFFIRMATIVE ACTION

Any discussion of equal opportunity (EO) or affirmative action (AA) in the classroom or the workplace tends to stir debate, sometimes heated debate. This is understandable, as EO and AA initiatives in government and the private sector have had a real effect in the market place. Therefore, some people are threatened and frightened by the existence of formal AA plans and their promotion.

As previously stated in practical terms, *affirmative action* simply means that an organization takes positive steps to ensure that their hiring practices are fair and do not disparately impact a targeted underrepresented group. AA is a more proactive remedy than EO for employment discrimination (Camp, Steiger, Wright, Saylor, & Gilman, 1997). AA as law has been used to promote the hiring of minority group members and white women.

But let us just begin this discussion by recognizing that a form of affirmative action has always existed in criminal justice employment. In the past an informal qualification for police, court, or correctional work with adult males (where most of the jobs were) was that the applicant be white and male. For instance, between 1925 and 1965 some police departments actually had quotas to restrict the hiring of women to one percent or less of the workforce (Roberg & Kuykendall, 1993). Moreover, the roster of minority group men on any police force, correctional staff, or attorneys' list was minuscule before the civil rights movement. Thus, there was a plan, albeit informal at times, but out in the open at others, that only white males would be hired to work in criminal justice.

For example, the state of California did not start hiring female correctional officers to work in male prisons until the early 1970s, or after the Civil Rights Act of 1964 had been amended, in 1972, to apply to gender discrimination in hiring. (*Pulido v. State of California et al. 1994*). The first woman police officer, with full police powers, was hired in 1968 in Indianapolis, Indiana (Roberg & Kuykendall, 1993). Women were excluded from most law schools until the late 1800s and from some until the mid-1900s. In 1970 only 3% of law students were female; today over 50% are (Merlo, Bagley, & Bafuma, 2000). Not so long ago, highly qualified women were discriminated against when they applied for positions as attorneys. For instance, retired Supreme Court Justice Sandra Day O'Connor, after graduating near the top of her law school class, was offered a secretarial position.

In all such cases, most women wishing to work in criminal justice were not hired before the gender provision of the Civil Rights Act was passed in 1972, and they had to sue to be hired and promoted (Martin, 1989; Merlo et al., 2000). In many cases these organizations and law schools did not hire women until they were sued, and many other criminal justice agencies continued for years to refrain from hiring women.

Mary Stohr was only the second woman hired at the prison she began work at in 1983. The first woman, a niece of a sergeant, had been hired only a month before Stohr; note this was more than ten years after the applicable statute passed and almost twenty years after the Civil Rights Act of 1964. The warden told Stohr in private that he had opposed hiring a woman and had fought the central office for five years before giving in. He also remarked that he had no intention of hiring African Americans, and he proactively worked to prevent the promotion of the one Hispanic officer. The warden's behavior was nothing, if not consistent: upon informing Stohr that she was to serve on the affirmative action committee, he also instructed her to do nothing to recruit minorities. (Stohr told him she could not serve on the committee with that stipulation.)

Discrimination against minority men and women has been just as difficult to overcome as it has been for women in general. As late as 1991 the General Accounting Office found that there was a "glass ceiling" in federal employment that kept minority group men and women and white women situated at lower salaries and lower grades in federal employment (U.S. Senate, *102nd Congress,* 1993). Though some real progress has been made in the hiring of minority group males into the criminal justice profession at the federal, state, and local levels, much remains to be done (Palacios, 2003). McCluskey and McCluskey (2004) found, for instance, after the review of hiring data for the 50 largest American cities that the employment of Latino officers has improved markedly for these police departments, but that the diversity of the department employees does vary by community served. Relatedly, Zhao, He, and Lovrich (2006) studied the influence of both internal institutional factors (e.g., affirmative action) and external environmental factors (e.g., city population, minority representation) on the hiring of female minority police officers. They found that the increased recruitment and hiring of African American and Hispanic female officers was due largely to the increase of minority representation within their respective cities. They also state that historically, affirmative action policies account for a portion of the initial increase in female officer employment, but those same policies have failed to sustain higher number of recruits due to the "differential retention patterns among male and female officers" (Zhao et al., 2006:479).

Discrimination in hiring, informal and sometimes formal, was common in American criminal justice until a few decades ago (Belknap, 2001; Martin, 1989; McCluskey & McCluskey, 2004; Merlo et al., 2000; Palacios, 2003; Walker, Spohn, & DeLone, 2003). To establish this fact, one need only examine the employment rolls for criminal justice agencies before the 1970s. Very few women or minority men worked in American criminal justice agencies before agencies were forced to hire them (Merlo et al., 2000). Those few included women staff in women's prisons (in a few women's prisons only female staff were hired because of abuses that had occurred) and women's sections of jails, who were hired as "matrons" (institutional supervisors) and typically paid less than the men, or some women police officers or probation officers working with delinquent girls and women on probation. As mentioned earlier, formal discrimination was eliminated only with passage of the Civil Rights Act of 1964 (and its amendment by Title VII in 1972) and numerous presidential executive orders (see Box 9.2) a few decades before that and since (by presidents Franklin Roosevelt, Kennedy, Johnson, and Nixon).

Civil Rights Legislation

Civil rights legislation first appeared in 1866 and 1871 and was concerned with employment discrimination against former slaves. Despite a series of executive orders barring employment discrimination in federal employment and in organizations having federal contracts, starting with Franklin Roosevelt in 1941, criminal justice entities remained largely unaffected. In 1961 President Kennedy's executive order imposed the first requirement for *affirmative action*. He required that federal agencies and those with federal contracts institute a "plan" and implement a program to ensure that the methods used for employment practices were nondiscriminatory. Affirmative action plans were also to address the methods used to make up for past discriminatory practices in employment. In other words, affirmative action plans were premised on fair employment in the present and providing a remedy for past employment discrimination. Both presidents Johnson and Nixon reaffirmed the importance of AA with their own executive orders.

The Civil Rights Act of 1964 (CRA) made it illegal to discriminate in voter registration requirements, public accommodations and facilities, and employment (for a brief social and political history of the CRA of 1964 and the movement that birthed it, see www.congresslink.org). The act also created the Equal Employment Opportunity Commission to review complaints, though the EEOC's ability to enforce change was weak. For our purposes, the most important title of the CRA, was Title VII, which came as an amendment to the act in 1972. Title VII essentially made it unlawful to discriminate in the hiring, maintaining, or discharging people because of their race, color, religion, sex, or national origin.

The Civil Rights Act of 1964 originally only covered employers of more than twenty-five persons, but was eventually extended to cover both private and public employment agencies, including those on the state and local level that employed fifteen or more people. With the passage of this act and its amendment in 1972, criminal justice agencies of any size were required to reform their hiring practices and to institute affirmative action plans. As Stohr's experience in 1983 in Washington State demonstrates, compliance with this law came only gradually and incrementally, from facility to facility. Several years passed and countless lawsuits were initiated to compel compliance.

BOX 9.2

EQUAL OPPORTUNITY/AFFIRMATIVE ACTION LAWS AS CITED BY
VARIOUS GOVERNMENT AGENCIES

The following laws embody some of the major legislation covering equal
opportunity, employment laws, anti discrimination laws, and affirmative action
laws. We present them here by. Sources and the description of these laws have
been directly quoted from several government agencies such as the Equal
Employment Opportunity Commission, the U.S. Department of Justice, and
U.S. Department of Labor websites. Each entry represents several pages of
condensed information. See the direct web links presented at the beginning of
each entry to explore these laws further.

Employment Law

Compensation discrimination in employment is prohibited by the Equal Pay
Act of 1963, Title VII of the Civil Rights Act of 1964, the Age Discrimination
in Employment Act of 1967, and Title I of the Americans with Disabilities Act
of 1990, all enforced by the U.S. Equal Employment Opportunity Commission.
Collectively, these statutes require employers to compensate employees without regard to race, color, religion, sex, national origin, age, or disability.

The law against compensation discrimination includes all payments made
to or on behalf of employees as remuneration for employment. All forms of
compensation are covered, including salary, overtime pay, bonuses, stock
options, profit sharing and bonus plans, life insurance, vacation and holiday
pay, cleaning or gasoline allowances, hotel accommodations, reimbursement
for travel expenses, and [other] benefits.

Source: http://www.eeoc.gov/facts/fs-epa.html, accessed January 4, 2007.

Equal Pay Act of 1963

The Equal Pay Act [EPA] requires that men and women be given equal pay
for equal work in the same establishment. The jobs need not be identical [for
this law to apply], but they must be substantially equal. It is job content, not
job titles, that determines whether jobs are substantially equal. Specifically,
the EPA provides: Employers may not pay unequal wages to men and women
who perform jobs that require substantially equal skill, effort and responsibility, and that are performed under similar working conditions within the same
establishment

Source: http://www.eeoc.gov/facts/fs-epa.html, accessed January 4, 2007.

Title VII of the Civil Rights Act of 1964

An Act:
To enforce the constitutional right to vote, to confer jurisdiction upon the district courts of the United States to provide injunctive relief against discrimination in public accommodations, to authorize the Attorney General to institute suits to protect constitutional rights in public facilities and public education, to extend the Commission on Civil Rights, to prevent discrimination in federally assisted programs, to establish a Commission on Equal Employment Opportunity, and for other purposes.

Source: http://www.eeoc.gov/policy/vii.html, accessed January 4, 2007.

Age Discrimination in Employment Act of 1967

An Act:
    To prohibit age discrimination in employment.

Source: http://www.eeoc.gov/policy/adea.html, accessed January 4, 2007.

Title I of the Americans with Disabilities Act of 1990

An Act:
    To establish a clear and comprehensive prohibition of discrimination on the basis of disability.

Source: http://www.eeoc.gov/policy/ada.html.

Discrimination—General

Executive Order 11246 and 11375 (1965 and 1967)

A four-part executive order, which enforces the following:

Part I, Nondiscrimination in Government Employment

Part II, Nondiscrimination in Employment by Government Contractors and Subcontractors

Subpart B—Contractors' Agreements

SEC. 202. Except in contracts exempted in accordance with Section 204 of this Order, all Government contracting agencies shall include in every Government contract hereafter entered into the following provisions:

During the performance of this contract, the contractor agrees as follows:

(1) The contractor will not discriminate against any employee or applicant for employment because of race, color, religion, sex, or national origin. The

contractor will take *affirmative action* [emphasis added] to ensure that applicants are employed, and that employees are treated during employment, without regard to their race, color, religion, sex or national origin. Such action shall include, but not be limited to the following: employment, upgrading, demotion, or transfer; recruitment or recruitment advertising; layoff or termination; rates of pay or other forms of compensation; and selection for training, including apprenticeship. The contractor agrees to post in conspicuous places, available to employees and applicants for employment, notices to be provided by the contracting officer setting forth the provisions of this nondiscrimination clause.

Part III, Nondiscrimination Provisions in Federally Assisted Construction Contracts

Part IV, Miscellaneous

Source: http://www.dol.gov/esa/regs/statutes/ofccp/eo11246.htm, accessed January 4, 2007.

Title VI of the Civil Rights Act of 1964

Title VI, 42 U.S.C. §2000d et seq., was enacted as part of the landmark Civil Rights Act of 1964. It prohibits discrimination on the basis of race, color, and national origin in programs and activities receiving federal financial assistance. As President John F. Kennedy said in 1963:

> Simple justice requires that public funds, to which all taxpayers of all races [colors, and national origins] contribute, not be spent in any fashion which encourages, entrenches, subsidizes or results in racial [color or national origin] discrimination.

Source: http://www.usdoj.gov/crt/cor/coord/titlevi.htm, accessed January 4, 2007.

Equal Employment Opportunity Act of 1972

An Act
To further promote equal employment opportunities for American workers.

Source: http://www.eeoc.gov/abouteeoc/35th/thelaw/eeo_1972.html, accessed January 4, 2007.

Title IX, Education Amendment Action of 1972

Section 1681. Sex

(a) Prohibition against discrimination;.... No person in the United States shall, on the basis of sex, be excluded from participation in, be denied the benefits of, or be subjected to discrimination under any education program or activity receiving Federal financial assistance...

Section 1682. Federal administrative enforcement; report to Congressional committees....

Section 1683. Judicial review....

Section 1684. Blindness or visual impairment; prohibition against discrimination....

Section 1685. Authority under other laws unaffected....

Section 1686. Interpretation with respect to living facilities....

Section 1687. Interpretation of "program or activity"....

Section 1688. Neutrality with respect to abortion....

Source: http://www.dol.gov/oasam/regs/statutes/titleix.htm, accessed January 4, 2007.

Disability Discrimination

Vocational Rehabilitation Act of 1973 and Rehabilitation Act of 1974

Section 503 of the Rehabilitation Act of 1973 prohibits federal contractors and subcontractors from discriminating against and requires affirmative action for qualified individuals with disabilities in all aspects of employment. Section 504 of the Rehabilitation Act of 1973 prohibits discrimination on the basis of disability in programs and activities that receive federal financial assistance and in federally conducted programs. Section 188 of the Workforce Investment Act of 1998 (WIA) prohibits discrimination against qualified individuals with disabilities in any WIA Title I-financially assisted program or activity.

Source: http://www.dol.gov/dol/topic/discrimination/disabilitydisc.htm, accessed January 4, 2007.

Vietnam-Era Veterans Readjustment Act of 1974

Prohibits discrimination against and requires affirmative action for qualified special disabled veterans, as well as other categories of veterans. This law is enforced by the OFCCP (Office of Federal Contract Compliance Programs).

Source: http://www.dol.gov/dol/topic/discrimination/disabilitydisc.htm, accessed January 4, 2007.

Other

Pregnancy Discrimination Act (1978 Amendment of Title VII)

An Act
To amend Title VII of the Civil Rights Act of 1964 to prohibit sex discrimination on the basis of pregnancy.

Source: http://www.eeoc.gov/abouteeoc/35th/thelaw/pregnancy_discrimination-1978. html, accessed January 4, 2007.

Immigration Reform and Control Act (1986, 1990, 1996)

In regards to immigration:
(h) Anti-Discrimination Provision.—(1)(A) For the purpose of applying the prohibitions against discrimination on the basis of age under the Age Discrimination Act of 1975 [42 U.S.C. 6101 et seq.], on the basis of handicap under Section 504 of the Rehabilitation Act of 1973 [29 U.S.C. 794], on the basis of sex under Title IX of the Education Amendments of 1972 [20 U.S.C. 1681 et seq.], or on the basis of race, color, or national origin under Title VI of the Civil Rights Act of 1964 [42 U.S.C. 2000d et seq.], ...

Source: http://www.usdoj.gov/crt/cor/byagency/doj1225a.htm, accessed January 4, 2007.

Americans with Disabilities Act of 1990

See Chapter 8, Box 8.1.

Civil Rights Act of 1991

An Act
To amend the Civil Rights Act of 1964 to strengthen and improve Federal civil rights laws, to provide for damages in cases of intentional employment discrimination, to clarify provisions regarding disparate impact actions, and for other purposes.

Source: http://www.eeoc.gov/policy/cra91.html, accessed January 4, 2007.

Intentional Discrimination

In an analysis of employment data provided in 1999 to the Equal Employment Opportunity Commission by employers of over fifty persons, and supported by the Ford Foundation, two Rutgers University law professors, Blumrosen and Blumrosen (2002), found that there is a continuing pattern of widespread intentional discrimination in employment that impacts both minorities (African Americans, Hispanics,

Asian-Pacific islanders, American Indians) and white women. What they found illustrates that discrimination in employment did not end with the institution of affirmative
action plans, though they noted substantial improvement in the employment of minorities and women since 1979. For this study, Blumrosen and Blumrosen (2002) declared
the existence of **intentional discrimination** when the employment of the minorities
and women fell 2 standard deviations below the average for employment for those
groups for that industry, job category, and metropolitan area.

As we might expect, they found that intentional discrimination differed by group
and by state. For instance, in Georgia there was a 33% chance that a minority group
member or white woman would face intentional discrimination in employment. But
the chance of discrimination was highest for minority Hispanics in Georgia a (45%),
Asians-Pacific islanders (42%), blacks (36% chance), and white women (25%). In
California minorities faced this risk of intentional discrimination in employment about
25% of the time, and white women faced it about 20% of the time. Specifically, blacks
were most at risk in California (29%), followed by Asians (28%), Hispanics (24%),
and white women (22%) (Blumrosen & Blumrosen, 2002; see the full text of their
report at www.eeol.com). Notably, when comparing just the two states of Georgia
and California, one sees that the risk of being intentionally discriminated against in
employment, though still high for some groups in our communities, can vary widely.

REVERSE DISCRIMINATION

The extent to which informal discrimination still occurs is not clear and presents some
difficulties in terms of research, although the Blumrosen and Blumrosen (2002) report
is more than suggestive. It is also not clear how often *reverse discrimination*, whether
informal or formal, occurs. **Reverse discrimination** *happens when a member of an overrepresented group is overlooked for jobs, promotions, college admission, or a related
opportunity because of race, color, religion, sex, or national origin.* Researching the
extent to which *reverse discrimination* occurs is quite difficult, though there is some evidence that it exists in college admissions (see Box 9.3 on the *Bakke* [1978] and *Grutter*
[2003] Supreme Court cases), and anecdotally the claim is not uncommon. Despite its
blatant unfairness, in some instances the courts have allowed *reverse discrimination* to
occur as a remedy for past discrimination. Courts also have used the reasoning that not
everyone is equally privileged because of current or past discrimination in housing, education and employment that sometimes is determined along race and ethnicity lines.

For instance, in the *Grutter* (2003) case described in Box 9.3, a white female
applicant to the University of Michigan's law school was denied admission based on
a policy that considered the race or ethnicity of its applicants as part of its mission
to increase the diversity of the student body. The Supreme Court agreed, ruling that
because of the compelling interest of promoting diversity in the university and the
community (a number of business organizations filed in support of the University of
Michigan's position), colleges and universities can use race and/or ethnicity as one
consideration in setting admissions policies.

How the *Grutter* case will impact employment in criminal justice is not completely
clear yet. It may mean that cases of reverse discrimination will continue to be given

BOX 9.3

UNIVERSITY OF CALIFORNIA REGENTS V. BAKKE (438 U.S. 265 [1978])
AND *GRUTTER V. BOLLINGER ET AL.* (288 F. 3D, AFFIRMED, U.S.
02–241 [2003])

The two most well-known reverse discrimination cases—because they are from the Supreme Court—are *Bakke* of 1978 and *Grutter*, decided in 2003. Both are concerned with admissions to professional schools at prestigious universities. In *Bakke*, a white male claimed that he was the victim of reverse discrimination because applicants with lower academic qualifications were admitted to a University of California (UC) medical school while he was denied admission. He alleged that this occurred because he was white and the less-qualified applicants were minority group members, some of whom were admitted to the school under a special admissions program that in practice was used to only admit minority group members. Justice Powell, writing for the majority, agreed in part with this assessment, and the Supreme Court ordered Bakke's admission to the medical school at UC Davis and invalidated the special admissions program. But the court did not say that race as a consideration in admissions was illegal. Indeed, Justice Stevens noted, that more than academic credentials may be considered when developing criteria for admissions.

In the more recent *Grutter* case (2003), Grutter, a white female applicant to the University of Michigan's law school, maintained that she was denied admission because of her race, again while applicants with lesser academic credentials were admitted. As women, particularly white women, now make up about 50% of law school entrants, they are rarely now accorded protected status requiring affirmative action. Justice O'Connor, writing for the majority, wrote that the consideration of race as one factor in admissions policies was lawful. She noted that the law school's admission policy, which places a value on diversity, does not define that term only in relation to racial and ethnic origin. She argued that the majority opinion in this case was in keeping with the *Bakke* decision, which allowed some consideration of race and ethnicity in admissions policies.

Note: These cases are available in law libraries and can be accessed on the Internet by going to the Supreme Court Collection of the Legal Information Institute of Cornell Law School (www.supct.law.cornell.edu.).

"strict scrutiny" by the courts, but that race and ethnicity of applicants can be considered in the making of employment decisions. In fact, since the *Bakke* decision in 1978 there have been relatively few claims of reverse discrimination in employment before the federal courts, and very few of them have been found to have merit. In a study for the U.S. Department of Labor's Office of Federal Contract Compliance Program, Blumrosen (1995), found that in federal district or appellate courts between 1990 and 1994, there were fewer than 100 cases (out of 3,000 discrimination opinions) involving reverse discrimination in employment, or about 1 to 3% of cases involving discrimination. Of these 100 opinions, only 6 ruled that discrimination had occurred, and the rest were dismissed as without merit (Blumrosen, 1995). Of course, most folks do not report discrimination in employment, even if they are aware of it.

Some have argued, as more minority group members join the middle class and as white women have gained a more equal footing in the work world and in colleges and universities, where women typically make up at least 50% of the student body, that affirmative action should exist for those who are poor or for those who come from an impoverished background. In fact, in the *Bakke* case it was noted that poverty was one of the qualifications for admittance via the special program. However, it was not noted how this factor was taken into consideration. Using poverty as a measure of disadvantage that merits remedy with affirmative action seems fair on its face; it cuts across racial and ethnic lines and gets at the disadvantage that poor people experience because of decrepit neighborhoods, underfunded schools, and reduced opportunities. Since minority group members are usually overrepresented among the poor in this country, there would be some consideration of minority status if poverty was used as a gauge for affirmative action. The difficulty lies, however, in establishing credentials as "poor" for anything but college admissions. College applicants could establish their "poverty" simply by supplying their parent's income tax returns. Even then there can be difficulties as, people's income tends to fluctuate from year to year. Also there is relative poverty across this country insofar as someone who would be deemed middle class in a rural community could barely afford an apartment in a marginal neighborhood of a big city. How can relative poverty and these income fluctuations be accounted for in the process to make it "fair"?

Also, how would a person establish their "poverty" when applying for jobs? By describing current circumstances? The poverty experienced as a child? Many college students are relatively poor; as are those who do not yet have a steady income or a job, but does this mean they were disadvantaged by poverty when they were younger? Maybe, but maybe not. Clearly, there are some difficulties inherent in using economic disadvantage as a consideration in school admissions, let alone employment decisions in criminal justice.

Finally, using AA only for those who would qualify as "poor" ignores the discrimination based on race or ethnicity that minority group members have experienced in employment based on their skin color. As indicated by the findings of Blumrosen and Blumrosen (2002), job discrimination based on race and ethnicity has not disappeared in this country. Given this fact, AA may still be needed to ensure that all qualified persons are considered for employment in criminal justice.

FOOD FOR THOUGHT

Many people believe that affirmative action programs formally provide advantage for some groups over others. In our classrooms, such opponents of AA tell us they are least likely to see the benefit for themselves of these programs. What opponents of AA may not consider, however, is that as our country becomes increasingly diverse, there will be a shift in advantage from group to group. California and New Mexico are already dominated numerically by "minority" groups, and other states, particularly in the Southwest, are moving in that direction. Remember those Workforce 2000 reports and the Census Bureau information that was presented earlier in this chapter indicating that the diversity of the American workforce and population will continue to grow. Consider these facts in tandem with the knowledge that women make up about 50% of most college majors and you have to conclude that formal plans in the future may tend to favor white males, who may increasingly become a "minority group" in terms of their representation in the workplace.

It is also possible that in their opposition to affirmative action some groups may be overestimating the opportunities it provides for minority group members. For instance, in two studies of affirmative action and personnel practices in the Federal Bureau of Prisons, Camp et al., (1997:313) and Camp and Langan (2005) found that "white correctional officers tend to overestimate minority opportunities" provided by the existence of affirmative action policies. In the second study the researchers replicated the first finding and also found that white men tended to overestimate job opportunities for women in the Bureau of Prisons as well (Camp & Langan, 2005). In the period during which Camp et al. focused on African American officers and women (1991–1994), these populations were sometimes overrepresented among those promoted but in other years were not. The authors conclude that "[i]t is probably more accurate to say that the playing field has been leveled [by affirmative action] for all races rather than to say [given the slight differences between racial groups] it favors any particular race" (Camp et al., 1997:330).

Of course, in and of itself, and beyond the self-interest of individuals, there is value for the community in having a diverse workforce. Particularly, in the criminal justice environment where the clientele tend to be very diverse, both racially and in terms of ethnic background. Affirmative action and equal employment opportunity initiatives have served to increase the complementary diversity of staff and to bring a sense of balance and fairness in employment.

CONCLUSIONS

In this chapter we discussed one of the most divisive issues of our day—affirmative action—and the related issues of equal opportunity in employment and reverse discrimination. These are the issues that our students, and the rest of the country for that matter, are most sensitive to. Everyone can agree that we want the best qualified applicants to fill criminal justice jobs. But some argue that minority status should not be one of those qualifications. Our personal belief is that affirmative action is a necessary evil to ensure that the occupants of public and private sector jobs, but public sector jobs particularly, reflect as much as possible the communities they serve. It would be nice to believe that criminal justice organizations would hire minorities and women without the push that AA gives them, but our experience in this country is that they did not.

But AA is an evil as it can lead to reverse discrimination in hiring and promotion. However, the incidence of these cases and their substantiation, as was illustrated by Blumrosen's (1995) findings, are likely to be much smaller than most people expect. If you look around this country you cannot fail to notice that most of the better paying jobs are occupied by whites. Most administrators and managers in criminal justice, forty years after passage of the Civil Rights Act, are still white men, though women and minority group men have made some progress here because of AA. Moreover, many people in the majority (usually white males, but in some cases white females) fail to realize that they may someday benefit from the protections that AA offers. The diversity levels by race and ethnicity are only increasing in our country, and those in the majority today may be in the minority in the years to come.

EXERCISE: TRACKING CRIMINAL JUSTICE EMPLOYMENT

This exercise is useful in exposing students to the number and types of jobs available in criminal justice, locally and statewide, as well as nationally. We suggest dividing a class into groups of five and assign each group a locality in your state in which to do a job search (*Note*: The counties and/or cities assigned must be large enough to be hiring criminal justice personnel on a regular basis.) You might also consider assigning one group of students the state and one or two groups to the federal government. Alternately, each group could take a different state, to provide a spectrum across regions of the country or among neighboring states. Or you could assign them to garner information on jobs in policing, court,or corrections. The point is to expose students to the number and types of jobs available.

Have the students find descriptions of at least two criminal justice–related jobs for their locality/state. (If the locality is large enough, and/or sophisticated enough, this information should be available on the web.) Have each group write and present a brief summary report to the class. The class should note the similarities and differences between the advertised qualifications/pay and application procedures for these jobs.

DISCUSSION QUESTIONS

1. What do the Workforce 2000 reports predict for the future? How will you use this information in making your employment plans?

2. Should those predictions come true, how will employment in this country be affected? Explain your answer.

3. Why are Americans so "touchy" when they discuss affirmative action? How do you feel about it?

4. What is the difference between formal and informal affirmative action, and who tends to be hired under each? Explain your answer.

5. What benefits might we gain as a society if we were to base affirmative action on considerations of an impoverished background? Why is the basing of affirmative

action on "poverty" (either current or during childhood) problematic? Explain your answer.

6. What is reverse discrimination, and why is it so harmful? Give an example and explain your answer.

KEY TERMS

affirmative action: positive steps to ensure that an organization's hiring practices are fair and do not disparately impact a targeted underrepresented group.

intentional discrimination: according to Blumrosen and Blumrosen (2002), conditions under which the employment of the minorities and women falls 2 standard deviations below the average for employment for those groups for that industry, job category, and metropolitan area.

reverse discrimination: the result when an overrepresented group is overlooked for jobs, promotions, college admission, or a related opportunity because of race, color, religion, sex, or national origin.

NOTE

1. This number was provided by Gary Raney, Undersheriff at the Ada County Sheriff's Department, on April 27, 2004.

REFERENCES

Belknap, J. (2001). *The invisible woman: Gender, crime and justice* (2nd ed.). Belmont, CA: Wadsworth/Thomson Learning.

Bennett, W. W., & Hess, K. M. (2001). *Management and supervision in law enforcement* (3rd ed.). Belmont, CA: Wadsworth/Thomson Learning.

Blumrosen, A. (1995). *Draft report on reverse discrimination commissioned by the Labor Department: How the courts are handling reverse discrimination claims.* Daily Labor Reports, March 23.

Blumrosen, A., & Blumrosen, R. (2002). *The reality of intentional job discrimination in metropolitan America—1999.* Accessed at www.EEO1.com, April 2004.

Camp, S. D., & Langan, N. P. (2005). Perceptions about minority and female opportunities for job advancement: Are beliefs about equal opportunities fixed? *The Prison Journal, 85*(4), 399–419.

Camp, S. D., Steiger, T. L., Wright, K. N., Saylor, W. G., & Gilman. E. (1997). Affirmative action and the 'level playing field': Comparing perceptions of own and minority job advancement opportunities. *The Prison Journal, 77*(3), 313–334.

Civil Rights Coalition for the 21st Century (2004). *Civil rights and race relations.* Accessed at www.civilrights.org, August 2005.

Conover, T. (2000). *New Jack: Guarding Sing Sing.* New York: Random House.

Cox, T., & Beale, R. L. (1997). *Developing competency to manage diversity: Readings, cases & activities.* San Francisco: Berrett-Koehler.

Crouch, B., & Marquart, J. W. (1994). On becoming a prison guard. In S. Stojokovic, J. Klofas, & D. Kalinich (Eds.), *The administration and management of criminal justice organizations: A book of readings* (pp. 301–331). Prospect Heights, IL: Waveland Press.

Joseph, J., Henriques, Z. W., & Ekeh, K. R. (2003). Get tough policies and the incarceration of African Americans. In J. Joseph & D. Taylor (Eds.), *With justice for all: Minorities and women in criminal justice* (pp. 105–120). Upper Saddle River, NJ: Prentice Hall.

Lester, D. (2003). Native Americans and the criminal justice system. In J. Joseph & D. Taylor (Eds.), *With justice for all: Minorities and women in criminal justice* (pp. 149–160). Upper Saddle River, NJ: Prentice Hall.

Lombardo, L. X. (1989). *Guards imprisoned: Correctional officers at work* (2nd ed.). Cincinnati, OH: Anderson Publishing.

Maguire, K., & Pastore, A. L. (Eds.). (2004). *Sourcebook of criminal justice statistics.* Accessed at www.albany.edu/sourcebook/, April 12, 2004.

Martin, S. (1989). Women on the move?: A report on the status of women in policing. *Women & Criminal Justice, 1*(1), 21–40.

Mays, G. L., & Winfree, L. T. (2002). *Contemporary corrections.* Belmont, CA: Wadsworth/ Thomson Learning.

McCluskey, C. P., & McCluskey, J. D. (2004). Diversity in policing: Latino representation in law enforcement. *Journal of Ethnicity in Criminal Justice, 2*(3), 67–82.

Merlo, A. V., Bagley, K., & Bafuma, M. C. (2000). In defense of affirmative action for women in the criminal justice profession. In R. Muraskin (Ed.), *It's a crime: Women and justice* (pp. 69–90). Upper Saddle River, NJ: Prentice Hall.

Palacios, W. R. (2003). Where is Mayberry? Community-oriented policing and officers of color. In J. Joseph & D. Taylor (Eds.), *With justice for all: Minorities and women in criminal justice* (pp. 65–78). Upper Saddle River, NJ: Prentice Hall.

Roberg, R. R., & Kuykendall, J. (1993). *Police & society.* Belmont, CA: Wadsworth.

Salisbury, J., & Dominick, B. K. (2004). *Investigating harassment and practical guide, discrimination complaints*: A New York: Wiley.

U.S. Census Bureau. (2004). *U.S. interim projections by age, sex, race, and Hispanic origin.* Accessed at www.census.gov, August 2005.

U.S. Census Bureau. (2005). *State government employment and parole data: March 2005.* U.S. Census Bureau. Accessed at http://www.census.gov/govs/www/apesst05dl.html, January 2007.

U.S. Department of Labor. (2004). Labor statistics. Bureau of Labor Statistics. Accessed at www.bls.gov,August 2005.

U.S. *Senate,* 102nd Congress. (1991). *The Glass Ceiling in Federal Agencies: A GAO Survey on Women and Minorities in Federal Agencies: Hearings before the Committee on Governmental Affairs.*

Walker, S., Spohn, C., & DeLone, M. (2003). *The color of justice: Race, ethnicity and crime in America* (3rd ed.). Belmont, CA: Wadsworth/Thomson Learning.

Workforce Development Strategies. (2004). *State of the workforce report: Research reports, tables and charts.* Accessed at www.wdsi.org, August 2005.

Zhao, J., He, N., & Lovrich, N. (2006). Pursuing gender diversity in police organizations in the 1990s: A longitudinal analysis of the factors associated with the hiring of female officers. *Police Quarterly, 9*(4), 463–485.

CASES CITED AND LAWS/STATUTES

Pulido v. State of California et al. 1994

University of California Regents v. Bakke (438 U.S. 265 [1978])

Grutter v. Bollinger et al. (288 F. 3d, affirmed, U.S. 02–241 [2003])
Civil Rights Act of 1866, 14 Stat. 27 (1866)
Civil Rights Act of 1871, 17 Stat. 13 (1871)
Civil Rights Act of 1964, PL 88–352 (1964)
Equal Pay Act of 1963
Title VII of the Civil Rights Act of 1964
Age Discrimination in Employment Act of 1967
Title I of the Americans with Disabilities Act of 1990
Executive Order 11246 and 11375 (1965 and 1967)
Title VI of the Civil Rights Act of 1964
Equal Employment Opportunity Act of 1972
Title IX, Education Amendment Action of 1972
Vocational Rehabilitation Act of 1973 and Rehabilitation Act of 1974
Vietnam-Era Veterans Readjustment Act of 1974
Pregnancy Discrimination Act (1978 Amendment of Title VII)
Immigration Reform and Control Act (1986, 1990, 1996)
Americans with Disabilities Act of 1990
Civil Rights Act of 1991

REACHING BEYOND THE EXPECTED: MANAGING TREATMENT, FORCE, STANDARDS, AND ACCREDITATION

The police are legitimate, bureaucratically articulated organizations that stand ready to use force to sustain political order. Anglo-American policing (AAP) is democratic policing: It eschews torture, terrorism, and counter-terrorism, is guided by law, and seeks minimal damage to civility....

(Manning, 2005:23)

Drug court treatment plans are different because they are court-mandated and reviewed periodically by the court. The judge makes ongoing determinations based on the input of both probation and treatment personnel. The client who is not progressing as required faces the immediate threat of incarceration for the original offense. This threat provides a powerful tool for treatment providers....

(J. R .Brown, 2002:19).

Brutalization begets brutalization. Violence begets violence. In Santa Fe we had a system of penology that was all punishment.... When you take everything away from a human being, including his personal dignity, they become extremely dangerous.... John Salazar, former Secretary of Corrections in New Mexico, explaining what led up to the 1980 prison riot

(ABC News Broadcast, 1983)

The pains of life in contemporary prisons are real. There is no point in denying them. Nor does it make sense to see pain merely as an obstacle to correctional work, for it is an obstacle that can never be circumvented. Pain is an enduring feature of the correctional enterprise. We must accept this hard reality, and quite explicitly attempt to promote growth through adversity. This is a genuine correctional agenda. For men who cope maturely with prison, I will argue, are men who have grown as human beings and been rehabilitated in the process....

(Johnson, 1996:97)

INTRODUCTION: DISCIPLINE AND DECENCY

A few years ago when politicians were at the apex of their "lock' em up and throw away the key" rhetoric, there were calls to remove televisions and weight rooms from prisons, jails, detention centers, and long-term juvenile facilities. Many of these concerns emanated from the belief, fueled by the media and politicians, that inmates were being "coddled" in correctional institutions—by the presence of TVs and satellite dishes—and that they were bulking up with weights as a means of increasing their ability to intimidate staff and other inmates (Merlo & Benekos, 2000). To top it off, there was concern that taxpayer monies were being used to pay for such extravagances. So the solution was, take away the TVs, the satellite dishes, and the weight rooms.

Thankfully, sanity eventually prevailed. Once the public (and the politicians) were informed that the TVs, satellite dishes, and weights were paid for out of inmate funds (usually created from profits from the purchase of store items by inmates) and not from taxes, and that most correctional administrators considered the presence of TVs and weight rooms as essential to inmate management, the furor died down. Moreover, the argument can be made that inmates use the weight rooms to channel aggression, rather than to fuel it. But this tempest in a teapot did serve to illustrate how the ignorance of the public can be manipulated to drive criminal justice policy.

This kind of misrepresentation of facts is what we can expect when the public is ill informed in an atmosphere of little coverage or outside review of criminal justice activities, beyond the infamous cases. Rumors and myths perpetrated by politicians and the media can take root and flourish in such an environment (Merlo & Benekos, 2000). The most salient example of this is illustrated by the warm embrace given to DARE programs when they fit the political conception of how the drug war might be implemented in schools. It was not until years later, and the empirical evidence piled up, that it became clear that DARE programs do not appear to "work" in reducing the use of drugs by children (e.g. see Clayton, Cattarello, & Johnstone, 1996). The point is, when people do not know any better, politics can drive policy.

Of course, given the nature of criminal justice programs and policy, it would be naïve, and wrong, to argue that program operations can or should be divorced completely from politics. The devil on the other side of this divide, however, is that too much political control—recall the discussion of democratic accountability v. neutral competence—can render its own set of problems.

But like other jobholders, those who work in policing, courts, and corrections should attend, at least equally, to what is known from practice and research, for only thus will they be able to keep from falling for the latest passing political fad. Moreover, and relatedly, there is evidence that criminal justice entities that submit themselves to outside review by objective bodies are more able to ensure that there is decency, along with discipline, in their operations.

Therefore, in this chapter we review some aspects of client management that are particularly salient these days, namely: treatment programming, drug courts, use of force in policing and corrections, standards, and accreditation. By way of setting the stage for a discussion of these elements of client management, however, we first discuss the false dichotomy that appears to prevail vis-à-vis security and treatment in court and correctional management. Our argument is that rather than either treatment or security, or one first and then the other, true security *relies on* the provision of treatment and other amenities.

TREATMENT

The False Dichotomy: Treatment or Security?

In the book *Governing Prisons: A Comparative Study of Correctional Management* (1987), John DiIulio argues that before amenities and services can be provided in prisons, there must be order. There have been a number of critiques of the "control model" he proposes for both staff and inmates in prisons and its corollaries in policing (by James Q Wilson [DiIulio's mentor] & Kelling, 1982) (e.g., see Crouch & Marquart, 1990; Irwin, 1985; Stohr et al., 1994; Walker, 1984). Nevertheless, DiIulio makes a well-taken point about the importance of order. The problem is that his perspective, whether intentional or not, supports a logical fallacy that somehow security (order) and treatment are in opposition. In fact, it is often argued that treatment and the provision of amenities (such as those TVs and weight rooms) *are key* to maintaining order. To paraphrase an inmate of the New Mexico prison at the time of the riot in 1980, "You can't put a dog in a room with nothing to do for 24 hours a day and then let him loose and not expect him to bite you" (ABC News, 1983).

Research on other social processes and institutions, such as parenting and teaching in schools, indicate that positive outcomes results when children are not just kept busy, but engaged in productive activities, of meaning to them. (Wisconsin Education Association Council, 2004). One of those outcomes is that there tends to be more "order" in the home and at school. The research shows that kids involved in sports, academic pursuits, or other prosocial interests are the most well adjusted and least likely to be involved in problems at school or home or with the law (Gottfredson, 1997; Sherman, Gottfredson, MacKenzie, Eck, Reuter, & Bushway, 1997). It also helps if the parents are involved in the school activities.

This research, of course, has relevance for all correctional facilities and programming and may apply generally to community members and work. If juvenile detainees are kept busy with prosocial and meaningful activities, they are more likely to positively reengage in the larger society. It makes sense that when human beings are busy and happy they are less likely to be disruptive.

Though it would be nice to believe that inactivity and meaningless work, or lack of programming, are unique to the "prison experience" of the past and are no longer relevant, the evidence does not support that supposition. Our earliest conceptions of corrections include the depictions of inmates "breaking rocks" as a means of both punishing them and keeping them busy. Today only a small fraction of any given correctional budget is devoted to treatment or educational programming. For instance, in 1995 the director of corrections for the state of Idaho indicated in a speech one of the authors attended that only one percent of the adult corrections budget was devoted to treatment or other programming in prisons and in the community. As the economy has soured, some states, such as Florida, have been forced to cut back on their treatment options at the same time that inmates are added to the system (Royse, 2003). Yet reports produced by and for some states (e.g., New Hampshire, Pennsylvania, and Connecticut) indicate that every dollar in treatment programming has the potential to save the state money in current and future correctional costs by reducing recidivism and the required level of supervision (Gioia, 2004; Merrow & Minard, 2003). Merrow and Minard (2003:1) found that the New Hampshire Department of Corrections's community-based programs "saved the state and county governments as much as two dollars for every dollar they have invested in the programs, saving approximately $10 million over six years" and "helped hundreds of nonviolent offenders stay in their jobs and with their families as they worked successfully through treatment and counseling programs."

So both in institutions and on the streets there is a need for people to have something to do that allows them to either better themselves or to contribute in a meaningful

BOX 10.1

WHISTLING WHILE THEY WORK

One of the authors, who worked in a prison in the 1980s, noted ironically that there was not enough work to keep about a third of the inmates busy. In this prison half the men worked in the surrounding forests for the state's Department of Natural Resources. These jobs were generally prized, as it was meaningful work (planting trees, clearing trails, maintaining roads, fighting fires in the summer and fall). Such jobs also presented the chance for the men to get away from the prison and be out in the fresh air. Other than the GED program during the day, chapel on Sunday, and 12-step meetings (which were staffed by the inmates themselves and a few volunteers from the community) in the evenings, no treatment programs were provided. Once the kitchen, cleaning, and facility maintenance staffs were full, no other jobs or activities were available.

But because there were not enough jobs, and because this was a "work camp," where everyone, save a few trustees, were required to be off the bed and out of the TV and weight rooms during the day, many tasks were trivial and repetitive "make work," devised to keep people busy. For instance, one inmate was assigned to polish the brass door handles every day. Because the prison itself housed only about 110 inmates at that time, the inmate would often polish the same knob twice a day. Other inmates were continuously engaged in raking and reraking the facility perimeter, in part for security, but also for something to do. Other inmates were assigned to digg dirt for a garden that was never planted or to clear a trail around the prison perimeter for a fence that was never constructed.

At the time, it seemed surprising that so many inmates complained bitterly about being assigned such pointless tasks. Before working in this prison, the author had half bought into the popular perception that all inmates were lazy. This was certainly true of some, who by their actions did appear to prefer inactivity; but the vast majority wanted to work and wanted to do something, anything, that mattered. Such inmates always claimed that working made "their time" go faster.

way to their communities. In short, the most effective regiment in correctional client management is not order first and then the provision of services and amenities, but order and services and amenities *together.*

Mature Coping and Finding a Niche

Robert Johnson devotes one chapter of his book *Hard Time: Understanding and Reforming the Prison* (1996) to a discussion of the importance of inmates maturely coping and finding a niche during their incarceration. This idea, of course, is related to our discussion of the need for correctional clients not only to engage in activities but to find those that have meaning for them.

By **"mature coping"** Johnson (1996:98) means "[d]ealing with life's problems like a responsive and responsible human being, one who seeks autonomy without violating the rights of others, security without resort to deception or violence, and relatedness to others as the finest and fullest expression of human identity." Johnson argues that inmates, like all human beings, have a natural inclination to desire autonomy, security, and relatedness to others and that prison can build on or accentuate those proclivities.

Much like correctional staff member, inmates and correctional clients in general would do better if they had some sort of say about the circumstances of their lives (Toch, Adams, & Grant, 1989). Those who have such autonomy are less likely to be disruptive in the prison; and once they leave it they are also less likely to experience emotional and physical distress and illness because of their incarceration (Goodstein & Wright, 1989; Johnson, 1996).

Another point made by Johnson is that inmates, like most humans (remember Maslow's hierarchy) place a premium on security. Johnson (1996) notes that "mature coping" requires that inmates achieve this security without resort to deception or violence. Unfortunately, in the prison, as on some mean streets, deception and violence may be accepted, even *valued* practices "Indeed, not to take advantage of others is to show a kind of moral weakness, to advertise a potentially fateful failure of nerve in a social jungle. Correspondingly, not to be ready for violence at any time is a fateful— and often deadly—departure from prison norms" (Johnson, 1996:106). The problem is that if this primitive resort to violence and this trust-destroying deception are to flourish in the prison, people will not be prepared to live prosocially or to maturely cope in the prison or in the free world.

Thus Johnson (1996) advocates that inmates, and by extension all correctional clients, learn how to "self-actualize" by caring for themselves and others. Caring for others comes from the recognition that inmates in prisons and jails and juvenile facilities are part of a community that is interdependent. Johnson does not believe this will be a selfless caring, but a means of deserving this care from others. He believes that inmates should act as "altruistic egoists" who are generous to those in need around them, but are not saints. By acting in this way, they can form security niches composed of other inmates interested in helping each other in return for assistance when needed. Predatory inmates, even in prisons plagued by violence, are less likely to go after other inmates who are seen as part of a group. Unfortunately, though, this banding together for security purposes has been one of the reasons for the spread of gangs in prisons.

Johnson (1996) is not advocating the formation of gangs, however, when he recommends that inmates look for *niches*. Rather he defines a **niche** as a private world that inmates try to carve out to serve as a sanctuary that offers "[s]heltered settings and benign activities that insulate [inmates] from the mainline prison" (Johnson, 1996:120).

Barbara Owen (1998), in her book *In the Mix,* relates the findings from her study of the prison life for inmates in California's largest women's prison. She found that the inmates who adjusted best in prison were those who related to others in a caring way and avoided those areas (e.g., the yard) where the most deviance was likely to occur. Such niches might be found in living units for trustees or other work settings, or in the art, school, or drug and alcohol programs. Though Johnson and Owen were describing inmates in prisons, finding a welcoming and productive niche can happen for inmates of an institution or for clients on probation or parole. The point is to have a common and worthwhile purpose that binds people and allows them to care for and protect each other while also becoming more than they were.

TREATMENT PROGRAMMING

Treatment programming, in its broadest sense, has always existed in prisons and jails, but particularly in juvenile facilities and for probation and parole clientele. Beyond the juvenile court and a century-long focus on rehabilitation programming for juveniles, a newer twist has been the development of courts devoted to promoting treatment as an alternative to a correctional institution and often in conjunction with a form of probation.

But whether treatment is provided on the streets or in jails or prisons, there are many forms it can take. This is because treatment programming often encompasses work programs, education programs, counseling programs, and all manner of rehabilitation/habilitation programs. It is easy to see why this broad conception aligns treatment with work and school; for as we discussed with niches, these productive activities, can also be therapeutic. In this sense, the earliest jails where inmates worked, had therapeutic purposes attached with their requirements for work and a quiet life of penance that was believed to lead to reform. The juvenile court was formed with the "best interests of the child" in mind,and even the most primitive of juvenile ranches and reformatories included some form of school program. Probation and parole programs too were developed to assist the client to transition back into the community. Historically, this usually included assistance in finding a job, and these days it might call for participation in a salient rehabilitation program.

In other words, treatment, broadly defined, has always been an integral part of courts, but particularly, correctional operation. It has also been one aspect of client and inmate management that has spurred much debate and research. As criminal justice reforms have waxed and waned in popularity, so too has the belief in the integrity and validity of some such programs.

Death to All Programs (!), or the Nothing Works Mantra

From 1966 to 1970, a research team headed by Robert Martinson undertook to study rehabilitation for the state of New York (Lipton, Martinson, & Wilks, 1975; Martinson, 1974). They were asking "what works" in correctional reform (Martinson, 1974 [reprinted in 2001]). To answer this question, they reviewed all evaluations of rehabilitation programs that had been published in the English language from 1945 to 1967. They then eliminated studies that did not evaluate a treatment method and did not adhere to conventional standards of social science research. Dropped from the study, then, were programs without control or comparison group, those lacking an independent measure of improvement, and those that were divorced from the treatment method. The team was most interested in whether the treatment programming resulted in a reduction in recidivism of those engaged in the program versus like individuals who were not. In the end they included 231 studies in their analysis. These studies spanned the breadth of court-sanctioned or correctional rehabilitation programming, including education and vocational training, training programs for adult inmates, individual and group counseling programs, milieu therapy in institutions, medical treatment, the effects of sentencing and decarcerating inmates, psychotherapy in community settings, probation and parole supervision, intensive supervision for juveniles and adults, and various community treatment programs.

What Martinson and his colleagues (1974:270; Lipton et al., 1975) found was that "[w]ith few and isolated exceptions, the rehabilitative efforts that have been reported so far have had no appreciable effect on recidivism." They never said "nothing works" in correctional programming, but they came pretty close, and their study outcomes were interpreted that way in the popular press. In rehabilitation's stead, Martinson (1974) suggested that the value of deterrence and punishment merited greater attention and study by scholars.

This research was widely cited by politicians who were interested in shifting away from treatment programming to a greater focus on punishment and deterrence in corrections (Cullen & Gilbert, 1982). In fact, this shift directly tracked the larger societal shift to a conservative approach to crime in general. Given these findings and the effect they had on policy, it is indeed ironic that the Governor's Special Committee on Criminal Offenders that originally commissioned the Martinson study was organized on the premise that "[p]risons could rehabilitate, that the prisons of New York were not in fact making a serious effort at rehabilitation, and that New York's prisons should be converted from their existing custodial basis to a new rehabilitative one" (Martinson, 1974:268).

Despite the original intent of the Martinson study, the stage was perfectly set to misinterpret the findings as "nothing works" in correctional programming. The country was primed politically to disavow treatment as a legitimate approach to correctional reform, and the Martinson report was embraced widely and used to eliminate funding for, or justify the death of, a number of correctional programs that served clients on the streets and in the institutions (Andrews, Zinger, Hoge, Bonta, Gendreau, & Cullen, 2001; Cullen & Gilbert, 1982). Which is why when one of the authors worked in a prison in the 1980s, there were very few programs available in the institution and not many more available in the community for the men for whom she wrote parole plans (see Box 10.1).

But despite this abandonment by politicians, Cullen and Gilbert (1982) were able to demonstrate that the public never lost complete faith in "rehabilitation" as a justification for the existence of correctional institutions or programs. They noted over twenty years ago, and after the Martinson report had had a chance to sink in, that in a national survey administered in 1981 more respondents (37%) thought that rehabilitation should be the primary purpose of putting people in prison than respondents who thought punishment (31%) should be.

Of course, the Martinson report had its critics, especially in the decades following its publication (e.g., see Palmer, 1995). These critiques, called meta-analyses, were structured reviews of the major published reports in the area. Among their criticisms was an assertion that Martinson had misconstrued the findings from the recidivism studies he had written about. Palmer (1995) noted that although no single program had worked for all targeted offenders, some programs had reduced the recidivism of some offenders. In fact, Martinson himself later recognized that individual programs might work for targeted groups even when whole groups of programs do not (Palmer, 1995). Other meta-analyses of correctional programming (e.g., Antonowicz & Ross, 1997; Leukefeld & Tims, 1992; Logan & Gaes, 1993; Wright, 1995) have also raised serious questions concerning the veracity of claims of success by correctional program components.

Moreover, of the forty-four programs that had adequate research designs, only twenty were found to be "effective" (Antonowicz & Ross, 1997:313). The programs that achieved some success in this and other meta-analyses (e.g., see Andrews et al., 1990; McMurran, 1995) were stronger in the areas of conceptualization (programs with cognitive/behavioral models, structuring, and role-playing). The better programs included a greater variety of programming options and techniques; they also targeted factors that were actually related to criminal involvement and matched offender learning styles to complementary services.

Programs also falter because of external factors, some of which they have little or no control over. Leukefeld and Tims (1992) caution that programs must be given time to succeed or fail on their merits. That is, to succeed, programs must have sustained, adequate funding over a period of time, and they must be designed with evaluation in mind. Such a design should be realistic in scope and time line with respect to outcomes and subject participation. Lipton and his colleagues (1992) note that the history of the demise of therapeutic community programs over the past two decades was oftentimes tied to factors external to the programs such as administrative changes and funding reductions, not to the efficacy of the programs themselves.

Drug Courts

The nexus between drugs and crime is well established. At least 60% of jail inmates admit they were under the influence of drugs or alcohol at the time of their offense or were regular substance abuse users (James, 2004; Wilson, 2000). Drug courts, first developed in the 1980s at the local level, represent another strategy in the drug war, one that eschews locking people up without addressing underlying addiction issues. Drug courts were developed as a means of diverting people from jail or prison time by engaging them in the treatment process in the community, under the close supervision of the court (Brown, 2002). At the same time it is expected that drug courts would reduce the dependence on both courts and corrections for processing relatively-low level drug and alcohol offenders and/or people who commit crimes to sustain their drug use (Bell, 2005). A General Accounting Office report (2005) noted that there were 1,200 drug courts established in the United States by 2004 and another 500 planned.

Drug courts will either defer prosecution or order drug court involvement as a means of "encouraging" participants. Substance abuse treatment, mandatory drug testing, and involvement of court actors, particularly judges, are central to the operation of drug courts. Attendance at the regularly scheduled status hearings before a judge is considered a key element of drug courts. Typically one year of successful participation in drug court is required for participants to clear their sentence.

The participants in these programs and the programs themselves vary widely. According to the GAO (2005) report, participants usually have committed a nonviolent drug or property offense, although some had extensive criminal justice histories. Most substance abuse treatment is conducted on an outpatient basis. Some courts include participants with prior convictions, while others do not. Most programs, recognizing that addiction is a disease, will accommodate relapse with either increased sanctions or treatment rather than immediate termination.

What Works, or Using Science to Separate the Wheat from the Chaff in Programming

The truth is that many of the well-intentioned and even well-funded programs out there do not deliver much in the way of reform of clients or inmates. On the other hand, there are many programs that are outright successes and/or show much promise in these areas. The difficulty is dividing the wheat from the chaff in programming, an enterprise that necessarily requires a scientific approach to research on programs (e.g., see, Box 10.2).

In their meta-analysis, Andrews et al. (2001 noted that although it is true that no program "works" for all offenders in all circumstances, plenty of rehabilitation programs in fact help reduce recidivism. In other words, in rehabilitation and treatment programming, as in life, there are no easy answers or silver bullets that will "cure" everyone from engaging in criminality. But there are some programs that do appear to "work."

According to Andrews et al. (2001) such programs can be distinguished from less successful programs by three principles: *risk, need,* and *responsivity.* By "risk" the authors are referring to the risk level represented by the offender. Those programs that target higher-risk offenders are more likely to have an effect in reducing recidivism. Those programs that focus on "criminogenic needs" or factors that are associated with criminal involvement, such as substance abuse, antisocial attitudes, poor role models, and parenting, and are replaced with more prosocial attitudes and behavior, are more likely to be successful. Programs that have styles and modes of program service delivery, or "responsivity," such as modeling, cognitive self-change, role-playing, and behavioral and social learning, coupled with the following factors, are also likely to be more successful in reducing criminal involvement (Andrews et al., 2001:295):

- the use of authority (a "firm but fair" approach and definitely not interpersonal domination or abuse).

- anticriminal modeling and reinforcement (explicit reinforcement and modeling of alternatives to procriminal styles of thinking, feeling and acting).

- concrete problem solving and systematic skill training for purposes of increasing reward levels in anticriminal settings.

- high levels of advocacy and brokerage are also indicated as long as the receiving agency actually offers appropriate service.

- service deliverers relate to offenders in interpersonally warm, flexible, and enthusiastic ways, while also being clearly supportive of anticriminal attitudinal and behavioral patterns.

BOX 10.2

THE SCIENTIFIC APPROACH IN SOCIAL SCIENCES

The scientific approach in the social sciences is based on logic, rationality, and the collection or analysis of data (Babbie, 1992). If researchers want to know why some phenomenon occurs—for instance, why inmates join gangs—they first need to review any research that might exist on this topic. If research does exist, they might test a hypothesis that emanates from that research or replicate a test by other researchers. If there is no research, then the researchers will want to find some means (methods) to investigate the topic. In either case, whether replicating or testing hypotheses from the extant research or engaging in a new area of research where little has been done, researchers need to collect data or analyze existing data. Such data, in the case of gang studies, could come in the form of surveys/police records/observations, and so on.. There are many methods to employ when doing science! But whatever method is chosen, it needs to allow the researcher to test, support or refute, or develop, hypotheses. The researcher also reviews the data to determine whether any patterns or trends, noted or not noted, in other research, become apparent. After a period of study, and taking the body of research into consideration, the researchers might propose a theory about why inmates join gangs. That theory should include hypotheses that are testable, and the process begins again.

It is of the utmost importance that criminal justice managers have some basic understanding of research methodology. Managers are top consumers of research findings, and need the abilities to sort out valid and reliable findings, and to correctly implement policy changes that are directed by empirical evidence. Furthermore, as many managers can attest, outsourcing research jobs is a critical process for those who do not have the time or the in-house resources to evaluate, explore, describe, or explain the many questions that arise in day-to-day operations. The manager then becomes a contract monitor, and she must possess the necessary research skills to effectively supervise the job and, in the end, justify the research expenses.

Some programs that are showing particular promise in rehabilitation programming are substance abuse treatment in adult prisons (Peters & Steinberg, 2001), cognitive self-change coupled with hormonal treatment for sex offenders (Nagayama Hall, 2001), and academic and vocational correctional education programs (Gerber & Fritsch, 2001). In fact, the literature on substance abuse and related programming is replete with research evaluations indicating that successful treatment programming can be designed and implemented in the correctional environment (Andrews et al., 2001; Applegate, Langworthy, & Latessa 1997; Knight, Simpson, Chatham, & Camacho, 1997; Lipton, Falkin, & Wexler, 1992; Lipton, 1998; Wexler, DeLeon, Thomas, Kressel, & Peters,

1999).[1] The most successful programs are those that deliver substantive knowledge in an environment that is suited to therapeutic change (Inciardi, 1995; Lipton, 1998; Lipton et al., 1992). Research also indicates that cognitive attributes, positive modeling, behavioral redirection, emotional therapy, a treatment environment engendering trust and empathy, and intensive involvement in problem-solving by clients in their own treatment are also key to attaining actual behavioral change upon release (Andrews et al., 2001; Antonowicz & Ross, 1997; Gendreau & Ross, 1987, 1995; Henning & Frueh, 1996; Inciardi, 1995; McMurran, 1995; Smith & Faubert, 1990). Treatment programs directed at drug offenders also appear to achieve greater success in reducing recidivism when services were continued postrelease (Lipton, 1998; McMurran, 1995; Tims & Leukefeld, 1992).

In fact, research conducted by Pearson and Lipton (1999) indicates that there are positive outcomes associated with cognitive-based programs in changing criminal activity. There is also now a substantial body of literature that documents the success of prison-based therapeutic community (TC) programs in reducing substance abuse and recidivism, especially when combined with an aftercare component (Gendreau, 1996; Knight et al., 1997; Knight, Simpson, & Hiller, 1999; Linhorst, Knight, Johnston, & Trickey, 2001; Martin, Butzin, & Inciardi, 1995; Martin, Butzin, Saum, & Inciardi, 1999; Pearson & Lipton, 1999; Peters & Steinberg, 2001; Wexler, Melnick, Lowe, & Peters, 1999).

Many correctional agencies have come to believe in, and are attempting to implement, cognitive behavioral and social learning approaches because they suspect these treatment components answer the question "What works?" (Andrews et al., 2001; Peters & Steinberg, 2001). However, these jurisdictions may be frustrated in their ability to combine these "best practices" in a complementary continuum of services.

The preliminary research on drug courts is also quite promising. In its review of twenty-seven evaluations of adult drug courts, the General Accounting Office (2005:1) found that "[l]ower percentages of drug court program participants than comparison group members were rearrested or reconvicted" and that "[p]rogram participants had fewer recidivism events than comparison group members." Moreover the lower recidivism effect remained even for offenders with different offenses. The GAO study authors did not find, however, that one particular mode of operation in the drug court, such as the behavior of the judge, affected the participants' recidivism.

The Challenges of Managing Treatment Programming

Criminal justice managers in courts or corrections who are interested in providing and maintaining effective treatment programming, and research by a number of scholars indicate that there are many such folk (Ahn-shikk, Devalve, Devalve, & Johnson, 2003; Caeti, Hemmings, Cullen, & Burton, 2003), face several challenges. The greatest obstacle, by far, is that of garnering resources. In fact, most management difficulties associated with treatment programming are associated with the funding issue.

Almost every prison, jail, juvenile facility, and community of any size in this country has volunteers who provide 12-step programs or church-related activities. Undoubtedly, the attraction of such programming is that it can be provided either at no or a very low cost (institutions may need to provide space and supervisory staff), and it can be effective in turning around some offenders. But other kinds of programming, which meet the principles outlined by Andrews et al. (2001), are going to cost.

As governmental entities are rarely so flush with funds that all such treatment needs can be met, dollars for treatment or rehabilitation programming are usually narrowly targeted, primarily at education programs at the GED or high school diploma level, and at some limited work skills training programming. Substance abuse treatment, of late, however, has received a boost in terms of federal funding targeted at detainees in juvenile and adult facilities (e.g., see the National Institute of Justice website for summaries of programs and research funded by NIJ: www.ojp.usdoj.gov). Moreover, other federal agencies, such as the National Institute on Alcohol Abuse and Alcoholism, have provided resources for community-wide drug and alcohol prevention programs that are targeted at youth. The surge in drug court development has been spurred by the authorization of federal monies, beginning in 1994 with grants under Title V of the Violent Crime Control and Law Enforcement Act (GAO, 2005).

So there are some limited and targeted resources available from the federal government and states that have opened up programming options for administrators, particularly within the last ten years. But it is the rare agency that can match programming to all or even most of the criminogenic needs of offenders.

Related to cost considerations are other management challenges such as staffing and space. Staff, per the criteria of Andrews et al. (2001), need be qualified and trained to provide the programming effectively. In a fifteen-month process evaluation of a local therapeutic community substance abuse program, we found that too often programming was provided either by other inmates or by staff who had not received adequate training (Stohr et al. 2003). Of course, a collateral problem is the low pay for people assigned to staff such programming in some institutions. In treatment programming, as with any service, you get what you pay for, and too often that inadequately trained and paid staff, or worse yet, programming provided by inmates or offenders themselves, which violates the principles described by Andrews et al. (2001).

Space, usually in short supply in correctional facilities and in some communities, is another problem requiring management attention. If the programming is provided in the community, a local school or church might be used after hours; but correctional institutions with security concerns do not have such options. In some cases the space predicament can be solved by co-opting the chapel or recreational facilities (when such exist) in the off-hours and/or by the more costly, and thus less likely, option of building on to the facility to provide more programming space.

As with the cost and staffing challenges, there are no easy answers to the shortage of space for programming. It will take more than a recognition of the value of treatment by politicians, other policymakers, and citizens before these hurdles of cost, staffing, and space can be fully addressed. Research by Applegate, Cullen, and Fisher (2001), however, indicates that the public supports treatment for offenders. Therefore, it will take the political will, and the sacrifices necessary to fund treatment, before these matters can be addressed. In the interim, managers will need to be creative in their resolution of these issues.

Although we may not have time to address all of the creative ways in which we can resolve treatment and programming issues, one way that we can start is for managers to tap into their local college(s) or university(s) for help. Often, outside state agencies will tap a university for (relatively inexpensive) resources such as graduate research assistance. Many of our students have been hired as interns, with or without pay. Networking within this resource is one way in which criminal justice managers can be creative in getting good and economical help, and it benefits students as well by giving them valuable work experience.

USE OF FORCE

Managing the use of force in policing and corrections is at least as problematic as managing treatment and rehabilitation programming. After all, at the very heart of criminal justice is force; its existence, use, and constraint. The threat of force, and the willingness to use it, lie behind the willingness of community members, suspects, and offenders to comply with directives about what they can do, where they are housed, where they work, what they eat, what programs they attend, and who they associate with (Pratt, Maahs, & Hemmens, 1999).

Certainly there are social controls exerted by family and friends and and community moral beliefs that induce people to act lawfully. But the coercive power of the state in influencing behavior cannot be underestimated. Kids hanging around on the corner will move when asked to by an officer because they know he has the ability to bring more attention to their activities than they might like. People comply with court orders because they know that if they do not they may be fined or compelled into custody. People allow themselves to be supervised by probation and parole officers because they know that if they do not they will be forced to submit themselves (or be physically taken) to incarceration in a correctional facility. They allow themselves to be housed in a juvenile detention or prison facility or an adult jail, where offenders always outnumber correctional staff by anywhere from 10 to 100 or more to 1, because they know that they have no choice; if they resist, they will be restrained in some way. They also know that there are few avenues of escape from such facilities, and if they try, they are likely to be caught and probably will be punished more with a longer sentence.

Recall that power is the ability to get people to do what they otherwise would not. The ability to use coercive power or force is a big reason why people comply, despite what the correctional officers in Hepburn's study thought (see Chapter 6 for a review of the discussion of Hepburn's 1990 study and types of power). In other words, in the everyday operation of police, courts, and corrections, force is either implied or explicitly displayed, and it is useful.

The use of force has been problematic throughout criminal justice history, and its abuse is usually highlighted only in infamous cases (Alpert & Smith, 1999; Pratt et al., 1999), particularly for the police and corrections. The worst abuses of force have ranged across the gamut of human hell, including beatings, shootings, isolation, overwork, starvation, torture, rape, and murder. But other than isolation for disruptive behavior, most of these uses and abuses of force have been constrained or eliminated by statute from most police or correctional agencies. Of course certain organizations and programs have staff who abuse force, but this is by no means the norm.

Documenting the abuse of force in policing and corrections is difficult, if at times impossible. As Thibault et al. (2004:255) indicate, police violence takes place in an environment typified by "secrecy, solidarity and social isolation," descriptors that certainly apply to correctional work as well. There are indications, however, that the use of excessive force is not as rare as one might think. For instance, the American Civil Liberties Union in 2005 alone complained about police practices entailing the use and abuse of force in Boston, Santa Fe, and Denver (ACLU, 2005a, 2005b, 2005c). In all three cities the police engaged in the questionable use of lethal and "nonlethal" force, specifically stun guns, that resulted in the death of citizens. Relatedly, the Department of Justice signed an agreement with the City of Cincinnati, Ohio, in 2002 that limits the use of force by police officers in that city (CNN, 2002). The city signed this agreement when the DOJ was threatening to sue over departmental practices related to the police shootings of young black men in Cincinnati. The death immediately preceding the agreement was that of an unarmed black man shot by a Cincinnati police officer, an incident that spurred four days of rioting in the city.

The U.S. Attorney General's Office typically handles over a hundred cases of civil rights violations of institutionalized persons every year. The attorney general can investigate such violations in accordance with the Civil Rights of Institutionalized Persons Act (CRIPA). "Since May 1980, when CRIPA was enacted, through September 2001, the Department investigated conditions in 355 jails, prisons, juvenile correctional facilities, and nursing homes" (U.S. Department of Justice, 2004:1). In 2001 alone, 187 facilities were involved in CRIPA cases, and 11 facilities were investigated, 53 investigations were continued, and monitoring continued over 105 facilities. These cases in 2001 existed in 33 states, the District of Columbia, and U.S. territories. In a number of these cases one issue was the abuse of force, or at least the protection from harm (U.S. Department of Justice, 2004). For instance, the complaint in a case involving five jails in Maricopa County (Phoenix), Arizona, which was filed in 1997 and settled in 2001, alleged

> that the defendants used excessive physical force and restraints in violation of the constitutional rights of individuals detained in the jails. The settlement agreement provided for adequate staffing; staff training, particularly in use of force issues; prohibition of "hogtying" procedures; revised policies on pepper spray and stun guns that prohibits their use where hands-on control can be used; proactive measures to prevent excessive use of force and restraints; and procedures to receive and investigate inmate grievances. (U.S. Department of Justice, 1998:2)

As this example illustrates, the appropriate use of force in criminal justice settings is shaped by the circumstances. Typically, policies allow the use of force only when there is real or potential danger, and even then there is a preference for a graduated use of force or progressive behavior control. For instance, item 804 of the Arizona Department of Corrections Policy (#804) regarding the use of force in prisons states in part that:

> [f]orce shall only be used after every other reasonable attempt to neutralize the real or potential danger has been considered and determined ineffectual. The use of force is reserved for situations where no other reasonable alternative is available to prevent escape, imminent death, serious bodily harm, or the taking of hostages. Verbal abuse by inmates does not constitute cause for the use of force. The use of force shall never be used as punishment or retaliation... Physical force shall be used only

when persuasion, direct orders, counseling and warnings are found to be insufficient to obtain cooperation from the inmate: Only the amount of force necessary to gain control of the inmate and minimize injury to staff and the inmate shall be used; once an inmate becomes cooperative, the physical force control techniques shall be consistent with the inmate's amended behavior. However, staff safety shall continue to be the governing consideration; No unorthodox, radical or extreme control techniques that might cause positional asphyxia or bodily injury to staff or inmates is to be used. (www.adc.state.az.us)

The policy even delineates the maximum use of force in given circumstances. Furthermore, according to the department's policy, staff who violate the use-of-force policy, or fail to report a violation, or a suspected violation, are subject to disciplinary action.

The Minnesota Department of Corrections Field Services Policy for community services staff also details the precise steps that staff should take and matters they should consider when a use-of-force incident occurs (Division Directive no, 201). Unlike the Arizona Department of Corrections use-of-force policy for institutions, however, the Minnesota policy for parole officers focuses more on identifying danger and putting some distance between themselves and the offender who may be endangering them or others. If, however, the officiers cannot leave they are authorized to use force to defend themselves and others:

Staff must avoid or leave any situation in which they do not feel safe or in which they are threatened. In the event that staff find themselves in a situation in which the offender or others appear to present a potential or immediate threat to the staff's safety or the safety of others, and the staff are not able to leave or have those presenting the threat leave, staff are authorized to respond in their own defense and the defense of others according to the Use of Force Continuum as defined in this directive and to the extent that they have been trained. The best protection against potential harm comes from:

A. Recognition and awareness

B. Preventive practices

C. Self protection plans and skills (www.doc.state.mn.us/DocPolicy2)

In the Minnesota policy, the *use of force continuum*, explicitly links the type of behavior with the appropriate response (e.g., see Figure 10.1). For instance, noncompliance with a request that an offender leave should be paired with a request by staff for an offender to leave, then a directive for the person to leave, then a command. If none of these actions by the staff induce the offender to leave, the officer should leave and get assistance and allow the offender to leave as well. But, if the offender should threaten the officer, "either verbally or physically," the officer is justified in using chemical spray and/or physical self-defense tactics.

Alpert and Smith, in their review, note that some police use-of-force continuum policies are adjusted based on the suspect's resistance and the officer's response level. Therefore, the officer would merely use verbal commands if the suspect resistance level included was characterized by just verbal resistance. However, the officer's response or "level of control (force)" would necessarily adjust to the use of physical tactics and/or weapons should the suspect resist physically (Alpert & Smith, 1999:61).

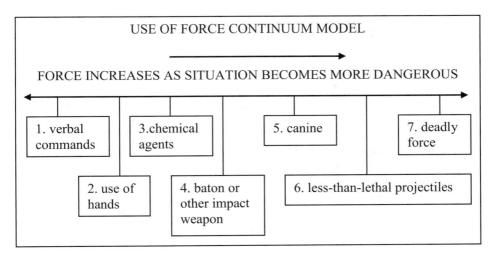

FIGURE 10.1 Basic use of force continuum model.

As you can see from these examples, the abuse of force is formally prohibited by criminal justice entities and actors. Rather, the use of force is carefully prescribed and delimited by policy and statute. But those who work in and manage police and corrections departments have to be concerned most with ensuring that the informal abuses are not occurring. As much of this abuse is hidden, the best way to stop abuse of force is to engage in preventive measures:

1. Ensure that your policies and procedures are appropriate and sufficient to cover regular and reoccurring interactions between staff and community members/suspects/clients/inmates.

2. Engage in progressive personnel practices that include hiring and maintaining the best people and training them well initially, and throughout their careers, about what constitutes the acceptable use of force.

3. Monitor the use of force carefully and consistently to ensure that staff are complying with policies and statutes.

4. Provide a reporting or whistleblowing mechanism and process so that staff and community members/suspects/clients/inmates can report the abuse of force by staff without repercussions (see Box 10.3 for a discussion of whistleblowing)

5. Develop an "early warning" system to identify officers who have received excessive use-of-force complaints or incidents (Thibault et al., 2004).

6. Investigate all reports thoroughly and according to established procedures.

7. Discipline violators of the policy.

In sum, there is nothing wrong with using force in criminal justice operations; it comes with the territory. The problems arise when that force is abused. A number of the CRIPA settlements by the U.S. Attorney General's Office included requirements

BOX 10.3

"THE ANSWER MY FRIEND, IS BLOWING IN THE WIND"

The answer to some management prevention issues is indeed blowing in the wind of the organization, and if employees feel they can report on problems without getting punished they will do just that. The idea of whistleblowing probably originated from sporting analogies—that the official blows the whistle on wrongdoing in a game (Miceli & Near, 1992). An employee who has observed wrongdoing in an organization can "blow the whistle" on the person or persons responsible, by reporting the improper action.

A definition of the term **whistleblowing** offered by Miceli and Near (1992:15) is: "[t]he disclosure by organization members (former or current) of illegal, immoral, or illegitimate practices under the control of their employers, to persons or organizations that may be able to effect action." As these authors note in their book *Blowing the Whistle: The Organizational and Legal Implications for Companies and Employees,* whistleblowing is a courageous and necessary act if any organization is to remain as free of corruption as possible. But since whistleblowing can be hazardous to the career of that employee, the authors advocate the creation of organizational mechanisms for anonymous reporting, the protection of whistleblowers, and the rewarding of whistleblowing that saves the public money or preserves its safety or health.

regarding the need for agencies to adequately staff facilities and to train personnel on the appropriate use of force (U.S. Department of Justice, 1998, 2004). The general sentiment seems to be that agencies that take proactive steps in this regard are much less likely to experience abuses of the use of force.

STANDARDS AND ACCREDITATION

Criminal justice standards have evolved over the centuries as a means of improving the professionalism of staff and the operation of agencies including the abuse of force. Standards typically cover all aspects of operation from prescribing the amount of training different classes of staff should have to drafting procedures for relating to community members to determining the amount of space an inmate needs in a jail to setting the ratio of staff to clients on probation. Accreditation is the process of determining whether an agency operates according to set standards. The best standards for criminal justice organizations are set by outside professional organizations. In turn, the best accreditation is done by these agencies. Such professional entities are best positioned to be aware of the level of standards necessary to operate the agency professionally;

ideally, they are also, hopefully, disinterested enough to provide an unbiased assessment, or accreditation.

Courts

State and federal courts, as loosely construed organizations, are not typically subjected to accreditation processes. The American Bar Association (ABA), however, rigorously accredits law schools and continuing legal education (CLE) credits, required by many states for practicing attorneys, are usually subjected to accreditation processes. The ABA also has a certification process for lawyers. Some states (e.g., Indiana) require certification of the courses in specialty areas like consumer bankruptcy (American Board of Certification), elder abuse (National Elder Law Foundation), and others (Indiana Commission for Continuing Legal Education, 2005). Generally speaking, court actors, particularly attorneys, are subjected to professional norms and standards through the American Bar Association, their law schools, and state requirements for CLEs; however these organizations are not always subjected to standards development and accreditation processes in the same way that police and corrections are.

However, in 1995, following an eight-year initiative (beginning in 1987), the Commission on Trial Court Performance Standards—composed of sitting judges, court clerks, and political scientists—along with personnel from the Bureau of Justice Assistance, the National Center for State Courts, and the Trial Court Performance Standards Project Staff developed standards for self-assessment of state trial courts (National Center for State Courts, 2001). The National Center for State Courts, with the funding assistance of the Bureau of Justice Assistance, created the commission to develop the standards. The standards were pre tested in twelve courts in the 4 states of Ohio, New Jersey, Virginia and Washington State by over a hundred personnel. The impact of the standards was intended to be narrow, and the self-assessment would not include the review of outside professional entities that might be more prone to objectivity: "The resulting measurement system is intended to be a versatile tool for self-assessment and improvement, and not a means for evaluating the performance of individuals or for drawing comparisons across courts" (National Center for State Courts, 2001:2). Having said this, the development of some standards is a step in the right direction. The 22 standards, with 68 measures, cover the following areas (National Center for State Courts, 2001:6):

- access to justice
- expedition and timeliness
- equality, fairness, and integrity
- independence and accountability
- public trust and confidence

Many of the measures under these five performance areas include a mix of data collection techniques, including surveys of staff and clients, observation, interviews, and the review of court documents. The point is to get a clear picture of how the court operates so that administrators can improve performance in problematic areas. It appeared that the commission intended that the standards be used in administrative decision making involving budgetary determinations and strategic planning.

In the more specialized area of courts and child abuse and neglect cases, the American Bar Association, the National Center for State Courts, and the National Council of Juvenile and Family Court Judges took four years to develop a "guide and toolkit" to measure court performance in this area (American Bar Association, 2005). The goal of these organizations was to provide tools for the assessment of performance and judicial workload, and to tailor the assessment to the capabilities for data collection of individual courts. The performance measures for courts dealing with child abuse and neglect cases incorporated national goals developed by the Adoption and Safe Families Act of 1997, namely, safety, permanency, and well-being for children. They added other performance measures for courts to these three, such as due process and timeliness (Amercian Bar Association, 2005). The methods or measures used to assess these performance areas are varied and include surveys, focus groups, case file review, and observation. Again, the process and performance areas were developed as a means for courts or court systems in the states to engage in self-assessment and to improve their performance without outside review.

It is not yet clear how many courts engage in these self-assessments developed by the National Center for State Courts and the ABA. Though time-consuming, such assessments are likely to be beneficial for courts that engage in them because they have the potential to systematize the available information and consequently to improve decision making.

Police

Police organizations have established voluntary accreditation through the Commission on Accreditation for Law Enforcement Agencies, or CALEA (CALEA, 2005). The International Association, of Chiefs of Police, the National Organization of Black Law Enforcement Executives, the National Sheriffs' Association and the Police Executive Research Forum established CALEA as an independent accrediting agency in 1979. CALEA is governed by a board composed of eleven law enforcement practitioners and ten members from the public and private sector. CALEA was established to improve and standardize service delivery by the police. There is a small staff and an executive director who produce a newsletter and workshops to explain the standards and the accreditation process. Accreditations are conducted by specially trained CALEA members.

CALEA claims that adherence to its standards, and thus accreditation, will reap benefits for police organizations including improvement of administrative and supervisory service and accountability, reduction in liability costs and lawsuit success (and insurance), and greater support from the community and political actors. The standards themselves address nine areas of law enforcement, running the gamut from operations to personnel structure to traffic operations. To earn accreditation, an agency must demonstrate compliance with 446 standards, although standard applicability varies by agency size and function. The accreditation process starts with an agency self-assessment that can take as long as two years and is followed by a visit by an assessment team. The accreditation lasts for three years.

It is not clear from the CALEA website whether all or most law enforcement agencies engage in voluntary accreditation through the commission. But a perusal of various agency websites indicates that several agencies around the country are proud of their accreditation status through CALEA or are interested in achieving it. For instance, the City of Mesa, Arizona, claims to be the 186th agency accredited by CALEA, in 1993; it was reaccredited in 2001 (Mesa Police Department, 2005). Similarly, the police department of the City of Plantation, Florida, earned accreditation in 1998. In Florida it is possible to also be state accredited, and Plantation achieved that the following year (Plantation Police Department, 2005). The Metro Police Department in Harris County, Texas, the Winston-Salem Police Department, in North Carolina, and the County Police Department in Arlington, Virginia all had accreditation requests soliciting community support/comment, postings on their websites at some point in the last five years (Arlington County Police Department, 2005; Metro Police and Traffic Management, 2005; Winston-Salem Police Department, 2005).

Corrections

As of 2004, most correctional agencies in this country were not accredited (see the American Correctional Association website, www.aca.org). The reasons cited for failure to seek accreditation typically include cost, time, and concern that the agency might not meet the defined standards of professional operation.

A number of corrections and related organizations provide information on the standards of care and operation of correctional entities. The American Probation and Parole Association, which was founded in 1975 by a group of probation practitioners and later joined by those in parole, has served as the professional entity for community corrections professionals. The organization's website (www.appa-net.org) indicates a history of trying to professionalize and standardize the delivery of services and the operation of agencies. For instance, in 1982 the APPA released position papers regarding organizational issues such as budgeting, workload, professionalization in general, and how best to use community resources. As a means of promulgating their message of professionalization, the association also publishes a newsletter, which includes research articles as well as, anecdotes and commentary on probation and parole practice and management. Currently, the APPA claims a membership of over 26,000 practitioners worldwide.

Like the APPA, the American Jail Association (AJA), founded in 1981, is heavily involved in training jail professionals at their annual training conferences and via their research/practice-based magazine, *American Jails*. According to the website (www.aja.org), the AJA instituted a certification program for jail managers that focuses on inculcating acceptable professional practice and standards for those who work and lead in the field. The managing editor of *American Jails*, Dr. Ken Kerle, has done extensive research on jail standards and has visited hundreds of jails nationally and internationally in an effort, to push for professional practice. In *Exploring Jail Operations* (2003:74), Kerle includes this comment regarding self-audits by jails:

> A self-audit would make it extremely difficult for a person to be objective about his own jail operation. Bias in an individual cannot be totally eradicated in such an exercise. This is somewhat analogous to a teacher giving the students an essay examination and then asking them to score their own papers; bias inevitably creeps in. A jail audit could be greatly improved and possess more credibility if the jail auditors came from outside the state with no prior knowledge of the jail's operation.

But the American Correctional Association (ACA), founded in 1870, with future U.S. president Rutherford B. Hayes as its first president, is the largest and most engaged organization in the standardization and certification of correctional personnel and organizations. With a worldwide membership in the tens of thousands, the ACA sponsors a number of training and knowledge enhancing opportunities at its annual meeting and in other venues. The ACA publishes the well-known *Corrections Today* and the more research-based *Corrections Compendium* to promulgate professional standards of practice and emerging research in corrections. The ACA is an emerging force in the academic publishing market, with a repertoire of scholarly books. The ACA is also heavily engaged in the accreditation of adult and juvenile prisons, jails, and community corrections agencies.

In fact, staff and facilities in the area of juvenile and adult corrections are audited for accreditation by the ACA. Although the ACA accreditation program is primarily focused on training and staff development programs for personnel, it also considers such characteristics of the agency as its physical plant, its mission, and the number of clients/inmates it is responsible for. Specifically, as part of accreditation, an ACA audit assesses matters that cover "[a]dministration and management, the physical plant, institutional operations and services, and inmate programs" (www.aca.org/standards/ benefits). The ACA believes that accreditation will allow a correctional organization to assess its strengths and weaknesses, better defend itself against lawsuits, establish criteria for improvement, and increase the professionalism of staff.

Because it is time-consuming and costly to get accredited by the ACA, many correctional agencies have not sought accreditation or have tried to improve standards by other means. For instance, as of April 2004, the ACA listed only 1,274 correctional agencies as accredited, which means that thousands of other facilities remain unaccredited (www.aca.org/searchfacilities). For instance, according to the ACA website, only one local jail (the Cumberland County Jail in Maine) and one federal prison (the FCI-Sheridan in Oregon) had completed accreditation; (yet each state has numerous county jails and detention centers, probation and parole departments, prisons, and work release programs that are not accredited). In contrast, 16 Illinois, 34 South Carolina, and 77 Texas juvenile detention centers, adult jails, adult transition centers, probation/ parole departments, work releases programs, and prisons, both public and private and at the local, state, and federal level, had been accredited by the ACA as of 2004 (www. aca.org/searchfacilities). Of course, these larger states have many more correctional entities than the small states so these raw figures may be misleading. For example, there might be proportionally more correctional entities accredited by the ACA in Idaho (the ACA currently lists only one prison in Idaho) than in Texas. Unfortunately, there is no easy way to determine this as there is no source listing all the correctional entities. But these ACA numbers, randomly selected from six states, appear to indicate that more accreditation is taking place in larger states, perhaps because the funding is there; but a tradition of valuing outside review by professional organizations may be more pronounced in larger states as well.

As a side note, we mention that accreditation by any agency, even an outside agency such as the ACA, is not perfect. An institution that wants to fudge the numbers or misrepresent facts probably can get away with it. For instance, in the early 1990s, while visiting a medium security prison in a southwestern state, one of the authors learned from a lieutenant that the officer's institution was able to get ACA accreditation despite being grossly overcrowded, by moving inmates around in buses from facility to facility within the substitute to avoid having them counted by ACA auditors.

CONCLUSIONS

In this chapter we discussed a number of issues related to the management of key issues in criminal justice organizations: treatment, use of force, and standards and accreditation. Each of these issues presents a special set of problems and concerns for those who work in and manage criminal justice agencies.

Treatment, broadly defined, has always existed in corrections and has been a focus of the courts for some time. It was integral to the genesis of correctional institutions as prisons for adults, and detention centers and juvenile facilities for children, and to the mission of probation and parole. Treatment has recently emerged as a central facet of courts as the popularity of drug courts has spread. Treatment still enjoys support from the general population and from correctional administrators, though that support has waxed and waned over the years. The good news is that empirically based research indicates that soundly structured treatment programs, can have a real and measurable impact on recidivism.

The use and abuse of force have concerned policing and correctional entities since their inception. By definition, these agencies are in the business of forcing people to do what they might not want to do and compelling them to be confined and/or supervised. Force is integral to the mission and operation of criminal justice organizations. The problems arise when organizational actors abuse force, something that history tells us is not uncommon. Criminal justice managers and workers interested in insulating their organization from the abuse of force should focus on standards, training, and reinforcement of positive and professional behaviors by staff.

Clearly, the development of standards is key to the professional management of criminal justice organizations generally, whether in the area of treatment delivery, the use of force, or some other sphere of operation. Because of the political nature of the operation of criminal justice entities, hence the need for objective assessment, the best method for managers to obtain a level of adherence to standards is to subject their agencies to regular accreditation audits by an outside professional agency. Such an audit is much more likely to be respected by the public, the courts, and policymakers than self-assessment or reviews by like agencies in a state. Outside accreditation is also much more likely to breed an environment of professionalism among those who labor in, and for, criminal justice agencies.

EXERCISE: TAKE AN INFORMAL POLL

Since one of the authors began teaching criminal justice classes over eighteen years ago, the attitudes of students toward rehabilitation programming have changed drastically. We both know this because we routinely engage in nonscientific polls. Faculty, students, and criminal justice practitioners might consider doing the same thing by polling their colleagues or students. Of course, as was mentioned in this chapter, to some extent those attitudes are based on how you define "treatment" and what kind of organization and population you are talking about. Here is how the version of our poll works. Before starting the discussion of treatment programs and rehabilitation generally, we ask students to respond, by raising their hands, to the following questions:

1. Do you support the existence of treatment programs for clients/offenders/inmates?
2. Do you support the existence of education programs (GED, High School diploma) for incarcerated persons?
3. Do you support the existence of drug and alcohol treatment programming for offenders in the community? How about via drug courts? How about in jails or prisons?
4. Do you support the existence of these programs for adults?
5. Do you support the existence of these programs for children?

Without giving away the game, you can imagine, and we believe you will find, that the level of support your students or colleagues will voice for treatment depends on a number of factors. But we have also found that the amount of support for treatment in general, and certain programs in particular, has increased markedly in the last few years. This change is perhaps a reflection of the growing support in communities as people become disillusioned with the "lock em up and throw away the key" philosophy of the 1980s and 1990s and as research emerges tallying the successes of some treatment programming. To test this last premise, that communities are supportive of treatment, students might consider doing a nonscientific poll of their friends and family to determine how much support there is for treatment and how that support varies by characteristics of the population and type of programming. They might also notice generational, gender, and other differences in the people they poll that *appear* to be related (remember that this is a nonscientific poll), to levels of support for treatment.

DISCUSSION QUESTIONS

1. Why is the dichotomy between treatment and security false? What would be a better way of viewing the relationship between treatment and security?
2. What does Johnson mean by "mature coping" in corrections? How might this concept apply to other areas of criminal justice? Explain your answer.
3. What is a niche, and how are niches related to mature coping? Give an example.
4. What attributes of a treatment/rehabilitation program are likely to "work"? Explain why.
5. How do drug courts operate? Briefly describe each step in the process.
6. Does the extant research indicate that drug courts "work"? Cite some examples in your answer.
7. What sorts of policies exist to determine when the use of force is appropriate in policing? How about in corrections? Explain your answers.

8. What are the best methods that can be employed in policing and corrections to control the abuse of force? Why? Give an example.

9. What are standards and accreditation? How are professional organizations involved in promoting standards? If you were a manager, would you want to go through the accreditation process? Why or why not?

10. What are the advantages that derive from the use of outside agencies to accredit criminal justice agencies? Given these advantages, why don't most criminal justice organizations get involved in the accreditation process? Explain your answer.

KEY TERMS

accreditation: the process of determining whether an agency operates according to set standards.

niche: a private world that inmates try to carve out that serves as a sanctuary that offers "[s]heltered settings and benign activities that insulate them [inmates] from the mainline prison" (Johnson, 1996:120).

mature coping: "[d]ealing with life's problems like a responsive and responsible human being, one who seeks autonomy without violating the rights of others, security without resort to deception or violence, and relatedness to others as the finest and fullest expression of human identity" (Johnson, 1996:98).

standards: typically cover all aspects of operation from prescribing the amount of training different classes of staff should have to drafting procedures for handling community members, to determining the amount of space an inmate needs in a jail to setting the ratio of staff to clients on probation.

whistle blowing: "[t]he disclosure by organization members [former or current] of illegal, immoral, or illegitimate practices under the control of their employers, to persons or organizations that may be able to effect action" (Miceli & Near, 1992:15).

NOTE

1. See also: Bowman, Lowrey, & Purser 1997; Brewster, 2003; Calco-Gray, 1993; Field, 1985, 1989, 1992; Finney, Moos, & Chan 1981; Gendreau & Ross, 1995; Hartmann, Wolk, Johnston, & Colyer, 1997; Henning & Frueh, 1996; Inciardi, 1995; Kelley, 2003; Lockwood, McCorkel, & Inciardi 1998; McMurran, 1995; Office of Justice Programs, 1998; Palmer, 1995; Rice & Remy, 1998; Siegal, Wang, Carlson, Falck, Rahman, & Fine, 1999.

REFERENCES

ABC News. (1983). *Death in a Southwest prison.* ABC News Special. Narrated by Tom Jarret.
ACLU. (2005a). *ACLU calls on Denver officials to deliver on promised police reform.* Accessed at www.aclu.org/PolicePractices, March 2005.

ACLU. (2005b). *In testimony before commission, ACLU of Massachusetts calls for change in Boston police department's lethal force policies.* Accessed at www.aclu.org/PolicePractices, April 2005.

ACLU. (2005c). *ACLU sues New Mexico sheriff's deputies for beating two young men.* Accessed at www.aclu.org/PolicePractices, May 2005.

Alpert, G. P., & Smith, M. R. (1999). Police use-of-force data: Where we are and where we should be going. *Police Quarterly, 2,* 57–78.

American Bar Association. (2005). *Building a better court: Measuring and improving court performance and judicial workload in child abuse and neglect cases.* Chicago: National Council of Juvenile and Family Court Judges. Accessed at www.abanet.org, May 2005.

Ahn-shik, K., Devalve, M., Devalve, E. Q., & Johnson, W. W. (2003). Female wardens. *The Prison Journal, 83*(4), 406–425.

Andrews, D. A., Zinger, I., Hoge, R. D., Bonta, J., Gendreau, P., & Cullen, F. T. (2001). Does correctional treatment work? A clinically relevant and psychologically informed meta-analysis. In E. J. Latessa, A. Holsinger, J. W. Marquart, & J. R. Sorensen (Eds.), *Correctional contexts: Contemporary and classical readings* (pp. 291–310). Los Angeles: Roxbury.

Antonowicz, D. H., & Ross, R. R. (1997). Essential components of successful rehabilitation programs for offenders. In J. W. Marquart & J. R. Sorensen (Eds.), *Correctional contexts: Contemporary and classical readings* (pp. 312–317). Los Angeles: Roxbury.

Applegate, B., Cullen, F. T., & Fisher, B. S. (2001). Public support for correctional treatment: The continuing appeal of the rehabilitative ideal. In E. J. Latessa, A. Holsinger, J. W. Marquart, & J.R. Sorensen (Eds.), *Correctional contexts: Contemporary and classical readings* (pp. 268–290). Los Angeles: Roxbury.

Applegate, B. K., Langworthy, R. H., & Latessa, E. J. (1997). Factors associated with success in treating chronic drunk drivers: The turning points program. *Journal of Offender Rehabilitation, 24*(3/4), 19–34.

Arlington County Police Department. (2005). *At a glance.* Accessed at www.co.arlington.va.us/Departments/Police/PoliceMain.aspx, September 2, 2005.

Babbie, E. (1992). *The practice of social research* (6th ed.). Belmont, CA: Wadsworth.

Bell, V. (2005). *A content analysis of adult drug courts in the Pacific Northwest.* Paper presented at the Western and Pacific Association of Criminal Justice Educators, Vancouver, BC, Canada.

Bowman, V. E., Lowrey, L., & Purser, J. (1997). Two-tiered humanistic pre-release interventions for prison inmates. *Journal of Offender Rehabilitation, 25*(1/2), 115–128.

Brewster, D. R. (2003). Does rehabilitative justice decrease recidivism for women prisoners in Oklahoma? In S. Sharp (Ed.), *The incarcerated woman: Rehabilitative programming in women's prisons* (pp. 29–48). Upper Saddle River, NJ: Prentice Hall.

Brown, J. R. (2002). Drug diversion courts: Are they needed and will they succeed in breaking the cycle of drug-related crime? In L. Stolzenberg, & S. J. D'Alessio (Eds), *Criminal courts for the 21st century* (pp. 5–37). Upper Saddle River, NJ: Prentice-Hall.

Caeti, T., Hemmens, C., Cullen, F. T., & Burton, V. S. (2003). Management of juvenile correctional facilities. *The Prison Journal, 83*(4), 383–405.

Calco-Gray, E. (1993). The dos pasos: Alternatives to incarceration for substance abusing women of childbearing age. *American Jails, 7*(4), 44–53.

CALEA. (2005). *CALEA Online.* Accesssed, at www.calea.org/newweb, September 2, 2005.

Clayton, R. R., Catterello, A. M., & Johnstone, B. M. (1996). The effectiveness of drug abuse resistance education (Project D.A.R.E.): 5-year follow-up results. *Preventive Medicine.* 25, 307–318.

CNN. (2002). *Cincinnati signs pact with U.S. over police.* Accessed at www.cnn.com/lawcenter, April 2005.

Crouch, B., & Marquart, J. (1990). Resolving the paradox of reform litigation, prisoner violence and perceptions of risk. *Justice Quarterly, 7*, 103–23.

Cullen, F. T., & Gilbert, K. E. (1982). *Reaffirming rehabilitation.* Cincinnati, OH: Anderson Publishing.

DiIulio, J. J. (1987). *Governing prisons: A comparative study of correctional management.* New York: Free Press.

Field, G. (1985). The Cornerstone Program: A client outcome study. *Federal Probation, 49*(2), 50–55.

Field, G. (1989). The effects of intensive treatment on reducing the criminal recidivism of addicted offenders. *Federal Probation, 53*(4), 51–56.

Field, G. (1992). Oregon prison drug treatment programs. In C. G. Leukefeld & F. M. Tims (Eds.), *National institute on drug abuse research monograph series: Drug abuse treatment in prisons and jails .* Rockville, MD: National Institute on Drug Abuse. Finney, Jhoos, & Chan (1981).

Gendreau, P., & Ross, R. R. (1995). Correctional treatment: Some recommendations for effective intervention. In K. C. Haas, & G. P. Alpert (Eds.), *The dilemmas of corrections: Contemporary readings* (pp. 367–380). Prospect Heights, IL: Waveland Press.

Gendreau, P., & Ross, R. R. (1987). Revivification of rehabilitation: Evidence for the 1980s. *Justice Quarterly, 4*, 349–407.

Gendreau, P. (1996). The principles of effective intervention with offenders. In A. Harland (ed.), *Choosing correctional options that work.* Newbury Park, CA: Sage.

General Accounting Office. (2005). *Adult drug courts: Evidence indicates recidivism reductions and mixed results for other outcomes.* Washington, DC: GAO.

Gerber, J., & Fritsch, E. J. (2001). Adult academic and vocational correctional education programs: A review of recent research. In E. J. Latessa, A. Holsinger, J. W. Marquart, & J. R. Sorensen (Eds.), *Correctional contexts: Contemporary and classical readings* (pp. 268–290). Los Angeles: Roxbury.

Gioia, P. (2004, March 23). State corrections needs comprehensive re-examination: Connecticut business and industry association report. *Norwich Bulletin.* Accessed at www.norwichbulletin.com, April 14, 2004.

Goodstein, L., & Wright, K. N. (1989). Inmate adjustment to prison. In L. Goodstein & D. L. MacKenzie (Eds.), *The American prison: Issues in research and policy* (pp. 229–51). New York: Plenum Press.

Gottfredson, D. (1997). School-based crime prevention. In L. W. Sherman, D. Gottfredson, D. MacKenzie, J. Eck, P. Reuter, & S. Bushway (Eds.), *Preventing crime: What works, what doesn't, what's promising. A report to the United States Congress.* National Institute of Justice by the Department of Criminology and Criminal Justice, University of Maryland.

Hartmann, D. J., Wolk, J. L., Johnston, J. S., & Colyer, C. J. (1997). Recidivism and substance abuse outcomes in a prison-based therapeutic community. *Federal Probation, 51*(4), 18–25.

Henning, K. R., & Frueh, B. C. (1996). Cognitive-behavioral treatment of incarcerated offenders: An evaluation of the Vermont Department of Corrections' cognitive self-change program. *Criminal Justice and Behavior, 23*(4), 523–541.

Hepburn, J. R. (1990). The exercise of power in coercive organizations. In Stojkovic, S., Klofas, J. and Kalinich D. (Eds.) *The administration and management of criminal justice organizations.* Pp. 249–265. Prospect Heights, IL: Waveland Press.

Irwin, J. (1985). *The jail: Managing the underclass in American society.* Berkeley: University of California Press.

Inciardi, J. A. (1995). The therapeutic community: An effective model for corrections-based drug abuse treatment. In K. C. Haas & G. P. Alpert (Eds.), *The dilemmas of corrections: Contemporary readings* (pp. 406–417). Prospect Heights, IL: Waveland Press.

Indiana Commission for Continuing Legal Education. (2005). *Independent certifying organizations for Indiana.* Accessed at www.in.gov/judiciary/cle/ico.html, September 2, 2005.

James, D. J. (2004). Profile of jail inmates, 2002. Bureau of Justice Statistics, Special Report. Office of Justice Programs. Washington, DC.: U.S. Department of Justice.

Johnson, R. (1996). *Hard time: Understanding and reforming the prison.* Belmont, CA: Wadsworth.

Kelley, M. S. (2003). The state-of-the-art in substance abuse programs for women in prison. In S. Sharp (Ed.), *The incarcerated woman: Rehabilitative programming in women's prisons* (pp. 119–148). Upper Saddle River, NJ: Prentice Hall.

Kerle, K. (2003). *Exploring jail operations.* Hagerstown, MD: American Jail Association.

Knight, K., Simpson, D. D., Chatham, L. R., & Camacho, L. M. (1997). An assessment of prison-based drug treatment: Texas' in-prison therapeutic community program. *Journal of Offender Rehabilitation, 24*(3/4), 75–100.

Knight, K., Simpson, D. D., & Hiller, M. L. (1999). Three year reincarceration outcomes for in-prison therapeutic community treatment in Texas. *The Prison Journal, 79*(3), 337–351.

Leukefield, C.G., Tims, F. M. (Eds.). (1992). *National Institute on Drug Abuse Research Monograph Series: Drug abuse treatment in prisons and jails.* Rockville, MD: National Institute on Drug Abuse.

Linhorst, D. M., Knight, K., Johnston, J. S., & Trickey, M. (2001). Situational influences on the implementation of a prison-based therapeutic community. *The Prison Journal, 81*(4), 436–453.

Lipton, D. S. (1998). Treatment for drug abusing offenders during correctional supervision: A nationwide overview. *Journal of Offender Rehabilitation, 26*(3/4), 1–45.

Lipton, D., Falkin, G. P., & Wexler, H. K. (1992). Correctional drug abuse treatment in the United States: An overview. In C. G. Leukefeld, & F. M. Tims (Eds.), *National Institute on Drug Abuse Research Monograph Series: Drug abuse treatment in prisons and jails.* Rockville, MD: National Institute on Drug Abuse.

Lipton, D., Martinson, R., & Wilks, J. (1975). *The effectiveness of correctional treatment: A survey of treatment evaluation studies.* Springfield, MA: Praeger.

Lockwood, D., McCorkel, J., & Inciardi, J. A. (1998). Developing comprehensive prison-based therapeutic community treatment for women. *Drugs and Society, 13*(1/2), 193–212.

Logan, C. H., & Gaes, G. G. (1993). Meta-analysis and the rehabilitation of punishment. *Justice Quarterly, 10,* 245–263.

Manning, P. K. (2005). The study of policing. *Police Quarterly, 8,* 23–43.

Martin, S. S., Butzin, C. A., & Inciardi, J. A. (1995). Assessment of a multi-stage therapeutic community for drug-involved offenders. *Journal of Psychoactive Drugs, 27,* 109–116.

Martin, S. S., Butzin, C. A., Saum, C. A., & Inciardi, J. A. (1999). Three-year outcomes of therapeutic community treatment for drug-involved offenders in Delaware: From prison to work release to aftercare. *The Prison Journal, 79*(3), 294–320.

Martinson, R. (1974). What works? Questions and answers about prison reform. *Public Interest, 35*(Spring), 22–54.

Martinson, R. (1974, reprinted in 2001)). What works?—Questions and answers about prison reform. In E. J. Latessa, A. Holsinger, J. W. Marquart, & J. R. Sorensen (Eds.), *Correctional contexts: Contemporary and classical readings* (pp. 268–290). Los Angeles: Roxbury.

McMurran, M. (1995). Alcohol interventions in prisons: Towards guiding principles for effective intervention. *Psychology, Crime & Law, 1,* 215–226.

Merlo, A. V., & Benekos, P. J. (2000). *What's wrong with the criminal justice system: Ideology, politics and the media.* Cincinnati, OH: Anderson Publishing.

Merrow, K., & Minard, R. A. (2003). *Under the influence. Part 2: Treating addictions, reducing corrections costs.* New Hampshire Center for Public Policy Studies: Concord, New Hampshire. Accessed at www.nhpolicy.org, April 2005.

Mesa Police Department. (2005). *Mesa Police Department accreditation.* Accessed at www.ci.mesa.az.us/police/admin/accred.asp, September 2, 2005.

Metro Police and Traffic Management. (2005). *Accreditation & professional standards.* Accessed at www.hou-metro.harris.tx.us/PDWebsite/standards.html September 2, 2005,

Miceli, M. P., & Near, J. P. (1992). *Blowing the whistle: The organizational and legal implications for companies and employees.* New York: Lexington Books.

Nagayama Hall, G. C. (2001). Sexual offender recidivism revisited: A meta-analysis of recent treatment studies. In E. J. Latessa, A. Holsinger, J. W. Marquart, & J.R. Sorensen (Eds.), *Correctional contexts: Contemporary and classical readings* (pp. 268–290). Los Angeles: Roxbury.

National Center for State Courts. (2001). *Trial court performance standards & measurement system.* Accessed at www.ncsconline.org. September 5, 2005,

Office of Justice Programs. (1998). *Residential substance abuse treatment for state prisoners.* Washington, DC: Department of Justice.

Owen, B. (1998). *In the mix.* New York: State University of New York Press.

Palmer, T. (1995). The 'effectiveness' issue today: An overview. In K. C. Haas & G. P. Alpert (Eds.), *The dilemmas of corrections: Contemporary readings* (pp. 351–366). Prospect Heights, IL: Waveland Press.

Pearson, F. S., & Lipton, D. S. (1999). A meta-analytic review of the effectiveness of corrections-based treatments for drug abuse. *Prison Journal, 79*(4), 384–410.

Peters, R. H., & Steinberg, M. L. (2001). Substance abuse treatment in U.S. prisons. In E. J. Latessa, A. Holsinger, J. W. Marquart, & J. R. Sorensen (Eds.), *Correctional contexts: Contemporary and classical readings* (pp. 268–290). Los Angeles: Roxbury.

Plantation (Florida) Police Department. (2005). *Accreditation.* Accessed www.psd.plantation.org/accreditation-section.html, September 2, 2005.

Pratt, T., Maahs, J., & Hemmens, C. (1999). The history of the use of force in corrections. In C. Hemmens & E. Atherton (Eds.), *Use of force: Current practice and policy* (pp. 13–22). Lanham, MD: American Correctional Association.

Rice, J. S., & Remy, L. L. (1998). Impact of horticultural therapy on psychosocial functioning among urban jail inmates. *Journal of Offender Rehabilitation, 26*(3/4), 169–191.

Royce, D. (2003). State prisons lock up 3,000 new inmates. *The Miami Herald* August 19, www.Miami.Herald.com.

Schuiteman, J. G., & Bogle, T. G. (1996). *Evaluation of the Department of Corrections' Indian Creek therapeutic community: Progress report.* Richmond: Criminal Justice Research Center, Virginia Department of Criminal Justice Services.

Sherman, L. W., Gottfredson, D., MacKenzie, D., Eck, J., Reuter, P., & Bushway, S. (Eds.). (1997). *Preventing crime: What works, what doesn't, what's promising. A report to the United States Congress.* Prepared for the National Institute of Justice by the Department of Criminology and Criminal Justice, University of Maryland.

Siegal, H. A., Wang, J., Carlson, R. G., Falck, R. S., Rahman, A. M., & Fine, R. L. (1999). Ohio's prison-based therapeutic community treatment programs for substance abusers: Preliminary analysis of re-arrest data. *Journal of Offender Rehabilitation, 28*(3/4), 33–48.

Smith, J., & Faubert, M. (1990). Programming and process in prisoner rehabilitation: A prison mental health center. *Journal of Offender Counseling, Services and Rehabilitation, 15*(2), 131–153.

Stohr, M. K., Hemmens, C., Baune, D., Dayley, J., Gornik, M., Kjaer, K., & Noon, C. (2003). Residential substance abuse treatment for state prisoners: Breaking the drug-crime cycle among parole violators. *NIJ Research for Practice-Web Only Document.* U.S. Department of Justice, Office of Justice Programs, National Institute of Justice. www.ncjrs.org.

Stohr, M. K., Lovrich, N. P., Menke, B. A., & Zupan, L. L. (1994). Staff management in correctional institutions: Comparing DiIulio's 'control model' and 'employee investment model' outcomes in five jails. *Justice Quarterly, 11*(3), 471–497.

Thibault, E. A., Lynch, L. M., & McBride, R. B. (2004). *Proactive police management* (6th ed.). Upper Saddle River, NJ: Pearson-Prentice Hall.

Tims, F. M., & Leukefeld, C. G. (1992). The challenge of drug abuse treatment in prisons and jails. In C. G. Leukefeld & F. M. Tims (Eds.), *National Institute on Drug Abuse research monograph series: Drug abuse treatment in prisons and jails.* Rockville, MD: National Institute on Drug Abuse.

Toch, H., Adams, K., & Grant, J. D. (1989). *Coping: Maladaptation in prisons.* New Brunswick, NJ: Transaction Publishers.

U.S. Department of Justice. (1998). Introduction and overview of CRIPA activities. *1998 CRIPA Report.* Accessed at at www.usdoj.gov, April 2005.

U.S. Department of Justice. (2001). Introduction and overview. *CRIPA Activities in FY 2001.* Accessed at www.usdoj.gov, April 2005.

Walker, S. (1984). 'Broken windows' and fractured history: The use and misuse of history in recent police patrol analysis. *Justice Quarterly, 1,* 57–90.

Wexler, H. K., DeLeon, G., Thomas, G., Kressel, D., & Peters, J. (1999). The Amity Prison TC evaluation. *Criminal Justice and Behavior, 26*(2), 147–167.

Wexler, H. K., Melnick, G., Lowe, L., & Peters, J. (1999). Three-year reincarceration outcomes for Amity in-prison therapeutic community and aftercare in California. *The Prison Journal, 79*(3), 321–336.

Wilson, D. J. (2000). Drug use, testing, and treatment in jails. Bureau of Justice Statistics. Office of Justice Programs. Washington, DC: Department of Justice.

Wilson, J. Q., & Kelling, G. L. (1982). Broken windows: The police and neighborhood safety. *Atlantic Monthly,* March, 29–38.

Winston-Salem Police Department. (2005). *Police department undergoing re-accreditation, public comment invited.* Accessed at www.ci.winston-salem.nc.us, September 2005.

Wisconsin Education Association Council. (2004). Great Schools Issue Paper: Parent and family involvement. Accessed at www.weac.org/greatschools, April 2004.

Wright, R. A. (1995). Rehabilitation affirmed, rejected, and reaffirmed: Assessments of the effectiveness of offender treatment programs in criminology textbooks, 1956 to 1965 and 1983 to 1992. *Journal of Criminal Justice Education, 6*(1), 21–41.

CHAPTER 11

STRATEGIC PLANNING AND BUDGETING

There is a connection between planning and doing....

Hrebiniak, (2005:65)

Zero-based budgeting sounds great in theory. But theory is not reality.
(Roger Simmons, County Commissioner of Ada County, Idaho, 2001)

Public budgeting involves making and carrying out decisions regarding acquisition, alloca-tion, and the use of resources, particularly money, by government. Although public and private budgeting are similar in many respects, public budgeting is often more controversial, more open to multiple influences, and more heavily regulated than private budgeting.

(Nice, 2002).

INTRODUCTION: STRATEGIC PLANNING AND BUDGETING ARE AT THE VERY CENTER OF ALL THINGS ORGANIZATIONAL

People tend to think of strategic planning, but particularly budgeting, as very dry top-ics. Many students hem, they haw, they yawn, when these topics comes up. As hard as we try, it is hard to raise the enthusiasm for budgeting or strategic planning to the level elicited by, say, selection! People who have not worked in criminal justice agen-cies before, or have not paid attention to organizational management and politics, often just do not see the relevance to themselves of strategic planning or of a budgeting discussion. That many should find planning and budgeting boring is not necessarily surprising; these can be much neglected areas of study and comment that have not been presented creatively. A scholarly lament on the "arid landscape" of the literature on budgeting (Key, 1940) remains applicable over a half-century later.

Of course, attitudes of boredom and nonchalance about strategic planning and budgeting are completely out of step with what these disciplines represent for pub-lic (and private) sector criminal justice organizations. For such organizations, and the people who work in and supervise in them, strategic planning and budgeting are, at the VERY CENTER OF THE ORGANIZATIONAL UNIVERSE. This is true, regardless whether it is recognized, because strategic plans spur and justify budgets. The budget, in turn, controls just about everything done by the organization as a whole, and by individual actors. Budgets determine pay, raises (or not), whether programs are funded, buildings built, computers and furniture purchased; budgets determine staffing levels, availability of promotions, training amounts, research, and on and on. Concomitantly, budgets and strategic plans affect stress levels, satisfaction with the job, and turnover of employees. In low-budget years or when budgets do not fit the strategic plan, even criminal justice agencies, with burgeoning numbers of clients, can be cut or, almost as bad, not funded at a level that allows them to continue operating as previously (Bryson, 1995; Campbell, 2003; Gaines, Worrall, Southerland, & Angell, 2003; Hrebiniak, 2005; Hudzik & Cordner, 1983; Royce, 2003; Smith, 1997; Swanson, Territo, & Taylor, 1998; Wallace, Roberson, & Steckler, 1995).

In short, for those who work in public and private criminal justice organizations, for those who have pursued such careers or want to, and for those who study such organizations, understanding strategic planning and budgeting is of paramount importance. Every topic that has been touched upon in this book is affected by how, or whether, an organization plans and budgets. In a very real sense, then, plans and budgets will influence who we are in any criminal justice organization and what we can become.

In this chapter, and keeping the proper recognition of the importance of planning and budgeting in mind, we explore some recent history on the following topics: methods of planning, effects of planning, types of budgeting, and innovations in budgeting. We will first, define strategic planning and budgeting and then, with politics ever on our minds, we will begin our discussion of budgeting with "some things to remember about public sector budgets," that are derived from the literature on this topic.

STRATEGIC PLANNING: DEFINITION, BENEFITS, AND THE DIFFICULTIES OF IMPLEMENTATION

According to Bryson (1995:4–5) **strategic planning** is "[a] disciplined effort to produce fundamental decisions and actions that shape and guide what an organization is, what it does, and why it does it." To plan well, managers of an organization must have valid and reliable information, be aware of viable alternatives, and consider the future implications of all planning decisions. Should the organization be in a position to engage in strategic planning, Bryson (1995:7) identifies the following benefits:

- the promotion of strategic thought and action
- improved decision making
- enhanced organizational responsiveness and improved performance
- benefit the organization's people [as policymakers and key decision makers can better fulfill their roles and meet their responsibilities, and teamwork and expertise are likely to be strengthened among organizational members].

In sum, the organization that engages in strategic planning consciously develops a map for organizational operation. (Figure 11.1 is a simplified flowchart for the strategic plan of a criminal justice system in Anytown, USA). As pointed out in Chapter 4, in our discussion of the systems perspective, most strategic plans will reflect the organization's overall goals and mission, which are influenced by environmental, external, and internal processes, inputs, outputs, and feedback. So again, the strategic plan as Bryson defined it explicates what the organization is and does, and the reasons for its actions.

In most locations, for instance, the defender's office can rationally choose to allocate its resources to certain types of cases while de-emphasizing others based on a plan. Bryson (1995) cautions, however, that there is no guarantee that a strategic plan

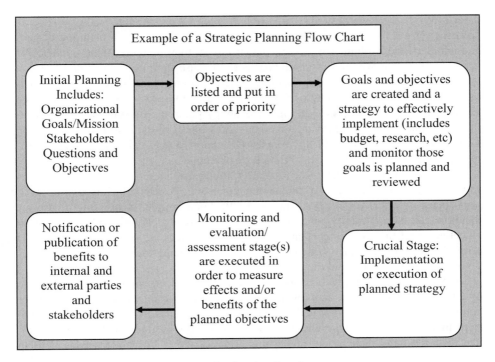

FIGURE 11.1: An example of a strategic planning flowchart.

will yield the benefits he lists, since for that to happen there must be leadership, the will to carry out the plan among organizational members, and the budget to implement the plan (Hrebiniak, 2005). Hrebiniak argues, in fact, that the planning, as arduous as it can be in some organizations, is actually the easy part. Execution or implementation is actually the most difficult part of strategic planning, and it is where most managers fail (Pressman & Wildavsky, 1973; Rothman, 1980). Therefore, that public defender's office may suffer politically (and potentially budgetarily) when it shifts resources to one type of case over others if the managers of the organization do not first persuade interested stakeholders (e.g., the police, courts, prosecutor's office, and community members) to buy into the plan.

Implementing the Plan

The execution of a strategic plan follows the layout of Figure 11.1 (also keep in mind how this planning process relates to the systems theory presented in Chapter 4). Notice that the "Crucial Stage" label is applied to the implementation section. It is here that all the plans are put into action. However, some very important steps must precede implementation if organizational goals are to be met. First, during the initial planning stage, representatives from the organization, key stakeholders, and all other individuals involved will come together and pose questions that feed into objectives, which (in theory) reflect the general goals of the organization (Welsh & Harris, 1999). This is done for several reasons; one is to flush out possible problems with planning design, and another is to explain why one particular design may be better than another. For example, if a state agency's ultimate goal is to increase funding for all treatment services available, the agency must gather information from several sources, both to help in the acquisition of more state or federal funding and to provide empirical evidence to guide and support decision making and policy planning. During the initial stage then, the state agency might bring together professionals in the field for advice in the form of technical assistance (TA), for research support, and to field and answer the all-important questions that will direct the plan's objectives.

During that initial meeting or thereafter, the managers and stakeholders responsible for overseeing all stages of the strategic plan will position objectives in order of importance or priority (Welsh & Harris, 1999). For example, in building a case for increased use of community policing, a planning group may prioritize a list of research objectives, and the most important will address or reflect the substantive question(s) posed in the planning stage (e.g., Does community policing increase positive interactions between the police and the public?).

Once the list of objectives, priorities and goals has been completed, a strategy to effectively implement and monitor those goals is planned and reviewed. The proper planning of this stage (which includes budget, research, etc.) is critical to the actual implementation stage for several reasons. Organizations often are faced with limited resources, and their proper management may make or break the whole planning process. (Organizations that have plenty of resources most likely achieved that status because of fiscal responsibility and success... so why waste it?). Therefore, budgeting the right amount of resources is paramount to success. The budget must cover all stages, and it must be understood that these resources will provide a *continuum of support* throughout the process. We shall return to this topic shortly.

We can also see that it is at this juncture that we map out how to effectively monitor and evaluate our plan. The evaluation may cover several key points in the plan at a variety of times (e.g., pre and post; multiple points during the progression of the plan), and it may include a strategy to effectively monitor and preassess the proposed time line for implementation, contracts and contracted employee oversight (deliverables), communication, budgeting, information gathering/data analysis/packaging and presentation, post assessment, and criteria for success (Welsh & Harris, 1999).

It is during the final decisive stage, implementing the plan, that all previous measures are put into action and must be effectively managed. Here monitoring and evaluation/assessment stage(s) are executed to measure effects and/or benefits of the planned objectives and notification or publication of benefits to internal and external parties and stakeholders. It is here, too, that the organization planning committee, stakeholders, and all relevant parties assess whether the objectives are being met.

Failure of Execution   The reasons for failure of execution are multifaceted (Hrebiniak, 2005). For one thing, managers are often trained on how to plan, but not on how to implement. Therefore, they may neglect to build support for programs and initiatives, and to restructure the culture to support the plan; they may not understand how power will shape and influence implementation; and they may continue to emphasize the importance of plan execution without having constructed control and feedback mechanisms to monitor implementation (Hrebiniak, 2005).

The very best of intentions by policymakers will not guarantee that a plan will be faithfully funded and implemented (Rothman, 1980). In fact, at times, as with the implementation of juvenile courts in the first half of the 20th century, just the opposite of the "best interests of the child" can play out when there is little oversight of powerful actors like judges (Rothman, 1980).

But even assuming that the money is there and there is widespread support for the strategic plan, "the best laid plans of mice and men," as John Steinbeck said, "often go awry."[1] Pressman and Wildavsky (1973) in a classic study of the failure to implement a well-funded and agreed-upon anti poverty program—economic development to increase minority employment in Oakland, California—found that it was the little things, the devil in the details, that stymied program implementation. Specifically, it was the lack of follow-through that kept this program from being adequately implemented. Agreements made for work, should have been maintained, approvals and clearances from all interested parties were needed. These are the small and ordinary, but important, matters that should have been attended to but were not. And these are the types of things, according to Pressman and Wildavsky (1973), that are often neglected in implementation. "Failure to recognize that these perfectly ordinary circumstances present serious obstacles to implementation inhibits learning. If one is always looking for unusual circumstances and dramatic events, he cannot appreciate how difficult it is to make the ordinary happen" (Pressman & Wildavsky, 1973:xviii). Thirty-plus years later, Hrebiniak (2005), makes a similar point, that achieving effective execution and change in organizations requires not just a plan and a budget, but sustained effort on the part of organizational members.

WHAT IS A BUDGET?

The implementation of a strategic plan is dependent on the development and execution of a **budget, that is**, a summary of expenses for a given program or organization. If as a student you were to devise a budget for your college education, you would likely list tuition and fees, books, rent, and food (or room and board), clothing, recreation, and miscellaneous items. Similarly, a transitional program for juvenile boys would budget for staff, housing, food, utilities, clothing, programming, school costs, recreation, maintenance, and miscellaneous. As with a personal budget, under each of these major headings for the transitional program would be subsidiary cost breakdowns, as in different salaries for the full-time and part-time staff positions, pay that varies by role (e.g., the director vs. the counselors), and health care and retirement benefits.

Table 11.1 gives a sample governmental budget. The proper planning (budgeting), implementation, and evaluation of an organization's goals and objectives takes fundamental, and in some cases advanced, mathematical and analytical skills, along with foresight and other managerial know-how. In the formation of fiscal policy and yearly budgets, most criminal justice organizations employ computer spreadsheets and other statistical software. A strong working knowledge of various computer programs (e.g., Microsoft Excel, Microsoft Access, and SPSS, [the Statistical Package for the Social

TABLE 11.1 Highlights of Recent Budget for the U.S. Department of Justice (millions of dollars)

Discretionary Budget Authority	Spending		
	2005 Actual	2006 Estimate	2007 Estimate
Federal Bureau of Investigation	5,208	5,669	6,040
Drug Enforcement Administration	1,696	1,665	1,739
Federal prison system	4,751	4,919	4,962
U.S. Marshals Service	748	792	826
Bureau of Alcohol, Tobacco, Firearms and Explosive	878	912	860
Detention Trustee	874	1,162	1,332
U.S. attorneys	1,544	1,580	1,637
General legal activities	625	653	684
National Security Division	—	—	67
Office of Justice Programs, COPS, Office of Violence against Women	2,795	2,414	1,228
Organized Crime and Drug Enforcement Task Force	552	483	706
All Other	779	722	628
Subtotal: Discretionary budget authority	20,450	20,971	19,451
Less crime victims fund rescission	—	—	−1,255
Total: discretionary budget authority	20,450	20,971	19,451
Memorandum: Budget authority from enacted supplements	267	229	—
Total: Discretionary outlays	21,343	20,839	22,247
Total: Mandatory outlays	1,408	1,505	2,491
Total: outlays	22,751	22,344	24,738

Note: Department of Justice budget cited directly January 7, 2007 from: http://www.whitehouse.gov/omb/budget/fy2007/justice.html
Source: Adapted from Department of Justice Budget January 7, 2007, http://www.whitehouse.gov/omb/budget/fy2007/justice.html.

Sciences]) is a must at the managerial level and, in some instances, the day-to-day operations of the whole organization. Technological tools such as these provide the manager and the organization with the ability to both plan and implement objectives, goals, services, and research within the organization and then interpret and benefit from the use of that information.

The Four Stages of the Budget Process

There are at least four stages in the budget process for organizations (Graham & Hays, 1986; see Figure 11.2 for a chart of the budget process and Box 11.1 for an example). The first stage involves the *preparation of the budget*. Often budgets are prepared with several objectives in mind, and they are not created out of whole cloth every year. Typically, the starting point for staff preparing the budget, are the previous years'

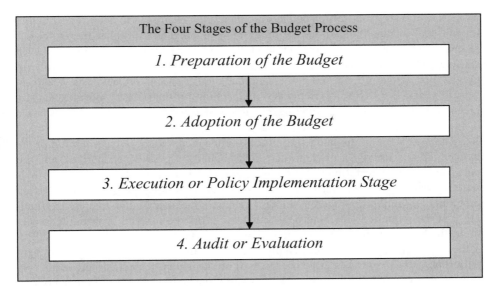

FIGURE 11.2: The four stages of the budget process.

BOX 11.1

REDUCED BUDGETS FOR JUVENILE CORRECTIONS IN FLORIDA

The budgetary crises that many states have confronted in the last few years have led some states to reduce their budgets for corrections and other services (Lauth, 2003). A case in point is the budget for the Florida juvenile justice system for fiscal year 2005 (www.djj.state.fl). According to the Florida Department of Juvenile Justice (legislative update), a total of 7 million was to be cut from juvenile facilities and community corrections. Detention would be cut by $934,235, probation and community corrections by $2,319,375, residential and correctional facilities by $1,047,898, and administration and executive direction by $895,033. Miscellaneous cuts of $2,587,706 were scheduled, as well. Across these areas, the cuts would affect jobs for staff and administrators, programs, placements, and secure and nonsecure beds for juveniles.

budgets. Staff will examine these budgets and allocate a similar amount of money to each item, while accounting for *inflation*. Briefly, the U.S. Department of Labor defines **inflation** as "the overall general upward price movement of goods and services in an economy." If new monies are likely to be available, they will be budgeted to account for the likely increase in expenses and/or used to fund new initiatives. The more discretionary parts of the budgets are then often examined to determine whether they fit, and further, the plan for the program or organization. In other words, for our juvenile transition program, housing, food, the cost of running the building, and even staffing remain somewhat fixed, if not requiring moderate increases from year to year. On the other hand, programming, recreation, and other special project costs vary from year to year—that is, are discretionary—depending on the budget priorities set in a given year, the availability of funding, the approval of the transitional program's board or funding agency, or the next step in the process.

The next stage in the budgeting process, after preparation, is the *adoption of the budget*. This is usually a process that is dominated by politics, economics, and the perceived and real performance of the program. If the current political actors, such as state legislators and the governor in the case of our transitional program, support such programs for youth, think there is enough money in the state budget to continue funding it at the requested level and believe it fills an important need in juvenile corrections, the budget proposed by our transitional program director will be approved. But if these important people think such programs are unnecessary, or disagree with them philosophically, then the funding request will be slashed or denied. If there is a recession, or if tax collections have decreased or are projected to decrease in the upcoming year, our transitional program's budget request is also likely to suffer. Or if there is little evidence to indicate that our transitional program is successful in reducing the criminal engagement of troubled youth, or if it is perceived to have failed in some capacity, the budget request will not be approved, as submitted, by either the governor or by the state legislators.

Should our transitional program's budget remain somewhat intact for the next year, it will enter the third stage of the budgeting process, which is the *execution or policy implementation stage*. Note that this stage takes the whole year, as the budget is intended to fund a year's worth of operation. Many states, cities, and counties count their fiscal year from July 1 through June 30. The federal government's fiscal year runs from October 1 through September 30. The vast majority of operations in criminal justice continue from year to year, and so the implementation of the budget for these organizations holds few surprises. New staff might be hired or computers purchased in our transitional house for juvenile boys, but normal operations are not disrupted much by the implementation of the budget. It is when new programs are funded or initiatives pursued that the agency feels the jolt and then the urgency that an infusion of, or reduction in, money brings. If, for instance, our transition program was funded to add more treatment space and programming, staff will need to undertake a number of tasks to ensure that expansion is accomplished. For instance, implementation of the budget will possibly require the construction of the space, and hiring and scheduling of new staff (e.g., see also Winkler & Smith, 2006). The development of a curriculum or curriculums may also be necessary. Usually all this activity will happen within the span of that budget year, if so specified in the budget plan.

The final stage in the budget process is *the audit or evaluation*. Typically, organizations of any size will employ internal or external financial auditors to go over their books to ensure that money budgeted for certain programs and activities was spent as intended. Even small organizations, if they are wise, will subject themselves to this kind of review.

BOX 11.2

JUDGE BOZZA ON BUDGETING, A SYSTEM IN USE

By Judge John A. Bozza

In Pennsylvania each county equals roughly one district. The Pennsylvania Supreme Court has administrative authority over courts. But each county provides most, but not all court functions. And this is a problem for budgeting. Different courts are funded in disparate ways by states. Pennsylvania has this dual system. Overall administrative control of the courts is by Supreme Court as per its constitution, but funding for most, but not all, court services is provided by the county. Then the county does gets reimbursed for some services.

Each year the president judge submits a proposed budget to the county council. The council decides whether to appropriate monies or not. Generally, these budgets are based on the budgetary history (line item) to determine what should be funded in the future. As the court supervises court operation, adult probation, juvenile probation, and family court, among other units, the court is a rather large administrative unit with a budget to match. So the administrative and president judges solicit a budget from each department, then review it and submit it to the council.

If the court and its various units do not spend all the money in one year, then that money goes back to the county general fund. As president judge, I made sure that we returned money every year to the county. I believed that doing so built good will with the county and allowed us to ask for more allocations when needed.

The biggest challenge I found when formulating budgets in the courts is that they do not always have performance standards to drive budgets. No one (meaning, in Erie County's case, the county council) asks us how we are doing. Essentially, we don't have to accomplish anything in terms of our service. For example, probation officers don't have to do anything differently from year to year to earn the same budgetary allocations, and that practice permeates throughout the court.

The Erie County Court developed performance standards for all units when they adopted the policy-based budget system. We have asked departments that want additional money to show us what they are planning on doing differently next year, as opposed to the current year. We want evidence to indicate what will be done in the upcoming year to justify an increased budget allocation.

An additional concern is the political nature of budget approvals for courts and other public services. People who make decisions about allocations in government are interested in not spending money each year or in spending less money. They will spend more money if they are convinced they will accomplish something good by doing so. But their standard for determining if it will accomplish something good is not objective and is really loose. In short, the budgeting process is very subjective, but that is understandable in a political world. Political decisions are often based on a feeling. They are also too often relational decisions and based on who is standing in front of you at any given time.

See Box 3.10 for a biography of Judge Bozza.

Some criminal justice organizations will also employ program auditors who, after examining the operation of a program, will make an assessment of its relative success. Both financial and program auditing are very important for at least the following reasons: they can help catch, reduce, or prevent corruption; they can improve financial and program records; they give successful programs some leverage in making their budgeting case to their funding agency; and they provide the organization with the information it needs to make valid budgeting decisions.

SOME THINGS TO REMEMBER ABOUT PUBLIC SECTOR BUDGETING

According to several authors of articles and books on budgeting, there are at least these four central facts to remember about all budgets in the public sector that have remained true for some time (Blomquist, Newsome, & Stone, 2004; Ebdon & Franklin, 2004; Graham & Hays, 1986; Key, 1940; Lauth, 2003; Nice, 2002; Poulson, 2001; Pyhrr, 1977; Schick, 1966; Whisenand & Ferguson, 1996, 2002):

1. As budgets are created in a political and economic environment, they are products of that environment.
2. Budgets are a mix of science and art.
3. Budgets, as political documents, reflect to some extent public priorities.
4. There is always more demand for public resources, than there are resources.

Item 1 means that decisions about the funding of criminal justice agencies are always done by political actors (Nice, 2002). For instance, budgets for sheriff's departments are typically determined and appropriated by elected county commissioners (usually based in large part on agency head proposals). Likewise, budgets at the county and city level for police, city and county courts, jails, detention centers, juvenile probation, and parole organizations (often through the county courts) are mulled over and funded by county commissions and city councils/city managers who are either elected or politically appointed.

For much of the 20th century, funding criminal justice agencies was not always seen as politically popular, and some agencies were underfunded. As a result, inmates languished in overcrowded facilities, people received little meaningful supervision by community corrections officers, police were unable to investigate all serious crimes, court dockets were overflowing, there were few programs or staff in juvenile or adult institutions, pay was poor, and facilities were nonexistent or falling down. Not surprisingly, these factors led to infamous abuses in any number of agencies and allowed serious offenders to remain on the streets to wreak additional havoc and pain. In the 1980s, as political priorities shifted and lawsuits forced funding, a building and hiring boom in many agencies began and continues today (Austin & Irwin, 2001; Campbell, 2003; Wallace et al., 1995).

Relatedly, as mentioned in item 2, budgets are a mix of science and art (Nice, 2002). The science these days lies in basing the budget on some definable, and even measurable, public good. If a jail is double- or triple-bunked with serious and repeat offenders, then some public good, such as continued public safety, would be achieved by floating a bond to fund construction of a new jail or expansion of the current one. The science comes in when the jail and those who oversee and set its budget (often county commissioners), study its practices, and those of related entities, such as the courts and the police, to determine whether that need for space (population forecasting) and funding, is real or whether some changes could be made to avert putting more money into the jail (e.g., see also Surette, Applegate, McCarthy, & Jablonski, 2006). Similarly, if that jail is interested in adding a drug and alcohol program for its long-term residents, it might seek funding at the local level or a grant from the state or the federal government, which in turn may allocate such money based on reigning political priorities (balancing treatment and security concerns, for instance). The "art" in all this is related to negotiating in the political realm to get the funding that is needed for current programs and priorities, while not neglecting to garner funds for any initiatives on the horizon.

Which means, as was noted in item 3, that budgets reflect public priorities (Blomquist et al., 2004; Ebdon & Franklin, 2004; Nice, 2002). Politicians, though often beholden to powerful political interests that are not aligned with everyday citizens, still have to be elected. When jockeying for votes, political actors will tend to shape their message to fit what they believe the public views as important. If the public is concerned about crime, as many polls indicated in the 1980s and 1990s (Merlo & Benekos, 2000), the politicians will respond by funding criminal justice agencies more. It is not a coincidence that a building boom in corrections and increased hiring in police and prosecutor's offices in the 1980s and 1990s (and continuing in some jurisdictions) tracked public support and concern about crime control (Austin & Irwin, 2001; Wallace et al., 1995).

Lipsky (1980) made a point similar to our item 4: that there is always *more demand for resources* in the public sector than there are resources. This is a point that particularly applies to public sector criminal justice agencies, as the clients of these agencies tend to be poor, to have less education than is the norm, and to be "nonvoluntary": that is, they usually did not ask for contact with a criminal justice actor, though the actions of offenders have dictated their entrance into the system. In other words, putting aside what the clients of criminal justice agencies did, this population is relatively powerless and sometimes cannot vote, even when released from incarceration. The clients' relatives and friends may be able to vote, but often they do not. So with a public good like safety prominently on voters' and politicians' minds, coupled with more recent concerns about the costs, criminal justice funding and practice can be affected.

For example, according to data provided by the National Center for State Courts (2003), the number of court filings involving criminal cases increased by 19% from 1993 to 2002. Add this to an across-the-board increase in court filings (civil, 12% domestic relations, 14% juvenile, 16%), and you get the sense that the workload of the courts at the state level has increased exponentially. In fact, overall the court filings have increased an average of 15% from 1993 to 2002 (NCSC, 2003:10). At the same time that the workload was increasing, however, the number of judicial officers in state courts from 1993 to 2002 increased by only 4.9% (NCSC, 2003:11). As of 2002, the average judge in the United States handled 1,568 filings per year, and about 15% of total state trial court filings involved criminal cases (NCSC, 2003:12, 37).

Large caseloads appear to be a theme not just for the courts, but for other sectors of the system as well. According to the American Correctional Associations *Probation and Parole Directory* for 2001–2003, there was an average caseload of 166 parolees for every parole officer in California (www.aca.org/publications: 2). This figure is an average, so the caseloads of some of the officers were much smaller, and for others much larger. But in reality what this means is that most offenders represented in these caseloads are not being supervised with any regularity. These are parole caseloads, not probation, and thus the matter becomes more serious, as by definition all these offenders have committed at least one serious enough felony to have put them in prison. Some will never commit another crime, or may do something that is a less serious threat to public safety, but with recidivism rates for parolees standing at about 41% (Glaze, 2003), we know that many of these offenders will recommit, sometimes violently. In other words, public safety is compromised by the politically, and economically, determined decision to increase the number of crimes that require a prison sentence (drug crimes come to mind), but also by the decisions to release people from overcrowded prisons, not to build more prisons, and then to release offenders out onto the streets with virtually no supervision. Based on all these complicated reasons, the status of clients, the politics of crime, the tightness of budgets, the input of a public both concerned for public safety and balking at more taxes, there is always more demand for resources than there are resources.

RECENT HISTORY OF BUDGETING AND PLANNING

Given the foregoing budgeting maxims, let us consider some recent history on the topic. Recall that before the reform of public agencies, contracts, and hiring ushered in by the civil service reforms, public sector agencies were openly ruled by the politics of the day (see the discussion of this matter in Chapter 2). Political ideology and connections before the 20th century had a much greater impact on the operation of public sector agencies than is true today, though as mentioned earlier, that influence is still quite apparent in budget determinations. Corruption and misspending of public funds made the need to control budgets and prevent their abuse a major concern for those in the policymaking and management spheres (Schick, 1966). An adherence to Taylorism in management, with its emphasis on control, also influenced the reformation of budgeting determinations. Budgeting was to be done by rote, in a dry and objective fashion. This approach is known as **line item budgeting**, which we will discuss shortly. Tradition has some influence in determining what was funded: if it was funded last year, then it should be funded this year with perhaps a bit more thrown in to cover inflation. In other words, formally, budgeting was very controlled and was regarded as a very staid and predictable process; the political and economic influences that inevitably intruded were little recognized in the literature on budgeting.

Key (1940) writing over sixty years ago, lamented what he regarded as "a lack of budgetary theory" in his article by the same name. He noted that the prevailing thought about budgeting at the time was consumed with a concern over technique (i.e., forms and their structure), with little attention or recognition of the influence of politics and economics. In contrast, he defined the budgetary process and document as "[a] judgement upon how scarce means should be allocated to bring the maximum return in social utility" (Key, 1940:117). He argued that determining the "social utility" of a given public program was not that difficult, but that budget analysts and managers needed more standardized ways to evaluate and guide choices. He urged such folks to consider the merits or return in social utility of a program and to not be afraid to decrease or end programs that do not yield such benefits.

Schick built on the work of Key when he wrote more than twenty years later that budgeting should be a systematic process that is related to *planned* objectives: "In this important sense there is a bit of PPB (planning, programming, budgeting) in every budget system" (Schick, 1966:300). He thought that budgeting should involve strategic planning, which considers the objectives and resources of the organization in tandem, as well as the policies that govern the resources. He also believed in management and operational control to ensure task efficiency in operation, to monitor resource acquisition and to avert the misuse or abuse of resources. He thought the "watchdog" approach taken by managers married to line item budgeting was an understandable reaction to the graft and corruption that prevailed in the public sector in the 19th century. Because the potential for abuse still exists, Schick did not advocate that public sector agencies abandon the controls and oversight of budgets, hence his emphasis on operational and management control; but he did think the agencies should lighten up a bit. He thought the line item analysis and work-cost assessments were appropriate tasks for the mid managers, but that top-level managers in the organizations should take a "big-picture" approach to planning and budgeting. Keep in mind that the big-picture approach is analogous of the systems perspective we discussed in Chapter 4 in that top-level managers must be able to understand and react to environmental, external, and internal demands or processes, output, and feedback, and then make adjustments according to such information.

Schick (1966) notes that as we became more sophisticated in economic analysis and informational acquisition in the 1960s, *long-range planning* for organizations became more doable. His central message was that managers needed to *plan and analyze more*, or pay attention to the forest as well as the trees.

In the 1970s an innovation in budgeting, perhaps reflective of the fiscal crisis looming at the national level, became popular and was premised on the ability to effectively analyze budgetary and program data. That innovation, which was wildly popular at first, was **zero-based budgeting**. Two questions are addressed under zero-based budgeting (Pyhrr, 1977:496):

1. Are the current activities efficient and effective?
2. Should current activities be eliminated or reduced to fund higher-priority new programs or to reduce the current budget?

The appeal of this approach to budgeting was its fiscal conservatism and its related emphasis on limiting governmental growth. Every program would be examined for its social utility (as Key would have defined it) and for its performance as that related to cost. Programs that did not pass muster or produce results would be eliminated or reduced in funding. Zero-based budgeting requires that program managers defend their entire budgetary appropriation for each year.

Zero-based budgeting became a true budgeting fad in that it was first adopted by Texas Instruments in 1969 and then by Governor Jimmy Carter for the state of Georgia (Pyhrr, 1977). After Carter was elected president in 1976, the use of zero-based budgeting spread to the federal government, and several other states and localities eventually adopted its principles (see Box 11.3).

Then reality set in. Despite its appeal, zero-based budgeting has a number of problems, the most damning of which is the lack of an easy way to know whether a program is "working." There are problems in defining performance (what is good, what is bad, what is mediocre) and appropriate costs for public sector or public sanctioned programs, such as the courts. Moreover, though part of the appeal of zero-based budgeting was its promised limits on government, doing thorough evaluations of program performance is ironically very costly. Moreover, an outcome evaluation requires good solid data on every program, and such information does not always exist in the real world. Finally, some pieces of programs are not measurable. How does one define and measure "justice" in the courtroom, for instance? How about rehabilitation? Is the true measure of rehabilitation only absence of recidivism? What about new programs? Are they likely to produce outcomes in the span of months or a year that would justify their continued existence?

Imagine a court administrator or a judge who could avoid budget cuts only by defending all her programs, every year, for funding (see Box 11.2). Imagine the funding bodies having to review every little program to determine its value. Imagine the redundancy and tedium in this whole process. Simply put, zero-based budgeting was great in theory, but in practice it was unintentionally costly and time-consuming. Not surprisingly, it was quickly abandoned by most organizations once these realities set in, although it is still used, at least to some extent, in some communities.

In the 1980s and 1990s budgeting continued to emphasize controls, as represented by line item budgets and audits, but with planning, when *planning, programming, budgeting systems* (PPBS), became key to the process (Graham & Hays, 1986; Whisenand & Ferguson, 2002). *Budgeting by objective* (BBO) also became popular as the sister of the managing by objective movement (as described in Chapter 4) during this time period. As with MBO, BBO involves greater input from organizational members into a central part of organizational operation: developing, implementing, and evaluating the budget.

BOX 11.3

ONE COUNTY'S EXPERIENCE WITH ZERO-BASED AND EXPENDITURE CONTROL BUDGETING

In Ada County, Idaho, the county commissioners have used both zero-based and expenditure control (aka mission-driven) budgeting systems. For several years, ending in 1992, the county used zero-based budgeting, and according to a former county commissioner, Roger Simmons, it didn't "work" very well (Simmons, 2001:8). "Zero-based budgeting sounds great in theory. But theory is not reality. There are several reasons why zero-base hasn't worked in government budgeting. Zero-based requires department supervisors to start at zero each year and justify every expenditure to the county commissioners. The reality is that any qualified supervisor knows their department's needs far better than the commissioners. Meanwhile, each supervisor, in hopes of funding what they consider to be legitimate needs, argues furiously for every expenditure. That, unfortunately, puts them in an untenable position when it comes to saving. As they approach the end of the fiscal year, they start looking for ways to spend their entire budget. They do that, not because they are bad people, but they are stuck in a system that encourages it." Because, as Commissioner Simmons argues, if they don't spend that money then they won't be believed when they ask for the money again next year. Moreover, should they save their money, it is pooled and may be given to departments that are less frugal. Commissioner Simmons (2001:8) concludes by saying, "In all the years Ada County used zero-base, we saved nothing—nothing."

In contrast, he notes that after the county moved to an expenditure control budgeting system, it did save money. "Under expenditure-control budgeting, each department is allowed to roll over 75 percent of its savings into the next budget year, thus eliminating the 'spend it or lose it' philosophy that prevails in zero-base. In Ada County, under expenditure control, we have been rolling over on average of about $3 million in savings each year" (Simmons, 2001:8).

Both initiatives, PPBS and BBO, represent an attempt to rationalize budgets and to tie them to the strategic plan and identifiable and measurable objectives (BBO). As such, both represent an attempt to insert more science, and less art, into the budgeting process.

Another initiative, *mission-driven budgeting* (aka *expenditure control budgeting*), is touted as a way of combining some of the science of the PPBS and MBO approaches with the input of workers, while rewarding frugality and keeping the realities of taxpayer revolts and worker calculations in mind (Whisenand & Ferguson, 1996). Under a mission-driven budget, each unit and its actors engage in developing a budget that is submitted to a department head. The budget for the organization will be allowed to grow only by the amount of inflation and the amount of community growth. Units that save money from year to year are allowed to keep all or a portion of those savings to reinvest in program activities. As funding is allocated in a lump sum, not line item, determination of how the money is to be spent rests with each unit, or those closest to the program delivery.

The beauty of this approach is that it averts the well-known problem of federal or state managers and workers trying to spend all their allocation by the end of the budget year to ensure that their budget request for next year can be at the same or a higher level. One cannot blame these workers. They know that they might well need the extra funds next year, even if they did not spend their whole allocation this year. But they will not be able to justify a budget request in the same amount if they had money left over this year. Mission-driven budgeting allows these workers to hoard their funds for next year, thus rewarding frugality, and allowing them to use the funds where they were most needed.

Whisenand and Ferguson (2002), in their book on police management, nicely summarize six budgeting approaches used by both public and private agencies.

1. Line item budgets: These are budgets that are largely based on previous budgets. Each unit of an organization may have input about a given line item. This budget approach is focused on keeping costs down, or at least stable. There is not much attention paid to performance or to public need, and ongoing program costs are allowed to continue.

2. Performance budgets: This approach is focused on measuring the performance of a program. Unfortunately, the output of some organizations is not easily quantifiable, though output for some programs may be.

3. Planning, programming, budgeting systems: This approach ties all parts of the organization, its present and future plans, together with its budget proposal, funding, and implementation. The difficulty with this system, as with performance budgets, is that it requires the generation and review of so much data on programs that it can become overwhelming to use a full-scale PPBS approach for an organization. Also, good data may not be available. This process tends to put budgeting in the hands of technically oriented people who collect and analyze data (i.e., those who can generate and examine statistics).

4. Program or outcome budgets and/or budgeting by objectives: This approach allows for much more input by each unit in the development of the budget or that pesky human element again (recall this discussion as part of the management theories reviewed in Chapter 4). Activities are related to outcomes, but decision making is also allowed at the unit level.

5. Zero-based budgeting: This approach requires that you start with a clean budgetary slate every year. Much data must be collected every year to justify the continued funding of each program. The approach is time-consuming and costly, hence very difficult to implement.

6. Mission-driven budgeting or expenditure control budgeting: This approach, suggested by Whisenand and Ferguson (1996), focuses on limiting expenditure growth

to inflation and community growth, retaining year-end savings in organizations to encourage frugality, and basing funding on lump sums, not line items, to allow program employees some decision-making autonomy. These authors like it because they believe it "[p]romotes sound management, simplifies the budget process, focuses on the big picture, restores trust in the budget process and promotes savings" (Whisenand & Ferguson, 1996:314–315). The problem with mission-driven budgeting is that there appears to be no formal approach to performance or outcome evaluation. Despite the difficulty of these activities, the truth is that in an environment of tight budgeting, program performance cannot be ignored, even as one acknowledges that it can't always be assessed effectively, either. But the problems in evaluation of effectiveness don't justify the skirting of the issue altogether.

In reality most budgeting processes include a mix of these approaches. Because of accounting principles, it is difficult to believe that the basis for most budgets should be anything but line item. Indeed, line item budgets can be the rampart for other budgets that are more focused on performance, planning and outcomes and that allow for more employee input (Blomquist et al., 2004: Ebdon & Franklin, 2004). Many governmental agencies use a form of zero-based budgeting for some limited types of programming, however, despite the problems (Simmons, 2001).

BUDGET STRATEGIES

At the beginning of his book *Public Budgeting*, Nice (2002:10–13), outlines ten different strategies that organizations and interested stakeholders adopt to increase their success in influencing budgetary decisions. These strategies, which may come in handy for managers and/or for those who study criminal justice organizations, are briefly discussed next.

Cultivating Client Support

The first strategy mentioned by Nice (2002), is *cultivating client support*. As a democratically operated organization presupposes some client input, some organizational scholars believe that both support *and input* by clients are just a given in the development of a healthy budget (Blomquist et al., 2004; Ebdon & Franklin, 2004). The *clients* of criminal justice enterprises in this case, and as defined by Nice, might be conceived broadly. They could include community members, suspects, clients, inmates, and supervisees; in budgetary matters, however, they are more likely to include employees and administrators, the pertinent elected representatives in both the legislative and executive branches of government and the general public. For instance, if the department of corrections in a given state were interested in building a work release facility in a community, it would behoove the administrators to solicit the support, and input, of those most affected by it. At a minimum the DOC would need to garner support from the larger community, but particularly prospective neighbors, state legislators in that district, and the governor's office—not necessarily in this order.

Gaining the Trust of Others and Documenting a Need

It should be a given in public service that one acts with honesty and integrity in all interactions (see the discussion of ethics in Chapter 3). Unfortunately, experience teaches us that this expectation of the "honest broker" is not always realized in either public or private sector work. Ideally and over the long term, however, being honest and upfront about factual matters usually pays off in a number of ways. In our work release example, the DOC should bring together all the affected "clients" and discuss with them the need for, costs of, and likely consequences of building and maintaining the work release. After all the facts are on the table, and the DOC has brought all the arguments and evidence to bear, the department may well fail to convince the appropriate parties that a work release is necessary at this time. But in subsequent discussions on the need for a work release, and other topics, the DOC is more likely to be believed and supported because its representatives are thought to operate with integrity.

Looking for Sympathetic Decision Makers

That said, there is nothing wrong with approaching the decision makers who are most inclined to be receptive and are willing to advocate for your organization's budgetary initiative. As Nice indicates, if one branch of government is not likely to be supportive, there are always the other branches and/or the public support to solicit. Nice (2002:11) points out that, "With many decision-making arenas and many decision makers, people may shop around for the decision they want."

Coping with Painful Actions and Minimizing the Risk of Future Cuts

In tight budgetary times, when all levels of government are forced to consider and reconsider funding options, Nice (2002) argues that agencies tend to develop strategies to avoid or reduce cuts. When painful cuts are threatened, he notes that agencies may tend to blame others for the budget crisis. They may also cut less visible positions or programs and/or do the opposite, and cut those that are popular to raise the ire of the program supporters. Another strategy organizations sometimes employ to minimize the risk or threat of cuts at such times is to quickly spend the monies they have to avoid having to return them to the state. Another option is to pad the original budget proposal with the understanding that less essential items may have to be cut later.

The Camel's Nose

A different budgetary strategy might be employed when an organization is starting or enhancing a program. Nice (2002) observes that in such instances some organizations may tend to de-emphasize the eventual cost of a program by asking for a small amount in the first couple of years and escalating the amount of their requests later. This tactic is premised on the belief that a small allotment is less likely to alarm decision makers and that incremental increases in funding will be the norm.

Making the Program Appear to be Self-Supporting

Funding for a program/policy or agency may be justified if it is partly self-funded. For instance, adding state patrol officers might appear more palatable budgetwise to decision makers if the director can argue that the new hires salaries will be partly supported by increased tickets paid by traffic violators.

Capitalizing on Temporary Circumstances

Some programs and organizations can effectively argue for more money in their budgets in the immediate aftermath of a crisis (Nice 2002). This phenomenon has occurred in corrections on many occasions in reaction to such events as riots and court orders to remedy conditions of confinement and practices. Correctional managers are quite cognizant of the advantages that such events can produce. For instance, one of the authors attended a conference organized by the National Institute of Corrections for progressive jail managers in 1992. Some of the participating managers wondered aloud how they could get the staff, training, capital influx for buildings, and programs for inmates from their county budgets if the ability of inmates to sue the jail was decreased. This is not to say that they liked being sued per se, but the prospect of lawsuits gave them leverage to argue for the funds they needed to properly run their jails.

Deception and Confusion

Though he does not recommend such strategies for garnering more resources, Nice (2002) recognizes that some organizations will engage in deception and confusion to increase or maintain their budget. To that end, agency representatives may hide information in their budget, provide misinformation, or engage in doublespeak by telling decision makers that the money will be used for something other than what they intend it for. In this sense, the ignorance of those in the public and among the decision makers about the agency or organization can be used to advantage to conceal budget priorities unlikely to meet with general approval.

CONCLUSIONS

Those unfamiliar with organizational operations often regard strategic planning and budgeting as dry and irrelevant exercises. If you have ever gotten a raise, or not gotten one, because of the political or economic environment, or if your program funding was cut or increased for the same reason, you quickly begin to appreciate the relevancy of these organizational functions. How does one, as a political leader or a policymaker, make a bureaucracy more responsive? The answer is cut, or threaten to cut, the agency's budget, forcing a change in plans. Bureaucrats, or wannabe bureaucrats, are also positively influenced by budget increases. Planning and budgeting really are at the center of all things organizational.

The types of budgeting discussed in this chapter reflect the various approaches and techniques that have been attempted over time. The attempts to both control and evaluate budgeting decisions in the 20th century were a laudable improvement over public sector operation of the 1800s. Criminal justice organizations interested in 21st century practice and with improved access to information will likely be increasingly called upon to evaluate and assess their programs' success, and to tie each budget to a strategic plan that outlines the organization's future.

Part of that plan, if even at the informal level, involves strategies to maintain or increase the organizations budget. Some of these strategies, as outlined by Nice (2002), are recognizable from real-world efforts to secure funding for criminal justice agencies.

EXERCISE: DEVELOP A CRIMINAL JUSTICE BUDGET

The goal of this group exercise is to acquaint participants with the likely costs of doing business in criminal justice. Here is one thing to remember: it almost always costs more than you think! Unless, of course, you happen to be familiar with police, courts, or corrections budgets! The following steps will allow folks to reconcile their projections with reality.

1. Divide the participants into manageable groups of four or five. This always seems to work best if people in each group choose specific tasks (there can be more than one person assigned to each task) and are held responsible for them. In this exercise, specific tasks might include doing the web research, writing the report, and presenting the report.

2. Choose a type of criminal justice agency, institution, or program in a city or state, and devise a budget for it. (The group may need to choose more than one city or state, as not all have their budgets available on the web). *Hint*: States and large cities and counties are more likely to post their budgets on the web.

3. Make an extensive and detailed list of likely expenses for the chosen agency, institution, or program (there should be 20–40 items listed).

4. Assign yearly costs to each of these budget items. To do this for some items on their list, it may be necessary to figure out the daily costs and then project the amount for the year. For instance, a group could calculate the costs of supervising one client on probation, multiply that by 365, and then multiply the product by the number of clients supervised in that community. Costs of buildings,and so on, can more easily be estimated by year. It is okay to make a reasonable guess. That is part of the fun!

5. Search the website chosen for the state or locality, and locate the posted budget. Again, not all states and localities post this material, so the group may have to use more than one resource. Also remember that some agencies and facilities are managed only by a certain level of government. Usually cities do not manage prisons; and with few exceptions, states do not manage jails. Cities, counties, states, and the federal government all have some form of law enforcement. Adult probation and parole usually are handled at the state or federal level, and juvenile probation/parole and detention at the county or city level. Courts are funded at the local, state, or federal level, depending on type.

6. Examine the most recent posted budget and compare the items to the preliminary budget. Make changes in item categories of the preliminary budget so that they are comparable with the "real" budget, but do not change the figures.

7. Write a brief report (3–5 pages) on the "budget development process" that your group engaged in and include an analysis of the preliminary and real budgets. Be sure to note the differences and similarities between the budgets and try to explain them. Also report on whether there were any surprises for the group upon examining the two budgets in tandem.

8. Present the report to the larger group and discuss.

DISCUSSION QUESTIONS

1. What are the four stages of the budgeting process, and how might politics intrude in each? Give an example for each one.

2. Why is budgeting regarded as both a science and an art? Explain your answer.

3. Where is planning likely to falter and why? Explain your answer and offer some examples.

4. What are the four things to remember about budgeting, and how are they related to the four stages of budgeting and the budgeting approaches discussed in this chapter?

5. What do you think are the most important matters to consider in the development of a plan and a budget for a criminal justice organization? Why?

6. What groups do you think are most represented in the development of criminal justice plans and budgets? Why? Explain your answer.

7. What groups do you think are least represented in the development of criminal justice plans and budgets? Why? Explain your answer.

8. Which budgeting approach appeals to you? Why?

9. Why is auditing and/or evaluation important in the operation of public and private sector criminal justice? Explain your answer.

KEY TERMS

budget: a summary of expenses for a given program or organization.

inflation: "the overall general upward price movement of goods and services in an economy" (U.S. Department of Labor (2007: www.dol.gov/dol/topic/statistics/inflation.htm).

line item budgets: budgets largely based on previous budgets. Each unit of an organization may have input about a given line item. This budget approach is focused on keeping costs down, or at least stable. There is not much attention paid to performance or to public need, and ongoing program costs are allowed to continue.

mission-driven budgeting or expenditure control budgeting: an approach suggested by Whisenand and Ferguson (1996) that focuses on limiting expenditure growth to inflation and community growth, retaining year end savings in organizations to encourage frugality, and funding on the basis of lump sums, not line item, to allow program employees some decision-making autonomy.

performance budgets: budgetary approach focused on measuring the performance of a program. Unfortunately, the output of some organizations is not easily quantifiable, though some programs might be.

planning, programming, budgeting systems: an approach that ties all parts of the organization, its present and future plans, together with its budget proposal, funding, and implementation.

program or outcome budgets and/or budgeting by objectives: this approach allows for much more input by each unit in the development of the budget or that pesky human element again. Activities are related to outcomes, but decision making is also allowed at the unit level.

strategic planning: "[a] disciplined effort to produce fundamental decisions and actions that shape and guide what an organization is, what it does, and why it does it" (Bryson, 1995:4–5).

zero based budgeting: the approach that requires starting with a clean slate every year. Much data must be collected every year to justify the continued funding of each program. This time-consuming and costly approach is very difficult to implement.

REFERENCES

Austin, J., & Irwin, J. (2001). *It's about time: America's imprisonment binge* (3rd ed.). Belmont, CA: Wadsworth/Thomson Learning.

Blomquist, G. C., Newsome, M. A., & Stone, D. B. (2004). Public preferences for program tradeoffs: Community values for budget priorities. *Public Budgeting and Finance, 24*(1), 50–71.

Bryson, J. M. (1995). *Strategic planning for public and nonprofit organizations.* San Francisco: Jossey-Bass.

Campbell, R. (2003). Dollars and sentences: Legislators' views on prisons, punishment, and the budget crisis. *The Vera Institute of Justice.* Accessed at www.vera.org/publications, December 1, 2006.

Ebdon, C., & Franklin, A. (2004). Searching for a role for citizens in the budget process. *Public Budgeting and Finance, 24*(1), 32–49.

Gaines, L. K., Worrall, J. L., Southerland, M. D., & Angell, J. E. (2003). *Police administration* (2nd ed.). New York: McGraw-Hill.

Glaze, L. E. (2003). Probation and parole in the U.S., 2002. *Bureau of Justice Statistics Bulletin.* U.S. Department of Justice, Office of Justice Programs, Washington, DC.

Graham, C. B., & Hays, S. W. (1986). *Managing the public organization.* Washington, DC: Congressional Quarterly Press.

Hrebiniak, L. G. (2005). *Making strategy work: Leading effective execution and change.* Upper Saddle River, N.J.: Wharton School Publishing.

Hudzik, J. K., & Cordner, G. W. (1983). *Planning in criminal justice organizations and systems.* New York: Macmillan.

Key, V. O. (1940). The lack of budgetary theory. In J. M. Shafritz & A. C. Hyde (Eds.), *Classics of public administration* (pp. 116–122). Chicago: Dorsey Press.

Lauth, T. P. (2003). Budgeting during a recession phase of the business cycle: The Georgia experience. *Public Budgeting and Finance,* 23(2), 26–38.

Lipsky, M. (1980). *Street-level bureaucracy: Dilemmas of the individual in public services.* New York: Russell Sage Foundation.

Merlo, A. V., & Benekos, P. J. (2000). *What's wrong with the criminal justice system: Ideology, politics and the media.* Cincinnati, OH: Anderson Publishing.

National Center for State Courts. (2003). *Examining the work of state courts.* Williamsburg, VA: NCSC. Accessed at www.ncsconline.org, September 07, 2005.

Nice, D. (2002). *Public budgeting.* Belmont, CA: Wadsworth/Thomson Learning.

Poulson, B. W. (2001). Surplus expenditures: A case study of Colorado. *Public Budgeting and Finance,* 21(4), 18–43.

Pressman, J. L., & Wildavsky, A. (1973). *Implementation* (2nd ed.). Berkeley: University of California Press.

Pyhrr, P. A. (1977). The zero-base approach to government budgeting. In J. M. Shafritz & A. C. Hyde (Eds.), *Classics of public administration* (pp. 495–505). Chicago: Dorsey Press.

Rothman, D. J. (1980). *Conscience and convenience: The asylum and its alternatives in progressive America.* Glenview, Illinois: Scott, Foresman.

Royce, D. (2003, August 19). State prisons lock up 3,000 new inmates. *The Miami Herald.* Accessed at www.MiamiHerald.com, April 14, 2004.

Schick, A. (1966). The road to PPB: The stages of budget reform. In J. M. Shafritz & A. C. Hyde (Eds.), *Classics of public administration* (pp. 299–318). Chicago: Dorsey Press.

Simmons, R. (2001). Zero-based budgeting hasn't worked well for Ada County. *The Idaho Statesman* June 8. Local: 8.

Smith, C. E. (1997). *Courts, politics, and the judicial process* (2nd ed.). Chicago: Nelson-Hall.

Surette, R., Applegate, B., McCarthy, B., & Jablonski, P. (2006). Self-destructing prophecies: Long-term forecasting of municipal correctional bed need. *Journal of Criminal Justice,* 34, 57–72.

Swanson, C. R., Territo, L., & Taylor, R. W. (1998). *Police administration: Structures, processes and behavior* (4th ed.). Upper Saddle River, NJ: Prentice Hall.

Wallace, H., Roberson, C., & Steckler, C. (1995). *Fundamentals of police administration.* Englewood Cliffs, NJ: Prentice Hall.

Welch, M. (1996). *Corrections: A critical approach.* New York: McGraw-Hill.

Welsh, W. N., & Harris, P. W. (1999). *Criminal justice policy and planning.* Cincinnati, OH: Anderson Publishing.

Whisenand, P. M., & Ferguson, R. F. (1996). *The managing of police organizations* (4th ed.). Upper Saddle River, NJ: Prentice Hall.

Whisenand, P. M., & Ferguson, R. F. (2002). *The managing of police organizations* (5th ed.). Upper Saddle River, NJ: Prentice Hall.

Winkler, G., & Smith, J. (2006). Long-term budgeting for operations in construction and design planning for jails. *American Jails,* 20(4), 53–55.

CHAPTER 12

DECISION MAKING AND PREDICTION

To be, or not to be,—that is the question:—Whether 'tis nobler in the mind to suffer the slings and arrows of outrageous fortune, or to take arms against a sea of troubles, and by opposing end them?

Hamlet, act iii scene 1, quoted in Shakespeare (1975:1088).

Ours is a time of uneasiness and indifference—not yet formulated in such ways as to permit the work of reason and the play of sensibility. Instead of troubles—defined in terms of values and threats—there is often the misery of vague uneasiness; instead of explicit issues there is often merely the beat feeling that all is somehow not right. Neither the values threatened nor whatever threatens them has been stated; in short, they have not been carried to the point of decision. Much less have they been formulated as problems of social science.... The great sociologist C.Wright. Mills commenting on the failure of social scientists to focus on core issues of "our times." Mills laments the jettisoning of reason and the failure to connect larger movements to individual existence.

(Mills, 1959:11)

INTRODUCTION

One of the most representative titles of a criminal justice textbook, in terms of its content, is *Screwing the System and Making It Work* (Jacobs, 1990). In essence this not so well known book is about a juvenile probation officer faced daily with no-win decisions regarding resources and his clients. Jacobs routinely had to decide how to reconcile his desire to help his clients with the fact that he had limited time, too many probationers to supervise, and too few programmatic options to refer them to. What to do? What to do? Or, not whether to be or not to be a probation officer, (as Hamlet might ponder), but how to be an effective one.

Ultimately, the probation officer's decision was to "screw the system to make it work," or to truly focus his time and talents on only the few clients he deemed most in need of his services, reluctantly ignoring the rest. By making this Solomonic choice, he believed that he might be "screwing" the system, and perhaps his more neglected clients, but "making it work" for the youths he could focus attention on. He was not necessarily "happy" or "satisfied" with this decision, but he believed it was the best he could do with limited resources.

Such a scenario—scarce resources and too many clients—is emblematic of social service work for SLBs, as discussed earlier with reference to the work of Lipsky (1980). This reality fits the work of criminal justice practitioners today as much as it did more than twenty-five years ago, when Lipsky published his classic work. As Mills wrote almost fifty years ago, there is a tendency in human history to fail to make the logical connection between what happens globally and the individual experience; yet the phenomena are inextricably intertwined: "Neither the life of an individual nor the history of a society can be understood without understanding both" (Mills, 1959:3). One global truth that fits public sector work with few exceptions is that resources are always short and demand is always great; and the SLB must make a determination, a decision, about how to reconcile these conditions.

So given these constraints, how do criminal justice practitioners and managers make decisions? What sorts of influences are likely to affect how they make those decisions? Do they always act as our erstwhile juvenile probation officer did, focusing their resources on the most deserving/hard cases? What sorts of factors are likely to hamper effective decision making, and to improve it?

In this chapter we review the act of decision making: what it is, obstacles to effective decision making, and how that act might be improved. In addition, and relatedly, we will discuss decisions of one type, namely, predictions, exploring how they are made and the typical errors associated with them. On this note we will touch on how brain cognition, and thus decision making, may be influenced by biology and environment and the implications of these connections for criminal justice actors and their work.

DECISIONS, DECISIONS, DECISIONS: WHAT THEY ARE AND WHO MAKES THEM (THE DECISION MAKERS)

A **decision** is simply a choice made by a thinking being. There can be alternate options available to the decision maker, or it may be that no other choices are apparent. In our example, the juvenile probation officer made a decision to concentrate his time and resources on certain probationers, rather than spreading himself too thin. But what if he had not done this? What if he had tried to serve all his clients by rationing out limited time and resources to offer a little bit to everyone? In other words, what if he had maintained the status quo? Would this have been a decision? The answer is yes, it would. People in the criminal justice system, and in all other aspects of their lives, are forever making decisions to maintain the current operations, even when they might be flawed.

Effective Decision Making

Of course, all criminal justice agency managers and actors are interested in making what we will define here as "effective" or "good" decisions or those most likely to further the ends of justice. It is useful here to repeat the definition of *justice* of the American Heritage Dictionary (1992:456) as stated in Chapter 2: "[t]he quality of being fair; fairness. 2. The principle of moral rightness; equity. 3. The upholding of what is just, especially fair treatment and due reward in accordance with honor, standards, or law." Distinctions between formal and natural justice (law and morality) and how justice is precisely and fully defined are matters best left to philosophers. However, in this text justice means that those who are guilty are caught, processed, and sanctioned, as befits community, professional, and moral standards, by system actors. We think that justice, for our purposes, also means that those who are innocent are given ample opportunity, and the due process necessary, to ensure that if they are caught up in the system, they do not remain there long and are not sanctioned. In terms of internal organizational operations, justice might also mean that employees are treated fairly and honestly by management and given the opportunity to develop and "give back" to their community. Effective or good decision making in criminal justice agencies, then, and in our view, has to do with furthering the ends of justice for those processed by the system, and for the criminal justice actors who work in it.

To Act or Not to Act: That Is But One of the Questions!

The decision *not to act* is perhaps the most common decision of all. The police choose not to ticket or arrest, the prosecutor chooses not to prosecute, the community corrections officer or correctional officer in the jail or prison chooses not to pursue violations of rules. The truth is that we who study the behavior of criminal justice actors really have no idea how often such decisions *not to act* are made, since they usually do not come to official notice. Given the number of cases that flood the system each year, and are sifted out, plus the official review that often accompanies decisions to act, it is likely there are more decisions not to act than otherwise (Bohm & Haley, 2005). Judicial decisions made inside courtrooms or in front of legal actors, even concerning the least important of matters, are usually recorded for posterity. But so many other decisions by criminal justice actors, especially when they involve the decision not to act, are never reviewed or reviewable, simply because they are not known. For instance, police officers often do not file reports detailing why they did not write certain tickets for speeding. So the police organization, the public, and sometimes the alleged speeders, do not know why the decisions were made, or even that there were decisions; only the officers know.

Yet when a police officer does write a ticket, any number of people will know of that decision and some will review it, not the least of whom will be the alleged speeder! Such a decision to act, then, presents the greatest risk for the officer organizationally and therefore must be supported with ample evidence that a real violation occurred (through observation, but better yet because of unbiased evidence as provided, e.g., by a radar reading). Notice, however, that if the officer thinks, based on comparable evidence, that a speeding violation occurred but chooses not to act, there is usually no need to justify that decision even though the dispatcher and perhaps a video recorder in the police car, may document that the officer made the stop. But whatever way you look at it, it is just easier for an officer who witnesses a minor offense, absent organizational pressure to do otherwise, to decide not to act. This is the reason why, of course, criminal justice organizations, particularly police organizations that may stand to receive revenue from each traffic ticket, will pay careful attention to how many tickets are written by individual officers. In fact, they will often include that information in the officer's performance appraisal as a measure of how much work she is accomplishing on her shift.

Such organizational surveillance or pressure regarding decision making may be both beneficial and detrimental to the ultimate goal of "good" decision making. Obviously, we want criminal justice actors to decide *to act* when there has been a violation of the law. But we also want them to have the discretion, as professionals, to determine when that is likely to have happened and to weigh the value of acting. So, of course, it is necessary for the criminal justice organization managers to watch and monitor how and why decisions are made, although an organization that applies too much pressure to make a decision one way or the other may thereby impose an obstacle to "good decision making."

OBSTACLES TO GOOD DECISION MAKING: LET US COUNT THE WAYS

Obstacles to "good" or effective decision making can come in many forms and from several sources. As we have seen, *the realities of the work* of street-level bureaucrats can force criminal justice actors to make less than optimal decisions. In essence, our juvenile probation officer was "screwing" not the system, but most of the clients, in order to "make it work" for those deemed most deserving or needy.

As was discussed in Chapter 7, *groupthink* has derailed many a decision-making process, and thus it constitutes a second and serious hindrance to effective decision making (Janis, 1972). A prosecutor surrounded by only "yes people" who fail to challenge the status quo (or at least to question it), and who provide no alternative routes for action, will often make decisions that do not achieve the best interests of justice for the community.

A third obstacle, as illustrated by police officers faced with ticket-writing decisions, indicates that *organizations can be both obstacles to, and facilitators of, effective decision making.* To repeat, because inertia, or inaction, is easier for officers in many cases of minor offenses—they do not have to do the paperwork and have it reviewed by others—organizational pressure to act may be inappropriate in some situations. Discretion with respect to minor offenses gives the officer the leeway she would not have with major offenses, where she would be compelled to act by law, practice, or conscience—or some combination of these. If the organization pressures her to act, to write the ticket, when she otherwise would not, this can be an obstacle to good decision making only if the ticket was not warranted. As mentioned in Chapter 3 on ethics, organizational pressure can also lead to decisions, involving *organizational deviance* that violate the laws or professional practices one would expect from criminal justice actors and thus constitute poor decision making (Lee & Visano, 1994).

Another, and fourth, obstacle to good decision making is the *politics of organizational operation.* As we have discussed in several chapters, starting with Appleby's conception of the nature of public organizations early in the text (Chapter 2) through the later treatment of budgeting and planning (Chapter 11), we have established that criminal justice agencies are centered in a political context. Laws and budgets that are formulated through give and take by political actors, wrangling among themselves, guide the actions of criminal justice organizations. What this means is that courtroom actors, facing known time and resource constraints, will tend to process cases more expeditiously than they might if there were more courtrooms, more judges, more prosecutors, more defense attorneys (Blumberg, 1984). The numbers of those actors and those courtrooms are determined by political actors, presumably acting in the public interest, and they will allocate funding at the level that would allow that more cases be given more time, or not.

Of course, central to this discussion of politics is *money*, another, fifth, potential obstacle to good decision making, particularly when it is lacking. The example given of the courts and their processing of cases is really about both money and politics, or politics determining how much money will be allocated for criminal justice operation. An organization that is strapped for funds may decide, like our intrepid juvenile proba- tion officer to "screw the system" and focus on "making" only a part of it "work." Thus courts might focus most resources on only the most serious cases. Or system-wide policy may be to plead down even the most serious cases, to diminish prosecutorial or courtroom time expended on them.

Relatedly, *space constraints* in jails and prisons, and extremely heavy defense and prosecutorial caseloads and court dockets, represent a sixth obstacle to effec- tive decision making for criminal justice actors. In Idaho, the lack of berths in treat- ment programs in the community has meant that judges sentence some offenders to prison,where they can in fact get treatment. Why is this a "poor" decision? Because it does not serve the ends of justice as we defined it. Judges in such cases will admit that some of the offenders did not *need* to go to prison for punishment, but they *desperately needed* substance abuse treatment. Why wasn't there substance abuse treatment avail- able for indigent offenders in the community, one might ask? Because establishing and funding such programs is a political decision. So the state, courtesy of the taxpay- ers, ends up spending much more to incarcerate low-level offenders ($20,000 for adult males) so that they can receive treatment. In turn, many offenders are more severely punished than their crimes warranted, according to the judges, and they are separated from their families and jobs, thus leading to a harder transition into the community once they parole.

Which gets us to the point, and the seventh obstacle, that a *lack of available alter- natives*, or knowledge of such alternatives, can also hinder good decision making. If judges have alternative sanctions or means of handling addicts—and in Idaho and other states drug courts are providing such an alternative in large urban centers— then they might be able to improve their decision making and in turn better serve the ends of justice. Unfortunately, information about such alternatives, regardless of whether they "work," is sometimes sorely lacking in the criminal justice system. There are problems with getting up-to-date and applicable research on criminal justice practices, programming, and processes, and undoubtedly such a gap in knowledge impairs the criminal justice decision maker's ability to make good decisions (we will discuss the value of research a bit more in the following).

The last obstacle, the eighth, also relates to information as it affects decision making. Rather the problem is that *there is too much information* for the decision maker to sift through and use effectively. For example, there is now a plethora of infor- mation about the relative effectiveness of treatment programming. So the criminal justice planner reviewing that information for the first, or even the sixth, time could be overwhelmed by its complexity and depth. Yet somehow people who make deci- sions about the content and duration of treatment programming will need to determine what information to pay the most attention to. A rule of thumb, in terms of review- ing scientific research as in this instance, is to look for studies that are well designed

(Babbie, 1992). That is, do they fit their subject, use multiple sources of both qualitative and quantitative data (also known as triangulation), and include enough subjects, and are they replicated?

However, when science cannot come to the rescue, so to speak, the decision maker will tend to evaluate the usefulness of information based on both logical and illogical factors. Illogical factors might include media presentations of infamous or nonrepresentative cases, the order in which conflicting statements are received (what is seen or heard first or last will be given most credence), the mode of delivery (people will better remember information put to a tune or dramatically presented vs. spoken in a lectures, or who delivers it (famous or infamous persons, or those who have a dramatic flare, are more likely to be "heard" than others) (Chiricos 2002; Dye & Zeigler 1989; Merlo & Benekos 2000). Other influential factors include who delivers the information (a trusted person or personality or someone with accepted expertise on a topic) and the mode of delivery (in a peer-reviewed academic journal vs. the popular press); it also makes a difference whether information fits the conventional wisdom or commonsensical notions about what is true and/or whether it is congruent with what has happened before.

People will also review information from the perspective of each individual's role as an organizational actor and make determinations about its truth and usefulness from that vantage point. Both the formal (training, official positions) and informal (subcultural and actual) practices of the organization will help people decipher the value of information. In other words, when faced with too much information, and absent any assurances about its validity from a scientific standpoint, the criminal justice manager and actor will try and sort through it using all sorts of filters; the danger arises when people are influenced by their own biases and predispositions, which may have been shaped by logical fallacies.

LOGICAL FALLACIES

One of the authors became acquainted with common logical fallacies in an undergraduate logic class. The professor was interested in preparing his students to "watch out for" and "beware" of failures in logic that frequently appear in public and private discourse and inevitably hampered the ability to make reasoned decisions. Classes on logic often include some discussion of logical fallacies or common errors in rhetorical arguments. Such fallacies are the refuge of the desperate and the deceitful, which is why we often see such tactics used in political discourse and over the airwaves. However, since criminal justice agencies and practices are guided mightily by the prevailing political winds, we often see such tactics used by those in, or those critiquing, criminal justice agencies or actors. The point of identifying common logical fallacies here is to prevent people from "falling" for them and thus making decisions that are influenced by the wrong conclusions they promote. Therefore, no discussion of decision making would be complete without touching on at least a few of the most common of these fallacies, including *ad hominem attacks, straw men, red herrings, begging the question or circular reasoning, the exception makes the rule, and appeals to patriotism/religion/emotion.* (Type "logical fallacies" into Google and you will be astounded at how many deceptive rhetorical tactics we humans have devised.)

Ad hominem attacks occur in arguments or discussions when the speaker or writer is attacked or slurred, without reference to the merits of what that person argued or stood for (Bassham et al., 2008). So, for instance, if a police chief were to argue *against* the establishment of a certain crime control program, a person launching an ad hominem attack would make disparaging comments either directly or indirectly about the chief, perhaps accusing the person and his or staff of being "soft" on crime, rather than addressing the merits of the argument. Whether the research or current practice supports the development of such a program is irrelevant for people who launch an ad hominem attack in this instance, because their goal is to influence the decision making of stakeholders (the public, but also the mayor, the city council, and others), and they do not want the facts to get in the way.

The **straw man** logical fallacy is used by those who want to divert attention from the merits of the real argument or situation (Bassham et al., 2008). To do this they will construct an argument that is as easy to "push over" as a "straw man" would be. A person using this tactic will set up a false or weak (straw man) argument and, once it is shown to be false, will act as if the opponent's argument is false in its entirety. To cite Wikipedia (2006:1), a straw man argument can take this, or many forms, including the following:

1. Present a misrepresentation of the opponent's position, refute it, and pretend that the opponent's actual position has been refuted

2. Quote an opponent's words "out of context"—that is, choose quotations that are not representative of the opponent's actual intentions.

3. Present someone who defends a position poorly as representative of its adherents, refute that person's arguments, and pretend that every upholder of the position, and thus the position itself, is wrong.

4. Invent a fictitious persona with actions or beliefs that are criticized, and pretend that the person represents a group of whom the speaker is critical.

Let's make our crime control program example more specific. Suppose a city council member who favored the establishment of a COMPSTAT program by the police department were to use a "straw man" argument (Chapter 13 discusses "the COMPSTAT phenomenon" in some detail). The council member might start by noting that failure to implement such a program will lead to greater crime in the streets. So an exchange between the police chief and the user of the straw man tactic, might go something like this:

Police chief: We should not develop a COMPSTAT program in the city until the research indicates that it "works" to improve our ability to control crime.

City council member: Drug dealing on our streets should be stopped. COMPSTAT is a proactive solution that can solve our drug and larger crime problem.

Now, of course, by opposing the adoption of COMPSTAT now, the chief is not arguing that drug dealing on the streets should be allowed to go on. This is the straw man portion of the argument, because nobody wants drug dealing to continue. Thus when the council member implies that to oppose COMPSTAT is to argue against a proactive crime control measure that will solve drug crimes, he deflates the chief's point about prudently waiting for research results and makes the chief appear to be reactive and perhaps "weak."

A **red herring** logical fallacy—the straw man fallacy could be a subgroup of the red herring—is also a diversionary tactic. As with all these tactics, it is used to divert attention from or mask the truth (Bassham et al., 2008). The difference is that the *red herring* tactic often entails an emotional twist, which is used to impair the listener's ability to make good decisions. Our police chief arguing against implementation of COMPSTAT now might have been educated at an elite Ivy League school, and his opponent might use this fact to argue that "the chief doesn't understand how things are done in this town." Now the police chief may in fact be well acquainted with how the department operates, having served in it for several years, but the person wielding this tactic is not interested in the truth, but in making an argument in a fashion designed to convince members of a community in which reverse snobbism about education is widespread. The city councilman is also playing to the emotions of his audience, intimating that the chief is an outsider and not "one of us." Therefore, group solidarity against those Ivy League outsiders requires that the community oppose what the chief wants to do in this matter. Where the police chief went to school, of course, has nothing to do with the merits of the COMPSTAT program.

Begging the question or circular reasoning involves restating in the conclusion the point on which the argument was based (Bassham et al., 2008). Thus the city council member might argue that "We know Compstat is effective in reducing crime, because it is successful in reducing crime." The latter part of this statement "begs the question" about the program's effectiveness by stating that the program should be used precisely because it is (said to be) effective.

Another common logical fallacy used in public discourse about crime is **the exception makes the rule,** or "If it happens once or was true once, it must happen all the time or be true in every case" (Bassham et al., 2008). We often see this argument used by practitioners who will tell an anecdote and then apply the lessons from that story to all like circumstances and clients/suspects/offenders. Such an anecdote might begin, "You can't trust such and such a type of offender, because this one time I did and the person violated that trust" or "This treatment program should be adopted everywhere because we have seen fewer offenders return after they graduated from it." The point is that both statements may well describe what happened in the instances related, and they might even apply to all like instances, as these practitioners imply. But we do not know for sure that the statements apply to like circumstances or offenders because each anecdote is only a single instance (the exception), there may be other explanations for what happened then or comparable circumstances in which the same outcome would not occur (make the rule).

Thus a proponent of COMPSTAT might use this logical fallacy by arguing that "COMPSTAT 'worked' to reduce crime in New York City in a given decade and so it should be adopted in all cities." Again, it may be true that COMPSTAT "worked" to reduce crime in New York City in the given decade. Alternatively crime may have dropped in New York for the same reasons (e.g., changing demographics, decline in violent drug trade, increased social supports for some offenders, increased income of the poor in the latter part of the 1990s, displacement of the poor from urban corridors, etc.) that led to its decline nationally over the same period, none of which had anything to do with COMPSTAT (Bureau of Justice Statistics, 2007). But the point is that one exception—the success of COMPSTAT in New York City, even if true—would not be a valid basis for making the rule for all cities. Of course, if scientific studies had empirically tested the relative worth of COMPSTAT programs, and the evidence indicated that the programs were instrumental in helping reduce crime, then the success of the program in New York City would no longer constitute an exception.

Finally, a very popular set of logical fallacies comprises those that have to do with **appeals to emotions/patriotism and religion**. These tactics can take many forms, but essentially they use emotional events or scenes (e.g., this child was made homeless because of drug crimes, so we must implement COMPSTAT), and appeals to God and country (e.g., people who don't support COMPSTAT are godless commie- lovers—this might also be considered an ad hominem attack) to make their point. Again, and obviously, decision making is improved when it is based on valid information, not name-calling of opponents, diversionary tactics, appeals to emotions, and nasty insinuations about opponents.

BIOLOGY AND COGNITION (SOCIAL INTELLIGENCE): A POSSIBLE UNDUE INFLUENCE

There is much emerging science that indicates that our biology and environment are constantly interacting to shape our behavior (Walsh, 2002; Walsh & Ellis, 2007). The reason a discussion of biology, as it affects cognition, fits in this chapter on decision making is obvious: cognition, or thinking and understanding, is central, or should be, to decision making. An important popular press book, *Social Intelligence: The New Science of Human Relationships*, describes how our reactions to each other and to our environment literally affect, and are affected by, our brain chemistry. As the author, Daniel Goleman (2006: 4) puts it:

> Neuroscience has discovered that our brain's very design makes it *sociable*, inexorably drawn into an intimate brain-to-brain linkup whenever we engage with another person. That neural bridge lets us affect the brain—and so the body—of everyone we interact with, just as they do us.

Clearly, there is much we do not know about the brain and how it interacts with its environment, but the current science tells us that *spindle cells*, which guide social decisions, are much more prevalent in the human brain than in the brains of other animals (Goleman, 2006). We also know that *mirror neurons* allow humans to anticipate the activity and emotions of others and to empathize with them, which probably explains why fallacious appeals to emotions are so persuasive for humans. According to Goleman, we "catch" the emotions of others and they have an effect on our own chemistry and, subsequently, our behavior. When those around us display anger or are upset at us, or others, we tend to feel it in a bodily sense, and our own well-being and attitude are affected. Luckily the opposite is also true: those who exhibit a happy, contented, or hopeful outlook are more likely to inspire such feelings in others.

The knowledge that our brains can be affected in such a manner, needless to say, has major implications for all criminal justice agencies and their management. Our conception of how best to lead, communicate, motivate, you name it, are all likely to be affected by a greater understanding of how the brain operates in this social context.

Understanding that decisions are often affected by the emotional impact of others is important because it means that decision makers need to be aware of this impact and account for it in their decisions. A judge, must think about whether his sentencing decision in a case is influenced by the actual crime committed or is being unduly affected by the community, and the victim's, emotions. If the case involves a heinous crime, where victim statements are taken into account in the sentencing, are we not agreeing that the sentencing decision should reflect some emotional affect? What about police handling of a suspected "cop killer"? How might the emotions of all involved affect the decisions made in that context? What about parole boards or correctional officials who are overly swayed by emotional appeals of an unrepentant inmate, who has every intent of committing the same types of crimes once released? In each case, the criminal justice actor must be aware that his own emotions, and those of others, are likely to have an effect on cognition, and that he may need to compensate for that effect.

PREDICTION

It is probably not an exaggeration to state that millions of decisions are made everyday in the criminal justice system. One key type of decision making is "prediction," or making a decision about what will happen in the future. As defined in Wikipedia (2007:1), a **prediction** in a scientific context is "[a] rigorous (often quantitative) statement forecasting what will happen under specific conditions, typically expressed in the form *If A is true, then B will also be true.* The scientific method is built on testing assertions which are logical consequences of scientific theories. This is done through repeatable experiments or observational studies."

As indicated by this definition, criminal justice decisions might be aided by the valid (true) and reliable (consistent) information that can be obtained through scientific investigation. Such investigations might be done qualitatively (e.g., using interviews or observations) or quantitatively (e.g., using surveys or agency data) (Babbie, 1992). Ideally, such methods should fit the subject under study and be designed to best determine what is true about theory or well supported about the practice. Criminal justice managers and actors who fail to use scientifically obtained information to inform their decisions risk making predictions that do not fit reality and do not further the ends of justice.

Having said this, there are two types of errors common to prediction: false positives (or overpredicting the occurrence of phenomena) and false negatives (or under predicting the occurrence of phenomena). It is likely, because of real-world concerns about safety and security, not to mention political and media influence, that criminal justice actors, with the possible exception of defense attorneys, are more inclined to make false positive mistakes than false negative. Police officers, prosecutors, judges, and community and institutional correctional officers are more likely to predict future offending by persons who have been accused and convicted than the opposite. Because the vast majority of people who enter the criminal justice system do not in fact commit another crime, if indeed they are guilty of the one they were apprehended for, the over-prediction of this outcome by criminal justice actors is likely.

Naturally, overprediction of reoffending or dangerousness leads to greater use of the whole criminal justice system, greatly enhances the monetary expenses of that system, and mars the ability to maintain a "just" system for those who are processed in it. On the other hand, if criminal justice actors were to commit the opposite error, that of false negatives or underpredicting reoffending or dangerousness, as sometimes happens as well, the outcome would be a threat to the safety and security of the community and impairment of justice, likewise. The "solution" to this tendency to commit either type of error in prediction is to focus on developing a system and a series of processes and practices that improve decision making generally, which will have the collateral effect of improving predictions specifically.

WAYS TO IMPROVE DECISION MAKING

Based on what we have presented in this text, and this chapter, we have come to believe that decision making in criminal justice agencies can be greatly improved by managers and other criminal justice actors. Generally speaking, the first step towards improvement is to *be aware of all the obstacles, errors, and rhetorical traps* (e.g., logical fallacies) that can impair effective decision making. Second, one must work to develop an atmosphere that *values organizational integrity* or one whose actors as a whole are honest, ethical, and can be trusted by the agency's members and by the community. An organization that has this reputation probably gained it by making effective decisions regarding its staff and the people they work with and for. Third, as much as is possible, one should work to *provide enough resources* so that staff can make the decision to devote the requisite time and effort to doing their jobs well. In addition to these more global ways to improve organizational decision making, the savvy criminal justice manager might also do the following:

- As much as is possible, insulate most criminal justice decision making, and decision makers, from political influence.
- Hire educated people, or support employees in educational endeavors that will prepare them for the complexity of their work (e.g., criminal justice or related classes that will give them the theoretical, historical, and research based information they need to contextualize their decision making).
- Emphasize professional practices as a guide to effective decision making.
- Focus on the validity and reliability of information that informs decisions. Concomitantly, make efforts to encourage and enhance research done in and for the agency.
- Be aware of, and account for, the biological processes that are at play in decision making.
- Foster creative and open decision-making processes, which encourage discussion and even dissent, and the consideration of alternative courses of action.

CONCLUSIONS

Criminal justice actors are constantly called upon to make decisions; yet often the information they have is incomplete or flawed in some way. Since at times that information is purposefully misleading, the criminal justice actor needs to be a wary consumer, and a thoughtful reviewer of the source and validity of information. It is always best if solid research on a topic has been done, and then done again and again, so that the decision maker has a good basis for making a decision. But most of the time, considering criminal justice decisions on any number of topics, such research does not exist or is not developed enough to give real guidance to criminal justice practitioners and managers.

In such cases, which are most cases, decision makers need to fall back on professional practices, training, education, and known and legitimate actions or decisions that "worked" in the past for themselves or their colleagues. Awareness of the logical fallacies used to bend the truth by those trying to illegitimately persuade and distract decision makers is also critical. As one of our undergraduate professors, who shall remain unnamed here, cautioned, "When you hear such crap [in the popular press], your shit detectors should be going off." Thankfully, and as noted in this chapter, there are ways to improve the organizational environment so that decision makers are not floundering alone or in some cases relying on a personal "shit detector" to determine whether a given piece of information is true or worth listening to.

EXERCISE: THE FALSE ARGUMENT

The point of this exercise is to better acquaint students with the failures of logic (logical fallacies) commonly used in arguments over criminal justice practices and policies.

1. Allow each student, or group of students, the opportunity to select an initiative from a list of criminal justice programs or practices (e.g., drug courts, therapeutic communities, community policing, the balanced approach in juvenile courts, unit management in corrections, problem-solving policing, parole, indeterminate/determinate sentencing, mandatory sentencing, human relations theory of management, traditional theory of management).

2. As a single-student exercise, assign a one- to two- page paper (to be written in or out of class) using each of the logical fallacies to argue for or against one of these initiatives. As a group exercise, have the group select a speaker and a scribe (writer of the group's notes), and have the whole group use each of the logical fallacies to argue either for, or against, one of the initiatives.

3. Have a few students, or all the groups, present their arguments (without naming the logical fallacy used) to the class, and have the class critique the arguments and identify each logical fallacy used.

DISCUSSION QUESTIONS

1. What is a decision? What do you think are everyday decisions made by criminal justice actors?

2. Why is the decision *not to act* often easier for criminal justice actors? When is it appropriate.

3. Provide some current examples of logical fallacies used by policymakers. Can you think of any that are specifically directed at criminal justice agencies or actors?

4. What are some common obstacles to effective decision making? How might these obstacles be overcome?

5. Why should scientifically derived information be weighted more heavily by the decision maker than information from other sources?

6. What are the types of common errors associated with prediction? Which error is most common for criminal justice decision makers, and why is that error more ubiquitous?

7. How might the decision-making environment in criminal justice organizations be improved? Is the ability to make such improvements solely in the hands of criminal justice managers? If not, why not?

KEY TERMS

ad hominem attacks: occur in arguments or discussions when the speaker or writer is attacked or slurred, passing over the merits of what that person argued or stood for.

appeals to emotions, patriotism and religion: these tactics can take many forms, but essentially they use emotional events or scenes and appeals to God and country to make a point that is not supported in logic.

begging the question or circular reasoning: restating as the conclusion a point in the argument.

decision: a choice made by a thinking being.

exception makes the rule: a logical fallacy that states that if *it* (i.e., the focus of the discourse) happens once or was true once, it must happen all the time or be true in every case.

prediction: in a scientific context "[a] rigorous (often quantitative) statement forecasting what will happen under specific conditions, typically expressed in the form: If A is true, then B will also be true. The scientific method is built on testing assertions which are logical consequences of scientific theories. This is done through repeatable experiments or observational studies" Wikipedia (2007:1).

red herring: a logical fallacy—the straw man fallacy could be a subgroup of the red herring—and is also a diversionary tactic, since like all these tactics, it is used to divert attention from the truth or mask it. The difference is that the *red herring* tactic often entails an emotional twist, which is used to impair the listeners' or readers' ability to make good decisions.

straw man: a logical fallacy used by those who want to divert attention from the merits of the argument or the facts of the situation.

REFERENCES

American Heritage Dictionary. (1992). *American heritage dictionary* (3rd ed). New York/ New York: Delta/Houghton Mifflin.

Babbie, E. 1992. *The practice of social research.* (6th ed.). Belmont, CA: Wadsworth.

Bassham, G., Irwin, W., Nardone, H. & Wallace, J. M. (2008). *Critical thinking*: A student's introduction (3rd ed). Boston: McGraw-Hill.

Blumberg, A. S. (1984). The practice of law as a confidence game: Organization cooptation of a profession. In G. F. Cole (Ed.), *Criminal justice: Law and politic* (pp. 191–209). Monterey, Ca: Brooks/Cole.

Bohm, R., & Haley, K. N. (2005). *Introduction to criminal justice* (4th ed). New York: McGraw-Hill.

Bureau of Justice Statistics. (2007). *Crime characteristics.* Office of Justice Programs, U.S. Department of Justice. www.ojp.usdoj.gov/bjs/cvict.

Chiricos, T. (2002). The media, moral panics and the politics of crime control. In G. F. Cole, M. G. Gertz, & A. Bunger (Eds.), *The criminal justice system: Politics and policies* (pp. 59–79). Belmont, CA: Wadsworth/Thomson Learning.

Dye, T. R., & Ziegler, H. (1989). *American politics in the media age.* Belmont, Ca:Wadsworth.

Goleman, D. (2006). *Social intelligence: The new science of human relationships.* New York: Bantam Books.

Jacobs, M. D. (1990). *Screwing the system and making it work: Juvenile justice in the no-fault society.* Chicago: University of Chicago Press.

Janis, I. L. (1972). *Victims of groupthink: A psychological study of foreign-policy decisions and fiascoes.* Boston: Houghton Mifflin.

Lee, J. A., & Visano, L. A. (1994). Official deviance in the legal system. In S. Stojokovic, J. Klofas, & D. Kalinich (Eds.), *The administration and management of criminal justice organizations: A book of readings* (pp. 202–231). Prospect Heights, IL: Waveland Press. Inc.

Lipsky, M. (1980). *Street-level bureaucracy: Dilemmas of the individual in public services.* New York: Russell Sage Foundation.

Merlo, A. V., & Benekos, P. J. (2000). *What's wrong with the criminal justice system.* Cincinnati, OH: Anderson Publishing.

Mills, C. W. (1959). *The sociological imagination.* London: Oxford University Press.

Shakespeare, W. (1975). *The complete works: All the comedies, histories, tragedies and poetry, including the sonnets.* New York: Gramercy Books.

Walsh, A. (2002). *Biosocial criminology: Introduction and integration.* Cincinnati, OH: Anderson Publishing.

Walsh, A., & Ellis, L. (2007). *Criminology: An interdisciplinary approach.* Thousand Oaks, CA: Sage.

W Wikipedia (2007). http://en.wikipedia.org/wiki/prediction

ikipedia (2006). http://en.wikipedia.org/wiki/Straw_man

CHAPTER 13

MODEL MANAGEMENT PRACTICES

You will see at once why I believe that the Enlightenment thinkers of the seventeenth and eighteenth centuries got it mostly right the first time. The assumptions they made of a lawful material world, the intrinsic unity of knowledge, and the potential of indefinite human progress are the ones we still take most readily into our hearts, suffer without, and find maximally rewarding through intellectual advance. The greatest enterprise of the mind has always been and always will be the attempted linkage of the sciences and humanities. The ongoing fragmentation of knowledge and resulting chaos in philosophy are not reflections of the real world, but artifacts of scholarship.

(Wilson, 1999:8)

Today arbitrary treatment of citizens by powerful institutions has assumed a new form, no less insidious than that which prevailed in an earlier time. The "organization" has emerged and spread its invisible chains. Within the structure of the organization there has taken place an erosion of both human values and the broader value of human beings as the possibility of dissent within the hierarchy has become so restricted that common candor requires uncommon courage.

(Nader, 1972:3)

<u>Select a person, set expectations, motivate the person</u>, and <u>develop the person</u>: these are the four core activities of the "catalyst" role. If a company's managers are unable to play this role well, then no matter how sophisticated its systems or how inspirational its leaders, the company will slowly start to disintegrate.

(Buckingham & Coffman, 1999:61)

Those elements of COMPSTAT that correspond with existing bureaucratic structures are more likely to change organizational practice, while those that do not have a much more limited effect. Furthermore, rather than streamlining the organization, COMPSTAT's operation appears to be hindered by the same bureaucratic features that it purportedly transforms.

(Willis, Mastrofski, & Weisburd, 2004:490)

INTRODUCTION: CRIMINAL JUSTICE AGENCIES IN A CONTINUING CRISIS IN NEED OF A SOLUTION

Ever since we started working in, and studying criminal justice, some thirty plus combined years now, justice system agencies have been in crisis. Of course, these problems did not start when we began to pay attention to them! The history of criminal justice agencies and institutions indicates that there has always been a crisis of varying proportions in evidence. Common themes of crises occurring for at least the last two centuries include understaffing, burgeoning numbers of clientele, dilapidated facilities,

300

brutality and other abuses, a lack of professionalism, inadequate training and pay, funding shortfalls, a lack of adequate or effective programming, and so on and so on.

Unfortunately, these problems have only been exacerbated as the number of people coming into contact with the criminal justice system has boomed. The latest figures from the Bureau of Justice Statistics (BJS) and the Federal Bureau of Investigation (FBI) indicate that except for arrests over the last ten years, there are more people adjudicated, sentenced, supervised, or incarcerated, in one form or another, by the criminal justice system than ever before (BJS 2004, 2005; FBI, 2005; Harrison & Karberg, 2003). This increased demand for services has only served to strain agency resources and personnel already grappling with a changing and dynamic environment.

Surprisingly, however, a number of criminal justice agencies are weathering these crises rather well. Yes, there are manifestations of problematic behavior in many forms. Stories of brutality and abuse by the police or in the courts leak out and then explode on the national news. Harassment of inmates and staff, by employees and by other inmates, is hidden behind the screen of officialdom and becomes evident only as lawsuits reach the courts. Serious disturbances may fester for years on the streets and in institutions and then reach the tipping point as demands for service are not met. The accused and the guilty sometimes leave the system no better off, and at times much worse, than when they entered. Moreover, turnover, stress, and dissatisfaction with the work plague some criminal justice staff and ultimately their agencies.

What is amazing about this whole cycle of crises that afflicts the adult and juvenile criminal justice system, however, is that somehow, and despite the challenges presented from the external and internal environments, many agencies, institutions, and programs are managing to sustain operations. Some are flourishing and innovating and have created enjoyable places to work, if not to live in. Clearly, there is a vast difference between a well-run agency and a poorly run agency. As the capstone chapter in this book, we are going to focus on the former, or the elements that contribute to success in a criminal justice operation: the "solutions" rather than the all too evident factors that can lead to failure.

All things being equal, and assuming some level of reasonable support for criminal justice operation in a state or locality, or at the national level, the following factors are likely related to its success: human relations management practices, a professional staff, proactive and shared leadership, an embedded subcultural belief in ethical practice, the availability of "best practices" programming, and an engaged and informed community. In this chapter we revisit and explore these factors, which are part and parcel of model management practices, but first let us note that such practices derive from several sources.

SALVATION THROUGH CONSILIENCE

The discipline of criminal justice is perhaps the most *consilient* of all. Harvard professor and author of two Pulitzer Prize–winning books Edward O. Wilson (1998) describes **consilience** as a *unity of knowledge* among seemingly disparate disciplines. Criminal justice was birthed in part from several other disciplines (sociology, psychology, social

.k, political science, public administration, business, chemistry, history, english, the arts and, more recently, biology) and continues to be influenced by them; these ideas, in combination with our own, forge a cogent understanding of crime, justice, and the associated practices (Guarino-Ghezzi & Trevino, 2005). We mention this here because a true understanding of criminal justice, or any management for that matter, requires the melding of many disciplines and a creative utilization of the knowledge they provide. This book presents but a sampling of the vast knowledge that one might employ in criminal justice management.

So as we begin the discussion of a "model criminal justice manager and model management practices," we merely note that the best managers are well educated, either formally or informally—and really both—and are tempered by experience. This statement is true because knowledge is a prerequisite to the understanding and practice of management. Experience is often valued in criminal justice practice, so it needs no defense here; but education is not always similarly valued.

Effective and just criminal justice management is impossible if managers have no, or little, exposure to the literature on the origin and nature of crime (sources include the disciplines of criminal justice, but also sociology, psychology, biology, and world literature). How will managers know what is likely to "work" if they do not study the history of institutions/agencies and solutions tried in the past (as discernible from sources on criminal justice, but also history, sociology, public administration, and business)? How will managers know how to evaluate practice if they do not understand principles in this area or know why programs are successful (from sources including not only criminal justice, but also psychology, sociology, social work, business, the arts, public administration, and chemistry)? How will managers know how to work well with other human beings, either their staff or clients, if they do not understand what motivates people (using as sources criminal justice, but also business, psychology, public administration, biology, and the humanities)? Finally, and perhaps most importantly, how will managers appreciate, and distinguish between, procedural and substantive justice in their organizations without the knowledge one can garner only from a number of disciplines (e.g., criminal justice, but also political science, public administration, philosophy, social work, literature, and history). Only with such knowledge and understanding can the criminal justice manager avoid the dangers inherent in all organizations (as briefly identified by Ralph Nader in the quote at the beginning of this chapter), and troubles that are particularly problematic for criminal justice agencies (as was discussed in Chapter 3).

In sum, effective criminal justice management requires vast knowledge of many topics. The best managers are of a Renaissance frame of mind, in that they either have the knowledge themselves or make it their business to acquire it, and use the brainpower of their colleagues in collaborative processes.

COMMUNICATION, LEADERSHIP, AND CULTURE CHANGE

The intersection of communications, leadership, and culture change is clear; their relationship is clearly dialectic. Leaders interested in changing their organization's culture, beyond approaching the work with a well-rounded education, use communication channels to convey that message. Yet the culture shapes the leader and the mode and style of the communication. In this way there is an interplay between the three, and all must be considered, and calibrated, when cultural change is attempted.

Cultural acceptance of the change will depend on any number of factors, such as the substance of the change, the extent of the change, the perceived and real effects of the change, leadership, and norms in the workplace. When the proposed change involves a movement from a sole focus on incapacitation for corrections to the inclusion of rehabilitation programming based on "best practices" (as discussed in Box 13.1), enormous effort is needed to effectuate such change. On many levels this need for change must be "sold" to the organizational members by leaders; but then, if it is to be successful, other members must be persuaded to "buy in."

Currently, police agencies are faced with the latest effort at organizational change, the COMPSTAT phenomenon. COMPSTAT, which stands for either "computer-statistics meetings" or "compare stats," was first implemented by New York City Police Commissioner William Bratton (Raney, 2005; Willis et al., 2004:464). It is heralded for sparking the huge decrease in crime in the city in the 1990s, and because of its perceived success in a city where crime was regarded as particularly intransigent, COMPSTAT has attained a number of acolytes in police departments around the country.

Integral to the COMPSTAT philosophy are the following six elements: "mission clarification, internal accountability, geographic organization of operational command, organizational flexibility, data-driven analysis of problems and assessment of department's problem-solving efforts, and innovative problem-solving tactics" (Willis et al., 2004:465–466). Some of these elements would appear to contradict each other. For instance, how does internal accountability, highly prized in bureaucratic organizations, coexist with an emphasis on organizational flexibility? How does one engage in innovation, where risks and chances are taken, when practices must also be both accountable and data driven? Such questions were also raised by Willis and his colleagues (2004) when they tried to reconcile the elements of COMPSTAT with its practice in a small bureaucratically organized police department. Simply put, they found that at times the bureaucracy got in the way of true COMPSTAT implementation (see the quote from the authors at the beginning of this chapter).

But then COMPSTAT implementation presents the real challenge of change in organizations that are bureaucratically arranged and are shaped by paramilitary practices. How to reshape the culture so that it prizes progress, innovation, excellence, and ethics is not always clear. It would appear that most organizations, public or private, that are interested in organizational change are struggling with just these issues. Willis and his colleagues (2004:493) conclude their article on a pessimistic note vis-à-vis COMPSTAT implementation: "Most significant, COMPSTAT'S reinforcement of the bureaucratic hierarchy of policing stifles creative problem-solving approaches." However, this pessimism regarding COMPSTAT does not mean that leadership cannot effectuate positive cultural change via communication; rather, it just means that these authors are not optimistic about this program in these types of agencies, in particular. Change might well be more possible if an agency has a less paramilitary structure (e.g., is fatter and flatter) and is more amenable to engagement of the workers, who construct the culture, in the change. For example, Box 13.1 presents a manager's account of an attempt at culture change of a corrections department.

BOX 13.1

MAKING A CULTURE CHANGE AS WE MOVE TOWARD EVIDENCE-BASED "BEST PRACTICES"

by Gary Barrier,

Prison culture change can be slow, and seeing change, when you are immersed in the organization, can be even harder. The IDOC Idaho Department of Corrections embarked on a remarkable era of change—matching what national researchers were saying was a needed diversion from "Nothing Works" to a "What Works" perspective in corrections. The latter concept is based on evidenced-based "Best Practices" and the shift to this began in the early to mid-90s for the IDOC.

The Idaho Department of Corrections has always been viewed as an agency which assures public safety by locking up dangerous criminals. Reducing offender risk and providing opportunities for the offender to change is part of our mission. Because the vast majority of those who are incarcerated in Idaho prisons will someday be in our communities, this is reason enough to ensure inmates leave the institutions better than when they entered them. The following facts are quite sobering in this regard:

- 3,237 incarcerated offenders were released from Idaho prisons in 2003
- 6,235 offenders were incarcerated
- 97% of all offenders will leave prison and return to our communities

I have personally worked in the corrections field for approximately 28 years. I began my career in corrections as a juvenile probation officer and counselor in the late 70s and graduated to adult supervision of probation and parole in the early 80s. I have served in programs and treatment, been a deputy warden, a warden and am currently serving in an administrative capacity with Programs/Education. My experience with prisons began in the early 90s. It was then I realized the problems and conflict day-to-day prison management was having with prison programs. We conducted and completed some research on prison ethics in partnership with BSU professors Dr. [Mary] Stohr and Dr. [Robert] Marsh. This was the starting point for IDOC to take a look at the problems we had with a number of areas (e.g., communication and culture) and provided an impetus to gear our efforts toward cultural change. Part of this shift in focus would be used to standardize programs into researched-based Best Practices for the IDOC.

In relation to these efforts, and national recognition and support for correctional change, in 2001 the governor, Dirk Kempthorne, initialed and signed into law the Substance Abuse Initiative Act. As a result of this act, [authorization for] 47.5 FTEs[full-time employees], along with $2,500,000 for substance abuse assessments, treatment and program evaluations was signed into law. Unfortunately, subsequent budget cuts in 2002 and 2003 negated these funds and positions. This initiative, however, served as another catalyst for a philosophical shift in the IDOC, which resulted in the implementation of new research-based programs and the enhancement of our existing programs. Being consistent with legislative intent, IDOC formulated partnerships with Health and Welfare and community treatment providers. These collaborations and partnerships have continued to grow with judicial and other state agencies, such as Idaho Housing, Vocational Rehabilitation, faith-based community services, and many others.

IDOC has been committed to provide research-based programs. In 1998 the IDOC opened up it s first of four therapeutic communities. We built on that success to develop a core program continuum of treatment which begins with a battery of assessments, and a personalized offender treatment/release plan. As a result of a comprehensive update of our data system and better documentation, IDOC is now able to process outcome research reports.

The need for offender programs continues to be evaluated through many analytical and aggregate reports. A research project is currently under way with the University of Idaho. The results [were] made available in early 2007.

The foundation has been successfully built. The average rate of Idaho offenders revoking parole and returning to prison from 1996–2003 was 39%. But our population continues to surge, with court commitments rising for violent and nonviolent offenders. Idaho has one of the fastest growing populations in the U.S. with an average rate of a yearly growth exceeding 10% for new inmates.

Clearly, we are at a crossroads. A bulging prison and community supervision population threatens our ability to deliver effective programs and, to fulfill our mission and vision for making our communities safe, while providing offenders opportunities to change. It will be our challenge to work together with our state and community partnerships to continue our efforts to ensure that we do not lose sight of the need to continue with these changes.

Gary Barrier is administrator of programs for the Idaho Department of Corrections.

HUMAN RELATIONS MANAGEMENT PRACTICES

As we discussed in Chapter 4, there has been a movement in both the private and public sectors toward the adoption of a more human relations management practice. Much like the other management theories discussed in Chapter 4, human relations management derived from the work of scholars and practitioners in a number of disciplines. In that sense, it is consilient, and thus it renders interrelated practices, as should become evident in the following.

The latest manifestations of the human relations movement come in the form of the push for "learning organizations" and "teaming" in businesses and governmental agencies. These initiatives of themselves represent a unity of knowledge from the disciplines of education, public administration, business, psychology, and of course, criminal justice. But beyond these current thrusts in management, styles of leadership, personnel practices, and processes and types of budgeting are all fitted, to some extent, to either a more traditional or a more human relations perspective of management.

The reality is that a human relations perspective on management could never be fully adopted in criminal justice organizations. Given their multilayered mission, their bureaucratic shape, and the need for accountability and some privacy protection, the implementation of this perspective, much like that of COMPSTAT, must always be relative to the mission of the organization. So the extent to which a human relations management perspective could be implemented in criminal justice agencies depends on the primary mission for that organization and the situation it finds itself in. For instance, traditional management is better fitted to correctional institutions that must be more secure. But a juvenile halfway house and an adult maximum security prison can and should be managed differently. The maximum security prison is more likely to need hierarchy, bureaucracy, rule of law, and para military apparatus in its organization than is the halfway house. The halfway house, on the other hand, might benefit from less structure, more open communication lines, greater flexibility, and empathy—characteristics that are aligned with a human relations perspective.

Moreover, all criminal justice agencies, whether police departments, courtrooms, or halfway houses for juveniles, must be concerned with accountability. Recall the discussion of Appleby's (1945) thesis that "government is different" from private sector work in part because of the need for accountability. Since it is the agencies' business to legally deny liberty to citizens in a democracy, managers and workers need always be accountable for their actions to ensure proper use of this awesome power.

Having said this, there is room for a human relations perspective of management in every criminal justice facility, though it should be adjusted for circumstances. We say this because one thing remains constant whether we are discussing a maximum security prison or a halfway house, a police department or a courtroom, and that is the need to manage human beings, as both clients and staff. As we found from our discussion of management theories in Chapter 4, human beings have motivating needs, some of which are fulfilled, or not, at work. If these needs are not fulfilled, there is a real chance that workers will not be motivated, that production will decrease, and that problems with negative stress, turnover, and job dissatisfaction will increase.

Recall the six basic tenets for those adopting a modern version of human relations theory, as noted in Chapter 4:

1. A fatter and flatter organizational structure, or a less pyramidal shape to the organization traditional than is.
2. Shared decision making by all sectors of the organization.
3. A mechanism or mechanisms for sharing in decisions.

4. Empowered employees who are willing and able to participate fully in decision making that affects their workplace.

5. Enhancement of top-down communication with bottom-up, horizontal, and diagonal communication avenues.

6. Acceptance and expectation that the organization and its members must adapt, grow, and even take risks, if they hope to achieve objectives.

The theory is that the organization and manager who can employ these tenets are more likely to avoid a number of the maladies common to unsuccessful management practice (Stohr, Lovich, Menke, & Zupan, 1994; Wright, Saylor, Gilman, & Camp 1997). It is also thought that an organization that can successfully employ all these tenets, given the twin concerns of security and accountability, is likely to experience positive outcomes, such as a highly motivated and engaged staff, a willingness to innovate by staff, and excellence in service delivery to clients.

IT IS THE PEOPLE AND THEIR GOALS THAT MATTER

Appleby's powerful argument that "government is different" from the private sector not withstanding, we can learn a great deal from studying business management practices (Raney, 2005). For example, Buckingham and Coffman (1999) interviewed over eighty thousand managers, primarily in the private sector. The study continued for almost twenty-five years, beginning in 1975. The managers hailed from large and small companies and agencies of all stripes. Each manager was interviewed for an hour and a half about his or her work, employees, reaction to situations, and recommendations. Their answers were audiorecorded. The responses of the "best" managers were separated from those who had been identified by others as "average" managers, and the two sets were compared.

The researchers found that the "best" managers were diverse demographically and stylewise. In most senses of the word they differed wildly from each other. However, Buckingham and Coffman were able to isolate and present some gems of wisdom that they distilled from the thousands of hours of tapes. These gems regarding workers in organizations included the following (Buckingham & Coffman, 1999:57):

- People don't change that much.
- Don't waste time trying to put in what was left out.
- Try to draw out what was left in.
- That is hard enough.

In other words, choose carefully who will to work in your agency. Train and develop those persons to their fullest potential. If you have employees who are not going to work out, and you are sure of that, do not waste your time and the company's resources trying to make them something they are not, or cannot be.

Such wisdom fits the perspective that criminal justice agencies should focus considerable resources at the selection and development end of personnel processes so that talented people will be identified, selected, and promoted. In their quote appearing at the beginning of this chapter, Buckingham and Coffman's indicates that if a manager does not select well, set expectations, motivate, and develop the personnel, then the organization will not long survive with any degree of effectiveness intact.

Once good people have been hired, they must be motivated. Sirota, Mischkind, and Meltzer (2005) analyzed 4 million survey responses as well as a mix of focus groups, interviews, and observations of mostly business, but some public sector organizations, in over eighty countries over a period of thirty years. They concluded that employee enthusiasm for work is tied directly to management practices. One startling finding from the research was that morale declines significantly for most employees in most companies after six months on the job. The authors claim that this decline is not just attributable to the novelty of the job wearing off, but that it is tied to management practices. They find that in 90% of companies management kills enthusiasm, but this does not happen in the other 10% (Sirota et al., 2005:xxix). Their question is, What distinguishes the 10% from the 90%. Their answer, as one would expect, is multifaceted and has to do with what people want from work.

What they found was that most employees in most cultures have three basic goals for their work: "equity, achievement and camaraderie" (Sirota et al., 2005:9). They think that organizations that provide the opportunities for workers to achieve these goals will benefit in the form of heightened morale and better performance. To set the stage for this achievement, management must establish policies and practices that promote these goals. Of course, these three goals closely mirror what Maslow identified as needs that motivate people in the workplace, Sirota and his colleagues (2005) merely provide some empirical evidence to support Maslow's theory.

A CONSILIENCE OF TOPICS TOO: THE UNITY OF KNOWLEDGE IN CRIMINAL JUSTICE MANAGEMENT PRACTICE

Did you notice? All of the management topics discussed in this book are interrelated, not just because they derive from several disciplines, but because excellence in one area, or lack of it, inevitably influences the other areas.

Of course if a human relations approach allows staff and clients to be more engaged in decision making and in shaping the agency in a positive way, the agency will inevitably succeed. Organizational success, in turn, effects many areas, as we have seen:

- The management of trouble, or unethical pratice, becomes less problematic when the organization is more open internally and externally (Chapter 3).
- There are improvements in ability and willingness to communicate (Chapter 5).
- There are changes in how people are socialized into the roles they adopt and in their use of power (Chapter 6).
- The leadership styles people adopt and respect manifest personal growth (Chapter 7).
- The understanding of the importance of selection, performance appraisal, and training in building and shaping the workforce and culture is increased (Chapter 8).

- The organization's openness to, and appreciation of, the need for diversity are enhanced (Chapter 9).
- Standards in treatment and the use of force, and general practice, are seen as necessary conditions to creating a professional workforce (Chapter 10).
- Efforts are made to conduct strategic planning and budgeting in the most effective way (Chapter 11).
- People learn how to make positive and effective decisions in light of all the obstacles that are present (Chapter 12).

In several chapters we used the extant research and knowledge on management, from a number of sources, from several disciplines, to formulate suggestions for improving criminal justice management. All these topics are interrelated, not because of some grand scheme orchestrated by the authors, but because management practices in one area necessarily affect practices in another. The management theory adopted by an organization, whether it is closer to human relations or to a more traditional focus, and the ways focus become translated into practice by all organizational members via the leadership and the culture, in turn affects everything.

Based on the literature in this area (as cited throughout the book), and using our six basic tenets noted earlier, here are some suggestions for incorporating a human relations–flavored version of model management practices into the criminal justice workplace:

1. Maintain and respect civil service rules and protections.
2. Uphold and respect the due process rights of staff and clients.
3. Increase training hours on all aspects of the organization (what it is and how it operates) and the role (what it involves and how to practice it) so that the role at least matches that of a profession.
4. Ensure that the substantive portion of training includes such topics as leadership and supervisory techniques, problem solving, interpersonal and communication skills, participatory management, ethics, diversity and cultural issues, and innovation/creative thinking, as well as the typical and necessary topics related to security, accountability, report writing, and the legal aspects of practice.
5. Make it a priority to hire people with a college degree and to support employees working to earn college credits.
6. Pay to all employees a livable wage that is commensurate with their professional status.
7. Select, evaluate, and promote based on formal and informal adherence to ethical practice.
8. Establish a whistleblowing program so that staff have a safe and anonymous means to report wrongdoing.
9. As much as possible, open the agency to scrutiny by outsiders, including researchers, the media, citizen groups, and other interested stakeholders.
10. Maintain the appropriate professional standards for operation, and submit the organization to an accreditation regimen.

BOX 13.2

THE IACP AND THE ROLE OF POLICE EXECUTIVES

In 1999 the International Association of Chiefs of Police held a conference entitled *Police Leadership in the 21st Century: Achieving and Sustaining Executive Success*. The roles of police executives were discussed and analyzed by conference participants, who later developed several recommendations. Notably, many of the recommendations from the IACP conference fit our own recommendations regarding model management in criminal justice agencies generally. To summarize how to foster key leadership attributes and activities for police executives and within police organizations, the attendees listed the following (IACP, 1999:i-ii):

- The profession is obligated to ensure the continuing presence of an abundant pool of candidates who possess the personal attributes, academic preparation, and formal training to meet the demands of the 21st century leadership.
- Competition for chief executive positions will increase among younger and better educated generation of professionals.
- Executive development education and training capacity must multiply to produce this pool.
- Police executives must become more intensely involved in framing executive development curricula, especially with the premier national training institutions.
- Forming and constantly reinforcing ethical values and behavior are paramount in leadership preparation and performance.
- Communities, governments, and especially the workforce look increasingly to a chief for clarity and precision in setting forth a vision and mission for the department, and constructing a framework of shared values.
- Chiefs are increasingly expected to conceptualize systematically—to define the role and place of policing and the police officer in society and the community.
- Transition to participatory management seems irreversible. In the empowerment milieu of contemporary organizations, chiefs must work collaboratively with members of many hierarchical levels and stakeholder centers, especially to constructively effect change.
- Mutual expectation guidelines, fashioned jointly by mayors, city managers, and chiefs, are paramount for building and sustaining executive success and tenure.
- In striving to prioritize customer service and satisfaction, traditional and unalterable obligations to victims and crime prevention and control must be diligently pursued and guarded.

- Numerous and complex issues and the changing environment demand that 21st century police leaders bring special passion for the workplace—that they regard their obligations as a calling that requires total commitment— not just a job.

11. Encourage and support innovation and the implementation of new ideas in the workplace.

12. Increase the avenues for communication, input, and involvement of staff in the workplace:
    - develop a newsletter with regular contributors from all ranks
    - organize work teams that include a mix of ranks and perspectives (e.g., security and treatment personnel), and do not neglect support staff
    - solicit input regarding management decisions, optimally before decisions are made
    - have some joint training sessions that include management and line workers
    - as needed, organize formal problem-solving sessions that involve a mix of ranks
    - involve all ranks in personnel processes (e.g., let entry-level workers sit in on some selection interviews or be involved in the development of a new performance appraisal instrument)
    - engage in regular discussion of the value of policies, the ethics code, and the budgetary process

13. Improve the management of clients:
    - provide meaningful opportunities for clients to work, participate in treatment programs, and grow
    - develop a newsletter for clients/the community with contributions from them
    - periodically survey or interview clients/the community about their needs and the services with which they are being provided
    - ensure that grievance procedures are fair

These suggestions for model management practices are not, of course, comprehensive, and their implementation is likely to vary from agency to agency (see also Box 13.2). But if employed with care to the degree necessary and possible, the organization and workers and clients should benefit in an enriched and more productive work environment (Buckingham & Coffman, 1999; Drucker, 1954; 1964; Gaines, Worrall, Southerland, & Angell, 2003; Heil, Bennis, & Stephens, 2000; Kiekbusch, Price, & Theis, 2003; Maslow, 1961, 1998; McGregor, 1957; Ouchi, 1981; Parker Follett, 1926; Patenaude, 2001; Peters, 1987, 1995; Schein, 1992; Slate, Vogel, & Johnson, 2001; Sirota et al., 2005; Stohr et al., 1994; Whisenand & Ferguson, 2002; Wright et al., 1997).

CONCLUSIONS

It has been our contention from the onset that there are very powerful reasons why criminal justice organizations should move further in the direction of a human relations perspective on management in the workplace. Our hope is that these pages have cogently conveyed this argument, along with the concomitant case for greater professionalism and funding. The gist of this book is that criminal justice agencies, and their actors, need not fall into the "big" and "bad" of management. There is much that is "beautiful" about the best-managed criminal justice entity, and management practices can be fashioned to showcase and promote that beauty.

DISCUSSION QUESTIONS

1. How are all the management topics covered in this book related? Give an example.
2. Why are all the management topics covered in this book related?
3. How do criminal justice organizations benefit from traditional management practices? Give an example and explain your answer.
4. Are any traditional management practices included in the model management practices listed in this chapter? If so, which ones are they?
5. How do criminal justice organizations benefit from human relations management practices? Give an example, and explain your answer.
6. Identify the human relations management practices included in the model management practices listed in this chapter. List them and give examples to show why each one is important.

KEY TERM

Consilience: a *unity of knowledge* among several seemingly disparate disciplines (Wilson, 1998).

REFERENCES

Appleby, P. (1945, reprinted in 1987). Government is different. In J. M. Shafritz, & A. C. Hyde (Eds.), *Classics of public administration* (pp. 158–163). Chicago: Dorsey Press.

Austin, J., & Irwin, J. (2001). *It's about time: America's imprisonment binge* (3rd ed.). Belmont, CA: Wadsworth/Thomson Learning.

Buckingham, M., & Coffman C. (1999). *First, break all the rules: What the world's greatest managers do differently.* New York: Simon & Schuster.

Bureau of Justice Statistics. (2004). *Probation and parole statistics.* Bureau of Justice Statistics, Office of Justice Programs, U.S. Department of Justice. Accessed at www.ojp. usdoj.gov/bjs/panp, April 5, 2004.

Bureau of Justice Statistics. (2005). *Courts and sentencing statistics.* Bureau of Justice Statistics, Office of Justice Programs, U.S. Department of Justice. Accessed at www.ojp. usdoj.gov/bjs/stssent.htm, November 16, 2005.

Drucker, P. F. (1954). *The practice of management.* New York: Harper & Row.

Drucker, P. F. (1964). *Managing for results.* New York: Harper & Row.

Federal Bureau of Investigation (2004). *Persons arrested.* FBI, U.S. Department of Justice. Accessed at www.fbi.gov.ucr.cius_arrested/index.html, November 16, 2005.

Gaines, L. K., Worrall, J. L., Southerland, M. D., & Angell, J.E. (2003). *Police administration.* Boston: McGraw-Hill.

Glaze, L. E. (2003). Probation and parole in the United States, 2002. *Bureau of Justice Statistics Bulletin.* U.S. Department of Justice. Washington DC: GPO.

Guarino-Ghezzi, S., & Trevino, A. J. (2005). *Understanding crime: A multidisciplinary approach.* Florence, KY: Anderson Publishing.

Harrison, P. M., & Karberg, J. C. (2003). Prison and jail inmates at midyear 2002. *Bureau of Justice Statistics Bulletin.* U.S. Department of Justice. Washington DC: GPO.

Heil, G., Bennis, W., & Stephens, D. C. (2000). *Douglas McGregor revisited: Managing the human side of the enterprise.* New York: Wiley.

IACP. (1999). *Police leadership in the 21st century: Achieving and sustaining executive success.* International Association of Chiefs of Police: Recommendations from the president's first leadership conference, May 1999. Alexandria, VA: IACP.

Kiekbusch, R., Price, W., & Theis, J. (2003). Turnover predictors: Causes of employee turnover in sheriff-operated jails. *Criminal Justice Studies, 16*(2), 67–76.

Maslow, A. H. (1961, reprinted in 1998). *Maslow on management.* New York: Wiley.

Maslow, A. H. (1998, first published in 1961). *Maslow on management.* New York: Wiley.

McGregor, D. (1957, reprinted in 2001). The human side of enterprise. In J. M. Shafritz & J.S. Ott (Eds.), *Classics of organization theory* (5th ed.) (pp. 152–157). Fort Worth, TX: Harcourt College Publishers.

Nader, R. (1972). An anatomy of whistle blowing. In R. Nader, P. J. Petkas, & K. Blackwell (Eds.), *Whistle blowing: The report of the conference on professional responsibility* (pp. 3–11). New York: Grossman.

Ouchi, W. (1981). *Theory Z: How American business can meet the Japanese challenge.* Reading, MA: Addison-Wesley.

Parker Follett, M. (1926, reprinted in 2001). The giving of orders. In J. M. Shafritz & J. S. Ott (Eds.), *Classics of organization theory* (pp. 152–157). Fort Worth, TX: Harcourt College Publishers.

Patenaude, A. L. (2001). Analysis of issues affecting correctional officer retention within the Arkansas Department of Correction. *Corrections Management Quarterly, 5*(2), 49–67.

Peters, T. (1995). *Two complete books: Thriving on chaos and a passion for excellence (with Nancy Austin).* New York: Random House.

Peters, T. (1987). *Thriving on chaos: Handbook for a management revolution.* New York: Harper & Row.

Raney, G. (2005). *Shining the star: Identifying priorities, processes and outcome goals of a strategic plan for the Ada County Sheriff's office.* Boise, ID: Unpublished master's project, Boise State University.

Schein, E. H. (1992). *Organizational culture and leadership* (2nd ed.). San Francisco: Jossey-Bass.

Sirota, D., Mischkind, L. A., & Meltzer, M. I. (2005). *The enthusiastic employee: How companies profit by giving workers what they want.* Upper Saddle River, NJ: Wharton School Publishing–Pearson Education.

Slate, R. N., Vogel, R. E., & Johnson, W. W. (2001). To quit or not to quit: Perceptions of participation in correctional decision making and the impact of organizational stress. *Corrections Management Quarterly, 5*(2), 68–78.

Stohr, M. K., Lovrich, N. P., Menke, B. A., & Zupan, L. L. (1994). Staff management in a correctional institution: Comparing DiIulio's 'control model' and 'employee investment model' outcomes in five jails. *Justice Quarterly, 11*(3), 471–497.

Whisenand, P. M., & Ferguson R. F. (2002). *The managing of police organizations* (5th ed.) Upper Saddle River, NJ: Prentice Hall.

Willis, J. J., Mastrofski, S. D., & Weisburd, D. (2004). COMPSTAT and bureaucracy: A case study of challenges and opportunities for change. *Justice Quarterly, 21*(3), 463–496.

Wilson, E. O. (1999). *Consilience: The unity of knowledge.* New York: Knopf.

Wright, K. N., Saylor, W. G., Gilman, E., & Camp, S. (1997). Job control and occupational outcomes among prison workers. *Justice Quarterly, 14*(3), 525–548.

INDEX

Bold page numbers indicate material in figures and tables. n indicates material in chapter endnotes.

War, Peace, and the Social Order

FOUNDATIONS OF SOCIAL INQUIRY
Scott McNall and Charles Tilly, Series Editors

War, Peace, and the Social Order, *Brian E. Fogarty*

Faces of Feminism: An Activist's Reflections on the Women's Movement, *Sheila Tobias*

Criminological Controversies: A Methodological Primer, *John Hagan, A. R. Gillis, and David Brownfield*

Immigration in America's Future: Social Science Findings and the Policy Debate, *David M. Heer*

What Does Your Wife Do? Gender and the Transformation of Family Life, *Leonard Beeghley*

FORTHCOMING

Race, Gender, and Discrimination at Work, *Samuel Cohn*

Social Change: The Long-Term View from Sociology and Anthropology, *Thomas D. Hall, Darrell La Lone, and Stephen K. Sanderson*

War, Peace, and the Social Order

Brian E. Fogarty

College of St. Catherine

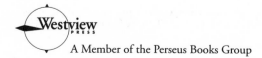

Westview
PRESS

A Member of the Perseus Books Group

Copyright © 2000 by Westview Press, A Member of the Perseus Books Group

Published in 2000 in the United States of America by Westview Press, 5500 Central Avenue, Boulder, Colorado 80301-2877, and in the United Kingdom by Westview Press, 12 Hid's Copse Road, Cumnor Hill, Oxford OX2 9JJ

Find us on the World Wide Web at www.westviewpress.com

Library of Congress Cataloging-in-Publication Data
Fogarty, Brian E.
  War, peace, and the social order / Brian E. Fogarty.
    p.   cm.
  Includes bibliographical references and index.
  ISBN 0-8133-6659-3 (hc).—ISBN 0-8133-6660-7 (pbk.)
    1. War.   2. Peace.   I. Title.
U21.2.F63   1999
355.02—dc21
                                                                99-41891
                                                                CIP

The paper used in this publication meets the requirements of the American National Standard for Permanence of Paper for Printed Library Materials Z39.48-1984.

10   9   8   7   6   5   4   3   2   1

For Cheryl, Stephanie, and Joe

Contents

Illustrations

Preface

As I write on this quiet Sunday morning, the conflict between Serbian Yugoslavia and ethnic Albanians is intensifying. Today's paper included its usual front-page photo of Kosovar refugees fleeing Serb troops and paramilitary police (it also contained a map of Europe in 1360, showing Serbs and Albanians in conflict even then). President Clinton continues to justify bombing cities and towns in Yugoslavia even in the face of disastrous mistaken attacks on the refugees themselves. The Serbs have made small incursions into neighboring countries, it appears, which threaten to widen the conflict. More worrisome still, Russia seems to be taking sides with the Serbs, which threatens to bring us back into the Cold War.

Like anyone else, I look at the pictures of the brutality and the suffering and I ask myself how people can do these things to one another. The atrocities being committed seem inhuman; the acts of people different from any I've encountered. But as a sociologist I know better. Kosovo is not a unique event, and if I want to attribute it to the wickedness of its participants I will also have to attach the same wickedness to those who have participated in all wars. That list will have to include the kindly uncles and other old men who still remember World War II, my high school friends who went to Vietnam, the sons and daughters of friends who served in the Gulf War of 1991, and millions of other ordinary people from virtually every country who have fought in a hundred wars great and small. It will also have to include myself, not as a combatant but as a citizen who has participated indirectly in war through taxes, citizenship, and acquiescence.

If I want to understand this conflict, I will have to try to understand war as a social structure, and if I want to take part in promoting peace, I'll have to understand that in the same way. Fortunately, I have studied the sociology of war and peace for some years now and I feel a little less perplexed, if no less glum, about what is happening in Kosovo. I first encountered the sociology of war and peace in 1987. I had been asked to teach "The Sociology of Peace," a required course for the minor in Peace Studies at Briar Cliff College in Sioux City, Iowa. I knew little of the topic at the time, but I had just spent six years working as a civilian for the army as an aircraft buyer and cost analyst and had lots of new questions to which my sociological training might be applied. As I set to the task of schooling myself in peace studies, I made several discoveries that have had a real impact on my professional and personal life. The first was that the field of peace studies is a world of fascinating ideas, offering powerful explanations for humankind's nastiest problem. As had happened so many times before in my intellectual upbringing, I enjoyed the thrill of understanding phenomena that had previously seemed imponderable.

The second discovery was that these wonderful ideas were couched in terms of various disciplines—some were "owned" by philosophy, some by the social sciences, some by the humanities—and some just seemed to be astute observations, without a disciplinary home at all. So while I reveled in the bits of understanding that peace studies had given me, there remained a certain frustration that came from an inability to grasp the problem of war and the prospect for peace as a whole.

The third discovery was that sociology had given me the tools to construct a coherent framework on which to hang a great many of these bits of understanding. It seemed nearly every important idea in peace studies could be expressed in terms of basic sociology; better still, the controversies in peace studies often mirrored the controversies of sociology. The relative primacy of the individual versus the community, the nature of the "social contract," the role of cooperation versus the role of conflict in social progress, the meaning of "progress" itself—these are all the stock in trade of the sociologist as well as the peace scholar.

The final discovery was that there was no well-integrated text in peace studies. Most people teaching in the field were using one or another reader, or assembling their own favorite collections of readings from various journals and popular media. As I taught my own course a few times the lack of a coherent text in the field became increasingly frustrating. It wasn't that students didn't learn or that I wasn't able to teach without such a text; in fact we all did fairly well. But the course seemed to lack integrity somehow, and I sensed the students took it to be both less rigorous than other courses and too unconnected to them.

Most courses in peace studies are highly experiential in their methods, and that in itself can contribute to a lack of integrity. Teachers wish not only to impart knowledge to students but to incite them to action, but it is easy to stray too far from the academic side of peace studies, to forget intellectual development as long as personal involvement pays such rich dividends. In my classes, some students had the memorable experience of getting arrested at the local air force base in protest of nuclear weapons targeting. However, I got the uncomfortable feeling that few of them understood how the air force had come to be what it was in the first place.

That is why I have written this book. Collections of disparate readings and experiential activities simply are not enough to make a coherent college course. The field of peace studies is a wide-ranging one, and students and instructors alike need a text that can bring this knowledge together. I have set myself the task of translating what I know of peace studies into the language of sociology, so that the former can be grasped as a more complete whole. As part of a course in peace studies it should help the reader better integrate the varied ideas and findings of the peace studies literature into his or her own knowledge base.

I also hope to increase interest among sociologists in issues of war and peace, because it seems clear that war and peace provide a good deal of food for sociological thought. As a discipline, sociologists can take a greater role in helping students and scholars alike to make sense of war and peace as social phenomena. I hope the book is successful in these goals.

I am most grateful to William E. Knox, associate professor emeritus of the University of North Carolina at Greensboro, for encouraging submission of this manuscript and for many hours of diligent editorial help. Grateful thanks go also to Scott McNall and Charles Tilly for including the book in the *Foundations of Social Inquiry* series, and to Andrew Day of Westview Press for his skill in shepherding the project through production. Paul Wehr and Echo Fields were also very generous with their advice and criticism, and for that I am in their debt. I am also indebted to the reference librarians at the College of St. Catherine for their assistance with various aspects of the research. Finally, thanks to my former colleagues at Briar Cliff for turning me on to peace studies.

Brian E. Fogarty
St. Paul, Minnesota

Acronyms

AMC	Army Material Command
CBD	civilian-based defense
EU	European Union
FORSCOM	Forces Command
HSWP	Hungarian Socialist Workers' Party
IRA	Irish Republican Army
MAD	Mutually Assured Destruction
NASA	National Aeronautics and Space Administration
NATO	North Atlantic Treaty Organization
NGO	nongovernmental organization
OAS	Organization of American States
PD	Prisoner's Dilemma
PLO	Palestine Liberation Organization
PMO	Project Management Office
R&D	Research and Development
RPV	Remotely Piloted Vehicle
SALT	Strategic Arms Limitation Talks
SDI	Strategic Defense Initiative
START	Strategic Arms Reduction Talks
TRADOC	Training and Doctrine Command
SSEB	Source Selection Evaluation Board
WHO	World Health Organization

Western Hemisphere

SOURCE: National Council for Geographic Education and Arizona Geographic Alliance.

Eastern Hemisphere

SOURCE: National Council for Geographic Education and Arizona Geographic Alliance.

Why Study War and Peace?

Discussions about war and peace, when carried to sufficient depth, tend to divide people into two schools of thought. The first approach is based on the assumption that humans are inherently violent creatures and that the civilizing veneer of society is all that saves us from chaos and self-destruction. We need restrictions imposed by strong government, authoritarian religion, and other institutions to protect us from each other, for the natural human impulse (so amply demonstrated by a glance at any newspaper) is to compete, exploit others, and generally act in absolute self-interest.

By contrast, the second approach rests on the assumption that humans are inherently peaceful beings, endowed by nature or God with an innate desire to cooperate and nurture. Those who take this view consider the social order and its attendant coercion, inequality, and injustice to be responsible for humanity's fall from grace. Violence and war are unnatural behaviors for humans, and could be reduced or even prevented if only the evils brought on by civilization could be undone. In short, society is the source of humanity's problems, not the solution to them. These two positions reflect, incidentally, a point of debate among the "social contract" philosophers of the seventeenth and eighteenth centuries, specifically Hobbes and Rousseau.

Each view advances a dangerous fiction. The first implies that peace can be purchased only at the expense of freedom and human dignity; the natural tendency to struggle against one another must be controlled by increasingly oppressive social and political structures. Indeed, one might argue that as the human population continues to grow, these controls must be tightened to accommodate ever greater scarcity and competition. Thus warfare can be expected and possibly even welcomed as one means to establish increasing control, or at least as an inevitable by-product of the process.

The second view inhibits one's understanding of the human condition by denying that war and violence are natural phenomena that can be understood. Instead, there is a tendency to treat the reality of war as if it were an exception to the natural way of things; a cosmic mistake that somehow might be rectified simply by realizing that war and violence are bad. This school of thought typically views war as the result of self-serving elites, worldwide communism, or worldwide capitalism—in short, the bad intentions of bad people who have acquired enough power to corrupt and lead other people to war. Such a view defeats the goal of ending war by rendering it unfathomable.

Neither assumption is acceptable. The pursuit of peace must begin with the faith that real peace can be achieved without increased enslavement and impoverishment. Humans are, after all, generally decent to one another given the chance. They voluntarily establish friendships, marry, and raise families. Parents may make lifelong sacrifices of their own comforts and opportunities, just to provide for the betterment of their children.

At the same time, one must recognize that ordinary people are capable of the most horrifying acts. War and violence are also a part of the human condition, and they can be understood as natural social processes, just like crime, racism, disease, and other human ills. Bemoaning war and violence is simply not enough; they ought to be acknowledged squarely as a side of human existence.

This book is based on a third assumption, that humans are not "inherently" anything. Everything we are, we have made ourselves, and whatever we want to be will likewise have to be a human construction. Both war and peace are cultural inventions, and each can lay claim to equal importance in human affairs. It is a bitter truth that human nature seems to often be characterized by both extremes: peace and violence, cooperation and competition, love and hate. Most striking, much of human behavior consists of both at the same time. To the sociologist these ironies have a familiar ring, for they manifest old dualities: that freedom comes partly through constraint, that conflict involves cooperation, that the self is created through others, that "we" are partly defined in terms of "them."

This dualistic assumption about human nature leads to two general principles. First, war is to be regarded as a natural social process that can be understood in the same way as other familiar social ills. This means that war itself must be given attention as one of humanity's creations. I believe strongly that the study and advancement of peace, without an understanding of war, is doomed to failure. Those who dismiss war as an incomprehensible aberration, or as the evil work of wicked people, cannot hope to disassemble the machinery that produces it.

Second, war and violence are not inevitable simply because they are natural social processes. The human world is human made, and real peace—with freedom, dignity, and justice—can be had if people set themselves the task of learning how to bring it about. It is a sad irony that much of what makes war possible is ignorance of the possibility of peace.

The Use of Sociology

The discipline of sociology has something unique to offer students of war and peace. I do not mean that sociology is the only discipline that can explain war and peace, or even that it is the "best" one. On the contrary, there should also be basic texts in the economics of war and peace, as well as in theology, philosophy, and literature. But the study of war and peace is the study of paradox, of which three specific examples come to mind. And as it happens, each of these paradoxes constitutes one of the most basic issues that sociology addresses.

Paradox One: Nobody Wants Wars, Yet We Keep Having Them. This reflects the simple but profound truth that the behavior of societies is not explainable in terms of the motivations or desires of the individuals that make them up. This is basic systems thinking, expressed most conveniently by saying that the whole is more than the sum of its parts. Yet this fundamental sociological truth is easily forgotten when scholars ponder war and other violence, and this creates dangerous blind spots. For example, it makes it easy to assume that since one's own society is composed mainly of peaceful people, any wars it becomes involved in must be of a purely "defensive" nature, or at worst, regrettable but necessary actions in defense of humankind. This of course is one of the myths that most effectively leads to war, because it allows participants to nurse the belief that God is on their side.

Paradox Two: The Problem of Determinism. One of the fundamental premises of sociology is the idea that beliefs, values, desires, and morals are acquired through participation in a community. Powerful institutions including family, church, economy, state, education, mass media, and a host of others combine to socialize people into some degree of conformity with established customs. This raises an important question: If individuals are controlled by the larger society, then what freedom does one have to change it?

The question becomes one of responsibility for one's own society. In a sense, individuals are the constituent parts of the society they live in, and so ultimately control it. Yet society is within each individual as well, so the control is circular. Ultimately, the paradox can be addressed by resolving to examine the myths by which humans are controlled and attempting to create more truthful ones.

Everett Hughes (1961) addressed this problem in his examination of the responsibility of German citizens for the Holocaust. When he interviewed ordinary citizens, Hughes found a remarkable capacity to rationalize, to gloss over, and even to forget much of the lurid reality that must have been inescapable. At the same time, Hughes raised the question: What else might have been expected of these people? They lived within a social order that provided ready denials for the "final solution," as well as plenty of explanations and rationalizations when denial failed.

For that matter, one can as easily point to the behavior of the American citizenry as it has turned its collective head from government policies that, though perhaps less flagrant, illustrate the same principle. A glimpse of newspaper and magazine stories from the nineteenth century reveals a striking lack of sympathy for American Indians as they underwent a similar holocaust lasting several centuries. Even in the 1950s, when I was a boy, the phrase "the only good Indian is a dead Indian" was a cute aphorism that little boys shouted as they played cowboy.

More recently, relatively few Americans allowed themselves much awareness of the national atrocity of Vietnam, until several years of military failures and effective antiwar activism at home forced the issue. And only a few columnists raised questions about the "strategic bombing" campaign that helped save the lives of so many American soldiers in Iraq in 1991—at the cost of many thousands of Iraqi civilian lives. Would the average American respond any differently to Hughes's questions than did the German people in recollecting the Holocaust?

Paradox Three: Action versus Knowledge. Finally, there is the problem of the uses to which knowledge can and ought to be put. On the one hand, it can be said that knowledge for its own sake is a sterile, even decadent, pursuit. What good is knowledge without action? On the other hand, one might object that knowledge conceived with action and application in mind is inherently prone to distortion, ideology, and dogma. In this view, only "value-neutral" science can amount to anything of worth.

Sociology finds itself in a unique position with respect to this paradox, for sociological knowledge can actually change the nature of society, its very subject matter. What would happen, for example, if Americans really understood that social inequality is legitimated by powerful ideologies promulgated by the elite? Or that humans are neither inherently violent nor inherently docile? Or that nuclear deterrence has not kept the peace over the past fifty years? Or that the human condition is not a struggle characterized by survival of the fittest? In the end, sociological knowledge *is* action, and its dissemination is always a political act.

The understanding of sociology itself calls for a deep appreciation of paradox, and that is what draws students to war and peace. For they are but two sides of the greatest paradox of all, the dual nature of human existence.

Our Involvement in War

We cannot avoid involvement in war, or at least in the system of war. In the first place, each individual is a potential victim of war. The very existence of the human species is threatened by the warmaking capabilities possessed by three or four of the world's Great Powers, not to mention the increasing destructive capability of smaller states and factions.

Nor should the "end of the Cold War" bring much comfort. Despite highly touted reductions in nuclear warheads and the missiles that deliver them, the United States alone continues to maintain more than 2,300 warheads on alert—the equivalent of about 44,000 Hiroshimas (Hall 1998). These are not solely targeted at Russian strategic sites anymore; today's flexible targeting software makes it practical to target Iraq, Iran, Libya, Korea, or other "trouble spots" in minutes. Of course, the U.S. military is only the largest of many such forces in the world, part of a system of nations that some scholars believe is less stable today than before the Soviet Union collapsed in 1991 (Betts 1994b; Huntington 1994; Mearsheimer 1994). Meanwhile, the cost of lethality has declined over the decades; even marginal groups can now afford land mines, handheld surface-to-air missiles, and a wide variety of compact explosives, not to mention the renewed interest in biological and chemical weapons among lesser military powers. You don't have to be a country to have an army.

Even if such appalling destructive potential did not exist, there would be plenty of cause for concern. Suter (1996) counted thirty-two ongoing conflicts in the world at mid-decade, each of which produced 5,000 or more casualties annually. Table 1.1 shows the world's roster of active conflicts as of 1997, and it does not include recent Balkan conflicts and others that have erupted since then (major regions of recent conflict are shown in Map 0.1). Kaldor (1996) noted that the Bosnian conflict alone has produced some 200,000 deaths. The Hutu-Tutsi conflict in Rwanda is estimated to have produced a staggering 500,000 deaths.

The fact that few war casualties in recent years have been American seems to comfort some people, but it does not argue that the world has become any less hazardous. Though only a few Americans were killed in the Gulf War of 1991, that adventure was made safe to Americans at great cost to Iraqi civilian life and social order. And it is easy to forget that Americans *have* died in military action within the past couple of

6

TABLE 1.1   Armed Conflict Around the World, 1997

Europe
   Govt. of United Kingdom | Provisional IRA

Middle East

Govt. of Iran	Mujahadeen e-Khalq
Govt. of Iraq	Supreme Assembly for the Islamic Revolution in Iraq (SAIRI)
Govt. of Israel	Various non-PLO groups
Govt. of Turkey	Kurdish Worker's Party

Asia

Govt. of Afghanistan	Jumbish-i-Milli-ye Islami
	Jamiat-i-Islami
	Hezb-i-Wahdat
Govt. of Bangladesh	Chittagong Hill Tracts People's Coordination Association (JSS/SB)
Govt. of Cambodia	Party of Democratic Kampuchea (Khmer Rouge)
Govt. of India	Kashmir insurgents
	Bodo Security Force
	United Liberation Front of Assam
Govt. of India	Govt. of Pakistan
Govt. of Indonesia	Revolutionary Front for an Independent East Timor
Govt. of Myanmar	Karen National Union
Govt. of the Philippines	New People's Army
Govt. of Sri Lanka	Liberation Tigers of Tamil Eelam

Africa

Govt. of Algeria	Islamic Salvation Front
	Armed Islamic Group
Govt. of Burundi	National Council for the Defense of Democracy
Govt. of Congo	United Democratic Forces
Govt. of Senegal	Casamance Movement of Democratic Forces
Govt. of Sierra Leone	Revolutionary United Front
Govt. of Sudan	National Democratic Alliance
Govt. of Uganda	Lord's Resistance Army
Govt. of Zaire	Alliance of Democratic Forces for the Liberation of Congo-Kinshasha (Rwanda)

Central and South America

Govt. of Colombia	Revolutionary Armed Forces of Colombia
	National Liberation Army
Govt. of Peru	Shining Path
	Tupac Amaru Revolutionary Movement

SOURCE: Stockholm International Peace Research Institute 1998, pp. 26–30.

decades: 300 marines in Beruit in 1983 and handfuls in Grenada (1983), Panama (1989), Somalia (1992), and Haiti (1994). Between 1961 and 1973, 56,000 Americans died in the Vietnam War, and unknown thousands were permanently disabled physically, mentally, or spiritually by that war.

We are also economically involved in war. The U.S. government currently spends nearly half its tax revenues on the military to maintain a large standing army, support a huge military procurement bureaucracy, design, purchase, and upgrade ever more sophisticated weapons, and to provide instantaneous and assured nuclear deterrence. Through these taxes everyone participates in the national war effort, and the more spent on the military, the less is available for the national betterment. In a speech of 1953, President Dwight Eisenhower recognized the problem, remarking that "Every gun that is fired, every warship launched, every rocket fired signifies in a final sense a theft from those who hunger and are not fed, those who are cold and are not clothed." The military is a part of everyone's life, and concern about any social problem is a concern about the problem of war.

One problem individuals have in thinking about military spending and its consequences is that because the United States is a large and wealthy country, we deal with large numbers. Talk about billions of dollars spent on one weapons system or another desensitizes a person to the size of the numbers. How much money are they talking about?

One way to grasp the size of the military budget is to compare it to what Americans spend as a society on other valued goods and services. To begin simply, the national defense is paid for out of the federal budget, and its revenues come from the taxes citizens pay. In 1997, that budget was just over a trillion dollars; or one thousand billion; or a million millions.[1]

Arguments abound as to the proportion of the budget actually spent for military purposes. The *Statistical Abstract of the United States* put it at about $270 billion in 1997, or roughly a quarter of the total budget. But this figure fails to count several items of military-related spending, including foreign military aid, training of foreign military forces, and Department of Energy development and maintenance of nuclear weapons. So the actual direct costs of the military is about $288 billion. It also excludes veterans' benefits and the defense budget's portion of interest payments on the national debt. In 1997, that interest payment was about $356 billion, of which $188 billion, or about half, should be considered defense's "share."

The commonly-cited figure also *includes* Social Security payments (over $300 billion) as part of the budget, and hence part of the total base

---

[1]This amount does not include Social Security and other trust funds, as noted later.

FIGURE 1.1   The Federal Budget

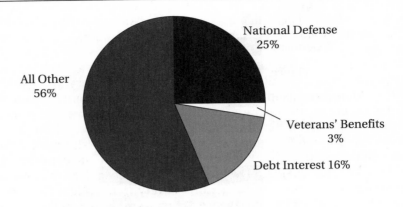

All Other
56%

National Defense
25%

Veterans' Benefits
3%

Debt Interest 16%

SOURCE: Friends Committee on National Legislation 1998.

from which the military's portion is calculated. This does not make sense because Social Security payments are made from the Social Security trust fund, which gets its money not from income taxes but from the Social Security contribution withheld from paychecks. Therefore, it is misleading to include that amount as a part of the tax base (Friends Committee on National Legislation 1998).

As Figure 1.1 shows, counting the military's share of interest payments and veterans' benefits, and excluding Social Security from the total, the United States spends about 44 percent of each tax dollar on the military. Everything else that the federal government provides—highways, bridges, national parks, education, scholarships, aid to sick babies, Head Start, space exploration, health care assistance, medical research, air traffic control—*everything* comes from the remaining 56 percent.

The 44 percent spent on the military is the highest in the world, by the way, unsurpassed by countries either actively involved in war or major threat of war. As Figure 1.2 shows, the closest rivals are nearly all Middle Eastern states, except for the Russian Federation. Comparable democracies such as Japan and those of western Europe spend far less of their public wealth on the military.

It does not take a sophisticated analysis to determine that dedicating such large sums of the common wealth to war must have tremendous impact on the rest of the social system. How does a government get its citizens to hand over that kind of money? It seems clear that the state must exercise a great deal of power and coercion to do so, either directly or indirectly. Fear of enemies, foreign or domestic, must be cultivated.

FIGURE 1.2 Military Spending as Percentage of Total Budget, Selected Countries

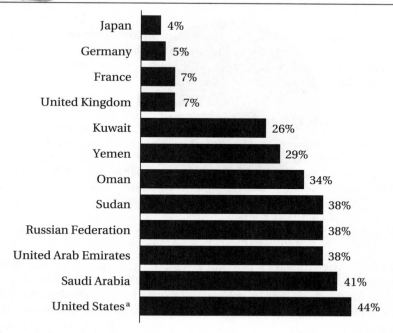

aFigure for United States is from Friends Committee on National Legislation 1998.
SOURCE: World Bank 1998.

Mass media must be harnessed to keep the population ignorant of the possibility of peace and keenly aware of even the most remote threats to normalcy. Genuine problems within society—from racial inequality to poverty to economic development—are swept under the rug for fear they will draw resources away from the more critical matters of "national security." In the name of that security, basic constitutional rights tend to be violated.

If for no other reason, personal involvement in war obliges a person to better understand war and one's role within it. To do so, one should begin with the assumption that war and peace have equal status as social phenomena. War and peace are natural social processes, and both can be understood by sociological theory. It is a liberating assumption that allows for a fresh view of events customarily seen in conventional terms. It also draws attention away—only temporarily, for purposes of analysis—from the values they are given, and this too provides a fresh perspective. There is a tendency within the peacemaking community to emphasize the peaceable nature of humankind, and to regard war as a corruption of that nature; an unnatural aberration caused by economic inequality, oppressive political regimes, or simply moral weakness. But to dismiss war as "unnatural" is to reject the possibility of understanding it. Only by facing squarely the reality that humans are inherently capable of both violence and peace can society learn how to tilt the balance away from the former and toward the latter.

Chapter Summary

Neither war nor peace is the sole "natural" state of humankind. The human experience includes both of them, and acknowledgment of this fact is the first step toward a deeper understanding of the problem of war and the hope for peace. Sociology can play an important role in developing such an understanding, because the sociological perspective has always been a useful one for understanding the dualities of human nature.

War and peace do not just pose an interesting intellectual problem, however. On the contrary, as citizens we are all involved in war as targets, as potential soldiers, and as taxpayers. This personal involvement alone obliges us to better understand how war is made and how peace can be increased.

Questions for Review

Many people approach peace studies with skepticism, claiming that "we have always had war and always will." How does this chapter dispute that claim?

In what ways have Americans been "good people" doing "dirty work"? What are some social processes that make it possible for ordinary citizens to ignore injustice?

In what ways do ordinary citizens participate in war in an ongoing way?

How is the military's share of the federal budget often understated?

For Further Research

Arendt, Hannah. 1963. *Eichmann in Jerusalem: A Report on the Banality of Evil.* New York: Viking Press.

Friends Committee on National Legislation. 1998. *How Much of Your 1997 Federal Income Tax Supports Military Spending?* (http://www.clark.net/pub/-fcnl/tax97doc.htm)

Hughes, Everett. 1961. "Good People and Dirty Work." *Social Problems* 10: 3–10.

Lorenz, Conrad. 1966. *On Aggression.* New York: Harcourt, Brace.

Mead, Margaret. 1973. "War Is Only an Invention—Not a Biological Necessity." Pp. 112–118 in *Peace and War*, ed. Charles R. Beitz and Theodore Herman. San Francisco: Freeman.

The National Budget Simulator. URL: http://garnet.berkeley.edu:3333/budget/budget.html.

2 | *The Social Structure of War and Peace*

Both war and peace are uniquely human inventions. Both have evolved apace with the development of culture in general, as human ingenuity has devised its usual stunning variety of forms for them. Most people recognize the ways in which warmaking has evolved technologically, and lament that "progress." But we are less aware of the *social* evolution of war—the invention of ever more abstract and elaborate justifications for it, for example. Most people are even less aware of the evolution of peace, which includes the development of all the systems of cooperation and sharing that the human genius has devised. It is seldom recognized that the evolution of peace is far more historically significant than the evolution of war. Pursuit of peace has involved more humans more of the time than war, including as it does such inventions as the family, law, democracy, capitalism, communism, taxation, bureaucracy, labor unions, medicine, public education, science, and a galaxy of other endeavors.

However they have been construed over the ages, war and peace have occupied the attention of social thinkers since the ancients. The reasons are not hard to see. The scourge of war has presented humanity with its most intractable social problem, and ever since there has been such a thing as civilization, war has loomed as a possibility. The thinkers of ancient Greece were perhaps the first to systematically consider war as a social problem per se. Herodotus had already characterized war as a pathology, a violation of the "natural order of things," when Thucydides began to contemplate it in what could be called political science terms (Jowett 1900; Paley 1989).

War has interested thinkers through the ages also because it is the greatest of human spectacles. Through it, all the dramas of human life are played: heroism, triumph, and altruism, but also alienation, ignominy, and barbarism. Many of Shakespeare's dramas are set against a backdrop of war; it is often the central dramatic ingredient. Countless novels, short stories, plays, operas, and myths are about war as the resolver of conflict, killer of heroes, ennobler of cowards, and destroyer of decency. Whether war is regarded as noble or ignoble, it commands attention in every intellectual sphere.

A third reason for the classical interest in war and peace is that they are inherently *moral* phenomena. No person in the "civilized" world (the term is used here in the popular sense) can escape thinking about the morality of killing and dying for abstract and collective goals. For that matter, most people in the civilized world (speaking now in the anthropological sense) have at one time or another been directly confronted with the moral dilemma of their own participation in war, directly or indirectly. Again, one need not look far for ancient treatments of this moral dimension. The pages of the Old Testament, for example, run red with the accounts of wars recounted, explained, justified, and condemned. If for no other reason, war is of interest to humans because it is, in the words of one sage, "humanity's greatest crime, and also its punishment."

The classical thinkers did not have the theoretical tools available today. In the modern age the social sciences have "discovered" social structure as an entity in itself rather than as the purposeful contrivance of human will. Instead of simply arguing the virtue or evil of social institutions, scholars now analyze their structure, identify causal factors in their development, and make predictions about their effects. What this means for the study of war and peace is that the existence of both are explained as social process, not only as moral choices.

What's Social About War?

War seems on its surface to be a distinctly antisocial enterprise. After all, the goal of the warrior is to destroy social order among the enemy; to kill, injure, and disrupt. But to dismiss war from theories because it is detestable is to ignore a phenomenon that occupies a great deal of human effort and interest. One might argue that war is antisocial, but it certainly cannot be argued that it is asocial. To leave it at that would be to miss an opportunity for understanding an important aspect of social action. Much of what is considered fundamental in social theory is "antisocial" in this sense. For example, Durkheim made sense of crime not by dismissing it (as most people do) as the actions of immoral people against society, but rather by including it within the realm of natural and understandable social processes. It may likewise seem curious at first to think of the mayhem of war as a social enterprise, but in fact, war is intensely social in a number of ways, observable from the microsocial level to the macro.

The Social Psychology of Combat

The very act of fighting in a war involves fundamental interaction processes that are well explained by sociological theory. Imagine that you are a member of a World War II infantry rifle team somewhere in a European forest. Your team has been ordered to assault a machine-gun position; success will enable your army to accomplish its objective with minimum danger.

In combat, there is strength in organization; a team of four soldiers acting together is much more effective than the sum of the efforts of four individual soldiers. Assume that if all four members of your team jump out of their foxholes simultaneously and rush the machine-gun position, you will overwhelm the defenders and succeed. However, there is a fair probability that one of your team will be killed in the attempt. On the other hand, if only two or three soldiers rush the position, the enemy will be able to kill you all easily. When the leader of your team yells, "Let's go!" you must make a split-second decision: Do you jump up and rush ahead, or remain in the protection of your foxhole?

Before arriving at an answer, consider the various possibilities. If you fail to participate in the assault, you are certain to survive, but your comrades are almost certain to die. Conversely, if you join your comrades, one of you will probably die anyway. Worse yet, that person might be you. Which course of action is favored by a rational, self-interested person? One might argue that participating in the assault is the most reasonable course of action, since only one will die instead of the three who will die if you do not participate. But if you stay behind, *your* life is spared, which ought to count for something (assume that no one finds out about your cowardice and has you executed).

But is this the only problem? Clearly not, because it fails to consider the risk that *one of your comrades* may not join the assault. In that case, if you participate your death is virtually guaranteed, and because the mission will fail, you will not even be awarded a posthumous medal. The problem is, the chances of your survival depend on what your comrades do. Consequently, the decision to go "over the top" or not depends on what you *think* they will do. If you believe that one of them is likely to hold back, you would be foolish to participate. Obviously, you will join the assault only if you believe the others will too.

This is what sociology takes as its central concern: The social order, whether a society, a family, a classroom, or a military unit, is made up of *expectations* that individuals have of each other. Military units maintain cohesion, and therefore survival, only so long as individual members believe that *other* members will go over the top when called upon. The military unit under fire can be thought of as a simplified, microcosmic model for the social order itself.

Consider the task of the military commander. Clearly, a commander's main concern is for every soldier to obey orders automatically. Given the opportunity to consider an order, some soldiers may think better of the matter and stay behind, which would surely increase casualties overall. More subtly, even a *few* soldiers holding back would sow doubt in the minds of the other soldiers—that their comrades might "chicken out" on them—and that doubt could become epidemic. In fact, this is exactly what happens when a military unit is overwhelmed or collapses in the field: It has enough demoralized members or casualties that the remainder of the unit is convinced that they can no longer count on their comrades. At that critical point, surrender (or in many cases, massacre) occurs.

This explains why military commanders are so concerned with morale. Contrary to popular belief, morale is really not simply a matter of "psyching up" soldiers to want to kill the enemy (although that may help). Rather, morale is the belief among soldiers that the *other* soldiers are enthusiastic about killing, or that they are fearless, or at least that they are unquestioning of orders. This is the reason that discipline—blind obedience to orders—is so highly instilled in soldiers in every army. It is not so dangerous for a few soldiers to fail to obey; the danger is that the other soldiers might find out.

Consequently, basic military training—boot camp—is almost wholly devoted to automating the soldier. Looking at what is actually taught in basic training reveals that relatively few combat skills are acquired there; they are covered in advanced training later. Rather, boot camp concentrates on drill, depersonalization (through uniformity and psychological stress), and developing dependency on comrades, and this goal is largely the same in the training of modern armies the world over. Many of the activities in boot camp stress a couple of overriding themes: (a) an individual must achieve the same feats as his buddies, else he will let them down; and (b) an individual is absolutely dependent on his buddies for his own survival and success. Virtually all of the training activities are aimed at making soldiers predictable to one another.

The organization of military units can have a positive or negative effect on this cohesion. For example, near the end of the World War II the U.S. military replaced combat losses by adding fresh new recruits to existing platoons and companies, rather than replacing whole units. This had devastating effects on morale, as combat-hardened troops who had grown to depend on each other were disdainful of the "reppls" they had been saddled with. Rather than a welcome addition to the unit, the replacements were often regarded as just another mouth to feed, or worse, a useless and therefore dangerous burden that could cause more trouble than they were worth. Samuel Fuller's film *The Big Red One* dramatizes this phenomenon well; the grizzled veterans repeatedly assign the new replacements the most dangerous patrols, out of both self-preservation and unit cohesion. In Joseph Heller's novel and Mike Nichols's film *Catch-22*, there is a more sympathetic treatment. The principal character feels mostly pity for a replacement who was killed before they ever met; later, though, he cynically conspires with his buddies to impersonate the dead man during a visit by his uninformed parents.

The Organization and Disorganization of Combat

The social construction and maintenance of morale also forms the basis for combat tactics at the intermediate level. If success and survival in combat depends on maintaining cohesion of one's own unit, it follows that destruction of the enemy unit's cohesion is a main objective of combat. In fact, it is actually the prime objective of combat, to which killing and maiming are secondary. There is no advantage to be gained in the killing of enemy troops except in the destruction it wreaks on the cohesion of those units (or the strategic value of making them unavailable for later reorganization). Hence, the doctrine of combat throughout the history of warfare has been to "sow disorder" in the ranks of the enemy, and to maintain order in one's own (Collins 1989).

It is a fundamental rule of military tactics that a relatively small number of well-organized troops can defeat far larger numbers that are poorly organized. This makes sense for a number of reasons. First, the essence of combat has always been to overmatch the enemy with larger numbers of troops or weapons. Yet to accomplish this with armies of roughly equal size, one side must concentrate its force in one area while leaving other areas thinly guarded. Thus, if one army intends to attack another, it seeks weakly-defended points along the front, masses troops in those areas, and attacks there. This leaves other points along the front relatively weak, but since defense is generally easier than offense, those weakly-held areas go safely on the defensive.

To manage an effort of concentrating troops in one place while thinning them out elsewhere requires centralized control. This applies at all levels of military organization, from the battalion of 1,000 men to an entire theater of operations such as Europe in 1944. Control consists of a number of elements. For one, there must be means of communication in both directions between headquarters and troops in the field. Commanders must be able to gain intelligence about the situation from the front, and they must subsequently be able to send orders back. In the Gulf War, the United States and its allies spent weeks bombing command and control centers of the Iraqi army to disrupt their communications.

Maintenance of control over troops has always been the primary goal of military commanders, because it constitutes the very essence of victory and likely survival, or defeat and likely death. In the "metal age" of combat, when the main implements of war were sword, shield, and armor, military order and organization consisted largely of maintaining a unified line of troops, such that all of them faced the enemy squarely with shield in one hand and sword in the other. By maintaining close ranks in this way, they formed a relatively impenetrable line and could withstand a formidable assault. The object of the assault, then, was to break holes in such a line. Doing so would allow the attackers to penetrate the line, running around behind the men-at-arms to stab or bash them from the less-protected rear. Of course, a defender that turned to ward off such an attack became more exposed in front. In the end, a breach in the line led to hideous slaughter as heavily armored infantrymen stumbled to the ground in panic to re-form the line, unable to get up because of their own weight, ultimately to be killed by stabs in the joints of their armor and the eye-slits of their helmets. Such was the nature of the action at Agincourt, the decisive English victory immortalized in Shakespeare's *Henry V* (Keegan 1976).

The same principles hold roughly for modern battle. Like the medieval man-at-arms, the modern tank is protected more heavily in front than in its rear. This is not simply an oversight by designers; it would be foolish, given a finite limit on weight, to armor equally on all sides. In addition to individual weapons, whole formations of troops, tanks, and machines are deployed so as to best protect the front, since that is the side facing the enemy. Like Henry at Agincourt, the goal of the modern commander is to maintain the integrity of the line.

The goal in attack is to breach the enemy's line so as to threaten troops from their less-protected rear. The effects of doing so are manifold. First is the obvious effect of killing large numbers of weakly-defended enemy troops and destroying tanks and other equipment. But more important, such a penetration affords the opportunity to disrupt communications, block supplies, and otherwise compromise the defender's social organization. Even more effective, penetrating the defender's formations can cause panic and general disorder as troops try to escape the danger. At Agincourt, dismounted French cavalry were trampled by their own infantry retreating from the line in panic. On the road leading out of Kuwait City in 1991, the technology was different, but the result was the same bloody thing: Iraqi troops created a massive traffic jam in their attempt to escape allied bombing and strafing, only increasing the rate of slaughter.

The Gulf War is actually a rare contemporary case of organized, "formal" warfare between two states. Table 1.1 in Chapter 1 shows that most wars today are less organized affairs, consisting of guerrilla raids by makeshift armies against the state or conversely, of state-sponsored aggression against emerging political or ethnic parties. In both cases civilians may be the principal targets of the fighting. The government attacks civilians as a means of rooting out and repressing "criminal" or "terrorist" elements, while the insurgents might attack civilian groups or institutions as a way of reducing confidence in the government's ability to maintain control. In some cases the government simply targets whole ethnic groups for expulsion so as to gain territory while obtaining an instant ethnic majority within it. This is the general pattern of recent warfare in Yugoslavia, as Serbian nationalist forces have made themselves the majority by expelling rival groups.

These "new wars" are characterized by different tactics than the conventional interstate ones, but at bottom the same goals are at stake. Each side seeks to reduce the cohesion of the other through a combination of combat, terror, and disruption. In some ways this is easier for the smaller, less-organized group to accomplish, since the established government relies more heavily on fragile formal organization. Communications, supplies, and other means of troop support are more centralized and more vulnerable. Moreover, the troops often fight with cumbersome mechanized weapons more suitable to larger-scale combat. The insurgents, on the other hand, are harder to disrupt because their organization is looser in the first place.

Thus military strategy in all kinds of warfare involves attacking social order and integrity. Getting the enemy's soldiers to stop obeying orders is the essence of victory in battle. Killing is only one means to this end; it is effective because it sows doubt and fear in those not killed. Armies will often use "psychological warfare" as a cheap way to demoralize the enemy. Leaflets and propaganda broadcasts typically aim to convince the enemy that his cause is hopeless by emphasizing or fabricating stories of stunning defeats, mass surrender, or political capitulation of one's own leaders. In each case, the goal is to weaken the individual soldier's conviction that his comrades will behave automatically; to disrupt the soldier's ability to "take the role of the other." If the seed of doubt can be sown that comrades in other places are giving up, the soldier may begin to think twice about continuing the fight. Although such efforts seldom have much effect on their own, they can facilitate an enemy's unraveling. For example, leaflets dropped on Iraqi troops in the Gulf War gave instructions for safe surrender, and also conveniently served as white flags.

The Macrosociology of War

Finally, the sociology of warfare can be considered at the macrosocial level as well, for it is the destruction of an adversary's overall political organization that is at the heart of international war. For an illustration, consider how wars end: There may be a negotiated settlement, a stalemate, or a collapse or surrender of one side in the face of overwhelming force applied by the other. The latter was the case at the end of both theaters of World War II, for example.

But what does a "negotiated settlement," a "surrender," or a "collapse" mean? In the most extreme case, the total collapse, the war is over when the defeated society no longer has any cohesion as a political, or perhaps even a social, unit. When Hitler shot himself in his Berlin bunker, German society no longer had an effective political organization. In fact, Germany ceased to exist as a unified political state until 1990, when the Berlin Wall came down and unification ensued.

The case of surrender is illustrated by the Japanese capitulation in 1945. In this case, the political identity of Japan and its personification in Emperor Hirohito survived the war, albeit in very changed form as dictated by the Allies. In the case of negotiated settlements and surrender (which is no more than a settlement on very unfavorable terms), there is an attempt by the "losing" side to retain some control over the society; that is, to maintain some level of social cohesion. Such settlements are undertaken when it becomes clear to the loser that further fighting will result in the total collapse described above. Thus it is advantageous to sue for peace and salvage something. Hence the use of nuclear weapons on Japan was intended to convince the Japanese government that all would be lost unless a surrender was offered. Similarly, the United States and its allies in the Gulf War achieved a collapse of Iraq's army almost entirely by the èclat of air power, thus avoiding much (American) bloodshed on the ground.

Such are the outcomes of what have come to be called "total" wars; conflicts in which no victory is acceptable other than the dissolution of the enemy's political organization. Of course, there are plenty of "limited" wars as well, but the goals of each are of the same nature: to sufficiently threaten a regime's control over its populace (or a portion of it) as to force it to capitulate to one's demands. Similarly, states may contest borders, in effect competing for political control over segments of populations.

If definitions of victory and defeat are based on the existence of macrosocial order in a society, then it follows that the ability of a government to conduct a war is based on maintaining such order. Thus societies at war (or those that expect to be at war often) tend to exert more rigid social control over their citizens. Martial law is an explicit recognition of the need for such control; normal rights and freedoms are typically suspended when such law is invoked. Conversely, this may explain the tendency for democracies to be less warlike than undemocratic states: It is simply harder to get the citizenry at large to agree on military action than for an oligarchical leadership to do so. Certainly this seems to have been the case in Imperial Japan, whose government was dominated by a small clique of militarists in 1941. This faction needed little political support to start a disastrous war with the United States.

Nor is this to say that government institutions are the only sources of control. Much of the censorship and other forms of control are self-imposed or imposed by other institutions. The church, for example, is often in the vanguard of the war effort. Thus President Bush called for a "national day of prayer" to support the Gulf War, and millions of Americans responded enthusiastically at their weekly services. Meanwhile, the FBI "interviewed" Arab Americans during the war to ensure against various forms of subversion, spying, and insurrection. Some American airlines barred American residents of Iraqi citizenship from their flights, and Arab Americans found themselves subject to discrimination of various kinds. Rallies and marches in support of the troops shouted down, and petitioned to eliminate, rallies and marches for peace. Newspaper letters to the editor called for a ban on peace groups and on pacifist sentiments expressed in other letters to the editor.

This sort of informal "martial law," and the formal varieties as well, have become more essential to belligerent societies because war has become an increasingly inclusive social activity. As the nature and conduct of warfare has evolved, an increasingly greater proportion of a society's people have become directly involved in it. In the medieval period, war was conducted generally by a cadre of noblemen who were appointed, or appointed themselves, as officers, and who raised enlisted men from the ranks of their serfs. Though battles were bloody, they were largely confined to combatants. This is not to say civilians did not suffer from war. They were often its passive victims, killed by massacre, starvation, or disease when towns were besieged.

It was the aftermath of the French Revolution and the First Republic that saw the invention of organized, national military conscription. Napoleon Bonaparte implemented this first draft, raising 770,000 men to carry the French dream of empire to fruition (Dyer 1985). By this time, a good-sized battle could be expected to cover an area of many square miles and result in the razing of any small villages that happened to be in the way. The American Civil War was worse; photographs from many of the battles still shock the senses, depicting not only massive casualties but total devastation of the physical and natural surroundings.

In World War I civilians of the modern era became more directly involved in war. Dyer identifies as the major turning point a Zeppelin bombing raid on London in 1915. In it, seventeen civilians were killed or injured at their barstools as a German bomb crashed through the roof of the Dolphin Pub. At the time, the world was shocked at the barbarism of a nation that would purposely target civilian noncombatants (Dyer 1985).

But this was only the most flagrant of such attacks. German U-boats had already by this time attacked civilian merchant ships as they sought to deprive the British of imported materials with which to wage war. What the Allied press had failed to realize was that it had become difficult to distinguish between combatants and noncombatants, because the war had become a contest of economies as well as of armies. With the invention of the machine gun, trench warfare, aircraft, and high explosive artillery, the ability to outproduce one's opponent in bullets, shells, fuel, and boots had become the deciding element of battle. To keep a million men in the field required tremendous organization, not only of the armies themselves, but of the factories and markets and warehouses and railways back home. And especially since the war had ossified into a static slugging match between two huge armies, the advantage belonged to the side with the best and the most supplies. The opening of the Battle of the Somme, for example, was prefaced by the firing of a *million* shells by Allied artillery.

So it was no particular act of barbarism that caused the German army to go after civilian targets. It was simply the recognition of civilians as a part of the war effort. Nor was this "crime" lamented for long. Only twenty-five years later, the Allied Eighth Air Force attempted to shorten the war in Europe through "strategic bombing." Devised by American general Curtis LeMay and his British counterpart Arthur "Bomber" Harris, the strategic bombing campaign sought to reduce the German people's willingness to support the war. The hope was that they would either quit producing weapons and matériel, or possibly overthrow Hitler, thereby ending the war abruptly.

It didn't work, which might have been expected since Hitler had tried and failed to do the same thing to Britain just a few years earlier. But it was not for lack of trying. In the course of the campaign, Allied bombers reduced much of urban Germany to rubble. Cities like Hannover, Dresden, and Hamburg were subjected to firebombing raids so intense that oxygen was literally sucked out of the air by the intense draft of the firestorms. From the shocking raid on the Dolphin in World War I, war had "progressed" in just a couple of decades to wholesale killing of entire cities. It had taken all day and relatively few lives for Henry V to win all of France for the crown of England. In Dresden, 70,000 died in an evening, to little advantage to the Allies. And this was not the worst of it, for only a year later, a like number perished in an instant in Hiroshima, and again in Nagasaki. This time it worked; the emperor was convinced that his cause was lost.[1]

Nor is that the end of the march of military "progress." Today, strategic nuclear weapons can target nearly any significant population or strategic center on earth. Estimated civilian casualties in the event of a full-scale nuclear exchange between, say, the United States and Russia run from a low of tens of millions to as high as several hundred millions, depending on the scenario. And in spite of variations in specific doctrine that include intentions to destroy enemy missile silos, or air defense capabilities, or even incoming missiles by "star wars" technology, the main target of these weapons is the social structure of the society itself. Nuclear doctrine is little more than a technical modernization of Le May's strategic bombing campaign: to bomb enemy cities until the underlying cohesion of the society is destroyed.

And so this examination of the sociology of war has come full circle. At every level of analysis, from the four-man infantry rifle team, through the medium-size battalion or regiment, through the full-scale theater of operations, all the way up to the level of the society as a whole, warfare is waged through the destruction of the enemy's social cohesion and the maintenance of one's own. This applies as well to civil and insurgent conflict as it does to interstate war, as each side often uses terror and civilian violence as a means to disrupt the opponent. The killing, the destruction, the maneuver, the intelligence, the propaganda—all military endeavors—are aimed at this overall social objective.

What Is War?

We must conclude that warfare is a distinctly social enterprise. Margaret Mead (1965) recognized this explicitly in her attempt to define war in social and cultural terms. For Mead, war is something more than violence, for violence can be found among peoples who do not "have the idea of war." For example, Eskimo cultures allowed for violence in the stealing of women and acts of revenge for it. The well-studied Yanomamö of Brazil institutionalized violence in many forms. American culture is rife with violence of all sorts; a glance of any newspaper will settle the point. But it seemed to Mead that to equate violence with war was to miss the essential reality of war. For murderers and robbers and barroom brawlers seem engaged in something qualitatively different than sol-

---

[1]That Japan had already made overtures for peace before the atomic bomb attacks raises another issue altogether.

diers. Similarly, there is a difference between the attack of an Eskimo man upon another for stealing his wife and the organized combat of military units, however technically primitive. For Mead, that difference was profound, and could best be reflected by the concepts of culture and social organization. War is distinguished from other forms of violence, according to Mead, by five essential characteristics.

First, war, as opposed to other forms of violence, involves two or more groups of people participating *as groups*. That is, the individuals that are involved fight because they belong to and are loyal to their group. Typically this sense of belonging is a bond of selfless loyalty: patriotism in the modern era, but it may instead consist of clan or kinship ties, regional or ethnic identity, or other form of primary or secondary group membership. Thus the soldier in, say, World War II was motivated by a national call for participation in a heroic struggle; this was emphasized by the widespread use of conscription and by low pay. The importance of low pay in sustaining morale was symbolized by the popularity of one World War II hit song, titled "Twenty-one dollars a day (once a month)."

To say that soldiers are typically motivated by collective ideals rather than by material rewards is not to say that such participation is necessarily noble. They are the sorts of ideals that motivated the Nazis as well as the Free French, Hutus and Tutsis, Serbs and Croats, Iraqis and Americans. These motives—nationalism, ethnic identity, religious fidelity, historic destiny—are easily inculcated into the typical twenty-year-old during basic training, and even earlier via state manipulation of the mass media. The sense of adventure, self-respect, and patriotic duty pandered in military recruitment advertising is a case in point. And even if the recruit is a conscript, it is only a matter of time before extreme loyalty to one's unit, if not to the state, is firmly imbedded.

Although altruistic motives are the typical means of binding individual combatants to the goals of a larger group, they are not always necessary. Many armies have been raised on the promise of pay or, more tempting, loot and rape. It was not uncommon for medieval lords to recruit sizable forces by assuring them that victory would win for them whatever goods and women could be carried off. And there is some evidence also that the sheer joy of guiltless killing can be a motivation. In the World War I battle of Gallipoli, for example, Allied soldiers actually offered bribes to those in the front lines so that they could get in a few shots at the vainly charging Turks (Moorhead 1956). For that matter, such evidence can be found today. Interviews with American pilots in the earliest phases of the Gulf War often revealed a sense of glee and fun in the "real life video game" that modern air war has become.

Second, war, as opposed to other forms of violence, involves a willingness on the part of participants to kill and to die. This element is necessary to distinguish war from, say, football, in which participation is also of a group nature and violence is the rule. What distinguishes war from football is that real harm is intended, and the "supreme sacrifice" is an accepted possibility. This does not mean necessarily that soldiers *want* to die—although suicidal fervor is not unknown. But every soldier comes to accept that one's own death, abhorrent as it may be, will be justified by the conflict. In the Civil War General Sherman's famous dictum, "War is hell," became the definitive statement of this acceptance.

Third, an understanding is achieved in war that the killing that goes on is not to be considered murder. It goes without saying that norms against killing are suspended for the killing of combat. For example, the Judeo-Christian commandment that thou shalt not kill is handily suspended in wartime, even to the extent that military chaplains are able to pray for the success of the troops. In the same way, Muslims can engage in holy wars without concern for incongruity. The more subtle notion here is that war is, *by definition*, that kind of killing which is approved, rather than condemned, by the group.

In the modern age it is the state that most effectively legitimates killing, but it is not the only group capable of doing so. Political factions within states often challenge the state's monopoly, sometimes to the extent of raising armies. Where the state's authority is weak these armies can amount to the ruling government in local areas; this was the case in Somalia early in the 1990s, and in ethnic enclaves within Bosnia and Croatia after the breakup of Yugoslavia. Where the state is stronger, factional wars may be carried out by less-organized paramilitary groups, as in Kosovo or Northern Ireland. On a smaller scale, the drug gangs of American cities have become more powerful and have acquired some of the force of a government among their members because they can define the killing of rival gang members as legitimate, and can make those definitions stick. Thus the ability of a group to define violence as war may actually enhance the group's authority, and may help to legitimate its hold over members.

Fourth, war is distinguished from other forms of violence in that killing is done in the name of abstract goals. These goals are typically couched in moral terms like "freedom" or "democracy" or "socialism." *Islam* They can, however, be more palpable, including ethnic political rights, traditional homeland territory, or personal obligation to the king or emir. On the other hand, war goals can reach a level of abstraction that boggles the mind: U.S. forces have "fought for peace" both in Vietnam and in the Cold War (official air force stationery includes the phrase "Peace . . . is our profession" at the bottom). Other armies have fought for and against Zionism, the Gihad, the revolution, the Union, states' rights, and nearly every ideology imaginable.

Whatever the goals are, Mead's conceptualization counts as war only those fights that are conducted in the name of some collectively-held end. This eliminates bands of brigands, terrorizing the countryside for booty alone, and certainly individuals on a spree. But more important, it reiterates and reaffirms the collective nature of warfare as an inherently communal phenomenon. No matter how violent, one person cannot make a war, any more than one person can make a religion or a government.

Fifth, Mead distinguished war from other forms of violence in that warfare actually involves a relationship between the warring factions. There is an agreement between warring states, for example, on the legitimacy of the killing. Diplomats representing states at war do not get incensed or indignant at the casualties inflicted by the enemy, so long as those casualties are the result of "fair," mutually-legitimated killing. It is easy to detect a difference in diplomatic language directed at enemy states when the conventions are violated. Curious as it seems, the Geneva Convention on the "rules" of war is an explicit recognition of the ongoing relationship that exists between warring parties.

The importance of Mead's contribution to understanding war cannot be overstated. In a single stroke, she not only offers a definition of the concept, but in the best social science tradition, she has forced a rethinking of a concept that was thought to be already understood. Although everyone has a working idea of what war is, the lay definition of the concept is inadequate when scholars seek to study war's causes and effects. For Mead, war is perhaps the most intensely social event there is.

The Social Structure of Peace

It makes more intuitive sense to speak of the social nature of peace than of war. Peace must be "social" because it involves cooperation and understanding. But what does one really know of peace? For one thing, there is little agreement on what peace actually is, much less on whether and how it can be achieved. Some think of peace solely in terms of the relationships between states; as the absence of war. Others, by contrast, regard peace as an all-encompassing utopia in which humankind reaches its highest state of cooperation and harmony. These two extremes form the poles of a continuum of thought about the meaning of peace; they have been labeled "negative" and "positive" peace, respectively (Barash 1991).

Thinking of peace in negative terms has important consequences for the way in which one seeks to understand the phenomenon. Because peace is viewed simply as the absence of war, and since war is made by the state, there is a tendency toward macrosociological thinking.

Thinkers in the "negative peace" tradition tend to view peace as achievable through diplomacy and other foreign policy efforts. Peace (that is, warlessness) can be achieved in a number of ways, depending on one's point of view and on the kind and duration of peace one requires. For some, peace is made by maintaining a "balance of power" among rival states. Such a balance ensures that no one power in a region will be tempted to make war on its neighbors. Thus the United States declared its intention in the Gulf War (at least for a time) of reducing the excessive military might possessed by Saddam Hussein (which, incidentally, the United States had vigorously helped to build), so that the Gulf states could keep Iraq's ambitions in check.

Others in this mode explicitly regard peace as achievable only through force. They point to the way societies and states have been formed throughout history: by the conquest of weaker groups by stronger ones, the former being absorbed by the latter. In these circumstances, larger and larger numbers of people come to cooperate with one another in the same society. William Graham Sumner regarded this as a natural ecological process; he actually referred to it as the continual expansion of the "peace group" (1911). The rise of the nation-state in the Middle Ages is a good example of this process, in which the rule—that is, the imposition of law and order—of powerful noblemen was extended through conquest to cover ever larger groups of people, until one of them was powerful enough to call himself king.

[handwritten margin note: disagree]

The modern variant of this sort of thinking justifies the existence of empires as a means of maintaining order among rival nations. Levy (1996) puts this in Hobbesian terms, noting that a well-run empire removes subordinate nations from the "state of nature" by placing a higher authority above them. A more benign manifestation would be the United Nations, a sort of world government whose reliance on force has increased dramatically in scope and intensity over the past decade or so (Diehl, Druckman, and Wall 1998).

"Negative" conceptions of peace can be troubling, because using them to understand the human condition seems to lead to a paradox: that peace can be achieved through war. This rationale was offered by many for the Gulf War: The war was necessary to restore equilibrium to the balance of military powers in the region. In fact, war is often justified as a means of achieving peace "through strength." Conversely, the "bad" peace of World War I is thought to have been responsible for creating the conditions that brought about World War II.

"Positive" definitions of peace seek to be more comprehensive. The mere prevention of war, or negative peace, is viewed as a limited goal at best, because it does not address many of the other forms of structured violence that are so prevalent in the world. Many countries are not at war, yet they are ruled by cruel despots or are exploited by corrupt elites or distant empires. These, it is argued, should not be considered societies at "peace." Others are so poor and dis-integrated that they are rife with violence, crime, and self-destruction. Even in the absence of war, it violates the sensibilities to think of such places as peaceful. It is worth an ironic note, too, that these are frequently the conditions in societies where "peace" has been imposed by a foreign power.

The trouble with expanding the definition of peace is that it is difficult to know where to stop. When I teach the sociology of medicine, it is common practice to engage students in a discussion of what "health" is. We often begin with the simple definition of health as the "absence of disease," but it soon becomes apparent that such a definition is of little use. Discussion progresses to social definitions, such as "ability to carry out normal role obligations" and social "normalcy." Before long the class has progressed all the way to the World Health Organization's (WHO) definition of health: "a state of complete physical, mental, and social well-being and not merely the absence of disease or infirmity" (World Health Organization 1958).

The problem with this sort of definition is that it is so inclusive and so general that it becomes difficult to distinguish health from any number of other desirable things. Health, according to the WHO, seems to be goodness and truth and justice and equality and beauty and self-fulfillment, all rolled into one. No doubt this could serve fairly well as a definition of peace, too. And this is the kind of problem encountered in defining peace: Ideas about peace become so imbued with one's own values that one is unable to distinguish it from other desirable states. Consequently, "positive" definitions of peace tend toward vagueness. Attempts to arrive at a positive definition of peace have ranged from the introspective to the cosmic, and include "universal responsibility" (Brenes 1990), "global cooperation" (Fischer 1996), and "respect for life" (Harris 1990).

But the most troublesome problem with defining "positive" peace is that its confusion with other valued states creates a strong tendency toward ethnocentrism. To even use the term "positive" is to engage a system of values in thinking about the concept. Thus students of peace in Western societies tend to define peace in terms of democracy, social equality, and "justice." In a roundtable discussion in the *U.S. Institute of Peace Journal,* Carl Gershman asserted:

> It should be self-evident that a society organized democratically according to the principles of consent, the rule of law, and respect for the rights of the individual will behave more peacefully in its foreign relations than a society governed by force and repression. The case for this view . . . should not need to be restated. (United States Institute of Peace 1990)

In the same discussion, R. J. Rummel concluded that "In sum, democracies are the least violent regimes, totalitarian states the most."

This sort of thinking is expressed in religious terms as well. For example, Catholic social teaching asserts:

> The Catholic tradition has always understood the meaning of peace in positive terms. Peace is both a gift of God and a human work. It must be constructed on the basis of *central human values:* truth, justice, freedom, and love. (Second General Council of Latin American Bishops 1970, italics mine)

culture clash

But are these really "central" human values? Would these all be held in equally high esteem by Muslims, Hindus, or devotees of nontheistic or animistic religions? Or more pointedly, would they be defined in the same way? The appeal to freedom may mean individual, personal liberty to a Westerner, but quite another thing to peoples of more traditional cultures, in which individuals are deeply rooted in kinship and community obligations. And "truth" may be even more difficult to pin down as scientific, religious, and ideological knowledge systems alternatively lay claim to truth in various of the world's cultures. Finally, justice may be the most problematic of all, for it is clear that ideals of justice vary widely from one culture to the next. In contemporary American society, for example, one basic tenet of justice is that all people should have equal opportunities for success or failure, but that neither success nor failure should be guaranteed (the extent to which this ideal is practiced is another matter). But there have been, and still are, many cultures in which this definition would be considered a grave injustice, or a nonsensical ideal. In some cultures tradition may specify that birthright or religious status, or age, or gender justly ascribes status and confers privilege on some, subservience on others. In a cross-cultural survey, Pen (1971) identified twenty-one different views of economic justice alone.

The problem with many positive conceptualizations of peace is that they are at best value-bound, hopelessly tied up in a variety of Western cultural beliefs and values. Defining peace in terms of "truth" or "justice" ignores real differences among cultural ideals. At worst, these ways of thinking about peace are little more than ideological slogans. Either way, they exert very strong influence over the kinds of questions asked about peace, and also over the sorts of actions people are likely to undertake to make it.

Some scholars have attempted to avoid value-centered definitions of peace by developing empirical measures. For example, a composite scale of peacefulness might be computed from the following indicators, among others:

- amount of interpersonal violence
- amount of intergroup violence
- prevalence of nonviolent conflict resolution
- level of personal satisfaction
- level of satisfaction with status and perception of society
- amount of international (or intertribal) war
- expenditures on military
- proportion of population imprisoned

These all seem at first to be useful indicators of the level of peace in a society. That they can be observed "objectively," that is, in the same terms by various observers, is a great help.[2] But the existence of a measure does not constitute a definition. Even though these points might be valid indicators of peace, one does not know what peace "is" until one can explain *why* these measures are good ones. In the end, a good multi-trait measure of a social concept should possess an underlying order; a "common denominator" that connects all the individual indicators together, and this is what is needed to complete this definition of peace. In a sense, this is an operational definition without a conceptual definition underlying it.

The definition of peace ought to possess the following characteristics:

1. It should be culture-neutral. Any adequate definition of peace ought to be universally applicable, or at least applicable to a wide variety of societies and cultures. Whether a society is at peace or not should not be measured in terms of culturally-specific values. For example, the peaceability of a society should be judged independent of whether it incorporates a democratic political system, a monarchy, or a tribal council. Certainly it should be independent of the precepts of any particular kind of religion. The definition should apply with equal sensibility to the Yanomamö and to the French.
2. The definition should avoid reductionism. Peace should be thought of as a characteristic of groups or societies and not of individuals. One of the great beauties of Mead's definition of war is that it makes sense of the capability of otherwise quite ordinary, mild individuals to engage in warfare. The definition of

---

[2]Still, there are some inherent validity problems. For example, it seems likely that people might express the most positive feelings of satisfaction with both their personal lives and with the society in highly oppressive states where opinion is effectively controlled through mass media. The same might be true of highly militaristic societies, or those undergoing periods of military adventure. One is reminded of the bubble or euphoria that existed in the U.S. during the Gulf War.

peace ought to do the same; making sense of the ability of "inherently" aggressive humans to engage in peaceful social interaction.

3. The definition should not conflict with commonsense ideas about what a peaceful world must look like. Societies defined as peaceful should be characterized by relatively little violence, for example. There should be relatively less human suffering, disease, or death than in less peaceful societies. In short, it should be consistent with those empirical indicators listed above. It should also be a concept separate from war; that is, it should be something other than merely the absence of war. This would be consistent with the notion of "positive" rather than "negative" peace.

4. Finally, the definition ought to be consistent with major ideas in sociological theory. Only in this way will it makes sense in terms of what is already known about the social order.

Such a definition is possible, and can be derived from the most fundamental principles of social psychology. But for purposes of exposition, I wish to develop the definition inductively, by inferring it from examples.

A Social Definition of Peace

What does a peaceful society look like? It seems possible to agree on some examples of peaceful and "peaceless" societies. First, it is easy to agree that a society at war with a foreign state is without peace. This was certainly true of the citizens of London and Hamburg and Hiroshima during World War II. The Vietnamese knew little peace for decades during which the French, then the Americans, sought to gain political control. The Iraqis, Israelis, and Saudis have seen the peace disrupted for a generation as ancient homelands, and now valuable oilfields, are disputed.

But a state engaged in war elsewhere is also relatively peaceless. Those too young to have experienced American life during World War II or Vietnam can now witness for themselves the costs of war, even on the "home front." In the Gulf War, families were disrupted as fathers and, more commonly in the nineties, mothers as well, were suddenly shipped out to the front. Many Americans were shocked to learn that there were no provisions in place to supplement the incomes of these families or to provide child care or other needed services for them. The cloying sentimentality of news stories about soldiers at the front and their families and lovers back home only thinly disguised the reality that war is about separation and disruption of the normal social order.

The Gulf War also saw a sudden polarization of American society, reminiscent of the Vietnam era. One's attitudes toward the war became almost overnight a centrally-important aspect of one's character, defining one's place on the political, social, and moral spectra. Meanwhile, a strong resurgence of nationalist fervor, manifested in flag-raisings and national prayer days, brought on a wave of informal censorship and self-repression. Rallies in support of the troops clashed with rallies against the war. That support of the troops and opposition to the war had become contradictory only drove home the point that reason and tolerance are among the first casualties of war.

Societies rife with internal political violence must also count as peaceless; for example, Rwanda, the Ivory Coast, Sri Lanka, Haiti. In fact, many of the bloodiest wars are civil wars or wars of the state against a segment of the population, and these latter have been rife in the twentieth century (Krain 1997). This is probably because civilians are often the primary targets in civil wars, and they are much easier to kill in large numbers than armed and trained soldiers. Whatever the casualties, internal war breaches the peace in large part by disrupting the normal social structures that make for cooperation and interaction. Industries are destroyed, shops close, roads and telephones and power grids go unrepaired. Health and medicine and education become low priorities.

There are also large segments of American cities that are, to some extent, without peace. It is in these urban ghettos that many of the nation's violent crimes are committed. These neighborhoods are thought to be "dangerous" areas, so police forces spend much of the public's resources trying to keep order. Since the residents themselves are most likely to be victimized by crime, they are torn between the benefits of greater police protection and the demoralization of living under what amounts to martial law. Moreover, such authoritarian approaches to geographically-concentrated crime prevention only furthers the stigmatization and ghettoization of residents.

Domestic and other kinds of interpersonal violence, to which Americans have become inured, should also be considered. Physical, sexual, and psychological abuse, usually directed against women, children, and the elderly, appall but no longer surprise us. Compared with many other societies, America is startlingly lacking in domestic tranquillity. This, too, is a breach of the peace.

It might also be agreed for the moment that societies undergoing wrenching economic change are peaceless places. Germany in the 1920s, for example, saw an inflation of the currency so explosive that bushel baskets of money could not buy a day's groceries. The United States in the 1930s was victimized by a different economic disruption: depression, crop failure, and bank insolvency had dried up the supply of cash, such that few could finance production of goods or the planting of crops.

If it is agreed that all these circumstances are examples of peaceless societies, what is the resulting definition of peace? Put another way, what do all these illustrations have in common? They are not all examples of societies threatened by an outside enemy. Not all of them are characterized by wholesale violence and organized killing. Certainly they are not all at war, in the sense that Mead described.

What these examples do have in common is that they are all circumstances in which people experience personal insecurity. They are *afraid*, of foreign enemies, internal insurrections, their own neighbors, their spouses and parents. They are uncertain about their futures, which might be altered politically by war, or economically by depression, shortage, or currency instability. They are no longer confident in their judgments as to which streets are safe to walk at night, or which people can be trusted. Their own government may be the source of their fears, or it may be viewed as their only protection from them.

Put another way, life is simply *unpredictable* in these examples. People in peaceless societies are less able to predict the actions of their fellows, in a variety of ways. Where there is a great deal of crime, people are suspicious of one another, and they bar their doors and windows for protection. Where there is economic instability, people are unable to save, borrow, or even work for wages because there is no consensus on the value of currency. Political unrest makes it necessary for people to know which "side" each other is on, in order to carry on normal social discourse. Suspicion and distrust, rather than communication and cooperation, prevail.

Predictability is the very basis of society, for it is the ability to predict the actions of others that makes it possible for humans to interact at all. Alfred Schutz was the first to express this view in explicitly sociological terms. Borrowing from Dewey, Schutz characterized all human action as a series of "projects," the scope of which could range from buying groceries to planning a career or raising a family. Each project, in order to have a chance for success, involves from the actor's point of view a series of predictions about the future. Thus an act as mundane as catching a bus to work really requires a series of predictions: I will not be accosted on the sidewalk, cars will confine themselves to the street, if I wait at a certain corner a bus will soon arrive, when it does I will be invited to board it, the fare will be seventy-five cents, the bus will go to my place of work, and when I get there, I will have a job. And the very idea of a "job" of course implies myriad intersecting predictions between employee, supervisor, fellows, and many others. One only has to consider the consequences of being unable to make even one of these predictions to understand their importance.

The essential fact of social life is that these sorts of predictions are grounded in a vast array of taken-for-granted assumptions. For Schutz, this taken-for-grantedness is a "primary characteristic" of human experience (Gurwitsch 1966). People really do not need to ponder whether the bus will arrive, or whether the possibility that an approaching stranger will assault or beat and rob them. People take for granted that spouses, children, and parents will behave toward them in the "usual" way, and that they in turn will be able to fulfill their roles. People also rest assured that the larger social structure will continue to function from day to day: The currency will not change drastically in value; the roads will be repaired; the trash will be collected. People feel "secure" because they can count on a million assumptions about the way the world works. Berger and Luckmann observed that much everyday conversation is aimed at reaffirming this taken-for-grantedness. Thus a commuter on the way to the office might announce, "Well, it's time for me to get to the station," and receive the response "Fine, darling, have a good day at the office"; this implies an entire world that makes sense to both participants. They contrast this with the following exchange: "Well, it's time for me to get to the station." "Fine, darling, don't forget to take along your gun" (Berger and Luckmann 1966 : 140).

What happens when assumptions are violated, when the world cannot be taken for granted? Certainly Berger and Luckmann's straphanger is on the way to a relatively peaceless environment, one in which people are unpredictable. But the situation would not be much different if instead it is an Israeli commuter being reminded to bring along her gas mask, or an Iraqi having no workplace left to go to and no transportation to get there. Berger and Luckmann's scenario is also a reminder that there are indeed people who carry weapons on a regular basis. In the United States, for example, a good many women find it wise to carry handguns or mace in their purses.

Peace, then, is nothing more than the ability to predict, or to "count on" the behaviors of others. In peaceful communities, members are usually able to "take the role of others"; to see things from others' point of view. They do not fear one another because they know what others are thinking. They act kindly because they expect kindness will be reciprocated. They work and loan and borrow because they believe the future will look much the same as the present. They raise their children carefully because they believe their own experience will still be of value when the children grow up. In short, under peaceful circumstances, people trust one another and their social institutions.

This sort of predictability is a matter of social structure, and may be likened to what Aquinas called the "tranquillity of order." Societies and the people within them are predictable when there is a high degree of consensus among citizens on most of the taken-for-granted assumptions of everyday life. These assumptions include two general kinds of knowledge: role expectations, on the one hand, and cultural values, beliefs, and norms on the other.

In the first place, peaceful societies are characterized by a high degree of consensus on the ways people should behave in certain roles. An excellent contemporary example is offered by gender roles in American society. Rapid changes in these roles (for both men and women) over the past few decades have disrupted consensus on the appropriate way to be a man or a woman. In the long run, this has had and will continue to have a liberating effect on both sexes. But the immediate result has been a certain level of anomie, a normlessness by which both men and women grope for identity, order, and predictability.

Second, peace also requires consensus on at least core ideas about what is true, what is good, and what is allowed. This sort of consensus makes it possible for people to take for granted that others will abide by mutually-understood rules, and that they will do so because they possess the same values and beliefs. Such consensus may be compromised, for example, where stratification creates social classes with fundamentally different ideologies and worldviews, but no structural or ideological means to integrate them. For example, a traditional stratification system like India's castes may exist peacefully as long as Hindu religious precepts "make sense" of the society's inequality. By contrast, American social inequality, so clearly rooted in race and sex, cannot be made sense of by traditional notions of "merit" rewarded through fair competition. Too many people simply do not buy it, and the result is a deep-rooted alienation among people of different classes and ethnicities. People of these various groups do not feel a sense of consensus on many core values, or, more pointedly, on the legitimacy of the social and political order. In the end, they simply do not trust or understand one another.

It is worth noting that "consensus" in this sense is something different than simple agreement among people on roles, values, and norms. The distinctly social nature of consensus was illustrated by Thomas Scheff (1967), who described it in terms of three discernible levels:

Agreement. The most rudimentary level of consensus exists when the people in a community possess the same idea about a belief, value, norm, or set of role expectations. To illustrate, if everyone believes that it is wrong to kill, then this sort of agreement exists.

Awareness. But simple agreement is not by itself social consensus. The parties to the agreement must be *aware that they agree*. That is, not only must everyone possess the belief that it is wrong to kill, but each individual must know that the others possess the same belief. People must be aware that they are not alone in their beliefs, alienated from the mainstream of society. Such a condition is expressed by the phrase "It's not just my opinion—ask anybody; they'll tell you the same thing!"

It should also be noted that there can be agreement without awareness, and conversely, a "false" awareness can exist without agreement. The first case can be illustrated by ethnic or class boundaries. It is a matter of fact, for example, that American blacks and whites agree substantially on most core beliefs and values: the value of hard work, the meaning of success, the importance of family, for instance. Yet it also seems true that whites and blacks both are generally unaware of their agreement. Their stereotypes about each other suggest that the "others" have a different view; that they do not care about the same things or think in the same way.

The opposite circumstance—the awareness of agreement that does not really exist—is illustrated by Irving Janis's notion of "groupthink." Janis observed that many "catastrophic" decisions made by groups are made because individual members are afraid to dissent from what they think is unanimous opinion. Yet in many groups this unanimity is an illusion. Janis used the Bay of Pigs invasion to illustrate this point; the group that made the decision to invade Cuba included several members whose own views were against the invasion. Yet because each thought himself a minority of one, none spoke up.

This phenomenon can be observed not only at the small-group level but at the macro level as well, for it is the goal of advertising, and especially political advertising, to create a "false consensus"; the illusion that the majority agree that one's product (or one's candidate) is the better choice. Poll results thus become important weapons in political campaigns, and each candidate will use them to claim the lead or, at least, a respectable showing among the voters. And in an even larger sense, belief in agreement that does not really exist is at the core of the Marxian concept of "false consciousness." In this case, it is a false belief in agreement between classes on mutual interests and destinies.

Understanding. Yet there is one more level of consensus, which Scheff described as an understanding that others are also aware of this mutual agreement: Not only do we agree that killing is wrong; not only do I know that we agree; but I also know that *you* are aware that we agree. This level of consensus is expressed by the phrase "We all understand each other on this. Just ask anybody; they'll tell you I feel the same way as they do." In this respect, consensus is fully "intersubjective"; it exists not simply in people's minds but between them.

This is exactly the effect that Durkheim recognized when he noted the importance of ritual as a community-building mechanism. Rituals (public prayer, song, pledges of allegiance, and the like) serve not simply as a rote exercise by which each participant is lulled into agreement with the other participants. What ritual does is to demonstrate to each participant that he or she is *not alone* in love of God, or country, or alma mater, or other symbol of the community. And moreover, ritual gives each participant an opportunity to demonstrate to the others his or her own agreement. Thus, when I sing a hymn or chant a mantra or raise a clenched fist with the others of my group, I reassure them of my membership and commitment, and of our mutual consensus. This is critical, as can be shown by simply refusing to pray or cheer or raise the clenched fist at the appropriate moment.

One objection that might be raised here is that defining peace simply as "predictability" and justice as "justification" can lead to an extreme sort of cultural relativism. Even the most heinous oppression could be regarded by this view as peaceful, as long as it is seen as normal and reasonable within the culture in which it occurs. A colleague who read an earlier version of this chapter called this a "Holocaust problem": If German society had been sufficiently convinced of the justness of the Final Solution, would one then have to conclude that the Holocaust was the policy of a peaceful society?

The answer is no, insofar as the Holocaust was not an institutionalized and accepted element of German society. The state propaganda apparatus had to go to great lengths to convince the populace that the camps were simply resettlement centers, and in any event that the Jews deserved harsh treatment. And whatever the citizens' views on whether the Jews deserved their fate, few took the mass executions *for granted* as the natural outgrowth of German values. On the contrary, the extermination of the Jews was at least regarded as an extraordinary event, undertaken under political duress, real and imagined, and made possible partly by a great deal of secrecy, subterfuge, and threat. Remember, too, that much of this occurred in the midst of an all-out war effort, which offers the despot a powerful set of tools for coercion and fear.

One might also object that clearly violent but orderly social systems might be considered peaceful under this definition; for example, a brutal prison where inmates are beaten and tortured. Such a scenario does begin to stretch the utility of the definition, but it is also hard to imagine that such a system could be understandable and predictable to its participants. A prison is not peaceful just because inmates can count on being beaten by the guard. What is required is that an overall consensus exists in which participants, including the inmates themselves, understand that beatings are normal.

The Maintenance of Peace

If peace is a state of predictability made possible by community, then it is clear that the creation and maintenance of peace is a social process. Each person is predictable to others only to the extent that people behave in patterned, ordered, and understandable ways. But what makes this happen? Why do people behave predictably? From a traditional sociological point of view, they are compelled to do so by powerful norms, beliefs, and values.

The earliest social theorists regarded this sort of peace as a state of cooperation, achieved voluntarily and rationally. Hobbes and the other "social contract" theorists viewed society as a rationally contrived enterprise, by which people entered into a rational agreement to surrender individual freedom in the name of the public good. For some, including Hobbes, this was a great achievement, as the "natural" state of humanity (before society was created) was characterized by a "war of every man against every other man." Under such conditions:

> There is no place for industry because the fruit thereof is uncertain: and consequently no culture of the earth; no navigation nor use of the commodities that may be imported by the sea; no commodious building; no instruments of moving and removing such things as require much force; no knowledge of the face of the earth; no account of time; no arts; no letters; no society; and, which is worst of all, continual fear and danger of violent death; the life of man is solitary, poor, nasty, brutish, and short. (Hobbes 1958: 82)

For Hobbes, then, cooperation is a social invention that makes possible virtually all of humankind's achievements. Without it people would still live as savages. It is worth noting that Hobbes actually used the term "war" to refer to this anarchic "state of nature" that he presumed to exist before modern civilization took place. Though it does not correspond to the definition adopted here, Hobbes certainly meant it to refer to the opposite of "peace."

Indeed, many of what are called "peace systems" are examples of Hobbesian contracts among people and groups of people. Examples of peace systems include international agreements on air traffic control, maritime law, highway regulations, and similar conventions. But it is not necessary to assume a rational agreement or contract among people in order to recognize peace as social cooperation. In fact, such an assumption is usually quite difficult to accept, since no individual can actually remember entering into any such bargain. This is exactly the question Durkheim addressed: Although he recognized that people could be seen to give up willingly their own prerogatives to the group, he could not identify the source of the original contract. He concluded and demonstrated that there must be a "pre-contractual solidarity" that binds people together. That is, where Hobbes saw individuals as the creators of society, Durkheim saw society as the shaper of the individual (Durkheim 1893/1964).

Durkheim's distinction is important; it allows for the recognition of values, ideals, religion, and the whole repertoire of human cultural ingenuity as the material that really holds the community together. Society is not held together by the rational self-interest of individuals. It is the product of a deeper sort of consensus, by which individuals share *faith* in something larger than themselves; an intuitive recognition of the community as the legitimate shaper of their lives. Of course, the community takes many forms in modern societies through various roles: family, the state, God, the workplace, and so forth.

By and large, people are not as calculating as the Hobbesian view suggests. Rather, they simply have faith in others. And this, it seems, is consistent with commonsense views of peace. Peace amounts to trust in one's fellows, one's institutions, one's society. For many people, it amounts to trust in God, which is to say much the same thing.

Things like "trust" and "faith" are characteristics of peaceful social structures, for they are maintained by keeping the values, beliefs, and norms by which people live highly understandable and even "taken for granted." But how is this accomplished? One way might be to impose strict, authoritarian rule over a community. In this way, every person understands perfectly the rules and conventions for behavior, and further, punishments for violations are so severe that no one dares break them. This certainly makes people highly predictable, and so it should enhance the peace.

This is not an outlandish proposition, and in fact there is plenty of evidence to support it. The invention of law itself was simply the reduction of intergroup conflict by the imposition of a higher authority, backed by force. Thus medieval landholders solved the problem of conflict among groups and individuals by subsuming them under authoritarian rule. In a more modern context, the state is an elaborate structure for regulating the relationships among individuals through the force of law. Individuals trust each other (more or less) to behave in a "civil" manner because of the force of civil law. And at an even higher level, empires like the former Soviet Union imposed a kind of peace among rival ethnic and nationalist groups. Strife among these groups is erupting on a large scale now that the overarching rule of the Soviet Empire is gone (see Katz 1996; Mearsheimer 1994). More dramatically at the moment, it seems the death of Tito began the unraveling of the former Yugoslavia into several independent and feuding states.

Peace and Justice

This sort of thinking leads, though, into a troubling paradox. If predictability is the social basis for peace and if the force of law creates predictability, then it seems to follow that the most authoritarian and even cruel regime will bring the greatest peace. For those who seek a more peaceful world, this is indeed an unappealing prospect; further, it implies a kind of peace that violates the commonsense notion of what peace should look like.

There are several considerations, however, that offer a way out of the paradox. First, like many good arguments, this one has less validity as it is carried to its extreme. Just because law is a good thing, it does not follow that all-pervasive and oppressive law is a better thing. The peaceful society is the one that is governed by "just the right amount" of law. More subtly, oppressive and militaristic police states are not more peaceful than less authoritarian states, because they do not in fact make life any more predictable. For one thing, the state tends to become less and less predictable as power becomes more absolute. Leaders are able to change policies at whim, or enforce laws capriciously. Thus merely obeying the law might not guarantee that one is able to stay out of trouble.

Such states typically abandon the rule of law altogether, maintaining control instead by terrorizing the opposition or even the citizenry at large. They also frequently divide the citizenry by infiltrating it with party members, secret police, and the like, thereby making it more difficult for individuals to predict and trust one another.[3] Thus citizens are suspicious of one another, and life reverts to what Hobbes called the war of all against all.

An even more fundamental consideration is the problem of consistency. Authoritarian states may be capable of enforcing a wide array of restrictions on the populace, in an effort to keep them "peaceful," and people might endeavor to follow them as best they can. But laws handed down from above, imposed on a society by an authoritarian regime, are not likely to be consistent with other social and cultural institutions, or for that matter, even with other laws handed down by the regime. It is

---

[3]The former Ceaucescu regime of Romania is a case in point. At the height of the state's oppression there, some members of opposition political groups were certain that 50% of their members were actually government infiltrators! While this was surely a wild overstatement, it indicates the level of distrust and paranoia the regime was able to maintain among its citizens.

even possible that in order to obey one law, a citizen might be forced to violate another.

Whether or not this is literally the case, it is almost certain that many of the laws so imposed will conflict with deeply-held cultural beliefs and values, which have evolved slowly over the long history of the society. For example, Marxist-Leninist doctrine could not coexist with the Orthodox Church, which undergirded much of Russian cultural life. In American society, official law providing social and political equality is inconsistent with the unequal structure of the U.S. economy. Merton saw in this contradiction the source of a good deal of criminality among the poor (Merton 1968).

In principle, it is possible to create the peace of predictability through force. But in practice, it is very difficult. Social systems are so complex that there are simply too many deeply-held customs, beliefs, structures, and values that might run counter to the regime one hopes to impose. Some regimes try to address this problem by various means, for example by controlling the schools so as to help the next generation "unlearn" the past. But by and large, it simply doesn't work very well. From the point of view of the citizenry, the regime is simply "unjust." The laws and regulations handed down are not *justified* by custom, tradition, or divine scripture. In short, they are arbitrary and probably even contrary to collective notions about what is right.

A peaceful society—that is, a predictable one—is better maintained when necessary laws are consistent with ongoing customs, structures, and beliefs. In such societies, the laws make sense, and can be derived from custom and convention. To paraphrase Mark Twain, when law is consistent with the rest of one's social world, "you don't have to remember anything." You simply do what comes naturally out of your own internalized principles. Further, in such a society, the various cultural institutions are consistent with one another. For example, property and wealth are distributed in a manner consistent with religious, moral, and political doctrine. Thus in a society that values equality of opportunity, wealth would be distributed according to merit rather than by luck, race, or class.

In the end, the society that is described here might best be called a *just* society; that is, a society in which norms are justified by values, beliefs, and other structures. In such a society the various spheres of life in which one participates are consistent and integrated with one another. The kinds of values required for effective performance at work, for example, are not contrary to those required to be a good husband, wife, or parent. Life is a relatively seamless fabric, which is understandable to people. In short, a great many things may be "taken for granted."

Peace is, in the end, mutually shared security, made possible by community and consensus. It is most often found in societies that are well integrated, that change slowly, and in which citizens perceive the social order as natural and uncontrived—that is, in just societies.

This is a definition of peace that can satisfy social scientists. It is a social definition, in the same way that Mead's definition of war is social. It places the determination of peacefulness in the structure of communities, because the human ability to predict—or understand, or empathize, or trust—one another is made possible by coherent and cohesive social structures. One can trust only to the extent that one can expect people to behave in certain ways, according to certain conventions. The definition is culturally neutral in the sense that, at least in principle, it can be applied sensibly in much the same way to any community or society. This coherence is a characteristic that can be assessed for any community, from a street gang to a hunter-gatherer band to a nation. Communities that have it are peaceful; those that do not are less so.

Cultural neutrality has important consequences for the way people think about peace and peacemaking, for it forces the concession that cultural practices and social structures people regard as morally reprehensible may still be peaceful. For example, a society with a strongly unequal class system might be a peaceful one, if the class system is justified by (that is, consistent with) religious, economic, kinship, and political institutions. For example, the value of individual rights and social mobility based on achievement might have been considered a ridiculous idea to the twelfth-century serf. Hindus may live peaceably with the caste system, so long as it remains undergirded by consensually-held religious beliefs about reincarnation.

The medieval serfs or the Hindu untouchables would likely regard their position, albeit unpleasant, as justly deserved, or at least understandable. If this is a difficult assertion to accept, one need only ask the question: In a coherent, integrated society, what evidence would be available to them to suggest otherwise? The fact is, well-integrated social systems provide plenty of consistent, commonsense information and knowledge that serves to *justify* the status quo.

This is bothersome to many people, because they are accustomed to thinking of peace and justice in terms of their own cultural values. Humans want the "peaceful" society to be that society in which all their own cherished values are realized. This is an error, both intellectually and morally. It is an intellectual error because it presumes that there are "universal" values that can provide a basis for the study of peace. Such a presumption fails to account for the profound differences that exist among cultures. It is a moral error because it masks an ethnocentricity that resembles the zeal of colonial missionaries. Few people today would think of bringing Christianity to natives as a means to their salvation, yet many people find it entirely reasonable to expect that Western "justice" must always be a welcome introduction. It cannot be both ways. People may well view the practices of many other cultures as morally reprehensible and may wish to take action against such "injustices." Yet those people cannot at the same time claim to be acting in the name of "universal" values, and certainly cannot claim always to be bringing peace.

What this means is that peace is not everything. From a moral standpoint, a little peacelessness might even be preferable to a morally unacceptable social order, although such a view is most often taken by colonial or missionary intruders into "primitive" foreign cultures. The fact is, peace is a characteristic of relatively stable cultures. A look at Fabbro's "peaceful societies" shows that societies without war are generally traditional ones that have not changed very much in a very long time. Peacelessness is, in fact, a nearly inevitable by-product of social change itself.

Change in social structures, whether "good" or "bad," comes often at the expense of peace. Sometimes it takes violent form, like revolution, civil war, or imperial intervention. More often, however, social change is more gradual; although it is not particularly violent, it still disrupts the peace. Rapid technological change such as Western society has witnessed in this century is a good example. Consider the consequences to stability and predictability—to tradition—that have resulted from the birth control pill, the automobile, the computer, television. The latter alone has radically altered American politics, the consumer economy, family life, the socialization process. The "information age" has made it possible for the state and capital to investigate and target citizens for a variety of purposes. Medical "advances" have created at least as many problems of morality, access, expense, and equity as they have solved. Each of these elements of technological change have created inconsistencies, structural strains, frictions, and challenges to the public consensus, and this is independent of whether they have been "good" or "bad" innovations.

Of course, there are many other kinds of change: economic, social, political, and so on. American life has seen much of all these kinds of change, and frankly, American life has not been very peaceful. Even the ostensibly "positive" economic expansion of the 1980s created strains in the underlying structure of society which, like a geological fault, will erupt in violent shaking when the stress gets too great. The poor are poorer, the rich are richer, the economic "infrastructure" has corroded, school funding has shrunk, and in a hundred other ways, the United States may be heading for a major social earthquake. It is no wonder that drug use, crime, abuse of women and children, and many other social ills have flourished as consensus has become more and more difficult to find in American society.

This definition of peace, then, seems consistent with commonsense ideas about what a peaceful society should look like. Peaceless societies tend to be violent societies. Where change is rapid and unpredictable, increasing numbers of people become alienated (that is, they find little in the culture that can be taken for granted). Sometimes people attach themselves to deviant subcultures as a source of integration with a larger community. More often they simply drop out or are left out of the social and cultural mainstream, to fall victim to a variety of social ills. Either way, the aggregate result becomes something very much like what Americans live with today: a violent society at war with itself, much of the rest of the world, and ultimately, with the very idea of peace.

Finally, this definition of peace has a substantial place in the body of sociological theory. It is a measurable concept (at least in principle) and is capable of being related to other concepts central to the discipline. It is a distinct concept from war, which satisfies the desire to think of peace in positive terms, rather than simply as the absence of something. In fact, peace defined in this way represents a different "level of measurement" than does war. Whereas war is a discrete and nominal concept (you either have it or you don't), peace is a continuum. A society can be more or less peaceful than another. One can seriously think about quantifying the concept, perhaps by measuring the extent to which people "take for granted" certain important socially-constructed realities.

War, Peace, and Social Disorder

War and peace are not two sides of a coin, but rather two different kinds of social phenomena. War is the collective action of organized groups, galvanized by communally-held ideals to vanquish an outgroup, for goals as varied as territory, religious dominance, or revenge. The causes of war are diverse, as will be seen in the next chapter, not only because there are many kinds of wars but also because there are many ways to think about them. But what all wars have in common is that the groups involved possess a high degree of cohesion and control. This cohesion is so strong that individual participants sacrifice their interests and even safety for the collective effort. In short, war is made possible by social organization.

Peace, too, is made possible by social organization. The peace of predictability is characteristic of societies in which people behave as they should, events occur as expected, government rules as it is supposed to, and the future is expected to look much like today. All of these traits are made possible by social organization, either through the rule of authority and control or the rule of justice.

Peacelessness is actually the opposite of both war and peace, because it embodies a lack of order altogether. In peaceless societies neither peace nor war is possible because the population is incapable of pursuing collective goals or providing for collective needs in an effective way. Thus the discussion ends with a triangular set of antonyms—war, peace, and social disorder—each of which is the opposite of the other two.

Chapter Summary

Although war seems on the surface to be an antisocial phenomenon, it is actually a highly social process. From the small military unit to the level of the whole society, the conduct of war depends on social organization. The very goal of combat is to disrupt the social organization of the enemy, and only secondarily to kill and destroy. War is at least as dependent on cooperation as it is on conflict.

Rather than simply the absence of war, peace is likewise a social process. Peaceful societies are characterized by the ability of citizens to successfully predict the actions of each other and of the social order itself. This predictability can be achieved to some extent through force and coercion, but in the long run it is most effectively maintained through justice—the integration of society and the consistency of its culture.

Questions for Review

How is war "social"? What is meant by "social" in this context?

How are civilians and civilian institutions involved in modern war?

What is the role of force in making and keeping peace? What are its uses and drawbacks?

What does a soldier's "morale" consist of? How can it be increased? How can it be reduced?

To what extent is the United States a peaceful society, according to the definition offered in this chapter? What about China, Israel, or Mexico? If you have traveled abroad, how peaceful was the society you traveled to?

In what ways is American society a just society, according to the definition offered in this chapter? In what ways is it unjust?

Can peace be had without justice? How does justice contribute to peace?

For Further Research

Dyer, Gwynne. 1985. *War*. New York: Crown.

Keegan, John. 1976. *The Face of Battle*. New York: Vintage.

O'Loughlin, John, Tom Mayer, and Edward S. Greenberg, eds. 1994. *War and Its Consequences*. New York: HarperCollins.

Solomon, Robert C., and Mark Murphy. 1990. *What is Justice?* New York: Oxford.

3 Explaining War

The Cultural Evolution of War

Humans have not always engaged in war as it is now defined. This statement should not be surprising, since humans have not always engaged in *any* of the activities assumed to be inherent in their nature. All of the cultural institutions that seem so naturally to form a part of human existence had to be invented by human ancestors; there was a time in human history before the idea of government was invented, before nations and schools and writing and laws. There was a time before humans had arrived at the idea of planting crops or domesticating animals.

Anthropologists refer to this time in human history as the Paleolithic era; the Old Stone Age. It is so called because the most important technology of the time was the fashioning of tools from stone, using nothing but wood, bone, and other stones. The ability to make such tools and hunting weapons kept a community alive, for it was the hunting of animals and their processing (cutting meat, scraping hides, and the like) that kept people alive.

These cultures are called foraging, or alternatively, hunter-gatherer, cultures. Foraging was the only way of making a living that humans knew for most of human history. From the time of the earliest hominids, about 2.5 million years ago, until roughly 10,000 years ago, every culture took for granted that the way to live was to hunt meat and gather wild vegetation. Not that these cultures were alike in every respect, for there were many other circumstances that determined how people could live. For example, woodland peoples developed elaborate techniques to trap and hunt small mammals and rodents and to build shelters out of forest products. Plains Indians, on the other hand, hunted buffalo and processed the animals for use of virtually every piece in some way. Pacific Island peoples fished and navigated, and Arctic peoples lived mostly off the seal and whale.

Yet there were commonalities among foraging cultures. Despite their varying ecological circumstances, they tended to develop fairly similar systems of social control, kinship structures, and religions. Their overall worldviews were markedly similar. For one thing, foragers tended to view themselves as coequal inhabitants of the world with other species. Their animistic religions reflected this view, emphasizing as they did the spiritual nature of animals, plants, and even inanimate natural objects.

Social organization showed similarities too. Because they hunted for a living, foragers needed tremendous amounts of room to support themselves. Consequently, humans lived by necessity in very small bands, seldom greater than fifty in number. When a band's size became too large because of natural population growth, a group would split off from the band (possibly precipitated by an argument over leadership) and move on to another territory. It should come as no surprise that the languages of many foraging peoples today still use terms like "the people" or the "human beings" to refer to their society; they may well have thought they were the only humans on earth.

For practical purposes, they were. There were very few humans around in the Paleolithic—only a few hundred thousand the world over, and widely scattered—so people generally had little knowledge of other humans outside their own bands. There was so much land and so few people that it was seldom necessary to contest hunting grounds. Further, population growth was extremely slow during the Paleolithic, owing to nutritional deficiencies, disease, the hazards of predators and the elements, and low birth rates.

Because they had to range widely to hunt and forage, these peoples traveled light. Few items were privately owned, since the more one owned the more one had to carry and tend to. Consequently, foragers were sharers. This does not mean that foragers were inherently docile or altruistic. Rather, they developed strong norms of sharing and reciprocity because such norms were functional for the survival of the group. The need to share was essentially a form of credit and banking that helped avoid the waste of perishable resources. If one hunter was fortunate enough to bag a large animal, he would share the meat with others, creating an obligation against the day when he would be less lucky. Having shared a kill was money in the bank, which could be claimed later if necessary. In this way, meat was completely consumed while fresh. Similarly, the sharing of tools and other commodities meant that not everyone had to have a particular tool of his or her own. Only the minimum necessary supplies needed to be carried around.

Moreover, the hunting of larger animals was by necessity a group activity. Buffalo hunts, for example, required cooperation of the group in stalking, then stampeding a herd either into a gauntlet of waiting archers or, more simply, over a cliff. Seal hunting by Arctic peoples involved a large group of hunters to man all of the seal's breathing holes in the ice. In this way, one hunter would be sure to get a shot when the seal came up for air. Since the seal's choice of breathing hole was beyond the control of the hunters, it was a matter of pure chance who got the kill; thus, no one could reasonably claim the result for himself.

When these characteristics of foraging cultures are summarized, it comes as no surprise to learn that hunter-gatherers were generally free of war as has been defined here. First, since enemies were few and far between, competition for hunting grounds was rare. Second, intragroup conflict was fairly easy to settle, since bands could split up and go their separate ways. Third, there was a general tendency to cooperate rather than compete, solely because cooperation was of greater survival value in such small groups. Fourth, people possessed few personal items to fight over; in fact, one might say the concept of "possession" was largely unknown since nothing could be locked up or hidden anyway. Finally, all the people in a band were typically kinspeople, related in one way or another by blood. Even the authority of a chief or "big man" was more like the authority of a parent than a magistrate or president. Since social control was imposed by relatives rather than strangers, the enforcement of that authority was informal, through humiliation or shame rather than punishment.

This should not be taken as evidence that humans were inherently less violent or aggressive then than now. On the contrary, there is ample evidence that people fought and killed for many reasons. Among many peoples, for example, infanticide was one of the methods by which populations were kept low. But organized, collective killing for abstract goals was not often practiced. Nor should it be assumed that foraging is a "dead" way of life. Even today foraging cultures are distributed around the globe, still thriving with cultural tools they developed hundreds of thousands of years ago. These peoples provide modern-day evidence of the relative peacefulness of the foraging way of life. David Fabbro (1978) made use of this evidence in attempting to determine the characteristics of peaceful and warlike societies. What he found was that most peaceful societies in existence today are hunter-gatherers, held together in relatively small groups through kinship bonds.

About 10,000 years ago, an earth-shaking change took place. As the world's human population slowly grew and the best food supplies began to dwindle, humans reluctantly took to growing food themselves, "reluctantly" because the evidence seems clear that the foraging life really was a much easier way of living than was growing food (as many farmers will agree). Communities hard pressed for subsistence began to collect seeds from what they ate and to cultivate the seeds to produce food. They also began coaxing animals to live with them, probably by feeding them scraps and then penning them in. Diamond (1997) suggests that the transition to horticulture was a gradual one. He notes that there are cultures even today that are living somewhere between foraging and horticulture, encouraging the growth of wild plants by clearing nearby brush and overhanging branches or directing water toward them.

The consequences of these developments changed the world profoundly. For one thing, the planting of seeds and the keeping of animals made staying in one place a necessity.[1] Consequently, the land in which one's seeds were planted had to be tended and left undisturbed until the crop came in. This meant that members of other bands had to be prevented from taking the crop themselves. In short, the idea of ownership had been invented. This must have been a period of tremendous upheaval, as foragers spying a nice dog or goat inside a crude fence were inexplicably confronted by a stranger pressing the claim that it "belonged" to his people.

Even though growing was more arduous than hunting and gathering, it was a much more efficient source of food for large groups (Diamond 1997). It was almost as easy to grow lots of food as it was to grow a little, and this was especially true if there were many hands to help. Consequently, the human population exploded in these regions, because larger bands had become more efficient than small ones. Where roaming hunters had to keep their populations low so as to travel, farming people found that a larger group could grow a bigger crop. In fact, each new member of the community had become an extra pair of hands, rather than another mouth to feed.

Suddenly (by cultural evolution standards) the world had changed. People now found it expedient to live in ever larger communities, clustered around the best growing or grazing regions. Because one person could produce more food than was necessary to feed him- or herself, it was possible—and in fact necessary—for many people to perform tasks other than getting food. Specialization of tasks in a division of labor arose, with some people farming, some making tools, others milling or trading. Some specialized in performing religious functions, because the new way of living had given rise to new, more formally-organized forms of religion as well. And since some people were performing roles other than growing food, they became dependent for their livelihood on those who did. Food became a commodity that was traded. It could be owned, and was used to control other people. This and the division of labor were

---

[1]Actually, pastoral cultures (those that live by herding animals) tend to be nomadic, following seasonal changes in pastureland. But these lands typically are recognized as the territory of one group or another.

prerequisites to social inequality, whereby some people owned much and others owned little.

The final component of this change in human organization was the result of both the complexity of the social order (consisting now of many specialists rather than just hunters and gatherers) and the increasing density of populations. This was the rise of government by strangers. No longer was social control achieved by the word of the patriarch or chief. Now there were too many people to control, and most of them were not kinfolk. Further, there were too many disputes to settle: who owned a patch of land, the worth of a bushel of wheat, determining the miller's fair share. Clearly, people needed a new way to organize themselves.

The result was the rise of specialists in social control; political rulers whose task it was to tell people what to do and to enforce those orders. Their rise was probably not orderly. Rather, the ruler of the new urban community was probably created through bloody fighting among rival family heads. As kinsmen fought other clans over territory or goods, victors took control of the vanquished. Gradually, warlords consolidated ever larger populations under their rule, until whole cities were formed into autonomous communities under a single ruler or ruling family. This was the case of the Mississippian cultures of North America, for example, where very large cities were established around the production and trade of corn. Impressive evidence of this culture can be found in the Cahokia Mounds, just outside St. Louis. The Mayans also are well known as a large urban culture, which integrated far-flung cities into a regional empire. The pyramids and other monuments of the Nile valley are evidence of even greater feats of social integration by the Egyptians.

Nisbet (1973) refers to this development as "the fall of kinship," and identifies it as the beginning of the age of war. Where social identity had previously been based on family heritage, it now came to be based on residence on a given piece of territory. Consequently, social organization came to be rooted not in a network of kinship obligations among groups of people but in the loyalty of individuals to leaders unrelated to them.

The rise of agriculture and the need for dense living also created what must surely be considered the greatest ecological disaster ever, for this was the real beginning of the human population explosion. Prior to the rise of agriculture, humans were but minor players on the world scene; a rare species, thinly spread over the globe, and having insignificant impact on it. But the agricultural revolution changed all that. Humans now are so dense in population that there is scarcely a place on earth where one does not see evidence of human presence. A substantial proportion of the world's surface has been converted from natural prairie, rain forest, or pampas to monoculture, the growth of a single crop in place of the dense variety that naturally arises. The view from the typical airline flight across the American Midwest will confirm this, as one gazes down at perfect rectangles and circles of agricultural production, bounded by straightened rivers and streams and punctuated only by the occasional town or city. Evidence of human habitation is visible even from space: At night the lights of large cities can be seen, and the Great Wall of China (itself an artifact of citification and the control of territory) is visible. The very temperature of Earth is rising as a result of human activities on it. This is not to mention the elimination of many species of plants and animals, and also the radical modification of others through selective breeding and, more recently, genetic engineering.

When people became growers rather than gatherers, their view of the world and their role in it changed. Because they now controlled the reproduction of plants and animals rather than letting nature take its course, they developed cultural beliefs and practices that viewed it as "natural" that humans should dominate the earth. Their religions reflected these beliefs in the recognition of gods who controlled the human world and, by extension, the recognition that governments could impose laws and sanctions on individuals. They also included the doctrine that it is all right to kill people when at war. In the end, it is the development of civilization—the urbanization of humankind made both possible and necessary by the invention of agriculture—that is responsible for the development of war. It is the close connection between civilization and war that moved Dyer to refer to them as "Siamese twins" (1985). In light of the Gulf War and its aftermath, it is a sad irony that the origin of agricultural living and urbanization—the "Cradle of Civilization"—lies between the Tigris and Euphrates Rivers, roughly in the area of Baghdad.

Approaches to Explaining War

Functional Theories

Early sociologists pondered war in light of its contribution to and origin in cultural evolution. Functionalism has deep roots in sociological theory and remains a useful intellectual tool for thinking about war, for the beauty of functionalist thinking is that it attempts to make sense of otherwise irrational and even nonsensical human behaviors and institutions. Why do people commit suicide? Why is there deviance in all societies? Why do societies keep having wars? Functionalism is a powerful paradigm for thinking about social evils, because it begins with the assumption that such evils must do some good.

The earliest and crudest forms of functional thinking began with the social Darwinist assertion that societies evolve through an ongoing struggle with their environments and competing societies. Those societies best suited for their ecological niche thrive; those ill-suited either die out or are conquered or absorbed by others better adapted. Like biological organisms, a process of natural selection governs the predominance of one society over another, of one way of living over another.

One consequence of this selection process is that societies that are best able to dominate other societies tend to survive, whereas those less aggressive die out. Nisbet's description of the decline of kinship is a more spohisticated version of this. In his view, the command structure of military organization was always able to defeat the traditional clan organization when the two came into conflict, and the military community gradually overtook the kinship community as the primary means of organization in the Western world.

Thus there is a process of natural selection by which militaristic societies proliferate. It follows that the most successful societies maintain value systems, religions, and social institutions that encourage and justify militarism and aggression. Herbert Spencer took this approach explicitly, arguing that the struggle among societies had naturally favored the most militant, because the more peaceful societies had over time been conquered by them. Only in the modern era had peacefulness acquired survival value.[2] Others extended the logic to suggest that even the inherent characteristics of the human species would be affected over time, as evolutionary forces gradually favored the more aggressive individuals over the meek, in a reversal of the promise of scripture.

William Graham Sumner (1911) took a subtler approach, for he recognized that the real survival skill that humans have over other species is the ability to contrive cooperative, not competitive, systems. He began with the observation that there seemed to be a natural tendency for human groups to increase in size, because larger groups are better able to survive than smaller ones. Larger groups could provide better mutual protection against predators and enemies than smaller groups, and they could produce a greater food surplus and allow for greater division of labor. Thus there were ecological pressures for humans to form ever larger "peace groups" as he called them; groups of people who cooperated with one another in competition or conflict with other groups.

But by what processes are groups enlarged? For one, increased birthrates could enlarge groups. Of course, ever-larger groups might sooner or later erupt in conflict, which could be resolved by the application of force by a strong leadership. But a second way groups grow larger

---

[2]Spencer was actually a strong opponent of the militarism he saw in contemporary Britain. A particularly clear discussion of the inconsistencies in his position can be found in Wiltshire (1978).

is by subsuming other groups within them; that is, by conquest of rival groups.

Either kind of growth could bring about warfare. Force employed to hold large groups together may be viewed as one or another form of internal strife, civil war, oppression, or simply social control. And of course, force used to incorporate other groups within one's own amounted to intergroup warfare, which generally would be followed by a process of assimilation by which the conquered group is incorporated into the victorious one. After a time, the social structure of the incorporated group gradually dissolves, its members identifying themselves as members of the larger group.

Generally, this is the way warfare has historically assembled nations and empires. The states of Europe, for example, were formed in the Middle Ages when powerful landholders fought each other for land and consolidated ever-larger holdings until one could claim dominion over all others in a region. This process came to its ultimate conclusion in 1648 with the Westphalian system, which formalized the idea of the state, defined by geographical boundaries and headed by a sovereign. Japan was formed in much the same way, but more recently. The United States, for that matter, can be viewed as a large "peace group" (in Sumner's sense) formed from thirteen original independent units that found it advantageous to band together for their mutual protection and the advancement of joint interests. Even that consolidation required in the end a bloody civil war, further expanded by the mostly violent annexation of other territories in the west.

Historical evidence suggests that there are limits to how large a peace group can become. The decline of various empires—the Roman, Holy Roman, British, and recently the Soviet—may be viewed as the result of an inability to assimilate, or "digest" groups previously subsumed. This can have many causes: The various parts of the empire may be too widely scattered geographically, as was the case of the Roman and British Empires. They may be so diverse culturally that they cannot be made to dissolve into the larger group's culture. In the case of the Soviet Union, for example, it is possible that there were simply too many subcultures and ethnic groups to incorporate at one time (scores of languages were spoken in the various republics of the former Soviet Union). Further, there is always the possibility of rival empires attracting away the various components of one's own, of which the reunification of Germany is a good example.

The expansion of the North Atlantic Treaty Organization (NATO) as a coalition of European states is an interesting hybrid case. It has grown over the past decade mostly through peaceful means, by inviting former Warsaw Pact states to become members. The recent bombing campaign waged by NATO against Serbian forces in Kosovo adds a new dimension, however. Although those in the West are encouraged to regard the war as an attempt to persuade the Serbs to stop "ethnic cleansing" and displacement of civilians, the Russian government views the bombing as a bald territorial grab by NATO itself; that is, an attempt to enlarge its "peace group."

The social Darwinist approach to war, then, suggests that violence and large-scale killing are simply the ugly but inevitable by-products of cultural evolution. War is the means by which societies are "selected" by the environment for survival; peace is a loser's strategy. It is an appealing perspective for pessimists. It implies a certain inevitability to the increasing militarism of societies, as the evolutionary process seems to favor the aggressive. And it does seem to fit well with the facts: Societies appear to have become more militarized over the centuries. They have evolved ever more destructive technologies, and their conflicts have come to involve ever greater numbers of noncombatants. It certainly seems that the unavoidable direction of human history is toward self-destruction.

But there are weaknesses as well. First, some of these "self-evident" observations might not be true. Have societies actually become more militarized? For example, it is true that the United States spends a high proportion of its Gross Domestic Product on the military, but what percentage of the production of medieval England or France was spent for war? Or of the Roman or Egyptian empires? Moreover, it might be more appropriate to take the average military expenditure of *all* the world's nations as the baseline for comparison. In such a case, it is at least possible that the world overall does not spend substantially more of its effort on warfare than it did in the past.

Nor is violence the only way that peace groups are enlarged. Many nations have been formed more peaceably. There is the contemporary example of the European Union's consolidation of what some are calling a "United States of Europe" by entirely peaceful means, despite the occasional outburst of nationalist fervor by constituent states. Other peace groups have been formed out of mutual interest, arising from advantageous trade patterns, for example. More common, such groups sometimes band together for common defense against an outside enemy.

Further, there is evidence that people are not really more aggressive than they used to be. Barbara Tuchman's (1978) fascinating account of life in the fourteenth century reveals a level of violence that will shock even the most world-weary reader. The day-to-day treatment in those times of women, children, animals, criminals, heretics, and of course enemies is enough to actually encourage faith in the progress of humankind. Mueller (1994) has suggested, in fact, that cultural evolution has moved steadily toward more peacefulness, and that warfare is moving into "terminal disrepute."

A further weakness of social Darwinist theory is that it is inherently historical in nature; that is, events are thought to be caused sequentially by those preceding them. This is the very nature of evolution: Change occurs by the system's adaptation to what has come before. So while it is strongly implied that the historical trend will continue indefinitely—for example, that the world will move toward increasing militarization— there is no reason to assume that this *must* be so. There could be an interruption in the evolutionary process of change; a revolutionary change could take place. An observer in the Paleolithic could not have imagined the agricultural and civil revolution that was coming. For that matter, few imagined in 1980 that the Cold War would be forgotten by 1999.

Finally, these theories fail to account for the role of purposeful human action in changing human destiny. It is reasonable to make this objection: If it is known that social evolution favors the militaristic societies, why can't something be done about it? Why not, for example, create a real "world order" like a United Nations, but with the recognized authority to enforce peace universally? Why could humankind not construct a universal "peace group"? The human race is not totally manipulated by history, and it is for this reason that students of peace find social Darwinist theories unappealing and useless.

A more useful application of functionalism to the problem of war goes beyond the "natural selection" idea, beginning with the assumption that since war is so prevalent (even though everyone hates it) it must serve latent functions for societies. Thus William James suggested in his famous essay "The Moral Equivalent of War" that war enhances cohesiveness in societies and moreover helps encourage the "ideals of hardihood" that every society must have. For James, war's "dread hammer is the wielder of men into cohesive states, and nowhere but in such states can human nature adequately develop its capacity. The only alternative is 'degeneration'" (1910/1985).

The solution, says James, is to find a substitute that will serve the same important functions of war without the carnage and waste. In the end, he actually suggested something like the Civilian Conservation Corps, a conscripted national service organization in which young men would work at hard labor for the public good as they developed their manly qualities.

Nisbet (1973) extended his analysis of the military community in this direction. Historically war has provided a means of social integration and solidarity at times when other institutions were too weak or undeveloped. The integrating effects of war and preparation for war, in this view, make mass-based society possible, and create the sense—or at least the illusion—of community.

Others have taken a similar tack. For example, some have suggested that war, or at least preparation for it, can be good for the economy (for example, Benoit 1972; 1973; 1978), although this is strongly contested by others (Deger and Smith 1983; Grobar and Porter 1989). It is even sometimes proudly announced by politicians that this or that weapon contract will bring jobs and investment to one's community. Others look favorably on military research and development as the source of valuable new products that sooner or later enhance the quality of life. The home computer is one example, but automotive, communication, navigation, medicine, weather forecasting, and food packaging technologies are cited as other less obvious innovations.

Marxian Theories

A second major sociological approach to explaining war springs from the theories of Karl Marx. For Marx, the whole of human endeavor, including the very creation and maintenance of the social order, is reducible to the struggle of people against one another for material advantage. This struggle has taken various forms through history: master versus slave, patrician versus plebian, lord versus serf. In the industrial age, it is between capitalists and those who work for them, and it is the ongoing conflict between the two classes that drives human history throughout this period.

It was V. I. Lenin who most clearly articulated the effects of this struggle on war and peace. This is not surprising since it was partly Russia's hardships in World War I that gave the final impetus to his revolution against the czarist Russian regime. The problem with capitalism, according to Lenin, is that it requires a constant drive to maximize profit and minimize costs. A simple, steady-state condition, in which a capitalist's cost to produce goods is a little lower than the price received for them, cannot be sustained because competitors will always enter the market and sell the same goods a little cheaper. This cost reduction is accomplished in two ways. The first is the use of labor-saving machinery (today, largely by information technology and computerized manufacturing), which makes it possible for fewer laborers to produce more goods. The "increased productivity" reduces the demand for workers overall, which reduces the market power of labor.

The second way the capitalist reduces costs is by finding new labor markets abroad, in countries where workers have lower living standards and lower expectations. When capitalism first evolved a few centuries ago, this process took the form of colonialism and empire. Holland,

Britain, France, Spain, and Portugal divided up much of the world among themselves, establishing colonies that supplied both raw materials and cheap labor for the newly-expanding industrial economy.

Today the exploitation of new labor markets is accomplished by slightly more subtle means. Most of the old colonies are politically independent now, but their economies may still depend heavily on the extraction of natural resources such as minerals or timber by foreign industries. Or they may be based on the exploitation of huge populations of laborers, who have been made available partly by having been removed from the very land taken by the miners and lumberers. This is the global economy, in which an American, German, or Japanese consumer is surrounded by the fruits of cheap Third World labor at the local shopping mall.

The consequences for peace are obvious. The capitalist economy, in its search for ever larger markets, has to involve itself in the economic and social affairs of other societies. In the name of "development" it drills for oil in the Middle East. It finds copper in Chile. It builds rubber plantations in Asia and tea and spice plantations in India. In doing so, the cultures of these areas are wrenched from their traditional moorings. Economies based on foraging, herding, or agriculture are suddenly (within decades) changed to urbanized, job-oriented cultures. This is the picture of "modernization": the congestion and pollution of Mexico City, the burning rain forest of Brazil, the astonishing poverty of Manila. Traditional cultures that had thrived for millennia are destroyed in a trice. Isbister (1995) gives an excellent account and explanation of this process in several modern instances.

These wrenching changes make for cultural and social instability—the very definition of peacelessness. There is political and social unrest, revolution is in the air, and the plantations, mines, and factories of the foreign capitalists are threatened. Before long, the capitalists are clamoring for something to be done about the insurgents, terrorists, revolutionaries, Communists, or whatever the current threat is called. Further, they are by now assisted by the wealthy elite and puppet government they have installed in the developing country. It is by this logic that the United States has supported brutal regimes in Chile, Iran, Iraq, the Philippines, Panama, El Salvador, and elsewhere. And it is by the same logic that half a million American soldiers were called on to defend Saudi Arabia and reclaim "our" oil in the Middle East, while Kuwait, the world's richest nation, cheered them on. Finally, military bases have to be established around the world to protect the national interests of the capitalist power—the resources, markets, and client governments that control them—and with these bases come a host of social ills, from prostitution to economic plunder to ecological abuses to the sheer insecurity of being a potential military target (Gerson and Birchard 1991).

Thus the Marxian view regards war as the result of the imperialism that is inevitable in a capitalist economy (Vigor 1975). Capitalists cannot mind their own business, because capitalist economies must continually expand. Parenti (1989) gives an especially detailed and clear discussion of this imperialism, observing that almost one out of every three employees of American multinational corporations live in foreign countries, and that many of the consumer goods most cherished—televisions, VCRs, stereos, motorcycles, and computers—are almost entirely manufactured by those workers.

The Marxian view has a compelling logic, well developed over the course of many volumes of the writings of Marx and Engels, as well as by a large following of contemporary scholars in many disciplines. Marxian and neo-Marxian theory remains one of the main thrusts of sociological thought today. This perspective also fits well with much of what can be observed empirically. There do often seem to be strong links between the interests of American corporations, for example, and American foreign policy. Oil companies are the most obvious example; refiners depend on a steady supply of foreign crude. Oil must also be regarded as an important resource on which the American economy depends. If oil were to double or triple in price, what would happen to the profits of auto manufacturers, airlines, trucking firms, plastics manufacturers, travel and tourism operators? Large agricultural and food-processing firms also have an interest in maintaining export markets, as do computer and software makers, aircraft manufacturers, and tobacco companies. It is no wonder that China retains its favorable trade status with the United States in spite of its poor record on human rights.

But there is contrary evidence too. Wars are sometimes fought on ideological grounds, rather than to protect economic interests. Vietnam, one notable example, offered no real natural resource or labor market, relative to what was spent trying to secure it. Of course, one could object that control of Vietnam by the United States was motivated by longer-range capital interests. The domino theory, widely held by pro-war administrations, hypothesized that if Vietnam "fell," more immediate and important economic interests would be severely threatened and ultimately would fall to Communist aggression. Nor did the war serve the interests of the defense industry—defense spending actually increased after the war's end, as production capacity was finally made available for development of new, more expensive, weapons.

Another problem with Marxian theory is that it does not account very well for the aggression of noncapitalist states. If war is caused by inevitable capitalist expansion, then why did the Soviet Union invade

Afghanistan? Why did China find it necessary to attack peaceful Tibet? And if the objection is raised that the USSR and China were really capitalists in Communist clothing, then one need only to look to history for more evidence. There was plenty of war in the classical period and in the Middle Ages, before capitalism was even invented. Alexander the Great was not driven by the corporate interests of the Macedonian elite.

In spite of these objections, Marxian theory remains a powerful means of explaining and understanding war, or at least some war. No theory, even one as grand and encompassing as Marx's, should be expected to explain every case. It is even possible that there are different types of wars, and that each type might require a different sort of explanation.

Feminist Explanations

Another approach to understanding war parallels closely the conflict perspective of Marx. Like the Marxian view, the feminist approach takes as its starting point the recognition that war is an instrument of domination by one group over another. The difference is that the two groups are classes defined not in economic terms but by gender, the oldest and most basic social division of all. It is the dominance of men over women, not of the bourgeoisie over the proletariat, that accounts for war.

There are many varieties of feminism; for example, the "liberal" type regards simple equity with men as its primary goal. Liberal feminists view the social order as fundamentally legitimate but the position of women in that order as disadvantaged, marginalized, and disempowered. Their agenda for change is simply to remove obstructions to parity that have held women back.

A much more powerful and comprehensive feminism asserts that the achievement of parity alone does nothing to bring the sort of fundamental social change needed to end violence and war. Gender inequity is, in this view, only one manifestation of a widespread pathology of the human condition, most often referred to by the shorthand term "patriarchy." Patriarchy is regarded as a fundamental organizing principle of all human institutions, or at least of Western institutions, which are characterized by domination, competition, and violence.

This ethos pervades life for both men and women, through virtually every social institution. For example, the family is a system of domination of men over women and children, enforced by both legal rights and traditional values and beliefs. The widespread incidence of domestic violence and child abuse are evidence of this, as is the unequal position of women in both the marriage contract and the dissolution of marriage in most societies.

The economy is another institution through which patriarchy is expressed. It amounts to a competition-based arena in which men—predominantly white men—exploit others in a rigged struggle for material as well as symbolic gain. The labor conditions in the Third World, particularly those of women, affirm this, but so does the existence of sexual labor in the pornography and prostitution industries worldwide.

Religion is both a tool and a symbol of the same human malady. Religions prescribe gender roles; for example, Islamic fundamentalism restricts the rights and activities of women, as do many elements of Christian and Jewish thought. Most religions divide clerical labor within their hierarchies; only the most recent and most progressive sects allow women to take on central clerical roles. Moreover, religion very strongly proscribes sexual behavior and obligations, and these proscriptions disproportionately restrict women.

Finally, the polity is handily dominated by men and more important, by male virtues and values. The state system itself is, in the feminist view, an inherently male formulation, founded on the assumption that every nation seeks to maximize power and domination over the others in a never-ending contest of force. The possibility of cooperation among states, or among people at all, is dismissed by the patriarchal system as sentimental idealism.

Reardon (1996a; 1996b) uses the term *war system* to refer collectively to the integration of all of social life under the ethic of oppression and domination. Under this system, war is but the ultimate expression of the ethos of sexism that lies at the very basis of social order:

> The profoundly sexist history of the human species indicates that the socially induced and prescribed separations and differences between the sexes . . . may well be the psychic origins of war, sexism, and all structures of violence and oppression. Various feminists have pointed to the oppression of women by men as the first and most fundamental form of structural oppression. . . . It is clear that for both boys and girls the first socially encountered other, a person they perceive as being different from themselves, is usually of the other sex; and our experience indicates that it is others, those different from us, who threaten us and instigate the fear that gives rise to the notion of enemy and, ultimately, the practice of war. (Reardon 1996a: 7)

The military institution builds on and benefits from the ethos of patriarchy in virtually every aspect of its operation. Enloe (1983) offers an exhaustive analysis of the importance of patriarchy and the exploitation of women to the maintenance of the military, both historically and in contemporary times. Women have been and still are widely used as "camp followers," for example. In earlier times women actually traveled with armies, providing important support services; today they still do in civilian and military positions as cooks, clerks, nurses, maids. They also are recruited or coerced to perform sexual services, since sexual exploitation is a deeply-imbedded military value. These services include the official and unofficial use of pornography as recreation for troops, as well as the establishment, often officially negotiated, of brothels adjacent to foreign bases (Enloe 1991).

Enloe also observed the supporting role of military wives as both emotional support and mechanisms of motivation and control of soldiers. They also provide unpaid labor for a variety of needs both of their husbands and of the military communities they inhabit. Finally, and perhaps most important, women account for much of the lower-paid industrial labor needed to keep the military machine running. The heroic image of Rosie the Riveter is carefully nourished not because it symbolizes the emancipation of women from traditional gender roles, but because it encourages women to make themselves available for the lowest paid defense work when the need arises. "Rosie the Engineer" and "Rosie the Executive" were less common than their famous counterpart.

In short, war and sexism go hand in hand. Militarism could not exist without sexism and the misogyny that elevates the explicitly male virtues above all others, and war could not be easily waged without the exploitation of women as military assets. This cannot be explained solely by social processes and actions in the economic or political sphere independently. According to Enloe, the idea of patriarchy is essential to explaining the existence of militarism:

> Disarmament may be too limited an objective. Militarism disarmed is militarism still. The structures of militarisation are only partially dismantled even if nuclear weapons are "frozen" and arms companies convert to more socially useful products. If ideas entailing men's dominance and women's subservience—patriarchy—remain, the victory over militarism may be surprisingly short-lived. Patriarchal militarism disarmed is only *temporarily* disarmed. (Enloe 1983: 208)

The beauty of the feminist synthesis is that it is able to tie war to virtually all social evils under the umbrella of patriarchy. War, violence, inequality, poverty, exploitation are clearly and persuasively shown to be manifestations of the same thing—the patriarchal system. It is a powerful generalization, more inclusive even than Marx's indictment of capitalism in its ability to tie social problems to one another. Furthermore, many of the *mechanisms* by which these evils are perpetuated are also identified. For example, early gender socialization creates a disdain in the male world for feminine values like accommodation and emotional thinking. The educational system of patriarchal society elevates rationalism as the legitimate way to address problems, rather than reflection, biography, and sentiment.

In some ways, this very inclusiveness is a weakness in feminist theory. The feminist view borders on tautology, a self-proving theory. There seem to be no contrary examples, at least since the beginning of civilization, to patriarchal societies. In fact, for most feminist theorists the history of humankind is always and essentially patriarchal. One is left with "thought experiments," hypothetical exercises in which one might ask "what would happen if women ran the world?" One answer to this question is that many women *have* held positions of great power—Queens Elizabeth I and Victoria, Margaret Thatcher, Indira Gandhi, Golda Meir, Madeleine Albright, and so on—and none has shown any less exploitative or aggressive qualities than their male counterparts. Feminist theory dismisses these as examples of women who have learned to excel in an inherently male system, and that it is the system and not the gender of the individual that matters.

Underlying this question is the assumption that the patriarchal world is rife with war, conquest, and violence because the males that run it are inherently warlike, competitive, and violent. The question is whether patriarchy is a characteristic of "maleness"; that is, whether the structure of societies is determined by the ideas and ideologies of their masters or vice versa. Enloe illustrates the first approach, which attributes patriarchy and militarism squarely to maleness itself:

> This approach conceives of militarism as somehow woven into the very fibre of maleness. Violence against women by men is so pervasive, across so many historical eras and cultural differences, that it seems only explicable by reference to something intrinsic in men *as* men, some fear, some insecurity or aggressiveness which also inclines men to sustain formal institutions—military forces—which embody and legitimate those violent attitudes and behaviours. Chinese footbinding, seventeenth-century New England witch burnings, 1980s "Yorkshire Ripper" assaults, the Falklands war and America's imposition of nuclear missiles on Europe all seem rooted in a common source: the intrinsically hostile character of men simply because they are men. (Enloe 1983: 209)

There is direct evidence, too, that men's experience of war is not interpreted as entirely negative. In addition to the comradeship and adventure shown in B movies, Broyles (1990) suggests that there are deeper satisfactions in combat. In fact, he suggests that it is the secret love of war, and not the horror of it, that makes it so difficult for veterans to discuss their combat experiences. Reflecting on his experience, he notes that war is an experience of great intensity, one in which anything might be witnessed. The thrill of seeing the unthinkable might be thought of as a parallel to the thrill of seeing car chases and various sorts of mayhem at the movies, but magnified hundreds of times. War can also offer a measure of freedom unattainable in normal life—the freedom to violate even the most deeply internalized prohibitions. And to make that freedom easier to handle, war also provides a clarity of purpose unseen in ordinary life. Enemies and friends are clearly defined and the soldier is given the means to deal with both.

Conversely, many feminists have asserted that peacemaking and nurturing are inherently female traits. This view has deep roots, tracing back as far as the first conference of the National Committee on the Causes and Cure of War in 1924. Building on Florence Allen's claim that women had "more consistent ethical standards" and a stronger sense of idealism and practicality, Carrie Chapman Catt, a suffragist and early peace activist, claimed that the "abolition of war is women's work" (Schott 1996).

But York (1996) says that this claim is built on two "hackneyed arguments": first, that women's role as mothers makes war antithetical to women's nature; and second, that the intrinsically "feminine" traits of caring and nurturing are better than the "masculine" traits of competition and aggression. She suggests that these arguments lead to acceptance of women's subordinate role as mothers and caregivers, and actually support patriarchy by characterizing the masculine world as the norm.

Further, this approach suffers from reductionism, attributing most elements of social structure to the psychological traits of men, and this raises problems. For one, it begs the question of how men get that way. Boys are *raised* to be men through the process of socialization; they are made as exploitative and aggressive as they are by a whole array of social institutions. To assert that those institutions are in turn male institutions because they are headed by males leads to the question of how *they* were raised with male values, and hence to an infinite regress of nested questions.

Such an approach also ignores the often active role of women in maintaining patriarchy. To attribute the participation of women in exploitation, competition, and aggression solely to their own victimization and exploitation by men is just too great a stretch, as Scheper-Hughes (1996) suggests. In times of crisis, bell hooks notes, women fight and "show no predisposition to be nonviolent" (1995: 63); she points also to the active role of women missionaries in spreading the domination of European culture throughout the world. She also recognizes the wide variation in the aggressiveness and bellicosity of men themselves, recalling that not all the men of her childhood glorified war. She concludes that feminist thinking must abandon the idea that women are inherently more life-affirming than men, and recognize that women and men alike are trapped in a social system that "embraces social domination in all its forms" (1995: 61). Tickner (1995) offers a resolution to the dilemma by suggesting that although militarism is "deeply gendered" this is not owing to the inherent traits of men. Rather, there is a cultural link between soldiering and masculinity that is rooted in history and tradition rather than in hormones.

The other problem with the reductionist approach is that, as Enloe recognizes, it offers no hope for change. She notes that "an approach which traces militarism back to patriarchy and patriarchy back to the fundamental quality of maleness can be demoralising and even paralysing," because it implies change can only come if the basic character of men is altered (Enloe 1983: 210).

If militarism is not caused by the imposition of inherently male qualities on social structure, why call it patriarchy? Why not simply call it "militarchy," and recognize that men are as trapped in it as women? Boys don't particularly enjoy being socialized into the machismo role they are stuck with; they don't like being pushed around by scoutmasters, coaches, and drill sergeants any more than anyone else. And it has been men themselves all these millennia who have suffered and died on the battlefields. Why not let them off the hook?

It's a legitimate question, but there is one powerful answer to it: The subjugation of women, through sexual violence and economic exploitation, does seem closely tied to military values. Military training really *is* loaded with misogynist content, from the use of sexually exploitative marching cadences to the demonization of women in drill and instruction. Foreign military bases really do encourage prostitution operations on their periphery. Rape really is a widespread act of terror and conquest by victorious troops. The U.S. Navy's "Tailhook" scandal is not a shocking exception to military virtue; it is shocking because it is unexceptional.

But this need not lead to the despair that Enloe suggests. Although there can be little doubt that military virtues are indeed male virtues, this does not mean they are inherently so. Miedzian (1991) observes that though males do seem to be more aggressive than females at a very early age, this is not the cause of violence and war. Rather, it is society's tacit acceptance of male behavior as the norm that is at fault. She makes the issue clear by asking what would happen if 90 percent of all violent crimes were committed by women—replying that violence would be regarded as a horrible aberration.

Militarism and maleness are correlated not because militarism is simply the expression of inherent male traits. Rather, they have proven to be mutually reinforcing value systems over the course of history. But as students learn in research methods classes, correlation does not imply causation. In fact, it is as likely that militarism causes patriarchy as it is that patriarchy causes militarism.

The practice of socializing boys to become aggressive, exploitative, calculating, and obedient to authority can be changed, and this will have a salutary effect on the level of militarism. Likewise, society can work to reduce war directly through economic, political, and cultural change—which will likely result in a reduction in the war socialization of boys. The two forces are intricately entwined, but probably neither has primacy in determining the structure of the social order.

International Relations Approaches

Another kind of explanation views war purely as an aspect of the relationships among states. This approach, called the "realist" paradigm in political science circles, regards states as if they were individuals, irreducible to any smaller component parts, and interested in their own aggrandizement (Betts 1994a; Levy 1996; Waltz 1994a). War and the events leading up to it can be explained in much the same way as conflicts that arise between individuals. In fact, principles from small-group theory are sometimes borrowed for the purpose.

One specific approach to the international relations of war is called "balance of power" theory. This has been the ruling paradigm in political science (Blainey 1994), partly because it has been the approach generally taken by modern political leaders in the conduct of foreign policy. Simply stated, this view regards war as the result of imbalances of power—economic, political, or military—between rival states. Thus, the Gulf War would be explained by the excessive buildup of Iraqi forces that led inexorably to the invasion of Kuwait.

This view has commonsense appeal. It certainly seems consistent with much of the history of states, inasmuch as a good deal of that history involves the conquest of powerless nations by more powerful ones. It is based on the assumption that possession of military advantage itself leads to its use. As it happens, there is evidence to support this assumption. Wallace (1979) used historical data to show that arms races between nations tend to lead to the outbreak of war. Of course, the question of which is the cause and which is the effect is a good one. Wolfson and Shabahang (1991) similarly conclude that economic competition tends to stimulate arms races, and that such races in turn can lead to open war. The most obvious specific example of this is World War I, which saw a tremendous growth in arms and armies during a period of intense industrial development in Europe. The mere existence of these huge and cumbersome armies made the war difficult to head off, as their mobilization plans required a hair-trigger response to the possibility of invasion.

Virtually all nuclear deterrence theory relies on this model. This idea is based on the view that parity in nuclear capability between the two great powers ensured against either one attacking the other. This point of view is clearly put by Saperstein (1991), who concludes that the bipolar era of the U.S.-Soviet Cold War really has preserved the peace since World War II. Huntington (1994) too has suggested that the world system is more unstable now than during the Cold War.

The clear implication of "balance of power" thinking is that peace can be kept by maintaining equity of military power among nations. What this implies for policy, then, is that peace can be maintained by bolstering the military power of the weaker nations in a region, or by reducing the power of the stronger ones. And this is pretty much the basis of foreign policy among the major world powers. Since it is generally in their interests to maintain peace among less-developed nations (Marxian theory provides a rationale for this assumption), it follows that stronger nations will spend a great deal of effort and resources to maintain the balance of power among them. So the powerful states send arms to their "clients" in troubled regions of the world, or they take the more indirect tack of sending economic aid that, in turn, frees up the client state's resources so it can purchase arms in the world market.

This sort of policy has the added benefit to the powerful nations of keeping the various states in a region fearful and suspicious of one another. To take the Gulf region for an example, the maintenance of a balance of power among Saudi Arabia, Iraq, Iran, Kuwait, Jordan, and Syria keeps them all wary enough of each other to prevent them from forming a strong alliance against U.S. interests. For that matter, this mutual distrust even helps keep them dependent on U.S. arms for their own security. This has been considered essential since the Arab oil "boycott" of the 1970s, which was the last time the Arab oil-producing states were able to form such an alliance and fix the price of oil. It should not be surprising, then, that the United States led the world in arms exports in the year following the Gulf War, much of it amounting to payoffs to allies in the region.

Similar considerations have guided American policy in its intervention in Croatia and Bosnia. Supporting the Croats against the stronger Serb army discouraged further incursions by the Serbs. The only problem, of course, is that the Serbs simply moved on to Bosnia and then to Kosovo.

There is an inherent problem in this approach as a way to maintain peace. On the one hand, it is relatively easy to get a client state to accept arms or money, especially if its neighbors are arming at the same time. But it is difficult to take arms away from a client. Even attempts to reduce the flow of arms can lead one's client into the "enemy" camp. For example, refusal by the United States to send weapons to one nation often led the nation to seek help from the former USSR. Since the only practical way to influence the balance is to add to the armaments of client states, there tends to be a "ratcheting" effect in the troubled areas of the world, whereby a number of regional powers engage in a vicious cycle of arms buildup. In the end, the "balance of power" approach to understanding or reducing war is self-contradictory, for it tends to imply ever-increasing levels of militarism and warmaking potential. This has certainly been the result in the Middle East, but the same principle applies to the global proliferation of nuclear weapons.

Curiously, there is a theory of war that proposes almost exactly the opposite hypothesis as the "balance of power" view, which may be called the "uncertainty" paradigm. In this view, imbalances in power are not a threat to peace, so long as they are clearly recognized by the competing states. Rather, it is *uncertainty* about relative military strength among states that is the cause of war. War becomes necessary when competing nations are unable to determine which is stronger than the other; the issue is "resolved" by the test of military strength. Quigley states this perspective by analogy:

> When two boys first come together, they have no idea of their relative power. Eventually, they will disagree about something, and this disagreement will be resolved in some fashion. They may fight each other, or they may simply square off and one will yield, or one may simply intimidate the other by superior courage and moral force. In any case, if there is no outside interference, some kind of resolution will demonstrate to both what is their power relationship, that is, who is stronger. . . . From that day on, they may be good friends and live together without conflict, each knowing that, when an acute disagreement arises and the stronger insists, the weaker will yield. Within and around this double relationship, each has the freedom to act as he wishes. It is this freedom of action within a framework of *power relationships which are clear to all concerned* that is security. (Quigley 1983: 17)

Note that this view places great emphasis on the *appearance* of power, for it is the mutual understanding that the two rival states share that presumably keeps the peace. One could paraphrase W. I. Thomas's famous dictum by stating that power relationships that are perceived as real are real in their consequences; that so long as both states agree on the nature of the relationship, the underlying "true" balance of power is irrelevant. This implies, of course, that appearances are important in the international arena, and this is consistent with much of what can be seen in international relations. In the early years of the Cold War, for example, the Soviet Union was "bluffed" into submission to U.S. demands by the belief that the United States had a much larger nuclear capability than it really possessed. Later, the Soviets were able to convince the Americans of a much faster buildup in their own arsenal than was actually the case.

In any event, this view does seem to explain the onset of certain kinds of war. Colonial relationships, for example, might tend to remain peaceful so long as the subordinate state remains clearly weaker than the dominant one. Problems arise, though, when the power relationship between the two states changes (for example, when the subordinate state becomes economically or militarily strong). When this happens, the consensus regarding the relationship between the states is called into question, and the two parties, "acting on different subjective pictures of the objective situation, come into collision" (Quigley 1983: 18). The outcome of the ensuing war reestablishes the consensus.

The Iran-Iraq war of 1980–1988 is a case in point. These two countries were of roughly equal military strength, or at least close enough so that neither could break the defenses of the other; thus their war dragged on for years with almost no exchange of territory but great loss of life. Had either side shown a clear superiority of power over the other, one expects the war would have ended quickly with a negotiated settlement, or perhaps would never have begun. World War I is a larger but similar case. It began with both Germany and France convinced of their own invincibility; the Germans were certain that they could enter Paris by autumn, the French that a swift counterattack would cut off the head of the German advance. Neither side was right, and Europe settled into a protracted war of attrition involving dozens of countries.

It seems curious at first that there can be two nearly opposite theories to explain the same thing. Such dilemmas can occur, however, for a number of good reasons. Often one theory provides a good explanation for one kind of war while the other fits a different kind. In this case, it appears that the relative effectiveness of "balance of power" theories and "uncertainty" theories depends on the offensive or defensive orientation of the states involved. "Balance" theories make the most sense when one assumes that the states in a region are worried about defending themselves from attack from the others. Where all states take this basically defensive stance in relation to one another, peace is kept by ensuring that neither can overwhelm the other.

But when states are most occupied with expansion rather than preservation, the "uncertainty" theory becomes more useful. When the parties involved are willing to take risks, then the only deterrent to war is certain defeat.

Because the international-relations approach regards states as rational individuals acting in their own interests, it has spawned a whole body of literature based on individual players' behavior as participants in various games (see, for example, Langlois 1989; Rapoport 1992; Bornstein, Budescu, and Zamir 1997). The games are metaphors for the forces and problems that states face in expanding or protecting themselves from the expansion of others.

The most commonly-used of these games is the "Prisoner's Dilemma." This game (referred to as "PD" by its devotees) presents two individuals with a paradox of cooperation. The game is very simple: Each participant is given two choices for behavior; to cooperate with the other player or to refuse to cooperate (without knowing what the other player's choice is). The two players' actions jointly determine the "payout" to each player, and of course since there are two players and two choices of action for each, there are four possible outcomes to the game:

Both players cooperate with each other
Both players refuse to cooperate
Player A cooperates; player B refuses
Player B cooperates; player A refuses

The payouts are structured in such a way that both players will benefit if they both cooperate, and both will suffer mildly if both refuse to cooperate. In the example shown in Figure 3.1, each player wins $1 if they both cooperate, and each loses $1 if neither cooperates. The trick, though, is that if one cooperates and the other does not, the noncooperative player wins big while the cooperative player suffers severe losses. In this example, the cooperating player loses $2 while the noncooperating player wins $2. Thus, cooperating promises rewards for all, but there is the risk of a big loss if the other player refuses. At the same time, if you refuse to cooperate, there is the likelihood of only mild suffering, but also the possibility that the other player will choose to cooperate, in which case you will reap the greatest reward of all. Thus, the rational choice is *never* to cooperate, and both players lose even though they both could win.

Prisoner's Dilemma is used in peace research to simulate the behavior of two states in the international relations arena. In its simplest sense, the payouts represent conditions of trust and distrust between nations. For example, the basic game may be used to simulate the Cold War relations between the United States and the former Soviet Union. The "mutual cooperation" outcome represents mutual adherence to an arms re-

FIGURE 3.1 Payout Scheme in a Typical Prisoner's Dilemma Game

	A cooperates	*A refuses*
B cooperates	Both win $1	A wins $2 B loses $2
B refuses	A loses $2 B wins $2	Both lose $1

FIGURE 3.2 Prisoner's Dilemma Applied to the Cold War

	United States *honors treaty*	*United States* *cheats*
USSR *honors treaty*	Both achieve security	United States dominates, USSR at risk of attack
USSR *cheats*	USSR dominates, United States at risk of attack	Arms race continues

duction agreement. As shown in Figure 3.2, both sides "win" here because they achieve security without the expense of arming to deter enemy attack. The asymmetric outcomes, in which one player cooperates while the other does not, represent adherence to an arms-control treaty by one country and violation of it by the other. This is the outcome most feared by policy makers, for it suggests that one country will be in a position to attack the other with impunity. The final possibility, in which neither player cooperates, represents the reality of the Cold War: Neither side enters into any arms control treaty. As a consequence, both countries suffer mild losses (they both must spend large sums on nuclear weapons) but neither risks attack by the other.

The game lends itself to surprising variation. The payouts can be tinkered with, to represent varying costs and risks to the two players so as to simulate varying international situations. The amount of information can be varied, so that players have partial knowledge of each other's actions. Players may be allowed to communicate to each other, which raises the possibility of lying and subterfuge. The number of players can be increased to add the complication of possible coalitions and greater uncertainty.

It is this latter possibility that is of greatest interest, for the real international relations arena never involves only two players. What happens to PD games as the number of players is increased just to three? Saperstein and Mayer-Kress recognized this complexity, and concluded that a "bipolar" world (dominated by two Great Powers) is inherently safer than a "tripolar" one (1988; see also Waltz 1994b). Georg Simmel had addressed the same idea in his pioneering discussion of small group theory. He noted that a triad, or group of three people, is qualitatively different than a dyad, or group of two. The dyad is inherently stable because each member is essential to the preservation of the group; if one leaves the group breaks down. The triad, on the other hand, is prone to all sorts of instabilities. Any two members can form a coalition against the third, for example (Coser 1956).

The addition of a third member to the international-relations arena introduces a new level of uncertainty. In Prisoner's Dilemma terms, each player now must evaluate not only the opponent's motivations and the opponent's perception of one's own motivation. Now there is the opponent's perception of the *third* player's motives and of the third player's perception of the other two. And of course one's own perception of the third player must be considered too. In short, a world of just three nations is already almost impossibly complex. But it is a much better reflection of the real world of international politics. In fact, even the Cold War relations between the two superpowers always involved each side's consideration of allies, opponent's allies, nonaligned nations, the U.N., and many other interests. To try to analyze such relationships is something like planning a move in a chess game involving a dozen players, each controlling a few of the pieces.

Whether through Prisoner's Dilemma simulations or by other methods, the international relations approach has developed and tested a formidable and systematic body of knowledge about the behavior of states. But it does imply a set of assumptions that strongly color the sorts of conclusions that can be drawn. Simply put, this approach to war takes for granted the idea that states can be viewed in the same way as individual people can; that they have motivations just as people do. In fact, the use of individuals to represent states in the game implies that states have the *same* motives as individual people.

This assumption—that states act as if they are persons—is not entirely nonsensical, especially if one considers that most states throughout history really were personified by individual people. The idea of monarchy is nicely represented by the concept of the "sovereign"; a person who embodies the state. The rise of the medieval European state was really the rise of individual landholders who consolidated ever larger regions under their protection and rule. The process was repeated in Japan into the nineteenth century, when warlords and shoguns were still only loosely confederated into an empire.

This sort of evolution can still be seen in the Middle East. Kuwait really is a monarchy in the most traditional sense. It is a piece of land owned by a royal family, who allow their subjects to live on it in safety in return for loyalty and tribute. Just a short distance down the Gulf, the United Arab Emirates is a confederation of similar lords (emirs) who have banded together for mutual protection and aid. In considering the behavior of such states, it is reasonable to think of these countries as individuals, for they are in many ways personified by individuals. The policies of Kuwait really are the policies of the al-Sabah family.

Or are they? As a matter of fact, the aftermath of the Gulf War probably weakened to some extent the authority of the Kuwaiti royal family, as their subjects began to complain about delays in restoring basic public services. It is possible that democratic reforms may be forced on the royal family, as dissident groups acquire a larger and stronger following. In the end, the emir of Kuwait may become a constitutional monarch, in the same sense as the British one, with real political power residing in the hands of an elected parliament. That would be consistent with the history of monarchies generally.

It appears, then, that even the absolute authority of the Kuwaiti monarch is not really absolute. Rather, the monarchy depends on the support of the governed, or at least on certain powerful sectors. It follows that to the extent that this is so, the motives of the state of Kuwait cannot be reckoned simply as the motives of the monarch. He must consider his political position, that is, the desires and motivations of his supporters, in deciding what to do in the international arena. If this is true of such an absolute ruler as Sheik al-Sabah, then it is easily true of the German prime minister or the American president.

Internal-Control Theories

These sorts of considerations lead to theories that explicitly account for the notion that governments rule only by consent of the governed, and conversely, that they use foreign policy to manipulate the governed. In their most extreme form, these "internal control" theories imply a grand conspiracy, by which political leaders use warfare as a means of controlling the political, economic, or social environments of their own nations. Orwell's fictional account in *1984* is probably the best-known example of this kind of thinking. It portrays a fictional future world in which citizens are demoralized and tightly controlled by the state, whose incessant propaganda promotes the constant state of war, or rumor of war, as a source of fear and acquiescence. Terry Gilliam's *Brazil* retells the tale in a more stylized way.

No doubt there are cases in which such conspiracy theories apply. But conspiracies are not a necessary premise, evidenced by a look at things from a slightly different angle. Under the assumption that governments depend on citizens for their power and legitimacy, it is clear that even in the absence of a conspiracy to instigate a war, certainly public approval makes it *possible* to engage in war. Political leaders might, under this view, actually be forced into war by a public driven by national pride or blood lust.[3] Conversely, the lack of support can make the decision to wage war politically risky, even for the most autocratic ruler.

Evidence for this perspective is easy to find close to home, the most persuasive of which is the Vietnam War. Lyndon Johnson's escalation of the war was motivated more by the fear of appearing soft on communism than by the prospect of gain, either political or economic. For that matter, many think that Vietnam was "lost" because the American public was not behind the war effort. And it is the vivid specter of that defeat that seems to have driven many of the decisions regarding the Gulf War. Thus President Bush made sure he had the support of Congress and kept a watchful eye on the polls at every stage of the conflict. In fact, Vietnam was so clear in the national memory that Bush officially declared, at the end of the fighting, that the United States had "put Vietnam behind us"—as if the Gulf War itself was little more than epilogue.

This approach to understanding war embodies two possibilities: Wars are instigated by the state (as embodied by political leaders), after which the public is "sold" on the idea. Alternatively, wars originate in the public demand, which is forced on political leadership. The reality is probably best thought of as a mixture of the two. Bush (as well as Reagan before him) won elections handily by running against the "malaise" of the 1970s, as exemplified in election rhetoric by the Carter administration. In this sense, one can argue that Americans have *demanded* a more hawkish stance in foreign policy. The election-campaign refrain "America is back!" roused voters to endorse Reagan's promise of a more activist and frankly imperialist role by the United States in world affairs.

Gene Sharp takes a much stronger view on the power of the citizenry to influence policy. He observes that even the most oppressive regimes depend largely on the acquiescence of the populace; even the power of dictators is largely illusory. For example, the occupying Nazi regimes in the conquered European countries were fairly impotent in cases where local citizens failed to cooperate actively with them. The deportation of Jews to the death camps was itself highly dependent on the active cooperation of local government leaders, average citizens, and even Jewish community leaders. Thus virtually no Danish Jews were taken by the

---

[3]Of course, "public" demands can be viewed as manipulated by powerful elites. Either way, the political leader's actions can be thought of as governed by the wishes of a constituency. Whether that constituency is democratic, aristocratic, or corporate is irrelevant for present discussion.

Nazis, simply because there were no Danes cooperative enough to give them over (Sharp 1980).

At the same time, it would be naive to conclude that American political leaders (or those of any state) simply reflect somehow the "will of the people." Those in positions of power have access to the tools that shape the public's desires and opinions. This was surprisingly explicit during the Gulf War, as pool reporters in the area were steered by military "information officers" from briefing to briefing, to interviews with pilots and officers, and generally, far away from scenes of death and destruction. In fact, M. Grossman (1995) asserted that reporters were never left unescorted for the duration of the war. After hostilities had ceased, Senator Alan Simpson of Wyoming mounted a sizable defamation campaign against CNN's Peter Arnett, the only major network reporter providing information on Iraqi losses from "eye level." The very reporting of the human misery of war was in Simpson's view "sympathizing" with the enemy.

Ultimately, the relationship between political leaders and those they lead, like that between the state and the individual, is complex. It is true that few leaders have the wherewithal to act for long purely on their own; a base of public acquiescence and legitimation is necessary for even the most autocratic leader. At the same time, political leaders—at least the successful ones—possess the means of gaining that acquiescence by controlling information, rewarding powerful elites, and centralizing and manipulating the economy. Some are also the religious leaders of their societies and thus have access to the very souls of their followers. But even in the most open democracies, it is probably fairly accurate to say that the people really do get what they want—as soon as they are told what it is.

Empirical-Inductive Approaches

An entirely different tack is taken by a growing number of researchers in war and peace. Led by historian Melvin Small and political scientist J. David Singer, this "inductive" approach begins with empirical data on wars and seeks to build theories from the "ground up" by identifying statistical patterns. Using data from their Correlates of War Project, a data-gathering and compiling effort comprising all the world's major wars since 1815, Small and Singer have been able to generate a number of provocative hypotheses. For one, major powers are far more prone to international war than lesser states (this may explain how major powers get that way). Moreover, and easily overlooked, a great many lesser powers have managed to avoid war altogether. They find too that the initiators of wars tend to be more successful militarily than the defenders

(Small and Singer 1989). Other inductive work has used other databases; for example, Gleditsch and Ward (1997) and Gleditsch and Hegre (1997) have used various databases to determine whether democratic states are more peaceful than nondemocratic ones.

The Correlates of War Project has a heritage in earlier work by Lewis Richardson (1960), Quincy Wright (1942), and even Pitirim Sorokin (1937), who included warfare in a general theoretical framework for sociology. The approach has much to recommend it. At the very least, it would seem that its dispassionate empiricism should be helpful in keeping discussion about war focused on the world as it is rather than on ideological formulas for a better one. An empirical approach forces one to look coldly at human activity, seeking solutions to problems in realistic understandings about the behavior of people and states. More important, this approach is useful for examining assumptions that can become truisms over time.

Yet there are problems, the most obvious involving the definition of basic terms. Decisions about what to "count" as war, for example, must be a matter of convention made on somewhat arbitrary grounds. To count as a war for Small and Singer's purposes, a dispute has to result in at least 1,000 battle-connected deaths (1989: 27). Further, the definition explicitly excludes internal unrest and civil war (as do most international-relations perspectives), and most of the "new wars" that characterize the current era are of this type (Kaldor 1996).

This is not to criticize the quality or the usefulness of the work that many scholars have accomplished in this area. On the contrary, such work is essential if progress can be made in understanding war as a social problem. Still, it is best to think of this sort of research, empirical as it is, as inductive and exploratory in nature.

Human Nature Approaches

During the Vietnam War, a popular poster found on college dormitory walls asked: "What if they gave a war and nobody came?" The poster represented a view of war that emphasized individual participation and responsibility for it, and suggested that in the end, wars are made up of individuals and thus could be prevented if only individuals would refuse to cooperate in it. As it happens, people do turn out for wars, often eagerly. The state seldom has difficulty in recruiting or conscripting soldiers, or in exacting loyalty and tolerance from its citizens in times of war. In fact, war frequently brings out the strongest feelings of community and nationalism in people. Perhaps people actually *like* war.

This is the basis for the simplest approach of all to the explanation of war. In this view, fundamental human traits, particularly the propensity toward aggression, are viewed as the ultimate cause of war. After all, when states go to war, it is really large masses of individuals who do the fighting and dying. Without their cooperation, war would not be possible. Thus, many investigators have looked to the fundamental human character as the cause of war.

The most important modern exponent of this approach was Konrad Lorenz, who looked to the aggressive behavior of other animal species for analogies to human violence. Lorenz observed that many species exhibited violent behavior, and concluded that such behavior must be of survival value to the species. For some species, aggression and fighting help space out populations so that they make maximum use of habitat. For others, fighting for mates helps ensure that only the strongest members procreate. For still others, attacking outsiders helps to strengthen bonds among mates (Lorenz 1966).

Two important assumptions underlie this view. First, there is the notion that aggression might be instinctive, or in some way inherent in the human psyche. After all, other animals fight instinctively; they do not reason or cogitate on the motives or consequences of their actions, so it stands to reason that the same might be true for humans. This assumption is strengthened by a good deal of psychological theory that shows that humans of all sorts can be made to exhibit aggression if given the right stimulus.

The other major assumption underlying human nature theories is that aggressive instincts are functional. Lorenz and the other human nature theorists actually represent a return to functionalist and social Darwinist thinking, for such traits must have evolved through a process of natural selection. Humans are inherently aggressive because aggression has, over the generations, improved survival chances for individual members of the species. The most aggressive people have survived and procreated.

The result is that humans have a certain level of aggressiveness programmed into them. It emerges under certain well-understood circumstances, and in some respects, may still (in this view) provide survival value for the species. The real problem is that if functionally appropriate channels of aggression are not available, then that instinctive aggression will spontaneously emerge, with dire and unpredictable consequences. This is unknown in the animal kingdom, because other species have evolved innate inhibitions against the inappropriate use of their natural weapons. Humans, on the other hand, have evolved artificial weapons for which no innate restraint has yet been evolved. In a sense, humans have a greater capability for violence than they are biologically equipped to handle. For Lorenz, the only solution is to find harmless channels for aggression: athletic competition, collective "wars" against social evils, and the like. In the end, this is almost exactly a restatement of William James's search for a "moral equivalent to war."

There are others who have similarly sought the cause of war in human nature. Freud proposed that the balance between community and conflict that can be seen in the human condition is reflected in a balance between two opposing instincts in the human psyche. These two instincts—one oriented toward preserving and uniting, the other toward destruction and death—interact in complex ways to create the mix of peaceful and violent behavior that humans exhibit. It is to Freud's credit that he recognized that much behavior might be motivated by *both* instincts at the same time, just as warfare is the product of both cooperation and conflict (Freud 1989).

Still others have stressed the adaptive value of aggression and violence in the evolution of the species. Edward O. Wilson, for example, suggests that while there may be no particular instinct toward aggression, it is such a common behavior pattern that it must have survival and adaptation value (Wilson 1975).

Although each of these views provides insight into the human mind, they are subject to a profound weakness in explaining war. The problem is that the conduct of war is really not dependent on a pool of aggressive individuals. Inherently docile people can be easily trained for war, and military officers will attest that anyone can be trained to kill, in even the most grisly and bloodthirsty ways. At the same time, it is clear that aggressive people live peaceably all the time. If people are inherently aggressive, then why don't they *always* engage in aggressive behavior? In the end, it does not seem to matter whether people are nasty or nice; war seems to have a life of its own.

This is just another way of saying that war and violence are not the same thing. Mead's definition of war makes the distinction nicely: War is a collective reality, irreducible to individual motivations or desires, and as such it must be understood in social terms. In the words of Creighton and Shaw, "aggression is not force, force is not violence, violence is not killing, killing is not war" (1987: 3). To take these as equivalent is to make the error of reductionism. War is a social, not a psychological, phenomenon.

It is an inconvenience when multiple theories claim to explain a phenomenon. It is understandable that one would want to know which theory is the right one. But there are good reasons why it is too much to expect that any one theory will suffice to explain something as pervasive and as varied as war.

First, there seem to be many kinds of war. Like cancer, it appears that war is not a single disease, but rather a whole family of diseases, related in certain ways but varied in many other ways. Even confining war to

Mead's definition, one can easily see that a good deal of variation is possible, as Barash (1991) concludes. Wars can be classified according to size, both in terms of number of troops, amount of territory, or the number of factions involved. They can be classified according to destructiveness in terms of deaths or property damage. Wars vary in terms of the goals of the combatants (territory, resources, ideological control, national pride, internal unrest) or the proportion of civilian involvement.

One useful categorization can be constructed according to the level of integration of the combatants, and this divides wars into just three fairly clear categories. International wars involve combat between two or more sovereign states, each controlling a military force in an effort to exact compliance from its foe or to destroy the foe's social integration. These include the clear examples of the world wars and more recently the several Arab-Israeli wars, Iran-Iraq, the Falklands, and the Gulf War. A variation on this type is the war between large nations conducted through smaller client states. Korea and Vietnam are two examples, the first involving the United States and China, the second involving the United States and the former Soviet Union.

A second type is the war of one state against a political or ethnic faction within it. These wars have predominated in the last couple of decades; the current examples are shown in Table 1.1 of Chapter 1. A variation on this type is the case in which the internal faction is large enough or strong enough to secede and form its own sovereign state. The American Civil War would be a case in point, as would the breakup of Yugoslavia into several independent states.

Finally, there is warfare between two or more factions within a state. Often one faction will be sponsored or indirectly supported by the state; for example, the Contras were endorsed by the Nicaraguan government and its sponsor the United States in their guerrilla war against the Sandinistas in the 1970s and 1980s. Recently the Tutsi-Hutu fighting in Rwanda and similar action between ethnic and clan groups in Somalia and the Ivory Coast provide bloody examples.

There are simply too many kinds of war to be explained by a single theory. But a second reason for multiple theories of war is that even a particular war may have multiple causes. Continuing the disease analogy, it is known that many diseases are caused by the presence of a particular virus or bacterium. But to call this the single "cause" of the disease is to ignore the question of how the germ is spread and what factors affect one's chances of exposure to it. Thus, although tuberculosis is caused by the tubercle bacillus, the disease is best explained in terms of air quality, living conditions, and population density. And this is not to mention the fact that many people harbor the germ benignly within healthy bodies. One must expect the same of war. At the very least, every war probably has immediate causes, antecedent causes, and something like "root causes" or "favorable conditions" underlying them. No one attributes, for example, World War I solely to the assassination of Archduke Ferdinand.

In the end, one should not be too uncomfortable with the idea that there are multiple theories of war, and that they all might serve to explain certain kinds of war, under certain kinds of circumstances. That many theories exist does not in itself imply that they are worthless, or that one should give up. On the contrary, a great deal is known about war, and every theory offers another approach toward explaining it.

Chapter Summary

War is not an inherent feature of the human condition. It came into being as the invention of agriculture gave rise to dense populations, division of labor, inequality, and government. Although people have always fought, organized warfare is dependent on the sort of social structure that came from the integration of large populations tied to particular geographic areas.

Sociology and other disciplines offer a variety of approaches to explaining war. According to early *functional* theories, militarism and aggression have survival value for states; thus the most belligerent states have thrived while peaceful ones have been conquered by them. Other functionalists view belligerence toward outgroups as the by-product of strong social cohesion or of useful social values.

Marxian theories attribute war to the pursuit of economic interests by self-serving elites. Much current warfare is caused by the global exploitation of new sources of labor and resources by capital interests.

Feminist explanations focus on the fundamental inequality of gender and its role in shaping all aspects of society and culture. The patriarchal form of social organization is responsible for war because its primary traits are domination, competition, and violence.

International relations theories explain war in much the same way as conflicts between individuals. According to *balance of power* theory, war results when one state acquires much more military power over a rival. The *uncertainty* paradigm takes nearly the opposite approach, suggesting that war occurs when two rival states disagree on their relative power. *Internal-control* theories depart from the international relations approach by recognizing the limited powers of heads of state.

Empirical-inductive approaches seek to develop explanations for war based on quantitative historical data. The general method has been to look for patterns in warfare without applying hypotheses developed from theory. Finally, *human nature* explanations take the reductionist tack of explaining war in terms of the human propensity toward violence.

Because war is a varied phenomenon, there will probably never be a unified or comprehensive theory of war. All of these approaches have strengths and weaknesses, and each is useful in explaining certain kinds of wars in certain kinds of circumstances.

Questions for Review

Why did the transition from foraging to agriculture lead to the invention of war? Do you think that as humanity moves into a "postindustrial" era we might see an end to war?

In what ways do each of these theories of war imply that war is inevitable? What does each theory imply is the way to end war? Do some theories offer more optimism than others?

Consider the strengths and weaknesses of the several kinds of explanations for war discussed in this chapter. Then consider which theory seems to best explain a war going on in the world today. Alternatively, you might apply them to various wars you have learned about in history courses.

Women are just now entering the ranks of fighting units in the American military, although they have fought in the armies of some other nations for years. How does this fit with feminist theories of militarism? Do you think American women will be effective fighters?

For Further Research

Amin, Samir. 1994. "About the Gulf War." Pp. 2189–2235 in *War and its Consequences*, ed. John O'Loughlin, Tom Mayer, and Edward S. Greenberg. New York: HarperCollins.

Betts, Richard K., ed. 1994. *Conflict After the Cold War Years: Arguments on the Causes of War and Peace*. New York: Macmillan.

Crocker, Chester A., and Fen Osler Hampson, eds. 1996. *Managing Global Chaos*. Washington, D.C.: United States Institute of Peace.

Diamond, Jared. 1997. *Guns, Germs, and Steel*. New York: Norton.

Enloe, Cynthia. 1983. *Does Khaki Become You?* Boston: South End Press.

_____. 1991. "A Feminist Perspective on Foreign Military Bases." Pp. 95–106 in *The Sun Never Sets: Confronting the Network of Foreign U.S. Military Bases*, ed. Joseph Gerson. Boston: South End Press.

Rapoport, Anatol. 1992. *Peace: An Idea Whose Time Has Come*. Ann Arbor, MI: University of Michigan Press.

Reardon, Betty. 1996a. *Sexism and the War System*. Syracuse, N.Y.: Syracuse University Press.

_____. 1996b. "Women or War?" *Peace Review* 8: 315–321.

Stoessinger, John G. 1990. *Why Nations Go to War*. New York: St. Martin's.

Sumner, William Graham. 1911. "War." Pp. 205–227 in *War and Other Essays*, ed. William Graham Sumner. New Haven, Conn.: Yale University Press.

York, Jodi. 1996. "The Truth(s) About Women and Peace." *Peace Review* 8: 323–329.

4 Militarism: Making War Possible

I grew up during the Cold War. In my elementary social studies classes I learned that the United States made more wheat than the Russians, more steel than the Russians, more milk, housing, electricity, movies— whatever was good, we had more of it than our counterparts in the Soviet Union. And whatever we had, we defined as good: our bread was white and refined; theirs brown and coarse. They made sugar from lowly beets, ours came from cane. Their children had to drink tea; we had Coke *and* Pepsi. We were better educated, more fashionable, and more sophisticated. Most of all, we had freedom and they didn't. What I learned was that a Soviet citizen was told what work he would do for a living, what kind of school he would go to, what sports he would play. And women did men's work there—you could see pictures of them sweeping streets, laying brick, pumping gas. They had to do this work because life was hard there. We simply had a better world than the unfortunate people behind the Iron Curtain, because democracy was a better system than communism. People risked their lives to escape the Communist world; I saw it myself in newsreel footage of people tunneling under or charging over the Berlin Wall.

When I was nine, I saw *Sputnik* orbit over my house on a clear and chilly fall night. My parents, like everyone else, were worried that this meant the Russians would be able to drop atomic bombs on us because they had long-range missiles. When I was eleven, Yuri Gagarin became the first human to orbit Earth, and the fears seemed more real than ever. A neighbor showed my father and me the fallout shelter he had built of concrete blocks in the basement. Other friends and neighbors stocked a corner of the basement with survival goods. Still others actually had underground shelters built; I watched one go into a backyard the school bus passed every day. This was an expensive project, involving excavating equipment and concrete work, probably costing several thousand dollars in today's currency. But it was not an extravagance; it was built by a middle-class family in a middle-class neighborhood. People genuinely believed that the bomb might very well be dropped.

Each day the Emergency Warning Broadcast System was tested. This was marked by an interruption of radio broadcasts during which an announcer would say "This is a test . . . this is only a test" and tell listeners what they should have done if a real national emergency had broken out. The first Monday of every month, at one P.M., the town's air raid siren was tested, and once or twice each school year students were let out of school early for evacuation drill. Children would pretend that a nuclear bomb had been dropped, "duck and cover," then get on special evacuation buses to take them home. Every public building of any size had a designated Civil Defense air-raid shelter, marked with a black and yellow triangular sign. *Fail-Safe* and *On the Beach* were best-selling novels.

When I was twelve my older cousin was called to active duty from the army reserve during the Cuban missile crisis. His unit was actually put on trucks and shipped south to stand by in case of war. I had had an uncle who was killed in Italy during World War II and my cousin was ready to follow in his footsteps.

In the 1980s Ronald Reagan referred to the Soviet Union as the "evil empire" and called on continued funding for the Strategic Defense Initiative, a "nuclear umbrella" that would protect us from waves of incoming missiles. The Soviets were ever more likely to send those missiles our way, he said, because previous administrations had allowed our guard to drop and failed to adequately fund defense acquisition budgets. But by then few of us believed an attack would really come.

Suddenly it all came to an end. The costs of the arms race finally became too great for the Soviet Union, which did not have the borrowing power to sustain budget deficits like the United States. The SALT and START (Strategic Arms Limitation Talks and Strategic Arms Reduction Talks) agreements were signed, and the spiral in nuclear weapons slowed. In 1989 people from Russia and other Warsaw Pact states found a leak in the Iron Curtain and began migrating to the West through Hungary. Seeing no point in maintaining the integrity of the border in Berlin, East German guards stood by as the Berlin Wall was symbolically and literally torn down by citizens of East and West Berlin amid delirious celebration. Mikhail Gorbachev's government negotiated settlements with several Soviet states, allowing them autonomy from the Soviet Union. With a faltering economy and the loss of international prestige, the reform movement Gorbachev had begun spun out of his control and ousted him from office. The new government adopted a new constitution, dissolving the Soviet Union and releasing the grip the Communist Party had exerted on the parliament and the bureaucracy. The Soviet Union was gone; the Cold War was over.

For a Cold War baby boomer, it was like waking from a dream. It seemed possible that the Cold War had never happened at all, the same way it had felt when the Vietnam War had ended, not with a bang but a whimper. There was no more air-raid siren; it had become a summer storm warning siren—when had that happened? The bomb shelters had been forgotten, turned into storage pantries or root cellars. The only vestige left was a reflexive habit of those who grew up during the Cold War: glancing at their watches when the storm siren sounds, to make sure it's the one o'clock test and not the real thing.

I grew up in a highly militarized society; that is, one in which much of ordinary civilian life was concerned with military activities and imbued with military values. It seemed most people, most of the time, were involved personally in the Cold War. Even if few people were building fallout shelters, they were keenly aware of the possibility of nuclear attack, the imperative of Communist aggression, and everyone's role in the national defense. In New York, citizens were even issued dog tags, just like soldiers.

The Cold War is over, or so it is said, but the military has worked hard at finding a new "mission." Today the U.S. military is charged with the global advancement of American interests and enforcement of American dictates. The ongoing Gulf crisis has helped justify that mission, while the military has also tried its hand at peace enforcement roles in Africa and eastern Europe. Because it has developed for itself these new missions while retaining at least part of the old one, and because it has managed simply to maintain its enormous size, the influence of the military in American civilian life seems as strong as ever. The United States continues to be a society organized for war, as exemplified by the permeation of military values into many of its most central institutions.

Militarism in Everyday Life

Chapter 3 described the many explanations that have been developed regarding why war occurs. But none of them addresses explicitly the question of what makes it possible. The existence of animosity between nations is not enough to lead to war, nor is the desire for territory, resources, or markets, nor even the need to protect them from encroachment by others. Even the large-scale theories of war offered by the functionalists and the conflict theorists are better viewed as theories of why, rather than how, wars occur.

In order for a state to make war it must possess the capability to mobilize resources, both material and social, for the actual conduct of warfare. In the modern age this means that large standing armies must be in a constant state of readiness for mobilization in case of conflict, and that large stores of weapons must be maintained. It also means that the industries that manufacture war materials must be ready to produce replacement materials on short notice and in enormous volume. In the Cold War military readiness was taken to the extreme, as fleets of bombers continuously patrolled the Arctic Circle with prearranged orders for the bombing of Soviet cities. They were poised to attack at the president's word, which could be delivered at a moment's notice from the "football," an electronic communications device carried at the president's side at all times.

But military readiness requires more than just a large and well-prepared military establishment. A society that maintains a large army and a ready weapons supply must have a sizable portion of the civilian population available as reserve forces. Still more people must be employed in weapons industries, and those industries have to be kept viable in case of national emergency. Further, the citizenry as a whole must be prepared to undergo the hardships of war; in fact, those hardships are best made an ongoing sacrifice through a program of heavy war taxation and defense spending.

And because war can break out suddenly and can be focused on an unexpected enemy, mobilization of public outrage and bellicosity cannot be delayed until the time of need. Rather, there must be a social consensus preestablished that justifies war, else the expense and hardship of maintaining such a large military readiness will be unacceptable to the population. A modern world power must therefore develop a culture of militarism; that is, military values and ideals must permeate civilian life.

This is accomplished by blurring the boundaries between the military component of the society and the civilian component; in this way the military can exert control over civilian life when the need arises. In a highly militarized society, the military sphere is not a special one peopled by distant professionals and governed by exotic and arcane values. It is as familiar as a football game and as friendly as first grade; the soldier is one's neighbor, teacher, or sister and the bomber is a child's toy. In contemporary societies this blurring can be found in virtually all of a society's institutions, but is most clearly seen in the education system, arts and entertainment, news media, sports, and the economy.

Education

Sociologists know that the educational institutions of modern societies exist not only to provide each new generation with the requisite intellectual skills to take on adult roles in the society, but to fulfill other functions as well. For one, education provides a "baby-sitting" service for families that, in industrial and postindustrial societies, require both parents to enter the paid labor force. For another, schools at every level inculcate the beliefs, values, and norms of the culture, or, in the case of pluralistic societies, of the dominant culture. But a third important function provided by the educational institution is the bonding of youth to the society at large, through rituals and ideas that engender commitment to the state as well as the creation and maintenance of outgroups, or enemies of the state. In short, one of the functions performed by the educational institution is to promote nationalism, and thus militarism, among the nation's youth.

This process is total in scope. My own experiences in elementary school, described at the beginning of the chapter, show that comparison between the free world and the Iron Curtain countries were a part of that process. Each day began with the Pledge of Allegiance, as well as the singing of "America." And this is not to mention students' overall immersion in a world of Americana, through literature, poetry, and song. For example, at a time when the World Series was always played during the day, one could expect at least some elementary teachers to bring a television to class so that students could take part in the national pastime. This was a significant ritual by which national identity was acquired.

This political and national socialization is of course not unique to American schoolkids. In prewar Japan, veneration of the emperor as a deity in human form was an integral part of public education; texts included chapters such as "The Emperor Meiji" and "Revere the Imperial Family" (Wataru 1989). At that time texts were approved by the Ministry of Education and used uniformly throughout the nation's schools; the following example comes from an elementary history text describing the Battle of Port Arthur of the Japanese-Russian war of 1904–1905. The most chilling observation is that the militaristic content is not far beyond the Cold War saber-rattling of the elementary education of my own memory:

> Our brave, loyal officers and men, resolved to repay His Majesty's benevolence with their lives, launched assault after assault and finally seized Hill 203. From there they sank all the enemy warships that were still hiding in the harbor. . . . Amid fierce winds and raging waves, our navy fought tenaciously. . . . It was the greatest naval victory of all time. (quoted in Ienaga 1994: 119)

The process of political socialization begins early and simply. Hess and Torney (1968) conducted a large-scale empirical project on the development of political attitudes of children, collecting data from 17,000 elementary students. They found that the process of bonding children to the national identity begins with the acquisition of simplistic attitudes toward vaguely defined symbols. For example, even in the earliest grades, 95 percent of kids say that "the American flag is the best flag in the world" and that "America is the best country in the world." These attitudes were not attached to any specific experience (with the mailman or policeman or other public official, for example), nor to any sense of common ideals or interests. Rather, these attachments were decidedly "non-rational and non-political" in nature.

As children progress through the system, they develop increasingly sophisticated foci of attachment to the state. Emerging from the first stage of attachment to the flag or the Statue of Liberty, their attachments acquire ideological content. They begin to justify their assertions of American superiority by citing American "freedom," the "right to vote," or an illustrious bit of history.

In the third stage, the United States is seen as part of a larger system of nations. By eighth grade, the United Nations comes to be viewed as the world's peacekeeper rather than the United States, and with a greater depth of study in history and social studies, some of the jingoism of the earlier grades seems to be moderated. But the emotional attachment to the nation remains, at a deeper level. Hess and Torney conclude that "The public school appears to be the most important and effective instrument of political socialization in the United States" (1968: 120). They might well have toned down that conclusion had they done their work thirty years later, when television had come to dominate the time and attention of the average child.

Arts and Entertainment

The contribution of the arts to militarism is complex in nature. In twentieth-century America the "high art" of museums and concert halls has largely been antimilitarist in its focus; in fact, modern art and music might even be thought a reaction against order altogether. But this is a relatively new phenomenon. Until the twentieth century—before World War I, to be more precise—art and music tended to reflect and support the virtues of order and discipline. In terms of thematic content, Tchaikovsky's *1812* is one of the most explicitly militaristic within music, portraying as it does the defeat of Napoleon before Moscow, replete with cannon fire and rocketry. But most art and music was, if not so explicitly martial in content, implicitly supportive of discipline, order, and conventional values.

All of this changed with World War I. Sociologists are accustomed to marking the beginning of the modern era here, as the Western world suddenly and cataclysmically lost its optimism. Where the future had previously appeared to be a steady march of social and technical progress, the war symbolized the real result of that social and technological evolution. What modern science had given people was not a cure for disease and a life of leisure but rather the machine gun and mustard gas. What social progress and capitalism had brought was not universal education but universal conscription and a world dominated by hair-trigger military machines too large to be controlled by rational government.

This loss of innocence was reflected in the arts, as the warmth and softness of impressionism gave way to cubism and ultimately a total abandonment of representation altogether. Picasso disassembled the human form and put it back together in ways that might better understand the structure beneath the surface, but which mostly suggested a flight from convention. In music, Stravinsky's *Rite of Spring* created a riot in the Paris concert hall at which it premiered. The music was so aggressive and so far from convention that concertgoers shouted, stomped, and pounded on the seats. And the ballet that it accompanied was not the customary glide of tutus on tiptoe, but a rendition of a prehistoric fertility dance, complete with sexually explicit gestures, some of them spontaneously added by the dancers.

But these are the "high" arts. The popular arts have played a more active role in acclimating people to violence and hence maintaining a warlike society in America. Films, for example, have played an important role in maintaining the political ideologies of the times. Sayre (1982) and Inglis (1991) point to such critical and box-office successes as *On the Waterfront, The Manchurian Candidate, Animal Farm, The Magnificent Seven,* and *1984* as examples of films that supported a Cold War mentality.

Film and television programming has done more than advance a nationalistic political agenda, however. It has also helped citizens overcome their revulsion to violence, and the increasing violence in both media has been well documented. Theaters and airwaves are drenched in blood, from slapstick eye-poking and cartoon explosions to rape, torture, and cold-blooded killing. In 1991 the Academy Award for Best Picture went to *Silence of the Lambs,* a thriller about the degradations of a cold-blooded cannibalistic killer and his threatening of a young female FBI agent. Another highly popular film of the same year was *Cape Fear,* an updated (that is, more explicitly violent) remake of a film about the terrorizing of a family by a revenge-obsessed killer. More recently, films like *Pulp Fiction* and *Scream* are part of a genre of cinema entertainment in which the audience is manipulated to laugh while witnessing the most gruesome acts of violence.

On television, dramatizations of violence have leveled off in recent years, although nonfictional portrayals have grown by leaps and bounds. Pioneering "reality-based" shows like *Cops* have been joined by such fare as *Exciting Police Chases, When Animals Attack,* and *Trauma:*

Life in the ER. These shows offer the spectacle of real-life suffering and death, more exciting and compelling than the dramatized and stylized version. These prime-time shows feature children being mauled by dogs, motorists burning alive in car crashes, the agony and death of gunshot victims, people leaping to their deaths from burning high-rises.

Meanwhile, a whole new genre of entertainment has arisen over the past few decades: Video games have evolved from the crude and harmless "Pong" of the seventies and "Donkey Kong" of the eighties to stunningly graphic adventures of intimate and brutal killing. "Street Fighter," "Dark Vengeance," and "Tomb Raider" (the latter featuring a woman protagonist) are a small sample of extraordinarily popular games in which the player personally shoots, stabs, bludgeons, and dismembers nameless enemies one after another, who pop up out of nowhere to threaten one's progress through the game. When killed, they splatter blood and viscera in what quickly becomes an orgy of carnage.

But what is the effect of this exposure? The question is usually couched in terms of whether exposure to violence in one form or another causes the viewer to behave more violently, and there is plenty of evidence that it does (Graves and Shreves 1990). But the more subtle and more substantial effect of this sort of vicarious violence is that it accustoms the viewer to associating violent acts with pleasure and entertainment. Viewers watch acts of the most horrifying degradation and suffering while munching popcorn and sipping a soft drink, perhaps while on a date with a boyfriend or girlfriend (D. Grossman 1995).

Grossman has studied the effects of vicarious violence from an unusual perspective: As a psychologist at West Point, he studied the techniques of military training and their effects on humans' ability to kill in cold blood. His work begins with the findings of military historian S. L. A. Marshall (1947), whose "after action" studies of World War II battles showed that only 15 to 20 percent of infantry soldiers who actually encountered the enemy fired their rifles at them. This remarkable finding flew in the face of common sense: The truth was, most soldiers managed not to fire their weapons, even when directly exposed to the enemy.

The military was naturally concerned about this, and consequently infantry training was changed after World War II. The major change was to de-emphasize physical skills in favor of psychological "motivation," that is, the ability and willingness to kill automatically. Many psychological techniques were used, but most took one of two simple forms. The first is a matter of drill and desensitization: chanting "Kill, kill, kill . . ." as a cadence while marching, for example. Or using the most explicit language possible when training to kill ("you want to *destroy* your enemy and send him home to his *mommy* in a *glad bag . . .* ").

The second technique was to make the training more realistic and more threatening to the recruit. For example, instead of learning marksmanship on a rifle range where the recruit aims dispassionately at a bull's-eye target, the new training puts the recruit in a foxhole while human-shaped targets pop up at random and fall satisfyingly when hit. The added tension of having the "enemy" appear out of nowhere puts a premium on reacting without thinking, and killing automatically. The consequences of this improved "quick-kill" training were clear. The firing rate of infantrymen increased markedly in Korea, and grew to 95 percent in Vietnam.[1]

There is a clear connection between the new training and the effects of violent entertainment: In Grossman's view, the increasing use of human suffering as entertainment exactly replicates the desensitizing forces of the new improved basic military training. Long-term exposure to explicit violence and human suffering takes the place of chanting "kill" every time one's left foot hits the pavement. It has the same desensitizing and distancing effect as the constant use of graphic language by drill instructors to dehumanize the enemy. Grossman compares this to a technique used in the Stanley Kubrick film *A Clockwork Orange*, in which the main character is conditioned to abhor violence through constant exposure to violent films while being made ill by drugs. In the real world the process is reversed: We are conditioned to enjoy violence by associating it not with nausea but with pleasure. One chilling bit of evidence: Grossman frequently asked his West Point classes how movie audiences react in "action" and "horror" films when a character is killed in an especially brutal way. Invariably, his students reported, the audience laughs.

Moreover, video games replicate the "operant conditioning" that soldiers undergo as they shoot human targets appearing suddenly on the firing range. The player learns to react instantly and aggressively lest he be eliminated from the game by a suddenly appearing enemy; further, success at the "quick kill" is immediately and graphically rewarded by a satisfyingly gory outcome. The difference between video games and infantry training, however, is that in infantry training there is the safeguard of military authority, which focuses aggression on an enemy and on the combat situation. In the video game there is no such control.

In short, the "safety catch" is being taken off the nation, according to Grossman, and people are training from childhood through adulthood for thoughtless killing, using the same techniques as the military but

---

[1]Grossman notes, though, that there were other consequences of this desensitization, including increased atrocities, civilian casualties, and alienation leading to a very high rate of Post-Traumatic Stress Syndrome.

without the controls. Whether this training makes a difference in behavior is not yet certain, although the apparent increase in violence by children offers at least anecdotal evidence. And whether this civilian training makes it easier for the military to produce a "motivated" soldier also remains to be seen. What seems certain is that this civilian training of military virtues constitutes an important blurring of the line between the civilian sector of society and the military; thus it is a substantial component of the militarization of American life.

There is evidence, too, that not all people outgrow the taste for violent pleasures. James William Gibson (1994) traced the growth since the Vietnam era of a paramilitary culture that affords adults the chance to play at death. This culture includes, at its lowest intensity, an explosion in military documentary series on television, from *Weapons at War* to *Tales of the Gun* to the more subtly titled *Our Century*. A steady increase in circulation of magazines like *Soldier of Fortune* and the debut of similar publications like *Eagle, New Breed, Gung Ho,* and *S.W.A.T.* suggest involvement at a higher level by an increasing number of citizens.

During the same period, Gibson notes, sales of military weapons to civilians rose sharply, including semiautomatic versions of the M-16 and the AK-47, but also kits to convert them to fully automatic mode. Today any sizable city is likely to host an annual gun show where enthusiasts can meet to buy, sell, and swap weapons without the restrictions placed on professional dealers. Many of these enthusiasts are likely to belong to one of the hundreds of paramilitary, "survivalist," or racist groups that represent the highest level of involvement in paramilitary culture.

The pervasiveness of these entertainments, organizations, and preoccupations show that the episodes of violence Americans witness from time to time—the school shootings, murder sprees, and the like—are not aberrations or departures from the norm. Rather, Gibson calls contemporary America a "war zone," where angry fantasies about the loss of American pride and the mongrelization of the white race are nourished by gun manufacturers, entertainment executives, and office seekers.

News Media

Among the many lessons learned by the U.S. military in Vietnam was a greater understanding of the importance of controlling press coverage of military operations. Although official statements continued to claim that the war was being conducted successfully, coverage on the evening news told a different tale. What Americans saw while they ate their dinner was the frustration, demoralization, and suffering of the military without evidence of any strategic or political progress.

In the Gulf War of 1991, the military got it right. In a ten-page memorandum titled "Annex Foxtrot," U.S. Central Command ordered that "News media representatives will be escorted at all times. Repeat, at all times" (M. Grossman 1995: 64). The need to control coverage was especially high because the Gulf War was the first to be televised live, in real time. There was no time to censor images prior to airing; moreover, the age of satellite communication meant that Iraqi citizens and officials had the same access to CNN's coverage as Americans. Thus news reporters were offered official briefings by military personnel showing the astonishing successes of modern high-tech weapons and not their failures, they were escorted to arranged interviews with photogenic soldiers and airmen, and they were fed military video of operations beyond the safe zone in which they were allowed to operate. Their cameras were placed strategically for background footage; one nice example was the placement of an American flag near the end of a runway so that it would enter the shot just as each departing fighter left the ground. One of the few noncontrolled reporters (at least not controlled by American authorities) was Peter Arnett of CNN, who broadcast scenes of destruction in Baghdad and environs. He was decried as a traitor by some in Congress; possibly he had been remembered as one of the star reporters in Vietnam.

Such manipulation was not confined to American authorities. In Great Britain, the BBC blocked the broadcast of a documentary on the export of British weapons to Iraq before the war. France summarily banned several publications critical of the war effort; Turkish authorities selected what it liked from CNN satellite transmissions for broadcast to its citizens (M. Grossman 1995).

It is easy to see the ways in which news media are manipulated during wartime, and by whom. Under normal circumstances it is less obvious, but the news media—particularly televised news—strongly shapes Americans' view of the national interest and the military's role in protecting it. The visual news is especially effective because, as Mimmo and Combs (1990) point out, people act on the basis of pictures in their heads, which are mediated by the television news.

> Accounts of the way things are conform to the pictures people have of these things, the way they imagine them, and thus the accounts reinforce instead of challenging the pictures in our heads. (Mimmo and Combs 1990: 2)

Pictures are assembled to form a consistent and coherent story, in which each element reinforces each other one. In working to maintain coherence, news coverage also tends to promote a consistent set of cultural values. In an empirical study of the content of television network and newsmagazine coverage, Herbert Gans (1979) observed that many network news stories promoted several "enduring values" between the lines. Often they used value-loaded verbs and adjectives when neutral ones were readily available. For example, a radical leader might be said to have "turned up" somewhere, while the president "arrived" somewhere else. At other times there are no value-neutral terms available at all; for example, newswriters might have to choose between the terms "draft evaders," "draft dodgers," or "draft resisters." According to Gans's observations, the latter was seldom used in the Vietnam era.

As for the actual values portrayed, Gans found a fairly small set of these "enduring values" consistently worked into news stories. One of the most consistent is ethnocentrism. Through the selection of adjectives as well as the simple choice of which stories to cover, the news media make a significant contribution to Americans' ethnocentrism. This is especially true during times of war; thus the North Vietnamese were consistently referred to as "the enemy." Atrocities committed against them by Americans were rarely covered; even the My Lai massacre saw the light of day only after the evidence was overwhelming. The citizens of an enemy country tend to be portrayed either as irrational radicals or more sympathetically as ignorant peasants under the thumb of their brutal leadership, because these images do not conflict with the main story of the nation's military intervention.

Even in peacetime it is clear that people of different cultures are almost always shown in stereotyped ways—Arabs are either machine gun–toting religious zealots or wealthy oil sheiks; Africans either starving tribesmen or insurgent military leaders; Asians willing slaves to capitalism. Sometimes individuals are given a tag line, like "terrorist leader" or "the Blind Sheik" or "African strongman," just to simplify things. Similarly, the globe is divided visually into the organized world and the chaotic Third World; this is a replacement for the free world-Communist world dichotomy of the past.

Individualism is another value promoted by the news, as it is in popular entertainment. This is done by selecting stories about individuals resisting the pressures of the group or succeeding on their own terms against difficult odds. But mostly, individualism is promoted simply by reducing complex issues down to individual stories. Thus a change in tax law is explained in terms of a particular couple's finances, or the impact of a war is shown by one soldier's typical day.

At the same time, the value of "moderatism" keeps rampant individualism in check by extolling the virtues of avoiding the extremes. People who consume too conspicuously are treated critically as wasteful or mindless, but on the other hand, those who consume too little are somewhat deviant. Most of all, moderatism compresses the political spectrum in such a way that even mildly leftist or rightist ideas are portrayed as extreme. This is done by covering them only in stories about the political spectrum itself, or by use of modifiers in introducing their proponents.

But the most important value promoted in the news is the value of social order itself. In fact, much of the emphasis of the news overall is on the preservation of order in the face of the threat of disorder. These threats include crime, civil strife, protest, strikes, economic crisis, and violence of various types. The media, according to Gans, generally portrays the white, male, capitalist version of the orderly society as the normal or default worldview, although oppressed people trying to enter it are treated with sympathy. Demonstrating that this order is being maintained and preserved is of paramount importance. For example, Gans cited a government commission's own findings in asserting that most news coverage of the antiwar riots of 1967 were devoted to the restoration of order, rather than to the cause, content, or action of the riots themselves (1979: 54).

In addition to the portrayal of social values in the news, there is also the simple need to gain ratings by using arresting visual imagery. Thus the media are much more likely to report war news than peace news, because it is more visual. Consequently, the world comes to look like a dangerous place, filled with enemies to the American way of life, because a skirmish between two quarreling factions half a world away is magnified on the evening news—if videotape is available. The weapons arsenals of potential enemies are reported, although their diplomatic peacemaking efforts are not, because war news makes for better ratings than peace news (Regan 1994).

In the view of Herman and Chomsky (1988) this adds up to a "propaganda model" by which the mass media are used by corporate and government elites to shape public discourse. This shaping is accomplished by "filtering" information according to several criteria. First, the large media companies are controlled by either small groups of large stockholders or even larger corporations. This is even more true today than when Herman and Chomsky did their research, since the major television networks have been bought by larger interests. For example, NBC is now owned by General Electric, one of the nation's largest defense contractors. Further, smaller outlets have been increasingly acquired by large media groups, a practice made easier since the relaxing of federal regulation since 1980. These companies also share members of their boards of directors with other components of the corporate world: Corporate executives, retired executives, and bankers accounted for over 60 percent of all media directors (1988: 11).

The second "filter" is the influence of advertisers on both content and presentation. Herman and Chomsky describe the death of the *Daily Herald,* a nineteenth-century London newspaper whose readership was working class. Although it had a larger circulation than any other paper in London, it strangled owing to lack of advertising revenues—advertisers simply did not want to waste money trying to sell to people who were not purchasers. Since then, the "quality" of an audience is recognized as important to advertising income; thus news media are careful not to offend affluent readers and viewers. The third "filter" is the role of the profit motive in gathering news. News gathering is expensive, and television networks are profit-making ventures. Thus it is no surprise that the majority of the stories that appear on the evening news are spoon-fed to reporters for free by official spokespersons at news conferences, briefings, or "exclusive" interviews. What isn't provided by the government is increasingly appropriated from newspapers or even tabloids, often without even a serious check of facts.

Finally, a fourth "filter" consists of the ability and willingness of offended advertisers or government information sources to punish news media outlets for unfavorable stories. This "flak" can consist of letters, petitions, lawsuits, or even congressional action. It can come from government offices directly; the White House itself, for example, or from corporate associations and institutes. It can also come from offended advertisers, who have the added clout of being able to withdraw their advertising from the network or magazine. And most advertisers are large corporations, many of them military contractors. Some of the most prominent advertisers on the evening news as of this writing are Lockheed-Martin, General Electric, and the military itself. Other groups with an interest in supporting military endeavors include the various international oil companies and manufacturers with sizable global interests.

By these means information regarding social and foreign policy is shaped to suit the interests of those who control its production. This is not to say that there is an active conspiracy among news media to misinform the public or to blur the distinction between civilian institutions and military ones. In fact, most of the evidence argues against it. Rather, the ostensibly "free" press is dominated by the state and its corporate constituents because that is the path of least resistance. It is easier to achieve maximum ratings with minimum effort, and thus to make a profit, by going along. Barker-Plummer (1996) summarizes by asserting that corporate media exert a "strong hegemony" on knowledge, particularly in marginalizing social change movements while making the status quo appear normal and rational.

Sports

Sports have become a central institution in the modern industrial world. They comprise, much like the arts, a world of symbolic meanings, played out collectively and reinforced through ritual games, through which participants and observers alike can find consensus on cultural ideals. These ideals vary from culture to culture, which accounts for the variations in popularity of particular sports and games from one society to another.

The pervasiveness and moral importance of sports in the United States would be difficult to overestimate. Today every child is required from an early age to participate in a variety of team and individual sports in school; significantly, this was codified into national policy by President Kennedy at the height of the Cold War. Legions of children play in organized leagues year-round, switching from sport to sport with the seasons.

By high school or even earlier, such activities are public spectacle. High school scores are reported in the local press and television news; in some rural locales the high school basketball or football game is the town's main focus of attention. Meanwhile, college sports are a multibillion-dollar business, commanding enormous resources and media attention. At the end of each year, national television networks broadcast a score or so of college football bowl games, each now with its own corporate sponsor, from the "Fed Ex Orange Bowl" to the enigmatic "insight.com Bowl."

At the professional level, sports constitute a significant sector of the economy. Their impact is not confined just to ticket sales and television revenues; they also affect local restaurant and entertainment sales in cities that are home to professional franchises, and increasingly, national sales of team clothing and athlete-endorsed shoes. Given the impact of sports on both local and national economies, it should be no surprise when major athletes are signed to nine-figure contracts. Conversely, the retirement of Michael Jordan caused a significant stir on Wall Street, amid concern that the departure of the greatest advertising icon ever might cause a significant reduction in sales, not only for Nike but across a variety of industries.

Sports accounts for dozens of hours of television programming each week, not even counting the all-sports cable networks, and they occupy their own section of the daily newspaper. They provide a good deal of the grist for everyday conversation, and a fair amount of turgidly moralistic writing and drama. Finally, a successful sports franchise can ignite civic pride and social cohesion among fans, and define clear boundaries between the ingroup of supporters and the outgroup of the opposition.

Sports play a central role in reinforcing militarism in several ways. First, competitive team sports are a model of conflict and warfare. The home team provides a metaphor for the combatants of "our side" as they do battle with those of the "enemy." It's an apt metaphor, especially considering the general lack of any real connection between the fans and the team: The home professional football or baseball team may change its roster substantially each year through trades and free agency. And college teams often are wholly unrepresentative of either the student body or even the fictive identity of the institution they represent—witness the "Fighting Irish" of Notre Dame: a nationally recruited team of semiprofessional athletes, most non-Catholic and far from Irish. Given this instability of team rosters, it is reasonable to ask: What exactly *is* it that the fans support? Since it is not represented by the players, might it be the coaches, or in the case of a professional franchise, the owner? This is occasionally the case, as when the St. Louis Cardinals were owned by paternalistic Anheuser-Busch, but mostly a team's owners are a group of distant tycoons, often despised as misers and gougers.

Clearly, loyalty to a team is seldom vested in persons at all (other than the occasional superstar), but rather in some collective identification. The home team is a totem of sorts by which fans can express their membership in a fiercely loyal ingroup as well as their disdain for the outgroup. This can grow to hostility, as evidenced by the fights that sometimes erupt at small-town Little League games as well as the great soccer riots of Great Britain and Latin America. More often this excess cohesion is manifested in rapturous celebration by the fans of the winning side—and sometimes this too results in riot and widespread violence.

The play of the game itself can also be metaphoric of militarist values. Football, for example, is almost an exact representation of warfare, involving two sides seeking to invade each other's territory. The method is decidedly military as well: Each side forms a line of "men-at-arms"; the attacking side tries to break through it and disrupt the enemy's organization in the rear. One can even see the problem faced by the medieval warrior in the actions of linemen as they try to protect the quarterback by always presenting their armored front to the attacking opponent. Notably, blocking a lineman from behind rather than squarely in front is a violation of the rules called "clipping."

Furthermore, football is hierarchical and corporate in its organization. Although individual talent is prized at certain positions, the success of the team is mostly grounded in the collective action of the team as a whole. The best running back goes to waste without an effective offensive line; it is not a platitude when a star quarterback gives credit to the linemen. Moreover, a staff of coaches act as generals, analyzing the situation and issuing orders from a safe position off the battlefield. No wonder General Schwartzkopf found the language of football so handy in describing the invasion of Iraq as a "gigantic end-around" play and the final assault as a "hail Mary."

Other sports are less violent and less militaristic in their organization. Baseball, for example, features individual performance more strongly and is not territorial. Basketball is also somewhat more oriented toward individual artistry and even rewards the subversion of order by occasional individual outbursts (the slam dunk, for example). And hockey is a curious hybrid—a game fundamentally rooted in complex skills of skating and puck handling, but with a superfluous layer of mayhem added, in which violent collisions and periodic outbursts of fighting are an integral part of the game. Although these sports vary in their violence or metaphoric militarism, they are all team sports and thus represent collective struggle against an opposing force in a zero-sum game. Further, the goal of the struggle is symbolic and collective—to win for "the fans," one's town, or one's school. Recalling Mead's definition of warfare, sports of all kinds fit the definition handily, with the exception that in sport, killing is not legitimated (although wounding is).

The ultimate manifestation of sports as symbolic warfare might be the Olympic Games. Here each team represents a nation, which makes it easy for fans to attribute success or failure to cultural or political differences in the origins of the teams. Thus during the Cold War strict medal counts were kept comparing the United States with the Soviet Union, or comparing "free world" with "Iron Curtain" states. The implied presumption was that one "system" or the other was better at producing athletes. The Olympics turn even individual sports into collective efforts, such that a single figure skater or swimmer or decathlete is able to represent an entire nation or culture. This is made visible when stadium audiences wave their national flags or wear the national colors in support, or when a winning athlete is handed his or her national flag during a victory lap.

The relationship between fans and their teams is central to the link between militarism and sports, for it represents the essential relationship between armies and the citizens in whose name they fight. If the importance of this relationship appears exaggerated, one need only look at the response of citizens and politicians alike toward the "support of the troops" in the Gulf War and subsequent military actions in Iraq and elsewhere. Even people strongly opposed to military action are expected to express support for fighting men and women, as Senate Majority Leader Lott did while condemning President Clinton's 1998 bombings of Iraq. In fact, in the Gulf War of 1991 there were explicit claims made that lack of support for the troops could undermine their morale and thus make them more vulnerable to danger. This view probably came out of

America's experience in Vietnam, interpreted by many as a defeat caused by a lack of support back home.

The implicit theory is that somehow the troops in the field can sense this lack of support and thus don't try as hard to "win." Soldiers are less strongly convinced in the righteousness of their cause, perhaps, so they are less aggressive in attack and adopt a more defensive, self-preserving orientation to the battle. This is exactly the same theory that is used to explain the relative success of athletic teams in the field. Fan support is thought to account for a substantial portion of the performance of one's team. This is why the "home field advantage" is highly prized in many sports, and why organized cheerleading is a staple of every college football and basketball game. In fact, athletes on the field can often be seen exhorting the fans to cheer louder so as to motivate the team to greater efforts. A failure to cheer can lead, according to this implicit theory, to demoralization of the athletes and loss of the game; in the same way a failure of citizens to cheer on their troops can lead to loss of the battle.

In this way the national involvement in sports is apt training for national involvement in military adventure. People become accustomed to cheering warriors on the battlefield through a lifetime of practice cheering athletes on the playing field. The development of this "spectator militarism" (Shaw 1988) is an important and growing part of Americans' socialization into their militaristic society. Ultimately, sports help provide "national integration" while serving as a "supporting institution of social control" (Vinocur 1988). Guttman relates sports even more deeply to culture, observing that modern sports has evolved over the past 150 years as capitalism has evolved, and that England, home of the Industrial Revolution, was its birthplace (1978).

Individual participation in sports is also a part of that socialization. Required involvement in team sports at an early age readies people for active participation in collective struggle. It is true that these activities are typically justified in the name of fitness, although there is no masking the moral and social intent of such experiences: the belief that sports "builds character" or "instills discipline" or in current parlance, "builds self-esteem."

Sports are also viewed as a means of maintaining a tough and well-disciplined population of potential soldiers. The mandatory program of physical fitness imposed on schoolchildren under President Kennedy was actually the result of a great deal of prodding by the army and air force. The latter had learned from its survival training program (a program that included training to withstand torture upon capture) that physical conditioning was an important factor in preventing collapse, both physical and emotional; this connection became generalized to apply to the population as a whole. Ultimately, physical fitness became connected to "moral stamina" as well; thus it was not a stretch for Kennedy to insist that America's youth should be trained more vigorously in the physical arts (Mrozek 1995).

Children learn through athletic competition the virtue of playing strictly-bounded roles for the common good; this subordination of the individual will to the collective is the virtue of teamwork or "being a team player." It is also a manifestation of obedience to the authority of the coach, whose role gradually evolves as the child grows, from teacher to taskmaster and strategist. Through team sports, the child learns to sublimate his or her own discomfort for the common good through arduous practice and later, by suffering and playing through injuries.

And the young athlete learns also a special role as representative of a larger community of fans. By high school, supportive parents are augmented by townspeople who have an interest not in the child's performance but in that of the team as representative of the town. Cheerleaders exhort the team from the sidelines and maintain the bond between fans and players throughout the game. In boys' sports, the athlete-cheerleader-fan connection also becomes a powerful device for reinforcing gender roles; the athlete taking on responsibility for the larger community while supported unconditionally by nonparticipating girls. And the prestige gained by the athlete in this way is traded for the romantic attention of girls as well.

Economic Dependence

A more basic mechanism by which the boundaries between military and civilian institutions are blurred is the economic dependence of most citizens on the military. In militarized societies, citizens depend on the military institution for their material needs in a variety of ways. In the first place, a large number of Americans earn their living directly from the military. This includes not only the million or so Americans on active duty in the military and the further 1.5 million in the reserves and National Guard, but also civilian military workers, either on bases or in administrative offices. These latter number about 732,000 at present (United States Bureau of the Census 1998). People directly dependent on the military economy also include those working for defense contractors and subcontractors. In 1992 there were 20,000 prime defense contractors in the United States and 150,000 subcontractors that received Department of Defense funds (Kirby 1992). In the early part of the century it was said that everyone in America had either a relative or a friend who worked for the railroad. Today the same might be said of the defense industry.

But this does not tell the whole story, because the rest of Americans are in one way or another indirectly dependent on the military to advance or protect U.S. economic interests. The most obvious example is military action to protect access to important resources; thus the strong military presence in the Middle East. The Gulf War and its sequels are only the visible manifestation of a lengthy history of diplomatic and military coercion in the region. Arms sales to various Arab states (including Iraq not long before the current difficulties), diplomatic and financial support of various political regimes (again including Saddam Hussein, but also the Shah of Iran, for example), and development of military bases (in Turkey, Saudi Arabia, and elsewhere in the region) have been largely aimed at ensuring a steady supply of cheap oil for U.S. industry. Secretary of State Baker's gaffe that the Gulf War was being fought "for your job" bore more truth than the administration could acknowledge.

Economic dependence of citizens on the military is probably the most pervasive way in which the boundary between the military and civilian sectors of society is blurred. In a highly militarized society like the United States, virtually every citizen is involved at some level in the military economy. This involvement predisposes the public to look favorably on the military and its activities, since it is not hard to see one's own involvement in them. When one's son or daughter is sent to the Gulf or Haiti or Yugoslavia, it becomes a natural thing to fly the Stars and Stripes in front of the house. When an air force base in one's community is slated to close, its importance to the national defense becomes apparent. When McDonnell-Douglas loses a large contract, the people of St. Louis become concerned about the readiness of the air force, and well they should, since dislocations and shutdowns can have substantial effects on employment, consumer spending, and the local tax base (Ettlinger 1992). And when Lockheed's stock declines in price, the loss shows up in the portfolios of investors and retirement funds all over the country. In short, Americans are *all* dependent in one way or another on defense spending.

Social and Cultural Suffusion

Finally, the boundary between civilian and military institutions is blurred simply by the suffusion of military structures and values into civilian life. One form of this suffusion is military service; in highly militarized societies a large portion of the population actually lives a military life, at least for a time. The clearest examples are countries with universal conscription such as Israel. There, everyone serves a period of active duty and is then placed in the reserves, making each citizen "a soldier on ten months' leave" (Ben-Eliezer 1997). In the United States military service is not universal and has declined since World War II, Korea, and Vietnam. Still, in the late 1960s it was true that most middle-age men—and most business, government, civic, and professional leaders—had served time in uniform (Donovan 1970).

Military service is often a powerful rite of passage for men and, increasingly, women. For many people, military service constitutes the most intense experience of their lives; its timing usually corresponds with the normal coming-of-age period when youths enter adulthood. The military can also be a means of achieving upward mobility; youngsters either in trouble or with little future find a respected and responsible role. Thus it should be expected that the military experience shapes attitudes and worldviews in a profound way, and the sharing of that experience among a generation's community and business leaders makes for a powerful social consensus.

Today the draft is dormant in the American scene, but hundreds of thousands of men and women choose military service as a step to adulthood and a career. Television advertising portrays the service as a fun adventure, and with benefits—particularly the acquisition of valuable career skills and funding for higher education later. In this way higher education is militarized too, as students earn part of their tuition through military service.

The permeation of boundaries between military and civilian life operates in both directions. According to Moskos (1993), the "postmodern military" has taken on a new role in society, beyond dealing with foreign threats and national interests. It now also serves as a "laboratory for social experimentation," taking on the task of dealing in an official way with the social issues of the day. This began, one supposes, with the racial integration of the military after World War II, a step that preceded integration in many sectors of the civilian world. Today the military is at the center of issues of gender equality, gay rights, sexual abuse, drug addiction, and other social concerns. This is certainly not to say that the military is at the vanguard of any of these movements; on the contrary, one is often shocked at how far behind the times the military world can be. What it does say is that the military is no longer isolated from the social world around it, or immune from the values and norms of the culture in which it is imbedded. It is becoming more like civilian society, and this is another measure of the blurring of the boundary between the two.

Finally, military personnel and interests are deeply imbedded in civilian government. After World War II hundreds of high government posts were occupied by military officers (the presidency, for one); though this has certainly declined since then there remains a good deal of spillage from the military to the civilian sector, Alexander Haig and Oliver North providing only the most visible recent examples. And the influence of defense contractors on government policy, both through lobbying and through infiltrating government offices, is great, as I discuss in Chapter 5.

In all these ways American society is militarized. Americans are drawn into the ongoing, permanent war effort from childhood on, through schooling, sport, entertainment, and the corporate-controlled press. U.S. citizens are made ready for military training by constant exposure to violence and human suffering and to jingoistic images of people who threaten material interests. Dependence on an economy influenced by weapons producers aligns individual's interests with those of the military. Moreover, dependence on the military to protect America's access to important resources such as oil renders protests against military adventures hypocritical.

It seems clear that where militarism is found, it is found throughout all of a society's institutions and not just in certain areas of life. The blurring of military and civilian values does not occur just in the public schools, nor in the arts or entertainment media or sports, because each of these facets of life reinforces and reflects the others. Violent movies are popular because people have been taught early on to accept violence as a way of asserting their position in the world. Militaristic sports make sense because they reflect the view of the world as a zero-sum competition for dominance. People accept the intrusion of military personnel and values into government policy because they have been shown by the media the military institution's capability to advance U.S. interests.

Militarism is all-pervasive, and this makes sense, because societies are integrated systems, made of interdependent parts that together form a whole. This view is most clearly articulated by functional thinking, which regards the constant movement toward integration and equilibrium of society's parts as the main impetus for social change and conflict. But the integration of society's parts is also recognized by conflict theory. Even while conflict thinkers emphasize the struggle among classes or groups for material gain, the flip side of conflict theory is that this struggle is largely a matter of dominant groups' efforts to integrate society in their image. Thus the military-industrial elite is able to inject military values into civilian life by controlling government, media, schools, and entertainment in a variety of ways. More fundamentally, it is able to predispose the citizenry to acquiescence by making so many people dependent on the military for the comforts of ordinary life.

Whatever the causation, it seems clear that militarism is an integral part of American society, and not just an adjunct to it, attached by history and accident to an otherwise peaceful culture. In fact, militarism seems an essential characteristic of any society that intends to play a role in the system of modern industrial or postindustrial states. The nature of modern diplomacy requires a readiness to use military force to advance a nation's aims; further, the use of modern military force requires the readiness of all sectors of society to participate in the war system.

The Post-Cold War Era

So what happened to the Cold War? How could such a massive threat to human existence simply have come to an end? Was it possible that the simple change from a Communist-dominated parliament to a multiparty parliament meant that the Russians no longer wanted to bomb us? And if so, why do the United States and Russia continue to maintain thousands of nuclear weapons? One answer is that the Cold War was always more than just a stalemate of will and weaponry between the superpowers. Cold War thinking and Cold War structures served a variety of functions and interests beyond the simple goal of each side to keep the other in check.

For one thing, the Cold War served the diplomatic and strategic interests of the two superpowers. As the two states with the most significant nuclear arsenals, the United States and the Soviet Union were able to jointly dominate world events, even as they competed bitterly with one another. Even other nations that had been world powers before the nuclear age found themselves having to become aligned with one of the two major players on the world scene. Thus the Cold War, with all its attendant risks, served each of the adversaries in pursuing their geopolitical interests.

A more troubling explanation for the Cold War lies in the interests of the military institutions within each nation. Both the United States and the USSR had emerged from World War II stronger than they had entered it, with enormous armies and stockpiles of weapons. The military institutions in both countries had dominated society through the war years and had penetrated civilian life to a significant degree, and both enjoyed widespread respect and gratitude. In the United States the economy had become addicted to weapons production, and emerging technologies like rocketry, nuclear engineering, and electronics promised ongoing business for weapons contractors. In the Soviet Union, the military had become a powerful political force.

The Cold War offered a continuation of World War II and further advancement of these interests. By virtue of what Regan (1994) calls political and economic inertia, the military sectors of the two societies simply became so strong that they were able to manipulate both the perception of foreign threat and the economic and political structures of their respective societies. Oakes (1994) gives a particularly clear account of how the former was accomplished, as the civil defense system became a primary means of reinforcing the public belief that an attack was imminent and that it could be survived.

The third and most encompassing explanation is that the Cold War was simply the ultimate expression of the war system, the culture of fear and violence with which the male world maintains its grip on humanity. The interests of defense contractors and the military, the technological imperative to develop ever more destructive weapons, the ability of government to scare the public of foreign aggression and possible annihilation—all were merely aspects of the larger reality of patriarchal dominance of societies worldwide, which reached its zenith in the industrial age.

Each of these explanations leads toward the conclusion that the Cold War was not only the means by which the forces of capitalism and the forces of communism squared off in the international arena. Rather, it was the visible representation of a system that institutionalized and focused militaristic values in both societies, and that served both to control the populace and increase the power of the state.

In the end, militarization and militarism are not only a response to the military needs of a society; they can become self-perpetuating elements of the social structure. War is today so encompassing and so sudden that the citizenry has to be kept at a constant state of readiness and bellicosity to ensure success when the time comes. But there is every reason to think also that high levels of militarism can make war more likely. It seems clear, for example, that the United States is much quicker to arouse to military action today than it was in the periods prior to the two world wars.

To the extent this is the case, the problem of war lies partly in the fundamental cultural realities of warlike societies, not simply in the relations between states. This problem must be addressed, some suggest, by changing the basic systems of organization of human societies overall. In Joseph's (1994) view, this requires development of "peace culture," amounting not to specific policies but a new set of inner beliefs and popular assumptions, including a greater attention to the environment, abandonment of "we-they" thinking, and an expanded time frame for making social policy. For others, the rise of women and women's ways of thinking are the solution.

This chapter has described many obstacles in the way of any such fundamental reform. The military institution of the large industrial state is deeply imbedded in social structure and cultural ideas, sometimes explicitly and sometimes subtly. But it is also closely attached to the economic and financial institutions of society, and this seems especially true in the modern age. The next chapter examines the financial impact of militarism on modern societies, and shows how the technological character of modern weapons as well as the bureaucratic nature of modern society encourages the growth of the modern military-industrial state.

Chapter Summary

The Cold War marked the high point of militarism in American society, as the boundaries between civilian and military values were highly blurred. The United States continues to be highly militarized because the instantaneous nature of military action in the modern age makes it impossible to mobilize armies and galvanize public opinion before engaging in war. Thus a ready military and a militaristic culture must be permanently maintained.

The blending of military life and civilian life can be found throughout the institutions of the modern militaristic society. The *education system* socializes children early to form emotional bonds with their country and to identify it as the best of all nations. In popular *arts and entertainment*, citizens are desensitized to violence and suffering in much the same way as military recruits are. *News media* allow themselves to be used by the state and its corporate constituents because it is easier and more profitable to do so, and besides, they are part of the corporate elite themselves. *Sports* are not only sometimes violent in nature, but are often metaphors for war itself, as the home team battles distant enemies for the sake of the fans and the community. Sports also help ready the young for possible military service. Finally, most citizens are dependent on the military for their *economic* comfort, either as employees in the defense sector, investors in defense industries, or as consumers of cheap commodities secured from Third World markets.

Questions for Review

The author describes his childhood during the Cold War as a time of fear and mistrust of foreign enemies. How have American attitudes changed since then? How have they remained the same?

What do schools do to encourage nationalism?

How do the experiences of young Americans prepare them to enter military service?

How do films and video games simulate military training?

If you wanted to raise a less militaristic child, what sports would you encourage your child to play? What ones would you discourage? Why?

In what ways are ordinary Americans dependent on the military?

For Further Research

Gibson, James William. 1994. *Warrior Dreams*. New York: Hill and Wang.
Grossman, Dave. 1995. *On Killing*. Boston: Little, Brown.

Herman, Edward S., and Noam Chomsky. 1988. *Manufacturing Consent: The Political Economy of the Mass Media*. New York: Pantheon Books.

Inglis, Fred. 1991. *The Cruel Peace*. New York: Basic Books.

Mimmo, Dan, and James E. Combs. 1990. *Mediated Political Realities*. 2d ed. New York: Longman.

Oakes, Guy. 1994. *The Imaginary War*. New York: Oxford.

Regan, Patrick M. 1994. *Organizing Societies for War*. Westport, Conn.: Praeger.

Vinocur, Martin Barry. 1988. *More than a Game*. Westport, Conn.: Greenwood.

Wiggins, David K., ed. 1995. *Sport in America: From Wicked Amusement to National Obsession*. Champaign, Ill.: Human Kinetics.

5 The Military-Industrial Complex

In 1961 President Dwight Eisenhower ended his two terms in office with a stern warning to the American people. In his farewell address, he described the extent to which the "partnership" that had been built between the government and large defense contractors (a partnership he had openly encouraged when he first took office) had become an independent political and economic institution. The "military-industrial complex," as he called it, was a conspiracy between government and industry to design and produce ever more exotic and expensive weapons for a military establishment that had become a powerful political force in its own right since World War II. In his address, Eisenhower noted:

> This conjunction of an immense Military Establishment and a large arms industry is new in the American experience. The total influence—economic, political, and even spiritual—is felt in every city, every statehouse, every office of the Federal Government. We recognize the imperative need for this development. Yet we must not fail to comprehend its grave implications. Our toil, resources, and livelihood are all involved; so is the very structure of our society.
>
> In the councils of Government we must guard against the acquisition of unwarranted influence, whether sought or unsought, by the military-industrial complex. The potential for the disastrous rise of misplaced power exists and will persist. (quoted in Cancian and Gibson 1990: 171)

Eisenhower had been elected on the strength of his military and organizational achievements as supreme commander of the entire Allied effort in Europe during World War II. It is a sad truth that even he could not control the monster he had created. And it is also true that every president since has failed to wrest even a little control over this enormous bureaucracy (some have tried harder than others).

This inability of civilian authorities to control the weapons acquisition system is important to understanding militarism in industrial societies. It shows how the military-industrial complex takes on a life of its own and thus promotes militarism without regard for the needs of foreign policy or military threat. It is partly because the civilian government cannot or will not control military acquisition that the military enters economic institutions and affects personal economic lives. The question for this chapter is a simple one: Why can't the government control military acquisition?

The answers to the question vary from one country to another. For one thing, weapons are produced by state-controlled industries in many countries. China, North Korea, and Iraq are familiar examples, although it is fair to say that components of the French and Italian aircraft industries are at least partly under state control or heavily subsidized. In other countries such as the United States, most weapons production is by private corporations, who negotiate prices and profits with the government. There are exceptions to the rule; the American space industry—the one that actually delivers satellites into space—is largely nationalized through the National Aeronautics and Space Administration (NASA).

Another way in which the military acquisition institution varies from country to country is the relative importance of domestic production and foreign imports. Some countries are heavy producers of their own systems, and thus also exporters to smaller states. Others rely extensively on the availability of weapons from larger producing states, which means that diplomatic relations figure more heavily in their weapons-acquisition decisions.

The military-acquisition apparatus will vary from country to country owing to these and many other factors. This chapter focuses on the U.S. military-industrial complex because it is somewhat unique in several ways. First, it is by far the largest military-acquisition system in the world. Figure 1.2 of Chapter 1 shows that the United States spends more on weapons than any other country. Table 5.1 shows that the United States also exports more weapons than any other nation.

Second, the American system is probably the most "privatized" in the world, at least on paper. Virtually all weapons development and production is performed by corporations under contract with the government purchasing system, which means that there are clear profit incentives to maximize both the sophistication of weapons and the number produced. It also means that foreign sales are encouraged and promoted by the same corporations, with only imperfect regard for foreign policy and national interest. The private character of U.S. military acquisition thus makes it more prone to excess and inefficiency. It thus offers a good model for understanding how the weapons-acquisition system itself can promote the insinuation of militaristic values and structures into civilian society.

TABLE 5.1   The Ten Leading Weapons Exporters, 1993–1997 (in millions of U.S. dollars at constant 1990 prices)

Suppliers	Amount
United States	$53,129
Russia	15,246
United Kingdom	9,423
France	7,760
Germany	7,177
China	3,531
Netherlands	2,178
Italy	1,781
Canada	1,339
Spain	1,230

SOURCE: Stockholm International Peace Research Institute 1998.

Scope of the Military Establishment

The U.S. military is one of the largest, most complex organizations that ever evolved. It maintains permanent bases around the globe, including a large standing army at the ready in Korea and bases all over the world. Large stores of equipment and arms are pre-positioned in various sites where warfare is, if not expected, contemplated. On the seas, aircraft carrier battle groups are on constant duty; under the seas submarines equipped with nuclear missiles patrol silently. Other such missiles are still kept at the ready in silos around North America, presumably to be fired as doomsday weapons at the first sign of nuclear attack. And only in 1991 did the Strategic Air Command (now called Strategic Command) order its fleets of B-1 and B-52 nuclear bombers to stand down from twenty-four-hour patrols near the borders of the former Soviet Union. In space, satellites keep watch over military and other developments around the world; others facilitate global communication among military units; still others provide precise navigation for ships, planes, and ground units.

Yet all of this activity constitutes only a fraction of the total military effort. For every soldier on the ground or plane in the air or ship at sea, the military must perform a variety of management, support, and supply services. For each actual combat soldier, sailor, and airman, there are as many as twenty military and civilian personnel performing these services. The result is that the Department of Defense employs over *1.5 million* people (United States Bureau of the Census 1998).

It is no wonder that the military consumes nearly half of America's federal taxes. Looking at the scale of the operation, it is easy to see how billions and billions of dollars might be required to keep such an organization going. But it is still difficult to get a feeling for how big these numbers are. Senator Everett Dirkson of Illinois expressed this years ago when he complained during a budget debate, "a billion here, a billion there—pretty soon you're talking about real money!"

One way to get an intuitive feel for the scale of military spending is to "build up" the defense budget in terms of the number of taxpayers needed to pay for it. How many taxpayers does it take to raise just $1 million for the Pentagon's coffers? For the sake of round numbers, one can guess that the average family pays something like $5,000 per year in income taxes. That means that it takes the total income tax burden of 200 families to generate $1 million. This could amount to the entire population of a rural midwestern town, or, for the more urban-oriented, perhaps everyone in a several-block area.

But $1 million is a very small amount of money in defense terms; budget numbers are most often quoted in billions. How many taxpayers does it take to generate $1 billion? When I worked for the army as a cost analyst, there was a general who was fond of ambushing young analysts with the question: "How much more than a million is a billion?" As often as not, the eager analyst would respond, "Ten times, sir!" And this is one of the things that underlies Americans' desensitization. A billion is not ten millions, of course, but a *thousand* times a million. This means that, in terms of the "taxpayer quotient," it takes *200,000 families* (probably close to 1 million people) to raise $1 billion. This would not buy even half of one B-2 bomber, at $2.6 billion each.[1]

Of course, even a B-2 is a drop in the defense bucket. That program alone is planned to produce a whole fleet of bombers. What if the defense budget were five times $1 billion? Then a million families would be needed to pay for it—the entire population of, say, Detroit. Put another way, the total B-2 fleet of twenty-one planes soaked up $54 billion, or a year's taxes from everybody in California (though they were not all bought in the same year). But even the entire B-2 fleet is only a small part of the defense budget. The air force alone has to fly and maintain many fleets of fighters, bombers, missiles, and satellites. The navy operates hundreds of ships every day. The army not only has thousands of tanks, trucks, and artillery, but boasts that it has more aircraft than the air force (in its helicopter fleet), and more watercraft than the navy (in its landing craft and other small vessels). This is not to mention the hundreds of thousands of men and women training, flying, sailing, shooting, typing, digging, building, and collecting pay every month. This is why the defense budget is not just $1 billion a year, nor even $5 billion. As

---

[1]Average for the total fleet of twenty-one aircraft, including research and development costs.

FIGURE 5.1   President Clinton's Proposed FY 2000 Discretionary Budget (in billions)

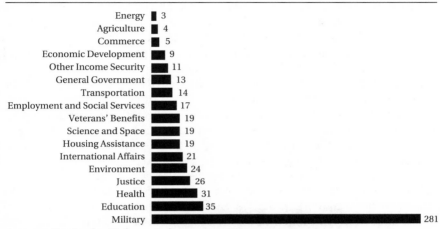

SOURCE: Center for Defense Information 1999.

Figure 5.1 shows, President Clinton's proposed FY 2000 budget includes *$281 billion* for defense—which amounts to the total income tax share of about 50 million families.

But these numbers do not add up. The defense budget is only about half of the total federal budget, which includes education and housing, highways, air traffic control, building maintenance, national parks, law enforcement—all of those "other" budget items lumped dismissively under the heading of "social programs." Adding in these items doubles the number of families, which amounts to a number greater than all of the taxpayers in the United States. What's missing?

Some of the difference is made up by corporate income taxes, federal excise taxes, import duties, and other sources of revenue. But a sizable portion is made up by the federal budget deficit. In most years, the government spends a great deal more than it takes in as revenue (the current budget surplus is a rarity, made possible by unexpected growth in revenues owing to the economic boom of the late nineties). This difference must be paid somehow—Boeing and Lockheed insist on being paid for the airplanes they sell to the air force—so the government borrows the difference. In 1997, the amount the government had to borrow to cover its expenses was about $107 billion, or the tax-burden equivalent of 21 million families.

Another way to understand the military budget is to compare what is spent for the military with what is spent on other federal programs; that is, what could be purchased with the same money. For example, the entire federal expenditure for transportation amounted to only $39 billion, or 2.5 percent of the budget in 1996. The entire education, training, and social services budget was $52 billion, or 3.3 percent of the total. The cost of the entire U.N. campaign to eradicate smallpox all over the world came to the cost of just two of the navy's F-30 class frigates.

It seems clear that defense acquisition is the place to look for federal budget reductions. As of November 1997, the House defense authorization bill included $331 million as a "down payment" on nine new B-2s. Assuming the production cost of each unit (not counting any more research and development costs) is about $1 billion, that small down payment would incur an obligation to spend about $9 billion in future years. That would be enough to cover the entire federal budget for agriculture, or nearly all the budget for health research.

Moreover, the purchase of a weapons system is only part of its cost, as anyone who owns a car will understand. Figure 5.2 shows the costs associated with a major weapons system over its life cycle. Before a system like a tank or helicopter can be purchased it must be designed, and the government pays every dollar of that cost to the contracting firm that designs it, plus profit and fees. Furthermore, each weapon requires maintenance personnel to keep it in working order. For exotic items like helicopters, every hour of operation can require many hours of maintenance, and that maintenance is performed by a soldier, sailor, or airman who must be paid, housed, and trained to do it. Each weapon also requires a ready source of spare parts, which means that a whole system of supply depots must be kept stocked. This is akin to operating a worldwide chain of department stores, except that customers never pay for what they buy.

Because operating and support costs actually comprise the bulk of a system's costs over time, it is likely that reductions in new acquisitions would lead to further savings in operation and maintenance in the future. It is for this reason that the acquisition of weapons systems is highlighted in the discussion of the workings of the military-industrial complex.

Explaining the High Cost of the Military

In the summer of 1989, Congress took its first tentative steps toward doing something about the B-2 (Stealth) bomber. A single week's headlines on the network news made the following revelations: The Stealth was planned to cost $600 million per aircraft (up $100 million from the projections made a month earlier); each Stealth would probably wind up costing closer to $800 million to $1 billion before the project was through; the Soviets probably already had countermeasures that would

FIGURE 5.2   Life Cycle of a Major Weapons System

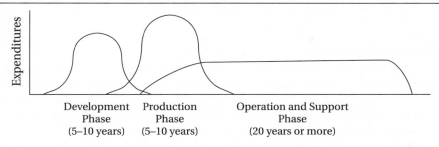

render the Stealth visible to radar; U.S. military doctrine did not really have a place for a bomber in a strategic role anymore, especially since the B-1 bomber was already in full-scale production; and Northrop, the builder of the Stealth, was under indictment for fraud in the pricing of Stealth contracts.

Faced with all this, the House of Representatives voted not to scrap production of the bomber, but rather to reduce the number to be produced that year from three planes to two. The end result of this was to actually *increase* the cost of each aircraft. Incidentally, in the same week, Congress was trying to restore to the budget funding for continued production of the F-14 fighter, which the Pentagon did not even want.

The Stealth is not a unique weapons system, at least not in terms of the way it was procured and the problems it developed. Virtually all major weapons systems run into many of the same difficulties. The army's M-1 Main Battle Tank turned out to be less reliable, less effective, and more than twice as expensive as promised (Oster and Ingersoll 1983). Maverick antitank missiles, at $70,000 a copy, are so expensive that troops never get to fire them in training. After all, firing one is like shooting a Mercedes. The navy's Aegis radar system, at $1 billion per ship, was supposed to identify, track, and prioritize dozens of targets at a time. In the first combat action seen by an Aegis-class destroyer, it shot down an Iranian civilian airliner.

Small systems are not immune. The army's M-16 rifle, introduced during the Vietnam War, was known to jam unpredictably in combat, costing many American lives (Fallows 1981). Congressional representatives received heartbreaking letters from soldiers recounting the deaths of comrades shot while trying to clean their weapons.

Further, some successes in military development have been suppressed. The M-16 described above, for example, was a modification of the AR-15, a highly effective and reliable rifle, changed by army brass to use a larger caliber bullet and the army's "traditional" gunpowder. The air force's A-10 attack aircraft is devastating to enemy tanks and cheap, but the air force does not like to perform combat support missions (a secondary, supporting role to the ground troops, and dangerous besides) so the army has largely taken over the role with its own helicopter fleet. The army cannot have its own A-10s because fixed-wing aircraft are the reserved bailiwick of the air force.

In short, the procurement system of the U.S. military establishment is structured in such a way as to virtually guarantee that the taxpayer will spend more than promised for weapons whose performance is less than promised. The examples given here are not unique, and in fact have become so typical that taxpayers and those who represent them have come to expect these sorts of problems. It is this typicality that makes one suspect that this is a structural problem, built in to the system rather than a "flaw" or "slippage" within it. How did it get this way? I explore here several different kinds of explanations for the waste that is found in the military acquisition process. These are not necessarily independent explanations; they operate at different levels of analysis and in fact could be mutually reinforcing.

Explanation One: Contracting and the High Cost of Saving Money

One reason the government overspends for weapons can be found in the cost-controlling procedures built into the acquisition system. The process by which the U.S. military buys weapons is one that has never been rationally planned or designed. Rather, it is a complex mixture of free enterprise and state socialism that has evolved over a hundred years or so by the accretion of layer upon layer of bureaucratic controls and procedures. The beginning of the "modern" military acquisition system can be traced as far back as the Civil War, when the Union first implemented a centralized system by which weapons and supplies are purchased from private industrial firms, or *contractors.*

Those days also saw the first large-scale abuses by contractors and military procurement officials. Thus began an endless cycle of regulations, followed by new contractor strategies, followed by more regulations. In each iteration of the cycle, the process has become ever more cumbersome, rigid, and costly. Each contracting difficulty has been met with a new layer of rules and procedures, each requiring more personnel to monitor and more paperwork to be filed. Ironically, this has increased the expense to the taxpayers in a number of ways, and has actually helped contractors increase their security and profits.

For one thing, the immense amount of paperwork and legalistic procedure has created huge entry barriers into military work. Only companies large enough to support a sizable government-sales bureaucracy can afford even to submit proposals for any but the most mundane procurement items. For example, an acquisition team on which I served received two competing proposals for a rotor blade to be used on the UH-1 helicopter, each of which formed a stack of paper roughly four feet high.

Furthermore, acquisition rules have developed that require the government to take into account the "track record" of a manufacturer in deciding whether to award a contract to it or to a competitor. This takes the form of judging the extent to which the contractor is "qualified" to produce the item—whether it has the capital, plant, and personnel to succeed. Again, one can imagine why the rule was made—in the past there were cases in which inexperienced or dishonest contractors submitted proposals priced unrealistically low. According to the rules, the government had to accept the proposal, it being the lowest bid, the contractor was unable to perform and went bankrupt, and the government was left holding the bag.

The creation of such entry barriers has tended to ensure the predominance of a handful of large corporations in supplying the government with its weapons. What this means is that the government and the contractors have become mutually dependent on each other. Lockheed-Martin, General Dynamics, and the other major defense firms would die without constant infusions of defense acquisition funds. But the government is also dependent on these firms for its supply of weapons. It cannot afford to let any of its big suppliers go out of business, for that would shrink the number of producers, creating monopoly conditions, or, even worse in the eyes of the military, it would eliminate suppliers of certain kinds of systems altogether.

The military's concern for this is expressed by its desire to maintain a "warm base" of manufacturers. Pointing to the stunning success of America's industrial establishment in mobilizing for World War II, procurement officials are quick to assert that multiple producers of aircraft, ships, tanks, and the like ought to be kept afloat in the event of some future mobilization. Thus Lockheed was "bailed out" of the financial losses it incurred on the air force's C-5A in the 1970s, even though the plane was beset with design and production troubles (Fitzgerald 1972). Similarly, three manufacturers of helicopters (Bell, Sikorski, and Boeing/McDonnell-Douglas), still generally share the few major contracts available in order to keep them all alive.

In addition to the entry barrier problem, the development of increasing layers of rules has also directly contributed to the costs of military hardware. The contractor's effort and personnel involved in following the rules—monitoring costs, producing paperwork, accounting, and the like—are all reimbursable as a part of the contract cost. Further, the calculation of the allowed profit margin in a contract may include all those costs in its base. That is, contractors not only get reimbursed for following bureaucratic rules, but they make a profit on it. In the end, the more red tape a contract involves, the more profit the contractor makes.

This is not to mention the cost the government incurs in the process of buying a major weapons system. A team on which I served to procure turbine engines for a new fleet of helicopters involved nearly a hundred people and lasted more than two years. Adding up the salaries, benefits, supplies, building space, travel, and the like gives an estimated total cost of about $15 million just to operate the team. Of course, this team amounts to only the tip of the iceberg, for there is also a large number of accountants, engineers, cost analysts, lawyers, and others whose task it is to plan, manage, and monitor the overall development and fielding of the system, and then to oversee the continued purchases of spare parts and replacement engines over the life span of the fleet. In the end, it is probably reasonable to suggest that the cost to manage the acquisition of a major weapons system amounts to 10 or 15 percent of the system's production cost.

The mutual dependence between government and defense contractor, and the resulting concentration of the defense business in a few large firms, has made it difficult for the government to strike a "hard bargain" with them. There are few serious competitors that the government can go to for aircraft, tanks, or ships. To counteract its disadvantage, the government has developed over time a variety of procedures and structures for purchasing major systems.

Each of the service branches—army, navy, and air force—is made up of a number of major "commands." Within the army, for example, three of the most prominent are Forces Command (FORSCOM), the organization that contains fighting troops, Training and Doctrine Command (TRADOC), which analyzes how best to fight, and Army Material Command (AMC), which is responsible for procuring and maintaining weapons and supplies. It is the mission of AMC to "put a gun in the hands of the soldier"; that is, to ensure that the fighting troops are supplied with whatever they need to defeat the enemy.

The actual process of acquiring a new major weapons system can begin at any level of the respective service's organization. In the army, the initial impetus for a new system can come from either of the three major commands discussed. Most commonly, analysts either at TRADOC or at AMC will initially develop the sketchy idea for a new system. This idea will usually take the form of a set of requirements for the new system— that it be able to carry a certain number of troops at a certain speed, or that it be able to shoot so many rounds per minute, or that it be able to penetrate armor of a certain thickness.

These ideas typically emerge from something called "threat analysis." TRADOC traditionally has used information gathered from the intelligence community and from combat experience to analyze the latest Russian weapons and combat techniques, and to develop ideas for either new weapons or new tactics by which U.S. troops can defeat the "threat." A typical threat analysis will analyze the new, thicker armor on the latest Soviet tank, for example, and determine whether or not (or more likely, the probability with which) U.S. antitank rockets can penetrate it. Simulation gaming and a great deal of statistical analysis are often used, detailing the grim probabilities of success or failure in terms of survivability, "kill ratios," and similar figures.[2]

The Research and Development Phase.   At some point, a decision will be made at the service level (secretary of the army, or secretary of the navy, for example) to begin the first stages of development for the system. This is the real "birth" of a weapons system, and the beginning of its acquisition cycle, a span of time that can run fifteen years or more. A typical acquisition cycle is diagrammed in Figure 5.3. Ideas for the system may be sketched out by government analysts (with the eager help of contractors) until there is enough detail to make a case for spending real money to have a contractor design it. At this point, congressional approval is required for funding.

This is the first of three major milestones for a weapons system, for it represents the military's first encounter with the legislative branch. If approved, Congress will release funds for the *Full-Scale Engineering Development* necessary to design the system. At this point, the military will select a contractor—Boeing, Sikorsky, or General Dynamics, for example—to design a system that meets certain specifications and to produce a prototype (a working model) of it. The simplest strategy here would be to simply pick a single contractor to design the system, but there are problems with that approach. For one thing, on what basis shall the contractor be selected? A fair competition among bidders would require that there be concrete standards by which each contractor's proposal can be judged. But since the system has not even been designed yet, such standards are difficult to come by, and besides, there is no way to judge whether a contractor has met the standards until the system is actually built. Thus, the only reasonable strategy for the competing contractors is to make extravagant claims about the high performance and low cost of the system they are going to design. Needless to

---

[2]With the dissolution of the Soviet Union, these analyses have often shifted to a focus on Middle East or terrorist threats—a good example of how military staffs always seem to prepare to fight the last war.

118

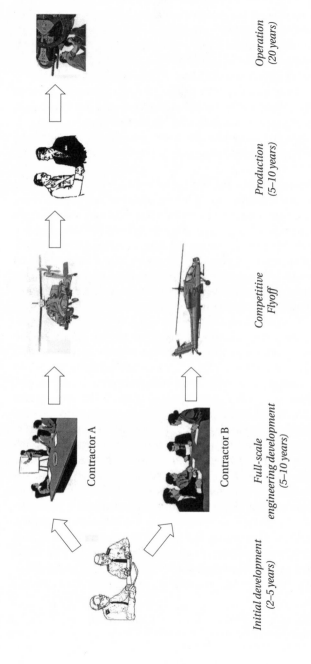

FIGURE 5.3 Typical Acquisition Cycle for a Major Weapons System
SOURCE: One Mile Up, Inc., and Corel, Inc.

say, the system is unlikely to live up to such claims in the end, and the government tends to end up selecting the contractor with the best sales force, rather than the one with the best system.

One might think that this problem can be avoided by refusing to pay the contractor until the system is designed and the prototype has been produced and tested. But even the largest contractors are unlikely to have enough capital to fund their own development efforts, and even those who do are usually unwilling to bear the risk of spending that much effort without the promise of a sure payoff.[3]

The government's solution to this dilemma has typically been to award *two* development contracts, to two separate contractors. Each firm then independently develops a system to meet the performance requirements, and each is free to use its own approach. At the end of the development phase, each contractor builds one or more prototypes and a "competitive flyoff" (or, one presumes, a "sailoff" or "shootoff") is held to determine which design is better. This decision is made by a Source Selection Evaluation Board (SSEB), an ad hoc government team composed of engineers, managers, lawyers, and cost analysts from various offices within the command.

The contractor with the winning design is awarded the production contract, which is the really lucrative part of the business. The promise of a production contract is usually incentive enough to make each contractor perform its best in designing the best-performing system. In the case of a transport plane, for example, each contractor might try to make a plane that would carry the largest load, fly the fastest, go the farthest, and land on the shortest runway (assuming that these characteristics are a part of the performance requirements). But this strategy of awarding two development contracts introduces new problems. First, a great deal of money is wasted on paying the losing contractor to develop the system that is not selected. As a matter of fact, the military still owns the prototypes of nonselected helicopters, airplanes, and vehicles never manufactured. In effect, the military pays double for development.

The bigger problem, though, is that the cost of manufacturing the system must also be considered here. Given a choice between two systems that perform equally well, it is not only fair but wise to buy the one that will have the lowest price tag. Unfortunately, while the competitive flyoff is a fine method for determining which of two systems performs the best,

---

[3]There are exceptions, though. Northrop spent its own money to develop the A-5 fighter (later designated the A-20), in hopes of selling it both to the U.S. Air Force and foreign countries. Northrop learned its lesson when the Carter administration reneged on an implied promise to buy a substantial quantity of the planes.

TABLE 5.2   Hypothetical Tank Production Schedule

Year	Quantity
1998	50
1999	150
2000	800
2001	800
2002	800
2003	800
2004	800
2005	800

it is a poor way to determine which is the most cost-effective. In fact, since only one or two prototypes have been built, it is difficult to determine which design is the more costly. The SSEB tries to estimate the cost of each system based on the cost of the prototypes and by other statistical methods, but such estimates are of course prone to considerable error. Besides, the data on which cost estimates are based come mostly from the contractor's own records. Therefore, it is in each contractor's interest to understate the cost of producing its system, and since the flyoff tests produce "real" results while costs are only "guesses," the government is likely to buy the top-performing but more expensive system.

The government tries to solve this problem by making the winning contractor actually produce the system for the low cost it claims. In this way, the contractor loses money if it understates its production costs. For example, Contractor A and Contractor B might design two tanks that perform equally well. But Contractor B claims it can produce its tank for $1.2 million each while Contractor A's price is $1.4 million. The government naturally gives the production contract to the lower-cost contractor, and in order to keep the contractor from understating costs, offers to pay only $1.2 million apiece.

This would work fine, except that production contracts are awarded for only a year at a time. The entire production schedule of, say, 5,000 tanks might stretch out for many years. Moreover, the first year's contract is usually for a relatively small number of units, as the contractor builds up to full speed. A typical production schedule might look like the example in Table 5.2.

It therefore becomes reasonable for the contractor to purposely take a loss on the first year's production of 50 tanks, in order to win the contract. This loss is more than recovered in later years when it has a monopoly on the production of the remaining 4,950 tanks, and can charge virtually anything it wants. This practice of taking a loss on the first year or two of a contract in order to win the competition is called *buying-in*.

The government has tried a variety of approaches to combating buy-in. The most straightforward is to attempt to estimate each contractor's production costs independently, to determine which of the competing systems will be the most expensive. This is fraught with difficulty since there is little information on which to base such estimates, and what little there is must be obtained from the contractor. Thus the contractor has many opportunities to create and pass along optimistic cost assumptions. A second and more novel approach is to award production contracts to both contractors, but to give the largest share of each year's production to the firm that quotes the lowest price for that year. For example, in the second year of production, the government might decide to purchase fifty aircraft. Contractor A might submit the lowest price, so it is awarded a contract for thirty of the aircraft while Contractor B receives a contract for the other twenty. This has the advantage of pitting the two contractors against each other in competition for the entire acquisition.

One drawback, however, is that the relative share of each contractor must be carefully determined beforehand, else both firms might decide the smaller share is not worth the trouble and thus both might submit excessively high prices. Another problem with this strategy is that both contractors are producing the same system, which was designed by only one of them. This means that the contractor that submitted the winning design must somehow be forced to share all of its design information with its competitor. This might seem easy enough in principle, since designs are documented in engineering drawings. But in practice it is very difficult because there remain many techniques and procedures that might work better in the original designer's plant, or with their tools, or even their management style. Thus, the losing designer is inherently disadvantaged in such a competition.

The Production Phase. Upon completion of the research and development of a system's design and the selection of a design based on performance of the prototype and cost estimates, the military returns again to Congress to seek funding for the system's production. This constitutes the second major milestone in a system's life cycle. It is here that the big money can be made, and at virtually no risk. For major systems like aircraft or tanks, production might run into hundreds or even thousands of units. The fleet of 132 B-2 bombers initially planned, for example, would have brought in over $79 *billion* to Northrop, its prime contractor. And at the 15 percent profit that is typically allowed on such a contract, $12 billion would be clear profit to shareholders. Clearly, much is at stake in winning a production contract for a major defense system, and it is no wonder that firms are often willing to "buy-in" to a program at a loss in order to reap profits later. It is also no wonder that the government goes to great lengths to try to avoid mistakes at this point.

The main risk in awarding a production contract is that once one or another contractor is selected to produce a system, that firm has a virtual monopoly from that point on. Whether the winning contractor has bought-in to the contract or not, that firm usually has a great deal of control over the price it charges for the system. The government has few options after the first couple of years, since it cannot go back to the losing contractor and start fresh. If the contractor quotes an unreasonably high price, the government could simply refuse to buy the tanks, planes, or ships altogether in an attempt to drive the cost down, but this is more difficult to do in practice than in theory. By this point considerable money has already been spent on research and development and on production, and many careers in both the military and Congress are at stake. Another possibility might be to take the design to another firm to build the system more cheaply, but it is probably true that the design is simply an expensive one, and another contractor would not be able to produce it any more cheaply.

The only reasonable approach is for the government to continue trying to estimate the cost of producing the system each year, and offer only that much. In fact, this is typically what is done. In the example of the 5,000 tanks, the government would assemble a *should-cost team* each year to participate in the negotiation of that year's production contract. The should-cost team normally travels to the contractor's plant and inspects its production records and methods to arrive at its estimate. However, it relies largely on historical costs—what the contractor has charged in previous years for the system—in determining what the current year's costs ought to be. The end result of this process is that each year's contract is based mainly on the cost of last year's production. Thus if the contractor is inefficient in production methods for the first couple of years, follow-on contracts will be negotiated at excessively high prices. If the contractor's efficiency is improved in following years, the difference is pure profit. Needless to say, this is frequently what occurs.

To make matters worse, the budget allowed for a project is a matter of public record, because Congress must pass an appropriations bill that funds the project before the military can negotiate the contract. In effect, the contractor knows how much the government has to spend on the system, and how high it is able to go in its negotiation. In the end, once the initial production contract is signed, the government has very little leverage over the contractor. Consequently, serving on should-cost teams can be demoralizing for a government cost analyst, for it becomes clear very early on that the contractor has the upper hand in the negotiations. In negotiating the contract to upgrade the CH-47 helicopter, the contractor's (Boeing-Vertol's) second proposal was priced *higher* than its first. In that negotiation, the two parties simply drifted further apart for weeks until the army agreed to give Boeing virtually all the money it asked for.

The Operating and Support Phase.   The final phase of a weapons system's life cycle is the longest, and the one in which the bulk of a system's costs are incurred. This is the operating and support phase, in which the system is "fielded"; that is, put into regular use in a fighting unit. Although it may first appear that spending for the system is largely finished at this point, it has actually just begun, for it is here that the costs of fuel, operating crew pay, maintenance, spare parts, and myriad other items are incurred. As shown in Figure 5.2, over the twenty-year life span of a typical major system (a helicopter, for example) the government will spend far more for these items than the total cost of developing and building the aircraft.

That operating costs are the bulk of the total cost of ownership is significant, because decisions regarding which of two systems to buy generally must be made in the absence of any real data on operating costs. For example, if two contractors design helicopters that perform equally well, the government naturally desires to buy the one that requires the least maintenance, the cheapest spare parts, and the simplest repair procedures. In fact, such considerations may well be more important than sheer speed or lift capacity or lethality; a high-tech helicopter under repair in a hangar is of no use at all.

Thus the military spends a good deal of effort attempting to estimate the operating costs of a system before it signs a production contract. But such estimates are fraught with even more error than production cost estimates, since they are based on gross assumptions about the way in which the system will perform. Moreover, what little information is available comes from the contractor's engineers and salespeople. In short, most of a system's costs are not known at the time of purchase. It is very much like deciding which car to buy based only on the purchase price and a test drive. One tries to get a feeling for how fuel-efficient each car is, and certainly how reliable it is, but hard information is lacking.

In the end, the procedures by which the government buys weapons are based largely on vague assumptions and unreliable data. It is no wonder, then, that these decisions are often influenced strongly by considerations other than rational calculations of cost, reliability, and performance.

Explanation Two:
Pork-Barreling and Acquisition Politics

A second major source of problems stems from the inherently political nature of defense acquisition. Congress has ultimate control over the spending of government funds, and the election of congressional representatives is the way in which citizens exercise power. But congressional representatives are elected not by national consensus, but by fairly small and geographically defined constituencies. Each representative must be reelected every two years in order to stay in office; for senators it is every six years. More significant, success or failure in office tends to be determined by whether the "home folks" believe their parochial interests have been well represented. It is especially good to have contributed to business expansion in one's district.

What this means for defense acquisition is that a representative whose district includes defense contractors had better protect the interests of those contractors. If the representative votes to fund an expensive weapons system that is manufactured within the district, then the economy booms, unemployment is low, and he or she will be difficult to beat in the next election. The tremendous force of this compulsion to vote for weapons systems lies in the fact that it comes from both the business community and from the average citizen. Should the representative vote against the purchase of the system, he or she is viewed as acting against the economic interest of nearly everybody—depriving the contractor of profitable business and depriving citizens of jobs. For both capital and labor to stand on the same side of an issue is unusual, and presents an irresistible force to an elected representative.

This is not a subtle undercurrent by which representatives are gently wafted along with the corporate tide. On the contrary, everyone involved in the process is perfectly familiar with the system, and plays it to the hilt. I once attended a briefing intended to convince an army official to approve the go-ahead for production of the AH-64 Apache attack helicopter. One of the charts included in the briefing was a map of the United States that showed, by different colors, the amount of money that would go into each state as a result of producing the system. Further, the biggest subcontracts would be awarded to manufacturers located in key congressional districts—that is, those represented by members of the committees which participate in acquisition decisions.

Former secretary of the navy John Lehman was frank about the realities of the acquisition game. One of his brainchildren was the "home port" system of basing the various naval fleets. This system dissolved the centralized port facilities the navy had used for decades and dispersed the fleets all over the American coastline. The dispersal added tremendous costs to the navy's operations, first in start-up construction costs at each new port, then in unnecessary duplication of facilities and personnel. Each port had to have complete maintenance and service facilities, even though the fleet based in that port might be gone to sea for months at a time.

The navy's public argument was that the United States was less vulnerable to a single devastating attack—like the one at Pearl Harbor—if the fleet was spread out. But Lehman's more candid view was that more members of important congressional committees could be rewarded with bases in their districts this way. More than a third of the members of the House Armed Services Committee were from states slated to receive new ports. And of the sixteen members of its military construction subcommittee, eight came from those states, moving the landlocked Senator Goldwater to quip that he had thought of having a home port in Arizona (United States Congress 1986: 474).

The results of pork-barrel acquisition politics are many. First, when decisions are made whether to go ahead with an expensive and ineffective weapons system or to discontinue it, congressional representatives and the military often find themselves on the same side of the debate. The military wants the system, even if ineffective, because it believes that problems can be worked out later. The representatives want the contracts and jobs in their home districts. Even representatives who do not stand to win contracts may support the system because of conservative or militaristic political leanings or to maintain friendly relations with the military for future use. Thus many systems are bought that are either too expensive, ineffective, or redundant.

A second problem is that decisions of which of two systems should be selected (at the beginning of the production phase, for example) will often hinge on the political support of each contractor. A helicopter contract will frequently pit the representatives and senators of Texas (home of Bell Helicopter) against those of Pennsylvania (home of Boeing-Vertol), Connecticut (Sikorsky), and California (McDonnell-Douglas, formerly Hughes Helicopter). And political pressures do filter down to the level of the decision makers. In 1982 Senator Weicker of Connecticut sent to an SSEB a particularly passionate letter of support for the proposal of Kaman Aircraft, which was competing against Bell Helicopter to make rotor blades for the UH-1 helicopter. It stands to reason that when source-selection decisions are made on political bases, inefficiencies are bound to result.

Finally, political influence on military acquisition encourages decentralization of production. Because congressional representatives benefit from contracts in their districts, the military goes to great lengths to reward as many representatives as possible. The way to do this is to favor contractors who propose to employ many subcontractors to build the system. This tactic reached its height in the production of the AH-64 Apache attack helicopter. The prime contract to build the aircraft was awarded to McDonnell-Douglas (which, incidentally, was also awarded funding for an entire new plant in Arizona in which to manufacture it). But McDonnell's only task was to assemble the aircraft from major components that would be manufactured by hundreds of subcontractors. Engines came from General Electric, entire airframes from Ryan Aircraft, targeting systems from Martin-Marietta, and so on. McDonnell actually "manufactured" almost nothing, but rather simply "integrated" and managed the final assembly.

Such practices run exactly counter to the kinds of business practices that a firm will undertake under "normal" competitive circumstances. Because each subcontractor will naturally make a profit on the work that it does, multiple levels of subcontracting adds layers of profit to the overall cost of the system. Thus when General Motors builds automobiles it does not subcontract its engines and transmissions; rather it seeks to integrate the process by manufacturing as much of the finished product as it can itself. In this way GM "captures" as much of the profit as possible. But in defense contracting, there are few incentives to contain overall costs since profit is virtually guaranteed under the terms of the contract. Thus the incentive is to do whatever is necessary to secure the contract in the first place.

Explanation Three: The "Moral" Imperative

Another underlying theme guiding military acquisition has to do with the appeal to cultural values that is made in the purchase of weapons. The moral foundation of American politics is rooted in militarism, often euphemistically expressed in the notion of the "strong defense." In fact, nothing less than the strongest of all military forces on earth is acceptable within the American political mythology. For evidence, one has only to look at the positions of the candidates in any presidential election since Roosevelt. In every case, both sides have sought to appear hawkish on defense (even George McGovern, who opposed the war in Vietnam, did so on grounds that it was not contributing to U.S. defense). Certainly the last three Republican victories have been won largely by characterizing the Democratic opponent as "soft" on defense.

Congress also is loath to appear ambivalent where military matters are involved. It is almost a sacred tradition within Congress to "stand behind" the president whenever he commits the U.S. military in an engagement. This tradition is so sacred, in fact, that Congress has even approved actions undertaken "behind its back" without prior consent or information. Only recently has this tradition begun to erode; for example, Senate Majority Leader Trent Lott criticized President Clinton's air attack on Iraq at the end of 1998.

It is simply easier to make a reasonable-sounding argument for more military spending to American voters than it is to argue for restraint and caution. First, it seems less risky to spend too much on defense than to spend too little. After all, the logic goes, if $100 billion more than necessary is spent to protect the United States, $100 billion has been lost. But if $100 billion too little is spent, all could be lost. This argument can appear especially compelling when the world is characterized as a dangerous place, full of enemies and "evil empires" just waiting to overrun American allies or even the homeland itself.

This argument is much like the one that unscrupulous insurance salespeople use on the elderly when they tout worthless cancer policies. They exaggerate the fear of a disease that, while particularly nasty and expensive, is not especially likely to strike. Then they overstate their ability to protect the customer if the unthinkable happens. The parallel is a close one. The defense establishment is fond of promoting fears of the bogeyman; variously the terrorist threat, nuclear attack, the domino theory, the takeover of western Europe, the new Hitler in Iraq, the even newer Hitler in Kosovo, and a variety of other threats. These all seem to be terrible eventualities indeed, but Americans seldom stop to think about how likely or real any of them are. The military's answer is that they are not just likely but inevitable if the United States lets down its guard, even for a moment.

Like the insurance huckster, the military exaggerates its ability to protect the country from each of these threats. The implication is that failure to keep spending for new weapons will result in dire consequences; conversely, lavish spending will guarantee security. But these claims are weak. Though American military might was successful in Iraq in 1991, it failed in Vietnam, has been both impotent and dangerous to civilians in Kosovo, and is simply not useful against terrorism. For that matter, the stupendous "victory" of the American military in the Gulf War failed to achieve any meaningful results in terms of advancement of U.S. interests. Saddam Hussein is still in power and the United States has fewer friends in the region than before the war.

It also came to light shortly following 1991 that the stunning success of America's high-tech weaponry was at least partly illusory. For example, the glowing official statistics on bombing effectiveness had referred not to the percentage of bombs that hit their targets but rather to the percentage that successfully dropped out of the aircraft. The vast majority of damage inflicted on enemy troops was, it turns out, inflicted not by "smart" weapons on pinpoint targets but by ordinary "dumb" bombs dropped en masse by ancient B-52 aircraft. The fallability of smart weapons has become more obvious in Kosovo, where the military has been unable to avoid repeated mistaken attacks on civilians, while showing little effect on Serb armed forces. Like the insurance customer, Americans live by the creed that "it is better to have and not need than to need and not have." The United States buys its military insurance policy without much examination of the fine print.

A second moral grounding of increasing defense costs lies in the way weapons have become increasingly reliant on high technology. Again, an analogy from the health field offers itself. In the 1960s a method was invented for keeping a person alive whose kidneys were not functioning. The miracle of kidney dialysis promised to save the lives of thousands of people by keeping them going until transplants could be arranged. The problem was that dialysis was hugely expensive; so expensive, in fact, that health insurers simply could not pay for their patients' dialysis without going bankrupt. In the end, the federal government stepped in and made dialysis available by using Social Security funds to pay for it.

Several principles of American values and beliefs are illustrated here. The most important is that no one must be allowed to die where there is a technology that might help. That is, no matter what the cost, each person has a right of access to that technology. Of course, dialysis is only one of many such medical "miracles" that people insist be made available. Open-heart surgery, transplants, exotic drugs, and many lesser miracles are considered appropriate treatment no matter how high the cost or how questionable the benefit.

Decisions to buy weapons follow much the same logic. In weapons technology, any capability that *can* be developed, *must* be developed. If a team of engineers claims it can devise an effective space-based laser weapon that can protect U.S. cities, who is to say no? There is a compelling moral logic that renders questions of cost unbroachable. In the same way that new medical technology must be employed, deadly weapons must be fielded. In war, as in medicine, Americans can't say no.

This "technological imperative" was well described by Jacques Ellul (1965), who asserted that the demands of technology ("technique," in his usage) drive the other institutions of society, rather than the other way around.

> First, technique is autonomous with respect to economics and politics. We have already seen that, at the present, neither economic nor political evolution conditions technical progress. Its progress is likewise independent of the social situation. The converse is actually the case, a point I shall develop at length. Technique elicits and conditions social, political, and economic

change. It is the prime mover of all the rest, in spite of any appearance to the contrary and in spite of human pride. (1965, p. 133)

Ellul's discussion is similar to Weber's analysis of the growing rational imperative in Western culture. In Weber's view, the insistence on efficiency above other considerations causes goals and values to be eliminated from decision-making processes. In weapons procurement, this means that "more bang for the buck"—or, even more simply, "more bang, period"—becomes the sole criterion for decisions, while questions about the actual need for a weapon are not raised. The division of responsibility for procurement between Congress and the military and between the various offices within the military only add to this goal-displacement because each decision maker sees only a small part of the "big picture."

Even worse, the compulsion to have the "state of the art" at all times further complicates the process of acquisition. Today, a major weapons system can take more than ten years to develop from early research and development (R&D) to full-scale production. In that time, literally hundreds of improvements are likely to be invented that would make it a more effective system. And the "threat" system is likely to be improved in hundreds of ways too, which renders the developing system useless.

What this means is that the design of the new system is constantly being revised and modified even as it is being developed, and this in itself is a major cause of cost increases. To understand why this is such a devastatingly costly phenomenon, imagine that you are designing an automobile. This vehicle is required to travel at eighty miles per hour, carry five passengers, and get twenty-five miles per gallon. After a year or so, the design team has worked out a preliminary design for the car, which may include drawings and specifications for the engine, transmission, brakes, steering, and other systems.

Now further imagine that a new requirement is added: The car is to be air-conditioned. The immediate response may be to simply install an air-conditioning unit under the hood. But there are problems. First, the body of the car was not designed to fit the bulky compressor and extra radiator under the hood. Also, increased electrical connections are needed to hook up the unit's controls. Further, a new pulley has to be added to the engine to turn the unit's compressor. Worse yet, the car no longer gets twenty-five miles to the gallon, nor will it go eighty miles per hour, because the air conditioner steals power from the engine. So the car will need a bigger engine to meet the requirements. This increases the car's weight and power, so a beefed-up transmission and drive train will be needed.

Of course, automobiles are relatively simple machines, and it would have been a simple matter to design the car originally with enough extra power and space to accommodate future requirements. But high-tech weapons systems are designed at the outset to be "cutting-edge" technologies. A new fighter for the air force, for example, cannot be designed with a little extra power and carrying capacity, because the requirements for the system are already just barely achievable. Even if this were not so, weapons are usually developed by two or more contractors competitively; no reasonable contractor is going to "design in" any more capability than is required by the contract.

One can imagine, then, how a constant tide of design changes—new requirements and capabilities—creates havoc in the process of developing weapons. The product of literally millions of engineers' labor hours may be crumpled up and thrown in the wastebasket during the design process.

The story of the army's "Aquila" remotely piloted vehicle (RPV) is a case in point. The RPV was intended to be a radio-controlled "drone" aircraft that could fly above the battlefield with a video camera and give the ground commander a view of the battle. The Israelis had had great success with their drones in earlier wars in the Middle East, using them to spot and draw fire from enemy surface-to-air missile installations.

The Aquila began life as a model airplane. In fact, the army actually hired an accomplished designer of hobby airplanes to participate in its development. It was to be powered by a McCulloch chainsaw engine. The whole idea was to make the Aquila so cheap that it would be expendable, so that a commander could afford to fly it into danger. But fairly early into the design process, requirements and capabilities began to be added to the design. In addition to a video camera, it was thought that other sensors would be good to have on board: infrared sensors to see at night, radar to see through clouds. Laser targeting devices would be good to have too. Soon the Aquila became expensive, and too valuable to fly into danger without protection. So armor plate was added, as well as electronic jamming and countermeasures equipment.

All of this made the Aquila quite heavy, so bigger wings were designed, and of course, a new engine. By this time, it had become so massive that the simple pole-mounted net that was to catch it when it returned from flight would be ripped to shreds in actual use. So the engineers set to work designing a much larger net that would "give" when the Aquila flew into it, thus saving itself and the plane. This turned out to be a much more complicated problem than designers had at first thought. It required a computer to control the amount of "give" in its recoil and, it turned out, a large truck to carry the net. What had begun as a model airplane with a jeep to carry it became a two-vehicle unit, complete with its own crew and computer. Moreover, the Aquila would now be a prime target to enemy troops; probably the first thing to be shot at. The Aquila was never completed; the army now has a scaled-down drone in use.

Explanation Four:
The Social Psychology of Acquisition

The fourth main theme running through the defense acquisition system involves the structure and culture of the organization that carries it out. Many analysts of defense acquisition problems regard them as the result of a conspiracy of greed among powerful individuals at the top of the defense and industrial establishment. For example, A. Ernest Fitzgerald, onetime management systems deputy for the air force, used White House and other memos to document his harassment and firing by the Nixon administration (Fitzgerald 1972). But conspiracy theories miss the point where this sort of ongoing, built-in malfeasance is found; even if one assumes that a small elite controls the system for its own benefit, how the system manages to cooperate with them is not explained. What Fitzgerald could not see from his high position was the incentive structure and belief system operating at the very lowest levels of the procurement hierarchy. At these levels, pervasive beliefs, values, and norms of military and corporate culture are at work.

The organizational structure of the acquisition system promotes and reinforces this culture. Early in the life of a weapons system, roughly at the beginning of full-scale research and development, the military establishes a project management office (PMO) whose task is to guide the system through development and production. It is the express task of this office to "advocate" for the system; that is, to do whatever is necessary to get the Pentagon and Congress to buy it. The PMO is responsible for working with contractors and potential contractors to establish the all-important requirements for the system (how fast it must go or how many troops it must be able to carry, for example). It is responsible for producing the request for proposal, the formal document that invites contractors to bid on the project. And during development and production, PMO managers and engineers oversee the contractor's work, making frequent visits to plants and headquarters. The PMO also develops the government's cost estimates, used to make decisions whether to go ahead in funding the system, and also to make decisions regarding which contractor is awarded the development and later the production contract.

Needless to say, the PMO becomes an unabashed cheerleader for the weapons system. This orientation is strongly reinforced by the composition and practices of the office. For example, PMOs for major systems are generally headed by a military officer, frequently a general. This makes the office highly autocratic, and this of course tends to discourage dissent or even unbiased analysis of costs and effectiveness. PMO staffs also tend to be dominated by engineers, with relatively few nonengineering contract and cost analysts. Given the interests of engineers, the result is a strong bias favoring high performance of the system over its cost. This is one reason why so many "bells and whistles" tend to be added to a system during its development phase, increasing costs tremendously. Finally, PMO offices often work longer hours, with unpredictable periods of overtime, out-of-town travel, and sudden crises when orders come from higher headquarters for one or another sort of study. This crisis mentality helps develop a high level of cohesion—esprit de corps in military parlance—which creates further pressures for conformity and against unbiased judgment.

Recognizing this, the military has established a system of "checks and balances" that check the PMO's analyses against the work of others. For example, at various milestones in the life of a developing system, the service branch assembles a committee of high-ranking military and civilian people to make the decision whether to continue work on the system. The most critical of these milestones occur just before full-scale development and again just before the production contract is awarded. This committee makes its "go/no-go" decision based on the information provided by the PMO and by a team of cost analysts assembled from independent cost analysis departments within the command. The critical basis for the decision is the system's estimated life-cycle cost—including development, production, and even operating costs.

The people in these departments refer to themselves as "honest brokers" whose task is to bring realism to the rosy estimates of the PMO staff. They even perform their cost analyses by different methods. The PMO typically develops its cost estimates from a "bottom-up" approach, counting up all the materials, parts, and labor hours needed to manufacture the aircraft or tank. The independent cost analysis team, by contrast, uses a "top-down" approach, estimating the cost of the system by statistical projections based on the costs of similar systems in the past.

In principle, the two cost estimates are used by the committee to make a determination regarding the future of the system. Ideally, they should agree. But what really happens is that there is often at first a wide disparity between the PMO estimate and the independent estimate. This is discovered before the estimates are presented to the committee (since the PMO and the independent team are usually just down the hall from one another), and because such a wide disparity reflects poorly on both sides, there is frequently an attempt to arrive at a compromise. But the compromise is not a single, agreed-upon estimate. Rather, the two sides seek to form two "realistic" estimates, just far enough apart to show that both sides worked independently and that both employed the appropriate biases in arriving at their number. At the same time, the estimates are close enough to lend credibility to both.

The PMO system therefore establishes an adversarial format for the military to make judgments about the continuation of weapons systems. At first glance this resembles the adversarial system of justice, by which the truth is found through the opposition of two sides in a dispute, each arguing their case as forcefully as possible. But this system is different, because the incentive structure of the military is such that neither side really has an interest in arguing against the promotion of a weapons system.

The weapons acquisition system is thoroughly immersed in the incentive structure of both corporate culture and the military. Rewards in both worlds are contingent on results and accomplishment, in the most concrete terms. In the contractor's corporate world, careers are advanced by successfully designing, manufacturing, and selling a product. And in this world, the virtue of these accomplishments is unambiguous: The task is to sell the product at greatest profit.

The remarkable thing is that the reward structure in the government world is strikingly similar. In the government, careers are made by successfully shepherding a system through the design, production, and fielding process. Rapid promotion comes to people who are associated with such successful programs; such associations become a pedigree. To have been a part of the original Apache attack helicopter team or the Bradley fighting vehicle team is to have won a battle to put a weapon in the hands of the soldier, possibly against stiff opposition from other weapons systems competing for scarce budget dollars. Conversely, to have been on a project that was canceled, such as the Cheyenne helicopter or the DIVAD air defense system, is to have known defeat. Luckily for government analysts, such experiences are extremely rare. Government procurement people know of and pay attention to this lineage; analysts are known by their colleagues in terms of the programs on which they've worked. And such teams typically sport icons of membership: coffee cups, tie tacks, and other tokens emblazoned with the product's picture or logo—handed out by the manufacturer—are the campaign ribbons of the civilian world.

Assignment to either PMO offices or special acquisition teams like source-selection boards or should-cost teams is highly desirable in the analyst community. Such assignments are a sign of favor from one's superiors. It is a vote of confidence from the boss that one is trusted to reflect well on the directorate and division. And favorable reviews from team leaders are virtual guarantees of quick promotion. There is a strong parallel to the military career: To have seen action in many procurement campaigns is comparable to the experienced combat veteran. And combat experience has always been the route to promotion.

It is no surprise, then, that there is a strong disincentive for members of such teams to criticize a weapons system or in any way to inhibit its progress through the procurement process. Even if there are hard-boiled skeptics among individual members—independent cost analysts, for example—the composition of such teams overwhelmingly favors engineers and PMO personnel with little interest in slowing the advance of military technology. Thus a collective conscience is formed; everyone understands that the promotion of the system is in the best interests of all. To further the Durkheimian metaphor, deviance from the accepted values and beliefs is roundly punished. The suggestion that there might be something wrong with the weapons system, or that perhaps it should not be bought, is simply never made.

The development of strong norms of conformity in this respect is made certain by the fact that, in the government, all work—even the smallest task—is carried out by teams and not individuals. Further, teams are always organized hierarchically, with a formally designated chief and one or more lower echelons; even a team of two people will have a chief. This way of organizing a task is virtually a recipe for what Irving Janis called "groupthink," a tendency for cohesive groups to rush toward consensus. When one analyzes a problem alone in order to make a decision or recommendation, the relevant information to be used is limited to the facts, theories, biases, and principles that make up one's model of what results can be expected from choosing various options. But when a group of other team members is involved, other information becomes relevant to the analyst. What do the other team members think? Do they have information I do not have? Is my opinion a minority opinion? What might be the consequences of voicing my views? Further, there are new risks involved in the decision. Not only might the analyst make or suggest the wrong solution to the task, he or she might make it *alone* in front of a group of peers and superiors. Thus the individual member's participation in the actual decision-making process may be diminished, or more likely, focused in an otherwise unexpected direction. That direction is typically toward what members perceive as the consensus of the group, and the result is a rush to conformity.

Another more pedestrian incentive is at work as well, at all levels of the institution. There is a great deal of occupational mobility on the part of managers, engineers, and analysts from the government to defense contractors. In fact, the Defense Department often serves as a training ground for many of the analysts, engineers, and salespeople on the contractor's team. This mobility has strong appeal, not only because the contractors are thought to pay better than civil service, but also because there is a great deal of prestige attached to working in the "real" world, in which people engage in the task of actually producing a product. People who work for the contractor are actually in day-to-day contact with the technology at hand.

Even among people who harbor no secret hopes to work for Boeing or General Dynamics, the contractor's personnel carry a certain mystique. They are viewed as more independent and thus more powerful than government analysts (who refer to themselves by such derogatory terms as "weenies" and "dog robbers"). Negotiating teams sent by the contractor are always compact, including only a dozen or so people, in contrast to the bloated hordes of weenies fielded by the government. And the contractor's team almost never includes women or minorities. Most important, the contractor's people work for the team that nearly always "wins," insofar as they are thought always to get the best of the government in negotiations. The desire to look one's best and even to ingratiate oneself before the contractor's people is therefore understandable. It is highly flattering to be thought well of by the "real men" of the contractor's world.

At the higher ranks, the career movement goes in both directions. Senior analysts and managers often retire from government to take high-prestige, low work jobs with contractors. This is especially common among retiring military officers. The project manager of the Apache helicopter, as a typical example, became a European sales executive for Martin-Marietta shortly after his retirement. Martin-Marietta had supplied much of the electronic gear for the Apache. In the other direction, a good many executives leave defense firms to take senior executive and politically appointed positions in the government. Many deputy secretaries and undersecretaries of defense and of the various service branches are recruited from these ranks.

One function of this "revolving door" policy is that it helps ensure that the Defense Department is led by people experienced in the management, production, and sales techniques of the major defense firms. Presumably, their experience is valuable both in instigating weapons programs and in negotiating with contractors. At the same time, it seems clear that this sort of boundary crossing creates inherent conflicts of interest. On one hand, military executives exert their greatest influence over negotiations with contractors and evaluations of their products just when they are about to retire, and are casting about for opportunities. This is exacerbated by the fact that most military officers retire at a relatively early age, fully expecting to work for another fifteen years or so.

On the other side of the coin, the upper ranks of Defense Department leadership are loaded with executives from the firms with which they are

TABLE 5.3   Weapons Systems Cost Terms

	• Recurring production
	  – engineering
	  – tooling
	  – manufacturing
	  – quality control
	  – profit and fees
		= TOTAL PRODUCTION COST

Plus:	• Engineering changes • Government-furnished equipment	= TOTAL HARDWARE COST
Plus:	• Nonrecurring production • System test and evaluation • Project management	= TOTAL FLYAWAY COST
Plus:	• Peculiar support equipment • Data • Operational/site activation • Training	= TOTAL WEAPONS SYSTEM COST
Plus:	• Initial spares and repair parts • Modification work orders	= TOTAL PROCUREMENT COSTS
Plus:	• Total research and development	= TOTAL ACQUISITION COSTS
Plus:	• Industrial facilities • Common support equipment • Operating and support costs	= TOTAL LIFE CYCLE COST

supposed to negotiate. They thus come to the job thoroughly immersed in corporate culture, imbued with the values and beliefs of the profit-making world. They have spent a lifetime viewing the government as a benevolent, bumbling adversary whose greatest fault has been the imposition of too many bureaucratic rules on the acquisition process, stifling the genius of capitalism. It is a case of the fox guarding the henhouse.

Explanation Five: The Bafflement of the Public

In addition to the general tendency to become desensitized to the huge numbers involved in understanding the cost of weapons, citizens are further kept in the dark about military costs because these costs are nearly impossible to report simply and clearly in the popular media. Table 5.3 shows the various cost definitions officially endorsed by the military. The lowest of these is "production cost," the price paid for the actual helicopter, for example. This does not begin to cover the government's full cost of buying the item. The government often has supplied the contractor with tools (government furnished equipment), or an entire factory to build the system, and this cost is not reflected in production cost. Nor are the costs of test-flying each helicopter (system test and evaluation) before the military accepts it. Further, the contractor charges an additional fee for managing the project (system project management)—separate from the cost of building the hardware and separate from profit—and this charge is not included in production cost. When these costs are added to hardware cost, the result is called "flyaway cost," ostensibly what it costs the government to actually take delivery of the aircraft.

But these costs are not all there is, either. Flyaway cost does not include "peculiar support equipment," the additional items needed to use and maintain that particular helicopter. This typically includes access ramps, work platforms, tools, ammunition and rocket loaders, transportation equipment, and other taken-for-granted items that are nonetheless necessary to actually using the system. These should not be assumed to be small items. One peculiar support item for the CH-47 helicopter was a "hoisting eye" that was used to pull the rotor shaft out of the helicopter for maintenance. It consisted of a small length of steel pipe, threaded at one end, flattened and drilled with a hole at the other end. Its price was $8,900.

Flyaway cost does not include "data," the manuals and other information needed to maintain the helicopter (typically produced at $8,000 per page), or the training of maintenance personnel. When these items are added to the system cost, they make up the "weapon system cost." But even the weapon system cost does not include the "initial spare and repair parts" needed to stock the maintenance shops found in army posts all around the world, so parts will be on hand when a helicopter comes in for repairs. When these expenses are added, the costs add up to "procurement cost."

Still, none of these costs include the tremendous expenditure for the research and development of the system in the first place. When R&D is included, it comprises "program acquisition cost," which fails to account for the operating and support cost for the lifetime of the system. When these costs are added up, the total is the "life cycle cost."

The cost figure reported in the news media might be any one of the above costs, and the citizen has no way of knowing which one. This is why people often receive apparently contradictory information about the cost of the latest controversial weapons system. In a political debate, people supporting the system will frequently report only the hardware cost while those against it might report the weapon system cost.

And there is more. The cost per unit of a weapons system varies over time, owing to a phenomenon called the "learning curve." When a contractor manufactures 100 helicopters, for example, the last one produced will cost a great deal less than the first, because the production line becomes more efficient with practice. This efficiency can come from gradual improvements in basic work techniques, finding new ways to organize the work flow, reducing wastage in the cutting or shaping of materials, finding or developing more effective tools, and a variety of other improvements. Learning curves are well understood in manufacturing and are known to follow a logarithmic curve. For example, an 85 percent learning curve is typical for helicopters, which means that the second aircraft produced will cost 85 percent as much as the first, the fourth will cost 85 percent of the second, the eighth 85 percent of the fourth, and so on (see Figure 5.4).

Learning curves are used in developing cost estimates for systems during the R&D and production phases of development. But learning curves also contribute to the public's confusion about the costs of weapons systems, because *the per-unit cost of the system depends on the number of units produced*. What this means is that the price per aircraft of the 21 B-2 bombers actually produced is much higher than the price per aircraft of the 132 originally planned. The result is a paradoxical increase in the per-unit cost of a system when the government decides to cut back on the number to be produced. Cutting the B-2 program in half, as was contemplated early in the program, would therefore have increased the cost of each bomber (assuming an 85 percent curve) from about $1 billion to about $1.23 billion. Thus the total cost of the production contract would not be cut in half, but "only" from $132 billion to $82 billion. The much deeper cuts that actually occurred created a steeper price increase because of an even greater loss of learning. Moving from a planned production run of 132 aircraft to 21 increases the cost by a factor of about 1.5, raising each aircraft's cost to $1.5 billion. Including research and development costs and averaging them across all 21 aircraft raises the per-aircraft cost to $2.6 billion (Brookings Institution 1998).

Needless to say, advocates of the system (the contractor, for example, and the congressional representative of its district) will proclaim loudly the cost savings to be realized by purchasing more copies of their system and the dire consequences of cutting back. Opponents of the system will ignore the unit-cost increases that come with reducing production.

FIGURE 5.4   Effects of Learning on Unit Cost (85 percent learning curve)

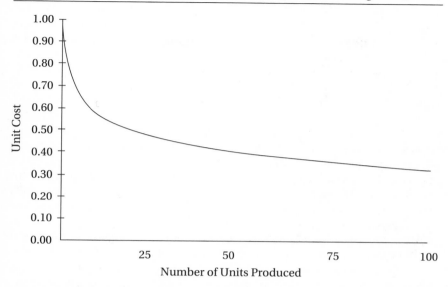

Either way, citizens are further alienated from the workings of the government by the variety of ways in which they can be baffled.

Macrosociological Views

Each problem outlined above offers a partial understanding of the deep-rooted inefficiencies of military procurement. It is likely that all the problems play a part in understanding how the system consumes so much of the national wealth. But an explanation is still missing for why these difficulties persist. As it happens, military waste provides useful illustrations of sociology's most basic theoretical perspectives: functionalism and conflict theory.

A Functionalist Explanation.   The functionalist approach to explaining intractable social problems is a powerful one. In fact, it might be said that the more intractable the problem or the more nonsensical a process seems, the more amenable it is to functional analysis. This sort of explanation relies on faith that social systems possess an underlying order, which may or may not be discernible at first glance because it may not make "sense" according to the conventions of a particular culture. Put another way, not all social structures or processes are "rational." The functionalist's article of faith is that there is some sort of "sense" to every persistent social process; every process serves some function for the social system.

By this reasoning, it is possible to explain why social processes that no one wants are able to persist. In what remains one of the most radical ideas in sociology, Durkheim posed a powerful explanation of the seeming constancy of deviance. Even though deviance is by definition considered undesirable in every society, every society seems to have a fair amount of it. Durkheim concluded that deviance must in some way help societies survive; he further suggested that it does so by enhancing social cohesion among the rest of the community and by reaffirming the values and norms of the group (1938). Other social ills have been explained by the same general method; for example, Gans offered a pointed and radical analysis of poverty (1972). In all of these analyses the thinking is the same: A structure or process that persists, especially despite efforts to eradicate it, must serve some function for society. The sociologist's task is to find that function.

Military waste is highly amenable to this sort of analysis. Waste is generally regarded as undesirable, no matter one's position on politics or militarism: Hawks and doves alike hate to waste money on defense. Hawks consider each dollar wasted a dollar that could buy more weapons; doves think it could buy something else entirely. Moreover, military waste has persisted despite apparently serious efforts to reduce it by any number of presidential administrations. In short, military waste may be viewed as a persistent social ill—like crime or poverty— that may be subjected to functional analysis.

It is not hard to think up possible functions of military waste. Most people recognize the argument that development of new weapons technologies, even if militarily questionable, can provide "spin-offs" of useful technological development. A good deal of aviation technology development can be attributed to military innovation, for example. Similarly, military waste employs many thousands of people who might otherwise appear on unemployment rolls; this may actually help buoy local economies in times of recession. One large defense contract to a local aircraft manufacturer or shipbuilder can keep a community afloat.

But there are less obvious functions too. In an earlier article (Fogarty 1991) I attempted to parallel Gans's explanation of the persistence of poverty by proposing several areas in which wasteful military spending might actually be functional for American society. *Social functions* are those that influence the structural characteristics of society. For example, wasteful military spending may actually be one mechanism by which Gans's permanent class of poor people is maintained. Considering the fact that even one sizable weapons system can cost more than the federal government's effort in public health, income assistance, or education, it seems clear that military waste is an excellent means of maintaining a class of poor people. And at the same time, the military provides its own safety valve by offering a social role to those it helps impoverish. The all-volunteer army is probably more effective in reserving the soldier's role for the poor than the draft deferments of earlier years.

Wasteful spending may also help strengthen social cohesion by legitimating outgroups and by enhancing what Kanter (1972) called "institutional awe." In the first place, the reporting of staggering military expenditures tends to make the foreign "threat" (until the 1990s, the Soviet Union) palpable. It is one thing to think about the "evil empire" in abstract terms, quite another to see the cost of defense coming out of one's paycheck. More tangible is the use of weaponry displays in military parades; in some cases they can provide a strong symbol of collective pride and identity. The annual May Day parade in Moscow under the Soviet regime was a case in point.

Political functions focus on the stabilizing effects of wasteful military spending. Large acquisition budgets can assist the government in maintaining control of the military. This can be a problem in highly militarized societies, but in the United States the government is seldom threatened politically by the military. Lavish spending on the military helps to curb its political ambitions, partly by creating opportunities for promotion through the fielding of new weapons systems. It is not uncommon for people to speak of a new aircraft or tank as a "career builder," offering new roles, new training, and new leadership opportunities for officers. Congressional representation is also stabilized by wasteful military spending, because incumbents are greatly advantaged by the ability to distribute large sums to contractors or bases within their districts.

The virtue of this sort of functionalist explanation is that it helps account for the apparent intractability of the problems of military waste. Functionalism provides an unseen "force" that discourages reform, which is helpful in understanding why reform fails to happen. At the same time, however, functional thinking fails to account for the mechanisms by which this force acts; the ways in which the system satisfies its needs. Thus, one is left with a radical interpretation of the circumstances, but no one to blame for them.

A Conflict Explanation. The conflict perspective offers a better chance of finding specific culprits in the promotion of waste. Taking as its fundamental premise the idea that social phenomena are best explained as the pursuit of material interests by groups or classes, it makes immediately clear where one should look for an understanding of wasteful mili-

TABLE 5.4   Boeing's Bill for Three Plastic Stool Caps[a]

1. Direct labor cost:		
Production labor hours	49.56 @ $12.35	$612.07
T&PP labor hours	2.86 @ $13.10	37.42
Tool labor hours	6.28 @ $12.80	80.38
Inspection labor hours	8.01 @ $12.93	103.57
Subtotal		$833.49
2. Indirect costs:		
Fringe benefits	41.5% of $833.49	$354.23
Manufacturer's overhead	66.71 hrs @ $15.33	1,376.83
Subtotal		$1,376.83
3. Material costs:		
Product material	$.26 x 3	$.78
Distributed material		53.52
Tool material		19.09
Subtotal		$73.39
4. Sum of 1, 2, and 3		$2,283.71
5. Direct charges: 43% of 4		$9.79
6. State and local taxes for 66.71 hrs.		$97.40
7. Total costs		$2,390.90
8. Profit fee @ 15%		$358.65
Total Charge for 3 Caps		$2,749.65

[a]Arithmetical errors are Boeing's.
SOURCE: Fitzgerald 1989: 158.

tary spending: the organized interests of corporate America, as expressed through the political system that serves it.

There is no shortage of evidence that these interests are advanced by military waste. The evidence takes two forms. First is the documentation of the detailed pricing structure that various contractors have used to generate inflated prices for weapons systems. Ernest Fitzgerald (1989) carefully documented many of these practices through his own experiences as a high official in the air force. For one example, Table 5.4 shows the pricing structure of "stool caps," those plastic feet that fit into the legs of a stool to keep it from scratching the floor.

There are also less direct methods. The price for one "alignment pin," a piece of support equipment used in the replacement of engine parts, was increased by specifying a level of precision in its manufacture that, while unnecessary, justified higher costs. The part is nothing more than a bit of stiff wire; simply by specifying its diameter to three decimal places its price was raised perhaps a hundredfold (Fitzgerald 1989: 212).

The sheer brazenness of the workups suggests that the defense analysts negotiating the contracts must have been either utterly incompetent or willing to do the bidding of corporate interests; Fitzgerald's analysis suggests the latter.

The second sort of evidence conflict analysts offer consists of documentation of the direct action of corporate lobbyists, negotiators, and executives to influence people making decisions for the military (see Figures 5.5 and 5.6). C. Wright Mills was, if not the first, the most memorable exponent of the idea that a power elite comprising corporate, political, and military leaders runs America (Mills 1956). His task was to demonstrate how these disparate groups interacted to serve common interests.

Excellent specific examples have been made available by the Project on Military Procurement, which published excerpts from the files of the Lockheed Corporation's lobbying efforts for the C-5 transport aircraft (Rasor 1983: 324–335). The "congressional contact tally" log was a listing of key members of Congress, including their committee appointments, contacts made by other defense contractors, and "further actions" planned; for example, "'Carlucci (deputy secretary of defense for acquisition) one-on-one' with Rep. Joseph Abbaddo," or "'Needs high level DoD/AF one-on-one" with Rep. Badham," or "'PAC committee wire' to Rep. Dornan."

Perhaps more graphic was Lockheed's "action/status" log of the same period, which laid out plans for contacts to representatives, senators, and executive branch and military decision makers. Examples: "Obtain White House L&L effort on house committees and member commitments"; "Draft letter to AF/CUA for White House use"; "Work on Dear Colleague ltr that other Committee Chairmen may be willing to sign"; "Energize all military associations & obtain leadership and 'back home' support." Such documents illustrate not only the contractors' efforts to exert influence directly, but also their role as hired guns in assisting one component of government in political fights with another. Thus, Lockheed drafted letters for White House officials to promote the C-5 to the air force. These accounts remain the most detailed and convincing descriptions available of the direct influence of corporations on the political and military decisions of the nation.

The close interaction of government with military and corporate interests should probably not come as too great a shock. As army chief of staff at the end of World War II, General Eisenhower proposed just such a cooperative relationship among these groups—and universities as well—as early as 1946 (Cancian and Gibson 1990: 167–169).

FIGURE 5.5   How It's *Supposed* to Work

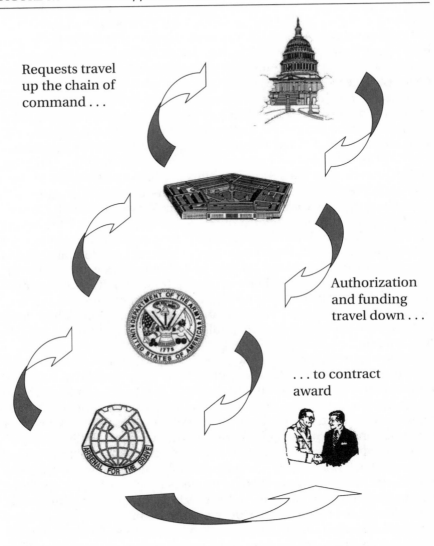

Requests travel up the chain of command . . .

Authorization and funding travel down . . .

. . . to contract award

SOURCE: One Mile Up, Inc. and Corel, Inc.

FIGURE 5.6   How It *Actually* Works

Contractor Representatives Lobby at Every Level
SOURCE: One Mile Up, Inc., and Corel, Inc.

One might think the end of the Cold War would outdate this discussion, but this is not the case. In fact, the apparent end of bipolar thinking has shaken the system very little. There has been a shift in the sorts of system demanded and developed by the military, as the long-range strategic capability becomes less important. The B-1 and B-2 bombers, the last of the Cold-War extravagances, are embarrassing anachronisms that came on line just as their usefulness was waning. However, there are plenty of new systems under development, most notably the X-22 advanced tactical fighter, the LHX helicopter, and a continuing growth in satellite communication and navigation systems. In some ways, times remain good for defense contractors as a larger variety of smaller systems are called for in the post–Cold War world.

It does not take a great deal of study to conclude that the military-industrial complex, so aptly named by Eisenhower after two terms as president altered his perceptions, is a powerful force in the U.S. political, economic, and social order. As such, it almost certainly pervades American culture as well. The previous chapter discussed the United States as a highly militarized society, having evolved over the past century or so from an agrarian nation of citizen-soldiers to an urbanized mass society ready for war. Part of that militarism comes no doubt from an economic dependence on the military so deep that the appropriation of a substantial portion of the national wealth for military use is taken for granted.

Much of America's dependence on the military is the result not of explicit policy nor of the exigencies of a foreign military threat. Rather, it is an artifact of the military-acquisition system, a curious dance of private corporate interests, congressional electoral politics, bureaucratic ambivalence, and nationalist mythology. One way to reduce the militarism of American society, and thus its propensity to war, might therefore be to restructure the way in which weapons are produced and purchased by the military, or to change the incentive structure by which contractors pursue military contracts. This is the approach taken by some peace activist groups. Jobs With Peace, for example, is an organization devoted to helping military contractors convert to peaceful production. It performs economic research to determine markets for alternative products, offers workshops and seminars to corporations, and seeks to inform communities of alternative ways of thinking about their local defense corporation.

My focus now moves away from understanding the problem of war toward understanding the prospects for peace. The three chapters that follow address the ways to peace on three successive levels. Chapter 6 approaches peacemaking as a matter of preventing or controlling war, a problem to be undertaken by states and even larger units. Chapter 7 addresses peacemaking from the point of view of the social movement or peace group; its approach is social-psychological. Finally, Chapter 8 approaches the problem of peacemaking from an individual and personal perspective.

Chapter Summary

The U.S. military consumes nearly half of each federal tax dollar. Its impact on the economy and government makes it one of the primary forces in the militarization of American society.

The defense acquisition process is an inherently wasteful one. Ironically, one of the major causes of its inefficiency is the evolution of *acquisition procedures* that have evolved over more than a hundred years. These have resulted in a concentration of a few large weapons producers on which the government has become dependent. A second cause of wastefulness is the *political process* by which acquisition funds are spent. Major weapons systems require congressional funding, and the political incentives for representatives and senators almost always favor spending over restraint. A third explanation for wastefulness is that American *cultural and political mythology* regards overspending for the military as the cautious approach to national defense. A fourth explanation is that citizens have *insufficient information* to exercise political control over the process. Finally, the *incentive structure* for government acquisition employees encourages them to promote spending for new systems rather than reducing costs.

These findings can be subsumed under more general sociological perspectives. *Functional theory* recognizes the intractable nature of military waste and explains it in terms of the latent functions it fulfills for society. *Conflict theory* focuses on the interests of the corporate elite, and how those interests are advanced by manipulating government to overspend on its products.

Questions for Review

What are some barriers to understanding the cost of a major weapons system?

A look at the history of major systems will show that costs that seem reasonable early in the acquisition process often double or triple by the time the system is produced. What are some causes of this?

How can competition among defense contractors actually increase the cost of weapons systems?

Why are congressional representatives generally hesitant to cut funding for weapons systems?

Much of American military involvement since the Cold War has been intervention in ethnic or partisan conflict. In what ways is the American military ill equipped for this kind of action?

For Further Research

Brookings Institution.*What Nuclear Weapons Delivery Systems Really Cost.* URL: http://www.brook.edu/FP/PROJECTS/NUCWCOST/DELIVERY.HTML.

Fitzgerald, A. Ernest. 1989. *The Pentagonists: An Insider's View of Waste, Mismanagement, and Fraud in Defense Spending.* Boston: Houghton-Mifflin.

Grossman, Mark. 1995. *Encyclopedia of the Persian Gulf War.* Santa Barbara, Calif.: ABC-CLIO.

Kirby, Andrew, ed. 1992. *The Pentagon and the Cities.* Newbury Park, Calif.: Sage.

Stockholm International Peace Research Institute. *SIPRI Yearbook.* URL: http://www.sipri.se/index/html.

United States Department of Defense. *Defenselink.* URL: http://www.defenselink.mil.

6   *Methods of Avoiding War*

Possibly the first and most fundamental idea that peace studies offers is that the cessation of war and the promotion of peace are two different things. War and peace are not simple opposites, where peace is defined as the absence of war. Rather, both war and peace are processes of interaction, conflict, and cooperation, involving the pursuit of collective and individual interests and rooted in a connection between the individual and the community. Both war and peace are collective endeavors made possible by the human desire to form and maintain community; Rapoport (1992) even asserts that war, at least participation in it by individuals, is motivated by the same ideals of selflessness as is peace. Yet war and peace manifest the polar opposites of human accomplishment, the one creative and life-affirming, the other destructive and murderous.

This way of thinking about war and peace carries with it the strong implication that the mere absence of war is a vaguely insufficient goal; that simply aspiring to a life without the fear of wholesale slaughter is a fatalist's vision (see, for example, Wagner 1988). Real peace-lovers, in this view, seek fundamental change in the way societies are organized, a utopian world in which conflict and cooperation are profoundly redefined. Yet there are millions of people who would settle gratefully for a mere cessation of hostilities in their corner of the world and who would happily return to the lives they once had of normal hardship, struggle, and injustice. This chapter discusses the means that have been used or proposed to achieve that limited sort of peace—reduction in the explicit and active conflict called war.

Deterrence

Probably the earliest and crudest means to avoiding war is deterrence, the prevention of aggression by threat of retaliation. Though the principle of deterrence is rooted in modern balance-of-power theories, one can imagine its practical use extending into conflicts in the earliest hu-

149

man societies. As a means of preventing war, deterrence relies on a nonobvious premise: The group seeking to maintain peace must be able to communicate to its adversaries a credible deterrent threat. This means that the symbols of retaliation are more important than the actual means of retaliation. Thus many warring tribal societies make great symbolic shows of force as a prelude to or substitute for combat. The practice of "counting coup" among the Cheyenne and certain other Native American peoples was a stylized and ritualistic means of symbolizing force.

American policy at the beginning of the Cold War offers an illustration of the role of symbol in deterrence. Though the United States had at the end of World War II only a few nuclear weapons, it had a large number of bombers available to carry them, so a conspicuous show was made of flying the bombers around North America and Europe. The Soviets had to err on the side of caution in guessing how many of them actually carried nuclear weapons. It is also the reason why, in spite of obsessive regard for state secrecy, it was never U.S. nor Soviet policy to hide nuclear arsenals.

Blainey (1973) showed the connection between deterrence and balance-of-power theories by noting that wars usually begin when two nations disagree on their relative strength. In such a case, one nation believes (either accurately or erroneously) that it is capable of overpowering the other, while the other disagrees. Note that at least one of the parties has to be wrong in order for war to break out and that they must disagree; if both parties understand that one of them can defeat the other then the weaker party will make whatever concessions are necessary to avoid war. Note also that the outbreak of war is not the same thing as the existence of conflict or tensions between the parties. Such hostility can exist indefinitely without producing war.

Deterrence, then, is the art of creating agreement between hostile parties on their relative strength, and there is some evidence that this has been effective not only in antiquity but in the nuclear age as well. In fact, some observers attribute the extended peace (that is, the recent period free of all-out interstate war) to the deterrent effect of nuclear weapons (Huth 1990; Mearsheimer 1994; Waltz 1994b). Others attribute it to the "bipolar" world of the Cold War era, in which it was easy for all parties to correctly assess their relative strengths, tied as they were to one or another of the Great Powers (Saperstein 1991).

But deterrence poses two problems as a means of preventing war. The first is that, although its effectiveness depends on agreement between parties as to relative strength, the rational and safe incentive is always to increase one's own strength. Thus deterrence as a policy of defense leads to arms races, and there is a good deal of evidence that arms races in themselves tend to precede the outbreak of war (Wallace 1979).

A second problem is that, although deterrence may reduce the likelihood of open warfare between states, it does nothing to reduce tensions or hostilities between them; in fact, it seems clear that one side effect of deterrence is that it actually increases hostility. Further, as discussed in Chapter 3, it contributes to militarism within the culture of each of the states involved, because their citizens are asked to pay for expensive offensive weapons that, if all goes well, will not be used. To get citizens to support such expenditures, the potential "enemy" has to be demonized as an "evil empire" that is kept at bay solely by the deterrent effect of increasingly expensive weapons.

This is not to mention the logical and moral problem of maintaining peace through warlikeness and bellicosity. Deterrence seems an inherently unstable strategy that sooner or later must break down, perhaps through a failure of intelligence by one side or the other, which causes a misperception of the parties' relative strengths. This is at least one contributing factor that led to the outbreak of World War I, according to White (1989). He claims the Austrian government erred not only in military overconfidence but also in underestimating the military resolve of its enemies.

The balance of deterrence can also break down because of a failure of states to act "rationally" as supposed by deterrent theory. It is possible that a government might simply be forced into a war on irrational grounds, to save face or to satisfy militaristic political factions within the state. Japan's attack on Pearl Harbor in 1941 might be considered such a case, although it might have been reasonably argued at the time that the attack would make the United States incapable of waging effective war for several years.

The escalation of deterrence into the nuclear age was thought to have addressed many of these problems, for the sheer unthinkability of nuclear war made it impossible for any state holding nuclear weapons to imagine a victorious outcome of their use.[1] The doctrine of "Mutually Assured Destruction" or "MAD" added a new twist to the doctrine of deterrence: the acquisition of such offensive capability on both sides that either could deliver a crippling blow to the other, even after absorbing a first strike. Since both sides possessed devastating destructive power, the relative strength of the combatants was irrelevant to decisions about whether to go to war. Thus no diplomatic affront or internal political pressure could any longer justify nuclear aggression, since self-destruction

---

[1]However, it wasn't unthinkable to everyone. General Curtis Le May, chairman of the Joint Chiefs at the time, advocated using nuclear weapons in Korea, for example.

was no longer a matter of doubt. Only the most desperate or maniacal government could entertain the possibility of nuclear engagement.

This is why President Reagan's insistence on pursuing the Strategic Defense Initiative (SDI, popularly known as "Star Wars") was so disconcerting to members of the peace community as well as to some military and diplomatic professionals. Development of a credible defense against nuclear missiles—a "nuclear umbrella" in Reagan's handy metaphor—would make it conceivable that the United States might be able to survive a nuclear exchange. This in turn would make it reasonable, under some circumstances, to initiate such an exchange. The deterrent effect of nuclear weapons and MAD would be lost. This was not viewed as a problem by those who shared Reagan's Hollywood image of the United States as the benign peacekeeper of the world. But those with a clearer view of history saw SDI as an advance of American imperialism and exploitation through nuclear terrorism, not to mention a whole new spiral of arms race spending.

In all, deterrence as a means of keeping peace is a dead end, or more accurately, a road with no end at all. There seems to be no way to stop the escalation of armaments, either in terms of sheer destructive power or better accuracy, intensity, mobility, or defensibility. When U.S. nuclear stockpiles far exceeded the strength needed to destroy every worthwhile target in the Soviet Union, designers turned to increasing the precision of the missiles' targeting capability. They also worked on making them more easily defended. The "dense pack" configuration of missile silos, in which all the missiles would be housed together in one superfortified underground location, was a much discussed possibility; use of mobile rather than fixed launchers was another.

But since even relatively low levels of nuclear capability are enough to deter aggression, it begs the question of why such developments are needed. This is exactly the question raised by Nalebuff (1988) and more recently by Hall (1998). Nalebuff suggests that arms spending is unnecessary once a nation achieves a minimal level of nuclear capability, since even a minimal nuclear capability is enough to deter attack. And Hall notes that even in 1998, with the Cold War "over," the United States maintains almost as large a nuclear arsenal as it ever did. Again one is reminded of the other functions of arms spending discussed in Chapters 2 and 5.

Arms Control

The natural successor to the excesses of deterrence is the attempt to limit the growth of arsenals. Although this seems most immediate and necessary in the nuclear age, arms control agreements are not new. In this century alone, there have been more than 100 arms control agreements achieved since The Hague Peace Conference of 1899 (Miller 1991).

The idea seems simple enough: Potential adversaries confer, either bilaterally or multilaterally, and establish specific limits on the number and types of weapons they will produce. Agreements typically focus on weapons of a "capital" nature; that is, the largest, most visible, and most expensive strategic weapons in use. For example, between the world wars the modern states agreed to limit their navies—the main symbol of strategic power at the time—in terms of both the number and size of ships.

But restrictions on smaller, tactical armaments are not unknown. The use of poison gas has been banned more or less effectively since its widespread use in World War I. And currently the international community has sought to restrict the use of land mines because of the danger they pose to civilian populations long after their use in warfare has passed. Notably, the United States has been the main impediment to this effort.

Experience of the past few decades highlights the most fundamental issue involved with arms limitation agreements: Like any treaty between adversaries, there is always the problem of ensuring that all the parties involved actually abide by the agreement. President Reagan's phrase "trust, but verify" symbolized this problem: What's the point of achieving an agreement to reduce armaments if it cannot be ascertained whether the parties are living up to it?

Moreover, even if verification is perfect—all parties having clear knowledge of the treaty violations of any of the other parties—what can be done about violators? When Germany violated the Treaty of Versailles by increasing its arsenal in readiness for World War II, the only recourse the Allies had was to use military force to exact compliance with the treaty. The same was true when Japan began to build battleships in excess of the size limits imposed by the Geneva Naval Disarmament Conference of 1927. The result was not a swift policing of the violation but rather protracted dithering, resulting in Japan's conquest of much of Asia and the Pacific, the attack on Pearl Harbor, and all the rest. The problem is further exacerbated because arms control treaties are intended to limit the very means by which states enforce treaties, thus making verification doubly important.

Even more troublesome, what can be done about parties refusing to sign on to arms limitation agreements? If one nation refuses to take part in an agreement to limit weapons, it would be folly for its potential adversaries to participate in it. This is more of a problem in agreements limiting small weapons, because a great many nations are capable of possessing them. Even the poorest Third World state can afford a sizable arsenal of land mines; thus agreements to limit their use must involve a large number of states with highly diverse interests.

But even nuclear weapons have become more difficult to limit for this reason. When the "nuclear club" included only a few states—all relatively wealthy and powerful—agreements were easier to achieve not only because there were simply fewer parties involved but also because they shared many common interests and values. Today there is a much more diverse nuclear community, including Third World nations like India and Pakistan. The military needs and political interests of such countries may be quite different from those of, for example, Russia and the United States. Where the latter are more interested in preserving an international status quo, the Third World nuclear powers may have specific territorial or cultural grudges, or may be seeking simply a measure of freedom from the tacit domination of the First World powers.

Yet even if these barriers are overcome, arms control might be an inherently flawed means of achieving peace. In a conference on approaches to peace hosted by the U.S. Institute of Peace, Miller (1991) concluded that arms control simply is not a path to peace. His historical discussion suggested that the arms control agreements of this century have neither prevented the outbreak of war (the two world wars being conspicuous examples) nor improved relations between nations. He attributed these failures to the demands of internal political factions and to the dominance of military interests in shaping such treaties in the first place.

On the other hand, it may be possible that past attempts at arms control have been carried out in the wrong way. Charles Osgood (1989) proposed a rationale for arms reduction that does not rely on mutual prior agreement among nations. Rather, Osgood's "Graduated Reciprocation in Tension-Reduction" is a unilateral process whereby one nation simply announces, then visibly executes, a reduction in its arsenal. It then invites its adversary or adversaries to do the same. The process begins with small reductions at first, so as not to weaken the nation's military capabilities disproportionately. But if these first reductions are reciprocated, then larger ones can follow until sizable reductions in weapons stockpiles are achieved.

The rationale for this "calculated de-escalation" is that it proceeds in the same way and by the same logic as the original escalation of weaponry: gradual, incremental action caused largely by the natural tendency to match the adversary's actions. If additions to one's arsenal are made in response to a perception of increased threat by one's adversary, then it seems reasonable to think that subtractions from the arsenal can be made in response to a perceived reduction in the threat.

Thus, while the arms race is a tension-increasing system, calculated de-escalation is a tension-reducing one.

The virtues of this approach are many. Although it does not guarantee any substantial reductions in arms (the adversary might not reciprocate), at least it doesn't cost very much. The worst that can happen is that an insignificant initial reduction in arms will not be matched by the other side, the process comes to an end, and nothing is lost. Both sides can then return to the prior state of uncontrolled arms competition. But the potential gains are great, since early successes can create an environment of optimism and trust between parties, where each perceives the process as beneficial to its own interests. Further, it does not contribute to increased tensions caused by negotiations over treaty restraints. Instead, each party can evaluate freely the actions of the other and respond freely in a manner that it believes will best contribute to the process. In a sense, this approach replaces a "legislated" process with a "free-market" process in which each side is free to act in its own interests.

This approach also benefits from the support of social-psychological research. Simulation of treaty compliance through the Prisoner's Dilemma game shows that a strategy called "Tit-For-Tat," in which each player simply matches the opponent's move, is the most consistently successful strategy (Rapoport 1992). Other strategies—for example, always cooperating or always refusing to cooperate—are losing strategies in even the short run. Using the Tit-for-Tat strategy, the player rewards an opponent's cooperation with cooperation, while punishing noncompliance with noncompliance. This tends to encourage compliance by one's opponent, which is profitable for both sides. This suggests that a Tit-for-Tat strategy applied to arms reductions would tend to encourage continued reductions, at least to the level of the minimum necessary for genuine deterrence.

It also seems possible that the internal barriers to arms reduction noted by Miller might be overcome by the unilateral approach. Nationalist political interests—for example, the right wing of conservative politics in the United States—wield considerable power in blocking arms reduction and similar efforts by promoting mistrust of adversaries and national pride through military strength. But a president could without too much political difficulty begin the unilateral process on his own by announcing some small reduction in weapons. If that reduction were reciprocated, it would be much more difficult for the right to block further reductions. Moreover, the treaty-less nature of the process means that Congress would not have to ratify any formal agreement between the United States and another nation.

The main shortcoming of unilateral arms reduction is that it seems most feasible when applied to just two nations. This approach made sense in the bipolar world of the Cold War, in which the "arms race" was a Tit-for-Tat game played by the United States and the Soviet Union. The world simply isn't like that anymore: There are so many players, even in the nuclear game, that it seems unlikely that any one state's actions would be reciprocated by all the others. For that matter, since the members of the nuclear community are so unequal with respect to the size and effectiveness of their arsenals, it would be impossible for all parties to reciprocate. How should Pakistan, with just a few weapons and no long-range delivery system, react if the United States unilaterally reduces its submarine nuclear missile fleet? Such considerations were simple when only the U.S.-USSR relationship needed to be considered because both nations had pretty much the same kinds and numbers of weapons. But in the present nuclear community it would seem this unilateral approach might have the simple effect of allowing the smaller nuclear powers to catch up to the larger ones—which of course is the last thing the larger powers want.

Still, the least that might be expected of arms reductions—whether unilateral or negotiated—is that they could reduce the costs of defense for the states that participate. And given the enormous redundancy in nuclear weapons among the principal nuclear powers, it is hard to believe that any significant reduction in deterrent capability would result.

Collective Security

A third general approach to avoiding war is collective security, the practice of forming alliances among individual states in order to pose a greater deterrent threat to their mutual adversaries. Current examples include the North Atlantic Treaty Organization (NATO) and the Organization of American States (OAS), founded purportedly to provide mutual security for all its members against aggression and coercion by the Soviet Union and its client states. The concept is an old one and includes military and political mutual defense alliances as old as the concept of the state itself. It may have reached its apotheosis at the beginning of the twentieth century as the whole of Europe, as well as the colonial possessions of the European powers, was enmeshed in a complex network of mutual defense alliances. These alliances were so dense and complex that a regional dispute between Serbian nationals and the Austro-Hungarian empire exploded into World War I as allies of the states involved, then the allies of allies, were committed to the conflict.

Although collective security arrangements have been effective in enhancing the deterrent capability of small nations, there are difficulties and risks inherent in this approach to maintaining peace. First, since collective security arrangements involve the loose federation of sovereign states, there is always the problem of guaranteeing the participation of each member in the alliance when participation violates its own self-interest. For example, with the end of the Cold War it is no longer as easy as it used to be to assume that the United States would commit troops to the defense of a NATO member. Even if all members participate nominally in the common effort, there is the possibility of suspicion among them that one or another member is dragging its feet. For example, the Soviet Union was convinced during World War II that the United States and Britain were stalling in their plans to invade France, allowing Soviet soldiers and civilians to bear more than their share of the burden. Similarly, many American strategists suspected the British (particularly General Montgomery) of being overly cautious in their conduct of the war while Americans bore the brunt of combat.

This "free rider" problem is less severe when a coalition is dominated politically or militarily by a single powerful member. In this case, participation may be enforced by the threat of retaliation by the dominant state, either by failing to support the deviant member in times of need, or by more subtle diplomatic, economic, or military means. This often makes for a stronger alliance, but at the same time the domination of an alliance by a powerful member carries its own risks. For one, the interests of the alliance may be channeled into the interests of the dominant state. The OAS is a clear example; through it the United States has exerted its own political and economic interests in Latin America, often by simple violation of the organization's charter (Rapoport 1992). It is not too great a stretch to think of NATO in the same terms, although the other members exercise a good deal more political, military, and economic power over the whole than do the members of the OAS.

Another difficulty faced by collective security arrangements is the question of inclusiveness: How large and how diverse a coalition is feasible? NATO faces this problem today as it begins to admit as members former Warsaw Pact nations. Even Russia has been considered for membership. One has to question whether such a coalition can actually work in practice; whether, for example, the United States, Britain, or Germany would actually commit itself militarily to the defense of Russia or one of its former client states.

Empire

The "collective security" model of war reduction involves a voluntary banding together of individual states into larger and more potent alliances. It is in these cases—for example, the formation of the United States—that the difficulties of maintaining the coalition are most pronounced. But the older and more common way that collective security arrangements have been achieved is by coercion and force; that is, through the building of empires.

One of the earliest and most primitive means of preventing warfare is the imposition of order on warring factions by a higher and more powerful authority. Since before the invention of the state, groups with the means to enforce their will have served their own interests by imposing peace on factions below them. This has the dual benefit for the warlord, prince, or emperor of making a more efficient realm and of making competing factions grateful to the higher authority for maintaining the peace.

It was by this means that the first city-states and then nation-states were created. In Asia, dynasties were built by warlords whose military and administrative powers were able to coalesce competing groups by both force and appeal to each group's interests. The exploitation of natural geographic and ethnic boundaries was often helpful as well, although sometimes artificial boundaries were necessary, hence the Great Wall. In Europe much the same processes were used, with the borders of empires ebbing and flowing across the continent with changes in economic, technological, and cultural realities. The Roman Empire was perhaps the most successful and longest lasting, partly because its administrative structure encouraged conquered peoples to become assimilated and integrated into Roman society while affording them a measure of regional autonomy.

Discussion of the assembly of factions into states and states into empires begs the question of the optimum size of the "peace group." For William Graham Sumner (1911) there was a natural limit to the size of the community; an equilibrium point at which it most efficiently divided its labor and provided for its defense against outgroups. This approach is of some use, for one can imagine that the historical trend toward ever larger communities has been driven by innovations in technology and social organization that have made larger groups possible. By this reckoning, the early hunter-gatherer cultures were limited in size by the carrying capacity of the land on which they roamed; large groups would have had to range too broadly to secure enough food to feed all members. The invention of horticulture and pastoralism made it possible and desirable to organize into larger groups; thus the city emerged. Later, the Romans built extensive road networks that enabled rapid communications—and thus control—across a vast empire comprising many cities. They also organized permanent legions of professional soldiers to police those far-flung regions. Similar processes occurred in the New World: The Anasazi in what is now the southwestern United States linked scattered settlements by roads, as did the Mayans and Incas.

One might imagine also that the current trend toward "globalism," characterized by the hegemonic spread of capitalism and Western culture, is similarly encouraged by an explosive growth in communications. Travel and shipping have become more rapid and better coordinated than ever; even the average citizen of Western societies finds an international bazaar of goods available in the local market. Middle-class Americans, Europeans, and Asians are found in their legions at the great historic and cultural sites of the world. And an Irish farmer in the most rural corner of county Mayo can check crop prices worldwide via cell phone or talk to his cousins in Chicago. Meanwhile, retailers in New York order goods from manufacturers in Singapore and publishers in Melbourne send text electronically across the world for printing. And most recently, people the world over have electronic access to newspapers and television from virtually any country. It would seem inevitable that the world will coalesce into a single cultural and economic entity, and that a similar worldwide political coalition cannot be far behind.

And yet this has not been the case. In Yugoslavia, a former nation has disintegrated into smaller states based on ethnic identity. The Middle East continues to pose apparently intractable differences between ethnic and religious groups. The same is true in sub-Saharan Africa, India and Pakistan, former Soviet republics, and other regions. Apparently technology alone does not dissolve barriers between outgroups; social barriers continue to be important. But what made Yugoslavia possible in the first place? There have been and still are plenty of multiethnic states, and smaller states continue to grow by inclusion of new ethnic groups. The world's recent experience with dis-integration ought not lead to the conclusion that worldwide integration is impossible.

World Order

The previous discussion leads to consideration of the possibility of coalescing of an ever larger collective-security alliance, one that might include all or virtually all the nations of the world. This has already been attempted several times; for example, the "peace of God" was sometimes invoked in medieval Europe to limit warfare between feudal princes. The League of Nations and later the United Nations are more recent attempts at achieving a system of world law and order. The ideal outcome of such a process is a world government that acts as a genuine government; that is, one that possesses the power to enforce a code of law on member states.

Katz (1996) notes that this amounts to a Hobbesian "social contract" by which individual states—currently living in the chaotic "state of nature" described by Hobbes—are brought under the rule of law by a higher authority. When empires are formed from individual states, they are brought out of the state of nature and under the authority of the empire. The problem, of course, is that the empires themselves remain in the state of nature, which means they are in conflict with one another; moreover, each is more powerful and more monolithic than the member states that comprise it. Still, if this process could be extended indefinitely to the point at which *all* states are within the "peace group" and all submit to the higher authority, then a more or less peaceful world might be achieved. This "world order" model of peace is often what beginners in peace studies imagine to be the principal path to peace.

But there are problems, as there must be, else such a world order would have been achieved by now. First, as Sumner implies, it is possible that a "peace group" including all the world is simply not the optimum size to efficiently provide economically and socially for all its people. Despite communications, transportation, and cultural diffusion, a social system that inclusive may not be governable. A second problem is that the cooperation inherent within the ingroup implies the existence of an outgroup. In fact, the existence and maintenance of an outgroup may be a requisite to maintaining the ingroup itself. When all the world is the ingroup, who is left to provide the common enemy?

A more subtle problem is that, as Durkheim teaches us, a rational "social contract" is not really the basis for social solidarity at all. For the social contract to be upheld, a "precontractual solidarity" must exist in the first place; that is, there must be an a priori understanding that the contract entered into will be followed. The world's nations may enter into a governmental body, but what is the reason for any one state to assume that the world government's laws will be observed by the others? This question is the very basis of theories of "political realism" or *realpolitik:* that every state acts entirely in its self-interest, without restraint of moral or ethical principle. Treaties are observed only so long as it is in the interests of the parties to observe them.

Moreover, such bodies work best when there is rough parity among members. When one member is much more powerful than most of the others, it is able to ignore the law of the group. The United States demonstrated this recently by its rejection of the establishment of a permanent world court to adjudicate crimes against humanity. Though the U.N. adopted the proposal, there is no reason to expect that the United States would submit to the court's judgment in the event that one of its military personnel were charged with such crimes. In fact, Senator Helms asserted that such a charge would be an unacceptable compromise of America's sovereignty. And the United States has a poor record of such compliance; for example, it dismissed a judgment of the U.N.'s World Court condemning its aggression in Nicaragua. It failed to agree to an international ban on land mines; it even failed to join the League of Nations after World War I—a body proposed by its own president. Even if the U.N. were a body with the "teeth" to enforce its laws on member states, it would not be difficult for a powerful member like the United States to withdraw its own troops from the U.N.'s police force and thus make it difficult to exact compliance.

In spite of these difficulties the U.N. has become more activist and more authoritative in recent years. Luck (1991) points to the U.N.'s diplomatic "breakthroughs" in the Afghanistan and Iran-Iraq conflicts as evidence that the organization will play a greater role in the future in making and preserving peace. And the U.N. conduct of peace-enforcement efforts in the Middle East, Somalia, and Yugoslavia certainly suggest a greater activism, not to mention its sponsorship of the Gulf War. In all, the U.N. has conducted more peacekeeping operations in the past decade than it did in the first forty-five years of its existence (Diehl, Druckman, and Wall 1998). And survey questionnaire data from various nations show that the U.N. has gained legitimacy in the eyes of many peoples as a result of its role in the Gulf War and the "explosion" of U.N. peacekeeping actions (Russet 1994). Whether these efforts are effective, or even a good idea at all, is of course another question, but they do at least represent a move in the direction of a more empowered world governance structure.

It seems likely that the end of the "bipolar" world order of the Cold War has freed the U.N. and its member states for greater activism, at least until a new alignment works itself out. Perhaps it will gradually acquire greater authority over the sovereignty of member states as those states see increasing advantage in the order it brings. Or perhaps it will become the instrument of a ruling cabal of First World capitalist powers whose will can be imposed on Third World "labor" states. The first alternative represents a metaphor for functionalist thinking about the rise and effectiveness of law; the second is a Marxian concept of domination by the powerful. Either could result in a fairly long period of stable relations between nations.

Finally, some people have suggested that the U.N. could be made a more effective body by making relatively small changes in its constitution. Hudson (1989) used the American Constitutional Congress as a model for suggesting ways in which the U.N.'s constitution could be strengthened so as to afford a stronger confederation among member states, thus making "a genuine peace system." His proposal involves two parts. First, the means by which the General Assembly passes a resolution would be changed. Whereas at present each nation has one vote, rendering every nation the equal of every other, Hudson's proposal would require three different kinds of majorities to pass a resolution. For a measure to be adopted by the Assembly, it would have to have the approval of not only two-thirds of the nations themselves, but also two-thirds of the populations represented by those nations and two-thirds of the financial contributions of those nations. Thus, although each state would vote only once, its vote would be counted three ways: its one vote as counted now, a number of votes based on its population, and a different number of votes based on its financial contribution to the U.N.

This "Binding Triad" voting system would give General Assembly resolutions more credibility because they would not be based solely on an unrealistic presumption of equality among nations. States representing more people would have more sway, as would states with the economic power to make larger membership contributions.

The second part of the proposal is to increase the power of the General Assembly relative to the Security Council by making its decisions binding on all parties, rather than recommendations. This would seem to be a major sticking point in the proposal since it would require the voluntary relinquishing of some of each nation's sovereignty to the common good. But the change in voting requirements might help in exacting the compliance of states by making the resolutions more credible and more legitimate.

At present, the General Assembly has little authority over members because its votes have little credibility. China's single vote is counted equally with that of Saint Christopher and Nevis, meaning that a citizen of the latter country has about 23,000 times as much representation than a citizen of China (Hudson 1989). The larger and more powerful states simply use their veto power in the Security Council to negate the actions of the General Assembly; thus the latter body is viewed as a mostly irrelevant soapbox for the small states. The Binding Triad proposal would increase the relevance of Assembly resolutions by weighting them somewhat in favor of larger and more powerful states. Although this is less egalitarian than the present arrangement, it might have the virtue of making the larger states take more serious notice of the resolutions, rather than dismissing them with a veto later.

What are the chances for a world peace through law? It is difficult to imagine powerful states like the United States or China relinquishing their sovereignty to a higher authority. Yet there is a great deal of international law already at work, and there has been for some time. Schachter (1991) asserts that there has been in fact a veritable explosion in new international law regarding trade, use of the seas, natural resources, copyright, space exploration, environmental protection, airwave use, and a variety of other activities. These have been prompted by increased interaction among states, the birth of new states, new technology, and rising standards of human rights.

But Schachter also notes that international law does not work in quite the same way as domestic law. It is not necessarily grounded in the threat of enforcement by a higher authority; the United Nations really does not have an effective, self-contained police force. In spite of this, most nations obey the law most of the time, owing in part to custom, in part to self-interest, in part to the fear of reprisal by other states, in part to the desire to be taken seriously by the international community. In fact, Schachter actually uses the term "internalization" to refer to the routine acceptance of the force of law by states—obeying the law becomes a taken-for-granted matter while violation, though certainly possible, becomes a weighty matter full of risk and import.

Ultimately, submission of one's own interests to the common interests of a group requires some sort of nonrational attachment to that group. Durkheim's insight into the bonding of individuals to the group might apply to states as well, if one can reasonably make the analytical leap from the individual psyche to national policy as the unit of analysis. Schachter's description of the compliance of states to international law does not sound so different from a description of how and why individuals comply to group norms and community law: partly out of self-interest, partly out of fear of punishment, partly out of an internalized moral code, partly out of sheer habit. And individuals sometimes violate the law, as states do—but this does not make the law irrelevant, so long as the community takes measures to reaffirm it through ritual and punishment.

It seems possible that the formation of a worldwide "peace group" might simply require a certain point in human progress to be reached. It might just have been too difficult to manage in the past, in the same way that the nation-state itself required certain social and technological advances to become practicable. It is said that the railroad and telegraph made it possible for the United States, and likewise Canada, to be forged into single cohesive nations; perhaps global communication and transportation can do the same for the world at large. It is only within the past few decades that the world's citizens have been able to see live images of each other, relatively unmitigated by the biases and agendas of others. Perhaps a kind of solidarity may yet emerge among the peoples of the world.

On the other hand, there is little evidence that the amount of conflict in the world is declining. Even if one ignores the two world wars, there seem to be about as many wars, involving as many people, as there ever were. In fact, the low cost of lethality—much lower, relative to other goods, than in the past—has made it easier for small conflicts to erupt into massive violence. Not that large-scale or high-tech weapons are necessary; the Hutu-Tutsi war in Rwanda was largely a rifle-and-machete affair.

It is possible, too, that the availability of instant global communications has made it easier to organize a population into a coherent and angry group. This has been the case of paramilitary and racist groups in the United States. Furthermore, it seems easier to solicit support for one's cause from outside, as ethnic and political factions can now get their story told via the Internet or by cable television.

In the end, establishment of a global governance system will require a rethinking of the idea of the sovereign state, a repeal of the Westphalian system. Individual national identities and boundaries will have to become at least partly irrelevant. But how will this happen? First, it will have to be economically advantageous for nations to pay less attention to their national identity. This is likely to come through very dense and widespread trade, and through a great deal of cross-boundary investment. This is what is happening in Europe at the present time, as the European Union (EU) moves toward a common currency and the elimination of trade barriers among members. There is already the example of the United States, which gave up independent sovereignty to form a national government with a common currency well after achieving independence.

Second, this economic interdependence will have to last long enough for the resulting "organic solidarity" to become sacred. The bonds uniting member nations will have to move beyond matters of expedience and take on the force of habit and tradition. Compliance with the world government will have to become the norm, and resistance to it a deviant act. This means that there must be a "critical mass" of compliant states, including the most powerful among them, such that deviant states cannot find powerful allies in their resistance.

This implies that there will have to be some measure of justice among the member states, so that they are not motivated to form coalitions in their own interests. This does not necessarily mean that there will have to be economic parity among all nations; in fact, that probably would not be a practical solution. Rather, the balance of wealth and power will only have to appear legitimate to member states. Without a common cultural or religious basis for legitimacy, this would likely depend on whether all members believe they *benefit* from cooperation—that it is better to participate than not to participate. The wealthy and powerful nations will disband the organization the moment they believe they are giving up more than they are gaining; at the same time, the poor and weak nations will continue to participate as long as their lot is marginally better by keeping within the group.

Whether these conditions will ever be met is difficult to say. It certainly seems that the world is fundamentally different today than at any other time, if only for the ease and density of communication and trade. It also seems likely that regional economic coalitions are beginning to lead the way already; in this regard the EU will be an important test for the future. The level of cooperation evidenced so far by its members is beyond what anyone could have imagined even fifty years ago. Finally, it is worth noting that cultural change, and even global change, can occur remarkably quickly sometimes. The Cold War seemed a permanent condition of the global system in its time; it came to an end with stunning suddenness.

The Limits of Sovereignty

A fundamental shortcoming of all the above methods for achieving peace among nations is that much of the peacelessness found at present is not between nations but within them (Ayoob 1996). In fact, of twenty-seven major armed conflicts occurring around the world in 1996, all but one were "internal," occurring between political or ethnic factions within a single state (Stockholm International Peace Research Institute 1997). Kaldor refers to these as "new wars," less dense but longer-running conflicts in which civilians play a greater role as targets, victims, and refugees (Kaldor 1996). It seems clear that whatever arrangements evolve between nations to maintain order among them, such arrangements are unlikely to bring about much peace to populations like the citizens of Somalia, Nigeria, Kosovo, the West Bank, Congo, or Northern Ireland.

The Problem of Ethnic Conflict

These "new wars" do not fit well into political, diplomatic, or strategic thinking if that thinking is restricted to sovereign states. The warfare of states is an easily identified act of diplomacy among well-defined groups and grounded more or less in a set of widely understood rules. Warfare between ethnic factions within states departs from this simple model in a number of ways.

Identity and Leadership. Sovereign states are usually well defined in terms of membership, territory, and leadership. There is a formally constituted government that includes diplomatic representatives able to speak for the state's interests and act on its behalf. Key, of course, is that a state has a monopoly on political power over its people in the international arena.

Ethnic factions within states, on the other hand, usually have a less formal leadership; in fact, it is common for such factions to be habitually undergoing a struggle for leadership and representation. The Intifadah, the uprising of Palestinians in Israel, was ended by an agreement reached by Yasir Arafat as leader of the Palestine people and the Israeli government. But Arafat did not have the complete mandate of Palestinians, nor did he possess the power to wrest that mandate from them. The result is that there remain factions within the Palestinian movement that refuse to recognize the agreement. They continue to fight the Israelis while Arafat is in the difficult position of having to use Palestinian police to stop them.

Even more loose is the leadership of the Catholic and Protestant factions in Ireland. It appears that the Sinn Fein Party largely speaks for Catholics, though it does so at least partly through the coercion of its armed wing, the Provisional Irish Republican Army (IRA). And the Protestant leadership is quite fluid, consisting of an ad hoc coalition of religious and fraternal groups ranging from the accommodating to the militant in their orientation to the other side. Moreover, even the membership of ethnic groups may be ill defined. Although it may be clear who is Irish Catholic and who is Irish Protestant by religious, language, or other cultural markings, the ethnic group does not have the power to compel individual commitment to the cause. Some Catholics are loyal to the IRA, some are lukewarm, and some are indifferent or hostile. To make matters worse, members of the warring factions may be geographically mixed together, removing residence as a marker of group identity.

Thus one problem in reducing ethnic or other internicene conflict is that the antagonist groups do not bear the legitimacy of states. That is, their leadership does not have the moral or coercive power to compel loyalty of its members, nor are the members themselves easy to identify. When it comes time to make peace, who speaks for each side? And just who are the sides, anyway?

Motives and Goals. A second difficulty in getting a grasp on ethnic conflict is that ethnic groups often fight for goals so abstract that it is difficult to envision any agreement that could make the fighting stop. Sometimes there is territory involved, as in Israel, but often the fighting is over a history of real or perceived oppression of one group by the other. The Northern Irish conflict fits this description, as Catholics resent being a minority to the more affluent and powerful Protestant majority. Sometimes the dispute seems to be over identity itself—the desire of one group to be recognized as a group, perhaps as a state in its own right. This is the case in Kosovo, where the Kosovo Liberation Army seeks political autonomy for the region.

In cases like these, the conflict with the outgroup is in part an attempt to solidify the cohesion and the very existence of the ingroup. For example, the Palestine Liberation Organization (PLO) represents Palestinians in the West Bank and Gaza partly because it defined itself as the enemy of Israel and fought against it for years. One could say that the Palestinian movement itself exists largely as the antithesis of Israeli authority in Palestine.

Higher Authority.   Finally, ethnic conflict occurs within the territory of a state, or of more than one state. This means that the conflict itself threatens the authority and therefore the survival of the state, and this puts the government in a difficult position. If the state wants to quell the disorder and restore its authority, it has to use force of some sort against its own people. The typical response is to side with one of the factions against the other; in fact one side usually has substantial control of the government in the first place. But this creates a problem, because it marginalizes one of the factions, often by declaring it a "criminal" or "terrorist" element. In this way it gives up any chance of gaining legitimacy with that element, which weakens its hold on perhaps a large fraction of its populace.

In fact, as was suggested earlier, weakening of the state's authority itself can be the cause of ethnic strife, or at least the factor that enables it to erupt into open conflict. Yugoslavia is a good example: under the Communist leader Tito, the country was regarded as one of the success stories of eastern Europe. Sarajevo was a vibrant and pleasantly livable city, so much so that it hosted the 1984 Winter Olympics. But the government's ability to control the many ethnic factions that constituted Yugoslavia had already begun to erode after Tito's death in 1980. Gradually the national Yugoslav identity gave way to regional and ethnic identity when the state was unable to use the economy to appease the bickering populations. It did not take many insults, slights, and injustices to allow for the rise of extremists and politicians; they further fanned the flames of identity and resentment.

It also often happens that one or both factions are supported or sponsored by a foreign government, adding another level of complexity to the problem. Thus the Russians supported the Afghan rebels in the seventies; the United States sponsored the Contras in Central America during the same period.

Civilian Involvement.   Finally, ethnic conflict generally involves a much higher proportion of civilian victims. Both warring sides use terror and massacre of civilians as principal strategies, partly because the distinction between civilian and combatant is blurred, but partly because achieving a numerical majority is often part of each group's goal. This was a primary goal of the Serbs in Kosovo: They sought to become a majority by chasing ethnic Albanians from the region.

It is not hard to see why ethnic conflict is so difficult to curtail. Even if it is clear that something ought to be done to stop the fighting, it is difficult to figure out who is responsible for doing so. It is certainly not clear to individual *states* why they should do anything to resolve or contain these conflicts. The doctrine of political realism by which states live relies on their rationality of acting in their own interests and their interests alone; thus it is often difficult for governments to respond to these new wars.

Still, such conflicts sometimes threaten the interests of other nations. Neighboring states may fear that the conflict could "spill over" into their own territory, as has happened in Albania and Macedonia (whence Kosovar refugees have fled) and in central Africa (where Hutu and Tutsi refugees continue their fighting). And more distant nations may find themselves involved by virtue of economic, political, or ethnic ties. Even where no specific connection exists between the interests of a strife-torn country and one far away, one might assume that the world at large has a general interest in maintaining peace among peoples, even those living within the borders of a particular state. The universal reach of news media, with real-time footage of atrocities and human misery, adds to the pressure of otherwise disinterested states to act, as their citizens clamor for an end to brutality and suffering.

This sort of conflict has created the need for a different type of collective security, as larger, richer, or more stable nations have sought to intervene in one way or another in the conflicts within or between smaller or emerging countries. Often the larger states have fallen into this pattern easily, as they have been called on to settle disputes within newly-liberated former colonies, or have found the need to support friendly regimes in client states. Thus the French became embroiled in Vietnam in the fifties and Algeria in the sixties, the Russians in Afghanistan in the eighties and Azerbaijan in the nineties, the United States in Asia and Latin America throughout.

Other cases are less immediately tied to the interests of the intervening nation. For example, the American-led coalition intervening in Yugoslavia probably is motivated more by a general desire to prevent instability in Europe than by the need to control access to any particular resource or market; contrast this with the U.S.-led coalition that went to war with Iraq in order to maintain access to Middle Eastern oil.

The motives of the intervening nation can almost always be characterized in two ways, depending on one's political and ideological bent. On the one hand, people sympathetic to the intervening regime view the intervention as a peacekeeping action, designed to help peace-loving citizens live normal lives by protecting them from armed insurgents with radical political, social, religious, or economic agendas. On the other hand, critics often view the same action as imperialist control over a helpless nation, designed to support a friendly and usually corrupt political regime, ultimately to maintain control of resources or labor markets. Parenti (1996) insists that these motives are invariably self-serving and seldom in the best interests of the citizens of the target country. Thus Ronald Reagan constantly referred to the Contras of El Salvador and Nicaragua as "freedom fighters"—and made it stick—even as they terrorized civilian populations and destroyed needed infrastructure. Even well-intentioned mediation efforts come with cultural biases that often favor Western cultural groups over others (Abu-Nimer 1996).

Nor should the motives of intervening nations be the only consideration in determining the value of their efforts. Despite whatever economic or geopolitical interests were at stake for the United States in Somalia, it would be difficult to think that the population, held hostage by warring political factions, could not benefit from the imposition of order even from a self-interested outsider. And the disruption of order in Yugoslavia can hardly be thought of as a good thing either, as formerly cooperative neighbors are pitted against one another and ancient towns and cities are torn by ethnic strife.

Other critics of intervention point to its questionable effectiveness. The very examples given above testify to this. U.S. intervention in Somalia in 1992 resulted in little resolution of that conflict. One problem is that military troops are just not the right resource for the job of creating or maintaining peace. Military forces are meant to kill and destroy social order as effectively as possible; thus their use as protectors or imposers of order is cumbersome at best. Falk (1996) cites the experiences of Vietnam, Afghanistan, and Northern Ireland in showing that while the military can inflict great civilian pain, it cannot even guarantee victory, much less peace. And the problems underlying the conflicts in the first place—historical ethnic hatreds, economic and political power differentials, postcolonial mistrust—are clearly beyond the military's purview.

Others suggest that intervention can be helpful to civilian populations and suggest that expectations may simply be too high. Although NATO intervention has not resolved the conflict between ethnic Serbs and Croats, it has at least made it possible for inhabitants of Sarajevo and other towns to resume life. And the inhabitants of Somalia were at least fed under U.S. intervention, short-lived as it was.

Discussion of the merits and shortcomings of intervention into domestic disputes by foreign nations invites absolutist thinking. Opposition to intervention tends to be rooted in a general aversion to the use of force to control conflict, or in a suspicion of the motivations of the intervening states. Views favorable to intervention are generally grounded in the hope, often unfounded, that intervention will resolve underlying issues and bring an end to the conflict. None of these offer solid grounds for argument about intervention. Force of one kind or another is often both effective and legitimate in controlling violence; at the very least, one might make the simple arithmetical argument that fewer people have died in Yugoslavia since foreign troops arrived than before. And it could also be argued that it does not matter whether intervening states have a vested interest, or exploitative intent, in their actions, so long as the outcome is greater peace. At the same time, it is clear that short-term intervention has a poor historical record of bringing about any permanent solution to the political problems of strife-torn countries.

Simplistic ideas about the value of intervention also tend to ignore the variety of ways in which states can intervene in the internal affairs of others. Diehl, Druckman, and Wall (1998) identified twelve different interventions, varying in military intensity, political intrusiveness, and collaborativeness. These include using armed troops with the permission of the host state(s) to separate opposing military forces, election supervision, humanitarian assistance, arms control verification, and the overthrow of oppressive regimes.

Ultimately, the intervention of collective security is the only approach available under the sovereign-state system for addressing the problem of "new wars." Yet even as it involves the actions of sovereign states in maintaining or reshaping other states, it represents a crack in the sovereign system; a step in the direction of world order. The most effective, and certainly the most legitimate, examples of collective security are those interventions carried out by coalitions of nations, acting either explicitly or implicitly with the approval of other nations or on the basis of widely-accepted principles of international justice. The history of U.N. intervention, mostly of a nonmilitary or at least nonaggressive nature, provides numerous examples, even as events in Yugoslavia have suggested a decline in the effectiveness of troops in some circumstances.

The cooperation of independent states in coalitions to intervene in conflict requires that each coalition member surrender a bit of its own sovereignty to the collective effort. This is a significant step, especially when the coalition is not defined in terms of a specific national enemy. It represents not only the germ of a larger "peace group" in the process of forming around perceived common interests and collective advancement. Such coalitions, if successful and long-lived, can over time also create the sense of the rule of law that transcends national interests or boundaries. It is worth noting that the United Nations was formed from the coalition of allies that emerged victorious from World War II; in fact, the term "united nations" was frequently used by Roosevelt and Churchill to refer to the alliance during the war.

It seems possible, then, that the gradual growth in the power and legitimacy of collective security arrangements might draw nations over time into a more solid world government after all. This seems more likely as the U.N. is called on to intervene in the "new wars" of internal conflicts rather than against specific aggressor nations or coalitions, for the perception of even moderate impartiality brings legitimacy. The main barrier to growth of this sort of world government, however, is the lack of a common enemy or outgroup. It has always been easier for political leaders to react to the threat of an outside enemy, and to articulate the rationale for such actions to their constituents, than to act for the good of a larger community. And this reflects what is known of the formation of many groups: Group cohesion and survival is enhanced by the definition of the ingroup in terms of a corresponding outgroup. It remains to be seen whether the diplomatic interests and actions of states will turn from reaction to enemy threats toward action in the common good. It is not at all clear whether this is any more likely today than when the League of Nations was formed after the War to End All Wars.

Nonsovereign Options

One way out of the dilemma of intervention is to look beyond the use of military or political force as the intervention mechanism. If populations suffer from intrastate conflict, there are ways of alleviating that suffering and even rebuilding community other than the imposition of foreign states. Such nonsovereign interventions are not new; the International Red Cross, Médecins Sans Frontières, and Amnesty International are only a few examples of civilian organizations that can be found in war-torn or chaotic countries.

Nongovernmental Organizations

Nongovernmental organizations (NGOs) like these can intervene in many of the ways that governments can: for example, monitoring ceasefires, supervising elections, providing humanitarian assistance, and rebuilding infrastructure. And NGO activity may be more effective as worldwide communication becomes more accessible, since much of what NGOs do is inform the outside world of activities within the troubled region. Most of all, these sorts of activities are explicitly nonmilitant and nonviolent, so they tend not only to reduce hostilities but to create social order and predictability. Thus they bridge the gap between "negative" peace (reduction of violence) and "positive" peace (building of order and community).

These efforts are not new. Moser-Puangsuwan (1996) examines the evolution of citizen-based intervention programs, beginning in 1932 with the Peace Army, a group formed to intervene in the fighting between Japan and China in Shanghai. These efforts, shown in Table 6.1, range widely in scope, from groups formed to intervene in a specific event (Sahara Protest Action of 1959–1960, organized to interrupt French nuclear testing) to Amnesty International and Greenpeace, whose missions are global both geographically and philosophically. Moser-Puangsuwan lists the following initiatives, but also names many others that were proposed but never got off the ground.

In addition to their manifest objectives, nongovernmental organizations also advance a less explicit goal by demonstrating the effectiveness of nongovernmental organizations in providing needed supplies and services where formal government has failed. On the one hand, this challenges the predominance of formal sovereign government in international affairs, and such challenges can be threatening. On the other hand, even as they demonstrate a challenge to established diplomatic powers, NGOs often unintentionally affirm the power of the First World in creating and maintaining order. Moreover, the attempt to restore order itself may be construed as support of the status quo, or at least the most powerful of the factions competing for power. Thus Bendaña (1996) argues that attempts to intervene in the conflicts of another state inherently tilt the balance of power against insurgents, radicals, and reformers. "Humanitarian" intervention can therefore become an attempt to maintain order—order that perhaps should be dissolved.

International media have also become important nongovernmental forces of intervention in international and domestic affairs. The role of CNN in shaping the public's view of the Gulf War is a prime example. It is especially significant that in the age of worldwide satellite television transmission, these images were available not only to Americans but to Europeans and Middle Easterners as well. This is not entirely new, of course—BBC Radio's World Service has been in operation for a good part of the century. In addition to CNN and other electronic media, many newspapers around the world now publish international editions. During the 1998 Iraqi arms-inspection crises, for example, one was able to read news features as well as opinions from the *Jordan Times*, the *Kuwait Times*, France's *Agence Presse,* and any number of others. And there is good reason to think that the portrayal of civilians suffering under oppression or aggression in foreign lands is a powerful impetus for governments to undertake intervention under pressure from their own

TABLE 6.1   Some Citizen-Based Intervention Programs

Dates	Organization	Action
1932–1939	The Peace Army	Intervention between Japan and China in Shanghai
1948–present	Volunteers for International Development/Peaceworkers	Peace actions teams in Suez Africa, Central and North America
1959–1960	A Shara Protest Action	Interruption of French nuclear testing
1960–1961	San Francisco-Moscow Walk	Protested nuclear testing
1961–1964	World Peace Brigade	Gandhi-inspired "peace army"
1966	Nonviolent Action Vietnam	Attempted to send volunteers to North Vietnam as a means to halt bombing
1966–1971	Quaker Action Group	Volunteers for various small overseas actions
1968	Support Czechoslovakia Actions	Ad hoc effort to support the "Prague Spring" resistance to Soviet invasion
1971–1973	Operation Omega	Marched, blocked arms shipments, and sent relief supplies to defuse India-Pakistan war
1973–1974	Cyprus Resettlement Project	Facilitated negotiations between Greek and Turkish community leaders
1977	Operation Namibia	Brought books banned by South African government into Namibia
1981–present	Peace Brigades International	Various activities, including protection of local activists from abduction and violence
1981–present	Witness for Peace	Border and conflict monitoring in Central America
1989–1991	Refugee Escort Services	Monitoring of safe return of refugees in Central America
1990–1991	Gulf Peace Team	Civilians camped on Saudi-Iraq border to try to stop the fighting
1990–1992	Mideast Witness	Placed teams to live with Palestinians in the Occupied Territories

(continues)

TABLE 6.1 *(continued)*

Dates	Organization	Action
1990–present	Christian Peacemaker Teams	Various activities, including working for hostage release in the Middle East
1991–1992	Peace Mission to East Timor	Sent a ship with students from twenty-one nations to challenge Indonesian sovereignty claims
1991–present	Memorial Human Rights Observer Missions	Sends observers to conflict spots in former Soviet Union to provide nonpartisan observers
1993	Mir Sada	Civilians camped in southern Bosnia to intervene in fighting
1993	Cry for Justice	Supported local grassroots organizations in Haiti prior to return of former president Aristide
1993–present	Balkan Peace Team	Assists refugees, residents, and community organizers in Yugoslavia
1995–present	Sipaz	Working with peasants in Chiapas, Mexico

SOURCE: Moser-Puangsuwan (1996).

sympathetic or outraged citizens. Such was probably the case in Somalia, for example.

Although it seems certain that news media have an effect on international affairs, one might question whether that effect is always—or ever—a beneficial one. The news agencies of many countries are nationalized mouthpieces of their governments; thus they must be regarded as doing the government's bidding. At the same time, the "free" press of other societies is suspect for two reasons. First, their interests are generally commercial in nature so they rely on attracting as wide an audience as possible. And since war, violence, and nationalism seems to do a better job of attracting viewers, this is what tends to be overrepresented in the media. Second, the freedom of the press, especially in times of international crisis, is somewhat overstated. During the Gulf War, for example, the media were very tightly controlled by the military. Even in normal times, the press finds it judicious to ingratiate itself with government officials and offices.

One sort of NGO is often overlooked as an important factor in non-governmental intervention: the actions of business, commerce, and capital. For good or ill, the multinational corporation—and increasingly, smaller businesses as well—have taken an increasingly large role in foreign affairs. Not that this is a new phenomenon; the imperialism of the colonial era as well as that of the modern and postmodern eras has always been fueled by the demands of business for markets, resources, and labor. This was as true of the exploitation of North and South America in the sixteenth century as it was of the Southeast Asian plantations of the nineteenth century, or the securing of Middle East oil resources in the twentieth century. Commercial interests in all of these cases exercised great influence over the activities of their governments to act, with military force if necessary, to protect investments overseas and to replace local governments with client governments of their own.

The difference in the present era is that capital increasingly exerts its influence over foreign societies, independent of the actions of either its home government or that of its host. American banks invest in Brazilian manufacturers; American shoe companies locate plants in Malaysia; Japanese and German car makers build plants in the United States. By these and myriad transactions they act directly on the economies and the cultures of societies other than their own. In some cases, the question of a corporation's "home" country becomes blurred altogether.

This phenomenon has been best described and most fully elaborated by Imanuel Wallerstein. His "World System" theory views the whole world economy as a loosely integrated system, in which economic functions are divided up by peoples of various regions and classes, in a worldwide division of labor. The world thus becomes divided into "zones": the "core" consists of the world's major consumers and capitalists, who exploit the rest of the system for their benefit. The United States would be considered the core at this point in history; going back through the centuries it has been located in Britain, France, and Holland in reverse order. The "semiperiphery" includes regions of laborers who work for the core corporations under relatively comfortable circumstances but with little control over the system. Much of present-day western Europe and the Pacific Rim would fit this description. Finally, the "periphery" includes what is generally thought of as the Third World; areas that provide raw materials and unskilled labor to the core, under heavy exploitation.

World System theory proposes that the world system itself drives the actions of the players within it, in the same sense that social systems theory takes "society" to be an organic whole, with needs of its own that it seeks to have fulfilled. In Wallerstein's formulation, this world system expands of its own evolution, incorporating more and more regions within it. Those regions so incorporated give up their identity, much of their state sovereignty, and their economy as they become subordinated to the larger system (Ritzer, 1992).

The question, of course, is whether and in what way the rise of global capitalism can reduce conflict among states. Wallerstein's analysis tends to focus on the disruptive and exploitative character of globalization, and there are certainly plenty of cases in which the influence of foreign capital interests have caused or exacerbated conflict. On the other hand, the capitalist mythology regards globalization of the world economy as a great move toward world peace. In this view, global capitalism creates a homogeneity of culture which, even as it destroys the cultural moorings of other societies, might ultimately promote a certain consciousness of kind among participants in the global economy. Industrial workers in Southeast Asia have more in common with workers in America than their agrarian parents had; in fact, they may have more in common with Americans than with their parents. One might consider the economic interdependence of workers, consumers, investors, and managers around the world as ultimately a good thing. Whether exploitative or paternalistic, the relationships among these participants represent alliances that may be stronger than the differences among their governments. As the largest and most powerful NGOs, corporations might well view themselves as ambassadors for peace, for peace is, after all, good for business.

One might almost be willing to accept the peacemaking role of global capitalism, were it not for the short-term effects of wrenching cultural change that capital brings to developing societies. At the personal level, the change from a rural life of farming or in some cases even foraging or herding means not only a different way of making a living. Rather, it turns making a living into a problem, a problem that had not been thought of under the old cultural traditions. Whereas economic life might have been solely a system of obligations among extended family members to share labor and the results of labor, the market economy makes it a matter of getting a job and earning money to purchase the means of existence. The transition to industrialism and capitalism means a shift from a community- or family-based life to one focused on the individual. It usually means moving to the city—that is, the slums of a city—from a rural village. It promotes the nuclear family over the extended family, and it makes one's living dependent on the decisions of strangers (Isbister 1995). Thus Amin (1994) concluded that the unification of the world through global capitalism is an "illusion," made believable by the militarization of global markets.

Even given the cultural destruction wrought by capital development, one might argue that this is a temporary disruption that will ultimately lead to a new, modern culture more in tune with the realities of the world's demography and history. Perhaps it is needed cultural change overall, and while change is always painful, the Third World will be better off in a few generations. But the problem is that capitalism is likely to be a mercurial presence in many of these countries. As their labor forces become more sophisticated and more consumer-oriented, they tend to become too expensive relative to the people of some other country, as yet undeveloped. Thus economies in Southeast Asia collapsed in the late 1990s because of the underlying strains in their newly developing economies, throwing millions of new industrial workers, as well as their managers, out of work. The cultural change brought by capitalism and industrialization is thus arrested in its earliest, most destructive stages while people are cast adrift without even their original cultural tools to keep them afloat.

Civilian-Based Defense

Perhaps the most explicitly nonsovereign means of avoiding war is civilian-based defense (CBD). As developed by Gene Sharp (1968; 1970; 1973; 1980), this method of avoiding war is a curious mixture of military deterrence and nongovernmental action. At its simplest, CBD is an organized national program of military decentralization, in which civilians are trained and equipped to resist invasion by a foreign aggressor. This resistance is not primarily military, however, but social—that is, the sort of organized noncooperation that would render the nation ungovernable by the invader.

Sharp observed that military occupation and oppression is made possible only through the cooperation, active or tacit, of the populace of the occupied country. In wartime France, Holland, and Poland, for example, citizens went about their daily tasks in as normal a way as possible, which was of great help to the occupying regime. Further, they were generally willing to staff governmental and administrative posts, which the Nazis would have never been able to staff with their own people, thus ensuring continuity and stability in spite of the disruption of war and occupation. In most places they passively or actively helped identify Jews and others for deportation to death camps.

It is not hard to see the ease with which citizens cooperated and the difficulties involved with noncooperation. At its simplest, the mere act of going to work and making a living is a powerful aid to the occupying forces, who depend on the existing infrastructure to ensure the availability of food, transportation, government administration, and the myriad everyday needs of the populace. Slightly more active cooperation is the adaptation of one's own activities to the needs and ideologies of the occupying regime. Running the trains according to the schedules imposed by the Nazis or staffing a ration program would be examples. At the more extreme end of the spectrum, one might cooperate even in odious activities out of the belief that one can do it more humanely than the occupiers. Thus *Judenrat* administrators actually participated in the selection process for deportations (Dawidowicz 1975).

Sharp also noted that there were exceptions to the cooperation of civilian populations. The Warsaw uprising of 1944 was a spectacular one; a military resistance by a relatively small number of minimally-equipped civilians that gave the Wehrmacht a lot of trouble. But more subtle were the instances of simple noncooperation carried out by groups of ordinary people. In Denmark, for example, Jews were not deported to the camps simply because citizens refused to participate in their identification and arrest. Even this activity failed to be carried out because the Nazis lacked the personnel. More subtle noncooperation was conducted in Norway, where schoolteachers refused to modify their curricula to conform to National Socialist ideology. They also conducted a successful "sports strike," first refusing to participate in events with German participants, then later boycotting events sponsored by the German-controlled Norway's Sports Association. Although these actions didn't drive the Nazis from the country, they did help to keep them out of the culture. Noncooperation is a powerful weapon because it is much more difficult to force a population to do something than to make it stop doing something. No matter how powerful a military regime, it cannot make people show up at the soccer match.

The idea of resistance and noncooperation is thus not a new one. Sharp's idea was to marry noncooperation to deterrence—to develop such an organized and widespread program of noncooperation that a would-be invader would think twice about making the attempt. In short, the perfect civilian national defense program makes the country not worth invading.

Sharp and many others have suggested a variety of ways in which civilians can resist violent usurpation. These include various forms of strikes and boycotts, underground publication and broadcasting, and such interventions as setting up parallel government. And the recent evolution of postindustrial societies renders them in some ways even more fertile ground for noncooperation. Successful administration of government and the economy depends heavily on an infrastructure of communication, transport, and energy delivery. If the workers in any of these sectors were to stage a strike, any occupying force or government would have a difficult time indeed.

These sorts of actions would have to be prearranged on a national scale, and further, they would have to be seen to be highly organized and effective in order to be of deterrent value. Through a process of "transarmament" civilians would be trained for various general and specific roles in the nation's defense. A "Department of Civilian Defense" might be created to train resisters and coordinate their activities, though the very nature of the project would require a good deal of civilian input from the beginning. Since the resistance program is decentralized, involving transportation, schools, lower-level administration, and the like, people working in these organizations would have to be involved in the planning itself.

Civilian-based defense has a compelling appeal. It depends on the active participation of citizens in a democracy as democracy's own defense, as it requires an apparently ideal mix of individual voluntarism and submission to the collective if it is to work. To be effective in the military sense, citizens would have to be confident and trusting of their neighbors in the same way soldiers must count on their comrades. An effective civilian defense would require a strong and genuine social cohesion, by which people of all walks of life understand that they are collaborators in their own collective security. In short, such a society would have to reduce barriers of class and race so that citizens could maintain these views of one another.

Sharp's proposal for defense is actually to create a society worth defending, and this is what takes it beyond mere military defense. The involvement of citizens themselves is a departure from the present situation, in which the American upper classes in effect hire the military to protect and expand their interests. Further, this "contracted" defense force is largely composed of members of the lower classes, who enter the military as a means of security or modest advancement in the social hierarchy. It is an inherently alienating model reminiscent of the military forces of colonial powers, whose armies were often filled with the very people being colonized.

Civilian defense removes the distinction between the "hired gun" of the military establishment and the interests it defends, thus making the question of genuine national interests relevant. When all are participants in the national defense, the interests to be defended might be defined more strictly and with more consideration.

The prime benefit of civilian defense is, of course, that it is strictly defensive in its posture. Such arrangements do not provide for a long-range "defense" by which client regimes across the world can be propped up by military force, or for the securing of key natural resources through military aggression. Thus the civilian-defended society is a more "peaceful" society in the terms defined in Chapter 2: It is both inherently less aggressive internationally, and it is more internally consistent, predictable, and cohesive than the professionally defended society.

But in a sense this is the catch. A nation whose citizens are so loyal, committed, and willing to serve the common good is already probably fairly immune to foreign invasion, and certainly to usurpation from within. Consequently it needs little defense in the first place. The subtle lesson of Sharp's formulation is that it calls into question the meaning of "national defense" itself. The civilian defense model ironically portrays a national defense that conforms with the mythology Americans have cherished all along—the civilian soldier, the "minuteman" who comes to the aid of his country out of a fierce sense of collective responsibility and a genuinely selfless patriotism. In a civilian-defended America, citizens would act together to defend their way of life, and would be motivated to that action through a sober and amicable loyalty to the country. The United States would, in short, be the country it fancies itself to be. Thus Sharp probably does more to explode the national mythology than to propose a practicable defense plan.

This is not to say that the idea of civilian defense is a pie-in-the-sky fabrication. On the contrary, elements of Sharp's formulation can be found in many industrialized countries today. It is best exemplified in neutral states like Sweden and Switzerland and in countries that have experience in noncooperation, like the Netherlands, Belgium, and Norway.

Switzerland provides a most ironic example, as it is perhaps the most heavily militarized country in Europe. Conscription is universal, and the presence of the military can be seen everywhere. One might see at a quiet restaurant a table of soldiers in uniform enjoying a *raclette* while their assault rifles lean against the wall. Or a rural train depot might be "defended" by an infantry squad dug in behind barbed wire, training on a Saturday afternoon. The mountains are honeycombed with weapons caches and artillery emplacements; the valleys necklaced with pocket airstrips and supply depots. Switzerland is the apotheosis of the *defensive* national defense, largely civilian in makeup and wholly oriented toward resisting foreign aggression.

Switzerland's geography and history have much to do with its defensive posture. It occupies the most defensible terrain imaginable, all mountains with only narrow valleys to accommodate an invasion, which would quickly stall as the first tanks were hit by presighted artillery. Airpower would be of limited effect, as strategic installations are scattered and decentralized. As for history, the Swiss have a tradition of militarism and warfare, culminating in a civil war in 1847. Partly as a result of this, the Swiss greatly value their nationality and cohesion, taking pride in a history of neutrality and resistance to outside interference.

The paradox of civilian defense, whether it involves military power or nonviolent resistance, is that it relies ultimately on a very strong sense of nationalism, which historically has been the sentiment most associated with warlikeness. Switzerland or Sweden might be expected to maintain a purely defensive posture because their geography is well suited to defense, or because they cannot afford military involvement abroad. But the same might not be expected of the United States, Germany, or Russia. Their geographic and economic situations might simply make a more "offensive" defense more practical and effective. The promotion of a militaristic nationalism for these countries might—indeed, has—led to a history of aggression and conquest.

The nonsovereign approaches to reducing war depart from traditional, state-sponsored methods not only in their tactics but in their goals. Many of the nongovernmental organizations described above aim not only to reduce open conflict but also to facilitate negotiation and empathy among factions, and ultimately to build communities. Civilian-based defense is more than a system of military resistance to invasion; it too is best thought of as a community-building and reaffirming force. These kinds of initiatives and organizations thus offer a transition between preventing war and promoting peace, to which I turn in the following chapter.

Chapter Summary

Although many peacemakers regard the avoidance of war as only a partial step toward genuine peace, it is a step that would surely improve the lives of many people around the world. Several approaches to avoiding war are identified, many of which have been employed with some degree of success.

Deterrence, the simplest and oldest approach, involves convincing potential adversaries that an attack will be met by overwhelming force. Its contemporary form is characterized by the amassing of large nuclear arsenals, so destructive as to assure mutual destruction of both sides in a nuclear war. *Arms control* is the natural successor to deterrence, as nations seek to reduce the costs and risks of deterrence. *Collective security* arrangements are alliances made between states for mutual protection. *Empire* is another form of collective security, where small states are brought into alliances involuntarily. The League of Nations and the United Nations are attempts to end war through *world order*. A successful world order would be achieved if the nations of the world surrendered a measure of their sovereignty to a central global government that had the power to enforce a code of international law.

These are just the actions that sovereign states may take toward the cessation of war. There are also many nonsovereign options, including the activities of *nongovernmental organizations*, like Amnesty International and Greenpeace. One could argue that global trade and business is a powerful NGO as well, for good or ill. Finally, *civilian-based defense* is a method of deterrence in which the civilian population, rather than the military, threatens such noncooperation with a potential invader as to discourage invasion.

Questions for Review

What are the principal weaknesses of each of the war-avoidance methods listed below?

> deterrence
> arms control
> collective security
> world order
> civilian-based defense

Give a historical example of each of the methods above.

What advantages does "graduated reciprocation in tension reduction" have over arms control treaties?

How might collective security arrangements actually make war more likely?

What are the arguments for and against military intervention for peacekeeping? Apply them to a contemporary example.

What are the barriers to an effective world order? What factors might make an effective world order more likely in the future?

How might civilian-based defense have been employed to deter a Soviet attack during the Cold War?

Against what sort of aggression will CBD not be effective?

For Further Research

Betts, Richard K., ed. 1994. *Conflict After the Cold War Years: Arguments on and Causes of War and Peace.* New York: Macmillan.

Crocker, Chester A., and Fen Osler Hampson, eds. 1996. *Managing Global Chaos.* Washington, D.C.: United States Institute of Peace.

Diehl, Paul F., Daniel Druckman, and James Wall. 1998. "International Peacekeeping and Conflict Resolution: A Taxonomic Analysis with Implications." *Journal of Conflict Resolution* 42: 33–55.

Fischer, Dietrich. 1996. "A Global Peace Service." *Peace Review* 8: 563–568.

Kaldor, Mary. 1996. "A Cosmopolitan Response to New Wars." *Peace Review* 8: 505–514.

Peacenet. URL: http://www.igc.org.igc/peacenet/.

Social Science Research Council Peace Studies Links. URL: http://www.ssrc.org/-search/ipslist.htm.

Thompson, W. Scott, and Kenneth M. Jensen, eds. 1991. *Approaches to Peace: An Intellectual Map.* Washington, D.C.: U.S. Institute of Peace.

United Nations Peacekeeping Operations. URL: http://www.un.org/Depts/-dpko/.

7 *Methods of Promoting Peace*

The previous chapter described a variety of ways in which states have tried, with greater or lesser success, to control war and violence among themselves. One general direction these efforts have taken is the application of deterrent force; military might sufficient to discourage the military adventures of potential adversaries. This is an approach fraught with risk, especially as weapons have become increasingly dangerous and increasingly available even to small nations.

A second form of this effort has been to expand the "peace group"—that is, to form larger states, coalitions, and empires that include larger populations within them. The collective security afforded by this approach both increases the strength of the group in question and reduces the potential number of adversaries. The problem with this approach is that such groups can only get so big before they are subject to irresistible internal strains among cultural, economic, ethnic, or religious subgroups. This limit on size and inclusiveness depends, one might suppose, on a number of geographical, technological, and other factors.

A third approach is to bypass the state as the sole actor in the conduct of war and peace. Citizen diplomacy and civilian national defense are ways in which the inherent barriers to peace posed by nationalism and statehood can be diminished. Instead of relying on the state apparatus for defense, ordinary citizens can interact with those of potential adversary states, undermining the polarizing tendency toward nationalism and xenophobia. Or citizens might be formed into a genuinely defensive force, protecting territory as well as culture and social structure. Such an approach promises both reduced violence in defense (being an inherently "defensive" approach) but also increased social solidarity and cohesion.

Although each of these historical methods for reducing war has shown a certain level of effectiveness, it is clear that none of them are really ways of achieving "positive" peace. In Chapter 2 this sort of peace was defined as a matter of predictability and trust both in one's fellow citizens and in the future. This trust is twofold: It is manifest first in the ability of people to take the role of the other to a high degree. In peaceful societies people enjoy a high degree of consensus; they agree on the most important values and understandings and they are aware of this agreement. Further, they take for granted that others are similarly aware of their agreement, because they can readily imagine what others are thinking. This "intersubjectivity" makes possible a sort of empathy and trust that is deeply internalized.

The second kind of trust has to do with perceptions of the world and its future. In peaceful societies people enjoy a clear perception of the world; they understand it and are able to anticipate the future accurately. Social structures, cultural ideas, and shared understandings are stable and comprehensible. This does not mean, by the way, that peaceful societies must be static or hidebound. It does mean that what change occurs is understandable within current conceptions of the world and that it comes at a pace that allows its incorporation into existing values and beliefs.

These two kinds of regularity and predictability are mutually reinforcing. It is the regularity and predictability of social structures and cultural ideas that make it possible for people to take each other's roles so easily; conversely, the wide sharing of cultural understandings helps the society appear solid and relatively stable. Not that such societies are immune to conflict. Individuals and groups within such societies still dispute material as well as ideological issues. In societies so integrated, the terms of dispute are usually clear, as are the bases for the different positions of the parties involved.

This sort of peace cannot easily be promoted by the methods described in Chapter 6. Certainly deterrence is an ineffective means of achieving peace, especially in the nuclear/biological/chemical warfare age, as the entire world has become unsure of any future at all. The growth of empires similarly brings a great deal of uncertainty, upheaval, and suffering even as it integrates larger populations into "peace groups." The nonsovereign methods of citizen diplomacy and civilian-based defense offer some promise of creating greater integration and consensus, but even these rest partly on the fear of enemies.

The reduction of war is only a partial step toward peace. In fact, it might be argued that ultimately war cannot be eliminated without the construction of genuine, positive peace. The question for this chapter is how "positive" peace is achieved.

The Peace-Justice Connection

Chapter 2 demonstrated that there are in principle two ways that peace can be promoted. The first way is through the coercion of a powerful state apparatus that so restricts both behavior and thought that there is little room for unpredictability. Such regimes generally fail because it is simply too difficult to create and enforce a contrived social order that does not conflict with deeper values and beliefs of the society. In spite of efforts to demolish vestiges of the old values through socialization and control of information, such regimes tend to seem artificial, inconsistent with more fundamental beliefs and values.

The second and more typical way to real peace is through the creation and maintenance of *justice*. This is not a universalistic or normative ideal, but rather a culture-neutral concept best described as consistency among values, beliefs, and norms. In just societies, each element of ideology, of belief, and of structure is *justified* by others. Life is coherent and comprehensible, and the human need to "make sense" of the world is satisfied. The ideal of justice in this sense seems elusive and even utopian. But it has not always been difficult to achieve; in fact, the very concept of "justice" has only become relevant in the modern age. It is the development of the modern, industrial society that has made justice problematic, because modernism itself is characterized by pluralism and rapid change. This can be understood as a consequence of the evolution of social order, which is the evolution of peace itself.

The Evolution of Peace

The creation of peace may be viewed as a matter of creating social solidarity itself; conversely, the evolution and development of societies is the evolution of peace. Put another way, the problem of human organization has been the problem of making the peace of predictability. The solutions to this problem have been varied throughout human history, but they can be characterized by three general methods. These are described in rough order of historical appearance, but all three solutions may be found in the contemporary world.

Functional Homogeneity.   The simplest way to solidarity and consensus is for all members of the society to play more or less the same roles. Many of the "peaceful societies" described by Fabbro (1978) are homogeneous in this way, characterized by a simple division of labor and few differentiated roles. Many are foraging peoples and their social structures afford few ways for people to differentiate themselves in terms of power, wealth, or prestige. These societies are characterized by what Durkheim called "mechanical solidarity," the consciousness-of-kind that comes from a taken-for-granted understanding of similarity. Although individuals might well develop personal animosities among one another, there are few structural means for persons or groups to develop collective animosities.

Cultural Homogeneity. As human communities have grown larger with the invention and growth of agriculture, it has become increasingly difficult to maintain a simple division of labor. Roles become specialized, societies become increasingly stratified, and consequently it becomes more difficult for people to easily understand and empathize with one another. But as functional homogeneity declines, a homogeneity of *identity* takes its place. Although people no longer view themselves as the same in terms of experience or role, they are encouraged or forced to view themselves as similar in cultural identity. Japanese society, for example, is often cited as one of racially and culturally similar people and thus more amenable to solidarity than pluralistic societies like the United States. And it is true that Japanese culture does emphasize conformity far more than American or most European cultures; it is likely too that perceived similarity among individuals accounts for some of this.

It is worth noting, though, that until a few centuries ago Japan was a land fragmented into warring shogunates, and that its highest values were military in nature. In fact, the samurai ideal is still cherished as a part of the Japanese mythology, much as the cowboy symbolizes deeply-held American values. Most of the homogeneity that characterizes Japanese culture today is thus a social creation, imposed by force but made "natural" over time. At the same time, Japan and societies like it are highly complex in terms of division of labor; thus the homogeneity of Japanese society is not a homogeneity of function or of experience, but of identity.

Civility. In highly pluralistic societies a certain degree of peace is attained by simple enforcement of peaceability; that is, by the rule of law and sanctions requiring cooperation. American society is a good example, and has been pretty much throughout its history. In the United States, successive waves of immigrants (both voluntary and forced) and successive conquests (Indians and Mexicans) have been construed as "other" than the dominant culture and have been segregated physically and culturally from one another. The "melting pot" ideal regards these groups as fundamentally different from the dominant culture, even as it overstates the power of assimilation and the tendency toward homogeneity. The notion of a single culture or race or even ethos is simply not a part of the American ideology. The peace of American society (what peace there is) is a peace of *law*; an imposed requirement of civility and equal justice that operates to minimize the effects of the "inherent" and taken-for-granted differences among people.

This is a fundamentally "rational" construction of peace, which departs substantially from more "traditional" ones that rely on a deep perception of similarity and empathy. Americans (and, to a greater or lesser extent, people in other modern societies) do not feel a particular empathy with fellow citizens of other ethnic traditions or social classes. Instead they feel (at best) an obligation to treat others fairly as individuals worthy of the protection of fundamental rights and freedoms, and perhaps also to recognize other cultural traditions as deserving of respect and consideration.

The Limitations of Civility

It is the rule of law, maintained by government and the force that undergirds it, that seeks to minimize conflict and violence in modern societies. But it does little to maintain genuine peace, in the sense of predictability and empathy. For example, Americans of different classes, cultures, races, and sexes are held, more or less, to good behavior by law and traditions of civility, but they do not find one another very predictable or understandable. There is a low and declining level of taken-for-grantedness in the expectations of others. For example, children are reminded to run from strangers making conversation with them, for fear that they might be kidnappers or molesters—as indeed they might. Handguns are widely viewed as a legitimate and effective form of protection from the possibility of attack, even as they are more likely to be used against a spouse or oneself. Meanwhile, husbands and wives find themselves in a constant process of negotiation of roles that change from year to year; geographic mobility only exacerbates the difficulties. And these difficulties lead to violence dismayingly often.

The idea of an evolution of social forms of peace is consistent with a long tradition in social theory. Basic anthropological theory rests on a theory of cultural evolution driven by the basic means of production; from foraging to horticultural to industrial and postindustrial. Marx regarded the evolution of the means of production as the fundamental engine of social and cultural change as well, asserting that capitalism was the product of earlier forms of economy and predicting that it would ultimately yield to a new form. Durkheim conceived of the history of human arrangements as an evolution of social solidarity from "mechanical" solidarity to "organic." Finally, Weber traced the history of human organization from "traditional" to increasingly "rational."

In many ways these various continua from classical anthropological and sociological theory are the same thing. Durkheim conceived the two forms of solidarity to solve the problem of developing a universal theory of social structure that would apply to modern as well as ancient societies. They explain how the modern world could fulfill the same functions as the ancient world, in spite of its dissimilarities to it. If all social structures require solidarity to survive, then such disparate worlds must perform this essential function in very different ways. Thus the simpler, traditional societies were held together by "mechanical" solidarity; modern, complex ones by the "organic" type.

Weber viewed the same process—the evolution of social order—in a parallel way. His generalization of history characterized social evolution as a process of increasing rationalization, by which human roles and interactions become increasingly fragmented and instrumental. Rationalization and its organizational manifestation, bureaucracy, are made necessary by industrialism because industrialism brings a more complex division of labor. A product comes to be made not by a craftsman, but by dozens of less-skilled workers whose efforts require supervision and coordination. And the manufacturing process is a metaphor for the social order itself, as society at large is characterized by a greater division of roles and functions, requiring coordination, supervision, and control. This is a formulation similar to Durkheim's, for the ultimate force behind modernism and rationalization is also the increasing complexity of the division of labor.

In the views of both Durkheim and Weber this evolution of social order has led to problems; in fact, they both lamented much the same problem. For Durkheim, the complex division of labor of modern society gives rise to anomie, a variably translated French term that actually might be a fair synonym for "peacelessness" in the sense used here. In societies characterized by anomie, norms are uncertain or of insufficient strength to provide a "common morality." This makes it difficult for individuals to "have a clear concept of what is and what is not proper and acceptable behavior" (Ritzer 1992: 85).

In Weber's view, the result of modernism's complexity is the "disenchantment" of the world. He spent his career demonstrating the loss of meaning and humanity in a wide variety of social institutions as they evolved over the centuries. The economy, religion, law, politics, even the arts—all had over time replaced the familiar taken-for-grantedness of tradition with a calculated, instrumental involvement based on the connection of means to ends. One way to characterize the rational approach to these institutions might be to note that in the rational world it becomes legitimate to ask "why." Why avoid sin? What is the rationale for a law? What makes a work of art "good?" Of what *use* is it?

Ritzer (1992) identified six basic characteristics of Weber's concept of rationality. These include a focus within organizations on calculability through counting and quantification. Further, rational organizations seek to gain *control over uncertainties*, through management, the collection and analysis of information, and record keeping. Finally, they commit a great deal of effort to ensuring *predictability*, through larger-scale organization and integration. In short, the essence of modernism is the rise of new, rational methods of maintaining predictability—the rule of law. As populations grow, diversify, and become more complex and dense, new ways evolve to make life more understandable and predictable. Tradition is replaced by reason, obedience by incentive, morals by law, faith by calculation.

In Weber's view it couldn't work in the long run. Aside from what he considered the dehumanizing aspect of rationalism, he also predicted that ultimately this way of organizing human life would find humans in an "iron cage" of their own making. This cage would consist of institutions of control that use force and coercion in order to maintain society, because the traditional, more "natural" forces no longer applied. And this is pretty much what has happened. The modern bureaucratic state and the corporation have replaced the clan and the church as the primary regulators and meaning givers of social life. People are no longer governed by familiars but by strangers, and the impersonal power they wield is the power of violence and the threat to material security.

It is no wonder that many people have come to think that peace and justice require individual freedom and a dissolution of social institutions generally. But this is an erroneous conclusion, for it relies on a conception of human nature that assumes the removal of social control will free up the inherent peacefulness of humankind. In fact, it is effective and meaningful social order—better called community—that unleashes the cooperative and constructive impulse. The problem in the contemporary world is that bureaucratic rationality is a poor system for achieving it.

Modern societies pose a historically new problem, then, for the creation of peace. Because the hallmark of modernism is reliance on rational, rather than traditional, bases for interaction and cooperation, modern societies tend to reject tradition as a foundation for civility. Where people in a traditional society cooperate simply because that is the way to live, those in modern societies cooperate because it is pragmatic, expedient, and reasonable. In short, one could say that the growth of increasingly complex layers of rational organization leads to a breakup of consensus on meanings and values. This in turn requires the imposition of force and coercion as a means of cooperation, and this tends to create injustice.

This has certainly been the case where modernization has come rapidly to traditional societies. At the very least, modernization has tended to lead to an erosion of what Pfeifer (1996) calls "indigenous knowledge" as development imposes "an ethnocentric and imperialist vision" on the local culture. John Isbister (1995) describes the disruptive effects of industrialization, modernization, and urbanization on traditional cultures, and makes a persuasive case that the poverty of the Third World is not an eternal fact of life there, but a new ill brought by the First World. He begins his discussion of the price of development with "Five Stories," a chapter that narrates the experiences of actual people in various Third World societies. One example is Shahhat, a young Egyptian *fellah*, or peasant, who lives on the banks of the Nile. Just during Shahhat's lifetime, the village way of life has changed dramatically.

> For millennia, the annual flood of the Nile River determined the rhythms of agricultural life. The river flooded each September to November, then receded, leaving a fertile layer of silt. Crops of wheat, barley and lentils were planted and harvested in April. There was just one crop a year, and summer was a time of rest.
>
> But in the region of Berat, the Nile flooded for the last time in 1966: thenceforth the flow of the great river was controlled by the towering Aswan Dam. The dam and its works provide continuous, planned irrigation of fields in place of the annual flood, and continuous cultivation is now possible, with up to three crops a year. (Isbister 1995: 9)

The consequences of this technological progress were immense. Now the *fellahin* had to work twelve months a year, and that disrupted the social and cultural calendar. Moreover, they had to use chemical fertilizers to supplement the soil's fertility. Motorized pumps had to be used in the irrigation process, so electricity and its concomitants came to the villages. Railways were laid to improve the shipping of crops for sale in the urban centers. New strains of crops were used to accommodate the new soils and growing seasons; these were introduced by the government. And salinity levels rose in the soil as it was overused and overirrigated.

Isbister concludes that, although Shahhat works more regularly than before, he is no more prosperous and even less secure about the future. His world is thus less peaceful than before. And in spite of having endured wrenching changes in his culture, he has gained nothing in return.

> In the old days the *fellahin* were dependent, as peasants always are, on the vagaries of the weather. Now they are still dependent on the weather and on much more besides—chemical processes, international market forces

and organizational structures that are far beyond their control or even comprehension. (1995: 9)

Similar stories are played out in a variety of developing countries around the world. They are the stories of people who used to be farmers or herdsmen but who are now tin miners, hotel maids, coffee plantation workers, or jobless urban slum dwellers. Some have been victimized by military or police or guerrilla forces as they have become a despised minority within the culture that has overrun them. All are poor, living in societies based on cash rather than obligation, and all are disconnected from the social and cultural realities that made for a sensible world. Isbister concludes:

> The poverty of the Third World is not "traditional"; it is not an ancient way of life. The traditional cultures of the Third World are rich and various, and they are closer to the surface of everyday life than traditions are in the industrialized world, where they have been suppressed. The great religions of the Third World—Hinduism, Buddhism, Islam—are not apologies for poverty; they are integral worldviews that bind the generations together. . . . The endless urban slums are not traditional; they are recent. (1995: 20)

This is not to say that modernization and development have not been resisted. Mohandas Gandhi, spiritual and political leader of India's movement for independence from British rule, preached maintenance of traditional Indian ways of living, from ox-powered farming to homespun clothing, as a means of warding off the problems of modernization. Islamic fundamentalism can be viewed as another form of this resistance. It explicitly identifies modernization as the cause of the Muslim world's ills, and calls for strict interpretation of scripture and adherence to tradition as a way of insulating the populace from modernization's pernicious effects: worldliness, sin, and loss of meaning. It is no surprise that Shahhat's Egypt is currently the site of a growing fundamentalist movement, which the Egyptian government is resisting.

The process of modernization is not unique to the Third World; it can be seen occurring in societies already quite modernized and rationalized. The process of change, accelerated as it is in the modern world, tends to cause inconsistencies and conflicts among the values and ideas of a society as people grope for new ideas consistent with new realities. The women's movement is a good example. When American society was an agrarian society, the role of women was fairly well understood by all. It was a role secondary in power and status, a role in which a wife was subservient to her husband economically and socially. Viewed in hindsight from today's perspective, it was an unjust role system. But viewed in its own time, the different role obligations of women and men made sense; the inequality they implied seemed natural.

American society changed in the second half of the nineteenth century. From the Civil War onward, industrial production caught up to and overtook agricultural production in importance to American life. People began moving to the cities in larger numbers, working in factories and bound to the company rather than working on farms and bound to the land. Family structure changed radically as families were separated for most of the day; children became an economic burden rather than an asset. The farm and household management skills that women had exercised in the old days were obsolete. In short, the functional elements of women's roles were changing.

But the social relations were slow to change. As the "natural" supremacy of men no longer seemed so natural, increasingly elaborate cultural justifications were invented to maintain that supremacy. Women began to be characterized as the weaker sex, a view helped along by male-dominated philosophical and scientific communities. The rising medical profession collaborated in promoting the idea that women (at least middle- and upper-class women) were inherently sickly, requiring medical attention for any number of peculiarly female ailments (Ehrenreich and English 1975). Just as the invention of racist ideology had helped justify slavery, sexist ideology was used to justify an unequal position of women that had become unjust. An inequality that had once been *justified* by functional differences and cultural consensus became *enforced* by oppression.

Justice and Justification

One tends to think of injustice in universal terms, as inequality or oppression or something else. Yet different cultures have different ideas of justice, and this is difficult to reconcile with dearly held "universal" principles. This conflict between the desire for justice as one's culture defines it and the norm of cultural relativism is one of the social scientist's enduring headaches. One wants to respect other cultural traditions yet project one's own conception of justice everywhere.

The remedy is to think of justice as an *inconsistency* between social realities and cultural values, or among cultural values themselves. Where individual freedom is valued, restrictions on those freedoms are unjust. Where equality is valued, gender oppression is unjust. But where the cohesion of the tribe or village is valued, individual independence or equality or initiative adds no justice and in fact may be a threat to it. Modern societies are more likely to be unjust in this sense because they are more complex and therefore include more opportunities for inconsistency among values.

This is a distinctly functionalist definition of justice, for it implies that societies work best when their component parts are consistent with each other. Injustice tears at the social fabric by reducing cohesion and confidence, and by increasing alienation and anomie. In short, it is in itself a breach of peace. It is for this reason that the pursuit of peace is linked with the pursuit of justice: genuine, positive peace is simply too difficult to achieve when values and structures are in so much conflict. It is too difficult for people to find their commonality and to take the role of the other when values and beliefs are inconsistent. If one wishes to make peace, then, one must reduce injustice—that is, social structures must be more consistent with the deep cultural values shared across social divisions. In other words, the structures and ideas of society must be more mutually justifying.

All of which raises the question of how this might be done. It is unlikely that government can accomplish the task; in fact, the overall trend among governments has been to erode the self-justifying character of societies by making them increasingly complex. This is the "iron cage" Weber warned of: the growth of government and other bureaucratic institutions whose need for efficiency and control leads to increasing inconsistencies among values, beliefs, and norms. These inconsistencies are in turn overcome by the application of oppressive legal and military control. This is why people interested in making peace are generally better off avoiding the bureaucratic channels of officialdom, with exceptions for specific opportunities to use government against itself.

In general, making a peaceful society must involve more fundamental change, in two ways. First, social structures that conflict with cultural values have to be dismantled. In this way the injustice of slavery, which conflicted with fairly fundamental American values, was an obvious target for social reform. Likewise apartheid became more clearly unjust in the eyes of the European world as it let go of racist ideologies that had supported colonialism of earlier eras.

More subtly, a society's values and beliefs are often in conflict. There is little doubt, for example, that American society is deeply racist and has been since the era of slavery and of Indian conquest, yet this racism coexists with ideals of democratic equality. The reason it is hard to dismantle the structure of racial inequality is that it is justified by these deeply-held racist values and beliefs. Thus peacemakers find themselves in a position not only of having to rid society of unjust structures, but also of trying to reconcile the very values and beliefs of the society. The culture itself must be changed, rid of less essential values that compete with those that are deeper and upon which the greater portion of society can find consensus. In this way, the peacemaker's task is cultural change.

This is a tall order, for cultural change is not easily rushed or directed. Still, it is achieved surprisingly often, sometimes on a global scale, by social movements. Slavery was largely ended worldwide over the past few centuries. In this century, colonial governments have been ousted in Africa, Asia, and Oceania. Just in the past few decades many oppressive political regimes have been deposed and replaced around the world.

These changes have mostly not been made by coercion or revolution, but rather by nonviolent social justice movements. The abolition of slavery in Great Britain, Brazil, and the Caribbean was largely the result of social reform pushed by citizen groups. (In the contrasting American case, slavery ended under decidedly violent circumstances; one legacy is that American race relations remain strained.) The extension of basic rights to women continues to spread via nonviolent means. The downfall of the Ceauçescu regime in Rumania was mostly nonviolent, as was the collapse of the Soviet Union. The "velvet revolution" in Czechoslovakia resulted in the establishment of two republics, one of them headed by the playwright Vaclav Havel. More astonishing, the end of apartheid in South Africa led to the creation of a new constitution and government, led by none other than the previous regime's star political prisoner, Nelson Mandela. More revolutionary still is the new South Africa's orientation toward the previous regime: Instead of facing criminal trials and retribution, former oppressors are invited to seek reconciliation with their victims.

These revolutions were achieved not by force of arms but by the force of nonviolent citizen action. It is this kind of force that has been most responsible for a good many of the fundamental changes in social structures and cultural beliefs, and I turn now to examining how this force works to create justice.

The Creation of Peace

Nonviolent action actually refers to a wide range of activities designed to bring about social change. Types of nonviolent action have been categorized according to motive, intentions toward opponent, the nature of the target, methods, characteristics of the parties involved, the amount of planning used, and of course, the goal of the action (Burgess and Burgess 1994). In all, Sharp (1973) identified 198 different nonviolent techniques. What all these forms have in common is that they are collective activities intended to bring about social change, and to do so in a way that uses the fundamental human tendency to create a coherent world. The other thing they have in common is that they all derive ultimately from the ideas of Mohandas Gandhi.

Gandhi was an Indian who grew up under British colonial rule. His nonviolent activism was first manifested in South Africa, where he worked for an Indian law firm. His exposure there to overt racism led him to work for a variety of social justice movements and to develop his theory of nonviolent resistance. After returning to India he got involved in labor organizing, which led to resistance to the British rule and the movement for Indian independence. It was leading this nationwide movement that made him a world figure, not only for its success but for its nonaggressive approach.

Gandhi was, of course, not the first to use nonviolent methods in working for social change. Nonviolence has always been a means of reducing injustice and promoting peace, as evidenced by earlier philosophical treatments (Henry David Thoreau, for example) and various social reform movements over the past several centuries. These have often come from religious sects (Quakers and Buddhists, for example), but not always; the women's suffrage movements in North America and Europe were largely secular ones, as is the contemporary women's movement.

Gandhi's contribution to nonviolence theory was to codify the various techniques, ideals, values, and doctrines of nonviolent action into a coherent philosophy, couched in terms of Hindu faith. Widely misunderstood as a "passive" method or one relying solely on a moral faith in the ultimate victory of good, Gandhi's process of *satyagraha* is actually a socially and politically sophisticated philosophy of conflict resolution and justice making. It was successfully used by Gandhi in South Africa and India, by Martin Luther King and others in the American Civil Rights movement, and by a variety of organizations in antiwar and antimilitarism movements around the world. In fact Sharp (1970) was able to cite eighty-five cases of nonviolent action used in this century up to 1970. It might well be historically the most effective method of real social change available to humankind.

The primary goal of satyagraha is to achieve a "change of heart" in one's opponent—the repressive regime, the unjust political system, the brutal police—through the application of "truth-force," nonviolence, and self-suffering (Bondurant 1965). By means of a variety of tactics such as demonstrations, civil disobedience, noncooperation, and boycott, satyagraha movements invite retaliation and repression by the opponent. The suffering endured by the satyagrahi as a result of these responses disarms the opponent by presenting an unexpected reaction to brutality, thereby throwing him off balance. This has been called "moral jiu-jitsu" by Gregg (1935/1968) and "political jiu-jitsu" by Sharp (1970).

The refusal to resist violence with violence amounts to a refusal to take part in a relationship that the perpetrator expects and often requires. It is by disarming the opponent and upsetting the oppressor/oppressed relationship that the nonviolent resister hopes to bring about the opponent's "change of heart."

Stubborn adherence to these principles made the Indian independence movement unique, and very likely made it effective. Years of persistent demonstration and self-exposure to police action and other official retribution gradually took its toll on British resolve and British legitimacy. It was by similar principles decades later that African Americans held sit-ins at segregated lunch counters (witnessing for and exposing the truth of segregation) and suffered both public scorn and arrest. Civil rights marchers voluntarily exposed themselves to police brutality in a variety of ways, as documented by grainy black-and-white films of peaceful marchers rendered unconscious by fire hoses and attacked by police dogs.

The Sociology of Satyagraha

Gandhi's formulation seems essentially individualistic and even mystical. The language of satyagraha is loaded with abstract ideals and articles of faith—the power of "truth-force"; the importance of *ahimsa,* an aspect of love as well as of nonviolence; the value of suffering. The connections to the teachings of Christ were not lost on Gandhi (he often referred to the Sermon on the Mount; see Gandhi 1951) nor on others (Johnson and Ledbetter 1997). Moreover, the principles of satyagraha seem oriented toward individual morality and action. The goal of satyagraha is expressed as encouraging "the opponent" to change "his" mind, and the means of doing so are often expressed as the behavior of the moral individual. One "does penance" for the injustice or violence of one's opponent; one fasts as a means of purification.

This religiously based orientation to action resulted in a widespread misunderstanding of satyagraha as a passive and defeatist strategy. It appeared that the whole enterprise was based on a faith in humankind; that good would eventually win over evil simply because it had to. Indeed, many later followers of Gandhi's principles did adopt fatalistic and, some might say, self-indulgent orientations to social action. These followers of "principled nonviolence" viewed nonviolent action not as a means to an end but as a way of life and an end in itself (Bond 1994). Rapoport (1992) called this "religious pacifism," and identified its main weakness as a belief that peace could be made only by each individual person becoming more peaceful.

By the 1960s new interpretations began to emerge, primarily from Gene Sharp (1968; 1970; 1973; 1980) and Joan Bondurant (1965; 1968). These views stressed the pragmatic use of nonviolence as a political and social change strategy rather than as a philosophy for living. Sharp especially focused on changing the language of nonviolence to an active, assertive one.

The strain between the "principled" and the "pragmatic" nonviolent resisters can be seen today in many peace and justice movements. Those focused on tactics and outcomes sometimes will be seen huddling in a strategy session while others are participating in a prayer service or purification ritual—after which both groups march out together to get themselves arrested. Usually both approaches are able to coexist for the sake of mutual support as in the case of the Honeywell Project, in which "strategists" and "witnesses" worked together in a "symbiotic relationship" (Rogne and Harper 1990). In some cases, though, the strain can be sufficient to break up the movement.

Despite these apparent divisions, the two approaches to nonviolence are not fundamentally at odds with each other. Sociological principles can reconcile the personal and mystical approach of Gandhi with the pragmatic and political approach of the moderns. At first glance, this might seem unlikely. In addition to its apparent focus on individual moral action rather than collective action, satyagraha seems also to imply universals—anathema to those accustomed to a culturally-relativistic point of view. The basis of action in "truth-force" implies fundamental truth, independent of culture or collective consensus. The use of "evil" and "good" as ways of characterizing action further implies universal, transcendent values. Moreover, the goal of bringing about a "change of heart" in the opponent implies a reductionist orientation toward social change: It sounds almost as if the satyagrahi hopes to change society one person at a time. One might suppose that the these ideas are impossible to understand in pragmatic, sociological terms.

But this is not the case at all. The language of nonviolent resistance, even in its purest Gandhian form, readily translates into sociological language. Each of the fundamental principles of satyagraha can be understood in concrete and demystified terms, as a system for making social change.

The "Change of Heart." Translating the philosophy of satyagraha into sociological terms might best begin with its fundamental goal—to bring about a "change of heart" in one's opponent. This aspect of the process is often illustrated in anecdotes about individual "changes of heart," for example, individual policemen being swayed not to beat and arrest demonstrators, or individual Klansmen sympathizing with civil rights demonstrators (Robbins and Robbins 1968). But changing the hearts of individual agents of a whole system of repression is a losing strategy, of sentimental but not pragmatic value. The police, soldiers, thugs, and goons only represent the tip of an iceberg of structure, interests, and ideology.

It is clear that, while such individual events are useful symbols that might encourage wider change, satyagraha movements have something larger in mind. At the very least, they seek to weaken the power of the social structures that oppress: not just one policeman but the police force; not just one Klansman but the Klan itself. But goals typically are broader still; the movement wants not only to stop the police from enforcing the law but to change the law itself or render it irrelevant. Disbanding the Klan is only an intermediate and symbolic victory if discrimination and racism persist.

Satyagraha movements operate on the recognition that unjust social structures ultimately thrive on the consent of the populace. According to Sharp (1980) even the most brutal and totalitarian regimes are dependent on public cooperation. He draws from Hannah Arendt (1963) in showing that even the Holocaust was made possible only by the tacit cooperation of ordinary citizens. In the end, then, no movement can bring about substantial social change without causing a "change of heart" in the community itself. Thus the movement's target is not individuals or even the structures that enforce injustice, but rather the established ideas that undergird the unjust regime.

The objective of a social justice movement is therefore to replace the beliefs, values, and norms that support the unjust status quo with different ones—typically older, deeper ones, closer to the core values of the society. Its general method is to demonstrate that the existing regime rests on ideas that are too complex and far removed from the community's "core" values. For example, the Civil Rights movement persistently pointed out the moral inconsistencies in American thinking about race. The simple act of sitting down at a lunch counter or in the front of a bus, and the often violent reaction, demonstrated the "wrongness" of discrimination to even the coldest observer. The simplicity and straightforwardness of such acts tended to focus the public's attention away from the violation of racial law, and instead on the meaning and illegitimacy of the law itself. People had to ask themselves *why* it was wrong to sit at an ordinary lunch counter or in the front of a bus, or to vote.

Demonstrations do not immediately bring about large-scale change in social ideas. There is usually a fair amount of backlash against them as the populace hangs on to the "old peace," the familiar rules and ideas that have made life livable up to then. The process of change is gradual, as the "change of heart" that amounts to a change in consensus occurs a few people at a time. A highly-publicized and well-conducted nonviolent demonstration might change the views of just a few observers. But these few "converts" actually count double against the status quo, because they not only are counted among the adherents to the new ideas but their support is also subtracted from the old order. They become just that many more examples that contradict the taken-for-grantedness of the old ideas. When just a relatively few people desert the taken-for-granted status quo, it becomes difficult for all to see it as natural, universal, and eternal.

Meanwhile, people hanging on to the old order find that they require increasingly elaborate justifications for it, in contrast to the simple justifications of the new thinkers. The justification for segregation is simply a greater intellectual and moral stretch than the justification for equality. Similarly, the case for peace ("thou shalt not kill") is easier to grasp than the convoluted and tenuous case that is nearly always made for war. Ultimately the new ideas have enough adherents to reach a sort of "critical mass" at which point they no longer can be viewed as marginal. They then become legitimated by mainstream literature and media—today, largely by television. In the nineties, for example, the portrayal of gays and lesbians as ordinary characters in film and television did much not only to reflect a change in norms but also to accelerate it. Some theorists have attempted to quantify the critical mass necessary to create a new norm, one study suggesting that when 5 percent of the population adopts a new idea, it becomes "imbedded" in the population; at 20 percent it is "unstoppable" (Brigham 1990).

In demonstrating this simpler, more "natural" world, the satyagrahi also forces the existing powers to do something active to enforce the status quo. Rosa Parks's sitting in the front of the bus was not a particularly "active" bit of resistance—rather, it was simply an act of noncompliance. It offered the city authorities the chance to do nothing; to simply let the action pass and thus bring an end to segregation on the buses. In order for segregation to continue, the city had to do something active; to arrest her or in some other way make a point of enforcing and maintaining the status quo.

It is typical that the status quo requires a lot of organization, effort, resources, and machinations to keep it running when threatened even a little. The deployment of National Guard troops in controlling demonstrations against the Vietnam War is a good example. The point was brought into sharp focus when the National Guard actually opened fire on demonstrators at Kent State University. This sort of overreaction further reduces the legitimacy of the old ideas, as it becomes clear to the populace that extraordinary efforts are being made to shore up a system that until then was thought to be the natural way of the world. Thus the law in all its complexity is invoked to keep the lid on, while demonstrators do simple things like sitting down in a public space or showing up someplace where they are not allowed. The inherent simplicity and clarity of the world they model is contrasted starkly with the cumbersome, overbearing, and often violent one that resists them.

"Truth" and "Goodness." A second fundamental principle of satyagraha is that the actions one takes must be in the pursuit of "truth," and that "evil" must always be met with "good." This too sounds like a spiritual notion based on a claim of universal values. One could raise the objection that there is no inherent reason why a movement for evil ends could not use the same methods and tactics. If Gandhi's methods work for people seeking "good" then why won't it work for those seeking evil?

Sociologists take claims of "good" and "evil" with a grain of salt. Students learn early that ideas about goodness are culturally shaped, and that attempts to evaluate cultural values according to a universal principle of goodness are fraught with problems. For example, one may dismiss the aggressive character of the Yanomamö as evil, but one does so from the point of view of one's own culture. Thus the condemnation of another culture's values is inherently ethnocentric. More subtly, it takes only a little reflection to recognize that modern industrial societies far outpace the Yanomamö in violence by any objective standard—it's just that they legitimate their mass killing as warfare.

How, then, can sociology make sense of satyagraha's call to fight evil with good? How can one know "good"? Gandhi addressed this problem by recognizing that good and evil are relative, yet collective and consensually defined; as in this discussion of what constitutes a wrong:

> The wrong act must be patent, accepted as such by all and spiritually harmful, and the doer must be aware of it. . . . Moreover, one should not do penance for an act, which one regards as wrong as his personal faith or opinion. It is possible that what one holds to be wrong today he might regard as innocent tomorrow. So the wrong must be such as is accepted by society to be so. (quoted in Bondurant 1965: 21)

In this way Gandhi adopted a social definition of evil: that which society clearly agrees is evil, and in fact, that which the evildoer himself would recognize as wrong. He might even have cited Scheff's (1967) definition of consensus—a matter of collective agreement, awareness, and understanding—had he been writing several decades later. In Bondurant's view, "While admitting truth to be relative, some objective standard is established" (1965: 21).

The satyagrahi's notion of good is not really a universal one, but a "practically universal" one. If one translates "goodness" to mean fundamental cultural values (whatever the culture being discussed), the satya-grahi's conception of justice becomes the adherence to those funda-mental values and the rejection of their erosion. Justice is therefore the achievement of consistency among values, of simplicity, of scrutability. In this way Gandhi's salt satyagraha demonstrated the right to make salt as a more basic value than the government's right to control the making of salt. Civil rights demonstrators in the United States demonstrated that the simple right to buy lunch at a cafeteria or to vote or to ride in the front of the bus was more basic and more valuable to Americans than the elaborately justified values of racism and segregation.

One of the ills of complex or pluralistic societies is that there may be fundamental values on which there simply is no consensus. In American society the issue of abortion rights would seem to be a good example, but one could add capital punishment, the proper role of government, drug use and individual rights, and sexual identity. These are clearly sources of peacelessness in American culture, and are likely to be so for a long time; perhaps forever. But time often does wear the edges off such issues, and it is easy to adopt too short a view. For example, dissensus over gender roles seems to have declined over the past couple of decades as a generation has come of age without having learned the re-strictions of their elders.

The philosophy of satyagraha does not assume a universally-accepted definition of what is good. It readily accepts that the satyagrahi's con-ception of truth and goodness might be wrong, which is why the satya-grahi is humble and open to the thoughts and beliefs of the opponent. But this also suggests that a satyagraha movement is unlikely to succeed if its aims are outside the deeper cultural values of the society it seeks to change. Put another way, it only works if it fights for "good."

It seems clear, then, that the perceived gulf between the "principled" and the "pragmatic" nonviolence activists is less substantial than may be thought. The satyagrahi's search for truth is really a search for the most consensually-held beliefs in the society. The definition of evil and the use of goodness to fight it is similarly a culturally-held definition, consisting of the identification of the society's most fundamental values. Finally, the aim of satyagraha, to bring a change of heart to the oppo-nent, can be viewed as an effort to reconcile conflicts among existing values and beliefs.

Beyond Satyagraha

In formulating his theories of nonviolent resistance, Gandhi envisioned an approach to social action that could take many forms. The nationalist movement in India, for example, included various forms of noncooperation (strikes, walkouts, resignation of offices), protest and persuasion, and interventions of varying degree. In the Vykom Road Satyagraha, satyagrahis escorted members of the untouchable caste down a road prohibited to them, suffering the beatings of brahmins along the way. In the salt satyagraha, Gandhi led a mass march to the sea to make salt in opposition to the Salt Act imposed by the British.

Even a casual review of the actions undertaken by Gandhi and his followers shows a tremendous variety of actions that can be taken by nonviolent resisters. It is no wonder that nonviolence theorists have tried many ways to categorize them and thus organize what is known of them. Moreover, there are many more sorts of activities that are not, strictly speaking, satyagrahas yet can reasonably be called methods of nonviolent action.

Lakey (1968) divided nonviolent action into three categories, according to the amount of discomfort inflicted on the opponent. *Persuasion* is a method aimed at making it "not worth the bother" of the opponent to enforce the status quo; in fact it could occur without even being very visible. The Quaker "invasion" of Massachusetts was an example in which a group regarded as a deviant minority simply grew over time through migration and birth, until it had become large enough to cease being unusual. This is one strategy of the contemporary gay rights movement as well. Encouraging gays and lesbians to "come out" is a way of achieving typicality or normalcy in the eyes of the majority, simply through numbers.

Conversion is Lakey's second level of intensity in action. Conversion involves the use of "patience and pacifism" to allow the unjust structure or regime time to see the "error of its ways" and to realign itself with the true values of the community. It is closest to what Gandhi meant by bringing about a "change of heart" in the opposition. The end of Communist rule in Hungary might be an example of conversion, although it is difficult to identify any one social movement that pushed it along. In Hungary, reform from hard-line state socialism to multiparty democracy had a "gradualist, evolutionary character (Batt 1990: 464). In the end, the Hungarian Socialist Workers' Party (HSWP) simply "lost confidence in its own right to rule." Edelstein's (1994) analysis of the Hungarian reform is illustrative in another way: It demonstrates that the "opponent" regime is never a single person, or even a monolithic body that behaves like one. The end of HSWP dominance came over the course of years of internal debate and conflict among party leaders, with the hardliners eventually losing their grip on party leadership.

Edelstein describes similar events in the fall of East Germany's Communist government. In fact, the fall of Hungary's government was the catalyst for change in East Germany, because the new government had begun to open its borders for travel to the West. When East German citizens vacationing in Hungary were permitted to cross into Austria instead of returning home to East Germany; an avalanche of emigrations ensued. This emboldened various reform movements to organize demonstrations and strikes. In Edelstein's words, "when a crack opened in an enforced consensus, a wave of discontent poured out" (1994: 114).

As in Hungary but at a faster pace, the East German government's various components struggled over how to react. Mikhail Gorbachev had stated a new policy of nonintervention in satellite states, which undermined the power of local governments to enforce their will. In East Germany, Communist Party leader Erich Honecker reacted with police beatings of thousands of demonstrators. When that failed to have the desired effect, he ordered the police to be prepared to shoot. But Egon Krenz, head of security, canceled the order, and the next day told Honecker in the Politburo meeting, "Erich, we can't beat up hundreds of thousands of people" (Edelstein 1994: 114). It was all over: the meeting ended a few days later with a declaration that the Politburo would "discuss all basic questions of our society." Ultimately the German Democratic Republic ceased to exist.

The third level of nonviolent action described by Lakey is *coercion*. This involves action that inflicts material hardship on the opponent, and includes strikes, boycotts, and disruptions of all sorts. The fall of the Communist government in Poland is an example. Years of economic stagnation had led to scattered strikes and protests by workers in various trades in the 1970s; these grew in 1980 into Solidarity, the first independent trade union in Poland or any other eastern European country. Efforts to reform the party and its government were reversed when Defense Minister Wojciech Jaruzelski staged a coup and imprisoned the leadership of the union. But the underlying economic problems only worsened, and ultimately the Communist Party in Poland decided to open the government to broader elections. It lost its dominance in the elections, and ultimately Solidarity, by then a political party, won control of the government.

Another form of coercion is economic sanction, including boycotts or blockades typically imposed by forces outside the society. The fall of the apartheid government in South Africa followed decades of sanctions by the United States and other Western nations; their effectiveness was hotly debated the whole time. Kaempfer, Lowenberg, Mocan, and Bennett (1994) have used empirical data to address this and other questions about the use of external sanctions in creating internal reform. Their results show that sanctions were effective in a complex and indirect way in South Africa. For one thing, although sanctions generally did not hurt the economic interests of the South African business community, they increased both the discomfort and the solidarity of protest groups, thus intensifying their political activities. The more sanctions were applied against South Africa, the more strikes were staged by black gold miners. But this effect was only temporary; after a year or so the miners had incurred such economic hardship by the sanctions and strikes that their political effectiveness was reduced.

Lakey considered coercion of these types to be the most extreme form of political action that could be called nonviolent. Others might go further, including actions like destruction of property and sabotage among nonviolent activities. On the other hand, Gandhi was opposed to such destructive actions, and in some cases even to inflicting economic pain. And at the extreme, some even propose nonresistance as a means of struggle: refusing to resist as a form of resistance.

Nor does Lakey's typology exhaust the categories of nonviolent action. But whatever their specific tactics or targets, they all seek to bring about social and cultural change by changing the taken-for-grantedness of the status quo and by demonstrating an alternative that makes more sense. Nonviolent action thus dismantles unjust social structures by the same methods that they are assembled: by operating on the image each individual has of the thoughts of the rest of the community. This can be demonstrated by reference back to the social psychology of combat described in Chapter 2. Recall that what makes combat possible is the assumption on the part of each soldier that all the other soldiers will follow orders without question and will risk their own lives when called upon. It is this assurance about one's comrades that makes it possible for an individual to take risks—and, incidentally, to violate even the most deeply internalized norms against killing.

Nonviolent resistance uses the same principle to make change. If one or a few citizens decide not to cooperate—that is, to reject the consensus belief or value or norm—then it will be more difficult for other citizens to assume that a meaningful consensus exists. It is clear that resisters must make their actions obvious and public for this to work; it is not their own refusal that creates change, but rather the contagion of new thinking that the action spawns.

Nonviolent resistance movements thus *demonstrate* an alternative to the status quo, taking on the responsibility to model a different order—a different reality. This is, one presumes, why it is called a "demonstration" when a group marches or protests or obstructs in order to make a point. The break-in to a military base is not really a threat to the functioning of the military, nor is it meant to be. Rather, it is a demonstration of what people can actually do in spite of the status quo, and of the fact that there are people who do not agree. It demonstrates that if one were inclined to resist, he or she would not be alone.

This is a powerful force in human behavior, as one learns from the most basic social psychology. Consider Solomon Asch's experiments on the effects of consensus on perception. Subjects were asked to judge which of three lines projected on a screen was equal in length to a comparison line. When they took their turn after several others (confederates of the experimenters) had already responded incorrectly, their answers frequently conformed to those of the others, even though the consensus answer was "obviously" wrong.

Asch's experiment, and many others in a similar vein, stands as a metaphor for social order: Individuals conform because the unanimity of the others lends legitimacy to the consensus view. What would happen in Asch's experiments if even one of the confederates departed from unanimity? Certainly this would embolden the actual subject to place more trust in his or her own perceptions, and the fiction created by the group would be on its way to demolition.

If just a handful of people can sway the perceptions of an individual in something as "objective" as the length of a line, then it is easy to imagine how a whole nation of "confederates" can sway the individual in matters less clear-cut. Who is to doubt racist ideology when everyone else in the community espouses it? Who can resist the institution of war and war making without some evidence of noncompliance and illegitimacy from others? Why reduce energy or resource use, or recycle, or conserve, if one is completely alone in doing so? It is the demonstration of an alternative that makes it possible for values, beliefs, and norms to change, and this is what nonviolent activists provide, even when they are few in number.

But why be nonviolent? Aside from the moral virtue of refusing to harm others, why should people interested in change exercise the patience and restraint of nonviolence? Experience suggests there is great reason to pursue change nonviolently, rather than through armed insurrection or military action. In the first place, nonviolent change tends to be more thorough change. Revolutions, coups, and other seizures of power almost invariably bring superficial change, of government or economic institutions only. Revolutionary governments recognize this and spend a great deal of effort in attempts to reform other institutions— family, religion, science, the arts, even sport. But these institutions are difficult to change through force. After more than six decades of Soviet government and ideology, for example, Russian literature and music continued to flourish, either underground or in disguise. For example, modern Russian playwrights often used the traditional form of the fairy tale to criticize both Soviet politics and Soviet repression of the arts. Even the Russian church sprang to life after 1990 as if little had happened. Change to these more deeply-rooted institutions probably can occur *only* nonviolently, through the more evolutionary and broad-based action of demonstrating and forming a new consensus.

A second virtue of nonviolent change is that it does not invite reprisal and counterrevolution as does violent change. Nonviolent change has a disarming effect that often lasts beyond the institution of change itself. The recent experiences in eastern Europe and South Africa are worthy examples, particularly the reconciliation process now under way in the latter. Violent conflict and change tends to increase polarization among factions; nonviolent conflict tends to reduce it.

Scarritt (1994) used historical data to study the effects of violent and nonviolent movements for independence from colonial rule in the various African states. He found that in general, countries that freed themselves from colonial rule nonviolently enjoy lower levels of ethnic grievances than those who threw off colonial rule through violence. Further, such countries see fewer human rights violations when grievances do occur.

Finally, nonviolent change involves more people, not only in the making of change itself but also in the conduct of the society afterward. This means that the new ideas and ideologies are likely to be internalized by more people, and thus shared more widely among them. Consequently, Scarrit's study also found that new nations that were established nonviolently showed greater democracy than those established through armed revolution. This is reiterated in the current experience of the new eastern European democracies as well.

The creation of peace is essentially a process of creating justice, construed as the consistency and mutual reinforcement of cultural ideas and social structures. In principle this can be accomplished by force and coercion; the People's Republic of China has probably gone the farthest in this direction in recent times. Through the Great Leap Forward, the Cultural Revolution, and other repressive initiatives, the governments of Mao Zedong and later Deng Xiaoping sought to undo traditional Chinese culture and replace it with modern Leninist principles. Compared with other revolutionary governments, they have been relatively successful. But nonviolent democracy movements eventually have arisen, most notably the 1989 student movement centered in Tiananmen Square. In recounting the experiences of that movement and the violent repression of it by the authorities, Thomas (1994) observes its failure with a measure of hope. He notes that China has a deep history of civil and political rights, and that the nonviolent character of the 1989 movement paved the way for eventual reform.

The maintenance of peace through force and repression is possible but is not suited to the modern age. Societies are simply too complex to be rationalized by intentional change of social institutions according to the will of a ruling party. Because societies are so diverse in terms of both division of labor and personal and cultural identity, maintaining solidarity by the old "mechanical" means—to use Durkheim's term—is simply too difficult. Where it has been tried, it has almost always failed—as can readily be seen in much of Africa today, for example. Instead, the peace of predictability is best achieved by the creation and maintenance of justice, and this is only achievable nonviolently.

Chapter Summary

The creation of *positive peace* requires the creation of predictability and trust. Historically, this has been established in three different ways: through *functional homogeneity*, *cultural homogeneity*, and *civility*. The latter is a "rational" means of violence control, characteristic of modern, pluralistic societies. Such societies are prone to peacelessness because complex and overlapping value systems contain many internal inconsistencies. This is also why modernization often brings peacelessness and injustice to developing societies.

The peacemaker's task is to create cultural change, such that structures and values are made more consistent with one another. This often means that inconsistencies are pointed out and reduced by a call to more basic social values. The most effective way of accomplishing this is through *nonviolent social action*.

Nonviolent action is rooted in the practice of *satyagraha*, a codification of social change strategies developed by Mohandas Gandhi. Its main goal is to fight injustice through "truth-seeking," by which is meant dismantling inconsistency by applying more basic, core values. The main tactic is the demonstration of an alternative to the status quo. In this way, social change activists dismantle consensus on the old ideas while demonstrating consensus on new ones.

Questions for Review

How has peace evolved? Why is it so difficult to achieve in modern, pluralistic societies?

Many people think justice is characterized by individual freedom and weak social institutions, but the author disputes this. Why?

How does modernization disrupt peace and justice?

How does satyagraha create change?

Why does satyagraha work only for "good"? What does the satyagrahi mean by "good"?

For Further Research

Ackerman, Peter, and Christopher Kruegler. 1994. *Strategic Nonviolent Conflict.* Westport, Conn.: Praeger.

Bondurant, Joan V. 1965. *Conquest of Violence: The Gandhian Philosophy of Conflict.* Berkeley: University of California Press.

Duncan, Ronald, ed. 1971. *Gandhi: Selected Writings*. New York: Harper and Row.

Hare, A. Paul, and Herbert H. Blumberg, eds. 1968. *Nonviolent Direct Action*. Washington, D.C.: Corpus Books.

Isbister, John. 1995. *Promises Not Kept: The Betrayal of Social Change in the Third World*. 3d ed. West Hartford, Conn.: Kumarian Press.

Marullo, Sam, and John Lofland, eds. 1990. *Peace Action in the Eighties*. New Brunswick, N.J: Rutgers University Press.

Sharp, Gene. 1980. *Social Power and Political Freedom*. Boston: Porter Sargent.

Wehr, Paul, Heidi Burgess, and Guy Burgess, eds. 1994. *Justice Without Violence*. Boulder, Colo.: Lynne Rienner Publishers.

8 Epilogue: People and Peacemaking

There is a parable in which a small boy is seen walking along an empty beach, periodically stooping to pick something up and throw it into the sea. A passerby stops and asks him what he's doing, to which he replies: "The tide has gone out, and these starfish will dry up and die if I don't throw them back." The passerby looks up and down the long strand and says, "But the sea is so vast—you can't even save all the starfish on this one beach. You'll never make much of a difference in the larger scheme of things." The boy picks up another starfish, tosses it into the water, and says: "True, but I just saved *that* one."

This little story draws a clear line between two perspectives on the role of the individual in the conduct of the community. The passerby views the boy's activities as insignificant; a harmless but childish and sentimental expenditure of time and energy. The boy knows he will never make much of a difference, but feels compelled to change "his little corner of the world" anyway out of a personal sense of responsibility.

Each character represents a polar position regarding the individual's role in effecting social change. The boy's "principled" involvement comes from the recognition that society is in the end made up of individuals and social action is ultimately the sum of a lot of individual actions. If *everyone* threw back all the starfish they saw, it would make a significant impact on the starfish-mortality problem. Similarly, if everyone acted more justly or peaceably, or if everyone recycled, or if everyone gave their fair share to charity, the world would be a better place. The boy knows that waiting for someone else or some institution to take care of the problem is a passive and defeatist approach: A better world starts with me.

But the passerby is right, too. The problem with the boy's sentimental approach is that everyone *isn't* going to take their part in building a better society, at least not on their own initiative. And it's not simply that people are too selfish to do the right thing—the problem is that their attention and energies need to be focused on the task to be done. Who is going to organize the Save the Starfish effort? How would people even be informed of the plight of the starfish in the first place?

This is not a problem new to modern life, for the story is actually an elaboration on the New Testament parable of the Good Samaritan. In it, a traveler encounters an injured man beside the road, the victim of robbers. The Samaritan's response is to bring the man to the next town and see that he is cared for, paying the costs out of his own pocket. The simple lesson, of course, is that each of us must assume responsibility for our fellows, without regard for who they are or what group they belong to or what their business. The value in the story is hidden, however, in the question of what the traveler should do if on his next journey he encounters several or a dozen wounded victims. Should he impoverish himself completely in an attempt to redress the wrong done to them? Worse yet, what if the traveler simply can't afford to serve all those he encounters? Should he make a glorious but vain gesture, even in the certainty of failure?

Each person faces a similar dilemma in judging for how, and to what extent, one should become involved in making a better world. On the one hand is a compulsion to act with a generosity of spirit in our dealings with the world; to give something of our own comfort to bring greater comfort to others. This might mean material sacrifice by way of charitable donations or charitable work, or it might mean living a simpler life altogether as a way of having a smaller impact on the world's resources. The phrase "Live simply, that others may simply live" is an embodiment of this spirit.

But at the same time one understands that, like the boy saving the starfish, one cannot alone make the world a better place. Although one recognizes that people have to act if the world is to be improved, one also recognizes that even a large personal sacrifice would be almost utterly inconsequential. And it would simply be dishonest to claim, even to oneself, that material comforts aren't important. One may not mind making sacrifices, but there is little sense in making them in vain. The question is, why should a person be an activist?

One answer is that a person should do good whether it makes a difference or not. This is the orientation of what Rapoport (1992) called "religious pacifists" and others whose activism is rooted in personal witness and virtue. Epstein (1990) referred to this as the "politics of example," noting that its practitioners often pay no attention to political strategy or outcomes, but use political action as a means of expressing conscience. Rapoport went a step further in observing that this kind of activist sometimes actually avoids organization altogether, for fear that collective action will lead to compromise of personal principles.

A second answer is that the effectiveness of social action is not always obvious in the short term. For one thing, it may take a long time for the activists' goals to come to pass. The early resisters of the Vietnam War must have felt quite powerless for a very long time, but their efforts created a foundation for the broadening of resistance that was to come later. Moreover, social action often has secondary effects beyond the immediate achievement of goals. Marullo (1990) notes that every social movement has the dual objective of not only pressing demands for change but also of mobilizing resources. That is, an activist group must generate growth in membership and finances while it pursues its political or social aims. Growth in membership is especially important; Oppenheimer (1968) noted that the size of the activist group is the most important factor in its success. It is so important, in fact, that some groups pursue innocuous goals so as to attract the most members (Brigham 1990). Finally, there may be worthwhile indirect effects of social activism. For example, Hine (1996) concluded that the student rebellion of the "Kent State era" led to the refocusing of an entire generation of scholars on militarism, racism, and sexism.

These observations suggest that there is a deeper answer to the question of personal involvement—that our responsibility to the community is not a solitary or heroic one. One is obliged not to save the world alone, but to join with others in making the world that should be. To vainly impoverish oneself in a futile, heroic gesture is both unhelpful and demoralizing. Better to build a community of caring in which small efforts by many can both directly address wrong and strengthen human ties.

The Good Samaritan should, on finding his own efforts too small to make a difference, go about the task of building an organization to address the problem of highway thievery. Perhaps it might police the road, or operate a free clinic in the area, or even devise a mutual-benefit society, a primitive form of insurance. Similarly, problems of peace and justice should be addressed by joining with others in the construction of stronger and more consensus-based communities. The eighteenth-century historian Alexis de Tocqueville recognized this when he studied democracy in America, concluding that the individual is more powerful as a subordinate part of a group or party than in casting his solitary vote alone.

One of the things that keeps many people from taking action against war and injustice is the belief that activism requires a kind of heroic effort that only a few extraordinary people can muster. This myth of the heroic activist takes two forms. The first is embodied by Gandhi, Mother Teresa, Martin Luther King, and other larger-than-life activist leaders. Surely not all of us can live as these luminaries did or achieve accomplishments like theirs. The second form is the nonfamous, ordinary peasant or laborer or housewife who, though not a leader, dedicates his or her life to a cause. This sort of activist, aptly described by Downton and Wehr (1997), takes activism as a major life role, as a means both to improving the community and to self-integration. Often these people can become recognized for their life work as well, as did Rigoberta Menchu and Jody Williams, head of the International Campaign to Ban Landmines, both ordinary people who received the Nobel Peace Prize for their work.

Both models offer a limited view of activism, one that tends to discourage participation. The fact is that the overwhelming majority of activists are not heroes, sacrificing their futures for abstract causes or for the advancement of others. On the contrary, most are ordinary people who have found cause to act against wrong, and usually in their own interests and those of their immediate fellows. And most are not leaders, but simply committed participants.

Numerous examples of this sort of activism can be found in this century. McManus and Schlabach (1991) detail more than a dozen successful peace and justice movements in Latin America, from peasant land actions in Honduras and Guatemala to war resistance in Nicaragua and Peru. The titles the editors give to the actions—"Labor holds the line in Brazil," "The nonviolence of desperation," "Argentina's mothers of courage"—are significant, as they remind us that it does not take any particular personal charisma or genius to become an activist, only a desire to work with others to make change. They also remind us of the honest value of having a personal stake in the outcome.

The United States has seen successful activism in the resistance to the Vietnam War, the Civil Rights movement, the women's movement, the American Indian movement, and the gay rights movement, to name the most visible. But there have been many less visible actions, on behalf of migrant farmworkers in the sixties and seventies, against the proliferation of nuclear power in the eighties, and against U.S. policy in Nicaragua and El Salvador in the eighties.

This is not to mention thousands of regional and local movements to save natural lands, protect waterways and their habitat, advocate for health care equity, force improvement of public housing, improve schools, establish citizen boards to oversee police, boycott exploitative employers, and dozens of other issues. And even this does not include the quiet citizen action involved in establishing, expanding, and staffing thousands of volunteer food pantries, homeless shelters, childcare co-ops, Habitat for Humanity chapters, refugee and immigrant settlement services, battered women's shelters—the reader can surely add plenty more to the list.

In short, there are more opportunities for activism than picketing and getting arrested. Meaningful citizen action can be undertaken at various levels of involvement, from the simple act of voting at the lowest level, to consuming and investing more conscientiously, to actively lobbying for legislation, to boycotts and strikes, all the way to serious illegal activity. Moreover, citizens can engage in activism on behalf of either specific focused issues on the one hand, or more broadly defined concerns, on the other. Many people begin their activist "careers" with involvement in an issue that personally affects them, such as a labor strike or a lobbying campaign for or against a particular bill. This involvement may raise the person's awareness of both the existence of other more general social problems and of the power he or she has to promote change. Others begin with concern for a more global problem, like the environment or energy consumption or weapons proliferation.

Figure 8.1 shows some of the kinds of action people can undertake to better their world, arranged in a twofold scheme according to the intensity of personal involvement required and the breadth of focus on particular issues. Of course there are many other ways for people to be involved; likewise there are many ways these actions might be categorized. But what seems clear is that almost none of these actions require heroism; for that matter most do not even require much sacrifice. What they do require is engagement with others and one's own time and effort.

But community spirit is not the only prerequisite to activism. Although one might exhort oneself and fellow citizens to become more active in shaping the community, one should not underestimate the importance of knowledge as a motivator to activism. Much of the evil that humans do—including the evil of passivity or acquiescence—is done on the basis of false, inaccurate, or slanted knowledge. More troubling, much of this evil is done because people don't *want* to know the truth about the effects of their actions.

In Chapter 1 a brief account was given of Everett Hughes's article, "Good People and Dirty Work" (1961). In it, Hughes recounted interviews with German citizens who had stood by during the Holocaust and participated in or failed to resist the brutality and killing that was occurring in their midst. In a search for answers to the question of how people could allow this activity, Hughes found that the "good people" of Germany were able to maintain a certain ignorance of what was going on around them. They did not know "for certain" that millions were being exterminated because of their ethnicity or religion or sexual orientation or politics. Of course there was plenty of evidence, from eyewitness accounts to smuggled photographs to official documents—but when a truth is unpleasant, a mountain of evidence is easily dismissed by even a

FIGURE 8.1   Dimensions of Activism

	Narrow ◄—————	Breadth of Focus —————►	Broad
High	Sabotage and other illegal activity	Militant activism (Greenpeace, etc.)	
		Arrest, legal consequences	
	Strikes	Travel for voluntarism or activism	Substantial lifestyle restrictions (vegetarianism, alternative living, etc.)
	Demonstration participation	Demonstration participation	Demonstration participation
	Boycott specific product in support of workers producing it	Human-rights voluntarism	
	Lobbying for specific legislation	Contribute to political action group	
	Write political representatives on specific legislation		Ethical investing, consuming
		Recycling and other community efforts	
Low	Voting	Voting	Voting

Intensity of Involvement (vertical axis, High to Low)

small official denial. The desire to believe a comfortable lie in the face of an uncomfortable truth is a powerful blinder, and it gives the official propaganda machine an enormous advantage.

Reading Hughes's article for the first time as a graduate student reminded me of the "truth wars" of the Vietnam era. Throughout the war, a wide variety of groups and individuals disseminated information about military failures, atrocities against civilians, demoralization of the troops, secret and illegal bombings in Cambodia, covert assassinations, political intrigue, and any number of other unsavory activities. At the same time, the government promulgated its own information, insisting the war was being won, the American soldier was welcomed by the populace and was committed to the righteousness of his cause, bombs only struck military targets, and most of all, that there were no military incursions into Cambodia or Laos. In short, the war was just, it was being conducted by the rules, and it would soon be won.

How easy it was to discount what was being said by the unauthorized, "marginal" groups criticizing the war. They had few resources and often relied on the word of individuals who were not only acting outside the official channels of communication, but were clearly hostile to them. Where photographs and video were offered as evidence, they were easily dismissed as "isolated incidents" or even "staged" events. By contrast, the government's information seemed to bear the weight of legitimacy: it had enormous resources and it was closer to the information—after all, it was actually conducting the war and therefore was in a better position to know the truth. And where the antiwar groups seemed shrill and extremist in their approach, the government was a sober, suit-and-tie organization of experienced managers and leaders.

But the government's greatest advantage was that it told the truth people wanted to hear. It was not until the press had turned against the war and began to broadcast a lot of negative images that the public at large began to acknowledge that these comfortable truths were not truths at all. To accept this bitter reality was not easy—it required not only that people change their thinking about the war, but also that they recognize that their government was lying and had been for years. The end of widespread public support came over a long period of steady accretion of contradictory and uncomfortable reality.

A quarter century later Saddam Hussein invaded Kuwait. Americans were told that Iraqi soldiers had cruelly pillaged their peaceful neighbor, going so far as to steal the incubators from hospitals, costing the lives of the newborns they protected. The Iraqi army, meanwhile, was portrayed as a legion of supermen who could only be defeated by the most disciplined, most virtuous, and most righteous liberation force. The decisive victory of that force was attributed to the miracle of modern weapons technology, which could drop a bomb down the chimney of an armaments plant while sparing civilian lives nearly completely. It was only cranks and leftists who pointed to the failures of the Patriot missiles in protecting against Iraqi missile attacks, or who mentioned the hundreds of thousands of civilian deaths that would result from the destruction of water purification, electric power, and other infrastructure facilities. And later, the story of the purloined incubators was found to be a lie, promulgated by a public-relations consultant employed by the Kuwaiti government.

As this is written, the United States continues its Iraqi adventure. Pinpoint attacks by smart bombs and cruise missiles are setting back Iraq's chemical and biological weapons programs by years, and Saddam's support is crumbling. All of this is being done in the name of the U.N. mandate to protect the world against "weapons of mass destruction" (a misnomer, but a catchy one that has stuck). As it happens, the U.N.

resolutions cited as legitimation for the current attacks do not authorize them at all, a fact not mentioned on the evening news. And Saddam's ravings that the U.N. weapons inspection teams were harboring American spies were dismissed by all but the most cynical anti-American critic—until the U.N. admitted it was true.

Like the German citizens during the Holocaust, Americans are encouraged at every turn to look away from evil conducted in their name. The centrally-consolidated news media make war appear as a normal, legitimate means of pursuing our interests. Citizens are predisposed to believe this because a lifetime of violent diversions have prepared them to regard human suffering with indifference and even pleasure. And everyday life is suffused with military ideals and military activities, from glamorous advertisements for the all-volunteer military aired during the football game to the presence of recruiters at the student union and at the mall. People are given to understand, like Candide, that they live in the best of all possible worlds.

This is easy to believe, as long as the path of intellectual least resistance is taken. People can allow themselves the impression of being informed by watching the news and reading *USA Today*. "Both sides" of every issue can be known by digesting the opinion page of the local newspaper. But in doing so Americans will still remain ignorant. One of Hughes's interviewees exemplified the problem in a particularly subtle way. He went to great lengths to observe that the Holocaust was a moral abomination; that it never should have happened and Germans would bear the guilt of it for generations. But still, he could understand why it had happened: One had to recognize that "there was a Jewish problem," after all. Even after the war against the Jews had mushroomed beyond any previous comprehension into a program of systematic annihilation, ordinary people could reserve this bit of justification.

Hughes's informant demonstrates that it was not inherent immorality or sadism that made German citizens acquiesce in the conduct of the Holocaust, but their deep acceptance that there was such a thing as a "Jewish problem." Given the acceptance of a "truth" like this, and the suppression of the unpleasant realities of the death camps, it was easy to go along. In fact, it was difficult not to. Until recently the United States had a worldwide communism problem; today there is an Iraqi problem. A North Korean problem is brewing and several African problems have been simmering for some time. Domestically, Americans have an immigration problem that justifies aggressive arrest and deportation activities on our borders, and a crime problem that justifies the death penalty and various suspensions of due process. There is a poverty problem, too, which has been characterized largely as a race problem and therefore not resolvable by social policy.

And so Americans, too, go along with injustice, helped to ignore much of what is unpleasant and to interpret the rest in a way that makes it palatable. Although Americans are not any more immoral than the German citizens of the thirties and forties, interests and ignorance help ensure our acquiescence in addressing the "problems" to be faced in today's world.

What this implies is that an important first step in working for peace and justice is removal of the blinders. If one wishes to be an activist—and an activist for the "truth" that Gandhi described—then the first task is to look behind the truths that justify comfort and seek out those less comfortable and less self-serving. This entails an obligation to undertake a personal kind of activism for one's own knowledge, and this can be pursued in several ways.

Seek Information from Marginalized Sources. One problem with "mainstream" sources of information and analysis is that, while they seek to provide "balanced" coverage of issues and "diverse" view, the range of diversity is a small fraction of the actual range of views. For example, a serious news analysis program like *Meet the Press* or the *Mc-Neil-Lehrer News Hour* will address a political controversy by hearing from congressmen of both the Republican and Democratic Parties. They may even include members from the most extreme wings of the parties. But those elected to Congress at all tend to be at the center of political thought generally, and certainly either a part of or obliged to the upper classes. They are overwhelmingly composed of lawyers, businesspeople, and military veterans. And they are elected by appealing to the political center of their constituencies, so as to capture votes from the other party.

This is why one is unlikely to hear much on *Meet the Press* that is sympathetic to Iraq or that explores the effects of class interests in waging war, or that explains the functions of military waste. The means to be critical of the status quo must be found outside its own information systems, in the alternative press, various academic and quasi-academic periodicals, and increasingly, the Internet.

Develop Critical Judgment. Recognize, too, that there is a lot of misinformation and genuine quackery around. The Internet, for example, offers a democracy of ideas that elevates the most ill-conceived and ungrounded assertions to the same level as the diligent work of teams of earnest researchers. Without a solid foundation in critical thinking—the kind that one seeks from higher education, for example—enthusiasm to do the right thing is easily perverted by the lure of movements pursuing false or evil ends. People are thus *morally obliged* to learn to separate wheat from chaff, lest they allow themselves to be used in the search for something other than the truth.

Seek Diverse Associations. A further cause of insularity and its attendant ignorance is our isolation from people whose ideas differ greatly from our own. In American society, it is easy to avoid people of a different race, social class, lifestyle, age, and level of education. Residential segregation, occupational stratification, religion, and even tracking in the public schools all help confine us to homogeneous communities in which the truth appears uniform and complete. This segregation probably becomes more acute as one gets older, since people are able with time to sort themselves more efficiently into like-minded communities through residence, work, and experience. This tendency can be resisted by establishing and maintaining connections with people different from oneself through joining associations or cultivating interests that appeal to a broader community.

These suggestions are a few ways in which one can resist the natural tendency to fall into a simplistic and limited worldview. Following them gives oneself the chance to resist cooperation with evil. I don't mean to suggest that knowledge alone will make for a better world. Being better informed will not automatically make anyone a social activist. Some of us are simply more courageous or more generous or more irritable than others, and those who are will locate themselves further along the continuum of social activism. But refusing to swallow the truths of the times is itself a first act of noncooperation, and it can be a powerful one. Its power is multiplied when one's own skepticism is expressed to others, for this begins the process of diffusion of new ideas into the community. It also leads to the formation of new communities of thought, as likeminded people begin to associate together and reinforce each others' beliefs and values. These communities can become powerful forces in the larger society, not because everyone in them is an activist, but because they endorse and legitimate the actions of those few who are.

I teach sociology, which is largely an exercise in getting comfortable people to look at uncomfortable truths. I have never found it necessary or useful to exhort students to do something about the social issues dealt with in class. People who undertake the challenge of critical examination of their society and their circumstance often do become activists at some level. But even among these intellectually active people, some are less predisposed to social action for reasons of temperament. What is certain is that the other students—the ones who refuse to see the uncomfortable realities, either by distancing themselves from them or quibbling over data or by sheer lack of intellectual engagement—never engage in any sort of action for social change.

Ultimately, the decision to become an activist for social change may be a matter of the heart, originating in deep feelings of empathy or responsibility for one's fellow beings. But it is possible that many people have the heart for activism yet have failed to find expression for it, owing to immersion in a culture of war and violence. An earnest attempt to throw off the lenses by which people have been invited to view the world is the first step in unlocking the energy they might possess for working toward its betterment. In short, while the decision to work for peace may be a decision of the heart, it begins with an effort of the mind.

Chapter Summary

The biblical story of the Good Samaritan raises the question of whether one should be an activist for the community good, even if it seems impossible to make a difference. One answer is that activism is a means of expressing one's conscience and one should take part whether it does any good or not. But another is that individual sacrifice and heroism is only one form of activism—most social change has been made by ordinary people acting collectively.

One of the most powerful barriers to becoming involved in creating social change is lack of knowledge of the need for change or of the potential for bringing it about. People are often kept in the dark about social evil by the authorities who perpetuate it, but people also collaborate in their own ignorance. One of the first steps toward activism, then, is the gaining of knowledge from *marginal sources*, associating with *diverse communities*, and developing *critical judgment*. Thus activism involves a commitment of both heart and mind.

For Further Research

Downton, James, Jr., and Paul Wehr. 1997. *The Persistent Activist*. Boulder, Colo.: Westview.

Hughes, Everett. 1961. "Good People and Dirty Work." *Social Problems* 10: 3–10.

Marullo, Sam, and John Lofland, eds. 1990. *Peace Action in the Eighties*. New Brunswick, N.J.: Rutgers University Press.

McManus, Philip, and Gerald Schlabach, eds. 1991. *Relentless Persistence*. Philadelphia: New Society Publishers.

Moser-Puangsuwan, Yeshua. 1996. "Grassroots Initiatives in Unarmed Peacekeeping." *Peace Review* 8: 569–576.

Schott, Linda. 1996. "Middle-of-the-Road Activists: Carrie Chapman Catt and the National Committee on the Cause and Cure of War." *Peace and Change* 21: 1–21.

References

Abu-Nimer, Mohammed. 1996. "Conflict Resolution in an Islamic Context." *Peace and Change* 21: 22–40.

Amin, Samir. 1994. "About the Gulf War." Pp. 2189–2235 in *War and its Consequences*, ed. John O'Loughlin, Tom Mayer, and Edward S. Greenberg. New York: HarperCollins.

Arendt, Hannah. 1963. *Eichmann in Jerusalem: A Report on the Banality of Evil.* New York: Viking.

Ayoob, Mohammed. 1996. "State Making, State Breaking, and State Failure." Pp. 37–51 in *Managing Global Chaos*, ed. Chester A. Crocker and Fen Osler Hampson. Washington, D.C.: United States Institute of Peace.

Barash, David. 1991. *Introduction to Peace Studies*. Belmont, Calif.: Wadsworth.

Barker-Plummer, Bernadette. 1996. "The Dialogic of Media and Social Movements." *Peace Review* 8: 27–33.

Batt, Judy. 1990, October 1. "Political Reform in Hungary." *Parliamentary Affairs*, pp. 464–481.

Bendaña, Alejandro. 1996. "Conflict Resolution: Empowerment and Disempowerment." *Peace and Change* 21: 68–77.

Ben-Eliezer, Uri. 1997. "Rethinking the Civil-Military Relations Paradigm: The Inverse Relation Between Militarism and Praetorianism Through the Example of Israel." *Comparative Political Studies* 30: 356–374.

Benoit, E. 1972. "Growth Effects of Defense in Developing Countries." *International Development Review* 14: 2–10.

———. 1973. *Defense and Economic Growth in Developing Countries*. Lexington, Mass.: Lexington Books.

———. 1978. "Growth and Defense in Developing Countries." *Economic Development and Cultural Change* 26: 271–280.

Berger, Peter L., and Thomas Luckmann. 1966. *The Social Construction of Reality*. Garden City, N.Y.: Doubleday.

Betts, Richard K. 1994a. "Introduction." Pp. 1–3 in *Conflict After the Cold War Years: Arguments on and Causes of War and Peace*, ed. Richard K. Betts. New York: Macmillan.

———. 1994b. "International Realism: Anarchy and Power." Pp. 63–65 in *Conflict After the Cold War Years: Arguments on and Causes of War and Peace*, ed. Richard K. Betts. New York: Macmillan.

Blainey, Geoffrey. 1973. *The Causes of War*. London: Macmillan.

———. 1994. "Power, Culprits, and Arms." Pp. 110–123 in *Conflict After the Cold War Years: Arguments on and Causes of War and Peace*, ed. Richard K. Betts. New York: Macmillan.

Bond, Doug. 1994. "Nonviolent Direct Action and the Diffusion of Power." Pp. 125–145 in *Justice Without Violence,* ed. Paul Wehr, Heidi Burgess, and Guy Burgess. Boulder, Colo.: Lynne Rienner.

Bondurant, Joan V. 1965. *Conquest of Violence: The Gandhian Philosophy of Conflict.* Berkeley: University of California Press.

_____. 1968. "Gandhi's Satyagraha Against the Rowlatt Bills." Pp. 31–46 in *Nonviolent Direct Action,* ed. A. Paul Hare and Herbert H. Blumberg. Washington, D.C.: Corpus Books.

Bornstein, Gary, David Budescu, and Shmuel Zamir. 1997. "Cooperation in Intergroup, *N*-Person, and Two-Person Games of Chicken." *Journal of Conflict Resolution* 41: 384–406.

Brenes, Abelardo. 1990. "Educating for Universal Responsibility." *Peace Review* (Spring 1990): 33–36.

Brigham, William. 1990. "Noncontentious Social Movements: 'Just Say No' to War." Pp. 155–166 in *Peace Action in the Eighties,* ed. Sam Marullo and John Lofland. New Brunswick, N.J.: Rutgers University Press.

Brookings Institution. 1998. *What Nuclear Weapons Delivery Systems Really Cost.* URL:http://www.brook.edu/FP/PROJECTS/NUCWCOST/DELIVERY.HTM (April 1998).

Broyles, William J. 1990. "Why Men Love War." Pp. 29–37 in *Making War/Making Peace,* ed. Francesca M. Cancian and James William Gibson. Belmont, Calif.: Wadsworth.

Burgess, Guy, and Heidi Burgess. 1994. "Justice Without Violence: Theoretical Foundations." Pp. 7–35 in *Justice Without Violence,* ed. Paul Wehr, Heidi Burgess, and Guy Burgess. Boulder, Colo.: Lynne Rienner.

Cancian, Francesca M., and James William Gibson, eds. 1990. *Making War/Making Peace.* Belmont, Calif.: Wadsworth.

Center for Defense Information. 1999. "The Fiscal Year 2000 Military Budget." *The Defense Monitor* 28(1): 1–2.

Collins, Randall. 1988. *Theoretical Sociology.* New York: Harcourt Brace.

_____. 1989. "Sociological Theory, Disaster Research, and War." Pp. 365–385 in *Social Structure and Disaster,* ed. Gary A. Kreps. Newark: University of Delaware Press.

Coser, Lewis. 1956. *Functions of Social Conflict.* New York: Free Press.

Creighton, Colin, and Martin Shaw, eds. 1987. *The Sociology of War and Peace.* Dobbs Ferry, N.Y.: Sheridan House.

Dawidowicz, Lucy S. 1975. *The War Against the Jews, 1933–1945.* New York: Holt, Rinehart.

Deger, Saadet, and Ron Smith. 1983. "Military Expenditure and Growth in Less Developed Countries." *Journal of Conflict Resolution* 27: 335–353.

Diamond, Jared. 1997. *Guns, Germs, and Steel.* New York: Norton.

Diehl, Paul F., Daniel Druckman, and James Wall. 1998. "International Peacekeeping and Conflict Resolution: A Taxonomic Analysis with Implications." *Journal of Conflict Resolution* 42: 33–55.

Donovan, James A. 1970. *Militarism, U.S.A.* New York: Charles Scribner's Sons.

Downton, James, Jr., and Paul Wehr. 1997. *The Persistent Activist.* Boulder, Colo: Westview.

Durkheim, Emile. 1893. *The Division of Labor in Society.* Reprint, New York: Free Press, 1964.

Durkheim, Emile. 1938. *The Rules of Sociological Method.* Translated by Sarah A. Solvay and John H. Mueller. New York: Free Press.

Dyer, Gwynne. 1985. *War.* New York: Crown.

Edelstein, Joel. 1994. "Nonviolence and the 1989 Revolution in Eastern Europe." Pp. 99–123 in *Justice Without Violence*, ed. Paul Wehr, Heidi Burgess, and Guy Burgess. Boulder, Colo.: Lynne Rienner.

Ehrenreich, Barbara, and Dierdre English. 1975. *Complaints and Disorders: The Sexual Politics of Illness.* Old Westbury, N.Y.: Feminist Press.

Ellul, Jacques. 1965. *The Technological Society.* New York: Knopf.

Enloe, Cynthia. 1983. *Does Khaki Become You?* Boston: South End Press.

——. 1991. "A Feminist Perspective on Foreign Military Bases." Pp. 95–106 in *The Sun Never Sets: Confronting the Network of Foreign U.S. Military Bases*, ed. Joseph Gerson. Boston: South End Press.

Epstein, Barbara. 1990. "The Politics of Moral Witness: Religion and Nonviolent Direct Action." Pp. 106–124 in *Peace Action in the Eighties*, ed. Sam Marullo and John Lofland. New Brunswick, N.J.: Rutgers University Press.

Ettlinger, Nancy. 1992. "Development Theory and the Military Industrial Firm." Pp. 23–52 in *The Pentagon and the Cities*, ed. Andrew Kirby. Newbury Park, Calif.: Sage.

Fabbro, David. 1978. "Peaceful Societies: An Introduction." *Journal of Peace Research* 15: 67–83.

Falk, Richard. 1996. "Grounds to Reject Intervention." *Peace Review* 8: 467–470.

Fallows, James. 1981. "M-16: A Bureaucratic Horror Story." Pp.85–101 in *More Bucks, Less Bang*, ed. Dina Rasor. Washington, D.C.: Fund for Constitutional Government.

Fischer, Dietrich. 1996. "A Global Peace Service." *Peace Review* 8: 563–568.

Fitzgerald, A. Ernest. 1972. *The High Priests of Waste.* New York: Norton.

——. 1989. *The Pentagonists: An Insider's View of Waste, Mismanagement, and Fraud in Defense Spending.* Boston: Houghton-Mifflin.

Fogarty, Brian E. 1991. "The Functions of Military Waste." *Peace and Change* 16: 162–175.

Freud, Sigmund. 1989. "Why War?" Pp.176–181 in *International War: An Anthology*, ed. Melvin Small and J. David Singer. Chicago: Dorsey.

Friends Committee on National Legislation. *How Much of Your 1997 Federal Income Tax Supports Military Spending?* URL: http://www.clark.net/pub/fcnl/tax97doc.htm. March 10, 1998.

Gandhi, M. K. 1951. *Non-Violent Resistance.* New York: Schocken Books.

Gans, Herbert. 1972. "The Positive Functions of Poverty." *American Journal of Sociology* 78: 275–289.

——. 1979. *Deciding What's News.* New York: Pantheon Books.

Gerson, Joseph, and Bruce Birchard. 1991. *The Sun Never Sets: Confronting the Network of U.S. Military Bases.* Boston: South End Press.

Gibson, James William. 1994. *Warrior Dreams.* New York: Hill and Wang.

Gleditsch, Kristian S., and Michael D. Ward. 1997. "Double Take: A Reexamination of Democracy and Autocracy in Modern Politics." *Journal of Conflict Resolution* 41: 361–383.

Gleditsch, Nils Petter, and Håvard Hegre. 1997. "Peace and Democracy: Three Levels of Analysis." *Journal of Conflict Resolution* 41: 283–310.

Graves, Kathy Davis, and Catherine Shreves. 1990. *Breaking the Cycle of Violence: A Focus on Primary Prevention Efforts*. Minneapolis: League of Women Voters of Minneapolis.

Gregg, Richard. 1935. "Moral Jiu-Jitsu." Pp. 328–341 in *Nonviolent Direct Action*, ed. A. Paul Hare and Herbert H. Blumberg. *Reprint*, Washington, D.C.: Corpus Books, 1968, pp. 328–341.

Grobar, Lisa M., and Richard C. Porter. 1989. "Benoit Revisited: Defense Spending and Economic Growth in LDCs." *Journal of Conflict Resolution* 33: 318–345.

Grossman, Dave. 1995. *On Killing*. Boston: Little, Brown.

Grossman, Mark. 1995. *Encyclopedia of the Persian Gulf War*. Santa Barbara, Calif.: ABC-CLIO.

Gurwitsch, Aron. 1966. "Introduction." Pp. xi–xxi in *Collected Papers III: Studies in Phenomenological Sociology*, ed. Alfred Schutz. The Hague: Martinus Nijhoff.

Guttmann, Allen. 1978. *From Ritual to Record: The Nature of Modern Sports*. New York: Columbia University Press.

Hall, Brian. 1998, March 15. "Overkill Is Not Dead." *New York Times Magazine*, p. 43.

Harris, Ian M. 1990. "The Goals of Peace Education." *Peace Review* (Spring 1990): 3–7.

Herman, Edward S., and Noam Chomsky. 1988. *Manufacturing Consent: The Political Economy of the Mass Media*. New York: Pantheon Books.

Hess, Robert D., and Judith V. Torney. 1968. *The Development of Political Attitudes in Children*. Garden City, N.Y.: Anchor Books.

Hine, Darlene Clark. 1996. "The Greater Kent State Era, 1968–1970: Legacies of Student Rebellions and State Repression." *Peace and Change* 21: 157–168.

Hobbes, Thomas. 1958. *Leviathan*. Indianapolis: Bobbs-Merrill, p. 107.

hooks, bell. 1995. "Feminism and Militarism: A Comment." *Women's Studies Quarterly* 23: 58–64.

Hudson, Richard. 1989. "An Open Letter to U.N. Chiefs." Pp. 344–352 in *International War: An Anthology*, ed. Melvin Small and J. David Singer. Chicago: Dorsey.

Hughes, Everett. 1961. "Good People and Dirty Work." *Social Problems* 10: 3–10.

Huntington, Samuel P. 1994. "The Errors of Endism." Pp. 33–43 in *Conflict After the Cold War Years: Arguments on and Causes of War and Peace*, ed. Richard K. Betts. New York: Macmillan.

Huth, Paul K. 1990. "The Extended Deterrent Value of Nuclear Weapons." *Journal of Conflict Resolution* 34: 270–290.

Ienaga, Saburo. 1994. "The Glorification of War in Japanese Education." *International Security* 18(3): 113–133.

Inglis, Fred. 1991. *The Cruel Peace*. New York: Basic Books.

Isbister, John. 1995. *Promises Not Kept: The Betrayal of Social Change in the Third World*. 3d ed. West Hartford, Conn.: Kumarian Press.

James, William. 1910. "The Moral Equivalent of War." Pp. 328–336 in *International War: An Anthology*, ed. Melvin Small and J. David Singer. Reprint, Chicago, 1985: Dorsey.

Johnson, Richard L., and Eric Ledbetter. 1997. "'Spiritualizing the Political': Christ and Christianity in Gandhi's Satyagraha." *Peace and Change* 22: 32–48.

Joseph, Paul. 1994. "Individualism and Peace Culture." *Peace Review* 6: 357–363.

Jowett, Benjamin. 1900. *Thucidides, Book V*. London: Oxford.

Kaempfer, William, Anton D. Lowenberg, H. Naci Mocan, and Lynne Bennett. 1994. "Foreign Threats and Domestic Actions: Sanctions Against South Africa." Pp. 191–215 in *Justice Without Violence*, ed. Paul Wehr, Heidi Burgess, and Guy Burgess. Boulder, Colo.: Lynne Rienner.

Kaldor, Mary. 1996. "A Cosmopolitan Response to New Wars." *Peace Review* 8: 505–514.

Kanter, Rosabeth Moss. 1972. "Commitment and Social Organization: A Study of Commitment Mechanisms." *American Sociological Review* 33: 499–517.

Katz, Mark N. 1996. "Collapsed Empires." Pp. 23–35 in *Managing Global Chaos*, ed. Chester A. Crocker and Fen Osler Hampson. Washington, D.C.: United States Institute of Peace.

Keegan, John. 1976. *The Face of Battle*. New York: Vintage.

Kirby, Andrew. 1992. "The Pentagon *Versus* the Cities?" Pp. 1–22 in *The Pentagon and the Cities*, ed. Andrew Kirby. Newbury Park, Calif.: Sage.

Krain, Matthew. 1997. "State-Sponsored Mass Murder: The Onset and Severity of Genocides and Politicides." *Journal of Conflict Resolution* 41: 331–360.

Lakey, George. 1968. "Mechanisms of Nonviolent Action." Pp. 381–393 in *Nonviolent Direct Action*, ed. A. Paul Hare and Herbert H. Blumberg. Washington, D.C.: Corpus Books.

Langlois, Jean-Pierre. 1989. "Modeling Deterrence and International Crises." *Journal of Conflict Resolution* 33: 67–83.

Levy, Jack S. 1996. "Contending Theories of International Conflict: A Level-of-Analysis Approach." Pp. 3–24 in *Managing Global Chaos*, ed. Chester A. Crocker and Fen Osler Hamson. Washington, D.C.: U.S. Institute of Peace.

Lofland, John, Mary Anna Colwell, and Victoria Johnson. 1990. "Change-Theories and Movement Structure." Pp. 87–105 in *Peace Action in the Eighties*, ed. Sam Marullo and John Lofland. New Brunswick, N.J.: Rutgers University Press.

Lorenz, Conrad. 1966. *On Aggression*. New York: Harcourt, Brace.

Luck, Edward C. 1991. "Interstate Organizations: Current Scholarship, Analysis, and Practice." Pp. 173–188 in *Approaches to Peace: An Intellectual Map*, ed. W. Scott Thompson and Kenneth M. Jensen. Washington, D.C.: U.S. Institute of Peace.

Marshall, S. L. A. 1947. *Men Against Fire*. New York: William Morrow.

Marullo, Sam. 1990. "Patterns of Peacemaking in the Local Freeze Campaigns." Pp. 246–263 in *Peace Action in the Eighties*, ed. Sam Marullo and John Lofland. New Brunswick, N.J.: Rutgers University Press.

McManus, Philip, and Gerald Schlabach, eds. 1991. *Relentless Persistence*. Philadelphia: New Society Publishers.

Mead, Margaret. 1965. "The Anthropology of Human Conflict." Pp. 65–69 in *The Nature of Human Conflict,* ed. Elton B. McNeil. Englewood Cliffs, N.J.: Prentice-Hall.

Mearsheimer, John J. 1994. "Why We Will Soon Miss the Cold War." Pp. 44–61 in *Conflict After the Cold War Years: Arguments on and Causes of War and Peace,* ed. Richard K. Betts. New York: Macmillan.

Merton, Robert. 1968. *Social Theory and Social Structure.* New York: Free Press.

Miedzian, Myriam. 1991. *Boys Will Be Boys.* New York: Doubleday.

Miller, Steven E. 1991. "Is Arms Control a Path to Peace?" Pp. 45–63 in *Approaches to Peace: An Intellectual Map,* ed. W. Scott Thompson and Kenneth M. Jensen. Washington, D.C.: U.S. Institute of Peace.

Mills, C. Wright. 1956. *The Power Elite.* New York: Oxford University Press.

Mimmo, Dan, and James E. Combs. 1990. *Mediated Political Realities.* 2d ed. New York: Longman.

Moorhead, Alan. 1956. *Gallipoli.* New York: Harper and Row.

Moser-Puangsuwan, Yeshua. 1996. "Grassroots Initiatives in Unarmed Peacekeeping." *Peace Review* 8: 569–576.

Moskos, Charles. 1993. "From Citizens' Army to Social Laboratory." *Wilson Quarterly* 17 (Winter 1993): 83–94.

Mrozek, Donald J. 1995. "The Cult and Ritual of Toughness in Cold War America." In *Sport in America: From Wicked Amusement to National Obsession,* ed. David K. Wiggins. Champaign, Ill.: Human Kinetics.

Mueller, John. 1994. "The Obsolescence of Major War." Pp. 19–32 in *Conflict After the Cold War Years: Arguments on and Causes of War and Peace,* ed. Richard K. Betts. New York: Macmillan.

Nalebuff, Barry. 1988. "Minimal Nuclear Deterrence." *Journal of Conflict Resolution* 32: 411–425.

Nisbet, Robert. 1973. *The Social Philosophers.* New York: Crowell.

Oakes, Guy. 1994. *The Imaginary War.* New York: Oxford University Press.

Oppenheimer, Martin. 1968. "Towards a Sociological Understanding of Nonviolence." Pp. 394–406 in *Nonviolent Direct Action,* ed. A. Paul Hare and Herbert H. Blumberg. Washington, D.C.: Corpus Books.

Osgood, Charles E. 1989. "Calculated De-Escalation as a Strategy." Pp. 337–342 in *International War: An Anthology,* ed. Melvin Small and J. David Singer. Chicago: Dorsey.

Oster, Patrick, and Bruce Ingersoll. 1983. "M–1." Pp. 34–39 in *More Bucks, Less Bang,* ed. Dina Rasor. Washington, D.C.: Fund for Constitutional Government.

Paley, Henry. 1989. "The Heroditus Solution." Pp. 309–313 in *International War: An Anthology,* ed. Melvin Small and J. David Singer. Chicago: Dorsey.

Parenti, Michael. 1989. *The Sword and the Dollar.* New York: St. Martin's.

_____. 1996. "The Myth of Good Interventions." *Peace Review* 8: 471–476.

Pen, Jan. 1971. *Income Distribution: Facts, Theories, Policies.* Translated by Treor S. Preston. New York: Praeger.

Pfeifer, Kimberly. 1996. "Modernization and Indigenous Knowledge: Ideas for Development or Strategies for Imperialism?" *Peace and Change* 21: 41–67.

Quigley, Carroll. 1983. *Weapons Systems and Political Security.* Washington, D.C.: University Press of America.

Rapoport, Anatol. 1992. *Peace: An Idea Whose Time Has Come.* Ann Arbor: University of Michigan Press.

Rasor, Dina, ed. 1983. *More Bucks, Less Bang.* Washington, D.C.: Fund for Constitutional Government.

Reardon, Betty. 1996a. *Sexism and the War System.* Syracuse, N.Y.: Syracuse University Press.

_____. 1996b. "Women or War?" *Peace Review* 8: 315–321.

Regan, Patrick M. 1994. *Organizing Societies for War.* Westport, Conn.: Praeger.

Richardson, Lewis. 1960. *Statistics of Deadly Quarrels.* Chicago: Quadrangle.

Ritzer, George. 1992. *Sociological Theory.* New York: McGraw-Hill.

Robbins, Jhan, and June Robbins. 1968. "Why Didn't They Hit Back?" Pp. 107–127 in *Nonviolent Direct Action,* ed. A. Paul Hare and Herbert H. Blumberg. Washington, D.C.: Corpus Books.

Rogne, Leah, and Bradley D. Harper. 1990. "The Meaning of Civil Disobedience: The Case of the Honeywell Project." Pp. 192–203 in *Peace Action in the Eighties,* ed. Sam Marullo and John Lofland. New Brunswick, N.J.: Rutgers University Press.

Russet, Bruce. 1994. "The Gulf War as Empowering the United Nations." Pp. 185–197 in *War and Its Consequences,* ed. John O'Loughlin, Tom Mayer, and Edward S. Greenberg. New York: HarperCollins.

Saperstein, Alvin M. 1991. "The 'Long Peace'—Result of a Bipolar Competitive World?" *Journal of Conflict Resolution* 35: 68–79.

Saperstein, Alvin M., and Gottfried Mayer-Kress. 1988. "A Nonlinear Dynamic Model of the Impact of SDI on the Arms Race." *Journal of Conflict Resolution* 21: 636–670.

Sayre, Nora. 1982. *Running Time: Films of the Cold War.* New York: Dial Press.

Scarritt, James R. 1994. "Nonviolent V. Violent Ethnic Political Action in Africa." Pp. 165–189 in *Justice Without Violence,* ed. Paul Wehr, Heidi Burgess, and Guy Burgess. Boulder, Colo.: Lynne Rienner.

Schachter, Oscar. 1991. "The Role of International Law in Maintaining Peace." Pp. 67–127 in *Approaches to Peace: An Intellectual Map,* ed. W. Scott Thompson and Kenneth M. Jensen. Washington, D.C.: U.S. Institute of Peace.

Scheff, Thomas J. 1967. "Toward a Sociological Model of Consensus." *American Sociological Review* 32: 32–46.

Scheper-Hughes, Nancy. 1996. "Maternal Thinking and the Politics of War." *Peace Review* 8: 353–358.

Schott, Linda. 1996. "Middle-of-the-Road Activists: Carrie Chapman Catt and the National Committee on the Cause and Cure of War." *Peace and Change* 21: 1–21.

Second General Council of Latin American Bishops. 1970. *The Church in the Present-Day Transformation of Latin America in Light of the Council, Volume II.* Bogota: Latin American Episcopal Council.

Sharp, Gene. 1968. "Types of Principled Nonviolence." Pp. 273–313 in *Nonviolent Direct Action,* ed. A. Paul Hare and Herbert H. Blumberg. Washington, D.C.: Corpus Books.

_____. 1970. *Exploring Nonviolent Alternatives.* Boston: Porter Sargent.

_____. 1973. *The Politics of Nonviolent Action.* Boston: Porter Sargent.

_____. 1980. *Social Power and Political Freedom*. Boston: Porter Sargent.

Shaw, Martin. 1988. *Dialectics of War*. London: Pluto Press.

Small, Melvin, and J. David Singer. 1989. "Patterns in International Warfare, 1816–1980." Pp. 26–37 in *International War: An Anthology*, ed. Melvin Small and J. David Singer. Chicago: Dorsey.

Solomon, Robert C., and Mark Murphy. 1990. *What Is Justice?* New York: Oxford University Press.

Sorokin, Pitirim A. 1937. *Social and Cultural Dynamics*. New York: American Book Co.

Stockholm International Peace Research Institute. 1998. *SIPRI Yearbook 1998*. Oxford: Oxford University Press.

Sumner, William Graham. 1911. "War." Pp. 205–227 in *War and Other Essays*, ed. William Graham Sumner. New Haven: Yale University Press.

Suter, Keith. 1996. "Globalism and Humanitarian Intervention." *Peace Review* 8: 515–520.

Thomas, Stephen C. 1994. "China's Movement to Resolve Citizen/Government Conflicts." Pp. 147–163 in *Justice Without Violence*, ed. Paul Wehr, Heidi Burgess, and Guy Burgess. Boulder, Colo.: Lynne Rienner.

Tickner, J. Ann. 1995. "Introducing Feminist Perspectives into Peace and World Security Courses." *Women's Studies Quarterly* 23: 48–57.

Tuchman, Barbara W. 1978. *A Distant Mirror: The Calamitous 14th Century*. New York: Ballantine.

United States Bureau of the Census. 1998. *Statistical Abstract of the United States, 1998*. 118th ed. Washington, D.C.: U.S. Government Printing Office.

United States Congress. 1986. *Congressional Quarterly Almanac*. Washington, D.C.: U.S. Government Printing Office.

United States Institute of Peace. 1990. "Conversations: Speaking about Democracy and Peace." *United States Institute of Peace Journal* 3: 1.

Vigor, P. H. 1975. *The Soviet View of War, Peace and Neutrality*. London: Routledge and Kegan Paul.

Vinocur, Martin Barry. 1988. *More than a Game*. Westport, Conn.: Greenwood.

Wagner, Richard V. 1988. "Distinguishing Between Positive and Negative Approaches to Peace." *Journal of Social Issues* 44: 1–15.

Wallace, Michael D. 1979. "Arms Races and Escalation." *Journal of Conflict Resolution* 23: 3–16.

Waltz, Kenneth N. 1994a. "The Origins of War in Neorealist Theory." Pp. 88–95 in *Conflict After the Cold War Years: Arguments on and Causes of War and Peace*, ed. Richard K. Betts. New York: Macmillan.

_____. 1994b. "The Spread of Nuclear Weapons: More May Be Better." Pp. 371–382 in *Conflict After the Cold War Years: Arguments on and Causes of War and Peace*, ed. Richard K. Betts. New York: Macmillan.

Wataru, Kurita. 1989. "Making Peace with Hirohito and a Militaristic Past." *Japan Quarterly* 36 (April–June 1989): 186–192.

White, Ralph K. 1989. "Misperception in Vienna on the Eve of World War I." Pp. 254–262 in *International War: An Anthology*, ed. Melvin Small and J. David Singer. Chicago: Dorsey.

Wilson, E. O. 1975. *Sociobiology: The New Synthesis.* Cambridge: Harvard University Press.

Wiltshire, David. 1978. *The Social and Political Thought of Herbert Spencer.* Oxford: Oxford University Press.

Wolfson, Murray, and Homa Shabahang. 1991. "Economic Causation in the Breakdown of Military Equilibrium." *Journal of Conflict Resolution* 35: 43–67.

World Health Organization. 1958. *The World Health Organization: A Report of the First Ten Years.* Geneva: World Health Organization.

Wright, Quincy. 1942. *A Study of War.* Chicago: University of Chicago Press.

York, Jodi. 1996. "The Truth(s) About Women and Peace." *Peace Review* 8: 323–329.

Index